A NEW VARIORUM EDITION

OF

SHAKESPEARE

EDITED BY

HORACE HOWARD FURNESS

VOL. VIII

AS YOU LIKE IT

———

PHILADELPHIA
J. B. LIPPINCOTT COMPANY
LONDON: 10 HENRIETTA STREET, COVENT GARDEN
1890

Copyright, 1890, by H. H. Furness

Westcott & Thomson,
Electrotypers and Stereotypers, Phila.

Press of J. B. Lippincott Company,
Phila.

v. 8

IN MEMORIAM

PREFACE

ALL needful information in regard to the scope and design of this Edition may be found on p. 439 of the *Appendix*.

The Text is that of the FIRST FOLIO, as accurately reproduced as a comparison almost letter by letter can make it.

There are many passages in SHAKESPEARE whereon it is desirable to have notes demanding no profundity of antiquarian research or archæological knowledge on the part of the annotator, but requiring solely keenness of intellect with clearness of thought or of expression. On such passages there cannot be, speaking for myself, too many notes nor too much discussion, provided only that we are fortunate enough to conjure into the circle such minds as DR JOHNSON'S, or COLERIDGE'S, HAZLITT'S, CAMPBELL'S, CHRISTOPHER NORTH'S, MRS JAMESON'S, or CHARLES LAMB'S ; or can summon to our aid the traditions of GARRICK, or of KEAN, or of MRS SIDDONS ; or listen to MRS KEMBLE or to LADY MARTIN. Indeed, the professions of 'love' and 'admiration' for SHAKESPEARE from those who can turn aside from such nights and feasts of the gods are of doubtful sincerity.

At the same time, to be perfectly fair, it must be confessed that we read our SHAKESPEARE in varying moods. Hours there are, and they come to all of us, when we want no voice, charm it never so wisely, to break in upon SHAKESPEARE'S own words. If there be obscurity, we rather like it ; if the meaning be veiled, we prefer it veiled. Let the words flow on in their own sweet cadence, lulling our senses, charming our ears, and let all sharp quillets cease. When AMIENS'S gentle voice sings of the winter wind that its 'tooth is not so keen because it is not seen,' who of us ever dreams, until wearisome commentators gather mumbling around, that there is in the line the faintest flaw in 'logical sequence' ? But this idle, receptive mood does not last for ever. The time comes when we would fain catch every ray of light flashing from these immortal plays, and pluck the heart out of every mystery there; then, *then*, we listen respectfully and gratefully to every suggestion, every passing thought, which obscure passages have stirred and awakened in minds far finer than our own. Then it is that we welcome every aid which notes can supply, and find, too, a zest in tracing the history of Shakespearian Comment from the condescending, patronising tone of the early critics toward the 'old bard,' with WARBURTON's cries of 'rank nonsense,' to the reverential tone of the present day.

It has been a source of entertainment, in this present play of *As You Like It*, to note, what I think has been but seldom noted, the varied interpretations which the character of JAQUES has received. With the sole exception of HAMLET, I can recall no character in SHAKESPEARE of whom the judgements are as diverse as of this 'old gentleman,' as AUDREY calls him. Were he really possessed of all the qualities attributed to him by his critics, we should behold a man both misanthropic and genial, sensual and refined, depraved and elevated, cynical and liberal, selfish and generous, and finally, as though to make him still more like HAMLET, we should see in him the clearly marked symptoms of incipient insanity. Indeed, so mysterious and so attractive is this character that, outside of England at least, JAQUES has often received a larger share of attention than even ROSALIND. So completely did he fascinate GEORGE SAND that in her version of the play for the French stage JAQUES is the guiding spirit of the whole drama, and is represented, by her, as so madly in love with CELIA that in a fit of jealousy he is only with difficulty restrained from fighting a duel with ORLANDO, and the curtain falls on the prettiest of ring-times between him and his adoration.

If all degrees of surprise had not been, for me, long ago exhausted concerning SHAKESPEARE, not alone at the poet himself, but at every circumstance howsoever connected with him, I should be inclined to wonder that the students of Anthropology, instead of adopting various standards, such as Facial Angles, Craniological Measurements, and the like, had not incontinently adopted one of SHAKESPEARE's comedies as the supreme and final test in determining nationality, at least as between the Gallic, the Teutonic, and the Anglosaxon races. I suggest a comedy as the test rather than a tragedy, because in what is tragic the whole world thinks pretty much alike; a fount of tears is in every human breast, and the cry of pain is sure to follow a wound. We are all of us like BARHAM'S Catherine of Cleves, who

'—— didn't mind death, but she couldn't stand pinching;'

it makes no difference whether the unshunnable outcry is in French, or German, or English, the key-note is the same in all. But in Comedy it is far different. We may all cry, but we do not all laugh; and when we laugh, we are by no means all tickled by the same straw. And it is just here wherein the difference of nationality or race consists. THÉOPHILE GAUTIER, in the short but good *Preface* to his translation of *Münchhausen*, has admirably explained the cause of this difference: 'Le génie des peuples,' he says, 'se révèle surtout dans la plaisanterie. Comme les œuvres sérieuses chez toutes les nations ont pour but la recherche du beau qui est un de sa nature, elles se ressemblent nécessairement davantage, et portent moins nettement imprimé le cachet de l'individualité ethnographique. Le comique, au contraire, consistant dans une déviation plus ou moins accentuée du modèle idéal, offre une multiplicité singulière de ressources; car il y a mille façons de ne pas se conformer à l'archétype.'

The 'beaded bubbles winking at the brim' of English wit may, therefore, be to German eyes merely insipid froth to be lightly blown aside.

Hence it is that such a sparkling comedy as this of *As You Like It* may be made to yield the test I have spoken of. It is through and through an English comedy, on English soil, in English air, beneath English oaks; and it will be loved and admired, cherished and appreciated, by English men as long as an English word is uttered by an English tongue. Nowhere else on the habitable globe could its scene have been laid but in England, nowhere else but in Sherwood Forest has the golden age, in popular belief, revisited the earth, and there alone of all the earth a merry band could, and did, fleet the time carelessly. England is the home of *As You Like It*, with all its visions of the Forest of Arden and heavenly ROSALIND; but let it remain there; never let it cross 'the narrow seas.' No Forest of Arden, 'rocking on its towery top, all throats that gurgle sweet,' is to be found in the length and breadth of Germany or France, and without a Forest of Arden there can be no ROSALIND. No glimpses of a golden age do German legends afford, and time, of old in Germany, was fleeted carelessly only by 'bands of gypsies.' Such a life as ROSALIND led in the Forest, which all English-speaking folk accept without a thought of incongruity, is to the German mind wellnigh incomprehensible, and refuge is taken, by some of the most eminent Germans, in explanations of the 'Pastoral drama,' with its 'sentimental unrealities' and 'contrasts,' or of SHAKESPEARE'S intentional 'disregard of dramatic use and wont,' &c. &c. ROSALIND ceases to be the one central figure of the play, her wit and jests lose all prosperity in German ears, and Germans consequently turn to JAQUES and to TOUCHSTONE as the final causes of the comedy and as the leading characters of the play. The consequence is that this almost flawless chrysolite of a comedy, glittering with ROSALIND'S brightness and reflecting sermons from stones and glowing with the good in everything, becomes, as seen through some German eyes, the almost sombre background for SHAKESPEARE'S display of folly; nay, one distinguished German critic goes so far as to consider the professional Fool as the most rational character of all the _Dramatis Personæ_. Indeed, it is to be feared that of some of the German criticisms on this comedy it may be truthfully said, that were the names of the characters omitted to which these critics refer, it would be almost impossible to discover or to recognise which one of all SHAKESPEARE'S plays is just then subjected to analysis; so difficult is it for an alien mind to appreciate this comedy of _As You Like It_.

Stress has been laid in these later days on the Chronological Order in which SHAKESPEARE wrote his plays, and attempts have been made to connect their tragic or their comic tone with the outward circumstances of SHAKESPEARE'S own life; it has been assumed that, in general, he wrote tragedies when clouds and darkness overshadowed him, and comedies when his outer life was full of sunshine.

For my part, I believe that SHAKESPEARE wrote his plays, like the conscientious playwright that he was, to fill the theatre and make money for his fellow-actors and for himself; and I confess to absolute scepticism in reference to the belief that in these dramas SHAKESPEARE'S self can be discovered (except on the broadest lines), or that either his outer or his inner life is to any discoverable degree reflected in his plays: it is because SHAKESPEARE is _not_ there that the characters are so perfect,—the smallest dash of the author's self would mar to that extent the truth of the character, and make of it a mask.

But assuming, for the nonce, that this belief of recent days is well grounded, and that from the tone of his dramas we may infer the experiences of his life, I cannot but think that it is an error to infer from his tragedies that his life was certainly sad, or that because his life was sad we have his tragedies. Surely, it was not then, when his daily life was overcast with gloom, and he was 'troubling deaf Heaven with his bootless cries,' that he would turn from real to write fictitious tragedies. Do we assuage real tears with feigned ones? From an outer world of bitter sorrow SHAKESPEARE would surely retreat to an inner, unreal world of his own creation where all was fair and serene; behind that veil the stormy misery of life could be transmuted into joyous calm. *If*, therefore, this belief of recent days be true, it was, possibly, from a life over which sorrow and depression brooded that there sprang this jocund comedy of *As You Like It*.

The extracts from KREYSSIG, who, of all German commentators, seems to have best caught the spirit of this play, have been translated for me by my Father, the REV. DR FURNESS, to whom it is again my high privilege and unspeakable pleasure to record my deep and abiding thanks.

H. H. F.

February, 1890.

As You Like It.

Dramatis Perſonæ.

DUKE of Burgundy.
Frederick, *Brother to the Duke, and Uſurper of his*
  Dukedom.
Amiens, ⎫ *Lords attending upon the Duke in his*
Jaques, ⎭ *Baniſhment.*   5

Dramatis Personæ] First given by Rowe (ed. i) and substantially followed by
all Editors. In Rowe (ed. ii), after the names Corin and Sylvius, there is added '*A
Clown, in love with* Audrey,' and '*William, another Clown, in love with* Audrey.'
Pope, Theobald, Hanmer, and Warburton followed Rowe (ed. ii). Capell added '*a
Person presenting* Hymen.'

5. **Jaques**] The pronunciation of this name has never been decisively determined.
A discussion in regard to it arose in the pages of *The Athenæum* for the 31st of July,
the 14th and 21st of August, and the 4th of September, 1880; by some of the par-
ticipants it was held to be a monosyllable, and by the others a disyllable. The discussion ended, as literary journalistic discussions generally end, in leaving the dis-
putants, as far as the public can judge, more firmly convinced than ever of the soundness
of the views with which they started. For the monosyllabic pronunciation no authority
was cited, merely personal preference was alleged. For the disyllabic pronunciation
the requirements of metre were urged when the occurrence of the name in the middle
of a verse shows that pronunciation to be indispensable, as in II, i, 29: 'The mel | an-
cho | ly Ja | ques grieves | at that,' and possibly in V, iv, 199: 'Stay, Ja | ques, stay.'
I have discussed in a note on II, i, 29, all the instances where the name occurs metri-
cally in Shakespeare, and beg to refer the student to that note, which supplements the
present. In *The Athenæum* for the 20th of May, 1882, H. BARTON BAKER gives of
this disyllabic pronunciation four examples from Greene's *Friar Bacon*, five from his
James IV, one from Kyd's *Spanish Tragedy*, another from his *Soliman and Perseda*,
and two from Beaumont and Fletcher's *Noble Gentleman*. The value of this list, for
our present purpose, is impaired by the fact that none of these characters is supposed
to be English, and in each case, therefore, 'Jaques' may possibly have received a
foreign pronunciation.

On the other hand, HALLIWELL says 'the name of this character was pronounced
jakes.' And FRENCH (p. 317) tells us that 'the name of the melancholy Lord Jaques
belongs to Warwickshire, where it is pronounced as one syllable; "Thomas Jakes of
Wonersh," was on the List of Gentry of the Shire, 12 Henry VI, 1433. At the sur-
render of the Abbey of Kenilworth, 26 Henry VIII, 1535, the Abbot was Simon
Jakes, who had the large pension of 100*l. per annum* granted to him. There are
still some respectable families of the name in the neighborhood of Stratford; John
Jaques and Joseph Jaques reside at Alderminster; Mrs Sarah Jaques at Newbold-on-
Stour; and families of the name are living at Pillerton and Eatington (1867).' The

Le Beu, *A Courtier attending on* Frederick.   6
Oliver, *Eldeſt Son to Sir* Rowland de Boys, *who
had formerly been a Servant of the Duke.*

Jaques,   }
          } *Younger Brothers to* Oliver.   9
Orlando, }

---

evidence which French adduces is sufficient, I think, to show that the name as a monosyllable was well known in Shakespeare's day. If more be needed in proof of this monosyllabic pronunciation it is settled beyond a peradventure by the coarse, unsavory anecdote with which Harington begins his *Metamorphosis of Ajax,* 1596 (p. 17 of Singer's Reprint), which need not be repeated here; Halliwell's word and mine may be taken for the fact. Assuming, then, this monosyllabic pronunciation, I think it is not impossible to reconcile it with the passages where the metre demands two syllables by supposing that, like many other words, such as *commandment* (see II, vii, 115 *post*), *England, children* and the like, there can be, when needed, the sub-audition of an extra syllable. The fact that *Jaques* was an old Warwickshire name takes it out of the rule which applies to foreign names, like *Parolles.* To me the evidence is conclusive that it was in general pronounced as a monosyllable, *Jakes,* and, when metre required it, there was, I believe, the suggestion of a faint, unemphatic second syllable.

Having thus discerned the right, let us be human and the wrong pursue. The name *Jakes* is so harsh, and so indissolubly associated with the old time 'Bowery boys,' that surely the fervent hope may be pardoned that the name *Jaques* will never be pronounced other than *Jaq-wes.*—ED.

6. Le Beu] This is the uniform spelling in the Folio, except in the Stage direction, I, ii, 88, which reads *Enter le Beau.*

7. Rowland de Boys] FRENCH (p. 316): It is very probable that Shakespeare took the name of his knight from an old but extinct family of great note in Leicestershire and Warwickshire, whose memory was long preserved in the latter county, Sir Ernald or Arnold de Boys, Arnold being easily transposed to Roland, and thence we have Orlando. The manor of *Weston-in-Arden* was held by Sir Ernald de Boys, *temp*. Edw. I, paying yearly to the Earl of Leicester 'one hound called a Brache, and seven pence in money for all services.' There were four generations in succession of the lords of the manor of *Weston-in-Arden*, each of whom is called Sir Ernald de Bosco, or de Boys.

9. Jaques] To avoid confusion with the 'melancholy Jaques,' WIELAND changed this to *Jakob*. LE TOURNEUR adopted *James* in his *Dramatis Personæ*, but by the time the Fifth Act was reached he had forgotten the substitution, and *Jaques,* not *James,* enters on the scene. It was Wieland, I am afraid, who started the custom in Germany, which has survived, I am sorry to say, even to the present hour, of translating, and of changing at will, the names of Shakespeare's characters. The infection spread even to that most admirable translator, François-Victor Hugo. Scarcely a play of Shakespeare's can be read in German wherein names with which we are all familiar from our childhood are not distorted and disguised beyond recognition, and however often they may occur in reading it is always an effort to recall the original. Who of us, however at home he may be in German, can recognize at first sight *Frau Hurtig ?* or *Schaal* and *Stille*, or those two associates lost to everlasting redemption under the disguise of *Holzapfel* and *Schleewein ?* Perhaps it may be urged that these

Adam, *an old Servant of Sir* Rowland de Boys,   10
    now following the Fortunes of Orlando.

Dennis, *Servant to* Oliver.

Charles, *A Wreſtler, and Servant to the Uſurping*
    Duke Frederick.

Touchstone, *a Clown attending on* Celia *and*
    Rosalind.

Corin, }
Sylvius, } *Shepherds.*   15

William, *a Clown, in Love with* Audrey.

Sir Oliver Mar-text, *a Country Curate.*   17

---

names, in that they have a meaning, ought to be translated, and there might be some justice in the plea if that meaning were always a key to the character. But it is rarely so. The names are simply those of the lower orders, and to bear, originally, a meaning is characteristic of all such names; the meaning, however, had long before ceased to have any special connection with the present owner of the name. In the play before us, in the translation of Dr Alexander Schmidt and in that of Herwegh, the two most recent translators and among the very best, mention is made of *Hannchen Freundlich;* who would recognise under this disguise Touchstone's *Jane Smile?* Touchstone himself figures as *Probstein,* and Audrey is *Käthchen;* and they come near to be married by *Ehren Olivarius Textdreher.* Perhaps we should be grateful that we are not called upon to read the tragedy of '*Dörfchen,* Prince of Denmark.' Would our German brothers relish the retaliation which should speak with delight of *Glitter's* 'Song of the Bell,' or of the tragedy of '*Faust* and *Peggie,*' or, better still, '*Fiſt* and *Peg*'? If this be wellnigh sacrilege, let them be gently reminded that our Shakespeare names have become a part of the language of our hearths and homes, and can be no more translated or changed than can the meaning at this late day be extracted from the Aztec name, *America,* and our country be referred to as *The Hills.* —ED.

17. **Sir Oliver**] JOHNSON: He that has taken his first degree at the University is in the academical style called *Dominus,* and in common language was heretofore termed *Sir.* This was not always a word of contempt; the graduates assumed it in their own writings; so Trevisa, the historian, writes himself *Syr* John de Trevisa. CRITICAL REVIEW (Dec. 1765, p. 409): Had Mr Johnson been more of an antiquarian, he would have been a much better editor of Shakespeare. He would then have known that this is no academical, but a pontifical style. The popes, not to be behindhand with our kings before the Reformation, arrogated to themselves a power of knighthood, both in England and Scotland; and the honour was sold by their legates or agents to churchmen who could pay for it, which great numbers did in both kingdoms. STEEVENS: We find the same title bestowed on many divines in our old comedies. NICHOLS: A clergyman, who hath not been educated at the universities, is still distinguished in some parts of North Wales by the appellation of *Sir.* Hence the Sir Hugh Evans in the *Merry Wives* is not a Welsh knight who hath taken orders, but only a Welsh clergyman without any regular degree from either of the universities. WRIGHT: The corresponding Latin 'Dominus' still exists in the Cambridge Tripos lists in its abbreviated form D^s.

Rosalind, *Daughter to the Duke.*   18
Celia, *Daughter to* Frederick.
Phœbe, *a Shepherdeſs.*   20
Audrey, *a Country Wench.*

Lords belonging to the two Dukes, with Pages,
     Foreſters, and other Attendants.

The SCENE *lyes firſt near* Oliver's *Houſe, and after-
     wards partly in the Duke's Court, and partly in*   25
     the Foreſt of Arden.

---

17. Mar-text] NEIL (p. 45): Martext was perhaps employed during the Marpre-
late controversy as a satirical designation for one who could not be expected to give
such expositions of Scripture as more learned vicars were able to do, with a *soupçon*
of puritanical reference to 'blind leaders of the blind.'

18. Rosalind] FLETCHER (p. 200): Few readers may now be aware that *Rosa-
linda* is, in truth, a Spanish name,—the adjective *lindo* or *linda* having no complete
synonym in English, but expressing beauty in the most exalted, combined with the
ordinary sense,—meaning, in short, *exquisitely graceful, beautiful,* and *sweet.* The
analogy will at once be seen which the image of the graceful rose bears to the
exquisite spirit of Rosalind, no less than to her buoyant figure in all its blooming
charms.

21. Audrey] HALLIWELL: 'Audry, Sax., it seemeth to be the same with Ethel-
dred, for the first foundresse of Ely church is so called in Latine histories, but by the
people of those parts, S. Audry.'—Camden's *Remaines,* ed. 1629, p. 77.   The name
was occasionally used in Warwickshire in the time of Shakespeare.   'Anno 1603, the
ix.th of May, Thomas Poole, and *Audry* Gibbes, were maried.'—*Parish Register* of
Aston Cantlowe.   Awdrey Turfe is one of the characters in Jonson's *Tale of a Tub.*

As you Like it.

Actus primus. Scœna Prima.

Enter Orlando and Adam.

Orlando.

S I remember *Adam*, it was vpon this fashion
bequeathed me by will, but poore a thousand
Crownes, and as thou saist , charged my brother on his blessing to breed mee well : and

5

Scœna] Scena F_3F_4.
An orchard. Rowe. Oliver's House.
Pope. Oliver's Orchard. Theob. Or-
chard of Oliver's House. Cap.

3. *fashion*] *my father* Warb. Han.
Cap. *fashion.* *He* Mal. Var. Coll. ii,
Ktly. *fashion ;—* Wh. *fashion,—*

Dyce i, Sta. *fashion,—he* Dyce iii,
Huds.

4. *me by*] *me. By* Johns. *me : By*
Steev.

poore a] *a poore* F_2. *a poor* F_3F_4,
Rowe+, Cap. Var. Steev. Coll. Sing.
Hal.

5. *Crownes*] *Crowns* F_3F_4.

As you Like it] TIECK, in Schlegel's translation (vol. iv, p. 308) suggests that the
title of this play, which may have been, he thinks, originally different, was adopted by
Shakespeare as a playful answer either to Ben Jonson's boastfulness in the Epilogue
to *Cynthia's Revels*, or else to his contempt for his audience expressed in the Induction to *Every Man Out of his Humour*.   In the former, the Epilogue himself, at a loss
to know how to characterise the play, bursts forth in the last line with, ' By —— 'tis
good, and if you like 't you may;' and in the latter, Asper, the poet, before he leaves
the stage to take his part as an actor in the performance, says : ' Now I go To turn an
actor, and a humorist, Where, ere I do resume my present person, We hope to make
the circles of your eyes Flow with distilled laughter: if we fail, We must impute it
to this only chance, Art hath an enemy call'd ignorance.'   Whereto, according to
Tieck, Shakespeare gives answer in the title to this play : 'As you like it, or, just as
you please, it is a Comedy.   Not in itself, but just as you, the spectators, choose to
pronounce it by your approval.'   ' This reference to Ben Jonson,' continues Tieck,
' can be discerned throughout the whole play by the attentive reader who is familiar
with the times and with the works of the rival dramatists.'   There seems to be no
foundation for Tieck's surmise; he overlooked the date of *Cynthia's Revels*, which
was first issued in 1601; and in *Every Man Out of his Humour*, Jonson in a foot-note
expressly disclaims any specific allusions either to the author, that is, to himself, or to
the actors.   LLOYD, in Singer's edition, thinks that this title was given in the same
spirit of idleness that pervades and informs so many of the scenes; 'it seems to

Enter Orlando and Adam.

reply carelessly to such a question as " How shall we entitle it ?" asked by men who
are fleeting the time after the fashion of the golden world.   " Laud it as you like it,"
it seems to say, or " as you like it allow it," and this is the tenour of the epilogue of
Rosalind, " I charge you, O women, for the love you bear to men, to like as much of
the play as pleases you," and so with little more strenuousness of exhortation it is left
to its fate, that could not be other than a kind one.'   In the ' Epistle Dedicatorie To
the Gentlemen Readers,' Lodge, referring to his Novel, says : ' If you like it, so.'
This phrase HALLIWELL surmises may have suggested to Shakespeare the title to the
play; and WRIGHT thinks ' it can scarcely be doubted ' that it is so.   Even if we
have to yield assent, as I suppose we must, surely a little fretting and fuming may be
pardoned over this filching, as it were, from Shakespeare of the originality of this title.
At any rate, the words were changed in the transfer, and *As You Like It* has a charm
which to *If You Like It* is denied—a charm which Shakespeare infused into all the
titles of his plays, affording therein a notable contrast to all his contemporaries.

Furthermore, HALLIWELL says : ' Braithwait, however, in his *Barnaby's Journal*
speaks of *as you like it* as a proverbial motto, and this seems more likely to imply the
true explanation of the title of Shakespeare's play.   The title of the comedy may, on
this supposition, be exactly paralleled with that of *Much Ado about Nothing*.   The
proverbial title of the play implies that freedom of thought and indifference to censure which characterizes the sayings and doings of most of the actors in this comedy
of human nature in a forest.'   It is well to remember that *Barnaby's Journal* was
not printed until 1648–50; in it ' drunken Barnaby ' finds the shop where ' Officina
juncta Baccho Juvenilem fere tobacco " Uti libet," tunc signata, Quæ impressio nunc
mutata, " Uti fiet," nota certa Quæ delineatur charta.'   Which is thus translated : 'A
shop neighboring near Iacco, Where Young vends his old tobacco : "As you Like it ;"
sometime sealed, Which impression's since repealed : "As you make it ;" he will have
it, And in chart and font engrave it.'—p. 57, ed. 1805.—ED.

3. The abruptness of this opening sentence, and the need of a nominative to be
understood before ' charged ' have occasioned some discussion, and several emendations.   WARBURTON pronounces the whole sentence as it stands ' confused and obscure.'
But the ' very small alteration in the reading and pointing ' which he is about to give
will ' set all right.'   It is this :—'As I remember, Adam, it was upon this *my father*
bequeathed me,' &c.   ' The grammar,' continues Warburton, ' is now rectified and
the sense also; which is this : Orlando and Adam were discoursing together on the
cause why the younger brother had but a thousand crowns left him.   They agree upon
it; and Orlando opens the scene in this manner—"As I remember, it was upon this,
i. e. for the reason we have been talking of, that my father left me but a thousand
crowns; however, to make amends for this scanty provision, he charged my brother,
on his blessing, to breed me well."'   This emendation CAPELL adopted with unwonted
alacrity, and asserted (*Notes*, i, 54) that there never was one more certain; seeing that
' it is pointed out and confirm'd by the context in so plain a manner as to need no
enforcing : The words " upon this " relate (probably) to some over-spirited action of
Orlando's first youth, that displeas'd his father, and occasion'd the bequest that is
spoken of, and the injunction concerning his breeding : a hint of it was proper; more
than a hint had been injudicious, as being foreign to the business in hand.'   ' There
is,' says JOHNSON, ' nothing but a point misplaced and an omission of a word which
every hearer can supply, and which therefore an abrupt and eager dialogue naturally
excludes.   I read thus : "As I remember, Adam, it was on this fashion bequeathed

[this fashion bequeathed . . . charged]

me. By will, but a poor thousand crowns; and, as thou sayest, charged my brother, on his blessing, to breed me well." What is there in this difficult or obscure ? The nominative *my father* is certainly left out, but so left out that the auditor inserts it, in spite of himself.' Sir WILLIAM BLACKSTONE pronounced Dr Johnson's reading 'awkward English,' and preferred to read thus: 'As I remember, Adam, it was in this fashion.—"*He* bequeathed me by will," &c. Orlando and Adam enter abruptly in the midst of a conversation on this topic; and Orlando is correcting some misapprehension of the other. As *I* remember, says he, it was thus. He left me a thousand crowns; and, *as thou sayest*, charged my brother,' &c. This same reading of Blackstone was also proposed by RITSON (p. 57) with, however, a different punctuation:—' it was on this fashion he bequeathed me by will,' &c. 'From the near resemblance,' says HEATH, p. 143, 'between "fashion" and *father*, it seems extremely probable that this last word was the word omitted, which led in consequence to the omission also of the possessive *my*. Read, therefore, "As I remember, Adam, it was upon this fashion; my father bequeathed me," &c.' CALDECOTT is satisfied with what he terms 'the following easy and natural interpretation: " It was upon this fashion bequeathed me by [my father in his] will, &c., and, as thou say'st [it was, or he there] charged my brother,"' &c. But it is not a question of interpretation; on that score the passage is perfectly plain, it is simply a question of grammatical construction; as LETTSOM says (ap. Dyce, ed. iii) from the use of 'it was' before 'bequeathed' and 'charged,' it is impossible to say whether these two words are aorists or past participles; if they are past participles we have no antecedent for the 'his' in 'his blessing'; if they are aorists a nominative is lacking to either the one or the other. DYCE (ed. iii) says that as 'fashion' is the last word of the line, he has little doubt that 'he' was omitted by a mistake of the compositor, wherein the present editor agrees with him, especially when it is remembered how easy would have been the omission if 'he' were expressed, as it often is, by the single letter, 'a.' At the same time, it is not to be forgotten that the nominative is sometimes omitted where it can be readily supplied from the context, as here.—See *Ham.* II, ii, 67; *Mer. of Ven.* I, i, 102, or Abbott, § 399.—ED.

4. **poore a**] CALDECOTT (and Dyce, ed. ii, cites the passage presumably with approval): *A* is *one*, a number. Suppose then the bequest had been two or five or ten, you see how insufferable would be this expression, 'ten *poor* thousand crowns.' But further—' a thousand crowns' are words of the Will, which the speaker quotes; and thereby makes them, as 'twere, a substantive to his adjective 'poor.' Cf. *Ant. & Cleop.* V, ii, 236: 'What poor an instrument May do a noble deed.' [There is, however, no necessity for explaining the construction as a quotation from the Will. WORDSWORTH (p. 12) points out a similar use in the Bible of the indefinite article prefixed to plural substantives. Thus in] Luke ix, 28, we read, 'It came to pass about an eight days after these sayings,' where the expression 'an eight days' has been retained from Tyndale's trans. in 1534. In like manner, in the Apocryphal Book, 1 Macc. iv, 15: 'There were slain of them upon a three thousand men.' WRIGHT and ROLFE apparently regard 'poor' as a simple adjective, and the present case as an instance of the common transposition of the article, and refer to Abbott, § 422; but Abbott himself refers this passage to § 85, and considers 'poor' as used adverbially; which is perhaps a little strained. To me the simplest explanation would be to consider it as a transposition not of the article but of the adjective, for the sake of greater emphasis; which is, after all, practically the same as Wright's and Rolfe's explanation.—ED.

AS YOU LIKE IT

there begins my fadneſſe : My brother *Iaques* he keepes   7
at ſchoole, and report ſpeakes goldenly of his profit :
for my part, he keepes me ruſtically at home, or (to ſpeak
more properly) ſtaies me heere at home vnkept : for call   10
you that keeping for a gentleman of my birth, that differs not from the ſtalling of an Oxe? his horſes are bred
better, for beſides that they are faire with their feeding,
they are taught their mannage, and to that end Riders
deerely hir'd : but I (his brother) gaine nothing vnder   15

7. *fadneſſe :*] *sadness.* Pope et seq.   10. *ſtaies*] *ſtayes* F_2F_3. *ſtays* F_4. *stys* Warb. Sing.

---

7. **Iaques**] Apart from the fact that in the introduction of this character here and at the close of the story Shakespeare merely follows Lodge, there may be, found, I think, an additional reason for it in the dramatic needs of the Fifth Act. In that Act it is needful that we should at once see how the changed fortune of the Senior Duke affects also the fortunes of Oliver and Orlando; and this connection in fortune is instantly suggested to us by seeing in Jaques, the messenger of good tidings, a brother of the two men in whom we are most interested. That the name Jaques was not only given to this character, but retained after the introduction of another and more promi-nent Jaques, is a proof either of haste (as Wright ingeniously suggests, and wherein I agree) or of careless indifference. But the character itself, a third brother, whatsoever his name, was retained, I believe, to meet the requirements of the close of the drama. Perhaps, too, it was to meet those same requirements that, in the tender treatment of a younger brother by Oliver, and in the latter's capacity to discern the fine traits in Orlando's character, we are to detect the elements of a better nature in Oliver, a soul of goodness in things evil, which will need but the refining influence of Celia's love to work a satisfactory reformation of his character, and thus go far to obliterate, or at least to soften, in this charming play 'the one smirch' therein, which Swinburne finds in the marriage of Celia and Oliver.—ED.

8. **schoole**] There was apparently no distinction drawn between a School and a University. Hamlet went to 'school' in Wittenberg.

10. **staies**] WARBURTON, whose *cacoethes meliorandi* was, of a truth, *insanabile*, here proposed to substitute *sties*, and, with more assurance than logic, asserts that the emendation is confirmed by the subsequent allusion to 'stalling of an ox.' Even Dr JOHNSON was overborne, and pronounced *sties* not only better, but more likely to be Shakespeare's word. MASON (p. 80) cogently observes that ' if *sties* had been the original reading the subsequent comparison would have been taken from hogs, not from oxen.' DYCE in his first edition pronounced Warburton's emendation 'very probable,' and asserted that there was 'not the slightest force in the objection urged against it by Mason,'—a note which Dyce withdrew in his third edition. There is no emphasis here, I think, on the word 'stays'; any emphasis on this word would in fact impair the antithesis between 'keep' and 'unkept,' which is meant to be of the strongest.—ED.

14. **mannage**] This good English translation (whereof see many examples in Schmidt s. v.) is now, I think, quite lost, and we have returned to its French original, *manège.*—ED.

him but growth, for the which his Animals on his   16
dunghils are as much bound to him as I : befides this nothing that he fo plentifully giues me, the fomething that
nature gaue mee, his countenance feemes to take from
me : hee lets mee feede with his Hindes, barres mee the   20

---

19. *countenance*] *discountenance* Warb.   20. *Hindes*] *hinds* F₄.
Han.

---

19. **countenance**] WARBURTON reads *discountenance;* JOHNSON pronounces the
change needless, 'a countenance is either good or bad;' and here it means, says
CAPELL, 'an evil countenance.' CALDECOTT interprets it, 'the mode of his carriage
towards me,' which DYCE cites with approval. WRIGHT gives its meaning as 'favour,
regard, patronage,' and SCHMIDT as 'appearance, deportment.' It is not difficult to
paraphrase it on these lines, so as to meet the requirements of an expression which
we all of us almost instinctively understand at once. And yet I cannot but think
that WALKER has here detected a refinement of meaning which has been hitherto
unobserved. He asks (*Crit.* iii, 59): 'Does not "his countenance" here mean
his entertainment of me, the style of living which he allows me? Selden's *Table
Talk,* art. *Fines:* "The old law was, that when a man was fined he was to be fined
salvo contenemento, so as his countenance might be safe, taking *countenance* in the
same sense as your countryman does, when he says, If you will come unto my
house I will show you the best countenance I can; that is, not the best face, but the
best entertainment. The meaning of the law was, that so much should be taken
from a man, such a gobbet sliced off, that yet notwithstanding he might live in the
same rank and condition he lived in before; but now they fine men ten times more
than they are worth." Such, I think, is the meaning of the word in Chaucer, *Per-
sones Tale, Remedium Luxuriæ:* "This maner of women, that observen chastitee,
must be clene in herte as well as in body and in thought, and mesurable in clothing
and in *contenance,* abstinent in eting and in drinking, in speking and in dede," &c.
Spenser, *Shepheards Calender,* Ægl. v [l. 81, ed. Grosart]: "But shepheards (as
Algrind used to say) Mought not live ylike, as men of the lay: With them it fits to
care for their heire, Enaunter ther heritage doe impaire; They must provide for
meanes of maintenaunce, And to continue their wont countenaunce." So understand,
Faerie Queene, Bk. v, cant. ix [l. 239, ed. Grosart]: "Then was there brought as pris-
oner to the barre, A Ladie of great countenance and place, But that she it with foul
abuse did marre;" &c.' Walker also cites an example from Ford, but it is not perfectly clear to me that in this case the meaning is the same; Dog, a Familiar devil,
in *The Witch of Edmonton,* says to Cuddy Banks (p. 263, ed. Dyce): 'Nor will I
serve for such a silly soul: I am for greatness now, corrupted greatness; There I'll
shug in, and get a noble countenance;' &c.—ED.

19. **seemes**] CAPELL thinks that 'we have here another example of that singular
usage of the common verb "seem" which is so conspicuous in' *Macb.* I, ii, 46: 'so
should he look That seems to speak things strange, and *Ib.* I, v, 27: 'Which fate
and metaphysical aid doth seem To have thee crown'd withal;' 'in both of which it
comprehends the idea of desire or intention; so here "seems to take from me" means
—seems as if it wished to take from me.' I think this is slightly over-refined. Give
to 'seem' its common meaning of *appear,* and is not then the *wish* or the *will*
implied?—ED.

place of a brother, and as much as in him lies, mines my   21
gentility with my education. This is it *Adam* that
grieues me, and the ſpirit of my Father, which I thinke
is within mee, begins to mutinie againſt this ſeruitude.
I will no longer endure it, though yet I know no wiſe   25
remedy how to auoid it.

Enter Oliuer.

Adam. Yonder comes my Maſter,your brother.

Orlan. Goe a-part *Adam*, and thou ſhalt heare how
he will ſhake me vp.   30

Oli. Now Sir, what make you heere?

Orl. Nothing : I am not taught to make any thing.

Oli. What mar you then ſir?

Orl. Marry ſir, I am helping you to mar that which
God made , a poore vnworthy brother of yours with   35
idleneſſe.

Oliuer. Marry ſir be better employed,and be naught
a while.   38

---

27. Scene II. Pope+.
Enter...] After line 30, Coll. et seq.
29. *a-part*] *apart* Ff.
30. Adam retires. Dyce, Coll. ii.

31. *heere?*] *heare?* F$_2$. *here;* F$_3$. *here?* F$_4$.
33, 34. *mar*] *marre* F$_2$F$_3$.
37. *be naught*] *do aught* Han. *be nought* Warb. Johns. Cap.

---

20. **Hindes**] SKEAT (*Dict.* s. v.) : "A peasant. The *d* is excrescent. Anglosaxon *hína*, a domestic; but the word is unauthenticated as a nom. sing., and is rather to be considered a gen. pl.; so that *hína* really stands for *hína man* = a man of the domestics. [I have heard an Irish farmer in this country constantly use the word when referring to farm-labourers.—ED.]

20. **barres**] ABBOTT, § 198: Verbs of ablation, such as *bar, banish, forbid,* often omit the preposition before the place or inanimate object. Thus, 'We'll *bar* thee *from* succession.'—*Wint. T.* IV, iv, 440, or '*Of* succession'—*Cymb.* III, iii, 102, becomes 'Bars me the place,' [in the present instance], and also in *Mer. of Ven.* II, i, 20.

21. **mines**] WRIGHT: Undermines the gentleness of my birth, and so destroys it.

31. **make**] STEEVENS: That is, What do you here? So, in *Ham.* I, ii, 164. CALDECOTT: We find the same play upon the word between the King and Costard in *Love's Lab. L.* IV, iii, 190.

34. **Marry**] WRIGHT: An exclamation from the name of the Virgin Mary, used as an oath. Here it keeps up a poor pun upon 'mar.'

37, 38. **be naught a while**] WARBURTON, after a fling at Theobald, says that this is a North-country proverbial curse equivalent to *a mischief on you.* So, Skelton [*Agaynste A Comely Coystrowne*, l. 62] 'Correct fyrst thy self; walk, and be nought! Deme what thou lyst, thou knowyst not my thought.' 'Or rather,' says CAPELL, 'Be hang'd to you! for that is now the phrase with the vulgar.' STEEVENS pronounced Warbur-

Orlan. Shall I keepe your hogs, and eat huskes with
them? what prodigall portion haue I ſpent, that I ſhould   40
come to ſuch penury?

Oli. Know you where you are ſir?

Orl. O ſir, very well : heere in your Orchard.

Oli. Know you before whom ſir?

Orl. I, better then him I am before knowes mee : I   45

---

44. *whom*] *home* F₃.

45. *I, better*] *Ay, better* Rowe.

45. *then*] *than* F₄.

45. *him*] *he* Pope +, Cap. Steev. Coll.
Sing, Clke, Ktly, Huds.

---

ton's explanation 'far-fetched,' and said that the words meant 'no more than this:
"Be content to be a cypher, till I shall think fit to elevate you in consequence." It
was certainly a proverbial saying, and is found in *The Storie of King Darius*, 1565 :
"Come away, and be nought awhile, Or surely I will you both defyle."' JOHNSON,
until he had learned the meaning from Warburton, supposed the phrase to mean : 'It
is better to do mischief than to do nothing.' WHITER affirms that the meaning is
manifestly : '*Retire,—begone,* or as we now say in a kind of quaint, colloquial language, *make yourself scarce,—vanish,—vote yourself an evanescent quantity.*' GIF-
FORD, in a note on Jonson's *Bartholomew Fair* (p. 421, where the phrase 'be curst
awhile' occurs), lashes, of course, Steevens and Malone ('from Mr Whiter,' he sighs,
'better things might be expected'), and then states that 'the explanation of Warburton is as correct as it is obvious, and may be proved " by witnesses more than my pack
will hold." It will be sufficient to call two or three : " Peace and be naught ! I
think the woman be phrensic "—*Tale of a Tub* [II, i, p. 160]; " If I stir a foot,
hang me ; you shall come together yourselves, and be naught "—*Green's Tu Quoque*
[p. 206, ed. Hazlett]. It is too much, perhaps,' he continues, 'to say that the words
" an hour," " awhile," are pure expletives, but it is sufficiently apparent that they have
no perceptible influence on the exclamations to which they are subjoined. To conclude, *be naught, hanged, curst,* &c. with, or without *an hour, a while,* wherever found,
bear invariably one and the same meaning ; they are, in short, petty and familiar male-
dictions, and cannot be better rendered than in the words of Warburton—a plague, or
a mischief on you !' DYCE (*Remarks,* p. 60): Since the origin of verbal criticism,
nothing more satisfactory has been written than the copious note of Gifford. . . . .
The first part of Warburton's note is wrong ; the expression was certainly not confined
to the 'North country.'

40. **prodigall portion**] This may be a case of prolepsis ; that is, 'what portion
have I prodigally spent ;' thus also 'the gentle condition of blood' in line 46, 'the
condition of gentle blood,' or as in 'two weak evils, age and hunger,' II, vii, 138,
and elsewhere. Schmidt's *Lexicon* (p. 1420) gives many instances. Or, since the
allusion is so clear to the Parable, it might be possibly the genitive of apposition, and
equivalent to 'what prodigal's portion have I spent ;' in this case the two words
should be joined by a hyphen.—ED.

45. **him**] For other examples of where 'him' is put for *he*, by attraction to *whom*
understood, see ABBOTT, § 208. Here the 'whom' precedes so closely that it might
be almost termed a case of attraction through proximity.

45, &c. The emphasis here is, I think : '*I* know you are my eldest brother, &c.,

know you are my eldeſt brother, and in the gentle con-   46
dition of bloud you ſhould ſo know me : the courteſie of
nations allowes you my better , in that you are the firſt
borne, but the ſame tradition takes not away my bloud,
were there twenty brothers betwixt vs : I haue as much   50
of my father in mee, as you, albeit I confeſſe your comming before me is neerer to his reuerence.

    Oli. What Boy.   ⟨this.
    Orl. Come, come elder brother, you are too yong in   54

47. *me :*] *me.* Johns.

50. *vs :*] *us.* Pope.

51. *mee, as you,*] *me ; as you,* F_2. *me, as you ;* F_3F_4, Rowe et seq.

51, 52. *your...reuerence.*] *you coming before me are nearer to his revenue* Han.

53. *Boy.*] *boy,*— Cap.

53. menacing him with his hand. Johns. strikes at him. Wh. ii.

54. collaring him. Johns. takes him by the throat. Wh. ii.

---

and *you* should so know *me.*' ' " So " is here,' says Allen, ' equivalent to accordingly, in pursuance of the same obligation : if *I* am to know *you* as a brother (the eldest), *you* are bound to know me as a brother (the youngest).' According to WORDSWORTH (p. 36), ' know ' is used here in the biblical sense of *acknowledge.*

    52. reuerence] WARBURTON : That is, The ' reverence ' due to my father is, in some degree, derived to you as the first-born. But I am persuaded that Orlando did not here mean to compliment his brother or condemn himself; something of both which there is in that sense. I rather think he intended a satirical reflection on his brother, who by letting him feed with his hinds treated him as one not so nearly related to old Sir Robert [*sic*] as himself was. I imagine, therefore, Shakespeare might write : Albeit your coming before me is nearer his *revenue*, i. e. though you are no nearer in blood, yet it must be owned, indeed, you are nearer in estate. CAPELL highly approved of this emendation, and added that ' Oliver's taking fire as he does, which gives occasion to his brother to collar him, was caused by something in the tail of this speech that gave him offence; and this he could not find in the submissive word " reverence." ' WHITER : Orlando uses the word in an ironical sense, and means to say that his ' brother by coming before him is nearer to a respectable and venerable elder of a family.' The phrase *His reverence* is still thus ironically applied, though with somewhat of a different meaning, and we frequently use the expression *your worship*, both with a grave and ludicrous signification nearly in the same manner. This sense will account for the anger of Oliver, and for the words which they mutually retort upon each other respecting their *ages* in the next two lines. It is extremely curious that Shakespeare has caught many words, and even turns of expression, belonging to the novel from which the play is taken; though he has applied them in a mode generally different and often very remote from the orig- inal. This has certainly taken place in the present instance, and the passage which contains it will likewise supply us with another example. Rosader or Orlando is introduced making his reflections on the indignities which he had suffered from his brother Saladine or Oliver. 'As he was thus ruminating his melancholy passions, in came Saladine with his men, and seeing his brother in a brown study and to forget his wonted *reverence*, thought to *shake* him out of his dumps.' Orlando says in

Oli. Wilt thou lay hands on me villaine?　　55

Orl. I am no villaine : I am the yongeſt ſonne of Sir *Rowland de Boys*, he was my father, and he is thrice a villaine that ſaies ſuch a father begot villaines : wert thou not my brother , I would not take this hand from thy throat, till this other had puld out thy tongue for ſaying 60 ſo, thou haſt raild on thy ſelfe.

Adam. Sweet Maſters bee patient , for your Fathers remembrance, be at accord.

Oli. Let me goe I ſay.

Orl. I will not till I pleaſe : you ſhall heare mee *;* my 65 father charg'd you in his will to giue me good educati- on : you haue train'd me like a pezant, obſcuring and 67

---

57. Boys] Rowe +, Cap. Mal. Cam. Rlfe, Wh. ii. Boyes Ff. *Bois* Steev. et cet.

　60. *puld*] *pull'd* F_3F_4.

　61. *ſo,*] *ſo ;* F_4. *so.* (shaking him) Coll. ii.

62. Adam.] Adam (coming forward) Coll. Dyce, Sta.

　62. *Maſters*] *Maſter* Ff, Rowe.

　67. *me*] *me up* F_3F_4, Rowe +. *pezant*] *peaſant* F_4.

Shakespeare : ' Go apart, Adam, and thou shalt hear how he will *shake* me up.' [It is evidently the irony in the tone, whatever the word, which inflames Oliver; as Whiter shows, that word may well be 'reverence.'—ED.]

53. **Boy**] COLERIDGE (p. 7): There is a beauty here. The word 'boy' naturally provokes and awakens in Orlando the sense of his manly powers; and with the retort of 'elder brother,' he graſps him with firm hands and makes him feel he is no boy.

54. STAUNTON : The obscurity in this line is at once cleared up by a passage in the original story : ' Though I am *eldest* by birth, yet, never having attempted any deeds of arms, I am *youngest* to perform any martial exploits.' Stung by the sarcastic allu- sion to his *reverence*, Oliver attempts to strike his brother, who seizes him, observing at the same time, ' You are *too young* at this game of manly prowess; in this, I am the elder.' NEIL : This play upon words has more in it than meets the ear. 'Elder' not only means ' one born before another,' but also the name of the plant *Sambucus*, the elder-tree or alder-tree, the *pith* of which is large, light, and little worth. Hence the Host calls Dr Caius contemptuously 'my heart of elder'—*Merry Wives*, II, iii, 3—as equal to 'faint-hearted one.' There was also a tradition ' Judas was hanged on an elder'—(*Love's Lab. L.*, V, ii, 610), and from this it became suggestive of treach- ery and deceit. The phrase therefore signifies, ' My faint-hearted, deceitful first-born brother, you are too young (you give me a title betokening rather fewer years than I have attained to) in this epithet " boy !" ' [The action here is so distinctly set forth that stage directions, and some editors have inserted them, are wholly superfluous, if not intrusive.—ED.]

55. **villaine**] JOHNSON : This word is used by Oliver in its present meaning for a worthless, wicked, or bloody man; by Orlando in its original signification, for a fellow of base extraction.

67, 68. **obscuring . . . qualities**] ALLEN (MS) : ' Qualities ' is equivalent to *qual-*

hiding from me all gentleman-like qualities : the fpirit 68
of my father growes ftrong in mee, and I will no longer
endure it : therefore allow me fuch exercifes as may be- 70
come a gentleman , or giue mee the poore allottery my
father left me by teftament, with that I will goe buy my
fortunes.

Oli. And what wilt thou do ? beg when that is fpent?
Well fir , get you in . I will not long be troubled with 75
you : you fhall haue fome part of your will , I pray you
leaue me.

Orl. I will no further offend you , then becomes mee
for my good.

Oli. Get you with him, you olde dogge. 80

Adam. Is old dogge my reward : moft true , I haue
loft my teeth in your feruice : God be with my olde mafter, he would not haue fpoke fuch a word. *Ex. Orl. Ad.*

Oli. Is it euen fo, begin you to grow vpon me ? I will 84

68. *from me*] *me from* Pope, Han.   iii.
74. *do ? beg*] *do—beg ?—* Dyce iii.   83. Scene III. Pope+.
79. *good.*] *good.* (releasing him) Coll.   84. *fo,*] *so ?* Rowe.

ifications. Perhaps : obscuring (ἀφανίζων) [*in* me] my own gentlemanlike qualities, and hiding *from* me those, which I might see and imitate, from *without* (*i. e.* in the persons of others). Cf. *1 Hen. VI :* V, i, 22, 'You have suborn'd this man Of purpose to obscure my noble birth.' *Hen. V :* I, i, 63, 'And so the Prince obscured his contemplation Under the veil of wildness.'

74, 75. **thou . . . you**] Throughout this quarrel between the brothers, and through-out the subsequent conference between Oliver and Charles, it is worth while to observe, and to appreciate if we can, the use of 'thou' and 'you,' which appears, at first sight, to be almost indiscriminate. Skeat's admirable and general rule, given in his *Preface* to *William of Palerne*, p. xlii, and cited in this edition at *Oth.* II, ii, 275, and at *Mer. of Ven.* I, ii, 35, should be borne in mind : '*Thou* is the language of a lord to a servant, of an equal to an equal, and expresses also companionship, love, permission, defiance, scorn, threatening; whilst *ye* is the language of a servant to a lord, and of compliment, and further expresses honour, submission, entreaty.' Abbott, § 235, says that in almost all cases some change of thought or some influence of euphony may be detected which will prove sufficient to account for a change of pronoun; and further-more (§ 232), when the appellative 'sir' is used even in anger, *thou* generally gives place to *you*. It is well worth while to ponder the varying shades of emotion thus indicated here.—ED.

76. **will**] Is there not a contemptuous emphasis on this word, which may bear a double meaning, in its reference to their father's Will which Orlando had invoked ? In a modern text, I think, it might well be printed with quotation-marks.—ED.

84. **grow**] COLLIER (ed. i) : This is probably right, in reference to the 'rankness' mentioned in the next line; but it has been suggested to me, that possibly Shakespeare

phyſicke your ranckeneſſe, and yet giue no thouſand   85
crownes neyther : holla *Dennis.*

Enter Dennis.

   Den.   Calls your worſhip *?*

   Oli.   Was not *Charles* the Dukes Wraſtler heere to
ſpeake with me ?   90

   Den.   So pleaſe you, he is heere at the doore, and im-
portunes acceſſe to you.

   Oli.   Call him in : 'twill be a good way : and to morrow the wraſtling is.

Enter Charles.   95

   Cha.   Good morrow to your worſhip.

   Oli.   Good Mounſier *Charles* : what's the new newes
at the new Court ?   98

---

89. *Wraſtler*] *Wraſtle* F₄.   *Wrestler*   93. Exit Dennis. Johns. et seq.
Rowe.

---

wrote, ' *growl* upon me,' following up the simile of the ' old dog,' which Oliver had just
applied to Adam.   [It is scarcely worth while to do more than to record this emendation, which Halliwell has adequately estimated by remarking that *growl* would refer
to Adam, whereas this speech clearly refers to Orlando. WRIGHT interprets ' grow
upon ' by *encroach,* and cites *Jul. Cæs.* II, i, 107 : ' Here, as I point my sword, the
sun arises, Which is a great way growing on the south.' HALLIWELL paraphrases :
' to increase in disobedience to my authority.' I think it means simply that Oliver is
beginning to find out that Orlando is growing too big on his hands to be treated any
longer like a boy. NEIL, however, asserts that ' grow ' is ' a provincialism for swell,
become sulky, murmur, repine.'—ED.]

   85. **ranckenesse**] WRIGHT : Luxuriant growth, exuberance ; hence, insolence.

   89. **Wrastler**] The pronunciation, as indicated by this spelling, is still general
among the common people in this country, as will at once occur to all who have read
—and who has not ?—Bret Harte's ' Luck of Roaring Camp.'—ED.

   97. **Good**] In one of Walker's excellent articles, which he rather infelicitously
names ' Omission by Absorption,' it is suggested (*Crit.* ii, 263) that the text here
should be ' Good *morrow*, monsieur Charles,' &c. I think there can be no doubt of
it. The *morrow*, however, was not ' absorbed,' but omitted altogether ; the compositor's eye was misled by the ' morrow ' directly above in the preceding line.—ED.

   97. **Charles :**] CAPELL (*Notes,* 55) says that the true punctuation here is a note
of admiration, and then ' the force of the speech, duly pronounced, will be : " Ah,
good monsieur Charles ! are you here ?—Well, what's the," &c.'

   98. **new Court**] I mistrust this ' new.' If Oliver was aware that there was a
' new ' court, Charles's information that the old duke had been banished (which fact
had created the ' *new* court ') would have been quite superfluous, and he would
scarcely have referred to this banishment as ' old news.' Moreover, in repeating a
question he who is questioned naturally repeats the very words. Charles's failure, in
the text, to do this when he repeats Oliver's question, not only casts an additional

Charles. There's no newes at the Court Sir, but the
olde newes : that is, the old Duke is banifhed by his yon-   100
ger brother the new Duke, and three or foure louing
Lords haue put themfelues into voluntary exile with
him, whofe lands and reuenues enrich the new Duke,
therefore he giues them good leaue to wander.

Oli. Can you tell if *Rofalind* the Dukes daughter bee   105
banifhed with her Father ?

Cha. O no ; for the Dukes daughter her Cofen fo
loues her, being euer from their Cradles bred together,
that hee would haue followed her exile, or haue died to
ftay behind her ; fhe is at the Court, and no leffe beloued   110
of her Vncle, then his owne daughter, and neuer two Ladies loued as they doe.

Oli. Where will the old Duke liue ?

Cha. They fay hee is already in the Forreft of *Arden*,   114

---

102. *into*] *into a* F_3F_4, Rowe.
103. *reuenues*] *vevenues* F_4.
105. *Dukes*] *old Duke's* Han. Johns.
Coll. iii.

107. *Dukes*] *new Duke's* Han. Warb.
Johns. Cap. Coll. iii.
109. *hee*] *he* F_2. *fhe* F_3F_4 et seq.
her] *their* F_3F_4, Rowe.

---

suspicion on 'new,' as I think, but also suggested to Lettsom (ap. Dyce, ed. iii) to
ask : ' Ought we not to read, There's no *new* news, &c. ?'—ED.

105, 107. **Dukes**] Hanmer's emendation (see Text. Notes), which is also found
in Collier's (MS), met with Johnson's approval as ' necessary to the perspicuity of the
dialogue,' and Dyce also considered it ' highly probable that Shakespeare so wrote.'
But in Malone's opinion the change is ' unnecessary; the ambiguous use of the word
" duke " in these passages is much in Shakespeare's manner.' Heath, also, disapproved of the change, ' which could proceed only from an itch of emendation. The
words which follow, " her cousin," sufficiently distinguish the person intended.' Unquestionably, Hanmer's emendation makes the passage clearer, but, I think, any editor now-a-days would be ' temerarious ' who should adopt it.—ED.

109. **hee**] A misprint easily detected.

109, 110. **to stay**] That is, in staying behind her. See II, vii, 182; III, v, 66;
V, ii, 103; also, for this indefinite use of the infinitive, ABBOTT, § 356, and Shakespeare *passim.*

114. **Forrest of Arden**] MALONE: *Ardenne* is a forest of considerable extent in
French Flanders, lying near the Meuse and between Charlemont and Rocroy. It is
mentioned by Spenser in his *Astrophel* [1596, line 93, ed. Grosart] : ' Into a forest
wide, and waste he came Where store he heard to be of saluage pray. So wide a
forest and so waste as this, Nor famous *Ardeyn*, nor fowle *Arlo* is.' But our author
was furnished with the scene of his play by Lodge's Novel. [The foregoing passage
from Spenser, Malone cited as from *Colin Clouts Come home againe.* The citations
by the earlier editors have to be so frequently corrected that I never think it worth
while to call attention to the trifling and venial misprints, which nevertheless do seem

[114. Forrest of Arden]

to have a mission when, as in the present case, they mislead subsequent editors, who, having 'conveyed' without acknowledgement the learning of their predecessors, stand betrayed by the adoption of errors.   In the present instance there is abundant excuse for Malone.   The running title of *Astrophel* is, as Grosart has pointed out, through a printer's error, *Colin Clouts Come home againe.*—ED.]   KNIGHT: Nothing can more truly show how immeasurably superior was the art of Shakespeare to the art of other poets than the comparison of Lodge's description [see Appendix] with the incidental scene-painting of *his* forest of Arden.   It has been truly and beautifully said (*Edin. Rev.* vol. xxviii) of Shakespeare: 'All his excellences, like those of Nature herself, are thrown out together, and, instead of interfering, support and recommend each other.   His flowers are not tied up in garlands, nor his fruits crushed into baskets, but spring living from the soil, in all the dew and freshness of youth.'   But there are critics of another cast, who object to Shakespeare's forest of Arden, situated, as they hold, 'between the rivers Meuse and Moselle.'   They maintain that its geographical position ought to have been known by Shakespeare, and that he is consequently most vehemently to be reprehended for imagining that a palm-tree could flourish, and a lioness be starving, in French Flanders.   We most heartily wish that the critics would allow poetry to have its own geography.   We do *not* want to know that Bohemia has no sea-board; we do *not* wish to have the island of Sycorax defined on the map; we do *not* require that our forest of Arden should be the *Arduenna Sylva* of Cæsar and Tacitus, and that its rocks should be 'clay-slate, grauwacke-slate, grauwacke, con-glomerate, quartz-rock and quartzose sandstone.'   We are quite sure that Ariosto was thinking nothing of French Flanders when he described how 'two fountaines grew, Like in the tast, but in effects unlike, *Plac'd in Ardenna*, each in other's vew: Who tasts the one, love's dart his heart doth strike; Contrary of the other doth ensew, Who drinke thereof, their lovers shall mislike' [i, st. 78, ed. 1634].   We are equally sure that Shakespeare *meant* to take his forest out of the region of the literal when he assigned to it a palm-tree and a lioness.   Lady Morgan tells us, 'The forest of Ardennes smells of early English poetry.   It has all the greenwood freshness of Shakespeare's scenes; and it is scarcely possible to feel the truth and beauty of his exquisite *As You Like It* without having loitered, as I have done, amidst its tangled glens and mag-nificent depths.'   We must venture to think it was not necessary for Shakespeare to visit Ardennes to have described 'An old oak, whose boughs were moss'd with age, And high top bald with dry antiquity;' and that, although his own Warwickshire Arden is now populous, and we no longer meet there 'a desert inaccessible,' there are fifty places in England where, with the *As You Like It* in hand, one might linger 'from noon to dewy eve,' and say, 'Ay, now am I in Arden.'   FRANÇOIS-VICTOR HUGO (p. 54): Apercevez-vous au bout de cette clairière cette forêt profonde dont l'automne dore les cimes mélancoliques?   C'est la forêt des Ardennes!   Mais ne vous y trompez pas, ce n'est pas la forêt historique à travers laquelle la Meuse conduit à la dérive le touriste charmé.   Vous ne trouverez dans ces halliers ni le manoir d'Herbeumont, ni le château-fort de Bouillon, ni la grotte de Saint-Remacle.   La forêt où nous transporte le poëte n'a pas d'itinéraire connu; aucune carte routière n'en fait mention, aucun géographe ne l'a défrichée.—C'est la forêt vierge de la Muse. Elle rassemble dans sa pépinière unique toutes les végétations connues: le sapin du Nord s'y croise avec le pin du Midi, le chêne y coudoie le cèdre, le houx s'y accli-mate à l'ombre du palmier.   Dans ses taillis antédiluviens l'Arche a vidé toute sa ménagerie; le serpent de l'Inde rampe dans les hautes herbes qu'effloure le daim

[114. Forrest of Arden]

effaré ; le rugissement de la lionne y fait envoler un essaim de cerfs.—Là la guerre et la vanité humaines n'ont jamais été admises à bâtir leurs demeures : là, ni palais ni forteresses. Tout au plus, sur la lisière du bois, quelque humble toit de chaume. [HALLIWELL notes Drayton's reference, in his Fifty-third *Idea*, to ' Where nightingales in Arden sit and sing, Amidst the dainty dew-impearlèd flowers,' and ' to " the rough woodlands " of Arden described in Poly-Olbion.' But this description in *Poly-Olbion* seems to me far more noteworthy than is the bare mention of the name as it occurs in the *Idea ;* the mere name Arden is to be found in other *Ideas* as well as in the Fifty-third. The first hundred and fifty lines, more or less, of the *Thirteenth Song of Poly-Olbion* are devoted to a description of the Forest of Arden in Warwickshire, and on this description Drayton dwells with especial affection, apostrophising Warwickshire as his own ' native country which so brave spirits hast bred.' Is this a gentle nod of recognition to Shakespeare ? The Song then goes on to say that of all the forests in Britain, this is the greatest, and that ' We equally partake with wood-land as with plain, Alike with hill and dale ; and every day maintain The sundry kinds of beasts upon our copious wastes That men for profit breed, as well as those of chase.' Here all birds are to be found, the ' throstel, with shrill sharps,' ' the nightingale hard by,' ' the woosel near at hand, that hath a golden bill ;' and here also are ' both sorts of season'd deer ; Here walk the stately red, the freckled fallow there : The bucks and lusty stags amongst the rascals strew'd, As sometimes gallant spirits amongst the multitude.' A hunt is then described, horns are sounded and the hunters cheer, and ' being then imbost, the noble stately deer When he hath gotten ground (the kennel cast arrear) Doth beat the brooks and ponds for sweet refreshing soil,' until at last, ' opprest by force, He who the mourner is to his own dying corse, Upon the ruthless earth his precious tears lets fall.' But this is not all, everything which sorts with solitude is to be found here. The hermit here ' leads a sweet retired life,' ' From the lothsome airs of smoky-citied towns.' ' Suppose twixt noon and night, the sun his halfway wrought,' ' the hermit comes out of his homely cell,' ' Who in the strength of youth, a man at arms hath been ; Or one who of this world, the vileness having seen, Retires him from it quite ; and with a constant mind Man's beastliness so loaths, that, flying human kind, The black and darksome nights, the bright and gladsome days, Indifferent are to him.' ' This man, that is alone a king in his desire, By no proud ignorant lord is basely over-aw'd ;' ' nor of a pin he weighs What fools, abused kings, and humorous ladies raise.' ' Nor stirs it him to think on the imposter vile, Who seeming what he's not, doth sensually beguile The sottish purblind world ; but, absolutely free, His happy time he spends the works of God to see.' I have given these extracts from Drayton, to which I am not aware that attention has ever been called, not only to show the deep impression on him which his friend Shakespeare's *As You Like It* had made, so that we seem to hear the very echo of the words of Jaques and of the Duke, but to show that to Drayton as well as to every listener at the play the ' Forest of Arden ' was no forest in far-away France, but was the enchanted ground of their own home. That Shakespeare intended it to be so regarded, and meant to keep his audience at home, no matter in what foreign country soever the scene be laid, may be detected, I think, in the allusion to ' Robin Hood,' a name around which clustered all the romance of forest life. Let that name be once uttered as a key-note, and every charm of a life under the greenwood tree, be it in the forest of Sherwood or of Arden, is summoned up and the spell of the mighty magician begins.—ED.]

and a many merry men with him ; and there they liue   115
like the old *Robin Hood* of *England* : they fay many yong
Gentlemen flocke to him euery day , and fleet the time
carelefly as they did in the golden world.

Oli. What , you wraftle to morrow before the new
Duke.   120

Cha. Marry doe I fir : and I came to acquaint you
with a matter : I am giuen fir fecretly to vnderftand, that
your yonger brother *Orlando* hath a difpofition to come
in difguis'd againft mee to try a fall : to morrow fir I
wraftle for my credit , and hee that efcapes me without   125
fome broken limbe, fhall acquit him well : your brother
is but young and tender, and for your loue I would bee
loth to foyle him, as I muft for my owne honour if hee   128

---

121. *came*] *come* F₄, Rowe, Pope, Han.

115. **a many**] For many other instances of the insertion of *a* before numeral adjectives, see ABBOTT, § 87.

115, 116. **and there . . . England**] Schmidt, in his admirable revision of Schlegel's translation, thus translates this sentence : ' und da leben sie wie Zigeuner-volk.'   Few examples could better illustrate than this how emphatically, how in-eradicably, Shakespeare belongs to England, and how impossible it is to transplant him to any foreign soil.   Surely never a foreigner lived who better mastered the lan-guage of Shakespeare than he to whom we all owe gratitude for the *Shakespeare-Lexicon*, and yet on his ears the name Robin Hood falls with a dull, unmeaning sound; and all that band of merry men, who ' in summer-time when leaves grow green, And flowers are fresh and gay,' with Will Scarlet and Little John fleeted the time carelessly,—all this band, the gods of every English-speaking boy's idolatry and summed up in the one name Robin Hood, is to the learned German merely ' a band of gypsies.'—ED.

117. **fleet**] WRIGHT notes this as ' an instance of Shakespeare's habit of forming verbs from adjectives,' and ROLFE says that it is only here used transitively by Shake-speare, though as ' an intransitive verb it occurs often.'   [Way (*Prompt. Parv.* s. v. *Fletyn*) cites Harrison, who in his *Description of England*, says ' the Lime water . . . . which commeth . . . . from the hils, fleting upon rockie soil, ... so falleth into the sea.'—*Holinsh. Chron.* i, 58.   Halliwell says that a vessel is said to fleet when the tide flows sufficiently to enable her to move.   Is it too fanciful to suppose that in the use of this word in this particular passage, where a gay, careless, happy life flows on from hour to hour without a ripple of annoyance, there was in Shakespeare's mind a dim association between this word to *fleet*, and the meaning to *float*, to *flow ?*—ED.]

122. **a matter**] For other instances where ' a ' is used for ' a certain ' see Abbott, § 81.

126. **shall**] ABBOTT, § 315 : That is, must, will have to.   WRIGHT refers to V, i, 14.   [See also II, iv, 92.]

come in : therefore out of my loue to you, I came hither
to acquaint you withall, that either you might ftay him   130
from his intendment, or brooke fuch difgrace well as he
fhall runne into , in that it is a thing of his owne fearch,
and altogether againft my will.

    Oli.   *Charles*, I thanke thee for thy loue to me, which
thou fhalt finde I will moft kindly requite : I had my   135
felfe notice of my Brothers purpofe heerein, and haue by
vnder-hand meanes laboured to diffwade him from it ;
but he is refolute. Ile tell thee *Charles*, it is the ftubbor-
neft yong fellow of France, full of ambition, an enuious
emulator of euery mans good parts, a fecret & villanous   140
contriuer againft mee his naturall brother : therefore vfe
thy difcretion, I had as liefe thou didft breake his necke
as his finger. And thou wert beft looke to't ; for if thou
doft him any flight difgrace, or if hee doe not mightilie
grace himfelfe on thee, hee will practife againft thee by   145
poyfon, entrap thee by fome treacherous deuife, and neuer leaue thee till he hath tane thy life by fome indirect
meanes or other : for I affure thee, (and almoft with
teares I fpeake it) there is not one fo young, and fo villanous this day liuing. I fpeake but brotherly of him,   150

---

137. *him*] *them* F$_4$.   146. *entrap*] *to entrap* F$_3$F$_4$, Rowe.
138. *Ile*] *I* F$_3$F$_4$, Rowe+.   150. *liuing.*] *living*, Var. '21.

---

130. withall] ABBOTT, § 196: Sometimes *this* is understood after 'withal,' so that
it means *with all this*, and is used adverbially : 'So glad of this as they, I cannot be,
Who are surprised withal'—*Temp.* III, i, 93, *i. e.* surprised with, or at, this. Here,
however, perhaps, and elsewhere certainly, *with* means *in addition to*, and '*with*-all
(this)' means *besides ;* as in, 'I must have liberty withal,' II, vii, 51 [of this present
play, and also in 'Marry, do, to make sport withal,' in I, ii, 26.] But [in the present
line] there is no meaning of *besides* and 'withal' means *therewith, with it.*

138. Ile tell thee] The same phrase occurs in IV, i, 206; and Lettsom questions
if it be not here a blunder for *I tell thee.* DYCE : It is not a blunder.

138. it is] The use of this impersonal phrase may be as various as the mood of
man. Here, as WRIGHT points out, its import is contemptuous. In 'It is a pretty
youth,' III, v, 118, there is a touch of coquettish familiarity.—ED.

141. naturall] HALLIWELL : This term did not formerly, as now, imply illegiti-
macy. '*Filius naturalis*, a natural or lawfully-begotten son.'—*Nomenclator*, 1585.

142. breake his necke] See the Tale of Gamelyn, in Appendix.

143. thou wert best] See ABBOTT, § 230, for this and other 'ungrammatical remnants of ancient usage.'

145. practise] DYCE : To use arts or stratagems, to plot.

but fhould I anathomize him to thee, as hee is, I muft   151
blufh, and weepe, and thou muft looke pale and
wonder.

   Cha.   I am heartily glad I came hither to you : if hee
come to morrow, Ile giue him his payment : if euer hee   155
goe alone againe, Ile neuer wraftle for prize more : and
fo God keepe your worfhip.   *Exit.*

   Farewell good *Charles.*   Now will I ftirre this Game-
fter : I hope I fhall fee an end of him ; for my foule (yet
I know not why) hates nothing more then he : yet hee's   160
gentle, neuer fchool'd, and yet learned, full of noble

---

151. *anathomize*] *anatomize* F₃F₄.   158. *Farewell*] Oli.   *Farewell* Ff et
   157. Exit. Rowe. After Charles, line   seq.
158, Cap. Dyce, Cam. Wh. ii.   160. *he*] *him* Han. Johns.

---

   153. **wonder**] MACDONALD (p. 126): If any one wishes to see what variety of
the same kind of thoughts Shakespeare could produce, let him examine the treatment
of the same business in different plays; as, for instance, the way in which the insti-
gation to a crime is managed in *Macbeth*, where Macbeth tempts the two murderers
to kill Banquo; in *King John*, where the King tempts Hubert to kill Arthur; in *The
Tempest*, where Antonio tempts Sebastian to kill Alonzo; [the present passage cited]
and in *Hamlet*, where Claudius urges Laertes to the murder of Hamlet.

   158 et seq. COLERIDGE (p. 107): This has always seemed to me one of the most
un-Shakespearian speeches in all the genuine works of our poet; yet I should be
nothing surprised, and greatly pleased, to find it hereafter a fresh beauty, as has so
often happened to me with other supposed defects of great men.—1810.

   It is too venturous to charge a passage in Shakespeare with want of truth to Nature;
and yet at first sight this speech of Oliver's expresses truths which it seems almost
impossible that any mind should so distinctly, so livelily, and so voluntarily have presented to itself, in connection with feelings and intentions so malignant, and so contrary to those which the qualities expressed would naturally have called forth.   But I
dare not say that this seeming unnaturalness is not in the nature of an abused wilfulness, when united with a strong intellect.   In such characters there is sometimes a
gloomy self-gratification in making the absoluteness of the will (*sit pro ratione volun-
tas!*) evident to themselves by setting the reason and the conscience in full array
against it.—1818.

   158. Gamester] STEEVENS: In the present instance and in some others, this does
not mean a man viciously addicted to games of chance, but a frolicsome person.   [The
meaning is probably more specific here, and Caldecott is nearer right in defining it as
'disposed to try his fortune at this *game*.'   In the story of *Faustina the Empresse* in
Painter's *Palace of Pleasure*, gladiators are said to be 'a certaine sort of gamsters in
Rome, which we terme to bee maisters of defence,' ii, p. 104, ed. Haslewood.—ED.]

   160. then he] See ABBOTT, § 206 et seq. for other instances of 'he' used for
him; 'she' for *her;* 'thee' for *thou,* &c.   And also I, ii, 17, 266.

   161. gentle] Cf. 'gentle condition of blood,' *supra.*

   161, 162. noble deuise] WRIGHT: That is, of noble conceptions and aims.   In

deuife, of all forts enchantingly beloued, and indeed   162
fo much in the heart of the world, and efpecially of my
owne people, who beft know him, that I am altogether
mifprifed : but it fhall not be fo long, this wraftler fhall   165
cleare all : nothing remaines, but that I kindle the boy
thither, which now Ile goe about.   *Exit.*

Scœna Secunda.

Enter Rofalind, and Cellia.

Cel.   I pray thee *Rofalind,* fweet my Coz, be merry.   2

Scœna Secunda.] Scene IV. Pope+.   before the Dukes Palace. Cap.
  The Dukes Palace. Rowe. Open walk   1, 3. Cellia] Celia Ff.
before the Dukes Palace. Theob. Lawn   2. *my Coz*] *Coz* Pope, Han.

a copy of F_4, which formerly belonged to Steevens, he has marked these lines as
descriptive of Shakespeare himself.

162. sorts] RITSON: In this place it means ranks and degrees of men.

162. enchantingly] CALDECOTT: That is, to a degree that could only be the
supposed effect of a spell or *incantation*. WALKER (*Crit.* ii, 88) compares for the
thought : 'such a holy witch That he enchants societies unto him; Half all men's
hearts are his,' *Cymb.* I, vi, 166.

165. misprised] WRIGHT: Cotgrave gives 'Mespriser. To disesteeme, contemne,
disdaine, despise, neglect, make light of, set nought by.'

166. kindle] STEEVENS: Cf. *Macb.* I, iii, 121, 'enkindle you unto the crown.'
NARES: To inflame, and thence to incite, to stimulate; that is, to inflame the mind.

1. Rosalind] MRS JAMESON (ii, 143): It is easy to seize on the prominent features
in the mind of Beatrice, but extremely difficult to catch and fix the more fanciful
graces of Rosalind. She is like a compound of essences, so volatile in their nature,
and so exquisitely blended, that on any attempt to analyze them, they seem to escape
us. To what else shall we compare her, all-enchanting as she is ?—to the silvery
summer clouds, which, even while we gaze on them, shift their hues and forms, dissolving into air, and light, and rainbow showers ?—to the May-morning, flush with
opening blossoms and the roseate dews, and 'charm of earliest birds' ?—to some wild
and beautiful melody, such as some shepherd-boy might pipe to 'Amarillis in the
shade' ?—to a mountain streamlet, now smooth as a mirror, in which the skies may
glass themselves, and anon leaping and sparkling in the sunshine—or rather to the
very sunshine itself? for so her genial spirit touches into life and beauty whatever it
shines on! BLACKWOOD'S MAGAZINE (April, 1833, p. 547. *Qu.* Thomas Campbell ?): But lo! One more delightful, more alluring, more fascinating, more enchanting, more captivating than Beatrice! In pure nature and sweet simplicity, more
delightful is Rosalind; in courteous coquetry and quaint disguise, more alluring is
Rosalind; in feeling, playing with fancy, and in fancy by feeling tempered, (ah! shall

Rof.   Deere *Cellia*; I fhow more mirth then I am mi-   3
ftreffe of, and would you yet were merrier : vnleffe you
could teach me to forget a banifhed father, you muft not   5
learne mee how to remember any extraordinary pleafure.

Cel.   Heerein I fee thou lou'ft mee not with the full
waight that I loue thee; if my Vncle thy banifhed father
had banifhed thy Vncle the Duke my Father, fo thou   10
hadft beene ftill with mee, I could haue taught my loue
to take thy father for mine ; fo wouldft thou, if the truth   12

---

4. *were*] *I were* Rowe ii et seq.   6. *any*] *my* F_3F_4, Rowe i.

---

we call her serpent?) more fascinating is Rosalind; in sinless spells and gracious glamoury, (what a witch!) more enchanting is Rosalind; and when to 'still musick' 'enters Hymen, leading her in woman's cloathes' and singing 'Then is there mirth in Heaven, When earthly things made even Atone together,' feelest thou not that more captivating is Rosalind—a snow-white lily with a wimple of dew, in bride-like joyance flowering in the forest!   LADY MARTIN (p. 409): What the courtly Le Beau had so plainly seen to be the state of the Duke's mind was not likely to have escaped Rosalind's quick, sensitive nature.   She feels the cloud of her uncle's displeasure hanging over her and ready to burst at any moment.   She will not pain Celia with her forebodings, who is so far from surmising the truth that these first lines she speaks are a gentle reproach to Rosalind for her want of gayety. . . . . It is obvious that Celia has no idea that Rosalind has fallen out of favour with the usurping Duke. . . . . Rosalind will hide from Celia the trouble she sees looming for herself in the not far distance.

   4. **and would you yet were merrier**] JOURDAIN (*Philol. Soc. Trans.* 1860-1, p. 143) proposes to allot these words to Celia, with an interrogation-mark after them. Although we can thus retain the text of the Folio and reject Rowe's emendation of '*I* were,' yet it is at the cost of an even greater change, without any corresponding improvement of the sense, as far as I can see.   COLLIER suggests that the original text might be intelligible if we suppose Rosalind to express a wish that Celia were yet even merrier than she appeared to be, an explanation which HALLIWELL says obscures the chief point of Rosalind's speech.   ALLEN thus paraphrases the text with Rowe's emendation: '"the mirth which I already *show* is more than I *really feel;* and do you *still* (nevertheless) insist I shall be merrier?"   Cf. for the transposition of "yet" line 165 *post:* "I come but in" for "I but come in."'   Rowe's emendation seems absolutely necessary.—ED.

   6. **learne**] This use of 'learn' for *teach* (see Abbott, § 291) is still common throughout New England.   WORDSWORTH calls attention to its use in the Prayer-Book version of Ps. xxv, 2: 'Lead me forth in thy truth, and learn me.'

   10. **so**] ABBOTT, § 133: *So* is used with the future, and the subjunctive to denote *provided that*.   The full construction is 'be it (if it be) *so* that.'   'Be it' is inserted in 'Be it so (that) she will not,' *Mid. N. D.* I, i, 39.

   12. **so wouldst thou**] ALLEN (MS): That is, 'so wouldst thou [have taught *thy* love to take *my* father for thine].'   We should *now* be obliged to write the *vice versâ* out in full.

of thy loue to me were fo righteoufly temper'd, as mine   13
is to thee.

Rof. Well, I will forget the condition of my eftate,   15
to reioyce in yours.

Cel. You know my Father hath no childe, but I, nor
none is like to haue; and truely when he dies, thou fhalt
be his heire; for what hee hath taken away from thy father perforce , I will render thee againe in affe&tion : by   20
mine honor I will, and when I breake that oath, let mee
turne monfter:therefore my fweet *Rofe*, my deare *Rofe*,
be merry.

Rof. From henceforth I will Coz, and deuife fports:
let me fee, what thinke you of falling in Loue?   25

Cel. Marry I prethee doe, to make fport withall: but
loue no man in good earneft, nor no further in fport neyther, then with fafety of a pure blufh, thou maift in honor come off againe.

Rof. What fhall be our fport then?   30

Cel. Let vs fit and mocke the good houfwife *For-*

---

17. *but I*] *but me* Han.   19. *heire;*] *heire?* Ff.

---

13. **so . . . as**] For other examples of *so* before *as*, which are not very common in
Shakespeare, see Abbott, § 275.

17. **but I**] See I, i, 160; and line 266 *post.*

17, 18. **nor none**] For double negatives, see Abbott, § 406, and Shakespeare *passim.*

25. See Lodge's *Rosalynde*, Appendix.

26. **withall**] See I, i, 130.

28. **pure blush**] WRIGHT: A blush that has no shame in it. ALLEN paraphrases :
thou may'st come off in (the possession of thy) *honor*, having *saved* (preserved) a
pure blush.

31. **mocke . . . wheele**] JOHNSON: The wheel of Fortune is not the *wheel* of a
housewife. Shakespeare has confounded Fortune, whose wheel only figures uncertainty and vicissitude, with the Destiny that spins the thread of life, though not indeed
with a wheel. [This is one of Dr Johnson's unhappy notes which must be offset by
a hundred happy ones. There was no confusion in Shakespeare's mind here nor anywhere else; he knew the symbolism in the wheel of Fortune quite as well as Dr
Johnson. Fluellen in *Henry V:* III, vi, 35 (as Wright points out) explains to Pistol
that ' Fortune is painted with a wheel, to signify to you, which is the moral of it, that
she is turning, and inconstant, and mutability, and variation.' HARNESS, whose original notes though few are good, well says: '*Good housewife* seems applied to Fortune merely as a jesting appellation, without any reference to the wheel on which she
stood. The wheel of Fortune was an emblem of her mutability, from which Celia
and Rosalind proposed to drive her by their wit, that she might ever after cease to be
inconstant.'—ED.]

tune from her wheele, that her gifts may henceforth bee   32
beftowed equally.

Rof. I would wee could doe fo : for her benefits are
mightily mifplaced, and the bountifull blinde woman   35
doth moft miftake in her gifts to women.

Cel. 'Tis true, for thofe that fhe makes faire, fhe fcarce
makes honeft, & thofe that fhe makes honeft, fhe makes
very illfauouredly.

Rof. Nay now thou goeft from Fortunes office to Na-   40
tures : Fortune reignes in gifts of the world, not in the
lineaments of Nature.

Enter Clowne.

Cel. No ; when Nature hath made a faire creature,   44

37, 38. *thofe...&c*] Om. Rowe i.
39. *illfauouredly*] *ill favouredly* F₂.
ill-favouredly F₃F₄. *ill favoured* Rowe
ii+, Coll. (MS), Dyce iii, Huds.

43. *Enter...*] After line 47, Dyce,
Sta.
43. *Clowne.*] Touchstone Theob. ii.
44. *No ;*] *No!* Theob. *No?* Han.

31. **houswife**] WHITE (ed. ii; note on *Oth.* II, i, 132): In Shakespeare's day,
and in some parts of England still, this word is pronounced *husif*, which has passed
into *hussy*. [The pronunciation *husif* is still quite general, I think, in this country;
and is always given to certain little pocket-books containing needles, thread, thimble,
&c. To call Fortune a *husif* is jocular, but to call her a *hussy* is a little too jocular;
nor do I imagine that White would have counselled that pronunciation here, though
it is appropriate enough in the passage in *Othello.*—ED.]

35. **blinde woman**] From many instances where rhythm obliges us to pronounce
as one word with the accent on the first syllable, such words as *wise man*, *true man*,
long man, &c., WALKER (*Crit.* ii, 139) suggests that these words be printed and pronounced *blíndwoman*.

38. **honest**] STAUNTON: That is, chaste. [See III, iii, 15, and V, iii, 5.]

39. **illfauouredly**] CAPELL (i, 55): Alter'd by the four latter moderns [*i. e.* Pope,
Theobald, Hanmer, Warburton] into *ill-favoured;* in order, as may be suppos'd, to
make the antithesis the rounder. But how if that roundness was dislik'd by the Poet,
as thinking it destructive of the ease of his dialogue? yet this he might think, and
with great reason. COLLIER (ed. ii): Strictly speaking, Fortune does not make the
honest 'ill-favouredly,' but ill-*favoured;* and the adverbial termination is erased in
the (MS).

40–42. MOBERLY: Shakespeare constantly harps on the motive powers of human
action; nature, destiny, chance, art, custom. In this place he playfully distinguishes
nature from chance; in *Wint. Tale*, IV, iii, he argues that the resources of art are
themselves gifts of nature : ' Nature is made better by no mean, But nature makes
that mean.' In *Macb.* I, iii, he shows that destiny can work itself without our help
(' if chance will have me king, why chance may crown me '), and in *Ham.* III, iv,
161, he splendidly exhibits the force of custom in ' almost changing the stamp of
nature.'

may fhe not by Fortune fall into the fire? though nature   45
hath giuen vs wit to flout at Fortune, hath not Fortune
fent in this foole to cut off the argument?

Rof. Indeed there is fortune too hard for nature, when
fortune makes natures naturall, the cutter off of natures
witte.
                                                                50
Cel. Peraduenture this is not Fortunes work neither,
but Natures, who perceiueth our naturall wits too dull
to reafon of fuch goddeffes, hath fent this Naturall for   53

47. *the*] *this* F₃F₄, Rowe+.   Cap. Steev. Knt, Coll. Sing. Wh. i, Sta.
48. *there is fortune*] *Fortune is there* Ktly, Rlfe, Dyce iii.
F₃F₄, Rowe i, Sing. *then is Fortune*   53. *hath*] *and hath* Mal. Dyce i, Cam.
Dyce iii, Huds.   Wh. ii.
52. *perceiueth*] *perceiving* Ff, Rowe+,

43. **Clowne**] DOUCE (i, 309): Touchstone is the domestic fool of Frederick, the
Duke's brother, and belongs to the class of witty or allowed fools. He is threatened
with the whip, a mode of chastisement which was often inflicted on this motley personage. His dress should be a party-coloured garment. He should occasioₙally
carry a bauble in his hand, and wear asses' ears to his hood, which is probably the
head-dress intended by Shakespeare, there being no allusion whatever to a cock's
head or comb. The three-cornered hat which Touchstone is made to wear on the
modern stage is an innovation, and totally unconnected with the genuine costume of
the domestic fool. [See Appendix, p. 309, 'Source of the Plot.']

44. **No;**] It is not easy to reject Hanmer's interrogation-point, which, indeed, has
been generally adopted. MOBERLY gives this good paraphrase of the whole speech:
'True that Fortune does not make fair features; but she can mar them by some accident. So Nature makes us able to philosophize, chance spoils our grave philosophy
by sending us a fool.'

52, 53. **perceiueth . . . hath sent**] MALONE suggested, and reads, '*and* hath
sent.' CALDECOTT, who never deserts his Folio, says that 'perceiveth' is equivalent
to 'who, *inasmuch as she* perceiveth.' DYCE in his first edition adopted Malone's
emendation, because, as he said, 'it is more probable that *and* was omitted by the
original compositor than that "perceiveth" should be a misprint for *perceiving;*' and
of Caldecott's defence he remarks that 'the general style of the dialogue is opposed
to the idea of Shakespeare's having intended such an ellipsis here.' But in his last
edition he adopts *perceiving* with the quiet remark that it is a correction of the Second
Folio. Dyce's vacillation, a quality in which he excels, is a proof not of thoughtless-
ness, but of extreme thoughtfulness; it is to be regretted that with it was not joined a
little more openness in confessing it, and a good deal less acrimony in criticising
others. The choice here is so evenly balanced between *perceiving* of F₂ and the *and*
of Malone that we can debate a long while over a very trifling matter. In the end, I
think, however, that the gray authority of the Second Folio should prevail.—ED.

53. **reason of**] That is, talk, discuss concerning. For the use of 'of,' as equivalent to *about, concerning,* see also V, iv, 59; or *Mer. of Ven.* I, iii, 54: 'I am
debating of my present store,' or Abbott, § 174. See also *Mer. of Ven.* II, viii, 30:
'I reason'd with a Frenchman yesterday,' that is, *talked.*

our whetftone. for alwaies the dulneffe of the foole, is
the whetftone of the wits.　How now Witte, whether　　55
wander you?

　　Clow.　Miftreffe, you muft come away to your farher.

　　Cel.　Were you made the meffenger?

　　Clo. No by mine honor, but I was bid to come for you

　　Rof.　Where learned you that oath foole?　　　　　60

　　Clo.　Of a certaine Knight, that fwore by his Honour
they were good Pan-cakes, and fwore by his Honor the
Muftard was naught : Now Ile ftand to it, the Pancakes
were naught, and the Muftard was good, and yet was
not the Knight forfworne.　　　　　　　　　　　　65

---

55. *the wits*] *his wits* Var. '03, Var. '13,　　　55. *whether*] *whither* F$_2$.
Var. '21.　　　　　　　　　　　　　　　　　　62. *Pan-cakes*] *Pancakes* Ff.
　　　Witte] Om. Rowe, Pope, Han.

---

53. **Naturall**] DOUCE (i, 293): Touchstone is here called a 'natural' [*i. e.* an
idiot] merely for the sake of alliteration and a punning jingle of words; for he is
undoubtedly an artificial fool.　[Cf. Touchstone's own use of the word in his conversation with Corin, III, ii, 31, whom he calls 'a *natural* philosopher.'—ED.]

55. **whetstone**] WHALLEY (p. 36): This is a proverbial term, denoting an excitement to lying, or a subject that gave a man the opportunity of breaking a jest upon
another.　And Jonson, alluding to the same when he draws the character of Amor-
phus, says: 'He will lie cheaper than any Beggar, and louder than most clocks; for
which he is right properly accommodated to the *Whetstone*, his page' [*Cynthia's
Revels*, II, i, p. 265, ed. Gifford.　I think Whalley is far afield when he traces any
connection between the present passage and the whetstone which was given at Fairs
as a prize to that clown who told the most impossible and enormous lies.　Why a
whetstone should have been selected as this prize has never yet been discovered.　It
is clear that Celia refers to the ordinary uses of the ordinary stone.　WRIGHT appo-
sitely cites the title of Robert Recorde's Arithmetic, 1557 : 'The Whetstone of Witte.'
—ED.].

55. **the wits**] In the Variorum of 1803 this was changed to '*his* wits.'　As no
reason was given for the change, nor even a reference to it, I am inclined to think
that it is a mere typographical oversight, precisely such a substitution of words as
WALKER (*Crit.* i, 309) conceived to have taken place in the second word 'wits,'
which he suggested should be *wise*, an emendation also proposed by SPEDDING;
DYCE (ed. iii), however, thinks the emendation doubtful, 'because it seems to be at
variance with what Celia says just before, " who, perceiving *our natural wits too dull*,"
&c.'; wherein, I think, all will agree.—ED.

55, 56. **How . . . you?**] STAUNTON: The beginning, probably, of some ancient
ballad.　WRIGHT: 'Wit, whither wilt,' was a proverbial expression.　See IV, i, 160.

65. **forsworn**] BOSWELL: The same joke ['such as it is'—Wright] is found in the
old play of *Damon and Pithias :* 'I have taken a wise oath on him, have I not, trow
ye?　To trust such a false knave upon his honesty?　As he is an honest man (quoth
you?) he may bewray all to the king, And break his oath for this never a whit.'　[ed.

Cel. How proue you that in the great heape of your   66
knowledge?
Rof. I marry, now vnmuzzle your wifedome.
Clo. Stand you both forth now : ftroke your chinnes,
and fweare by your beards that I am a knaue.   70
Cel. By our beards(if we had them)thou art.
Clo. By my knauerie (if I had it) then I were : but if
you fweare by that that is not, you are not forfworn : no
more was this knight fwearing by his Honor, for he neuer had anie ; or if he had, he had fworne it away, before 75
euer he faw thofe Pancakes, or that Muftard.
Cel. Prethee, who is't that thou means't ?
Clo. One that old *Fredericke* your Father loues.   78

68. *your*] *you* F$_2$.   78. Fredericke] *Ferdinand* Cap. conj.
77. *is't*] *is* F$_4$, Rowe +.   Coll. ii.

Dodsley, vol. iv, p. 60]. CALDECOTT: Richard, swearing by his 'George, his garter,
and his crown,' is answered in much the same way by Queen Elizabeth, who says he
swears ' By nothing; for this is no oath,' *Rich. III :* IV, iv, 374.

70. **sweare by your beards**] GREY (i, 163) refers to the oath of the porter 'by
goddes berde' in the *Tale of Gamelyn*, 295.

78. **old Fredericke**] In the last Scene of the last Act we are told that the name
of Celia's father is Frederick, and there would be no difficulty here in Touchstone's
reply were it not that Rosalind speaks as though the name of her father also were
Frederick. As it is impossible that the two brothers should both have the same name,
one of two changes must be made. Either the name Frederick must be changed,
or the answer given to Rosalind in line 79, must be given to Celia. This latter
emendation THEOBALD was the first to propose and to adopt, and it is the simpler
solution of the two. The instances are numerous, filling more than ten pages in
Walker (*Crit.* ii, 177–189), wherein speeches in the Folio are assigned to the wrong
characters; the present is in Walker's list. It is to be noted that it is Celia's question
that Touchstone is answering, and when he says 'your father,' must he not mean
Celia's father? CAPELL did not approve of Theobald's emendation, and preferred to
change the name, but Capell should be always allowed to speak for himself—he stands
solitary in style : ' Two of the Poet's editors [Theob. and Han.] have given this speech
[l. 79] to Celia; assigning for reasons, first—that she is the questionist; that the
answer therefore ought naturally to be address'd to her and reply'd to by her; and
in the next place—that " Frederick " is the name of *her* father. To the first of these
reasons, it may be reply'd, that Celia is effectually answer'd; but the matter of his
answer concerning Rosalind most, the Clown turns himself in speaking to her; to the
second, that " Frederick " is a mistake, either of the Poet's through haste, or of his
compositor's, as we shall endeavour to shew by and by; first observing that the speech
cannot be Celia's, for two very good reasons : we have no cause to think that she
would have been so alert in taking up the Clown for reflecting upon her father; who
(besides) is not the person reflected upon, that person being call'd " *old* Frederick."
Throughout all this play Shakespeare calls his two dukes "*Duke senior*," and "*Duke*

[old Fredericke your Father]

junior" [see II, i, 1], giving no proper name to either of them, except in this place, and in [line 228 of this scene, and in V, iv, 158] : his original makes them both kings, and kings of France; calling the elder, Gerismond; the younger, and the usurping king, Torismond : these names the Poet chose to discard (perhaps, for that he thought them too antiquated), putting " Frederick " instead of the latter; but not instantly hitting upon another that pleas'd him, when he had occasion to mention the former, he put down " Frederick " there too, with intention to alter it afterwards.　There is a name in the Novel, which might (possibly) be that intended for Gerismond; and this the reason why it was taken away from it's owner, Orlando's second brother; and " Jaques " bestow'd upon him for " Fernandine," his name in the novelist; however that may be, it can be no very great licence to put " Fernandine " [into the present line] or *Ferdinand* rather; and get rid of a name by that means, which will be for ever a stumbling-block to all those who read with attention.'　MALONE was evidently impressed with Capell's emendation, but he did not venture to adopt it (Collier was the only editor temerarious enough to do that).　' I suppose,' says Malone, ' some abbreviation was used in the MS for the name of the rightful, or *old* duke, as he is called (perhaps *Fer.* for *Ferdinand*), which the transcriber or printer converted into Frederick.'　He disapproves of giving the next speech to Celia instead of Rosalind, because ' there is too much filial warmth in it for Celia : besides, why should her father be called *old* Frederick ?　It appears from the last scene of the play that this was the name of the *younger* brother.'　Whereunto STEEVENS replies : ' Mr Malone's remark may be just; and yet I think the speech which I have still left in the mouth of Celia exhibits as much tenderness for the fool as respect for her own father.　She stops Touchstone, who might otherwise have proceeded to say what she could not hear without inflicting punishment on the speaker.　" Old " is an unmeaning term of familiarity.　It is still in use, and has no reference to age.'　This last observation in regard to ' old ' DYCE (*Remarks*, p. 61) pronounced ' just.'　CALDECOTT will neither renege Frederick, nor affirm Celia, nor turn his halcyon beak for one instant away from the First Folio.　' The Clown,' he urges, ' might turn towards Rosalind, though addressed by Celia; or might speak inaccurately; neither would it be out of character to make him do so.　The answer of Rosalind, at the same time, seems to shew that it was her truly respectable father that was meant.'　COLLIER (ed. i) made a bold suggestion that ' perhaps the name of the knight was Frederick, and the clown's answer ought to run " One old Frederick, that your father loves," which only changes the place of " that." '　This suggestion was not repeated in his next edition, where he upholds and adopts Capell's *Ferdinand* on the score that it ' makes the whole dialogue natural and consistent, and it does no violence to the poet's language merely to introduce a change of name '—a reason which applies with equal force to the change of '*Ros.*' to '*Cel.*'　In Collier's third and last edition Theobald's change is adopted in the text with the following note : ' In the old copies this speech is by mistake given to Rosalind.　Theobald was the first to detect the error, which has not been repeated ' —an oversight for which Collier's venerable age is an ample excuse.　DYCE quotes Caldecott's remark that the clown ' might speak inaccurately,' and affixes two exclamation-marks.　NEIL follows the Folio, and, supposing that Touchstone gives ' a jocular answer addressed first to Celia and then explanatorily to Rosalind,' thus prints line 78 : ' [*To Celia*] One that old Frederick [*to Rosalind*], your father, loves.'　[The many examples collected by Walker of speeches wrongly assigned in the Folio seem to me amply sufficient to justify Theobald's change here.　The error may be due, how-

Rof. My Fathers loue is enough to honor him enough;
fpeake no more of him, you'l be whipt for taxation one   80
of thefe daies.

    Clo. The more pittie that fooles may not fpeak wife-
ly, what Wifemen do foolifhly.

    Cel. By my troth thou faieft true : For, fince the little
wit that fooles haue was filenced, the little foolerie that   85
wife men haue makes a great fhew ; Heere comes Mon-
fieur the *Beu.*

Enter le Beau.

    Rof. With his mouth full of newes.

    Cel. Which he vvill put on vs, as Pigeons feed their   90
young.

---

79. Rof.] Celia. Theob. Han. Johns.
Steev. Knt, Sing. Hal. Wh. Dyce, Sta.
Ktly, Cam. Rlfe, Coll. iii.
    him enough ;] *him :—enough !*
Han. Johns. Steev. Sta. Cam. Wr. Wh.
ii. *him. Enough :* Mal.
    him enough] *him* Gould.

83. *Wifemen*] *Wife men* F_3F_4, Rowe.
86, 87. *Monfieur*] *Mounfieur* Ff.
87. *the* Beu.] Le Beu. Ff.
88. Scene V. Pope+.
    le Beau.] Le Beu. Ff.   After line
93, Dyce, Sta. Cam. Wh. ii.

---

ever, to Shakespeare himself, and be but another proof of that haste in composition
which Wright finds in the play.—ED.]

    79. **honor him enough ;**] This punctuation, which has been followed by a major-
ity of the Editors, COLLIER asserts to be 'in Shakespeare's characteristic manner,'
and adds, I think with truth, that Hanmer's punctuation, as well as Malone's, ' sacrifices the point of the reply.'

    80. **whipt**] DOUCE : This was the discipline usually inflicted on Fools. [See *Lear*,
I, iv, 105, where Lear says to the Fool : 'Take heed, sirrah ; the whip.']

    80. **taxation**] MALONE : That is, censure or satire. See II, vii, 74 and 89.

    83, 86. **Wisemen . . . wise men**] These two forms should be, I think, retained
in a modern text. See V, i, 34.—ED.

    84. **since . . . was silenced**] For other instances of the simple past for the com-
plete present with 'since,' see ABBOTT, § 347.

    85. **silenced**] JOHNSON : Shakespeare probably alludes to the use of Fools or
Jesters, who for some ages had been allowed in all courts an unbridled liberty of censure and mockery, and about this time began to be less tolerated. WRIGHT : Perhaps referring to some recent inhibition of the players. See *Ham.* II, ii, 346. FLEAY
(*Life and Work of Sh.*, p. 208) thinks that this ' alludes probably to the burning of
satirical books by public authority 1st June, 1599,' and holds this allusion to be an
important indication of the date of the play.

    90. **put on vs**] I doubt the need of analysing here the exact meaning of 'put,' or
of citing other passages where it is to be found. Its special meaning is plainly, almost
too plainly, conveyed by Celia's simile, which is distended to its fullest extent by the

Rof. Then fhal we be newes-cram'd.   92

Cel. All the better : we fhalbe the more Marketable.
Boon-iour, Monfieur le Beu, what's the newes?

Le Beu. Faire Princeffe,   95
you haue loft much good fport.

Cel. Sport : of what colour?

Le Beu. What colour Madame?   How fhall I aun-
fwer you?

Rof. As wit and fortune will.   100

Clo. Or as the deftinies decrees.

Cel. Well faid, that was laid on with a trowell.   102

---

94. Boon-iour, Monfieur] Boon-jour
Mounfieur Ff.
 what's the] *what the* F$_2$. *what*
F$_3$F$_4$, Rowe+.

96. *much good*] *much* F$_3$F$_4$, Rowe,
Pope, Han.
98. *Madame*] *Madam* Ff.
101. *decrees*] Ff, Rowe, Cam. *decree*
Pope et cet.

---

suggestion that they 'shall be more marketable,' because the heavier by the operation.
—ED.

96. **good sport**] COLLIER (ed. ii): From what follows this observation we learn
that Le Beau pronounced 'sport' affectedly *spot*, and Celia retorts it upon him in his
own way, '*Spot?* of what colour?' The old corrector of F$_2$ made this change in
order to render a point clear which has hitherto been missed by all Editors. [This
emendation is so specious that apparently it staggered Collier's opponents. Of course
they do not adopt it, but they do not exclaim against it. MOBERLY and NEIL are, I
think, the only avowed converts; nay, Moberly amplifies it, and suggests that 'with
a finicking pronunciation, the next line would end with "answer ye," rhyming to
"decree."' The best answer to Collier is given indirectly by WRIGHT, who shows
that 'colour' is 'used for *kind, nature*, in *Lear*, II, ii, 145: "This is a fellow of the
self-same colour Our sister speaks of:" where the Quartos actually read "nature."'
Apposite as this citation seems and satisfactory as it may appear to us, I am afraid
that Celia's use of the word was neither so satisfactory nor so clear to Le Beau. He
is evidently gravelled by it, and at a loss for a reply. His answer would have been
prompt enough had he at once thus understood the word 'colour.'—ED.]

101. **destinies decrees**] Another of the many instances where a final *s* is interpolated; see I, iii, 60. WRIGHT: It is by no means to be regarded as an example of
the old Northern plural in 's,' which, so far as Shakespeare is concerned, is a figment
of the grammarians.

102. **trowell**] GREY (i, 163): A proverbial expression for a great lie. See Ray's
Proverbs [p. 49, ed. 1817. The first ed. of Ray is dated 1670; it is useless therefore
as an unsupported authority for any phrase of Shakespeare's like this.—ED.]. JOHN-
SON: I suppose the meaning is, that there is too heavy a mass of big words laid upon
a light subject. RITSON: It means a good round hit, thrown in without judgment or
design. M. MASON: To do anything strongly and without delicacy. MOBERLY: Well
rounded off into a jingle; the lines being pronounced 'As wit and fortune will. Or as |
The destinies decree.' [I doubt if this last interpretation will gain many converts.

Clo.   Nay, if I keepe not my ranke.   103

Roſ.   Thou looſeſt thy old ſmell.

Le Beu.   You amaze me Ladies : I would haue told   105
you of good wraſtling, which you haue loſt the ſight of.

Roſ.   Yet tell vs the manner of the Wraſtling.

Le Beu.   I wil tell you the beginning : and if it pleaſe
your Ladiſhips, you may ſee the end, for the beſt is yet
to doe, and heere where you are, they are comming to   110
performe it.

Cel.   Well, the beginning that is dead and buried.

Le Beu.   There comes an old man, and his three ſons.   113

---

103. *ranke.*] *rank*— Rowe et seq.   113. *ſons.*] *sons,*— Theob. et seq.
104. *looſeſt*] *loſeſt* F$_4$.

The phrase carries its own explanation to every man, woman, or child who has ever
watched a mason at work. TIECK (p. 309), premising that the phrase, ' be it proverbial or not, is incomprehensible,' wonders if there be not herein ' a malicious allusion
to Ben Jonson, who, as all the world knew, had been, in his youth, a mason.' It is
to be feared that Gifford would have emptied the printer's case of exclamation-marks
after this suggestion of Tieck's, had he ever seen it.—ED.]

103. **ranke**] CALDECOTT : ' Rank ' is quality or place. The unsavory perversion
of Rosalind's is obvious. So also in *Cym.* II, i, 17. COWDEN-CLARKE : Touchstone
as the professional jester, uses this word ' rank ' to express ' rate of talking,' ' way of
following up one joke with another;' while Rosalind puns upon it in the sense of
' rancid,' ' offensively scented.'

104. **old smell**] NEIL : Holinshed says : ' The making of new gentlemen bred
great strife sometimes among the Romans, I meane when those which were *Novi
homines* were more allowed of for their virtues newlie seene and shewed, than the
old smell of ancient race latelie defaced,' &c.—*Description of England,* chap v.
[p. 162, ed. 1574]. Rosalind banters Touchstone by taking ' rank,' meaning own place,
to signify *true station* in one sense, and *strong-scented* in another, and so employs this
equivoque.

105. **amaze**] JOHNSON : This is not to astonish or strike with wonder, but to perplex, to confuse, so as to put out of the intended narrative. WRIGHT : The word
' amazement ' was originally applied to denote the confusion of mind produced by
any strong emotion, as in Mark xiv, 33 : 'And they began to be sore amazed, and to
be very heavy.'

110. **to doe**] ABBOTT, § 359 : The infinitive active is often found where we use
the passive, as in ' such a storm As oft 'twixt May and April is to see,' *Lov. Com.* 102.
This is especially common in ' what's to do ' (*Twel. N.* III, iii, 18) for ' what's to be
done.' So in ' Savage, extreme, rude, cruel, not to trust.'—*Sonn.* 129, that is, *not to
be trusted.*

113. **There comes**] ABBOTT, § 335 : When the subject is as yet future, and, as it
were, unsettled, the third person singular might be regarded as the normal inflection.
Such passages are very common, particularly in the case of ' There is.' See *Oth.* I,
i, 188 : ' Is there not charms.' See also V, ii, 76 of the present play.

Cel. I could match this beginning with an old tale.

Le Beu. Three proper yong men, of excellent growth   115
and prefence.

Rof. With bils on their neckes : Be it knowne vnto
all men by these prefents.   118

116. *prefence.*] *presence,*— Theob. et   117, 118. *Be...prefents*] Given to
seq.   Clown, Warb.
117. *With...neckes*] Given to Le Beu,   118. *prefents.*] *prefents,*— Theob. et
Farmer, Dyce, Huds.   seq.

---

115. **proper**] CALDECOTT : That is, of good figure and proportion.

117, 118. WARBURTON supposes that Rosalind and Touchstone are playing ' at a
kind of cross purposes,' and to serve out Rosalind for catching him up in line 104,
Touchstone now, ' to be quits with her, puts in—" Know all men by these presents."
She spoke of an instrument of war, and he turns it to an instrument of law of the
same name, beginning with these words : So that they must be given to him.'
FARMER says, ' " With bills on their necks " should be the conclusion of Le Beau's
speech.' [Thus between Warburton and Farmer no word of the speech is left to
Rosalind at all.] Farmer continues : ' Mr Edwards ridicules Dr Warburton, " As if
people carried such instruments of war as *bills* and *guns* on *their necks*, not *on their
shoulders !* " But unluckily the ridicule falls upon himself. Lassels, in his *Voyage
of Italy*, says of tutors, " Some persuade their pupils that it is fine carrying a *gun
upon their necks.* " But what is still more, the expression is taken immediately [from
Lodge's novel.' See Appendix, p. 362]. JOHNSON : Where meaning is so very thin
as in this vein of jocularity it is hard to catch, and therefore I know not well what to
determine ; but I cannot see why Rosalind should suppose that competitors in a
wrestling match carried *bills* on their shoulders, and I believe the whole conceit is in
the poor resemblance of *presence* and *presents*. CAPELL : The humour of Rosalind's
speech, such as it is, took it's rise from Le Beu's word ' presence.' ' Bills ' are—labels.
STEEVENS added others to Farmer's proof from Lodge's novel, of the practice of
wearing bills on the neck ; in Sidney's *Arcadia* [book i, p. 68, ed. 1598] ' Dame-
tus . . . . with a sword by his side, a Forrest bill on his necke.' Again in Rowley's
When You See Me You Know Me, a stage direction conveys almost the same idea :
' Enter King and Compton with bills on their backs ' [p. 28, ed. Elze]. M. MASON
(p. 81) believed that neither an instrument of war, nor one of law, was meant by
' bill,' but merely a label or advertisement, as we say a *play-bill*, a *hand-bill*. CALDE-
COTT : From the [foregoing] instances it is highly probable that an allusion is here
made to the undoubted usage of ' bills, forest-bills, and bats ' being carried on the neck ;
although the leading idea holden out is manifestly that of ' scrolls or labels,' with an
inscription running in a legal form, and for the purpose of a conceit between ' presence ' and ' presents.' ' The watchman's weapon,' says DOUCE (ii, 51), was the bill ;
but Stowe (*Annal.* p. 1040, ed. 1631) informs us ' that when prentizes and journey-
men attended upon their masters and mistresses in the night, they went before them
carrying a lanthorne and candle in their hands and a great long club on their necks.'
COLLIER (ed. i) is inclined to accept Farmer's distribution of the speeches. ' Lodge
calls the father " a lustie Franklin of the country " with " two tall men that were his
sonnes," and they would properly be furnished " with bills on their necks." ' DYCE
adopted Farmer's emendation in his first edition, and remained constant to it in his

3

Le Beu. The eldeſt of the three, wraſtled with *Charles* the Dukes Wraſtler, which *Charles* in a moment threw   120 him, and broke three of his ribbes, that there is little hope of life in him : So he feru'd the ſecond, and ſo the third : yonder they lie, the poore old man their Father, making ſuch pittiful dole ouer them, that all the beholders take his part with weeping.   125

Roſ. Alas.

Clo. But what is the ſport Monſieur, that the Ladies haue loſt ?

Le Beu. Why this that I ſpeake of.

Clo. Thus men may grow wiſer euery day. It is the   130 firſt time that euer I heard breaking of ribbes was ſport for Ladies.

Cel. Or I, I promiſe thee.

Roſ. But is there any elſe longs to ſee this broken   134

---

127. *Monſieur*] *Mounſieur* Ff.   134. *ſee*] *set* Theob. Han. Warb. Cap.
129. *this*] *this is* F₄, Rowe i.   *feel* Johns. conj. Walker, Dyce iii, Huds.
130. *may*] Om. Rowe, Pope, Han.   Coll. iii.
131. *heard*] *heard of* F₄, Rowe i.

---

subsequent editions, pronouncing it undoubtedly right; 'for if they [*i. e.* the words "with bills on their necks"] are spoken by Rosalind, the whole humour of the passage evaporates.' [This, I think, is somewhat too strongly expressed. And yet Farmer's suggestion is so ingenious that I am inclined to say ' Ditto to Dr Johnson,' and confess that ' I know not-well what to determine.'—ED.]

120. **which Charles**] ABBOTT, § 269: *Which* being an adjective frequently accompanies the repeated antecedent, where definiteness is desired or where care must be taken to select the right antecedent. This repetition is, perhaps, more common with the definite 'the which.' See *post* II, i, 36; II, vii, 125.

121. **that**] For the frequent omission of *so* before *that*, see Abbott, § 283.

126. **Alas**] COWDEN-CLARKE: It is often by such apparently slight touches as these that Shakespeare depicts the moral perfection of his characters and gives them their crowning charm. By this single word he shows us Rosalind pausing in the full career of her sportive word-bandying, struck with pity for the poor old father's grief. His women are always true women; not mere heedless, heartless wits, but witty from the very depths of their sweet and sensitive natures.

134–136. **But ... Cosin**] In the Cambridge Edition there is recorded an Anonymous conjecture whereby this speech is given to Touchstone as far as 'rib-breaking.' To Rosalind is given the rest: ' Shall we see this wrastling, Cosin ?'

134. **any else longs**] For the omission of the relative in this very elliptical phrase ('any *one* else *who* longs'), see ABBOTT, § 244, where many parallel instances are given.

134. **see this broken Musicke**] WARBURTON asserts that the pleasantry of Rosalind's repartee must consist in the allusion she makes to *composing in music*. ' It

Muſicke in his ſides? Is there yet another doates vpon   135
rib-breaking? Shall we ſee this wraſtling Coſin?
   Le Beu. You muſt if you ſtay heere, for heere is the
place appointed for the wraſtling, and they are ready to
performe it.   139

               138. *for the*] *for* Ff, Rowe.

necessarily follows, therefore,' so he says, ' that the poet wrote—*set* this broken music.'
This emendation received CAPELL'S approval. HEATH (p. 145): Possibly it might
be '*get* this broken music.' JOHNSON: If any change were necessary, I should write
'*feel* this broken music.' But 'see' is the colloquial term for perception or experiment. So we say every day: *see* if the water be hot; I will *see* which is the best time;
she has tried, and *sees* that she cannot lift it. In this sense 'see' may be here used.
CALDECOTT paraphrases: witness the crash made by his broken bones; get so rough
a handling. WALKER (*Crit.* ii, 299): *Feele*, surely; and so Johnson conjectures,
although he doubts whether any change is required. DYCE (ed. iii) adopted this
emendation, remarking that the error 'see' was evidently derived from the close of
the speech, ' Shall we *see* this wrestling, cousin?' It may be as Dyce says, but I
always mistrust these 'errors of anticipation.' What has once passed through a compositor's mind, and under his fingers, may, it is conceivable, readily recur. But the
case is altered when the error is in the future. Why is it not simpler to take Walker's
explanation that the error arose from the confusion, a confusion very, very common, of
the long *s* and *f?* Rosalind repeats her question with a variation; since the second
time she refers to the wrestler, and not to a spectator, it seems but natural that she
should have referred in the first question also to the wrestler—an additional reason
for adopting Dr Johnson's emendation.—ED.]

   134, 135. **broken Musicke**] WRIGHT: This was first explained by Mr Chappell
(*Popular Music*, &c, p. 246) as the music of a string band. But he has since altered
his opinion, and has kindly favoured me with the following explanation: Some
instruments, such as viols, violins, flutes, &c., were formerly made in sets of four,
which when played together formed a ' consort.' If one or more of the instruments
of one set were substituted for the corresponding ones of another set, the result is no
longer a ' consort,' but ' broken music.' The expression occurs in *Hen. V:* V, ii, 263,
' Come, your answer in broken music; for thy voice is music and thy English broken.'
And Bacon, *Essay* xxxvii, p. 156: ' I understand it, that the Song be in Quire, placed
aloft, and accompanied with some broken musicke.'

   136. **Shall . . . Cosin**] COWDEN-CLARKE suggests that this should be uttered in
a tone to indicate the purpose *not* to see it. BLACKWOOD'S MAGAZINE (April, 1833,
p. 549, *qu.* Campbell?): Ought Rosalind to have remained to see the wrestling after
having been told by Le Beau that Charles had thrown the three sons of the old man,
and left them lying on the ground with broken ribs and little hope of life? On hearing of the rib-breaking Rosalind only said, 'Alas!' Probably she would not have
gone to see the wrestling, for she asks Celia's advice; but Celia replies, ' Yonder, sure,
they are coming; let us now *stay* and see it.' And there is Orlando. ' Is yonder the
man?' asks Rosalind; and would you have had her to leave him, who, ' alas! is too
young, but looks successfully,' in the hold of the Duke's wrestler, without sending
strength to all his sinews from the sympathy shining in her troubled eyes? As for

Cel. Yonder ſure they are comming. Let vs now ſtay   140
and ſee it.

    Flouriſh.   *Enter Duke, Lords, Orlando, Charles,*
                and Attendants.

Duke. Come on, ſince the youth will not be intreated
His owne perill on his forwardneſſe.   145
   Roſ. Is yonder the man *?*
   Le Beu. Euen he, Madam.
   Cel. Alas, he is too yong : yet he looks ſucceſſefully
   Du. How now daughter, and Couſin:
Are you crept hither to ſee the wraſtling?   150
   Roſ. I my Liege, ſo pleaſe you giue vs leaue.
   Du. You wil take little delight in it, I can tell you
there is ſuch oddes in the man : In pitie of the challen-   153

---

142. Duke] Duke Frederick. Rowe.
Duke junior. Cap.
Scene VI. Pope+.
144. *intreated*] *entreated* F_3F_4.
149. *Couſin*] *Coſin* Ff.
151. *I*] *Ay*, Rowe.

152. *you*] *you*, Ff.
153. *in the*] *on the* Anon. (ap. Cam. Ed.)
   man] *men* Han. Warb. Johns. Cap. Steev. Mal. Sing. Wh. i, Dyce, Sta. Coll. (MS) ii, iii, Ktly, Rlfe, Huds.

---

the vulgarity of wrestling, 'tis a pretty pastime; and then Orlando could do nothing vulgar.

145. ALLEN (MS): Instead of 'his forwardness is at his own peril,' it is to be understood as 'his danger is based upon his own forwardness.'

150. **Are you crept**] For instances of some few intransitive verbs, mostly of motion, with which *be* and *have* are used, see ABBOTT, § 295.

153. **oddes in the man**] CAPELL pronounced Hanmer's change 'palpably necessary.' CALDECOTT evidently refers 'man' to Orlando; and paraphrases: 'the challenger is so little of a match.' COLLIER, in his first edition, agrees with Caldecott, in his second and third he was overborne by his 'old Corrector.' BLACKWOOD'S MAGAZINE (Aug. 1853, p. 197): We take leave to say that Hanmer was *not* right in altering 'man' to *men*. What is meant to be said is, 'there is such superiority (of strength) in the *man;*' and 'odds' formerly signified *superiority*, as may be learnt from the following sentence of Hobbes: 'The passion of laughter,' says Hobbes, 'proceedeth from the sudden imagination of our own *odds* and eminency.' DYCE defends Hanmer's change: 'If Shakespeare had here written "man" (meaning Orlando), he surely would not immediately after have written "*In pity of the challenger's youth,*" &c., but "*In pity of his youth,*" &c. Nor, on carefully considering the passage, can I think more favourably of the old reading, because a critic in *Blackwood's Magazine* confidently maintains [as above]. A little above [line 146] "man" is applied to Orlando, and a little below [line 168] to Charles: here the two *men*, Charles and Orlando, are spoken of.' [Caldecott is the only editor, I think, who refers 'man' to Orlando. Clearly it refers to Charles. WRIGHT agrees substantially

gers youth, I would faine diffwade him, but he will not
bee entreated. Speake to him Ladies, fee if you can 155
mooue him.

Cel. Call him hether good Monfieuer *Le Beu.*

Duke. Do fo : Ile not be by.

Le Beu. Monfieur the Challenger, the Princeffe cals
for you. 160

Orl. I attend them with all refpect and dutie.

Rof. Young man, haue you challeng'd *Charles* the
Wraftler?

Orl. No faire Princeffe : he is the generall challenger,
I come but in as others do, to try with him the ftrength 165
of my youth.

---

157. *hether*] *hither* Ff.
　　Monfieuer] *Mounfieur* Ff.
158. Duke goes apart. Theob.
159. *Princeffe cals*] *Princeffe calls* F$_2$
F$_3$. *princefs calls* F$_4$. *Princesses call*

Theob. Warb. Johns. Steev. Mal. Sing.
Sta. Huds. *princess' call* Dyce.
161. *them*] *her* Rowe, Pope, Han.
165. *but in*] *but* Ff, Rowe, Pope,
Han.

---

with Blackwood, and for ' odds,' in the sense of advantage or superiority, cites *Love's
Lab. L.* I, ii, 183 : ' Cupid's butt-shaft is too hard for Hercules' club; and therefore
too much odds for a Spaniard's rapier.'—ED.]

159, 161. **the Princesse cals . . . them**] WHITER : It is Celia only who calls
for him; and the answer of Orlando, ' I will attend *them*,' as Celia is accompanied by
Rosalind, does not invalidate the ancient reading. [See Theobald's change in Text.
Notes.] CALDECOTT interprets ' them ' as ' those of the princess's party, or the princesses.' KNIGHT observes : ' When Orlando answers, " I attend *them*," he looks
towards Celia and Rosalind;' and COLLIER and WHITE to the same effect. WALKER
(*Crit.* i, 263) gives this among his many instances where *s* has been interpolated or
omitted, and adds ' certainly " the *princesses call* for you," as some editions have it.'
In his *Vers.* 248, he again cites the passage, and asks ' Is there an erratum in both
these words, or merely in *cals ?* I think the former.' DYCE : I prefer ' the princess'
call for you :' the plural form *princess'* occurs in *Temp.* I, ii, 173, while *princesses* is
not once found throughout the whole of Shakespeare's works. Still, whether we
read ' the princess calls,' &c. or ' the *princess' call*,' &c., an inconsistency will remain.
Mr Lettsom not improbably conjectures that the speech now given to Celia, ' Call him
hither,' &c., should have the double prefix '*Cel.* and *Ros.*' : ' this notion,' he adds, ' is
in some degree supported by the Duke's immediately preceding words, " Speak to
him, *ladies ;*" as well as by the fact that Rosalind is the first to address Orlando,
which is not altogether consistent with Celia only requesting Le Beau to call him.
At any rate, it seems quite impossible, if " princess " is a singular, to explain " I attend
them," though Caldecott, Knight, and Collier have made the attempt.' WRIGHT : It
is Celia who gives the order, and it may be that Orlando in his reply is thinking of
Rosalind, and is made to say ' them ' designedly. [I agree with Dyce that the error
lies in the interpolated *s* in ' cals.' There was the sound of a plural in ' Princesse '
which sufficed for Shakespeare's ear, but did not apparently appeal to the composi-

Cel. Yong Gentleman, your ſpirits are too bold for   167
your yeares : you haue ſeene cruell proofe of this mans
ſtrength, if you ſaw your ſelfe with your eies, or knew
your ſelfe with your iudgment, the feare of your aduen-   170
ture would counſel you to a more equall enterpriſe. We
pray you for your owne ſake to embrace your own ſafe-
tie, and giue ouer this attempt.

Roſ. Do yong Sir, your reputation ſhall not therefore
be miſpriſed : we wil make it our ſuite to the Duke, that   175
the wraſtling might not go forward.

Orl. I befeech you, puniſh mee not with your harde
thoughts, wherein I confeſſe me much guiltie to denie   178

169, 170. *your eies...your iudgment*]   Johns.
our eyes...our judgment Han. Warb.   178. *wherein*] *Therein* Johns. conj.
Cap. Coll. (MS), ii, iii, Dyce iii, Huds.   *herein* Cap. conj. Dyce iii. Om. Sped-
your own eyes...your own judgment   ding (ap. Cam. Ed.) Huds.

---

tor's. The triple sound of *s* in *Princesses* is certainly harsh, which is sufficient, in the
present case, I think, to condemn it.—ED.]

169, 170. **your eies . . . your iudgment**] WARBURTON: Absurd! The sense
requires that we should read, *our* eyes and *our* judgement. The argument is, Your
spirits are too bold, and therefore your judgement deceives you; but did you see yourself with our more impartial judgement, you would forbear. JOHNSON: I cannot find
the absurdity of the present reading. If you were not blinded and intoxicated (says
the Princess) with the spirit of enterprise, if you could use *your own eyes to see, or
your own judgement to know* yourself; the fear of your adventure would counsel you.
[See Johnson's reading in Text. Notes.] HEATH (p. 145): A very modest proposal
truly [Warburton's reading] that Orlando, who must have been taught by experience
the measure of his own skill and strength, should rather refer himself to the judgement upon the first view of two ladies to whom he was till that moment a perfect
stranger! GRANT WHITE: It would seem very superfluous to point out that 'eyes'
and 'judgement' are the emphatic words here, were it not for Warburton's proposal. WALKER (*Crit.* ii, 7): Surely *our.* 'Your' occurs twice just before, and
three times immediately after, which probably helped to mislead the printer's eye.
COLERIDGE also says 'your' should surely be *our.* 'But,' says WRIGHT, 'the meaning is, "If you used the senses and reason which you possess"' [which is substantially the same interpretation as Johnson's, Heath's, White's, and Cowden-Clarke's,
and which I cannot but think the true one.—ED.]

172. **own safetie**] Is not this second 'own' suspicious ?—ED.

175, 176. **wil . . . might**] For other instances of the irregular sequence of tenses,
see Abbott, § 370.

178. **wherein**] CAPELL: This does not seem express'd with that neatness which
is so conspicuous in this play above any of the others; For with what propriety can
Orlando be said to be guilty in the ladies' *hard* thoughts? or why *confess* himself
guilty in those thoughts. He might indeed confess himself guilty, in denying their
request; and this leads to what (perhaps) is the true reading, *herein :* 'wherein'

fo faire and excellent Ladies anie thing. But let your
faire eies, and gentle wifhes go with mee to my triall ;   180
wherein if I bee foil'd, there is but one fham'd that vvas
neuer gracious : if kil'd, but one dead that is willing to
be fo : I fhall do my friends no wrong, for I haue none to
lament me:the world no iniurie, for in it I haue nothing :
onely in the world I fil vp a place, which may bee better   185
fupplied, when I haue made it emptie.

   Rof. The little ftrength that I haue, I would it vvere
with you.

   Cel. And mine to eeke out hers.

   Rof. Fare you well:praie heauen I be deceiu'd in you.   190

   Cel. Your hearts defires be with you.

---

187. *that*] Om. Rowe.   191. Cel.] Orlando. Theob. Han.
189. *eeke out*] *eek-out* F_3F_4.   Warb.

---

stands at the head of another period, only two lines below; which might be the occasion of its getting in here. [This conjecture of Capell's has been generally credited
to Mason, who also proposed it, probably independently.   The latter observes]:
As the word 'wherein' must always refer to something preceding, I have no doubt
but there is an error in this passage, and that we ought to read *herein*, instead of
'wherein.' The hard thoughts that he complains of are the apprehensions expressed
by the ladies of his not being able to contend with the wrestler. He beseeches that
they will not punish him with them. MALONE: The meaning, I think, is, Punish me not
with your unfavourable opinion (of my abilities); *which, however, I confess, I deserve
to incur*, for denying such fair ladies any request. [Staunton quotes this; and Caldecott's paraphrase is substantially the same.]   KNIGHT: Mason says 'the hard thoughts
that he complains of are the apprehensions expressed by the ladies of his not being
able to contend with the wrestler.' Hard thoughts! The tender interest which the
ladies take in his safety to be called 'hard thoughts'—to be complained of? Surely
the meaning is, Punish me not with your hard thoughts, *because* I confess me much
guilty to deny what you ask. 'Wherein' is decidedly used in the sense of *in that*.
WALKER (*Crit.* i, 309) suspects 'wherein,' and DYCE (ed. iii) adds that it is 'justly'
suspected. WRIGHT: The construction is loose, and we must supply as antecedent
some such expression as 'in this business,' or, as Malone suggests, 'of my abilities.'
Knight's interpretation would make very good sense, but [*because* or *in that*] is not
the meaning of 'wherein.'   Mr Spedding would omit 'wherein' altogether.

   178. me] For instances of 'me' used for *myself*, see Abbott, § 223.

   182. gracious] SINGER: Anciently used in the sense of the Italian *gratiato, i. e.
graced, favoured, countenanced;* as well as for *graceful, comely, well-favoured*, in
which sense Shakespeare uses it in other places.

   185. onely] This transposition is common in Shakespeare; we have another
instance in 'the onely prologues' in V, iii, 12. Compare 'Which touching but my
gentle vessel's side,' *Mer. of Ven.* I, i, 37, or line 50 in the same scene, 'Therefore
my merchandise makes me not sad.' Abbott, §§ 420, 421, gives other examples.
—ED.

Char. Come, where is this yong gallant, that is fo   192
defirous to lie with his mother earth ?

Orl. Readie Sir, but his will hath in it a more modeſt
working.   195

Duk. You ſhall trie but one fall.

Cha. No, I warrant your Grace you ſhall not entreat
him to a fecond, that haue fo mightilie perſwaded him
from a firſt.

Orl. You meane to mocke me after : you ſhould not   200
haue mockt me before : but come your waies.

Roſ. Now Hercules, be thy fpeede yong man.

Cel. I would I were inuiſible, to catch the ſtrong fellow by the legge.   *Wraſtle.*

Roſ. Oh excellent yong man.   205

Cel. If I had a thunderbolt in mine eie, I can tell who
ſhould downe.   *Shout.*

Duk. No more, no more.

Orl. Yes I befeech your Grace, I am not yet well
breath'd.   210

Duk. How do'ſt thou *Charles*?

194. *in it*] *it in* Var. '21 (misprint ?)   204. Wraſtle.] They Wraſtle F$_3$F$_4$.
201. *mockt me*] *mockt* F$_3$F$_4$, Rowe,   208. Charles is thrown. Rowe et
Pope, Han.   seq.

200. **You meane**] THEOBALD (*Lit. Illust.* ii, 329): Should not this be '*An*' you
mean,' &c. ? MASON (p. 82): I believe we should read, '*If* you mean,' &c. CAM-
BRIDGE EDITORS (to whom Theobald's conj. had occurred independently) remark
(*Note* v) : *And* for *an* is a more probable reading than *if*, as it may have been omitted
by the printer, who mistook it for part of the stage direction—'Orl. and' for 'Orland.'

204. **Wrastle**] In a notice (*Sh. Jahrbuch*, ii, 274) of certain performances of
Shakespeare's plays in Munich, Bodenstedt mentions that, on one occasion, this
wrestling-match was so arranged behind barriers that only the upper halves of the
wrestlers' bodies were visible to the audience. Whether or not this arrangement is
novel, or has been adopted elsewhere, I do not know, but it seems to be highly com-
mendable, as far as it goes. It is questionable if the barriers might not be made much
higher to advantage. Wrestling is a sport so unusual at this day and in this country,
and our stage Orlandos and Charleses are generally such feeble adepts in it, that this
match, as it is usually seen, is far from thrilling, and we are amazed not so much at
Orlando's prowess as at Charles's accommodating mortality.—ED.

204, 207. Note the imperative mood of these stage-directions, indicating a stage
copy.—ED.

207. **downe**] For the omission of verbs of motion before certain adverbs, see
Abbott, §§ 30, 41, &c.

210. **breath'd**] SCHMIDT: That is, in the full display of my strength. Equivalent
to *mis en haleine.*

Le Beu.   He cannot fpeake my Lord.   212

Duk.   Beare him awai e :

What is thy name yong man ?

Orl.   *Orlando* my Liege, the yongeſt ſonne of Sir *Ro-*   215
land de Boys.

Duk.   I would thou hadſt beene ſon to ſome man elſe,

The world eſteem'd thy father honourable,

But I did finde him ſtill mine enemie :

Thou ſhould'ſt haue better pleas'd me with this deede,   220

Hadſt thou deſcended from another houſe :

But fare thee well, thou art a gallant youth,

I would thou hadſt told me of another Father.

> *Exit Duke.*

Cel.   Were I my Father (Coze) would I do this ?   225

Orl.   I am more proud to be Sir *Rolands* ſonne,

His yongeſt ſonne, and would not change that calling

To be adopted heire to *Fredricke.*

Roſ.   My Father lou'd Sir *Roland* as his ſoule,

And all the world was of my Fathers minde,   230

Had I before knowne this yong man his ſonne,

I ſhould haue giuen him teares vnto entreaties,

Ere he ſhould thus haue ventur'd.

Cel.   Gentle Coſen,   234

213, 214. Prose, Pope et seq.	Theob.
215, 216. Roland de Boys] Rowland	224. Scene VII. Pope+.
de Boyes Ff.	226. *more*] *most* Han.
224. Exit...] Exit...with his train.	227. *ſonne,*] *son ;*— Cap.

219. **still**] That is, constantly. See Shakespeare *passim.*

220. **should'st**] An instance of the peculiar use of *should*, to which attention was
called in *Mer. of Ven.* III, ii, 289.   It is not the past tense of *shall*, nor does it suggest compulsion or 'bounden duty' (see Abbott, § 322).   Of course, at the present
time we should use *would.*—ED.

227. **yongest sonne**] MALONE suggests that some such phrase as 'than to be
descended from any other house, however high,' is to be understood.   It is almost
superfluous to remark that Capell's punctuation has been adopted since his day,
whereby the sentence is shown to be incomplete; 'such things,' says Capell, 'have
their beauty in a free dialogue.'

227. **calling**] STEEVENS : That is, appellation; a very unusual, if not unprece-
dented, sense of the word. [It is the only instance given by SCHMIDT with this meaning, who says that, in the sense of *vocation, profession,* 'it is always used of the eccle-
siastical profession, except in *Per.* IV, ii, 43,' where Pandar says, 'Neither is our
profession any trade; it's no calling;' it is just possible that even in *Pericles* there
is no exception to the general usage.—ED.]

Let vs goe thanke him, and encourage him :   235
My Fathers rough and enuious difpofition
Sticks me at heart : Sir, you haue well deferu'd,
If you doe keepe your promifes in loue ;
But iuftly as you haue exceeded all promife,
Your Miftris fhall be happie.   240
 Rof.   Gentleman,
Weare this for me : one out of fuites with fortune   242

237. *Sticks*] *Stickes* F₂.   239. *all*] Om. Cap. Steev. Dyce iii,
 me at] *at my* Han.   Huds.
238. *loue ;*] *love,* Ff. *love* Cap.   *promife*] *in promife* Ff, Rowe,
239. *iuftly*] *justly,* Cap.   Pope, Theob. Warb. *promise here*
 as...promife] *as you've exceeded* Ktly.
promise Han.   242. *fortune*] *fortune ;* Cap.

---

236. **enuious**] DYCE: Malicious.

237. **at heart**] This is, I think, an instance of the absorption of the definite article in the dental termination of 'at.' This absorption, originally adopted for the sake of ease in pronunciation, led gradually to the omission of the article in other cases, as in 'milk comes frozen home *in pail,*' or in 'spectacles *on nose* and pouch *on side.*'—ED.

239. **iustly**] KNIGHT: In the degree that you have gone beyond all expectation : but *as* justly. WRIGHT: That is, exactly. Compare the use of 'righteously,' line 13.

239. **exceeded**] WALKER (*Crit.* i, 288): Read, *metri gratiâ, excell'd.* I think, too, 'as y' have *here* excell'd,' &c. as an antitheton to 'in love.'

239. **all promise**] WHITE (ed. i, referring to 'in promise' of the Ff): But Orlando had not exceeded all in promise ; he, or his performances, exceeded all promise.

242. **Weare this**] THEOBALD (ed. i): There is nothing in the sequel of this scene expressing what it is that Rosalind here gives to Orlando. Afterwards, in the third Act, when Rosalind has found a copy of verses in the woods writ on herself, and Celia asks her whether she knows who has done this, Rosalind replies, by way of question, 'Is it a man ?' To which Celia again replies, 'Ay, and a *Chain* that *you* once *wore,* about his neck.' LADY MARTIN (p. 410): Rosalind needs not the prompting of her cousin to 'go thank him and encourage him;' but while Celia finds ready words, Rosalind's deeper emotion suggests to her a stronger token of the admiration he has roused. She has taken a chain from her neck, and stealthily kissing it—at least I always used to do so—she gives it to Orlando, saying (ll. 242, 243). Here she pauses, naturally expecting some acknowledgement from Orlando; but finding none come, and not knowing how to break off an interview that has kindled a strange emotion within her, she adds, 'Shall we go, coz ?' Celia, heart-whole as she is, has no such difficulty. 'Ay. Fare you well, fair gentleman,' she says, and turns away.

242. **suites**] JOHNSON: This seems an allusion to cards, where he that has no more cards to play of a particular sort, is *out of suit.* STEEVENS: It means, I believe, turned out of her service, and stripped of her livery. MALONE: So afterwards Celia says, ' but turning those *jests out of service,* let us talk in good earnest.' CALDECOTT: Its import seems equivalent to ' out of her books or graces.' HALLIWELL records the conjecture of ' an anonymous critic, " out of *sorts,*" that is, discontented with the blind goddess ; and another suggests the explanation " out of her favour," and not obtaining

That could giue more, but that her hand lacks meanes.   243
Shall we goe Coze?

   Cel.   I : fare you well faire Gentleman.   245

   Orl.   Can I not fay, I thanke you? My better parts
Are all throwne downe, and that which here ſtands vp
Is but a quintine, a meere liueleſſe blocke.   248

---

243. *could*] *would* Han. Dyce iii, Coll.
iii.

   meanes] *meane* F_2.

244. Giving him a chain from her

neck. Theob.

245. *I*] *Ay* Rowe.

248. *meere*] *more* F_4, Rowe.

   liueleſſe] *lifeless* Rowe ii.

---

the *suits*, the petitions, *she* addressed other.' WRIGHT also suggests 'one to whose entreaties Fortune grants no favours, with a play upon the other meaning of the word,' namely *livery*. [See Whiter's note on II, vii, 47.]

243. **could giue more**] CALDECOTT: That is, who could find in her heart to give more, were her ability greater. WRIGHT refers to what Anthony says of Fulvia, 'She's good, being gone; The hand could pluck her back that shoved her on,' *Ant. & Cleop.* I, ii, 131.

246. **better parts**] CALDECOTT: Compare 'it hath cow'd my better part of man,' *Macb.* V, viii, 18; that is, his spirit. We may therefore conclude that by these terms *spirit and sense* were meant here.

248. **quintine**] WARBURTON, to whom, despite his arrogant and offensive style, we must concede ingenuity, thus interprets this allusion, which he pronounces 'beautiful' : A quintain was a *post* or *butt* set up for several kinds of martial exercises, against which they threw their darts and exercised their arms. 'I am,' says Orlando, 'only a quintain, a lifeless block, on which love only exercises his arms in jest, the great disparity in condition between Rosalind and me, not suffering me to hope that love will ever make a serious matter of it.' Whereupon, GUTHRIE (*Crit. Review*, 1765, vol. xx, p. 407) called Warburton to task, and denied that the 'quintaine' was the object of darts and arms, in fact, 'it was a stake driven into a field, upon which were hung a shield and other trophies of war, at which they shot, darted, or rode, with a lance. When the shield and the trophies were all thrown down, the "quintaine" remained. Without this information how could the reader understand the allusion of "my better parts are all thrown down"? &c.' As there seems to be here a difference of opinion as to the exact nature of a 'quintain,' all the archæological resources of the commentators were summoned to the field 'to fight for a spot,' as Steevens says, quoting Hamlet, 'whereon the numbers cannot try the cause;' and the consequence is that we have page upon page of explanations, and quotations from Latin, French, Italian, and English sources, accompanied by many wood-cuts and engravings, all of which are extremely valuable as an archæological contribution to the subject, but throw little light on Orlando's allusion other than is revealed in the definition of a quintain as given by Strutt and quoted below. For ampler researches those who list may consult : Grey, vol. i, pp. 171–173; Whiter, pp. 9–13; Variorum of '21, pp. 514–519; Caldecott, *Appendix*, p. 4; Knight, *Illustrations*, p. 220; Brand, *Pop. Antiq.* i, 177; ii, 163 (Bohn's ed.; several other authorities are there cited, some whereof are quoted by Wright); Theobald (Nichols's *Lit. Illus.* ii, 329), who cites Stow's *Survay;* and Halliwell *ad loc.* The extract from STRUTT (p. 112, ed. Hone, 1841) is as follows : 'Tilting or combating at the quintain is certainly a military exercise of high antiquity,

Ros. He cals vs back : my pride fell with my fortunes,
Ile aske him what he would : Did you call Sir ?   250
Sir, you haue wraſtled well, and ouerthrowne
More then your enemies.   252

---

249. *fortunes,*] *fortunes* F$_2$F$_3$. *fortunes.* F$_4$.

---

and antecedent, I doubt not, to the justs and tournaments. The quintain, originally, was nothing more than the trunk of a tree or post set up for the practice of the tyros in chivalry. Afterward a staff or spear was fixed in the earth, and a shield, being hung upon it, was the mark to strike at; the dexterity of the performer consisted in smiting the shield in such a manner as to break the ligatures and bear it to the ground. In process of time this diversion was improved, and instead of the staff and the shield, the resemblance of a human figure carved in wood was introduced. To render the appearance of this figure more formidable, it was generally made in the likeness of a Turk or Saracen, armed at all points, bearing a shield upon his left arm, and brandishing a club or sabre with his right. Hence this exercise was called by the Italians "running at the armed man, or at the Saracen." The quintain thus fashioned was placed upon a pivot, and so contrived as to move round with great facility. In running at this figure it was necessary for the horseman to direct his lance with great adroitness, and make his stroke upon the forehead between the eyes or upon the nose; for if he struck wide of those parts, especially upon the shield, the quintain turned about with much velocity, and, in case he was not exceedingly careful, would give him a severe blow upon the back with the wooden sabre held in the right hand, which was considered as highly disgraceful to the performer, while it excited the laughter and ridicule of the spectators.' 'There were other kinds of quintains,' adds DYCE, 'but the words of Orlando, "a quintain, *a mere lifeless block*," seem to show that Shakespeare alludes to the kind above described.' The simile itself was suggested, as WHITER says in substance, not only by the feats of activity which were then going forward, but by the assault upon his own heart which he had just experienced; 'the phrases "thrown down" and "stands up" were impressed on Shakespeare's mind by the subject of *wrestling* which had just occupied his attention;' it is Whiter's endeavour, be it remembered, in his thoughtful book, to explain various passages on the principle of Locke's doctrine of the Association of Ideas.—ED.

250–252. BLACKWOOD'S MAGAZINE (April, 1833, p. 550, *qu.* Campbell ?) : Giving him a chain from her neck! How much worthier of a woman such frankness, not unaccompanied with reserve, than the pride that sat in the eyes of high-born beauty, as with half-averted face she let drop glove or scarf to her kneeling knight, with silent permission to dye it for her sake in his heart's blood! Not for all the world would Rosalind have sent her wrestler to the wars. But, believe us, she said aside to Celia, and in an undertone, though looking on Orlando, 'Sir, you have wrestled well, and overthrown More than your enemies.' She felt it was so, and could not help saying it, but she intended not that Orlando should hear the words, nor did he. All he heard was, 'Did you call, sir?' So far 'she urged conference,' and no farther; and 'twas the guileless hypocrisy of an unsuspecting heart! For our own parts, we see no reason in nature, had circumstances allowed it, why they should not have been married on the spot.

252. LADY MARTIN (p. 411): This 'more than your enemies' is very significant, and speaks plainly enough, though spoken as it would be, with great reserve of

Cel. Will you goe Coze? 253

Rof. Haue with you : fare you well. *Exit.*

*Orl.*What paffion hangs thefe waights vpõ my toong? 255
I cannot fpeake to her, yet fhe vrg'd conference.

Enter Le Beu.

O poore *Orlando*! thou art ouerthrowne
Or Charles, or fomething weaker mafters thee.

*Le Beu.*Good Sir, I do in friendfhip counfaile you 260
Te leaue this place ; Albeit you haue deferu'd
High commendation, true applaufe, and loue ;
Yet fuch is now the Dukes condition,
That he mifconfters all that you haue done : 264

---

257. Enter...] Re-enter... (after line　　261. *Te*] F$_1$.
259), Dyce.　　　　　　　　　　　　　264. *mifconfters*] *misconstrues* Pope.

---

manner, of the favorable impression which the young wrestler has made upon her.
We may be sure that, but for his modest demeanour, Rosalind would not have allowed
herself to confess so much.

253. LADY MARTIN (p. 411): Celia, amused, and disposed to rally her cousin
about what looks to her rather more than 'falling in love in sport,' accosts Rosalind
mockingly in the phrase she has used but a few minutes before, 'Will you go, coz?'
'Have with you,' Rosalind rejoins, quite understanding the roguish sparkle in her
cousin's eyes, but not deterred by it from giving to Orlando as she goes an earnest
'Fare you well.' But she is still slow to leave, hoping and longing for some words
from his lips addressed to herself. When Celia takes her hand and is leading her
away, Celia bows slightly to Orlando; but Rosalind in a royal and gentle manner
curtseys to him, wishing to show her respect for the memory of his father, the dear
friend of her father, and also her sympathy with his misfortunes. These she can give
him, if nothing else. This scene, you will agree, needs most delicate touching in the
actress. Rosalind has not much to say, but she has to make her audience feel by
subtle indications the revolution that is going on in her own heart from the moment
her eyes fall upon her future lover, down to the parting glance with which her farewell is accompanied. It is Juliet in the ball-room, but under conditions that demand
a far greater variety of expression. There is no avowal of love ; but when she linger-
ingly leaves the stage, the audience must have been made to feel that in her case, as
in Juliet's, her heart has made its choice, and that a change has come over her akin
to that which has come over Orlando. OXON (p. 49): When Celia sees that Rosalind has fallen in love with Orlando, she checks her desire to return and speak to
him once more, because she sees that her cousin's effusiveness is carrying her a little
too far; and she utters 'Will you go, coz?' in a *jam satis* tone.

259. Or . . . or] ABBOTT, § 136: There is perhaps a disposition to revert to the
old idiom: *other* . . . . *other*. The contraction of *other* into 'or' is illustrated by
whe'er for *whether* in Old English and the Elizabethan dramatists.

263. condition] JOHNSON: It here means *character, temper, disposition.* So
Anthonio, in the *Mer. of Ven.* is called by his friend 'the best condition'd man.'

The Duke is humorous, what he is indeede   265

264. **misconsters**] 'This form,' says DYCE (*Remarks*, p. 54), 'is common in our
early writers.' It represents the early pronunciation, which was probably in a transition state when the Folio was printing. We find this same form in *1 Hen. VI*: II,
iii, 73 (p. 103, *a*, F₁): 'Be not dismay'd, faire Lady, nor *mi∫con∫ter* The minde of
Talbot;' and also in *Rich. III*: III, v, 61 (p. 190, *b*, F₁): '*Mi∫con∫ter* vs in him and
wayle his death,' and again, 'I be *mi∫con∫terd* in the place I go,' *Mer. of Ven.* II, ii,
184; but in the only other passages where the word occurs we have the spelling *mis-
construe*: 'Alas, thou haft *mi∫con∫trued* euerything,' *Jul. Cæs.* V, iii, 84 (p. 129, *a*,
F₁); and 'So much *mi∫con∫trued* in his Wantonneffe,' *1 Hen. IV*: V, ii, 69 (p. 70, *b*,
F₁). See also *con∫ter* in *Oth.* IV, i, 118, and note in this edition, where all the
instances are given of the occurrence of that word in the Folio; from which list it
appears that it was spelled *conster* three times and *construe* eight times; in *R. of L.*
and in *Pass. Pilg.* it is spelled *conster*; so that the proportion stands five to eight, and
shows, I think, that the pronunciation was in a state of transition. See also Greene's
James the Fourth, p. 106, ed. Dyce; and Peele's *The Arraignment of Paris*, p. 24,
ed. Dyce, where Dyce cites a passage from Marston in which *conster* rhymes with
monster.—ED.

265. **humorous**] This is defined as *capricious* by Caldecott, Knight, Dyce, Staunton, Wright, and Rolfe; Dyce adds *perverse*, and Staunton to *perverse* adds *contrari-
ous*. Halliwell's first definition is *capricious*, but he continues, 'it is sometimes used
in the sense of *fantastic*, the meaning given to the word by Minsheu, or, perhaps,
peevish, *wayward*, as Coles has it, translating it by *morosus*. Cotgrave has, "*Averti-
neux*, moodie, humorous;" and again, "*Avoir le cerveau un peu gaillard*, to be
humorous, toyish, fantasticall, new-fangled."' Despite this general agreement, I
doubt if 'humorous' is here exactly defined by *capricious*, or if *capricious* exactly
defines the Duke. The Duke's predominant trait seems to be suspicion, bred of the
treachery to his brother. This suspicion blazes forth at times, as in such inconstant
starts as the banishment of Rosalind, but it is persistent and consistent, which can
scarcely be affirmed of a temperament that is *capricious*. Moreover, it would never
do to call the Duke's conversion and reconciliation to the Church, in the Fifth Act, a
caprice. Yet this humorousness, whatever it be, is emphasised as a characteristic of
the Duke. He is twice called 'humorous'; here by Le Beau, and again by old
Adam. The only other instance where 'humorous' is used in this play is where
Jaques thus characterises his melancholy; and surely if any melancholy were ever
ingrained and persistent, and less liable to freaks or caprices, it is Jaques's; he himself says expressly that it is not 'fantastic.' It behooves us, then, I think, to find a
meaning for 'humorous' somewhat nicer than merely *capricious*. Ben Jonson, in
the *Induction* to *Every Man Out of his Humour*, gives a definition of 'humour,'
which, contemporaneous as it is, is more likely to be exact than any modern attempt to
define it; from 'humour' the meaning may be presumably extended to 'humorous.'
Asper says to Mitis, 'When some one peculiar quality Doth so possess a man, that it
doth draw All his affects, his spirits, and his powers, In their confluctions, all to run
one way, This may be truly said to be a humour.' Such a dominant trait, then, as
this, it would be hardly correct to term a *caprice*, or a man thus dominated, *capricious*.
A man thus 'humorous' may be *headstrong*, *wayward*, and his 'humour' may
assume an odd, extraordinary turn, but it would be steady, persistent, and by no means
capricious; it might manifest itself unexpectedly, but all the 'humorous' man's
'affects would run one way.' Wherefore, I think, and I speak with diffidence,

More fuites you to conceiue, then I to fpeake of.   266
   Orl. I thanke you Sir ; and pray you tell me this,
Which of the two was daughter of the Duke,
That here was at the Wraftling?
   *Le Beu.*Neither his daughter,if we iudge by manners,   270
But yet indeede the taller is his daughter,
The other is daughter to the banifh'd Duke,
And here detain'd by her vfurping Vncle
To keepe his daughter companie, whofe loues
Are deerer then the naturall bond of Sifters :   275

---

266. *I*] *me* Rowe +, Cap. Mal. Steev.
Coll. Sing. Ktly.
  268. *the*] *these* Rowe.
    of the Duke] *to the Duke* F_3F_4,
Rowe.
  269. *was*] *were* Han. Cap. Dyce iii.

271. *taller*] Ff, Cam.   *shorter* Rowe
ii +, Cap. Steev. Cald. Knt, Coll. ii, Dyce
iii, Huds.   *smaller* Mal. Bos. Coll. i, Sing.
Wh. i, Dyce i, Clke, Rlfe.   *lower* Sta.   *less
taller* Ktly.   *lesser* Spedding, Wr. Wh. ii.
  272. *other is*] *other's* Pope +.

'humorous' in the present play is more nearly defined by *wayward, headstrong, obsti-nate,* than by *capricious.*—ED.

266. **then I**] See line 17 *supra,* and I, i, 160. ABBOTT, § 216 : After a conjunc-tion and before an infinitive we often find *I, thou,* &c., where in Latin we should have 'me,' 'te,' &c. The conjunction seems to be regarded as introducing a new sentence, instead of connecting one clause with another. Hence the pronoun is put in the nominative, and a verb is perhaps to be supplied from the context. Thus here, 'More suits you to conceive *than I* (find it suitable) to speak of,' *i. e.* 'than that I should speak of it.' [See also HUNTER's plea (i, 344) for retaining archaic forms, urged at a time when there was need of it; nor is it altogether needless now-a-days, when we find as good a scholar as Keightley changing 'I' to *me.*—ED.]

271. **taller**] See Text. Notes. MALONE : Some change is absolutely necessary; for Rosalind, in a subsequent scene, expressly says that *she* is 'more than common *tall,*' and assigns that as a reason for her assuming the dress of a man, while her cousin Celia retained her female apparel. Again, in IV, iii, Celia is described by these words, 'the woman *low,* and browner than her brother;' *i. e.* Rosalind. [As between *shorter* and *smaller,* Malone urges that the latter is much 'nearer to the cor-rupted reading.'] STEEVENS : Shakespeare sometimes speaks of *little* women, but I do not recollect that he, or any other writer, has mentioned *small* ones. MALONE : *Small* is used to express lowness of stature in Greene's *James the Fourth* [Act IV, ad fin.] : 'But my small son made prettie hansome shift To save the queene his mistresse by his speed.' KNIGHT : Shakespeare uses *short* with reference to a woman—'Leo-nato's *short* daughter,' *Much Ado,* I, i, 216. [This is one of the very rare omissions in Mrs Cowden-Clarke's *Concordance,* s. v. *short.*] COLLIER, in his First Edition, approves of Malone's *smaller,* and adds that '*shorter* and "daughter" read disso-nantly;' but in his second edition, influenced by his Old Corrector, he adopts the 'dissonant' *shorter.* WALKER (*Crit.* iii, 60) : I suspect this is a slip of Shakespeare's pen. The word he had in his thoughts was probably *shorter,* not *smaller,* which in this sense belongs to later English.

But I can tell you, that of late this Duke   276
Hath tane difpleafure 'gainſt his gentle Neece,
Grounded vpon no other argument,
But that the people praiſe her for her vertues,
And pittie her, for her good Fathers ſake;   280
And on my life his malice 'gainſt the Lady
Will ſodainly breake forth : Sir, fare you well,
Hereafter in a better world then this,
I ſhall defire more loue and knowledge of you.
 Orl. I reſt much bounden to you : fare you well.   285
Thus muſt I from the ſmoake into the ſmother,
From tyrant Duke, vnto a tyrant Brother.
But heauenly *Roſaline.*   *Exit.* 288

277. *tane*] *ta'en* Rowe.
 Neece] *Neice* F$_3$.
279. *her vertues*] *vertues* F$_2$.

284. Exit. Rowe.
285. *fare you well*] *fareyouwell* F$_2$.

283. **better world**] STEEVENS: So in *Cor.* III, iii, 135 : 'There is a world elsewhere.' WRIGHT: That is, in a better age or state of things. [Wordsworth (p.
300) interprets this as an expression of faith and hope, and as an allusion to the world
beyond the grave. To me Wright's interpretation is decidedly the true one; Wordsworth's interpretation (which is undoubtedly a mere oversight on the part of the
gentle and reverend author), would be singularly inappropriate under the circumstances.—ED.]

286. **smother**] WRIGHT: Out of the frying-pan into the fire. 'Smother' is the
thick, stifling smoke of a smouldering fire. Bacon uses 'to pass in smother,' for *to be
stifled*, in *Essay* xxvii, p. 112; and 'to keep in smother' for *to stifle*, in *Essay* xxxi,
p. 134.

288. MOBERLY: These words are said and prolonged with a burst of enthusiasm
which sweeps away all his gloomy reflections.

Scena Tertius.

Enter Celia and Rofaline.

Cel. Why Cofen, why *Rofaline* : *Cupid* haue mercie,
Not a word?

Rof. Not one to throw at a dog.

Cel. No, thy words are too precious to be caft away   5
vpon curs, throw fome of them at me ; come lame mee
with reafons.

Rof. Then there were two Cofens laid vp, when the
one fhould be lam'd with reafons, and the other mad
without any.   10

Cel. But is all this for your Father?

Rof. No, fome of it is for my childes Father : Oh
how full of briers is this working day world.   13

2. *Cofen*] *Cofn* F$_2$.
  Rofaline] *Rofeline* F$_4$.
5. *thy*] *my* F$_3$F$_4$.
  precious] *precoious* F$_2$.
6. *come*] *come,* Ff.

12. *childes Father*] *father's child*
Rowe ii, Pope, Han. Warb. Johns. Knt,
Dyce, Coll. (MS) ii, Clke, Ktly, Huds.
Coll. iii, Wh. ii.
  13. *day world*] *day-world* F$_4$.

1, 2. **Rosaline**] This spelling, and where it again occurs in this scene, lines 93 and 101, Walker (*Crit.* ii, 66) attributes to the frequent confusion in the Folio of the final *d* and *e*. It may be so; but the frequency with which it occurs (for these are not the only instances) indicates that, as was natural, in common pronunciation the final *d* was somewhat slurred. That the name was Rosalind is made sure by Orlando's verses and Touchstone's doggerel in the Third Act.—Ed.

9. **mad**] Is this word quite above suspicion? Is it not somewhat early for Rosalind to confess herself *madly* in love? Or is it that she is mad, thus to love without reason?—Ed.

11. **Father**] MOBERLY: The reason which Rosalind had given for her sadness in Scene ii. Imagine the ironical accent on this word.

12. **my childes Father**] THEOBALD: That is, 'some of it is for my Sweetheart, whom I hope to marry and have children by.' COLERIDGE (p. 108): Who can doubt that this is a mistake for 'my father's child,' meaning herself? According to Theobald's note, a most indelicate anticipation is put into the mouth of Rosalind without reason; and besides, what a strange thought and how out of place and unintelligible! [I do not care to discuss this passage. It is enough to give, as above, the two most eminent advocates on the opposing sides. Further discussion cannot but emphasise the thought, whereof the purity or impurity will depend on the bias of the reader; 'the worm, look you, will bite after its kind.' It is well, however, in this case, and

4

Cel. They are but burs, Cofen, throwne vpon thee
in holiday foolerie, if we walke not in the trodden paths   15
our very petty-coates will catch them.

Rof. I could fhake them off my coate, thefe burs are
in my heart.

Cel. Hem them away.

Rof. I would try if I could cry hem, and haue him.   20

Cel. Come, come, wraftle with thy affeftions.

Rof. O they take the part of a better wraftler then
my felfe.

Cel. O, a good wifh vpon you : you will trie in time
in difpight of a fall: but turning thefe iefts out of feruice,   25
let vs talke in good earneft : Is it poffible on fuch a fodaine, you fhould fall into fo ftrong a liking with old Sir
Roulands yongeft fonne ?   28

27. *ftrong*] *ftrange* F_3F_4, Rowe.   28. *Roulands*] F_2.

---

in all similar cases (which will, hereafter, in this play receive, in the Commentary, no
notice at my hands), to bear in mind that modes of thought and of speech, as well as
of manners, shift and change from age to age as widely as do the costumes, and that
every age must be measured by its own standard.   Moberly says, ' Shakespeare would
have smiled' at Rowe's emendation.   Mrs Jameson says wisely : ' If the freedom of
some of the expressions used by Rosalind or Beatrice be objected to, let it be remembered that this was not the fault of Shakespeare or the women, but generally of the
age.   Portia, Beatrice, Rosalind, and the rest, lived in times when more importance
was attached to things than to words ; now we think more of words than of things ;
and happy are we in these later days of super-refinement, if we are to be saved by
our verbal morality.'—ED.]

  20. **cry hem, and haue him**] According to WARBURTON, this is a proverbial
expression signifying ' having for asking ' ; WALKER also (*Crit.* ii, 168) thinks that ' it
must be a proverbial expression,' and adds, ' though I cannot find it in Ray,' wherein
the present editor also has looked for it in vain.   MOBERLY surmises that it is ' a game
like hunt-the-slipper.'   Is it, however, necessary, after all, to find any deeper meaning
than the merest play on words in ' hem ' and ' him ' ?—ED.

  24. **a good wish upon you**] Used where ' my blessing on you' would be too
strong.—ED.

  25. The page in the Folio, which begins with this line, is wrongly numbered 187 ;
it should be 189.—ED.

  26, 27. **such a sodaine**] WRIGHT : Shakespeare uses ' on a sudden,' ' of a sudden,' and ' on the sudden,' elsewhere, but not ' on such a sudden.'

  27. **strong**] As far as I know, WALKER (*Crit.* iii, 23) is the only critic who
approves of *strange* of F_3F_4, for which, I think, much could be urged here, apart
from the fact that confusion has elsewhere arisen between these two words (cf. ' O
strong and fasten'd villain' of Q_1 in *Lear* II, i, 77).   Rosalind, by pleading the old
mutual love of their parents, gives merely a reason for loving Orlando at all, and why

Rof.   The Duke my Father lou'd his Father deerelie.

Cel.   Doth it therefore enſue that you ſhould loue his   30
Sonne deerelie ? By this kinde of chaſe, I ſhould hate
him, for my father hated his father deerely ; yet I hate
not *Orlando*.

Rof.   No faith, hate him not for my ſake.

Cel.   Why ſhould I not *?* doth he not deſerue well ?   35

34. *not*] *nor* F$_2$.   35. *he not*] *not he* F$_3$F$_4$, Rowe i.
35. *I not ?*] *I ?* Cap. Dyce iii.

---

that love should not be *strange*, but she would scarcely urge this parental love in the
past as a reason for vehemently loving him now.—ED.

29. MOBERLY: A line of much resource for a good actress; capable of being
shaded from the purely sentimental into the convincingly logical.

31. **chase**] JOHNSON: That is, by this way of *following* the argument. WHITER
(p. 93): Can the reader doubt that Shakespeare fell into this expression by a combination arising from the similar sounds of ' dear ' and *deer ?*   That our ancient writers
have sometimes quibbled on these words may be urged as an argument to convince
the reader how easy and natural it is for our Author to be led into such an association; although, in the present instance, not the most distant allusion to this equivocal
meaning was intended by the Poet. [To the unconscious association of ideas suggested by Whiter, I think there may be fairly added the association arising from the
word ' ensue,' to which ALLEN calls attention in a brief marginal note : ' ensue = pursue (" seek peace and ensue it "). Therefore Celia adds : " by this kind of *chase* " =
pursuing = *following* (= logical sequence, inference.)'—ED.]

32. **deerely**] Cf. ' my *dearest* foe,' *Ham.* I, ii, 182, and notes in this edition,
where CLARENDON'S concise statement is given : ' *dear* is used of whatever touches
us nearly, either in love or hate, joy or sorrow.'

35. **should I not**] THEOBALD (Nichols, *Lit. Illust.* ii, 330) : Either the negative
should be expunged, or it would be clearer to read, ' Why should I *hate*.' [This
remark, which was in a private letter to Warburton, was not subsequently repeated in
Theobald's edition. Capell's omission of the negative was therefore original with
him.] MALONE : Celia answers Rosalind (who had desired her ' *not to hate* Orlando,
for her sake ') as if she had said ' *love* him, for my sake :' to which the former replies,
' Why should I *not* [*i. e.* love him] ?' So, in the following passage, in *Hen. VIII :*
' Which of the peers Have uncontemn'd gone by him, or at least Strangely neglected ?'
Uncontemn'd must be understood as if the author had written *not* contemn'd; otherwise the subsequent words would convey a meaning directly contrary to what the
speaker intends. [It is to be feared that Malone's ingenuity is misplaced.] CALDE-
COTT : Meaning to be understood by reference to that which had preceded, *i. e.* upon
a principle stated by yourself, ' because my father hated his father, does he not well
deserve by me *to be hated ?*' while Rosalind, taking the words simply, and without
any reference, replies, ' Let me love him for that,' *i. e.* for that *he well deserves.* DYCE
(ed. iii) followed Capell in omitting the negative ' as a manifest error, in consequence
of " not " occurring just before and just after.' The explanation given by WHITE
(ed. i), that ' doth he not deserve well ?' means doth he not deserve well *to be hated,*
Dyce pronounces ' utterly inconsistent with the declaration in Celia's preceding speech,

Enter Duke with Lords.   36

Roſ. Let me loue him for that, and do you loue him
Becauſe I doe.   Looke, here comes the Duke.
Cel. With his eies full of anger.
Duk. Miſtris, diſpatch you with your ſafeſt haſte,   40
And get you from our Court.
Roſ. Me Vncle.
Duk. You Coſen,
Within theſe ten daies if that thou beeſt found
So neere our publike Court as twentie miles,   45
Thou dieſt for it.
Roſ. I doe beſeech your Grace
Let me the knowledge of my fault beare with me :
If with my ſelfe I hold intelligence,   49

36. Scene IX. Pope +.   42, 43. *me... You*] *me,... You*, Rowe.
Enter...] In line 38, Coll.   43. *Coſen*] Om. Han.

" yet I hate not Orlando." ' [It must be confessed that by this omission of ' not ' the
text is rendered simpler, but at the cost of all archness or irony. Moreover, that most
wholesome rule, as wholesome as it is venerable, should never be lost sight of : *durior
lectio preferenda'st*, a necessity all the more urgent now-a-days, since it seems to be
about the very last rule which occurs, if ever it does occur at all, to the minds of the
emenders of Shakespeare's text.—ED.]

37. me . . . you] These are the emphatic words.

40. safest] SINGER suggests that this is probably a misprint for *swiftest*. COLLIER :
The Duke means by this epithet to refer to the danger which would attend Rosalind
if she delayed.   The (MS) has *fastest*, but change seems undesirable. BLACKWOOD'S
MAGAZINE (1853, Aug., p. 197) : ' Safest haste '—that is, most convenient despatch—
is much more probable than ' *fastest* haste,' inasmuch as the lady to whom the words
were addressed is allowed *ten days* to take herself off in. WHITE : In ' safest haste '
there is an unconscious anticipation by the Duke of his subsequent threat. Besides,
Shakespeare would not needlessly write ' *fastest* haste.' KEIGHTLEY : *Safe* is sure,
certain, a sense which it retains in the Midland counties. MOBERLY : That is, the
haste which is your best safety.

42. Vncle] ABBOTT, § 465, scans this line by ' dropping or softening ' the *le* final
in this word, thus : And gét | you fróm | our cóurt. | Me, úncl*e* ? | You, coúsin. Un-
questionably this dropping or softening of syllables containing a liquid, final or otherwise, in certain words, frequently takes place. But I do not think that we are to
expect to find it in broken lines.—ED.

43. Cosen] SKEAT (*Dict.* s. v.) : A near relative.   Formerly applied to a kinsman generally, not in the modern restricted way. . . . . Low Latin *cosinus*, a contraction of Lat. *consobrinus*, the child of a mother's sister, a cousin, relation.

44, 51. if that] For other instances of *that* as a conjunctional affix see *post*, line
122; II, vii, 76; III, v, 99; IV, iii, 121; or Abbott, § 287, or *Mer. of Ven.* III, iii,
35; or Shakespeare *passim*.

Or haue acquaintance with mine owne defires,   50
If that I doe not dreame, or be not franticke,
(As I doe truft I am not) then deere Vncle,
Neuer fo much as in a thought vnborne,
Did I offend your highneffe.

   Duk. Thus doe all Traitors,   55
If their purgation did confift in words,
They are as innocent as grace it felfe;
Let it fuffice thee that I truft thee not.

   Rof. Yet your miftruft cannot make me a Traitor;
Tell me whereon the likelihoods depends?   60

   Duk. Thou art thy Fathers daughter, there's enough.

   Rof. So was I when your highnes took his Dukdome,
So was I when your highneffe banifht him;
Treafon is not inherited my Lord,
Or if we did deriue it from our friends,   65
What's that to me, my Father was no Traitor,
Then good my Leige, miftake me not fo much,   67

---

50. *mine*] *my* Rowe+.   60. *likelihoods*] *likelihood* Ff, Rowe+,
Cap. Steev. Var. Cald. Knt, Coll. Cam.

---

56. **purgation**] A technical use of a legal term which seems to have escaped
RUSHTON, LORD CAMPBELL, and HEARD. Vulgar purgation, as distinguished from
canonical purgation, demanded not alone oaths, but ordeals by fire, or water, or combat.—ED.

60. **likelihoods**] See 'destinies decrees,' I, ii, 101. WALKER (*Crit.* i, 234): The
interpolation of an *s* at the end of a word, generally, but not always, a noun substantive, is remarkably frequent in the Folio. Those who are conversant with the MSS
of the Elizabethan age may perhaps be able to explain its origin. Were it not for the
different degrees of frequency with which it occurs in different parts of the Folio,
being comparatively rare in the Comedies (except perhaps in *The Wint. Tale*),
appearing more frequently in the Histories, and becoming quite common in the
Tragedies, I should be inclined to think it originated in some peculiarity of Shakespeare's handwriting. [See II, i, 54; or *Mer. of Ven.* II, ix, 35 and *Oth.* I, i, 31,
where several instances are given which had escaped Walker.—ED.] ALLEN paraphrases: 'Tell me on what depends your belief that I am likely to be a traitor.'

66. **no Traitor**] LADY MARTIN (p. 413): In speaking this I could never help
laying a slight emphasis on these last words. For what but a traitor had the Duke
himself been? The sarcasm strikes home. MOBERLY: Rosalind's brave spirit will
not allow her to defend herself at her father's expense or to separate her cause from
his. There are few passages in Shakespeare more instinctively true and noble than
this. She had *not* offended her uncle, even in thought, though every one else was
doing so. But the least suggestion that her father is a traitor rouses her in arms to
defend him.

To thinke my pouertie is treacherous. 68

Cel. Deere Soueraigne heare me fpeake.

Duk. I *Celia,* we ftaid her for your fake, 70
Elfe had fhe with her Father rang'd along.

Cel. I did not then intreat to haue her ftay,
It was your pleafure. and your owne remorfe,
I was too yong that time to value her,
But now I know her : if fhe be a Traitor, 75
Why fo am I : we ftill haue flept together,
Rofe at an inftant, learn'd, plaid, eate together,
And wherefoere we went, like *Iunos* Swans,
Still we went coupled and infeperable. 79

70. *we ftaid*] *we but staid* Pope +.   79. *infeperable* F₁.
73. Om. Rowe i.

67, 68. **so much, To thinke**] See II, iii, 8; also *Mer. of Ven.* ' so fond To come abroad,' or Abbott, § 281, for instances of a similar omission of *as.*

73. **remorse**] STEEVENS : That is, compassion. DYCE : Tenderness of heart.

74. **that time**] See Abbott, § 202, for instances of the omission of the preposition in adverbial expressions of time, manner, &c. Thus also ' all points ' in line 123, *post.*

76. **still**] That is, constantly, always; thus in Shakespeare *passim.*

77. **an instant**] For instances where *a* is used for *one,* see Abbott, § 81.

78. **Iunos Swans**] WRIGHT : No commentator appears to have made any remark upon this, but it may be questioned whether for ' Juno ' we ought not to read *Venus,* to whom, and not to Juno, the swan is sacred. In Ovid's *Metam.* x, 708, 717, 718, the same book which contains the story of Atalanta, who is mentioned in this play, and of Adonis, Venus is represented in a chariot drawn by swans. [That this over-sight should have escaped Shakespeare's notice is strange, but nothing so strange as that during all these many years it lurked undetected, full in the blaze of the fierce light that beats on every line of these plays. That it is a mistake there can be no doubt, and most probably Shakespeare's own. As Shakespeare's knowledge of myth-ology was, in all likelihood, mainly derived from Golding's translation of Ovid, my hopes were high that somewhere or other the slip of referring to ' Juno's swans ' might be found in that volume. Dyce once, half mournfully, half apologetically, referred to the ' hours he had wasted ' over old, half-forgotten books. Be his sigh re-echoed here. The expression ' Juno's swans ' is not in the Fifteen Books of Golding's Translation of Ovid.—ED.]

79. **inseperable**] COLLIER (ed. ii) : There is no reason for changing this to *inseparate,* beyond the fact that in the (MS) *inseparate* is inserted and ' inseparable ' struck out. Perhaps *inseparate* is a little more in Shakespeare's manner, but he also has ' inseparable ' in *King John,* III, iv, 66. WHITE (ed. i) : The F₂ has ' insepa-rate,' a reading so consonant with Shakespeare's phraseology, and so rhythmically advantageous to the line, that it would be acceptable without question, were not authority against it. [An oversight. White was thinking of Collier's (MS). F₂ and the rest have *inseparable.*—ED.]

Duk.   She is too subtile for thee, and her fmoothnes;   80
Her verie filence, and per patience, ·
Speake to the people, and they pittie her :
Thou art a foole, fhe robs thee of thy name,
And thou wilt fhow more bright, & feem more vertuous
When fhe is gone : then open not thy lips   85
Firme, and irreuocable is my doombe,
Which I haue paft vpon her, fhe is banifh'd.
Cel.   Pronounce that fentence then on me my Leige,
I cannot liue out of her companie.
Duk.   You are a foole : you Neice prouide your felfe,   90
If you out-ftay the time, vpon mine honor,
And in the greatneffe of my word you die.
                                          Exit Duke, &c.
Cel.   O my poore *Rofaline*, whether wilt thou goe?
Wilt thou change Fathers ? I will giue thee mine :   95
I charge thee be not thou more grieu'd then I am.
Rof.   I haue more caufe.
Cel.   Thou haft not Cofen,   98

81. *per*] F₁.	94. *whether*] *where* Pope+.
88. *Leige*] *Liege* F₂.	95. *Fathers*] *father* Ff.
91. *out-ftay*] *out-ftany* F₄.	96. *then*] *them* F₄.
93. Scene X. Pope+.	98. *Cofen*] *dearest cousin* Han.

79. MRS JAMESON (p. 153) : Celia is more quiet and retired; but she rather yields
to Rosalind than is eclipsed by her.   She is as full of sweetness, kindness, and intelligence, quite as susceptible, and almost as witty, though she makes less display of
wit.   She is described as less fair and less gifted; yet the attempt to excite in her
mind a jealousy of her lovelier friend by placing them in comparison [as in lines 80–
86] fails to awaken in the generous heart of Celia any other feeling than an increased
tenderness and sympathy for her cousin.   To Celia, Shakespeare has given some of
the most striking and animated parts of the dialogue; and in particular that exquisite
description of the friendship between her and Rosalind [lines 75–79].   The feeling
of interest and admiration thus excited for Celia at the first, follows her through the
whole play.   We listen to her as to one who has made herself worthy of our love;
and her silence expresses more than eloquence.

84. **seem**] WARBURTON: Doubtless the poet wrote *shine, i. e.* her virtues would
appear more splendid when the lustre of her cousin's was away.   JOHNSON: When
she was seen alone she would be more noted.

84. **vertuous**] CAPELL (57, *b*): This means gifted, not with *virtue*, but *virtues*,
virtuous and good qualities of all sorts.

94. **whether**] Undoubtedly contracted, as in many other instances, into *whe'er*.
See Walker (*Vers.* 106), or *Macb.* I, iii, 111; *Ham.* III, ii, 193; *Lear*, II, i, 53;
Mer. of Ven. I, i, 183; V, i, 329.

98. **Thou hast not Cosen,**] STEEVENS: Some word is wanting to the metre.

Prethee be cheerefull ; know'ft thou not the Duke
Hath banifh'd me his daughter?   100
  Rof. That he hath not.
  Cel. No, hath not? *Rofaline* lacks then the loue
Which teacheth thee that thou and I am one,   103

100. *Hath*] *Has* Rowe ii+.	103. *thee*] *me* Theob. Han. Warb. Cap.
102. *No, hath not?*] Ff, Rowe i. *No?*	Dyce iii, Huds.
hath not? Rowe ii+.	*thou*] *she* Cap. conj.
	am] *are* Han.

Perhaps our author wrote *Indeed,* thou hast,' &c. [I beg leave to doubt that in a
broken line a syllable or a foot is ever wanting, to complete the metre.—ED.]
    102. **No, hath not?**] In *Notes & Qu.* (vol. vii, p. 520) ARROWSMITH gave, for
the first time, a correct explanation of such phrases as *No did? No will? No had?*
&c. by citing ' a string of examples' showing that they were equivalent to *Did you
not? Will you not? Had you not?* &c. Whereupon SINGER (*Ib.* p. 593) inferred
that the present line was another illustration of this same idiom, losing sight of the
fact that to be exactly parallel Celia should say *No hath?* HALLIWELL, also, was
misled, and although neither he nor Singer made any change in the text other than in
erasing the comma after ' No,' yet Halliwell suggested that it would be better understood if printed, *no, ' hath not,'* which is true enough, but if Celia's question is a mere
quotation of Rosalind's remark, where is the ' singular idiom' which Halliwell says
is to be noticed here?—ED.
    103. **teacheth thee**] THEOBALD : 'Tis evident the Poet wrote ' teacheth *me ;*' for
if Rosalind had learnt to think Celia one part of her Self, she could not lack that
Love which Celia complains she does. [This emendation, such as it is, belongs to
Theobald, although it is generally attributed to Warburton, even in the Cambridge
Edition. Theobald proposed it in a letter to Warburton in 1729; see Nichols, *Illust.*
ii, 330. Wright correctly gives it to Theobald, but while correcting one oversight
commits another by giving to Theobald the change of ' am ' to *are,* which in reality
belongs to Hanmer. Singer proposed it, perhaps believing it to be original, in *Notes
& Qu.* vol. vii, p. 593, but did not adopt it in his subsequent text.—ED.] CAPELL :
The inexpressible sweetness of the sentiment contain'd in this line, and that before
it, is lost by the old reading ' thee '; which were alone sufficient to justify the corrector, and those who have follow'd him in his change. JOHNSON : Either reading
may stand. The sense of the established text is not remote or obscure. Where
would be the absurdity of saying, You know not the law which teaches you to do
right? KNIGHT thinks there is reason in the change of ' thee ' to *me ;* and WHITE
(ed. i), after quoting Johnson, adds : ' still, it remains true that Celia would naturally
reproach her cousin for the lack of that completeness of love which she herself possessed.' MOBERLY : That is, ' which ought to teach you as it has already taught me.'
The futurity is sufficiently expressed by the context; as in ' non dubito quin tibi
Chremes *det* gnatam.' [There seems to be no necessity for change. Johnson's illustration is pat. But if any change at all is adopted, it should be as thorough as that
proposed by Capell in the following note on ' am.']
    103. **am**] CAPELL : The freedom us'd with grammar in ' am ' has (perhaps) a
reason for 't; the diction, it will be said, is more forcible in that than in *are* : But is
either diction or pathos improv'd by the transition from Rosalind in the third person

Shall we be fundred? fhall we part fweete girle?
No, let my Father feeke another heire :   105
Therefore deuife with me how we may flie
Whether to goe, and what to beare with vs,
And doe not feeke to take your change vpon you,
To beare your griefes your felfe, and leaue me out :
For by this heauen, now at our forrowes pale ;   110
Say what thou canſt, Ile goe along with thee.
  Roſ.   Why, whether fhall we goe?   112

107, 112. *Whether*] *Whither* Ff.   Coll. ii. *the charge* Sing, Wh. i, Dyce
  108. *your change*] *your charge* Ff,   ii, Ktly, Rlfe.
Rowe, Pope, Theob. Warb. Han. Cap.   110. *now...pale*] In parenthesis, Ff.

in one line to Rosalind in the second in this? if they are not, 'thou' should give
place to *she*, as 'thee' has to *me*. KEIGHTLEY (*Exp*. 156): Such was the structure
of the time. 'My thoughts and I *am* for this other element'—Jonson, *Cynthia's
Revels*, I, i. It was the same in French: 'Ni la mort ni vous-même Ne me *ferez
jamais prononcer que je l'aime*'—Racine, *Bajazet*, IV, i. WRIGHT: No one would
now think of writing 'thou and I am,' but as it is an instance of a construction of
frequent occurrence in Shakespeare's time, by which the verb is attracted to the nearest subject, it should not be altered. See Ben Jonson, *The Fox*, II, i, 'Take it or
leave it, howsoever, both it and I am at your service.' WHITE (ed. ii): A disagree-
ment of words due to mere heedlessness.

  104. **sundred**] WHITE (ed. i): It is noteworthy that this is the form of the contracted participle, usually, if not always, found in books of Shakespeare's time; as,
for instance, in this play, 'seque*st'red*'; 'engen*d'red*'; 'mini*st'red*'; 'rememb'*red*';
'win*t'red*'. It seems more than probable that this uniformity is not accidental; and
it is quite possible that it represents the colloquial form of the contraction.

  108. **change**] MALONE: That is, to take your 'change' or reverse of fortune upon
yourself, without any aid or participation. STEEVENS: I have inserted this note, but
without implicit confidence in the reading it explains. WALKER (*Crit*. iii, 61): I
have no doubt that Shakespeare wrote *charge*, and so the F₂. The erratum *change*
for *charge* occurs frequently in the Folio. *Vice versâ, Tam. of the Shr*. III, i, 81,
the Folio reads, 'I am not so nice To *charge* true rules for old [*odd*] inventions.'
SINGER: Whoever glances at the passage must see that the printer has here again
mistaken *yᵉ charge* of the MS for *yʳ change*. [There is but little doubt in my mind
that *charge* is the true reading. To share her griefs with Celia would be no 'change'
to Rosalind, but to bear them all alone and leave Celia out could not but be a heavy
charge or burden, which Celia says she must not think of. To bear the 'reverse of
fortune' bravely is not what Celia is urging, but that they may still go coupled and
inseparable.—ED.]

  110. **pale**] CALDECOTT: This passage may be interpreted either 'by this heaven,
or the light of heaven, with its lustre faded in sympathy with our feelings;' or, 'for,
by this heaven, now we have reached, now we are at the *utmost verge* or *point*, in this
extremity or crisis of our fate,' &c. (for such it was) as this word is used in *Wint.
Tale*, IV, ii : 'For the red blood reigns in the winter's *pale*.' [This latter interpretation is extremely doubtful.—ED.]

Cel.   To feeke my Vncle in the Forreft of *Arden*.   113
Rof.   Alas, what danger will it be to vs,
(Maides as we are) to trauell forth fo farre?   115
Beautie prouoketh theeues fooner then gold.
   Cel.   Ile put my felfe in poore and meane attire,
And with a kinde of vmber fmirch my face,
The like doe you, fo fhall we paffe along,   119

115. *forth fo farre*] *for farre* F₂.   118. *fmirch*] *fmitch* F₂. *fmutch* F₃F₄,
                                              Rowe, Pope, Han.

---

113. **in the Forrest of Arden**] STEEVENS: These words are an evident interpolation, without use, and injurious to the measure : ' Why, whither should we go ?—To
seek my uncle,' being a complete verse.   Besides, we have been already informed by
Charles the Wrestler that the banished Duke's residence was *in the forest of Arden*.
KNIGHT : All the ordinary reprints of the text are here mutilated by one of Steevens's
hateful *corrections*.   [Knight here quotes Steevens's note, and proceeds :] And so
the two poor ladies are to go forth to seek the banished Duke through the wide world,
and to meet with him at last by chance, because Steevens holds that this indication
of their knowledge of the place of his retreat is ' injurious to the measure.'   WALKER
(*Vers.* 69) scans the line as it stands in the Folio by reading ' forest ' as a monosyllable.
     115. **farre**] WALKER (*Crit.* i, 189, Article xxx—*Far* and *near* used as com-
paratives) : *1 Hen. IV :* III, i, 256 : ' And givest such sarcenet surety for thy
oaths, As if thou never walk'dst further than Finsbury.'   I would read, 'As if thou
ne'er walk'dst fur' than Finsbury.'   Compare *Wint. Tale*, IV, iv, 440 : ' We'll bar
thee from succession ; Not hold thee of our blood, no, not our kin, Far than Deuca-
lion off.'   Quasi *farrer, furrer ?*   In Chaucer we have *ferre*, further ; *House of Fame*,
Bk. ii, line 92, ' But er I bere the much ferre, I wol the tel what I am.'   (Note, *As
You Like It :* ' Maids as we are, to travel forth so far !'   Does not Shakespeare's
instinctive love of euphony require that we should here pronounce, perhaps write,
fur ? πόρρω.)   [Walker's ear was so delicately attuned to the harmony of verse that
one should be exceedingly cautious in gainsaying him.   Yet I must confess that this
last query seems to me the weakest in an article which is otherwise admirable throughout, and one to which it is a pleasure to record obligations.   We must remember that
Walker did not live to see his notes in type ; indeed, did not even live to prepare
them for the press.   They are merely the jottings of a scholar, almost his private
adversaria, which accounts for their abruptness and their Greek and Latin short-cuts,
which some critics, oblivious of this fact, have severely criticised as pedantic.   Walker's
admirable editor, Lettsom, whose influence over Dyce, by the way, was marked, was
wise in preserving every scrap, however disjointed, of Walker's memoranda, albeit
Walker himself might have erased many a one when the heat was cooled with which
they were first struck out.   But whether wise or otherwise, no suggestion from a
scholar like Walker should pass unregarded by simple folk like us.—ED.]
     118. **vmber**] MALONE : A dusky, yellow-coloured earth, brought from Umbria in
Italy.
     118. **smirch**] See Text. Notes for other forms of this word, all of which, together
with *smudge*, WRIGHT says, are originally connected with *smear*.   Compare ' the chaste
unsmirched brows of my true mother,' *Ham.* IV, v, 115.

And neuer ftir affailants. 120

  Rof. Were it not better,

Becaufe that I am more then common tall,

That I did fuite me all points like a man,

A gallant curtelax vpon my thigh,

A bore-fpeare in my hand, and in my heart 125

Lye there what hidden womans feare there will,

Weele haue a fwafhing and a marfhall outfide,

As manie other mannifh cowards haue,

That doe outface it with their femblances.

  Cel. What fhall I call thee when thou art a man? 130

---

121. *Were it*] *Were't* Pope +.   124. *curtelax*] *curtelass* Cap.

123. *me*] Om. F$_4$.   127. *Weele*] *I'll* Han. Johns.

---

122. **Because that**] See I, iii, 44.

123. **suite**] DYCE: That is, clothe, dress; as in *Lear*, IV, vii, 6, 'Be better suited,' *i. e.* 'put on better clothes.'

123. **all points**] See line 74 *supra*.

124. **curtelax**] DYCE: A cutlass. WRIGHT: The termination is an instance of a frequent corruption by which a word is altered so as to correspond to a supposed etymology. Other forms of the word, due to the same tendency, are 'cutlace' and 'cutlash.' A curtleaxe was not an axe at all, but a short sword. The word is formed from a diminutive of the Latin *cultellus*. Florio (*It. Dict.*) has 'Coltellaccio, a cutleaxe, a hanger.' Cotgrave gives 'Coutelas: m. A Cut elas, Courtelas, or short sword, for a man at armes.' Compare Fairfax, *Tasso*, ix, 82: 'His curtlax by his thigh, short, hooked, fine.' And *Hen. V:* IV, ii, 21: 'Scarce blood enough in all their sickly veins To give each naked curtle-axe a stain.' Again, Lodge in his novel, 'To the Gentlemen Readers,' says, 'Heere you may perhaps finde some leaues of Venus mirtle, but hewen down by a souldier with his curtlaxe.' Spenser, supposing the weapon to be a short axe, wrote (*Faery Queene*, IV, ii, 42): 'But speare and curtaxe both vsd Priamond in field.' In DuBartas, *Historie of Judith* (trans. Hudson), book ii, p. 16 (ed. 1611), the word appears in the form 'curtlasse': 'And with a trembling hand the curtlasse drewe.'

125. **bore-speare**] Halliwell gives a wood-cut both of a curtleaxe and of a boar-spear. The latter, says FAIRHOLT, has a blade very broad and strong, with a cross-bar inserted immediately below it, to prevent its passing directly through the animal. 'Unlike the ordinary spear, it appears to have been seldom thrown, but the rush made by the animal on the hunter was met by a direct opposition of the weapon on his part.'

127. **swashing**] STEEVENS: That is, an appearance of noisy, bullying valour. [See *Rom. & Jul.* I, i, 55, with its superfluity of notes in this edition. The word is still current here in America. The line is thus scanned by ABBOTT, § 455, with an accent on *out* in the last word: 'We'll háve | a swásh | ing ánd | a már | tial oút-side.—ED.]

129. **it**] For other instances of this indefinite use of 'it,' which is as universal now as ever, see Abbott, § 226.

Rof.   Ile haue no worfe a name then *Ioues* owne Page,
And therefore looke you call me *Ganimed*.
But what will you by call'd?
   Cel.   Something that hath a reference to my ftate :
No longer *Celia*, but *Aliena*.   135
   Rof.   But Cofen, what if we affaid to fteale
The clownifh Foole out of your Fathers Court :
Would he not be a comfort to our trauaile ?
   Cel.   Heele goe along ore the wide world with me,
Leaue me alone to woe him ; Let's away   140

133. *by*] F₁.   140. *woe*] *wooe* Ff.   *woo* Rowe.
134. *hath*] *bath* F₄.

---

131. **Page**]   FLETCHER (p. 202) :   Mrs Jameson, amongst others, misled probably
by one of those hasty verbal mistakes which have been so often made by the exposi-
tors of Shakespeare, seems to have been betrayed by Rosalind's allusion immediately
after to '*Jove's* own page,' into talking of '*her page's* vest,' '*her page's* costume,' &c.
Now, *pages* of the banished Duke do appear in the course of the forest scenes, two
of whom sing, at Touchstone's request, the lively song introduced in the Fifth Act ;
but the accoutrements of a page would ill have supplied that '*martial*' exterior for
the sake of whose protection alone Rosalind has any inclination to put herself in
masquerade.   She is to wear *manly*, not *boyish*, habiliments.   The *curtleaxe* and
boar-spear are not the page's nor the shepherd's array, but the forester's, such as was
worn by her father and his exiled followers.   [But see Lodge's Novel, where Rosalynde says, ' I would very well become the person and apparel of a page,' &c., and
again, ' if any knave offer wrong, your page will shew him the poynt of his weapon.'
See further, Fletcher's note, III, v, 114.—ED.]

   132. **Ganimed**]   NEIL :   This name, which is that used by Lodge, would not be
the less acceptable to Shakespeare that it had acquired a fresh poetic interest in *The
Affectionate Shepherd, containing the Complaint of Daphnis for the love of Ganymede*, by Richard Barnefield, 1594.

   135. **Aliena**]   WRIGHT :   With the accent on the second syllable.   ROLFE :   But
surely ' Celia ' is a trisyllable, as in line 70 above, and 'Aliena' accented on the
penult, as it ought to be.   [This is the only line in the play where the rhythm can be
our guide.   Our choice, therefore, lies, I think, only between ' No lóng | er Cél | ya,
bút | Alí | ena,' and ' No long | er Ce | liá, | but Al | iéna.'   With Rolfe, I much pre-
fer the latter, because, as he says, Celia is elsewhere unquestionably a trisyllable,
namely, in 'Ay, Ce | liá, | we stáy'd | her fór | your sáke.'   Moreover, Shakespeare's
' small Latin ' was quite large enough for him to remember the quantity of *ălĭēna*.
—ED.]

   140. HUDSON (p. 16) :   It is curious to observe how the Poet takes care to let us
know from the first that beneath the affectations of Touchstone's calling some precious
sentiments have been kept alive ; that far within the Fool there is laid up a secret reserve
of the man, ready to leap forth and combine with better influences as soon as the
incrustations of art are thawed and broken up.   This is partly done [here in this
present passage], where we learn that some remnants, at least, of a manly heart in

And get our Iewels and our wealth together,   141
Deuife the fitteſt time, and ſafeſt way
To hide vs from purſuite that will be made
After my flight : now goe in we content
To libertie, and not to baniſhment.   *Exeunt.*   145

Actus Secundus. Scœna Prima.

---

*Enter Duke Senior : Amyens, and two or three Lords
          like Forreſters.*

Duk. Sen. Now my Coe-mates, and brothers in exile :
Hath not old cuſtome made this life more ſweete
Then that of painted pompe? Are not theſe woods   5
More free from perill then the enuious Court?
Heere feele we not the penaltie of *Adam*,   7

---

144. *in we*] Cald. Knt, Neil.   *we in*
Ff et cet.
  content] *cantent* F₄.
Actus] Actu F₂.
  1. Lords] Lorde F₄.

3. *brothers*] *brother* Ff.
7. *not*] *but* Theob. +, Cap. Steev. Mal.
Coll. ii, iii, Sing. Wh. Dyce, Cam. Clke,
Wr. Mob.

---

him have asserted their force in the shape of unselfish regards, strong as life, for whatever is purest and loveliest in the characters about him. He would rather starve or
freeze, with Celia near him, than feed high and lie warm where his eye cannot find
her. If, with this fact in view, our honest esteem does not go out towards him, then
we, I think, are fools in a worse sense than he is. [And the reflection of this devotion illuminates Celia, too, who kindled it.—ED.]

144. **in we**] MALONE: I am not sure that the transposition *we in* is necessary.
Our author might have used 'content' as an adjective. NEIL follows the Folio,
which means, he says, Now let us go in, contentedly. 'Perhaps,' he adds, 'the
reading, "Now go in; we consent," would give the author's meaning.'

1. **Duke Senior**] In a note on I, ii, 78, Capell says that 'throughout all this play
Shakespeare calls his two Dukes, *Duke Senior* and *Duke Junior.*' In a MS note of
Malone's, given by Halliwell, Malone says: 'This is not so. The younger brother is
never once called *Duke Junior*, throughout the play, in any one entry. He is always
called simply *Duke*. The other is called Duke Senior.'

3. **exile**] WALKER (*Vers.* 291) gives a list of many words, chiefly disyllabic, which
have 'an accent—though, of course, an unequal one—on both syllables, the principal
one being shifted *ad libitum* from the one syllable to the other.' Thus, in *Rom. &
Jul.* III, iii, 13: 'For exile hath more terror in his look,' yet within eight lines the
accent is shifted to the second syllable (as it is here in *As You Like It*): 'And world's
exile is death; then banished.' See also Abbott, § 490.

7. THEOBALD: What was the penalty of Adam, hinted at by our Poet? The
being sensible of the difference of the seasons. The Duke says, the cold and effects

---

[Heere feele we not the penaltie of Adam]

of the winter feelingly persuade him what he is. How does he *not* then feel the penalty? Doubtless the text must be restored as I have corrected it [see Text. Notes], and 'tis obvious in the course of these notes how often 'not' and *but*, by mistake, have chang'd place in our author's former editions. MALONE: As 'not' has here taken the place of *but*, so, in *Cor.* II, iii, 72, 'but' is printed instead of *not*: *Cor.* 'Ay, but mine own desire. *First Cit.* How! not your own desire.' [This is perhaps scarcely apposite. According to the excellent emendation of the Cam. Edd. *not* had simply fallen out of the line, and had not been changed into 'but': 'Ay, but *not* mine own desire.'—ED.] BOSWELL: Surely the old reading is right. Here we feel *not*, do *not* suffer, from the penalty of Adam, the season's difference; for when the winter's wind blows upon my body, I *smile*, and say— WHITER (p. 13): Theobald supposes that the penalty of Adam here expressed is 'the being sensible of the difference of the seasons.' I do not think that this is the allusion intended. I read the whole passage thus:

> 'Here feel we *not* the pena'ty of Adam:
> The seasons' difference, as the icy fang
> And churlish chiding of the winter's wind—
> (Which when it bites and blows upon my body
> Even till I shrink with cold, I smile and say
> This is no flattery;)—these are counsellors,
> That feelingly persuade me what I am.'

The penalty of Adam, here alluded to, may be gathered from the following passages in Scripture: 'Cursed is the *ground* for thy sake; in *sorrow* shalt thou *eat* of it all the days of thy life,' *Gen.* iii, 17; 'In the *sweat* of thy face shalt thou *eat* bread,' ver. 19; 'Therefore the Lord God sent him forth from the garden of Eden, to *till the ground* from whence he was taken,' ver. 23. We here plainly see that the only curse or penalty imposed on Adam which can have any reference to the condition of a country life is the toil of cultivating the ground, and acquiring by that labour the means of sustenance. The Duke therefore justly consoles himself and his companions with the reflection that *their* banishment into those woods from the *paradise of a court* (if we may be permitted to continue the allusion) was not attended with the penalty pronounced on Adam,—a life of pain and of labour; but that, on the contrary, it ought to be considered as a philosophical retirement of ease and independence. With respect to the minute inconvenience which they might suffer from the difference of the seasons—the biting frost and the winter's wind—*these* (he observes) should not be regarded in any other view than as sharp but salutary counsellors, which made them *feel* only for the promotion of their good and the improvement of their virtue. CALDECOTT: Wherever the course of thought admits it, Shakespeare is accustomed to continue the form of speaking which he first falls upon; and the sense of this passage, in which he repeats the word 'not,' appears to be, 'The penalty here, properly speaking, is *not*, or scarce is, physically felt, because the suffering it occasions, sharp as it otherwise might be called, turns so much to account in a moral sense.' The construction of 'which, when it blows,' is '*at* which, or which blowing.' *And* or *for*, instead of *which*, would have given a plain and clear sense; but the same forms and cold terms of reasoning would have clogged the spirited and warm flow of the sentiment; and the recurrence of *and* at the beginning of the line would have

[Heere feele we not the penaltie of Adam]

offended the ear. Still, the word 'feelingly,' used at the end of this passage in an affirmative sense, after 'feel' had been brought forward, coupled with a negative, certainly makes a confusion, if it be not said to favour Theobald's substitution. HARNESS: Theobald's alteration is not only unnecessary, but palpably wrong. The Duke's sentiment is as follows: Here we do not feel the penalty of Adam, the difference of the seasons, because the slight physical suffering that it occasions only raises a *smile*, and suggests a moral reflection. KNIGHT follows Whiter (except that after 'Adam' he puts a full stop instead of a colon), and urges in support that: Milton represents the repentant Adam as thus interpreting the penalty: 'On me the curse aslope Glanced on the ground; *with labour I must earn My bread;* what harm? Idleness had been worse.' The beautiful passage in Cowper's *Task*, describing the Thresher, will also occur to the reader: 'See him sweating o'er his bread Before he eats it. 'Tis the *primal curse*, But soften'd into mercy; made the pledge Of cheerful days, and nights without a groan.' 'The seasons' difference,' it must be remembered, was ordained *before* the fall, and *was in no respect a penalty*. We may therefore reject the received interpretation. But how could the Duke say, receiving the passage in the sense we have suggested, 'Here feel we *not* the penalty of Adam'? In the First Act, Charles the Wrestler, describing the Duke and his co-mates, says, they 'fleet the time carelessly as they did in the *golden world*.' One of the characteristics of the golden world is thus described by Daniel: 'Oh! happy golden age! Not for that rivers ran With streams of milk and honey dropp'd from trees; Not that the earth did gage Unto the husbandman Her voluntary fruits, free without fees.' The song of Amiens, in the Fifth Scene of this Act, conveys, we think, the same allusion: 'Who doth ambition shun, And loves to live i' the sun, *Seeking the food he eats, And pleas'd with what he gets*.' The exiled courtiers led a life without toil—a life in which they were contented with a little—and they were thus exempt from the 'penalty of Adam.' We close, therefore, the sentence at 'Adam.' 'The seasons' difference' is now the antecedent of 'these are counsellors'; the freedom of construction common to Shakespeare and the poets of his time fully warranting this acceptation of the reading. In this way, the Duke says, 'The differences of the seasons are counsellors that teach me what I am;—as, for example, the winter's wind—which, when it blows upon my body, I smile, and say, This is no flattery.' We may add that, immediately following the lines we have quoted from the *Paradise Lost*, Adam alludes to 'the seasons' difference,' but in no respect as part of the curse: 'With labour I must earn My bread; what harm? Idleness had been worse. My labour will sustain me; and lest cold Or heat should injure us, his timely care Hath unbesought provided, and his hands Cloth'd us unworthy, pitying while He judg'd. How much more, if we pray Him, will his ear Be open, and his heart to pity incline, And teach us further by what means to shun Th' inclement seasons, rain, ice, hail, and snow.' [Although COLLIER in both of his editions interpreted the 'penalty of Adam' as the 'seasons' difference,' yet at one time he followed the Folio, and at another Theobald; in the latter case he did so, despite the fact that his (MS) retained the old reading, merely changing 'as the Icie phang' to '*or* the,' &c.] HUNTER (i, 346): Read either 'not' or *but*, and still the passage is perplexed. Taking the text as we have it, I venture to suggest that the first part of this passage should be read as an interrogative appeal to the companions of his banishment: 'Here feel we not'—'Do any of you say that we do not feel the severity of the wintry blast?' But 'when it bites and blows upon my body, I, for my part, smile, and say This is no flattery,' &c. I do not say that this

[Heere feele we not the penaltie of Adam]

takes up every word, but I think it approaches nearer to the poet's intention than any-thing that has been suggested. That the 'penalty of Adam' is not the severities of winter, but the obligation to labour, or the being sensible to the difference between heat and cold, leaves the passage as perplexed as ever. In the idea of Paradise before the Fall has always been included that there was perpetual summer or at least perpetual genial seasons—no winter's cold. ANON. [ap. Halliwell]: It appears to me impossible to let 'not' stand in the passage at all without leading to utter inconsequence; whereas, if we substitute the word *yet*, sense and harmony are restored to the whole of the Duke's speech at once, without the necessity of our resorting to ingenious or elaborate speculation and research. The proposed reading will nullify the argument founded on the views of the 'seasons' difference' in the time of our first father; the correctness of which, by the way, appears to me to be rather invalidated than otherwise by anything I can find in the opening chapters of Genesis. WHITE (ed. i): 'Not' is clearly a corruption, because there was no pen-alty of Adam from which the speaker and his companions were exempt. Whiter suggested that the penalty of Adam was that he should get his bread by the sweat of his brow. So did the banished Duke; Adam, after his curse, might as well have lived by hunting as the Duke. Plainly, the penalty of Adam is the seasons' difference—eternal Spring being inseparably connected with the idea of Eden—and the com-mon misprint of 'not' for *but* took place. For what is the culminating thought of the whole passage?—'these are the counsellors That feelingly persuade me *what I am.*' The Duke finds the icy fang and the churlish chiding of the Winter's wind more truthful counsellors than those which buzzed about his painted pomp. They make him feel that he is a man. But how would they do this if he were exempt from any part of that heritage of all mankind—the penalty of Adam? It is to be observed, however, that the passage, although its meaning is clear, is written in a very free style, and will defy parsing criticism. STAUNTON: Neither 'not' nor *but* is satisfactory, nor do we think that 'not' is the only corruption in the speech; the word 'as' is equally open to suspicion. The passage, it is presumable, may have run thus in the original manuscript: ' Here feel we *yet* the penalty of Adam, The seasons' difference: *At* the icy fang,' &c. The Duke is contrasting the dangers and sophistications of a court life with the safety and primitive simplicity of their sylvan state; and glories in the privilege of undergoing Adam's penalty,—the seasons' difference. COWDEN-CLARKE: The speech seems to us to lose consecution if 'not' be retained; whereas, '*but* the penalty of Adam' (taking 'penalty' to mean the 'seasons' difference'), accords with that which follows, and also with other passages in the play, where the sharp yet salutary effects of open-air life are adverted to. KEIGHTLEY (*Exp.* 157): It does not appear that any writer anterior to Milton made the Ovidian change of season a part of Adam's penalty. The text may therefore be right, and a line, some-thing like this, have been lost, ' Here is no toil; we have only to endure.' INGLEBY (*Sh. the Man*, &c. i, 139) cites a letter to him from C. J. Munro, in which the latter suggests the making of the sentence interrogative, wherein he is anticipated by Hun-ter. Ingleby himself says that 'however we may regulate and interpret the passage, there is certainly a hitch, but it is very questionable whether the hitch be sufficiently great to justify verbal emendation.' ' Probably sufficient justification might be found for *now* in the place of 'not'; *now* referring to the present time of winter, after the "penaltie" would be no longer felt?' WRIGHT [adopting Theobald's *but*]: The Duke contrasts the happiness and security of their forest life with the perils of the envious

The feafons difference, as the Icie phange   8
And churlifh chiding of the winters winde,
Which when it bites and blowes vpon my body   10
Euen till I fhrinke with cold, I fmile, and fay
This is no flattery : thefe are counfellors
That feelingly perfwade me what I am :
Sweet are the vfes of aduerfitie   14

10. *bites*] *baits* F_3F_4.

court. Their only suffering was that which they shared with all the descendants of Adam, the seasons' difference, for in the golden age of Paradise there was, as Bacon phrases it, ' a spring all the year long.' . . . . If the blank left by Boswell were filled up, it would just contradict what he had said before—' These are counsellors That *feelingly* persuade me what I am.' The Duke's senses therefore did make him conscious that he was a man, though what he felt was only ' the seasons' difference.' Milton has the same idea of change of seasons after the Fall. See *Par. Lost*, x, 678, 9 : ' Else had the spring Perpetual smiled on earth with vernant flowers.' [Whatever be the ' penalty of Adam,' be it ' labour ' or ' the seasons' difference,' all critics seem to agree that the drift of the speech is to show that this present life takes from that penalty its bitterness. The penalty is here, but it is not really felt; we can even smile at it. In the same way, adversity is grievous, but here we can find that its uses are even sweet. We know that ' in the state of innocency Adam fell,' and was punished; if that punishment be removed, there is a return to the state of innocency; and it is that state of innocency which reigns here in Arden; and when the icy fang of the winter's wind bites till we shrink with cold, we know that there is no flattery here; our feelings, our outward senses, reveal the truth to us. ' Feelingly ' is not used in this connection in the same sense as ' Here feele we '; the former goes no deeper than the skin, the latter touches the heart. Thus interpreting the passage, as, I suppose, every one else interprets it, I think we can afford to disregard any specific definition, and hold, as ' the penaltie of Adam,' everything which tends to make this life unlike what it really is, be it the seasons' difference, labour, or the peril of the envious court.

See Capell's remark (line 20, *post*) on the change in the Duke's feelings when the chance came to him in the last Act.—ED.]

8. **as**] Here used in the sense of *to wit, namely*. See ' How all the other passions fleet to air, *As* doubtful thoughts,' &c., *Mer. of Ven.* III, ii, 115; also Walker (*Crit.* i, 127), or Abbott, § 113. See also *post*, II, vii, 151, where Walker with probability suggested that 'At' should be *As*. LETTSOM (ap. Dyce, ed. iii) refers to IV, iii, 149 as an example of the plural, followed by a single instance : ' Teares our *recountments* had most kindly bath'd, *As* how I came into that desert place;' but Capell and Malone conjectured that a line or more had been there lost, in which other circumstances were recounted.—See notes *ad loc.*—ED.

10. **Which**] For other instances of ' which ' used adverbially for *as to which*, see Abbott, § 272, or *Lear*, V, iii, 149.

10–12. **Which . . . flattery**] As a matter of punctuation note that Whiter, followed by White (ed. i), enclosed these lines in a parenthesis.

14. **the vses**] HARTLEY COLERIDGE (ii, 142) : There is a beautiful propriety in the word ' uses ' here, which I do not remember to have seen remarked. It is the

Which like the toad, ougly and venemous,   15
Weares yet a precious Iewell in his head:

---

use, not the mere effect of adversity, wherein resides the sweet. Whether adversity shall prove a stumbling-block, a discipline, or a blessing, depends altogether on the use made of it. There is no natural necessary operation of adversity to strengthen, to purify, or to humanise. Men may be made better by affliction, but they cannot be made good. From an evil heart, the harder it is wrung, the blacker the drops that issue. If perfumes are the sweeter for crushing, so are stenches more pestiferous. Even the average quality of mankind are much oftener the worse than the better for continued suffering. All, indeed, might be better for chastening; but that any individual will be better no one has a right to presume, for we know not what use he will make of the dispensation.

14. 'It is good for me that I have been afflicted.'—*Psalms*, cxix, 71.

15. **venemous**] That the toad was venomous has been a popular belief from the days of Pliny at least. In Holland's translation (Bk. 25, p. 231, *a*) we read: 'Frogs (such especially as keep in bushes and hedges, and be called in Latine Rubetæ, *i.* toads) are not without their venom: I my self haue seen these vaunting Montebanks calling themselues Psylli .... in a brauery .... to eat those toads baked red hot between 2 platters; but what became of them? they caught their bane by it, and died more suddenly than if they had bin stung by the Aspis.'

16. **Iewell**] STEEVENS: In a book called *A Green Forest or a Natural History*, &c., by John Maplett, 1567, is the following account of this imaginary gem: 'In this stone is apparently seene verie often the verie forme of a tode, with despotted and coloured feete, but those uglye and defusedly. It is available against envenoming.' Pliny, in the 32d book of his *Natural Hist.* [p. 434, l. trans. Holland], ascribes many powerful qualities to a *bone* found in the right side of a *toad*, but no mention of any gem in its head. This deficiency is however abundantly supplied by Edward Fenton, in his *Secrete Wonders of Nature*, 1569, who says: 'That there is founde in the *heades* of old and great *toades*, a *stone* which they call Borax or Stelon: it is most commonly found in the *head* of a hee *toad*, of power to repulse poysons, and that it is a most sovereign medicine for the stone.' Thomas Lupton, in his *First Booke of Notable Things*, bears repeated testimony to the virtues of the '*Tode-stone*, called *Crapaudina*.' In his Seventh Book he instructs us how to procure it; and afterwards tells us: 'You shall knowe whether the Tode-stone be the ryght and perfect stone or not. Holde the stone before a Tode, so that he may see it; and if it be a ryght and true stone, the Tode will leape towarde it, and make as though he would snatch it. He envieth so much that man should have that stone.' [It would be easy to fill page after page with allusions to this *toadstone* and with descriptions of it. Steevens refers to a passage in Beau. and Fl.'s *Monsieur Thomas*, III, i, p. 356, ed. Dyce, and he might have added another in *The Woman's Prize*, V, i, p. 199. Nares gives a reference to Jonson's *Volpone*, II, iii, p. 223, ed. Gifford, and another to Lyly's *Euphues*, p. 53, ed. Arber: 'The foule Toade hath a faire stone in his head; the fine golde is found in filthy earth; the sweet kernell lyeth in the hard shell; vertue is harboured in the heart of him that most men esteeme mishapen.' This sentence, by the way, was quoted by Francis Meres, in his *Wits Commonwealth*, Part 2, p. 161, but without naming the author—a duty which he performed in many instances, but which the purpose of his book did not render obligatory in all; the fact would not be worth referring to here, were it not that Halliwell failed to notice, when he cited both Meres

And this our life exempt from publike haunt,   17
Findes tongues in trees, bookes in the running brookes,
Sermons in ſtones, and good in euery thing.
   Amien. I would not change it, happy is your Grace   20

20. *I...it*] Given to Duke, Wh. Dyce, Cam. Ktly, Huds. Rlfe.

and Lyly, that the two were in reality only one, and other editors, who have followed Halliwell without verifying, have fallen into the same error. As for descriptions of it, which properly belong to the archæology of gems, and in no wise illustrate
Shakespeare's words here, where the simple existence of the jewel is alluded to, I
need merely refer the student to Douce, i, 294, or to the four folio pages of notes in
Halliwell's edition, or to King's *Natural Hist. of Gems*, cited by Wright, where the
origin of the belief in the existence of such a stone is ascribed to Pliny's simple
description of a stone as ' of the colour of a frog.' Douce suggests that it is not
certain in this present passage that there is an allusion to a *stone*, ' for Gesner informs
us that in his time, and *in England more particularly*, the common people made
superstitious uses of a *real jewel* that always could be found in a toad's head, viz.: its
forehead bone.' Lastly, CALDECOTT says: ' It is, perhaps, rather a figure of speech,
than a fact in natural history; and it is its eye, proverbially fine, that is the · precious
jewel in his head.' There can be no doubt, however, that a belief in toadstones and
their efficacy existed, and it seems equally sure that Shakespeare here alludes to that
belief, which, like everything that he touched, he ' gilds with heavenly alchemy.'—ED.]

   17. **haunt**] ALLEN (MS): A verbal noun, equivalent to *haunting;* exempt from
the *haunting* of the public.

   18. STEEVENS: So in Sidney's *Arcadia*, bk. i [p. 82, ed. 1598]: ' Thus both trees
and each thing else, be the bookes of a fancy.' [If this quotation from Sidney
had not been repeated by several editors, it would not be repeated here. There
is in it nothing particularly parallel to this speech of the Duke's. ' When,' says
Dorus, ' I meete these trees in the earth's faire liuery clothèd, Ease do I feel. . . . .
For that I finde in them parte of my state represented,' and, thereupon, with that
prolixity which at times outwearies the most enthusiastic lover of Elizabethan pastoral
poetry, he enumerates almost every tree known to the temperate, or even tropical, zone,
in each of which he discovers what may symbolise his passion. Shakespeare's Duke
accepts the lessons which the trees teach him; Sidney's Dorus sets the lessons that are
to be taught to the trees. It is perhaps worth while to mention, and merely to mention with the lightest touch, that emendation which suggests an exchange of places
between ' bookes ' and ' stones,' an emendation which, gray though it be with dry
antiquity and palpable to the dullest sense, is always propounded anew as the highest
stretch of wit, and accompanied with the demand that it be greeted with acclamation.
—ED.]

   20. **Amien**] ROFFE (*A Musical Triad from Shakespeare*, &c. 1872, p. 21):
Amiens is certainly to be considered as first and chief of the *Musical* characters in
Shakespeare, and it must assuredly be admitted, that if we require an idea in every
way pleasing and harmonious of a musical man, (as an accomplished amateur), that
idea has been wrought out for us in Amiens, who, indeed, shows as favorably even in
the few words which he is called upon to speak as when he sings his charming songs.
It is Amiens who makes reply to the Duke, and that reply is beautiful, worthy of an
amiable man of sense, and, indeed of a true gentleman. . . . . Amiens is willing, both

[Amien.]

for himself and for all his friends, to make the best of their lot, nay, even fully to accept it, and how felicitously is the idea expressed, of '*translating*' the stubbornness of fortune into a quieter and a sweeter style. In that *translation* lies the one thing, which, if we *could* only do, might, at the very least, make us all, if not perfectly *happy*, much *less unhappy* than we are. Such a man as Amiens is one who spreads around him an atmosphere of quiet and content, and we cannot but feel that he is beautifully placed in such a Pastoral as Shakespeare has here given us. The very earliest words then, spoken by Amiens, at once seem to give us the true intimation of his character and suggest to our minds the most pleasing thoughts concerning him. An evidently congenial spirit is the First Lord, and we find them taking their walk together in the Forest. .... In Music, we shall find that Amiens is accomplished in a degree and manner befitting his mental state; of his friend, the First Lord, we have no evidence that he is accomplished in Music, but it is clear that he is to be thought of as a most true and *feeling observer*, with all the power of painting his observations in words. In *that* power he may be even conceived of as *superior* to Amiens, and so *discriminated* from him; for which reason doubtless it is, that to this First Lord, Shakespeare assigns those interesting descriptions of what Amiens and his friend beheld together, such as that of the 'poor, sequestered stag.' .... At the banquet [II, vii] Amiens only sings, and the little address of the Duke to him still paints Amiens to us as the man who both *can*, and *will*, lay himself out to promote the pleasure of others. .... After the banquet Amiens is only *seen* with the Duke, and that in the last Act, and no more is set down for him either to sing or to speak. .... Possibly, Shakespeare might have deemed that dramatic considerations as to Amiens himself would show, that *after* the memorable banquet-scene, and the beautiful 'Blow, blow, thou Winter Wind,' it was not so well to let him appear again, *musically*, in the comparatively inferior position of one who is simply required to lead off the jovial Hunting Song and Chorus.

20. **I** . . . **it**] UPTON (p. 260): The Duke is speaking of the happiness of his retirement. How much more in character is it for the Duke to say, 'I would not change it,' than for Amiens! CAPELL (p. 58, *a*): But the reverse of this [Upton's remark] is true: Amiens, as a courtier, might make the declaration, being only a mode of assenting to the truth of what his master had spoken; but the Duke could not, without impeachment of dignity, of being wanting to himself and his subjects; accordingly, when occasion of 'change' presents itself at the end of the play, we see it embrac'd with great readiness: Add to this, that the following reflection of Amiens, 'Happy is your grace,' &c. would come in too abruptly, were the other words taken away. WHITE (ed. i): They are not only 'more in character for the Duke,' but the necessary complement of his thought. DYCE: It seems strange that no one before Upton should have seen that these words *must* belong to the Duke, and still stranger that, after the error was once pointed out, any editor should persist in retaining it. WALKER (*Crit.* ii, 187) made, independently, the same suggestion as Upton, and adds; 'Let any one read the passage as thus distributed, and he will perceive the propriety of the change.' [The phrase may be proper enough for the Duke, but is it improper for Amiens? Is there any reason why one of the circle of courtiers should not at once announce his sympathy with the Duke? The Duke has asked a question. Is no one to answer? Surely some response is needed of a more cordial and more personal character than a mere non-committal and courtier-like exclamation, 'Happy is your grace,' &c. Besides, some weight attaches to Capell's remark that the Duke

That can tranflate the ftubbornneffe of fortune   21
Into fo quiet and fo fweet a ftile.
   Du. Sen.   Come, fhall we goe and kill vs venifon *?*
And yet it irkes me the poore dapled fooles
Being natiue Burgers of this defert City,   25
Should intheir owne confines with forked heads

<hr>

25. *Burgers*] *Burghes* F₄.

<hr>

shows himself ready enough to ' change' his life as soon as the chance is offered to him
at the close of the play, and Shakespeare, who provides for everything, would not thus
have precluded the Duke from resuming his throne by making him here assert that
he would not exchange 'these woods' for the 'envious court.' Moreover, although
the printing of this line is the compositor's and not Shakespeare's, it is worth noting
that there is merely a comma after the phrase, not a full stop. This faint indication
of what the MS might possibly have been before the compositor's eyes, we may esti-
mate for what it is worth. On the whole, as far as the Folio's text is concerned, ' I
would not change it.'—ED.]

   21. translate] MOBERLY: This is one of the interesting passages in which a great
writer reflects upon his own expressions with pleasure or surprise. Dialogue gives
great opportunity for such reflections; as in Plato, *Rep.* 361: βαβαὶ ἦν δ'ἐγὼ, ὦ φίλε
Γλαύκων, ὡς ἐρρωμένως, ὥσπερ ἀνδρίαντα, τὸν τελείως ἄδικον ἐκκαθαίρεις! and *Iliad*,
ix, 431. A most striking instance is 2 Cor. vi, 11, where St. Paul, with a kind of surprise at the fervour of his own appeal, suddenly exclaims, τὸ στόμα ἡμῶν ἀνέῳγε πρὸς
ὑμᾶς, Κορίνθιοι, ἡ καρδία ἡμῶν πεπλάτυνται.

   24. irkes] WRIGHT: The Eton Latin Grammar has made us familiar with ' Tædet,
it irketh'; and *irksome* is still used in the sense of wearisome. Palsgrave (*Lesclar-
cissement de la langue Francoyse*) gives, 'It yrketh me, I waxe wery, or displeasaunt
of a thyng. *Il me ennuyt.*' [See also *Prompt. Parv.* p. 266; Stratmann, p. 338; or
Skeat, s. v.]

   24. dapled fooles] DYCE (*Strictures*, p. 68): Compare, 'Then he stroking once
or twice his prettie goate . . . . said thus, Lie downe, *pide foole*, by me,' &c.—Shelton's
Don Quixote, Part First, p. 556, ed. 1612.

   25. Burgers] STEEVENS: In Sidney's *Arcadia* the deer are called 'the wild *bur-
gesses* of the forest.' Again in the 18th Song [line 65] of Drayton's *Poly-olbion :*
' Where, fearless of the hunt, the hart securely stood, And everywhere walk'd free, a
burgess of the wood.' MALONE: A kindred expression is found in Lodge's *Rosalynde :* 'About her wondring stood The citizens of wood.' Compare line 59, *post.*
[It is probable that Steevens trusted to his memory alone in citing the phrase from
Sidney's *Arcadia*. The phrase, just as he has given it, cannot, I think, be there
found, and the nearest approach to it does not refer to a deer, but to a shepherd. In
Book ii, p. 220, ed. 1598, two young shepherds sing 'eclogue-wise' their rival complaints; and Strephon says: 'I that was once free burgesse of the forrests, Where
shade from Sunne, and sports I sought at evening,' &c. The next sestine is sung by
Klaius, and begins: 'I that was once delighted every morning, Hunting the wild
inhabiters of forrests,' &c. These two passages Steevens may have confounded, and
inadvertently omitted to give the exact reference, but unfortunately Steevens cannot
be always implicitly trusted.—ED.]

   26. forked heads] STEEVENS, COLLIER, and HALLIWELL define this as 'barbed

Haue their round hanches goard.   27

   I . *Lord.*   Indeed my Lord

The melancholy *Iaques* grieues at that,   29

---

arrows,' for which they have some authority, though they do not cite it, in Cotgrave, where it stands, ' Fer de fleiche à oreilles. *A forked, or barbed arrow-head.*' But WRIGHT (*Lear*, I, i, 143) cites Ascham, whose authority is weightier than Cotgrave's, as follows : ' Two maner of arrowe heades sayeth Pollux, was vsed in olde tyme. The one he calleth ὄγκινος, descrybynge it thus, hauyng two poyntes or barbes, lookyng backewarde to the stele and the fethers, which surely we call in Englishe a brode arrowe head or a swalowe tayle. The other he calleth γλωχὶς, hauing .ii. poyntes stretchyng forwarde, and this Englysh men do call a forke-head '—*Toxophilus*, p. 135, ed. Arber; again on p. 136 : ' Commodus the Emperoure vsed forked heades, whose facion Herodiane doeth lyuely and naturally describe, sayinge that they were lyke the shap of a new mone wherwyth he would smite of the heade of a birde and neuer misse.' ·SINGER defined the ' forked heads ' as the *antlers*, oblivious apparently of the physiological difficulty which stags would encounter in attempting to gore their own round haunches with their horns.—ED.

28, &c. In J. P. Kemble's Acting Copy, 1815, this speech is given to Jaques, beginning thus : ' Indeed, my lord, I've often griev'd at that, And, in that kind, think you do more usurp,' &c. Whether or not Kemble was the first to make this change I do not know. Of course the language throughout the rest of the scene is adapted to the change, and lines 68–70 are omitted. It is almost needless to remark that this sense-less change obliterates one of Shakespeare's artistic touches, whereby an important character is described and the key-note struck before he himself appears.—ED.

29. **Iaques**] WALKER (*Vers.* 3) : In French speeches or phrases the final *e* or *es*, now mute, is usually sounded. In *Jaques, Parolles, Marseilles* the same rule holds without exception. [According to Mrs Cowden-Clarke's *Concordance*, Jaques occurs sixteen times in these plays. Of these sixteen, ten instances are in prose or close a line, and are therefore useless as far as the pronunciation is concerned. Of the remaining six, one occurs in *Love's Lab. L.* II, i, 42; one is in the present line; two are in *All's Well* (III, iv, 4 and III, v, 98); and two are in *Hen. V* (III, v, 43 and IV, viii, 98). This last line Walker himself considers an exception, despite the fact that he had just said that the rule was without exception; it is ' Jaques of | Chatil | lon, ad | miral | of France.' This reduces the six instances of uncertain pronunciation to five. No less do I think the first instance in *Hen. V* is an exception, and that it must be thus scanned : ' Jaques Cha | tillon, | Rambu | res, Vau | demont.' This reduces the five to four. The two instances in *All's Well* both refer to the church of St Jaques, and I believe them to be in the genitive, like St Peter's, and that the *s* should be heard after the monosyllable *Jakes*, thus : ' I am | Saint Jaques' | *es*, pil | grim thi | ther gone,' and also : ' There's four | or five | to great | Saint Jaques' | *es* bound.' This reduces the four to two, and in both of them the name appears undeniably a dissyllable. Thus : ' Of Ja | ques Faul | conbridge | solem | nisèd,' *Love's Lab. L.* II, i, 42, and ' The mel | ancho | ly Ja | ques grieves | at that.' Nevertheless the conviction expressed in the note on line 5 of *Dramatis Personæ* remains unshaken, that the name was in general pronounced as a monosyllable, with, possibly, the faintest suggestion of a second syllable, such as we have in the word *aches*. Harington's anecdote and French's testimony are decisive to my mind that the name in Shakespeare's own day was a monosyllable. In our day it is to be hoped that, in this play

And in that kinde fweares you doe more vfurpe　　　　30
Then doth your brother that hath banifh'd you :
To day my Lord of *Amiens*, and my felfe,
Did fteale behinde him as he lay along
Vnder an oake, whofe anticke roote peepes out
Vpon the brooke that brawles along this wood,　　　35
To the which place a poore fequeftred Stag
That from the Hunters aime had tane a hurt,
Did come to languifh ; and indeed my Lord
The wretched annimall heau'd forth fuch groanes
That their difcharge did ftretch his leatherne coat　　　40
Almoft to burfting, and the big round teares
Cours'd one another downe his innocent nofe
In pitteous chafe : and thus the hairie foole,
Much marked of the melancholie *Iaques* ,　　　44

---

34. *anticke*] *antique* Pope.　　　　34. *roote*] *roope* F₂. *roop* F₃F₄.

at least, it will not be heard otherwise than as a dissyllable : *Jaq-wes*, which is as Mrs Kemble pronounced it,—for me an ample authority.—ED.

34. COLLIER (*Introd.* p. 5) has preserved the following note, 'made at the time,' from Coleridge's Lectures in 1818 : 'Shakespeare never gives a description of rustic scenery merely for its own sake, or to show how well he can paint natural objects; he is never tedious or elaborate, but while he now and then displays marvellous accuracy and minuteness of knowledge, he usually only touches upon the larger features and broader characteristics, leaving the fillings up to the imagination. Thus, he describes an oak of many centuries' growth in a single line : " Under an oak whose antique root peeps out." Other and inferior writers would have dwelt on this description, and worked it out with all pettiness and impertinence of detail. In Shakespeare the " antique root " furnishes the whole picture.'

34. **anticke**] Accented by Shakespeare on the first syllable. Steevens calls attention to Gray's *Elegy :* 'There at the foot of yonder nodding beech,' &c.

36. **the which**] See I, ii, 120.

39. WHALLEY (p. 57) compares this passage with Vergil's description, *Æn.* vii, 500 *et seq.*, a remote and almost pointless comparison, which, nevertheless, Malone and some other editors have repeated.

41. **teares**] STEEVENS : In one of the marginal notes to a similar passage in the 13th Song of Drayton's *Poly-olbion*, it is said that, 'The Hart weepeth at his dying ; his teares are held to be precious in medicine.' DOUCE (i, 296) : 'When the hart is arered, he fleethe to a ryver or ponde, and roreth cryeth and wepeth when he is take,' *Batman vpon Bartholome*, xviii, 30.

42, 43. **Cours'd . . . chase**] WHITER (p. 97) : Surely no reader of taste can doubt but that the 'stag' and 'the hunter' led the imagination of the poet to this beautiful metaphor.

43. **foole**] For many references to the use of this word where no reproach is implied, see the notes on *Lear*, V, iii, 306 : 'And my poor fool is hang'd !'

Stood on th'extremeſt verge of the ſwift brooke,   45
Augmenting it with teares.
    Du. Sen.   But what ſaid *Iaques ?*
Did he not moralize this ſpectacle ?
    1 .*Lord.*   O yes, into a thouſand ſimilies.
Firſt, for his weeping into the needleſſe ſtreame ;   50
Poore Deere quoth he, thou mak'ſt a teſtament
As worldlings doe, giuing thy ſum of more
To that which had too muſt : then being there alone,
Left and abandoned of his veluet friend ;   54

45. *th'extremeſt*] *the extremest* Han. Cap. Steev. Mal. Coll. Sing. Dyce i, Sta. Cam. Clke, Ktly, Wh. ii.

46. *it with*] *in the* F₄.

47. *ſaid*] *ſay* F₄.

50. *into*] *in* Pope+, Cap. Steev. Mal. Sing. Sta. Coll. iii, Ktly, Dyce iii.

53. *had*] *hath* Sing. Coll. ii, Ktly, Huds.

muſt] *much* Ff.

there] Om. Ff, Rowe+, Cap. Steev. Dyce iii.

54. *friend*] *friends* Rowe+, Cap. Wh. Dyce, Sta. Cam. Clke, Ktly, Rlfe.

48. **moralize**] WRIGHT: This usage of the word is well illustrated by Cotgrave : ' Moraliser. To morrallize, to expound morrally, to give a morall sence vnto.' Hence it came to signify, to expound or interpret generally.

50. **into**] Although it is not impossible to scan this line as it thus stands : ' First, for | his weep | ing in | to th' need | leſſe streame,' yet it is harsh, and needless too when we have so many instances of the use of *in* for ' into ' (see Abbott, § 159), and when, as Malone suggests, the second ' into ' was caught by the compositor's eye from the first ' into ' directly above it. I should not therefore hesitate to adopt Pope's change. But KEIGHTLEY, whose opinion carries weight, is of a different way of thinking. In his *Expositor*, p. 157, he says : ' Pope's change has been generally followed, but without the slightest reason, by the decasyllabists. I am almost ashamed to say that I have joined them from pure inadvertence.'—ED.

50. **needleſſe**] For a list of adjectives used both in an active and a passive sense see Walker (*Crit.* ii, 80), or Abbott, § 3. Caldecott refers to ' age is unnecessary,' *Lear*, II, iv, 151.

53. **had too must**] STEEVENS : Shakespeare had almost the same thought in his *Lover's Complaint*, 38 : ' Which one by one she in a river threw, Upon whose weeping margent she was set ; Like usury applying wet to wet.' Again, in *3 Hen VI :* V, iv, 8 : ' With tearful eyes add water to the sea And give more strength to that which hath too much.' [This latter extract convinced SINGER that ' had ' in the present line should be *hath*, and he accordingly so printed it. But, as WHITE (ed. i) says, ' the time of the action referred to is not the same in the two passages. Worldlings, in making their testaments, give to those who *had* too much *before*.']

53. **being there alone**] KNIGHT : It is wonderful how soon after Shakespeare's death his verse offered an opportunity for the tampering of those who did not understand it. [See Text. Notes.] The twelve-syllable verse, sparingly introduced, imparts a singularly dramatic freedom to the poetry, and makes the regular metre more beautiful from the variety. [Abbott accepts this line as a trimeter couplet.]

54. **of**] For instances where we should now use *by*, see III, ii, 332, Abbott, § 170.

'Tis right quoth he, thus miſerie doth part   55
The Fluxe of companie : anon a careleſſe Heard
Full of the paſture, iumps along by him
And neuer ſtaies to greet him : I quoth *Iaques,*
Sweepe on you fat and greazie Citizens,
'Tis iuſt the faſhion ; wherefore doe you looke   60
Vpon that poore and broken bankrupt there?
Thus moſt inuectiuely he pierceth through
The body of Countrie, Citie, Court,   63

---

55. *thus*] *this* Var. '03, '13 (a misprint?).

59. *greazie*] *grazy* F$_4$.
63. *of*] F$_1$, Mal. *of the* Ff et cet.

---

54. **veluet**] NEIL: 'Velvet' is the technical term for the outer covering of the horns of a stag in the early stages of their growth. Here 'velvet' seems to be equiv-alent to *delicate.*

54. **friend**] WHITER: The singular is right; it is often used for the plural with a sense more *abstracted,* and therefore in many instances more poetical. [CALDECOTT, KNIGHT, and HALLIWELL quote Whiter with approval, but DYCE in noting the fact affixes an exclamation-mark. The present is, I think, but another instance of the crooked nature of the crooked *s,* which persists in appearing where it is not wanted, and fails to appear where it is wanted; so marked is this peculiarity that, as I have frequently had occasion to quote, Walker (*Crit.* i, 234) suggests that it may have its origin in some characteristic of Shakespeare's handwriting. See I, iii, 60; also *Mer. of Ven.* II, ii, 181; II, ix, 35, &c.—ED.]

56. This line ABBOTT, § 495, gives as an illustration of the insertion of two sylla-bles at the end of the third or fourth foot. 'The flúx | of cómpany. | Anón | a cáre | less hérd.' [I do not think that lines like this with a pause in it, and line 53 above, should be formulated with unbroken lines.—ED.]

59. **fat . . . Citizens**] A tough phrase for our German brothers to translate. SCHLEGEL, followed by SCHMIDT, renders it thus: ihr fetten wohlgenährten Städter (wherein there is, I think, scarcely enough contempt). DINGELSTEDT: ihr Spiesser und Spiessbürger (which is, perhaps, a little too slangy, but still not bad). HER-WEGH: ihr fetten, feisten Herrn Philister (the best, perhaps, but, *eheu, quantum mutatus ab illo!*).

59. **greazie**] CALDECOTT: 'By other men's losses to enrich and greaze them-selves,' Newton's *Lemnie's Touchstone of Complexions,* 1581, p. 58.

59. **Citizens**] See the reference, at line 25 above, to Lodge's *Rosalynde.* See also Sidney's *Arcadia,* p. 34, ed. 1598: 'The wood seemed to conspire with them [*i. e.* the hunters] against his owne citizens.'—ED.

63. **body of Countrie**] STEEVENS: *The* is supplied by the Second Folio, which has many advantages over the First. Mr Malone is of a different opinion; but let him speak for himself. MALONE: 'Country' is here used as a trisyllable. So again in *Twelfth N.:* 'The like of him. Know'st thou this *country?*' The editor of the Second Folio, who appears utterly ignorant of our author's phraseology and metre, reads: [see Text. Notes]. STEEVENS: Is not 'country' used elsewhere also as a dissyllable? See *Coriol.* I, vi, 'And that his country's dearer than himself.' Besides, by reading 'country' as a trisyllable, in the middle of a verse, it would become rough

Yea, and of this our life, fwearing that we
Are meere vfurpers, tyrants, and whats worfe   65
To fright the Annimals, and to kill them vp
In their affign'd and natiue dwelling place.

  D. Sen. And did you leaue him in this contemplation?

  2. Lord. We did my Lord, weeping and commenting
Vpon the fobbing Deere.   70

  Du. Sen. Show me the place,
I loue to cope him in thefe fullen fits,
For then he's full of matter.

   1. Lor. Ile bring you to him ftrait.   *Exeunt.* 74

---

64. *of this*] *this* F$_3$F$_4$. *through this*   69. 2. Lord.] Ami. Cap.
Rowe i.   74. 1. Lor.] 2. Lor. F$_3$F$_4$.
66. *vp*] *too* Quincy (MS).

---

and dissonant. [Unquestionably we must here follow the reading of the Second Folio, which Malone himself would have at once adopted had it not been found in that edition whose authority was always a well-fleshed bone of contention between him and Steevens.—ED.]

 66. **kill them vp**] CALDECOTT gives five or six instances of the use of this phrase: 'Killed up with colde,' Adlington's *Apuleius's Golden Asse*, 1582, fo. 159; 'The remembraunce of theire poore, indigent, and beggerlye olde age, kylleth them vp,' Raphe Robynson's trans. of *More's Utopia*, 1551 (p. 159, ed. Arber); 'The Spanyardes . . . . were quyte slayne vp, of the turkes arrowes,' Ascham's *Toxophilus*, 1545 (p. 82, ed. Arber). HALLIWELL, also, in his *Essay on the Formation of Shakespeare's Text*, vol. i, p. 273, gives many more examples of what he says (erroneously, I think) is merely a redundant and not an intensive use of the particle. For many other instances from Shakespeare's own plays, see Schmidt, *s. v.* 7.

 69. **2. Lord**] CAPELL refuses to acknowledge this Second Lord, 'both because he thinks it a folly to multiply speakers unnecessarily, and is clearly of opinion that Amiens was the person intended.' [It seems a matter of so small moment that I confess I have not collated the modern editions in regard to it. I think no one has followed Capell, and several, among them Steevens and Malone, have followed the Third and Fourth Folios in giving the last speech, line 74, to the Second Lord.—ED.]

 72. **cope**] JOHNSON: That is, to encounter him; to engage with him.

 73. **matter**] WRIGHT: Good stuff, sound sense. Compare *Lear*, IV, vi, 178: 'O matter and impertinency mixed.' [As, also, where Jaques calls Touchstone, III, iii, 29, 'A material fool.'—ED.]

Scena Secunda.

Enter Duke, with Lords.

Duk.   Can it be poſſible that no man ſaw them?
It cannot be, ſome villaines of my Court
Are of conſent and ſufferance in this.
   1.*Lo.*   I cannot heare of any that did ſee her,   5
The Ladies her attendants of her chamber
Saw her a bed, and in the morning early,
They found the bed vntreaſur'd of their Miſtris.
   2.*Lor.*   My Lord, the royniſh Clown, at whom ſo oft,   9

---

7. *a bed*] *abed* F$_4$.

Scena Secunda] MOBERLY: The use of these short scenes deserves remark. The present one, with the usurper's troubles and suspicions, affords a strong contrast to the 'quiet and sweet style' of the banished Duke in the last scene. The same double progress of the plot is skilfully exhibited in III, i. Act II, ii and IV, ii, which have little to do with the plot, are still very effective, as showing the various aspects of the 'golden' life in the forest, and the pursuits in which days fleet away there.

4. **consent and sufferance**] MOBERLY: This is a quasi-legal term, applied to a landlord who takes no steps to eject a tenant whose term has expired. [Both words undoubtedly bear at times a technical legal sense, but it is doubtful if any relation of landlord and tenant can be in the remotest degree applicable to the present case. The use of the word 'villaines' would dispel any legal association with the words that follow.—ED.]

6. **her attendants of her**] This phrase is cited by Abbott, § 423, as an instance of the repetition of the possessive adjective, and as a modification of such transpositions as we find in 'your sovereignty of reason,' 'her brow of youth,' &c.; which is quite possible, but, at the same time, I think we can see how both sound and sense controlled the line. 'The ladies, *the* attendants' is unrhythmical, and the second definite article must be emphasised to avoid an elision: 'th' attendants.' On the other hand, the sense would have been obscure and uncertain in 'her attendants of the chamber.' So that I doubt if the present construction is peculiar either to Shakespeare or his times. Allen suggests, '*Her* ladies, the attendants,' &c., which, if change be needed, is unobjectionable.—ED.

8. **vntreasur'd**] BLACKWOOD'S MAGAZINE (Apr. 1833): We like his lordship for these words. ROLFE: Used by Shakespeare only here, and 'treasure,' *i. e. enrich*, only in *Sonn.* 6, 3.

9. **roynish**] STEEVENS: From *rogneux*, scurvy, mangy. See Chaucer, *Romaunt of the Rose*, 987: 'The foule croked bowe hidous, That knotty was, and al roynous.' And again, line 6193 [ed. Morris]: 'This argument is alle roignous.' Again, in

Your Grace was wont to laugh is alſo miſſing,   10
Hiſperia the Princeſſe Centlewoman
Confeſſes that ſhe ſecretly ore-heard
Your daughter and her Coſen much commend
The parts and graces of the Wraſtler
That did but lately foile the ſynowie *Charles*,   15
And ſhe beleeues where euer they are gone
That youth is ſurely in their companie.   17

10. *laugh...miſſing*] laugh,...missing: 11. Hiſperia] Ff, Rowe+, Cam. Mob.
Ff.   Wh. ii.   *Hesperia* Warb. et cet.
                                                  Centlewoman] F₁.

Harvey's *Pierce's Supererogation*, 1593 [p. 229, ed. Grosart]: 'Although she were
. . . . somewhat like Gallemella, or maide Marian, yet was she not such a roinish ran-
nell . . . . as this wainscot-faced Tomboy.'   HUNTER (i, 346): I conceive 'roynish'
to mean obtrusive, troublesome, a fault we may well suppose often belonging to the
poor unfortunates who were retained in the houses of the great.   This at least is one
of the meanings of the word, and it seems to suit the passage quite as well as the
disagreeable senses which all the editors, down to the latest, have given it.   Parkinson says of the Germander that on account of its disposition to spread, it must be
taken up and new set once in three or four years, 'or else it will grow too *roynish* and
troublesome,' *Paradisus Terrestris*, 1629, p. 6.   HALLIWELL: Hunter misinterprets
the passage in Parkinson; 'roynish' there means *coarse;* and 'troublesome' is used
in a somewhat peculiar sense.   'The slouen and the carelesse man, the roynish nothing
nice.'—Tusser [*Five Hundred Points of Good Husbandry, &c.*, p. 142, ed. 1614].
STAUNTON: It may, however, be no more than a misprint of *roguish.*   WRIGHT:
Cotgrave gives: 'Rongneux . . . . scabbie, mangie, scuruie.'   The contemptuous
phrase in *Macb.* I, iii, 6, 'the rump-fed ronyon,' had probably the same origin.
. . . . In the form 'rinish,' signifying 'wild, jolly, unruly, rude,' it is found among
the Yorkshire words in Thoresby's Letter to Ray, reprinted by the English Dialect
Society.   'Rennish,' in the sense of 'furious, passionate,' which is in Ray's *Collection
of North Country Words*, is perhaps another form of the same.   [I do not find it in
Skeat.—ED.]

   11. **Hisperia**] That Warburton should have changed this name to suit himself is
not surprising, but what excuse can his followers urge?   Of the conclusion of this
speech a writer in *Blackwood*, April, 1833, says: 'No unfitting conjecture for a Second Lord and First Chambermaid; but, though not wide amiss of the mark, as it happened, yet vile.   Hesperia would have left her couch at one tap at the window, and
gone with the Wrestler whom she overheard the young ladies most commend (though
we suspect, notwithstanding his mishap, that she would have preferred Charles), but
Hesperia did not at all understand their commendation; and had she been called on
to give a report of it for a Court Journal, would not merely have mangled it sadly, but
imbued it with her own notions of "parts and graces." '

   11. **Princesse**] For many other instances of the omission of the plural or possessive *s* after words ending in the sound of *s*, see Walker, *Vers.* 243, or Abbott, § 471.
See also 'Princesse,' I, ii, 159.

   14. **Wrastler**] A trisyllable.   See Walker, *Vers.* 7, or Abbott, § 477.

Duk. Send to his brother, fetch that gallant hither, 18
If he be abfent, bring his Brother to me,
Ile make him finde him : do this fodainly; 20
And let not fearch and inquifition quaile,
To bring againe thefe foolifh runawaies. *Exunt.* 22

Scena Tertia.

Enter Orlando and Adam.

Orl. Who's there?
Ad. What my yong Mafter, oh my gentle mafter,
Oh my fweet mafter, O you memorie
Of old Sir *Rowland*; why, what make you here? 5
Why are you vertuous? Why do people loue you?
And wherefore are you gentle, ftrong, and valiant?
Why would you be fo fond to ouercome 8

---

18. *brother*] *brother's* Cap. Ktly, Dyce   1. Oliver's House. Rowe.
iii, Huds.   5. Rowland;] Rowland? Ff.

---

18. **brother**] MASON: I believe we should read *brother's*. When the Duke says,
'Fetch that gallant hither,' he certainly means Orlando. [An emendation which
Mason may *possibly* have made independently of Capell; in whose text it is found.
It is almost demanded by the next line.—ED.]

20. **sodainly**] HALLIWELL: That is, soon, immediately. This meaning, formerly
prevalent, is not now used in colloquial language. In an advertisement appended to
Walker's *Treatise of English Particles*, 1679, we are told that 'the Whole Duty of
man . . . . is now printing, and will *suddenly* be finished.' WRIGHT: Compare
Psalm vi, 10: 'Let them return and be ashamed suddenly.'

21. **quaile**] STEEVENS: To 'quail' is to *faint*, to sink into dejection. DOUCE (i,
297): Here, however, it means to *slacken, relax*, or *diminish*. 'Thus Hunger cureth
love, for love quaileth when good cheare faileth.'—*The Choise of Change*, 1585.
SINGER: 'To quaile, fade, faile,' are among the interpretations Cotgrave gives of the
word *Alachir*. DYCE (ed. iii): Mr Lettsom observes that '*fail* [Mr Lloyd's con-
jecture] seems more appropriate here than "quail."'

4. **memorie**] STEEVENS: Often used by Shakespeare for *memorial*. MALONE
(note on 'these weeds are memories of those worser hours,' *Lear*, IV, vii, 7): Thus
in Stowe's *Survey*, 1618; 'A printed memorie hanging up in a table at the entrance
into the church door.'

8. **so fond to**] See I, iii, 68. WRIGHT: 'Fond' is contracted from 'fonned' or
'fonnyd.' The latter form occurs in Wiclif's version of 1 Cor. i, 27 (ed. Lewis),
where 'tho thingis that ben fonnyd' is the rendering of 'quæ stulta sunt.' The former
is found in the second of the Wiclifite Versions, edited by Forshall and Madden, 1

The bonnie prifer of the humorous Duke *?*
Your praife is come too fwiftly home before you.   10
Know you not Mafter, to feeme kinde of men,
Their graces ferue them but as enemies,
No more doe yours : your vertues gentle Mafter   13

---

   9. *bonnie*] *bonny* Ff, Rowe, Pope,   *bony* Johns. et cet.
Theob. Han. Wh. i, Cam. *boney* Warb.   11. *feeme*] *fome* Ff.

Cor. i, 20, ' Whether God hath not maad the wisdom of this world fonned ?' where the
Vulgate has ' nonne stultam fecit Deus sapientiam hujus mundi ?' Hence ' fonnednesse '
in the same version is used for ' foolishness.' ' Fonned ' is derived from ' fon,' a fool,
which occurs in Chaucer's *Reve's Tale*, l. 4087 : ' Il hail, Aleyn, by God ! thou is a fon.'
And ' fon ' is connected with the Swedish *fane*, and perhaps with the Latin *vanus*.

   9. **bonnie**] WARBURTON : We should read *bony*. For this wrestler is characterised for his strength and bulk, not for his gayety or good humour. HEATH (p. 146) :
' Bonny ' does not signify *gay* or *good-humoured* only, but *high-spirited, active*.
STEEVENS : ' Bonny,' however, may be the true reading. So in *2 Hen. VI:* V, ii,
12 : ' Even of the bonny beast he lov'd so well.' MALONE : The word ' bonny '
occurs more than once in Lodge's Novel. DYCE (ed. iii) : ' Bonny ' is retained by
some editors, most improperly I think. (As Charles is here called ' bony,' so in the
preceding scene he is called ' sinewy.') WRIGHT : It may be doubted whether in
Shakespeare's time ' bony ' signified *big-boned*, and whether a *bony* man would not
rather mean a thin and skeleton-like man.

   9. **priser**] WRIGHT : Prize-fighter, champion ; properly, one who contends for a
prize, as in Jonson's *Cynthia's Revels*, IV, i [p. 323, ed. Gifford] : ' Well, I have a
plot upon these prizers.' Again, *Ib.* V, ii [p. 334, and in at least three other passages in
the same scene].

   9. **humorous**] See I, ii, 265.

   11. **seeme kinde of men**] See *Lear*, II, ii, 96, or Abbott, § 412.

   11, 12. WALKER (*Crit.* i, 55) gives this, among others, as an instance ' of what
may, perhaps, be described as an instinctive striving after a natural arrangement of
words, inconsistent indeed with modern English grammar, but perfectly authorised by
that of the Elizabethan age.' ' Here a Greek would find no difficulty : Οὐκ οἶσθα,
ὅτι ἐνίοις τῶν ἀνθρώπων καὶ τὰ αὑτῶν καλὰ πολέμιά ἐστιν ; One may perhaps compare
Sidney, *Arcadia*, bk. iii, p. 323, l. 15, " The general concert of whose mourning performed so the natural tunes of sorrow, that even to them (if any such were) that felt
not the loss, yet others' grief taught them grief—.' ' ' So, too ' —let it then suffice To
drown one woe, one pair of weeping eyes,' *R. of L.* l. 1679. ABBOTT, although he
gives these lines under his paragraph (§ 414) which treats of redundant accusatives,
yet says that ' them ' is in a somewhat different case, probably because the inverted
order calls for a repetition for clearness' sake. The instance from Sidney's *Arcadia*
cited by Walker seems to me exactly parallel. Though the ' them ' is redundant, it
is not of the same kind of redundancy as in ' I know *you* what you are.'—ED.

   13. **No . . . yours**] ABBOTT, § 414 : That is, your graces are not more serviceable
to you. SCHMIDT (s. v. *more*, 5) says that ' *no less* would have been expected.'
Hardly, I think. If the service were a real service, we might say ' no less ' ; but the
service is false, virtues are traitors, and ' no more ' good service does Orlando get from
his graces than if they were his enemies.—ED.

Are fanctified and holy traitors to you :
Oh what a world is this, when what is comely   15
Enuenoms him that beares it ?
Why, what's the matter ?
    Ad.   O vnhappie youth,
Come not within thefe doores : within this roofe   19

---

17. *Why*] Orl. *Why* Ff et seq.   19. *within this*] *beneath this* Cap.
19. *within thefe*] *with thefe* F$_2$.   conj.

---

15. **when**] ALLEN (MS): Possibly, '*where* what is comely.' If 'when' be retained, then 'world' is taken in its most restricted meaning, as this life of our little domestic circle. If *where* is used, then the 'world' is equivalent to this wide world of man, this animate creation of God's. Cf. II, vii, 11: 'what a *life* is this That your poor friends must woo your company.' Also below, line 59: 'The constant service of the antique *world, When* service sweat for duty.' [A note, added later.—ED.]   Cf. De Quincey (*Suspiria*, p. 194): 'In what world was I living *when* a man (calling himself a man of God) could stand up publicly, and give God "hearty thanks," that He had taken my sister?' (Perhaps, therefore, in Shakespeare, the full meaning is, 'What *a pass* has this world come to, *when*,' &c. And so 'when' can stand.)

16. **Enuenoms**] WALKER (*Crit.* iii, 61): Was the shirt of Nessus in Shakespeare's mind? [The same reference occurred independently to Allen. See next note.]

16. **beares**] ALLEN (MS): The figure appears to be that of putting on a garment, like the shirt of Nessus or that sent by Medea to Jason's new wife. If so, 'bears' is, singularly, used like the French *porter* (il *porte* un bel habit), or we should read *wears*.

19. **within this roofe**] COLLIER (ed. ii): This may be right, and we do not alter it; but '*beneath* this roof' seems more proper, and that is the word in the (MS). Perhaps the old printer repeated 'within' by mistake. [This remark of Collier's, if needless, is, apparently, perfectly harmless, and yet it seems to have irritated Dyce greatly, who in his *Strictures*, &c., p. 68, writes as follows: 'It is most unwise in Mr Collier to commit himself, as here and in fifty other places, by thinking it necessary to *say something in favour of those very readings of his Corrector which he does not adopt.* "Roof" was often used for the house in general: "If time, and foode, and wine enough acrue Within your roofe to vs," &c., Chapman's *Homer's Odysses*, b. xiv, p. 216, ed. fo.' It is impossible for us, removed as we are by time and space from the animosities of the hour, to comprehend the reason for the sharpness of the criticisms on Collier. Thus, in the present case, I cannot, try as I may, see why it is '*most* unwise' to express a mild approval of an emendation, which is all that Collier has here done; he does not commit himself by changing the text, he merely says the emendation '*seems* more proper,' wherein I must say I agree with him; and if Dyce had only turned to Mrs Clarke's *Concordance* he could have found there three instances at least where reference is made to being 'underneath' or 'under' a roof, and there may be others: the point is not worth further time, because 'roof' is unquestionably used elsewhere for the whole house. Before Dyce issued his third edition he had learned that the same conjecture had been made by Capell, who is held by all

The enemie of all your graces liues   20
Your brother, no, no brother, yet the fonne
(Yet not the fon, I will not call him fon)
Of him I was about to call his Father,
Hath heard your praifes, and this night he meanes,
To burne the lodging where you vfe to lye,   25
And you within it : if he faile of that
He will haue other meanes to cut you off;
I ouerheard him: and his practifes :
This is no place, this houfe is but a butcherie;
Abhorre it, feare it, doe not enter it.   30
    Ad.   Why whether *Adam* would'ft thou haue me go?
    Ad.   No matter whether, fo you come not here.
    Orl.   What, would'ft thou haue me go& beg my food,
Or with a bafe and boiftrous Sword enforce
A theeuifh liuing on the common rode?   35
This I muft do, or know not what to do :
Yet this I will not do, do how I can.
I rather will fubiect me to the malice   38

21. *no, no brother,*] *no ; no brother,*   31, 32. *whether*] *whither* Ff.
Rowe ii+.   *no ; no brother;* Theob.   31. *would'ft*] *would* F_4.
Warb.   32. *fo you*] *for you* Ff.
    31. Ad.] Orl. Ff.

Shakespeare scholars in esteem, and although he still pronounced the conjecture 'very erroneous,' he did not repeat his remark about the unwisdom of expressions of approval.—ED.]

26. **faile of**] See Abbott, § 177.

28. **practises**] DYCE : Contrivances, artifices, strategems, treachery, conspiracy.

29. **place**] STEEVENS : 'Place' here signifies a *seat*, a *mansion*, a *residence*.   So in *1 Samuel*, xv, 12 : 'Saul came to Carmel, and, behold, he set him up a place,' &c. Thus 'Crosby place' in *Rich. III.*, &c.   MALONE : Compare *A Lover's Complaint*, 82 : 'Love lack'd a dwelling and made him her place.'   MASON (*Additional Comments*, &c., p. 21) : It appears to me that Adam means merely to tell Orlando that his brother's house was no place fit for him to repair to.   Compare Fletcher's *Mad Lover* [I, ii, 3], where Memnon says : 'Why were there not such women in the camp then, Prepar'd to make me know 'em ?'   To which Eumenes replies, ''Twas no place, sir.'   Meaning that the camp was not a place fit for them.   KNIGHT : But there could be no sense in saying this is no house—place—mansion; this *house* is but a butchery. It is clearly, this is no abiding-place.   DYCE follows Steevens.   NEIL : There is perhaps here an *aposiopesis*, or emotional interruption of the sentence, leaving the words, 'for you to approach,' unexpressed.

31, 32. **thou . . . you**] See I, i, 74.

38. **subiect**] Steevens, Malone, Dyce, in fact all editors who adopt accents in the

Of a diuerted blood, and bloudie brother.

   Ad.   But do not fo : I haue fiue hundred Crownes,   40
The thriftie hire I faued vnder your Father,
Which I did ftore to be my fofter Nurfe,
When feruice fhould in my old limbs lie lame,
And vnregarded age in corners throwne,
Take that, and he that doth the Rauens feede,   45
Yea prouidently caters for the Sparrow,
Be comfort to my age : here is the gold,
All this I giue you, let me be your feruant,
Though I looke old, yet I am ftrong and luftie ;   49

---

41. *your*] *you* Ff.   44. *age*] *age be* Ktly.
43. *lie*] *be* Han. Quincy (MS).

---

text, here accent the second syllable. The inference is that without this aid to the eye the unwary reader would pronounce the word 'súbject'; and Wright goes so far as to call attention to the fact that 'the accent is on the last syllable, as in *Temp.* I, ii, 114.' This is puzzling. Are we to infer that in England at the present day this verb is an exception to the rule that dissyllabic verbs accent the second syllable? As Rolfe says: 'This [*i. e.* subjéct] is the modern pronunciation of the verb, at least in this country; and it is the only one in Shakespeare.'—ED.

   39. **diuerted blood**] JOHNSON: That is, blood turned out of the course of nature. COLLIER: The line as it stands is intelligible enough; but it may be reasonably doubted whether the old compositor did not make a lapse, for the MS corrector instructs us to read: 'diverted, *proud*,' &c. 'Blood' was formerly often spelt *bloud*, and hence, possibly, the error of mistaking *proud* for 'bloud.' DYCE: 'The language is so strikingly Shakespearian, that nothing but the most extreme obtuseness can excuse the MS corrector's perverse reading.'—*Blackwood's Magazine*, Aug. 1853, p. 198. WRIGHT: 'Blood' is used for passion in opposition to reason in *Ham.* III, ii, 74. Here it denotes natural affection, such as should accompany blood-relationship.

   41. **thriftie hire**] A singular use of the adjective. The thrift is neither the cause of the hire nor the effect of the hire. It cannot, therefore, I think, be exactly paralleled by 'weak evils' in II, vii, 138, which are evils caused by weakness, nor by the 'gentle weal' in 'Ere humane statute purged the gentle weal,' *Macb.* III, iv, 76, that is, 'purged the commonwealth and made it gentle.' Both of these examples have been adduced as parallel. It is more like 'youthful wages' in line 69 below, a *constructio pregnans*, to which the ordinary meaning of prolepsis scarcely, perhaps, applies. ALLEN (MS) paraphrases: 'that which by my thriftiness I saved out of the hire,' &c.—ED.

   44. In his paragraph (§ 403) on the 'Ellipsis of *It is, There is, Is*' ABBOTT gives this passage and thus prints this line: 'And unregarded age (? should be) in corners thrown.' To harmonise the construction and avoid this ellipsis HANMER substituted *be* for 'lie' in the preceding line, which is not only needless, but, I think, really injurious. There is a certain feebleness or helplessness in the old limbs *lying* lame in corners, which Hanmer's text obliterates.—ED.

For in my youth I neuer did apply   50
Hot, and rebellious liquors in my bloud,
Nor did not with vnbafhfull forehead woe,
The meanes of weakneffe and debilitie,
Therefore my age is as a luftie winter,
Froftie, but kindely ; let me goe with you,   55
Ile doe the feruice of a yonger man
In all your bufineffe and neceffities.

    Orl.   Oh good old man, how well in thee appeares
The conftant feruice of the antique world,
When feruice fweate for dutie, not for neede: 60
Thou art not for the fafhion of thefe times,
Where none will fweate, but for promotion,
And hauing that do choake their feruice vp,
Euen with the hauing, it is not fo with thee :   64

---

51. *in my*] *to my* Cap. conj.   60. *fweate*] *swet* Dyce, Clke.
52. *not*] *I* Rowe+.   *neede*] F₄, Rowe i. *meede* F₂F₃
59. *feruice*] *fashion* Ktly. *virtue* Neil   et cet.
conj.

    51.. **rebellious liquors in**] Malone suggested that the rebellion here is that against reason, but Steevens, with greater probability, I think, interpreted the reference as to liquors ' that *rebel* against the constitution.' In this case Capell's conjecture of ' *to* the blood' is rendered needless.—ED.

    52. **Nor did not**] For the double negative here, and ' I cannot goe no further,' in the eleventh line of the next scene, see Abbott, § 406, or Shakespeare *passim*.

    57. **businesse**] ALLEN (MS) suggests that this is the plural, *business*'.

    59, 60. **seruice . . . seruice**] WALKER (*Crit.* i, 293): I believe that the former 'service' is the corrupt one; yet I can imagine Shakespeare having written, ' When *duty* sweat for duty,' &c. [LETTSOM in a foot-note conjectures, ' The constant *temper*,' &c.] COLLIER (ed. ii): The (MS) corrector alters the former 'service' to *favour*, in the sense of likeness or appearance. HALLIWELL: One critic suggests that the second 'service' should be altered to *servants*. [It is to be confessed that in general the repetition of a word in the very next line is suspicious, but here there seems a need for the repetition. Moreover, in this speech there are other repetitions; see, as Rolfe points out, 'sweat,' in lines 60 and 62; and 'having,' in lines 63 and 64.—ED.]

    60. **sweate**] This form may be considered either as the perfect indicative with the *-ed* absorbed, for which see Abbott, § 341, or it may be a strong form and pronounced *swat*, or the spelling may be changed as Dyce has changed it.—ED.

    60. **neede**] An instance of variation in different copies of the First Folio. The original of Booth's Reprint and of Staunton's Photo-lithograph evidently read 'meede;' and so also presumably did that of the Cambridge Editors; they have recorded no variant. My copy reads unmistakeably 'neede.'—ED.

    64. **hauing**] JOHNSON: Even with the *promotion* gained by service is service extinguished.

But poore old man, thou prun'ſt a rotten tree,   65
That cannot ſo much as a bloſſome yeelde,
In lieu of all thy paines and husbandrie,
But come thy waies, weele goe along together,
And ere we haue thy youthfull wages ſpent,
Weele light vpon ſome ſetled low content.   70
   Ad.   Maſter goe on, and I will follow thee
To the laſt gaſpe with truth and loyaltie,
From ſeauentie yeeres, till now almoſt foureſcore
Here liued I, but now liue here no more
At ſeauenteene yeeres, many their fortunes ſeeke   75
But at foureſcore, it is too late a weeke,
Yet fortune cannot recompence me better
Then to die well, and not my Maſters debter.   *Exeunt.*   78

73. *ſeauentie*] *ſeventy* Ff. *seventeen* Rowe et seq.

---

65. rotten tree] MOBERLY: Orlando *says* melancholy things, as in I, ii; but his elastic mind rises instantly from such thoughts, and in a few moments he anticipates 'some settled low content.' A fine instance of the same manly temper is found in the *Iliad*, vi, where Hector at one moment dwells sorrowfully on his wife's inevitable doom of slavery at Argos, and the next thinks of her as a joyful Trojan mother welcoming back her victorious son (see vv. 447–465 and 476–481).

71. thee] Note the change of the personal pronoun with the changed personal relations.—ED.

73. seauentie] See Text. Note for the obvious correction.

76. a weeke] CALDECOTT. That is, a period of time, indefinitely. The calculation of time by this interval was not then confined, as it is at present, to small contracts or domestic engagements and a fixed period, but embraced a large and indefinite compass and extended to all things. 'To whose heavenly praise My soule hath bin devoted many a weeke,' Heywood's *Britaine's Troy*, 1609, p. 251. HALLIWELL adds also, from Heywood's *Workes* [Spenser Soc. ed. p. 74—ap. Wright]. 'And, amend ye or not, I am to olde a yere.' WRIGHT: But it seems more likely that 'a week' is an adverbial phrase equivalent to 'i' the week.' See 'a night,' line 49, in the next scene. VERITY: Perhaps *in the week* is the meaning; or, which seems to me more probable, '*by* a week.'

Scena Quarta.

Enter Rofaline for Ganimed, Celia for Aliena, and Clowne, alias *Touchſtone.*

Roſ. O *Iupiter*, how merry are my ſpirits?　　　　3

1. Rofaline...Touchſtone] Rosalind in Boys Cloaths for Ganimed, Celia drest like a Shepherdess for Aliena, and Clown.　Rowe.

3. *merry*] Ff, Rowe, Pope, Cald. Knt. *weary* Theob. et cet.

3. **merry**] THEOBALD : And yet, within the space of one intervening line, she says she could find in her heart to disgrace her man's apparel and *cry* like a woman. Sure, this is but a very bad symptom of the *briskness of spirits :* rather a direct proof of the contrary disposition. Mr Warburton and I both concurr'd in conjecturing it should be, as I have reform'd it in the text : 'how *weary* are my spirits.' And the Clown's reply makes this reading certain. [*Weary* was also suggested to Theobald in 1732 by an anonymous correspondent, L. H.; see Nichols's *Illust.* ii, 632.—ED.] GUTHRIE (*Crit. Rev.*, Dec. 1765, p. 407) : We think that Rosalind's rejoinder [lines 6, &c.] makes the original reading certain; from this speech (which we are to suppose Celia not to hear) Rosalind affects a merriness of spirits. MALONE : Rosalind invokes 'Jupiter' because he was supposed to be always in good spirits. So afterwards : ' O most gentle Jupiter !' The context and the Clown's reply render certain Theobald's emendation. WHITER (p. 16) : The context, however, and the Clown's reply, added to the comment of Mr Malone, establish the *original* reading and render Theobald's emendation *certainly wrong.* Does not the reader perceive that the whole humour of the passage consists in the word MERRY, and that Rosalind speaks thus ironically in order to comfort Celia? ' O Jupiter !' says she, ' what MERRY spirits I am in !' To which the Clown replies, ' I care not whether my spirits were good or bad, if my legs were not weary.'—' Indeed,' adds Rosalind, ' to speak the truth, tho' I pretend in my *mannish* character to be in *good* spirits, and *not* to be weary, yet I could find in my heart to disgrace my man's apparel and to cry like a woman; as it becomes me, however, to comfort the weaker vessel, I must assume a quality which I have not;— therefore, *courage*, good Aliena, bear fatigue as I do, good Aliena.' Nothing is more certain than this explanation. KNIGHT pronounces Whiter's explanation as marked ' with great good sense.' COLLIER : Why should Rosalind assume good spirits here to Celia, when in the very next sentence she utters she says that her spirits are so bad that she could almost cry? WHITE (ed. i) : If Rosalind were to say that her spirits were ' merry,' Touchstone's reply would have no point. In WALKER'S chapter (*Crit.* ii, 300) on ' *m* and *w* confounded ' this line is cited; and that Knight should have followed the Folio in reading ' merry' Walker marks with an exclamation. DYCE quotes Knight's note, printing in small capitals ' GREAT GOOD SENSE,' and adds at the conclusion : ' Surely such notes are quite enough to make any one " merry,"—absolute *Cordials for Low Spirits.*' [With all deference to my betters, I respectfully but firmly protest against making the cart draw the horse, and changing Rosalind's speech to suit the humour in Touchstone's. The confusion of *m* and *w*, on which Walker

Clo. I care not for my fpirits, if my legges were not
wearie.   5

Rof. I could finde in my heart to difgrace my mans
apparell, and to cry like a woman : but I muft comfort
the weaker veffell, as doublet and hofe ought to fhow it
felfe coragious to petty-coate; therefore courage, good
Aliena.   10

Cel. I pray you beare with me, I cannot goe no further.

Clo. For my part, I had rather beare with you, then   13

---

7. *to*] Om. Rowe+.
9. *to*] *to a* F$_3$F$_4$, Rowe.

11. *cannot*] *can* Ff, Rowe, Pope, Han.
Johns. Cap. Coll. Sing. Clke, Ktly.
11, 12. *further*] *farther* Coll.

---

relies, will do well enough in such words as *may* and *way*, *mind* and *wind*, *meek* and
week, &c., but a little too much confusion is demanded to justify the change of *merry*
into *wearie*. The *ductus literarum* is helpful where nonsense is to be converted to
sense, but is there any nonsense here ? Is it not clear that Rosalind is talking for
effect ? With Celia ' fainting almost to death ' and needing every possible encouragement, is it likely that Rosalind, the taller and stronger of the two, would utter such a
wail of despair as the substitution of *weary* for ' merry ' would make her sigh forth ?
Of course this merriment of hers is assumed, and that it is assumed, and that we may
know that it is assumed, she tells us, in an aside, by confessing that in her heart she
is ready to cry like a woman. This confession must be in an aside; at least Celia
must not hear it; if Celia heard it no syllable of stimulus would she have found in an
encouragement thus clearly and confessedly fictitious; she must believe Rosalind's
courage to be genuine if it is to impart any strength to her. Grant that this last confession of Rosalind's is an aside, then it is clear that in the first line, which cannot be
an aside, we must retain ' merry,' and with it the strength of Rosalind's character.
Deny that this confession is an aside, then we may adopt Theobald's *weary*, add a
feeble ray of humour to Touchstone's remark, reduce all that Rosalind says to a
whine, and weaken Celia's character by showing her capable of being encouraged by
a jauntiness confessedly and openly false and assumed.—ED.]

9. **therefore courage**] To indicate the termination of the aside, and that ' courage ' is the first word addressed to Celia, I think this should be printed ' Therefore,
——courage, good Aliena !'—ED.

11. **cannot goe no**] See line 52 of preceding scene. CALDECOTT regards this
double negative as so thoroughly Shakespearian that he cites the change in the Second
Folio (see Text. Notes) as one among many proofs of Malone's theory, that the alterations in that edition were ' arbitrary and made without a knowledge of the author's
manner.' But DYCE (ed. iii) says : ' I feel strongly tempted to read here, with the
Second Folio, " I can go no further," the very words of Adam in the first line of the
sixth scene below.' [However strong the temptation, it is unquestionably wise to
resist it.—ED.]

13, 14. **beare . . . beare**] A play on the same word is cited by Steevens in *Rich.
III:* III, i, 128 ; and by Wright in *Two Gent.* I, i, 125–128.

beare you : yet I ſhould beare no croſſe if I did beare
you, for I thinke you haue no money in your purſe.   15

Roſ.   Well, this is the Forreſt of *Arden.*

Clo.   I, now am I in *Arden,* the more foole I, when I
was at home I was in a better place, but Trauellers muſt
be content.

Enter Corin and Siluius.   20

Roſ.   I, be ſo good *Touchſtone*: Look you, who comes
here, a yong man and an old in ſolemne talke.

Cor.   That is the way to make her ſcorne you ſtill.   23

---

14. **crosse**] DYCE: 'The ancient penny, according to Stow, had a double cross
with a crest stamped on it, so that it might be easily broken in the midst, or in four
quarters.   Hence it became a common phrase when a person had no money about
him, to say, he had not a *single cross.*   As this was certainly an *unfortunate* circumstance, there is no end to the quibbling on this poor word,'—Gifford's note on *Johnson's Works,* vol. i, p. 134.   WRIGHT: A play upon the figurative expression in
Matthew, x, 38.

17. **Arden**] UPTON (p. 245): The Clown, agreeable to his character, is in a punning vein, and replys thus, 'Ay, now I am in *a den,*' &c.   HARTLEY COLERIDGE (ii,
141): Nothing can exceed the mastery with which Shakespeare, without any obtrusive or undramatic description, transports the imagination to the sunny glades and
massy shadows of umbrageous Arden.   The leaves rustle and glisten, the brooks murmur unseen in the copses, the flowers enamel the savannas, the sheep wander on the
distant hills, the deer glance by and hide themselves in the thickets, and the sheep-
cotes sprinkle the far landscape spontaneously, without being shown off, or talked
about.   You hear the song of the birds, the belling of the stags, the bleating of the
flocks, and a thousand sylvan, pastoral sounds beside, blent with the soft plaints and
pleasant ambiguities of the lovers, the sententious satire of Jacques, and the courtly
fooling of Touchstone, without being told to listen to them.   Shakespeare does all
that the most pictorial dramatist could do, without ever sinking the dramatist in the
landscape-painter.   The exuberant descriptions of some recent authors are little more
dramatic than the voluminous stage directions in translated German melodramas.   I
know not what share the absence of painted scenes might have in preserving our old
dramatists from this excess, but I believe that the low state of estimation of landscape-
painting had a good deal to do with it.   Luxurious description characterises the second childhood of poetry.   In its last stage, it begins, like Falstaff, to babble of green
fields.

21, 22. WALKER (*Crit.* i, 16): Arrange thus:

> 'Ay,
> Be so, good Touchstone;—Look you, who comes here;
> A young man and an old, in solemn talk.'

This, too, serves as a stepping-stone from the prose dialogue preceding to the conversation in verse between Corin and Silvius.

Sil.   Oh *Corin,* that thou knew'ft how I do loue her.

Cor.   I partly gueffe : for I haue lou'd ere now.   25

Sil.   No *Corin,* being old, thou canft not gueffe,

Though in thy youth thou waft as true a louer

As euer figh'd vpon a midnight pillow :

But if thy loue were euer like to mine,

As fure I thinke did neuer man loue fo :   30

How many actions moft ridiculous,

Haft thou beene drawne to by thy fantafie ?

Cor.   Into a thoufand that I haue forgotten.

Sil.   Oh thou didft then neuer loue fo hartily,

If thou remembreft not the flighteft folly,   35

That euer loue did make thee run into,

Thou haft not lou'd.

Or if thou haft not fat as I doe now,   38

---

29. *euer*] *ere* Ff.
30, in parenthesis, Pope et seq.
34. *neuer*] *ne'er* Rowe +, Coll.

35. *flighteft*] *slighted* Rowe.
38. *fat*] *fate* Ff, Rowe.

---

27. **wast**] ALLEN (MS): *Wert* seems to be required.   Silvius does not mean
to state or to recognise the fact that Corin *really had been* such a lover, but merely
to concede that *if* Corin had been, &c. he could not now, in his old age, guess,
&c.

32. **fantasie**] WRIGHT: The earlier form of the word ' fancy.'   ' Fantasie ' occurs
in Chaucer's *Merchants Tale,* l. 9451, in the margin of the later Wiclifite version of
Josh. xxii, 19, and perhaps earlier still.   ARBER, in the few words of Introduction to
his reprint of Dryden's *Essay on Dramatic Poesie* (*English Garner,* iii, 502), notes
four changes of the meaning of ' fancy.'   First, in the Elizabethan Age it was but
another word for personal *Love* or *Affection.*   Second, by the Restoration Age its
meaning had utterly changed.   Sir Robert Howard, who wrote it *Phancy,* Dryden,
and that generation understood by it, *Imagination, the mental power of Picturing
forth.*   Third, Coleridge, in his *Biographia Literaria,* 1812, endeavours yet further
to distinguish between *Imagination* and *Fancy ;* calling Milton an *Imaginative* Poet,
and Cowley a *Fanciful* one.   Fourth, it is now also used in another sense, ' I do not
fancy that,' equivalent to ' I do not *like* or *prefer* that.'

34. JOHNSON: I am inclined to believe that from this passage Suckling took the
hint of his song : ' Honest lover, whosoever, If in all thy love there ever Was one
wav'ring thought ; if thy flame Were not still even, still the same ; Know this Thou
lov'st amiss, And to love true, Thou must begin again, and love anew,' &c.

36. **into**] The second syllable receives an accent.   See Walker (*Crit.* ii, 173) or
Abbott, § 457, *a.*

37, 40, 43. ABBOTT, § 511 : Single lines with two or three accents are frequently
interspersed amid the ordinary verses of five accents.   These lines are often found in
passages of soliloquy where passion is at its height.   Thus in the madness of *Lear,*
IV, vi, 112–127.   So in this impassioned speech of Silvius.

Wearing thy hearer in thy Miftris praife,

Thou haft not lou'd.   40

Or if thou haft not broke from companie,

Abruptly as my paffion now makes me,

Thou haft not lou'd.

O *Phebe*, *Phebe*, *Phebe*.   *Exit.*

  Rof. Alas poore Shepheard fearching of they would,   45

I haue by hard aduenture found mine owne.

  Clo. And I mine : I remember when I was in loue, I

broke my fword vpon a ftone, and bid him take that for

comming a night to *Iane Smile*, and I remember the kif-

fing of her batler, and the Cowes dugs that her prettie   50

---

39. *Wearing*] *Wearying* Ff, Rowe+,
Cap. Steev. Mal. Coll. Clke, Ktly, Huds.
Wh. ii.   *Wear'ing* Wh. i.
44. Exit.] Exeunt. Ff.
45. *they would*] *their wound* Ff, Cald.
Knt.   *thy wound* Rowe et cet.

46. *mine*] *my* Rowe ii+, Cald.
  49. *a night*] *a nights* Ff, Rowe+.
o' nights Cap. *o' night* Mal. Wh. *anight*
or *a-night* Steev. et cet.
50. *batler*] *batlet* Ff, Rowe+, Cap.
Steev. Mal. Sing. Dyce.

---

39. **Wearing**] WHITER (p. 17) cites an old definition from Junius, *Etymol. Angli-can*, s. v. *Wear*, which shows clearly enough that *to wear* and *to weary* were formerly synonymous, and then adds : but the following quotation from Jonson's *The Gipsies Metamorphosed* [p. 419, ed. Gifford] puts the matter out of dispute : ' Or a long pre-tended fit, Meant for mirth, but is not it ; Only time and ears out-wearing.' SKEAT derives 'wear' from A.-S. *werian*, to clothe ; and 'weary' from A.-S. *wérig*, tired, connected with A.-S. *wórian*, to wander, a weak verb formed from the substantive *wór*, which probably meant a moor or swampy place ; so that *wórian* was originally ' to tramp over wet ground,' the most likely thing to cause weariness.

41. **broke**] For a list of similar participles that have dropped the *-en*, see Abbott, § 343.

43, 44. From Capell to Collier these two lines were printed improperly as one ; Collier restored the old division.

45. **searching of**] For similar instances of this preposition after present parti-ciples, meaning ' in the act of,' see Abbott, § 178. Cf. also II, vii, 5.

45. **they would**] See Text. Notes. Neither Caldecott nor Knight gives any justification of their text. Unquestionably Rowe's correction should stand.—ED.

46. **aduenture**] ALLEN (MS) : The ' adventure ' (or experiment, *periculum ?*) was not *in itself* a hard or painful one to Rosalind ; but by the chance of hearing Sylvius expose *his* state [of love-pains] *her* similar pains were brought out ; and the *hardness* was in the pain thus brought out.

49. **a night**] For many examples of adverbs with the prefix *a-*, which represents some preposition, as *in*, *on*, *of*, &c., contracted by rapidity of pronunciation, see Abbott, § 24.

49, 51. **the kissing of . . . the wooing of**] ABBOTT, § 93 : The substantive use of the verbal with ' the ' before it and ' of ' after it, seems to have been regarded as colloquial. Shakespeare puts it into the mouth of Touchstone.

50. **batler**] JOHNSON : The instrument with which washers beat their coarse clothes.

chopt hands had milk'd; and I remember the wooing   51
of a peafcod inftead of her , from whom I tooke two

HALLIWELL: Often spelt *batlet*.   It is also called a *batling-staff* or a *bat-staff*, and
sometimes a *batting-staff*.   WRIGHT [gives many forms of the word in various English dialects, and adds]: The two forms, 'batler' and *batlet* as diminutives of *bat*,
may be compared with 'lancer' (*1 Kings*, xviii, 28, ed. 1611), and 'lancet' as
diminutive of 'lance.'   The form 'lancet' is substituted in modern editions of the
Authorised Version.   [See also Skeat, s. v. 'battledore.']

51. chopt] WRIGHT: That is, chapped; as in *Sonn.* lxii, 10: 'Beated and chopt
with tand antiquitie.'   Both forms of the word were used, the pronunciation being
the same in each case.   Cotgrave gives: 'Crevasser, To chop, chawne, chap, chinke,
riue, or cleaue asunder.'   And in the Authorised Version of *Jeremiah*, xiv, 4 (ed.
1611), we find, 'Because the ground is chapt, for there was no raine on the earth.'

51. the wooing] HALLIWELL: Our ancestors were frequently accustomed in their
love affairs to employ the divination of a peascod, by selecting one growing on the
stem, snatching it away quickly, and if the omen of the peas remaining in the husk
were preserved, then presenting it to the lady of their choice.   According to Mr
Davy, speaking of Suffolk, 'the efficacy of peascods in the affairs of sweethearts is
not yet forgotten among our rustic vulgar.   The kitchen-maid, when she shells green
peas, never omits, if she finds one having *nine* peas, to lay it on the lintel of the
kitchen-door, and the first clown who enters it is infallibly to be her husband or at
least her sweetheart.' . . . . 'Winter-time for shoeing, peascod-time for wooing,' is an
old proverb in a MS Devon. Gl.   But perhaps the allusion in Shakespeare is best
illustrated by the following passage in Browne's *Britannia's Pastorals* [B. ii, Song 3,
ll. 93–96, ed. Hazlitt—*ap*. Wright]: 'The peascod greene oft with no little toyle
Hee'd seeke for in the fattest fertil'st soile, And rend it from the stalke to bring it to
.her, And in her bosome for acceptance wooe her.'   [Halliwell cites no authority for
this note, which is also to be found in nearly the same words in Brand's *Popular
Antiquities*, ii, 99, ed. Bohn, as noted by Wright.]   WHITER (p. 17) quotes the following proverb from Florio's *Second Frutes*, 1591, for no reason that I can discern
other than that the word 'peascod' is common to both passages: 'If women were as
little as they are good, A Peascod would make them a gowne and a hood.'

52. peascod] FARMER: In a schedule of jewels in the 15 vol. of Rymer's *Fœdera*,
we find: 'Item, two peascoddes of gold with 17 pearles.'   STEEVENS: The ancient
name for *peas* as they are brought to market.   So in Greene's *Groundwork of Cony-
catching*, 1592, 'went twice in the week to London, either with fruit or pescods,' &c.
Again, in *The Honest Man's Fortune*, by Beau. and Fl.: 'thou shalt wear gold, feed
on delicates; the first peascods, strawberries, grapes,' &c. [III, iii, p. 402, ed. Dyce].
DOUCE: The 'peascod' certainly means the whole of the pea as it hangs upon the
stalk.   It was formerly used as an ornament in dress, and was represented with the
shell open exhibiting the peas.   SKEAT: Cod is a husk, shell, bag; *peas-cod, i. e.* pea-
shell, husk of a pea.   [Cf. 'with leaues like unto the cich pease.   It beareth seed in
certain cods,' Holland's *Plinie*, 27th Book, p. 231.—ED.]

52. from whom] KNIGHT: That is, from his mistress.   He took from her two
peascods, that is, two pods.   STAUNTON: Touchstone surely means that he both took
the cods from, and returned them to, the *peascod*, the representative of his mistress.
In like manner he tells us, just before, he broke his sword upon a stone, and bid *him*,
his imagined rival, 'take that.'   [Unquestionably Staunton is right.—ED.]

cods, and giuing her them againe, faid with weeping   53
teares, weare thefe for my fake: wee that are true Louers, runne into ftrange capers; but as all is mortall in   55
nature, fo is all nature in loue, mortall in folly.

Rof. Thou fpeak'ft wifer then thou art ware of.

Clo. Nay, I fhall nere be ware of mine owne wit, till
I breake my fhins againft it.

Rof. Ioue, Ioue, this Shepherds paffion,   60

---

53. *cods*] *peas* Ktly.   60. Ioue, Ioue] *Love. Love!* Coll.
55. *as all*] *all* Rowe, Pope, Han.   (MS), ii, iii.
56. *mortall in*] *mortal to* Rowe i.   60, 61. Prose, Pope+, Mal.
58, 59. *till...it*] One line, Coll.

---

53. **cods**] JOHNSON: For 'cods' it would be more like sense to read *peas*, which,
having the shape of pearls, resembled the common presents of lovers. MALONE: In
the following passage, however, Touchstone's present certainly signifies not the *pea*,
but the *pod*, and so I believe the word is used here : ' He [Richard II] also used a *peascod* branch with the *cods* open, but the *peas* out, as it is upon his robe in his monument
at Westminster,'—Camden's *Remaines*, 1614. The *cods* and not the *peas* were worn.

53, 54. **weeping teares**] CAPELL: Here the Poet is wag enough to raise a smile at
the expence of his friend the novelist; who employs these words seriously in a something that he calls a sonnet, without once seeing the ridicule of them. [See Rosader's Sonnet, beginning, ' In sorrowes cell,' &c.] HALLIWELL: This pleonastic
expression is of so extremely common occurrence that there is no necessity for pre-
suming it to have been suggested to Shakespeare by its introduction into Lodge's
Novel. [Hereupon follow the titles of ten works wherein the expression is found.]

56. **mortall in folly**] JOHNSON: This expression I do not well understand. In
the middle counties, ' mortal,' from *mort*, a great quantity, is used as a particle of
amplification; as *mortal tall*, *mortal little*. Of this sense I believe Shakespeare takes
advantage to produce one of his darling equivocations. Thus the meaning will be,
so is all nature in love *abounding* in folly. CALDECOTT: That is, extremely foolish.
DYCE refers to Carr's *Craven Glossary : 'Mortal*, Exceeding, very; "he's *mortal*
rich," " I'se *mortal* hungry." ' STAUNTON: As the commentators appear not to suspect corruption here, the passage probably contains a meaning we have failed to discover. SCHMIDT: ' Mortal' is here equivalent to human, resembling man in folly.
[These explanations of ' mortal' in this particular passage are all so mortal weak
that I prefer to agree with Staunton that the meaning is yet to be discovered. If it
were not for Rosalind's reply I should think that we were looking too deep. Yet
Weiss's explanation (p. 113) is ingenious : ' That is, Nature can be foolish in love,
but the folly is mortal, as all the things of Nature are, and will pass away, leaving
love behind.' Therefore he'll have no jibes about it, and Rosalind justly replies,
' Thou speak'st wiser than thou art ware of.'—ED.]

57, 58. **ware . . . ware**] It seems almost needless to point out that Rosalind means
aware, and Touchstone means *cautious*.—ED. SINGER : Perhaps Rosalind takes the
Clown's equivoque seriously, and has in her mind that possession is the grave of love,
which expires in its own folly.

60, &c. COLLIER (ed. ii) here takes his text from his (MS) Corrector, who, he

Is much vpon my fafhion.   61

   Clo.   And mine, but it growes fomething ftale with
mee.

   Cel.   I pray you, one of you queftion yon'd man,
If he for gold will giue vs any foode,   65
I faint almoft to death.

   Clo.   Holla; you Clowne.

   Rof.   Peace foole, he's not thy kinfman.

   Cor.   Who cals?

   Clo.   Your betters Sir.   70

   Cor.   Elfe are they very wretched.

   Rof.   Peace I fay; good euen to your friend.

   Cor.   And to you gentle Sir, and to you all.

   Rof.   I prethee Shepheard, if that loue or gold
Can in this defert place buy entertainment,   75
Bring vs where we may reft our felues, and feed:
Here's a yong maid with trauaile much oppreffed,
And faints for fuccour.   78

---

61. *much vpon*] *too much on* Coll. (MS), ii, iii.

62, 63. *it…mee*] *It grows something stale with me, And begins to fail with me* Coll. ii, iii.

64. *yon'd*] *yond* Rowe. *yon* Cap.

70. *Sir*] Om. Han.

71. *are they very*] *they are* Rowe i. *they are very* Rowe ii+. *they're very* Han.

72. *Peace*] *Peace, fool,* Han.

good…friend] One line, Cap. Steev. Mal. Cald. Knt, Coll.

your] *you* Ff et seq.

---

says, 'must have had some foundation for the addition, unless it were a mere invention'; Collier suggests that we have fragments here of an old ballad, wherein, as far as lines 60, 61, and 'it grows something stale with me' of the Folio is concerned, Dyce (ed. iii, p. 26) agrees with him. His text is as follows:

> '*Ros.* Love, Love! this shepherd's passion
> Is too much on my fashion.
>   *Touch.* And mine; but
> It grows something stale with me,
> And begins to fail with me.'

Ellis (*Early Eng. Pronun.*, p. 949, *b*): Observe that the rhyme [*passi-on, fashi-on*] is here an identical one, on the final syllable *-on*, and that it is *not* a double rhyme, like the modern *pash-un fash-un*, as this would make each line defective by a measure. *Pas-si-on, fash-i-on* were really trisyllables. Allen (MS): The 'passion' of love is love conceived of as something like *suffering*.

72. **your**] One of the many instances where, in the Folio, *you* and *your* are confounded. See Walker, *Crit.* ii, 190.

77, 78. Abbott, § 403: Either *who is* is omitted, 'Here's a young maid (who is) with travel much oppressed,' or the nominative (cf. § 399) is omitted before 'faints.'

Cor.   Faire Sir, I pittie her,
And wifh for her fake more then for mine owne,   80
My fortunes were more able to releeue her :
But I am fhepheard to another man,
And do not fheere the Fleeces that I graze :
My mafter is of churlifh difpofition,
And little wreakes to finde the way to heauen   85
By doing deeds of hofpitalitie.
Befides his Coate, his Flockes, and bounds of feede
Are now on fale, and at our fheep-coat now
By reafon of his abfence there is nothing
That you will feed on : but what is, come fee,   90
And in my voice moft welcome fhall you be.
    Rof.   What is he that fhall buy his flocke and pafture?
    Cor.   That yong Swaine that you faw heere but ere-
        while,   94

82. *fhepheard*] *a shepherd* Rowe.   87. *Coate*] *Cote* Han.
85. *wreakes*] Ff, Rowe+, Cald. *recks*   90, 91, 93. *you*] *ye* Johns.
Han. Johns. et cet.

---

85. **wreakes**] STEEVENS : That is, heeds, cares for. So in *Ham.* I, iii, 51 : 'And recks not his own rede.' [Perhaps from the spelling here, and in *Ham.*, where it is *reakes* in the Qq and *reaks* in the Ff, we may, perhaps, infer that in pronunciation the sound of *e* was longer then than it is now. The assonance in Ophelia's speech would be thereby certainly more decided : 'and *reeks* not his own *reed*.'—ED.]

86. **hospitalitie**] WORDSWORTH (p. 218) : Flowing from a kindly and considerate disposition, the duty of hospitality is one which the Bible, we know, frequently enjoins and commends. See 1 Peter, iv, 9 ; Hebrews, xiii, 2 ; Romans, xii, 13. But there is a passage more solemn and impressive than any of these, spoken by our Lord Himself with reference to the great day of account : 'I was a stranger, and ye took me *not* in,' Matt., xxv, 43 ; which I cannot help thinking was present to our poet's mind when he made Corin [speak these words].

87. **Coate**] WRIGHT : Cotgrave has : '*Cavenne de bergier :* a shepheards cote ; a little cottage or cabine made of turues, straw, boughes, or leaues.'

87. **bounds of feede**] CALDECOTT : That is, range of pasture.

91. **voice**] JOHNSON : That is, as far as I have a voice or vote, as far as I have power to bid you welcome. ['Fortinbras . . . . has my dying voice,' *Ham.* v, ii, 343.]

92. **What is he**] For many other instances of the use of this phrase, see ABBOTT, § 254, where there is the thoughtful remark that 'in the Elizabethan and earlier periods, when the distinction between ranks was much more marked than now, it may have seemed natural to ask, as the first question about any one, " Of what condition or rank is he ?"   In that case the difference is one of *thought*, not of grammar.'

92. **shall**] ABBOTT, § 315, paraphrases this by *is to*, and classes it with I, i, 126 : ' He that escapes me shall acquit him well.'   It is difficult to distinguish these shades of meaning.   To me the present ' shall ' is not the same as Charles's ' shall.'   Here, I think, it is simple futurity.—ED.

That little cares for buying any thing.   95
 Rof.   I pray thee, if it ftand with honeftie,
Buy thou the Cottage, pafture, and the flocke,
And thou fhalt haue to pay for it of vs.
 Cel.   And we will mend thy wages :
I like this place, and willingly could   100
Wafte my time in it.
 Cor.   Affuredly the thing is to be fold :
Go with me, if you like vpon report,
The foile, the profit, and this kinde of life,
I will your very faithfull Feeder be,   105
And buy it with your Gold right fodainly.   *Exeunt.*

---

97. *pafture*] *and the pafture* F_3F_4. 100, 101. *I... Wafte*] One line, Rowe
99–101. Two lines, ending *place...it*, ii+.
Cap. et seq.

---

96. **honestie**] In the wide range of meanings which this word bears, extending from *chastity* to *generosity*, the meaning which best suits the present context is, I think, *honour*, that is, honourable dealing towards Silvius.—ED.

99, 101. Unquestionably, Capell's division is better than the Folio's, which in fact is not rhythmical at all. At the same time, an extra syllable in the third foot is objectionable : 'And we | will mend | thy wag*es :* | I like | this place.' To be sure, if the line *must* be of five feet, we may make it a little smoother by reading *wage*. But the thought closes so completely with 'wages' that I would close the line with it, and put a full stop after it. Let the next two lines divide at 'waste' : 'I like | this place, | and will | ingly | could waste ‖ My time in it.' All of which, after all, is merely scansion for the eye. An ear instinctively rhythmical decides such divisions for itself.—ED.

101. **Waste**] That is, simply *spend, pass*, as in *Mer. of Ven.* III, iv, 14 : 'Companions That do converse and waste the time together.' See II, vii, 141, *post :* 'And we will nothing waste till you return.'

105. **Feeder**] DYCE : A servant, a menial ; as in *Tim.* II, ii, 168, 'our offices .... oppressed With riotous feeders,' and in *Ant. & Cleop.* III, xiii, 109 : 'By one that looks on feeders.' WALKER (*Crit.* i, 311) : *Qu. factor ? Feed* occurs thirteen and sixteen lines above. '*Your factor,' i. e. your agent in buying the farm.* [Dyce (ed. iii) notes that Walker thus queries, and adds, 'wrongly, I believe.' Walker must have overlooked the instances of the use of 'feeder' cited by Dyce.] NEIL : Perhaps the word ought to be *Feodar* or *Fedary*, male representative undertaking the suit and service required by the superior from those holding lands in feudal tenure under him.

106. BLACKWOOD'S MAGAZINE (April, 1833) : How fortunate that the prettiest cottage in or about the Forest is on sale ! No occasion for a conveyancer. There shall be no haggling about price, and it matters not whether or no there be any title-deeds. A simple business, as in Arcadia of old, is buying and selling in Arden. True that it is not term-day. But term-day is past, for mind ye not that it is mid-summer ?

Scena Quinta.

Enter, Amyens, Iaques, & others.
Song.
Vnder the greene wood tree,
who loues to lye with mee,
And turne his merrie Note,   5
vnto the ſweet Birds throte :
Come hither, come hither, come hither :
Heere ſhall he ſee no enemie,
But Winter and rough Weather.

Iaq.   More, more, I pre'thee more.   10
Amy.   It will make you melancholly Monſieur *Iaques*
Iaq.   I thanke it : More, I prethee more,
I can ſucke melancholly out of a ſong,   13

Scene changes to a desart Part of the Forest. Theob.

3. Vnder] Ami. *Under* Cap. et seq.
   greene wood] *greenwood* F₃. *greenhood* F₄, Rowe i.
5. turne] F₂. *tune* Rowe ii+, Cap.

Coll. ii, iii, Dyce iii.   *turn* $F_3 F_4$ et cet.
8. he] *we* Cap. (corrected in Errata).
   Two lines, Pope et seq.
8, 9. Marked as a Chorus. Cap.
10, 14. *pre'thee*] *prethee* Ff.
12–14. Prose, Pope et seq.

---

5. **turne**] MALONE in support of the change to *tune* cites *Two Gent.* V, iv, 5 : 'And *to* the nightingale's complaining *note Tune* my distresses,' &c. STEEVENS : The old copy may be right.   To *turn* a *tune* or a *note* is still a current phrase among vulgar musicians.   WHITER corroborates Steevens : ' To *turn a tune* in counties of York and Durham is the appropriate and familiar phrase for' [correct singing].   SINGER : That 'turn' is right appears from the following line in Hall's *Satires*, Bk. vi, s. i [p. 157, ed. Singer] : ' Whiles threadbare Martiall turns his merry note.'   COLLIER (ed. ii) : It is altered to *tune* in the (MS).   It is misprinted *turn* in Hall's *Satires*.   DYCE (*Strictures*, &c., p. 69) : There is no reason to suspect a misprint in the line from Hall's *Satire*.   [Dyce, however, changed his opinion when he printed his third edition ; he there says that *turns* in this line from Hall] ' is manifestly an error for *tunes ;* so again in *The Two Gent.* IV, ii, 25, the Second Folio makes Thurio say to the Musicians : " Let's *turne*," &c.   To " turn a note " means only to " change a note " ; compare *Locrine*, 1595 : " when he sees that needs he must be prest, Heele *turne his note* and sing another tune." '   WRIGHT, after quoting this last note of Dyce's, adds : Even granting this, there appears to be no absolute necessity for change in the present passage, for 'turn his merry note' may mean adapt or modulate his note to the sweet bird's song, following its changes.

7. **Come**] From the references in the *Index* to Abbott, it is to be inferred that this ' come ' is considered by him as a subjunctive used optatively or imperatively.

As a Weazel fuckes egges : More, I pre'thee more.

Amy. My voice is ragged, I know I cannot pleafe   15
you.

Iaq. I do not defire you to pleafe me,
I do defire you to fing :
Come, more, another ftanzo : Cal you'em ftanzo's ?

Amy. What you wil Monfieur *Iaques.*   20

Iaq. Nay, I care not for their names, they owe mee
nothing.   Wil you fing ?

Amy. More at your requeft, then to pleafe my felfe.

Iaq. Well then, if euer I thanke any man, Ile thanke
you : but that they cal complement is like th'encounter   25
of two dog-Apes.   And when a man thankes me hartily,

15. *ragged*] *rugged* Rowe +, Cap.
17, 19. Prose, Pope et seq.
19. *Come, more*] *Come, come* Rowe +.
  'em] *them* Mal.

19. *ftanzo ... ftanzo's*] Ff, Rowe +,
Cam. Wh. ii, Huds.   *stanza...stanzas*
Cap. (conj.) et cet.
  25. *complement*] *compliment* Pope.
compliments Theob. Warb. Johns.

15. **ragged**] MALONE: That is, broken and unequal.   [For a dozen other instances
in Shakespeare where 'ragged' is thus used, see Schmidt, s. v. 3.]

19. **stanzo**] In Sherwood's *English and French Dictionarie*, appended to Cotgrave, 1632, we find, 'A stanzo (staffe of verses) *Stance*.   A stanzo (of eight verses)
Octastique.'   On turning to Cotgrave, under *Stance* we find, among other meanings,
'also, a stanzo, or staffe of verses.'   In the only other place where Shakespeare uses
the word, *Love's Lab. L.* IV, ii, 99, it is printed, according to the Cam. Ed., *stanze*
$F_1 Q_2$, *stanza* $F_2 F_3 F_4$, and *stauze* Q_1 (of course a misprint for *stanze*).   Jaques was
apparently a little doubtful as to the correctness of the term, which I think he used
in the sense of the second definition given by Sherwood.   If we divide ' Heere shall
he see no enemie ' into two verses, as every editor has divided it since Pope, the
song will be an *Octastique*, which Cotgrave again defines, 'Octostique : A staffe, or
Stanzo of eight verses.'—ED.

21. **names**] Used in a classical, legal sense.   Caldecott finds the allusion to the
Latin phrase, *nomina facere*, which we all know means to 'set down, or book the
items of debt in the account-book,' as the definition reads in Andrews's *Lexicon*.
But it seems to me that it is simpler to suppose that Jaques refers merely, as he says,
to 'the names,' for which the Latin is plain *nomina*.   In Cooper's *Thesaurus*, 1573,
the Dictionary which Shakespeare probably used (we are told that Queen Elizabeth
used it), the second definition of *nomina* is 'the names of debtes owen.'   Here, it is
possible, Shakespeare may have found the allusion which Jaques makes.—ED.

25. **that**] For the omission of the relative, see Abbott, § 244, or Shakespeare *passim*.

26. **dog-Apes**] DOUCE (i, 298) : Bartholomæus, speaking of apes, says : 'Some
be called *cenophe;* and be lyke to an hounde in the face, and in the body lyke to an
ape.'—*Lib.* xviii, c. 96.   WRIGHT : Topsell (*History of Beasts*, p. 8) says : 'Cyno-
cephales are a kind of Apes, whose heades are like Dogs, and their other parts like
a mans.'

me thinkes I haue giuen him a penie, and he renders me   27
the beggerly thankes.   Come sing ; and you that wil not
hold your tongues.

Amy.   Wel, Ile end the song.   Sirs, couer the while,   30
the Duke wil drinke vnder this tree; he hath bin all this
day to looke you.

Iaq.   And I haue bin all this day to auoid him :
He is too disputeable for my companie :
I thinke of as many matters as he, but I giue   35
Heauen thankes, and make no boast of them.
Come, warble, come.

Song.   *Altogether heere.*

Who doth ambition shunne,
and loues to liue i'th Sunne: 40

28. *not*] *not*, Ff.   38. Altogether heere] Om. Rowe+,
31. *drinke*] *dine* Rowe+.   Cap.
33–37. Prose, Pope et seq.   40. *liue*] *live* F$_2$F$_4$.   *lye* F$_4$, Rowe+.
34. *disputeable*] *disputable* F$_4$.

---

28. **beggerly**] That is, beggar-like.   The thanks are neither paltry nor mean ; but
the reverse.—ED.

30. **couer**] STAUNTON : That is, prepare the table; equivalent to our 'lay the
cloth'; compare *Mer. of Ven.* III, v, 55.

31. **drinke**] CAPELL (p. 58): The moderns have *dine* instead of 'drink,' but bid-
ding the attendants 'cover' was telling them the Duke intended to *dine* there;
'drink' tells them something more, that he meant to pass his afternoon there, under
the shade of that tree.

32. **looke you**] DYCE (ed. iii): I may notice that this is equivalent to 'look *for*
you.' Compare *Merry Wives*, IV, ii, 83: 'Mistress Page and I will *look* some linen
for your head.' [For many other instances of this omission, see Abbott, § 200.]

34. **disputeable**] MALONE: That is, disputatious. WALKER has a chapter (No.
xxix, *Crit.* i, 183) on examples of adjectives in *-able* and *-ible*, both positive and
negative ones, which are frequently used by old writers in an *active* sense. See also,
Abbott, § 3.

38. **Altogether heere**] It is almost needless to remark that this is a stage direction; and the stage direction of a play-house copy. Some of the early editors, even
Capell, omit it altogether here. See ROFFE, in Appendix, 'Music,' p. 434.

40. **liue**] TOLLET : To 'live i' th' sun,' is to labour and 'sweat in the eye of
Phœbus,' or *vitam agere sub dio ;* for by *lying* in the sun, how could they get the food
they eat?   CAPELL (p. 58): To *lye i' the sun* is a phrase importing absolute idleness,
the idleness of a motley (see *post*, II, vii, 17), but 'live i' the sun' imports only a
living in freedom; a flying from courts and cities, the haunts of 'ambition,' to enjoy
the free blessings of heaven in such a place as the singer himself was retir'd to;
whose panegyrick upon this sort of life is converted into a satire by Jaques, in a very
excellent parody that follows a few lines after. CALDECOTT: Othello refers to his

> *Seeking the food he eates,*　　　　41
> 　　*and pleas'd with what he gets :*
> *Come hither, come hither, come hither,*
> 　　*Heere ſhall he ſee.&c.*

Iaq.　Ile giue you a verſe to this note,　　　　45
That I made yeſterday in deſpight of my Inuention.
Amy.　And Ile ſing it.
Amy.　Thus it goes.

> *If it do come to paſſe, that any man turne Aſſe :*
> *Leauing his wealth and eaſe,*　　　　.　　　　50
> *A ſtubborne will to pleaſe,*
> *Ducdame, ducdame, ducdame :*　　　　52

44. Heere] Cho. *Here* Cap.
　he] *you* Rowe.
　&c.] no enemy, But Winter and
rough Weather. F₃F₄ et seq.
45, 46. Prose, Pope et seq.

48. Amy.] Iaq. Ff et seq.
49. Two lines, F₃F₄ et seq.
52, 55. Ducdame, ducdame, ducdame
...*Ducdame*] *Duc ad me, Duc ad me,*
Duc ad me...Duc ad me Han. Wh. Mal.

'unhoused, free condition.'　WHITE (ed. i): To 'live i' the sun' was to live a profit-less life.　WRIGHT: A life of open-air freedom, which, as opposed to the life of the ambitious man, is also one of retirement and neglect.　Hamlet seems to have had this in his mind when he said (I, ii, 67): 'I am too much i' the sun'; and Beatrice in *Much Ado*, II, i, 331: 'Thus goes every one to the world but I, and I am sun-burnt,' that is, exposed and neglected, like the bride in *Canticles*, i, 6.　See also *Tro. & Cress.* I, iii, 282.

46. **Inuention**] MOBERLY: As imagination would do nothing for me, I spited it by the following choice composition.

52. **Ducdame**] JOHNSON: Hanmer, very acutely and judiciously, reads *duc ad me*, that is, *bring him to me*.　CAPELL (p. 58): The words 'Come hither' are Latin-iz'd by the composer; but not strictly, for then his word had been *Hucdame ;* and the Latin words crouded [*sic*] together into a strange single word of three syllables, purely to set his hearer a staring; whom he bambouzles still further, by telling him, ''tis a Greek invocation.'　The humour is destroy'd, in great measure, by decom-pounding and setting them right, and giving us *duc ad me* separately.　FARMER: If *duc ad me* were right, Amiens would not have asked its meaning, and been put off with a '*Greek invocation.*'　It is evidently a word coined *for the nonce.*　We have here, as Butler says, 'One for *sense*, and one for *rhyme.*'　Indeed, we must have a *double rhyme*, or this stanza cannot well be sung to the same tune with the former.　I read '*Ducdamè, Ducdamè, Ducdamè*, Here shall he see Gross fools as he, An' if he will come to *Ami*.'　That is, to Amiens.　Jaques did not mean to ridicule himself. STEEVENS: That Amiens, who is a courtier, should not understand Latin, or be per-suaded it was Greek, is no great matter for wonder.　In confirmation of the old read-ing, however, Dr Farmer observes to me, that, being at a house not far from Cam-bridge, when news was brought that the hen-roost was robbed, a facetious old squire who was present immediately sung the following stanza, which has an odd coincidence

7

[Ducdame, ducdame, ducdame]

with the ditty of Jaques: '*Damè*, what makes your ducks to die? *Duck, duck, duck.* —*Damè*, what makes your chicks to cry? Chuck, chuck, chuck.' 'Ducdàme' is a trisyllable. WHITER tells us he was 'favoured' with one or two more stanzas of the same song which Dr Farmer thinks sheds so much light on this passage, and Whiter, in turn, 'favours' us with them, though it is not easy to see how Shakespearian criticism is advanced by learning that the cause of the ducks' death was 'eating o' Polly-wigs,' howsoever valuable the fact may be therapeutically. Be this, however, as it may, the stanzas seem to have imparted aid to Whiter, who says: 'In the foregoing stanzas it is of no consequence, either as to the sense or the metre, whether "Dame" be read in its usual way or whether we pronounce it Damè, with the accent on the last syllable. They are all, however, manifestly addressed to the Dame, the good housewife of the family, under whose care we may suppose the poultry to be placed; and it may be observed that the *Ducks* are particularly specified on account of the alliteration with *Dame*. I therefore see no difficulty in the derivation of the word "Ducdame," which has so much embarrassed our commentators. What is more natural or obvious than to suppose *Duc Dame* or *Duc Damè* to be the usual cry of the Dame to gather her Ducks about her; as if she should say, "Ducks, come to your Dame," or "Ducks, come to your Damè." .... The explication here given of this passage is the only one which at all properly corresponds with the context.' In justice to Whiter it must be said that he appears conscious of the ridiculousness of such shallow profundity by the final remark: 'If Shakespeare is to be explained, neither the writer nor the reader should become fastidious at the serious discussion of such trifling topics.' KNIGHT: It was not in the character of Jaques to talk Latin in this place. He was parodying the 'Come hither' of the previous song. The conjecture, therefore, that he was using some country call of a woman to her ducks appears much more rational than his Latinity. COLLIER: Hanmer's alteration is probably right; but *duc ad me* being harsh, when sung to the same notes as its translation 'Come hither,' it was corrupted to *duc-da-me*, a trisyllable, which ran more easily. Farmer observed that 'if *duc ad me* were right, Amiens would not have asked its meaning.' Why not, if Amiens be supposed not to understand Latin? When Jaques declares it to be 'a Greek invocation,' he seems to intend to jeer Amiens upon his ignorance. [Collier adds, in his second edition]: We may conclude, with tolerable certainty, that it was the burden of some old song, although none has been pointed out that precisely agrees with 'ducdame' or *duc ad me*. HALLIWELL (*Sh. Soc. Papers*, 1844, vol. i, p. 109): Hanmer's change is forced and unnecessary, I admit, but not quite so absurd as to suppose Jaques was using some country call of a woman to her ducks. .... I have recently met with a passage in an uncollated MS of the *Vision of Piers Plowman* in the Bodleian Library, which goes far to prove that *Ducdamè* is the burden of an old song, an explanation which exactly agrees with its position in the song of Jaques. The passage is as follows: 'Thanne set ther some, And *sunge* at the ale, And helpen to erye that half akre With *Dusadam-me-me*.'— *MS Rawl. Poet*, 137, f. 6. To show that this is evidently intended for the burden of a song, we need only compare it with the corresponding passage in the printed edition: 'And holpen ere this half acre With *How, trolly lolly*.'—*Piers Ploughman*, ed. Wright, p. 124. Making allowances for the two centuries which elapsed between the appearance of *Piers Ploughman* and *As You Like It*, is there too great a difference between *Dusadam-me-me* and *Duc-da-me* to warrant my belief that the latter is a legitimate descendant of the more ancient refrain? At all events, it must be borne

[Ducdame, ducdame, ducdame]

in mind that the commentators have not produced any old word equally near it in their dissertations on its meaning. This word may also possibly be intended by *Dmee! dmee! dmee!* in Arnim's *Nest of Ninnies* (*Sh. Soc. Reprint*), p. 32. Mr Collier, however, thinks it 'most likely an abbreviation of *Dear me!*' [With a few verbal alterations Halliwell repeated this in his edition.] STAUNTON: After all that has been written in elucidation of 'ducdame,' we are disposed to believe the 'invocation,' like the Clown's: 'Fond done, done fond' in *All's Well*, is mere unmeaning babble coined for the occasion. DYCE: The attempts made to explain this 'burden' are, I think, alike unsatisfactory. A. A. (*Notes & Qu.* 2d S., viii, Oct. 8, '59): Is it not literally as written *duc dà me*, 'lead him from me'? Amiens has been describing the generous soul 'who does ambition shun,' and welcomes him with a 'Come hither.' Jaques describes the opposite character, and goes on with his parody 'keep him from me,' instead of 'come hither.' *Da* is the Italian preposition *from*, answering to the Latin *a, ab, abs*. TREGEAGLE (*Ibid.* 5th S., x, July 20, '78): It seems not improbable that this word may be intended to represent the twang of a guitar. [In *Notes and Qu.* 5th S. ix, June 29, '78, DR MACKAY has a note which was afterwards substantially repeated and enlarged in his *Glossary of Obscure Words*, &c., 1887. From the latter I extract the following:] Amiens, puzzled by the phrase, asks Jaques what it means. Jaques replies, ''Tis a Greek invocation to call fools into a circle.' By 'Greek' he appears to have meant *Pedlar's Greek*, the popular name for the cant language of the beggars and gypsies of his day, which is not wholly disused in our own. . . . . No one has discovered or even hinted at the 'circle' to which Jaques alludes. Perhaps the old game of Tom Tidler's Ground may throw some light on the matter. [After stating that Brewer in his *Dictionary of Phrase and Fable* maintains 'Tom Tidler' to be a corruption of *Tom th' Idler*, Dr Mackay continues:] This derivation has hitherto passed muster; but the true derivation is from the Keltic, and proves the game to have been known to British children before the Saxon and Danish irruptions and conquest. *Tom* signifies 'hill' or mound, a word that enters into the composition of the names of many places in the British Isles; and *tiodlach*, gift, offering, treasure; so that *Tom-tiodlach*, corrupted by the Danes and Saxons into *Tom-tidler*, signifies the hill of gifts or treasure, of which the players seek to hold or to regain possession. It was the custom for the boy who temporarily held the hill or *tom* to assert that the ground belonged to him of right, and dare the invaders to dispossess him by the exclamation of '*Duc da mè.*' This phrase has puzzled commentators quite as much as the name 'Tom Tidler' has done. The phrase, however, resolves itself into the Gaelic *duthaich* (the *t* silent before the aspirate, pronounced *duhaic*), signifying a country, an estate, a territory, a piece of land; *da* or *do* signifying to, and *mi*, me—*i. e.* this territory or ground is to me, or belongs to me; it is my land or estate. This old British phrase continued to be used in England by children and illiterate people long after the British language had given way to the Saxon English, and was repeated by boys and girls in the game now called 'Tom Tidler's Ground' so lately as forty years ago, when I heard it used myself by children on the Links of Leith and the Inches of my native city of Perth. . . . . A correspondent of the *Pall Mall Gazette*, signing himself 'Welshman,' says, 'Clearly, the critics are at fault in their endeavour to give a reasonable rendering to "ducdamé."' Admittedly, it had its origin in a prehistoric game. . . . . Whether Shakespeare knew it to be good Welsh or not is little to the purpose. However, there is no doubt he did. . . . . In point of fact Jacques was but verbally repeating the selfsame invitation which . . . .

Heere ſhall he ſee, groſſe fooles as he,   53
And if he will come to me.

Amy.   What's that Ducdame?   55

Iaq.   'Tis a Greeke inuocation, to call fools into a circle.   Ile go ſleepe if I can : if I cannot, Ile raile againſt all
the firſt borne of Egypt.   58

---

53. Two lines, Pope et seq.   54. me] *Ami.* Farmer, Steev.
54. And] *An* Cap.   56. *inuocation*] *invocarion* F$_4$.

---

had been twice given in the vernacular, "Come hither." . . . . For the "Greek" rendering which accompanied it was good, honest Welsh, as nearly as the Saxon tongue
could frame it.   Its exact Cambrian equivalent is *Dewch da mi,* "Come with (or to)
me."   It is jargon no longer.   In early times the Sassenach, no doubt, often heard
this "Challenge" ("Come, if you dare!") shouted to him by the Kymri from the
hilltop or the embattled crag.   Hence it was perpetuated in the mimic warfare of
their children's game.'   'The Kymric derivation,' adds Dr Mackay, 'is ingenious, but
does not meet the case so clearly and completely as the Gaelic.'   In *Notes & Qu.*,
5th S., 5 Oct. '78, V. S. LEAN suggests *Duct-àmi; ami* being the abbreviation for
Amiens as well as French for friend.   [The phrase having been thus proved, satisfactorily to the provers, to be not only Latin, but Italian, and French, and Gaelic, and
Welsh, and Greek (surely Jaques ought to know), and a 'twang,' we are prepared for
the sensible and conclusive note which I have reserved for the last.]   WRIGHT: It is
in vain that any meaning is sought for in this jargon, as Jaques only intended to fill
up a line with sounds that have no sense.   There is a bit of similar nonsense in Cotgrave, s. v. Orgues : 'Dire d'orgues, vous dites d'orgues.   You say blew; how say
you to that; wisely brother Timothie; true Roger; did am did am.' . . . . Mr Ainger
has suggested to me that we should read : '*Ducdo′me, Ducdo′me, Ducdo′me,* to rhyme
with '*An if′* he will′ come to′ me.'

56. **to call fools into a circle**] for the purpose of etymologically and linguistic-
ally investigating the meaning of ' Ducdame,' says MOBERLY, dryly.

58. **first borne of Egypt**] GREY (i, 174) : Alluding to *Exodus,* xi, 5.   JOHNSON :
A proverbial expression for highborn persons.   NARES : Perhaps Jaques is only
intended to say that if he cannot sleep, he will, like other discontented persons, rail
against his betters.   WORDSWORTH (p. 70) : One feels somewhat at a loss to determine whether of the two pieces of criticism [Grey's and Johnson's], though very different in kind, is the less satisfactory.   The play in which this passage occurs turns
upon two incidents, in both of which an *eldest* brother is mainly concerned, in the one
as suffering, in the other as doing, injury.   And the reflection, therefore, naturally
presents itself to the moralising Jaques, that to be a *first-born son* is a piece of good
fortune not to be coveted now, any more than it was in the days of Pharaoh, when all
the *first born of Egypt* were cut off, but rather to be 'railed at.'   In Act I, Sc. i,
Orlando says to Oliver, ' The courtesy of nations allows you my better in that you are
the *first born.*'   If it be objected that Jaques was not yet aware of what had happened to Orlando, still, I think, the poet might have put the sentiment into the mouth
of such an one as Jaques, to be as a kind of waking dream, half experimental in
regard to what he already knew, half prophetical of what he would soon discover;
but, at all events, the reference to ' the old Duke,' who had been ' banished by his

Amy.   And Ile go feeke the Duke,
His banket is prepar'd.   · *Exeunt*   60

Scena Sexta.

Enter Orlando, & Adam.

Adam.   Deere Mafter, I can go no further:
O I die for food.   Heere lie I downe,
And meafure out my graue.   Farwel kinde mafter.
   *Orl.*Why how now *Adam*?   No greater heart in thee: 5
Liue a little, comfort a little, cheere thy felfe a little.

1–21. Prose, Pope et seq.   6. *comfort*] *comfort thee* Anon. conj.
                                              (ap. Cam. Ed.).

younger brother, the new Duke,' will hold good.   And he 'rails at' him, not only as
showing sympathy, after his quaint manner, with the old Duke's banishment, but as
reflecting upon his own folly in becoming voluntarily a partaker of the banishment,
and thereby forfeiting all his 'lands and revenues' to the usurper; as he had sung
just before in the verse, which (he says), 'I made yesterday in despite of my invention': 'That any man turn ass *Leaving his wealth and ease A stubborn will to please,*
Here shall he see, Gross fools as he, An if he will come *to me.*'

   60. banket] GIFFORD (Massinger's *City Madam*, II, i, p. 29): A 'banquet'
was what we now call a *dessert;* it was composed of fruit, sweetmeats, &c., 'Your
citizen is a most fierce devourer, sir, of plumbs; six will destroy as many as might
make A *banquet* for an army.'—*The Wits.*   The banquet was usually placed in a separate room, to which the guests removed as soon as they had dined; thus, in *The
Unnatural Combat*, Beaufort says (III, i): 'We'll *dine* in the great room, but let the
musick And *banquet* be prepared here.'   The common place of banqueting, or of eating the dessert, among our ancestors was the garden-house, or arbour, with which
almost every dwelling was once furnished; to this Shallow alludes in *2 Hen. IV:* V,
iii, 2.   [See *Rom. & Jul.* I, v, 120.   Dyce refers to *Tam. the Shr.* V, ii, 9: 'My
banquet is to close our stomachs up After our great good cheer.']

   2, 3.   WALKER (*Crit.* i, 18) divides these lines, which, he says, 'the Folio prints as
verse in a scrambling sort of way,' at ' O,' and reads: 'I die, *I die* for food.   Here
lie I down.'   [Walker has a chapter (*Crit.* ii, 141) on the 'Omission of Repeated
Words.']   DYCE (ed. iii) quotes Walker, and adds: But the speech which immediately follows this, and which is stark prose, is so printed in the Folio as to look
like verse.   [See note, line 21.]

   4. grave] STEEVENS: So in *Rom. & Jul.* III, iii, 70: 'fall upon the ground,
.... Taking the measure of an unmade grave.'

   6. comfort] WRIGHT: We must either take ' comfort' as equivalent to ' be comforted' or ' have comfort,' or else regard ' thyself' as the object to ' comfort' as well
as ' cheer.'   ALLEN (MS): I suppose ' comfort' *may* be used *absolutè*, just as ' cheer

If this vncŏuth Forreſt yeeld any thing ſauage,   7
I wil either be food for it, or bring it for foode to thee :
Thy conceite is neerer death, then thy powers.
For my ſake be comfortable, hold death a while   10
At the armes end : I wil heere be with thee preſently,
And if I bring thee not ſomething to eate,
I wil giue thee leaue to die : but if thou dieſt
Before I come, thou art a mocker of my labor.
Wel ſaid, thou look'ſt cheerely,   15
And Ile be with thee quickly : yet thou lieſt
In the bleake aire.   Come, I wil beare thee
To ſome ſhelter, and thou ſhalt not die
For lacke of a dinner,
If there liue any thing in this Deſert.   20
Cheerely good *Adam*.   *Exeunt.*

---

11. *heere be*] *be here* Rowe +, Cap.   Var. Cald. Sing. Sta. Ktly.
Mal. Dyce iii, Huds.   15. *cheerely*] *cheerily* Reed, Var.
13. *I wil*] *I'll* Pope +, Mal. Steev.   '21.

---

up' is.   It is, however, in favour of the anonymous emendation, 'comfort thee' (Cam.
Ed.), that the *thee* may have been pronounced like *tee* (*more Eboraco*, as Walker says),
and then the second *t* was dropt in pronunciation, as in 'all but mariners,' *Temp.* I,
ii, 210.

   9. **conceite**] DYCE : Conception, thought, imagination, fancy.

   10. **be comfortable**] CALDECOTT : That is, be comforted, become susceptible of
comfort.

   11. **heere be**] Let Walker's chapter on the *Transposition of Words* (*Crit.* ii, 246)
with its long list of examples be read and pondered, and after that there will be no
hesitation, I think, in deciding that we have an instance of transposition here.   See
Text. Notes.—ED.

   11. **presently**] ABBOTT, § 59 : Equivalent to *at the present time, at once*, instead
of, as now, 'soon, but *not* at once.'

   15. **Wel said**] COLLIER : This was often used for '*Well done.*'   WHITE (ed. i) :
But Orlando seems to refer to what he himself has said.   [Cf. *Oth.* II, i, 192.]

   21. The last line of this Scene is, in the Folio, the last line of the page, and I
strongly suspect that the division into verse of what Dyce calls 'stark prose,' is due
simply to the effort of the compositors to spread out the lines in order to avoid the
necessity of having the heading of a Scene at the foot of the page, that is, the heading *Scena Septima* merely, with, perhaps, not a line of text.—ED.

Scena Septima.

Enter Duke Sen. & Lord, like Out-lawes.

Du. Sen.   I thinke he be transform'd into a beaſt,
For I can no where finde him, like a man.

  1. *Lord.*   My Lord, he is but euen now gone hence,
Heere was he merry, hearing of a Song.   5

Du. Sen.   If he compaƈt of iarres, grow Muſicall,
We ſhall haue ſhortly diſcord in the Spheares :
Go ſeeke him, tell him I would ſpeake with him.

Enter Iaques.

  1. *Lord.*   He ſaues my labor by his owne approach.   10

Du. Sen.   Why how now Monſieur, what a life is this
That your poore friends muſt woe your companie,
What, you looke merrily.   13

1. Out-lawes] out-lawes Ff.	9. Enter...] After line 10, Dyce, Sta.
A table set out. Rowe.	13. *What,*] *And cannot have 't?*
2. *be*] *is* Pope +.	*What,* Cap.

2. **think he be**] See Abbott, § 299, for instances of ' be ' used after verbs of think-ing.   The standard example, to which all others might be referred, is that mnemonic line : ' I *think* my wife *be* honest, and *think* she *is* not,' *Oth.* III, iii, 443.—ED.

4. **euen now**] ABBOTT, § 38 : '*Even* now ' with us is applied to an action that has been going on for some time and *still* continues, the emphasis being laid on ' now.' In Shakespeare the emphasis is often to be laid on ' even,' and ' *even* now ' means ' *exactly* or *only* now,' *i. e.* ' scarcely longer ago than the present.'

5. **hearing of**] See II, iv, 45 or Abbott, § 178.

6. **compact**] STEEVENS : That is, made up of discords.   DYCE : Compacted, composed.

7. **Spheares**] See *Mer. of Ven.* V, i, 74 and notes in this edition, where the music of the spheres is discussed.   WRIGHT : Compare Batman *vppon Bartholome* (ed. 1582), fol. 123, *b :* 'And so Macrobius saith : in putting & mouing of the roundnesse of heauen, is that noyse made, and tempereth sharpe noyse with lowe noyse, and maketh diuers accordes and melodie : but for the default of our hearing, and also for passing measure of that noyse and melodie, this harmony and accord is not heard of vs.'

13. The comma at the close of the preceding line led CAPELL to suppose that the sentence was not complete ; he thereupon supplied the omission (see Textual Notes), and thus justified the addition in his notes : ' Which circumstance [the comma after ' company '] alone indicates an omission ; but it further appears from the sense, if a little attended to : For what great crime is it, that Jaques must be *woo'd* for his com-pany ? but that he makes his friends *woo* it, and won't let them *have* it after all, is an accusation of some weight.   The words now inserted carry this charge.'

Iaq. A Foole, a foole : I met a foole i'th Forreſt,
A motley Foole (a miſerable world :)   15

---

14. *foole i'th*] *fol i'th* F₄.   15. *world*] *varlet* Han. Warb.

---

15. A motley Foole] DOUCE (ii, 317) : The costume of the domestic fool in
Shakespeare's time was of two sorts. In the first of these the coat was motley or
parti-coloured, and attached to the body by a girdle, with bells at the skirts and
elbows, though not always. The breeches and hose close, and sometimes each leg
of a different colour. A hood resembling a monk's cowl, which, at a very early
period, it was certainly designed to imitate, covered the head entirely, and fell down
over part of the breast and shoulders. It was sometimes decorated with asses' ears,
or else terminated in the neck and head of a cock, a fashion as old as the fourteenth
century. It often had the comb or crest only of the animal, whence the term *cockscomb* or *coxcomb* was afterwards used to denote any silly upstart. This fool usually
carried in his hand an official sceptre or bauble, which was a short stick ornamented
at the end with the figure of a fool's head, or sometimes with that of a doll or puppet.
To this instrument there was frequently annexed an inflated skin or bladder, with
which the fool belaboured those who offended him or with whom he was inclined to
make sport; this was often used by itself, in lieu, as it would seem, of a bauble. . . . .
It was not always filled with air, but occasionally with sand or pease. . . . . In some
old prints the fool is represented with a sort of flapper or rattle ornamented with bells.
It seems to have been constructed of two round and flat pieces of wood or paste-
board, and is, no doubt, a vestige of the *crotalum* used by the Roman mimes or
dancers. This instrument was used for the same purpose as the bladder, and occasionally for correcting the fool himself whenever he behaved with too much licen-
tiousness. . . . . In some old plays the fool's *dagger* is mentioned, perhaps the same
instrument as was carried by the *Vice* or buffoon of the Moralities; and it may be as
well to observe in this place that the domestic fool is sometimes, though it is presumed
improperly, called the Vice. The dagger of the latter was made of a thin piece of
lath, and the use he generally made of it was to belabour the Devil. It appears that
in Queen Elizabeth's time the Archbishop of Canterbury's fool had a wooden dagger
and a coxcomb. . . . . The other dress, and which seems to have been more common
in Shakespeare's time, was the long petticoat. This originally appertained to the
idiot or natural fool, and was obviously adopted for the purpose of cleanliness. Why
it came to be used for the allowed fool is not so apparent. It was, like the first, of
various colours, the materials often costly, as of velvet, and guarded or fringed with
yellow. A manuscript note in the time of the Commonwealth states *yellow* to have
been the *fool's colour*. This petticoat dress continued to a late period, and has been
seen not many years since in some of the interludes exhibited in Wales. But the
above were by no means the only modes in which the domestic fools were habited.
The hood was not always surmounted with the cockscomb, in lieu of which a single
bell, and occasionally more, appeared. Sometimes a feather was added to the comb.
. . . . A large purse or wallet at the girdle is a very ancient part of the fool's dress.
Tarlton, who personated the clowns in Shakespeare's time, appears to have worn it.
. . . . We may suppose that the same variety of dress was observed on the stage which
we know to have actually prevailed in common life.

  15. world] WARBURTON : What, because he met a *motley fool*, was it therefore *a
miserable world?* This is sadly blundered; we should read 'a miserable *varlet.*'

As I do liue by foode, I met a foole,   16
Who laid him downe, and bask'd him in the Sun,
And rail'd on Lady Fortune in good termes,
In good fet termes, and yet a motley foole.
Good morrow foole (quoth I :) no Sir, quoth he,   20
Call me not foole, till heauen hath fent me fortune,
And then he drew a diall from his poake,   ·   22

His head is altogether running on this fool, both before and after these words, and
here he calls him *a miserable varlet,* notwithstanding he 'railed on Lady Fortune in
good terms,' &c.   JOHNSON : I see no need of changing 'world' to *varlet,* nor, if a
change were necessary, can I guess how it should certainly be known that *varlet* is
the true word. 'A miserable world' is a parenthetical exclamation, frequent among
melancholy men, and natural to Jaques at the sight of a fool, or at the hearing of
reflections on the fragility of life.   CAPELL : [It was a miserable world] in the estimation of Jaques and others equally cynical, who disrelish the world ; arraigning the
dispensations of Providence in a number of articles, and in this chiefly—that it has
created such beings as fools.   HUNTER (i, 347) acknowledges that there is no real
need of disturbing the text, and that the meaning, as given by Capell, is not unam-
biguous, but, he continues, 'if this be not thought a satisfactory explanation of the
passage, there is a word which would suit it so well if substituted for "world," and
which might so easily become changed into "world" that I cannot but think that it
may have been what Shakespeare wrote. . . . . The word is *ort.* "A motley fool ! a
miserable *ort !*" "Ort," says Tooke, "means anything vile or worthless " ; but it
seems to contain the idea of remnant or fragment.   Shakespeare uses it thus in *Tro.
& Cres.* V, ii, 158, and in *Timon,* IV, iii, 400.   Fragments of victuals were *orts ;* so
that the word may have led to the idea which next entered the mind of the poet : "As
I do live by *food,* I met a fool," and in the course of what he says of him he still
keeps to the idea which the word *ort* would naturally introduce, and speaks of the
clown's brains as "being dry as the remainder biscuit After a voyage," which was
eminently an *ort.*'   [Whenever we wish to think of the excellent Hunter at his best,
let us wipe from our memory every vestige of an ort of this emendation.—ED.]   COW-
DEN-CLARKE : A parenthetical exclamation, whereby Jaques for the moment laughs
at his own melancholy view of the world, having just heard it echoed by a professional jester.   Moreover, he seems to exclaim, ' This a miserable world !   No, it contains a fool and food for laughter.'

   21. fortune] REED : *Fortuna favet fatuis* is, as Upton observes, the saying here
alluded to, or, as in Publius Syrus : *Fortuna, nimium quem fovet, stultum facit.* So
in the Prologue to *The Alchemist :* ' Fortune, that favours fooles, these two short hours
We wish away.'   Again, in *Every Man Out of his Humour,* I, i [p. 38, ed. Gifford] :
'*Sogliardo.* Why, who am I, sir ? *Macilente.* One of those that fortune favours.
Carlo. [*Aside*] The periphrasis of a fool.'   HALLIWELL : ' Fortune favours fools, or
fools have the best luck.'—Ray's *Proverbs.*   MOBERLY : The proverb, Coleridge wittily and wisely suggests, has something the same meaning as Sterne's saying, ' God
tempers the wind to the shorn lamb.'   WEISS (p. 115) : Thus, indeed, like the wise
men, Touchstone will have a social chance to show, as they do, what his folly is.

   22. diall] KNIGHT : ' There's no clock in the forest,' says Orlando, and it was not
very likely that the Fool would have a pocket clock.   What, then, was the ' dial ' that

And looking on it, with lacke-luftre eye,   23
Sayes, very wifely, it is ten a clocke :
Thus we may fee (quoth he) how the world wagges :   25
'Tis but an houre agoe, fince it was nine,
And after one houre more, 'twill be eleuen,
And fo from houre to houre, we ripe, and ripe,   28

---

27. *one*] *an* Var. '03 (misprint?) Var.   27. *eleuen*] *a eleuen* Cap. (corrected in
'13, Harness.   Errata).

---

he took from his poke? We have lately become possessed with a rude instrument.
. . . . It is a brass circle of about two inches in diameter; on the outer side are
engraved letters indicating the names of the months, with graduated divisions; and
on the inner side the hours of the day. The brass circle itself is to be held in one
position by a ring; but there is an inner slide in which there is a small orifice. This
slide being moved so that the hole stands opposite the division of the month when
the day falls of which we desire to know the time, the circle is held up opposite the
sun. The inner side is of course then in shade; but the sunbeam shines through the
little orifice and forms a point of light upon the hour marked on the inner side. HAL-
LIWELL: The term 'dial' appears to have been applied, in Shakespeare's time, to
anything for measuring time in which the hours were marked, so that the allusion here
may be either to a watch or to a portable journey-ring or small sun-dial. . . . . Ring-
dials were manufactured in large number at Sheffield so lately as the close of the last
century, and were commonly used by the lower orders. [Halliwell gives three or
four descriptions of various patterns, accompanied with wood-cuts; the frontispiece
of his volume is an engraving of an ivory 'viatorium or pocket sun-dial.']

   22. **poake**] If the Fool were habited in the orthodox fashion, this pocket was
probably the 'large purse or wallet' referred to above by Douce.—ED.

   25. **wagges**] See Schmidt for instances of both its transitive and intransitive sense.
Hamlet's use of it is noteworthy: 'I'll fight . . . . Until my eyelids will no longer
wag.'—V, i, 255.

   28. **ripe**] Thus, 'stay the very riping of the time,' *Mer. of Ven.* II, viii, 43. Used
as a verb in only two or three other instances, according to Schmidt. MOBERLY:
Probably most readers of the play will have remarked that the Fool's utterances, as
here given, are not in Touchstone's style. He is not the kind of fool who rails 'in
good set terms,' which are ridiculous from their grave senselessness. It would appear
that the Poet allowed himself to turn aside for a moment here to satirize and parody
some of the current dramas of the day. The original of these lines seems to have
been *The Spanish Tragedy* of Kyd, where a father, finding his son hanged on an
apple-tree, vents his grief by saying of it, 'At last it grew and grew, and bore and
bore; Till at the length it grew a gallows.' The pun on 'gallows' and 'thereby
hangs a tale' is quite Shakespearian. [But we must remember that it is Jaques who
reports Touchstone's words. We hear Touchstone only through Jaques's ears. And
as for the parody on Hieronimo—it is not impossible. Kyd's fellow-dramatists found
in that tragedy a rich vein of Termagant o'erdone, and worked it with ridicule merci-
lessly. It was not, however, at the substance, the plot of the tragedy, that they
laughed, it was only at the wild rant of the expression, such as 'What outcry plucks
me from my naked bed?' 'let my hair heave up my nightcap,' &c. And so it seems

And then from houre to houre, we rot, and rot,
And thereby hangs a tale.   When I did heare   30
The motley Foole, thus morall on the time,
My Lungs began to crow like Chanticleere,
That Fooles fhould be fo deepe contemplatiue :
And I did laugh, fans intermiffion
An houre by his diall.   Oh noble foole,   35
A worthy foole : Motley's the onely weare.

33. *deepe contemplatiue*] *deep-contemplative* Mal. Steev. Knt, Dyce, Cam.

---

to me doubtful that there can have been here any thought in Shakespeare's mind of
The Spanish Tragedy : it comes too near ridiculing the very substance of that drama,
which was a bitter tragedy, to have compared the 'hanging of a tale' with the
hanging of an idolised son in his own father's orchard.—ED.]

30. **tale**] A phrase used several times by Shakespeare. WEISS (p. 115) : What
tale ? Why, the everlasting tedious one of over-accredited common-place behavior.
Only a Touchstone, with his sly appreciation, can lend any liveliness to that.

31. **morall**] This is generally interpreted as a verb, equivalent to *moralise*. But
SCHMIDT, *s. v.*, says it is 'probably an adjective,' a view which is strengthened, I
think, by the preposition 'on.' If the verb, *moralise*, needs no preposition after it (cf.
'Did he not moralize this spectacle ?'—II, i, 48), it is not easy to see why 'moral,'
if used as an equivalent verb, should need one. Had Shakespeare intended to convey the force of *moralise*, would he not have used the word ? there is no exigency
of rhythm to prevent it. The line, 'The motley Fool thus moralise the time,' runs
smoothly.—ED.

32. **crow**] WRIGHT : That is, to laugh merrily. Cf. 'You were wont, when you
laughed, to crow like a cock,' *Two Gent.* II, i, 28, [From what Speed says to Valentine it is to be inferred, I think, that this 'crowing' was laughter, not so much, perhaps, of a merry, as of a boisterous, kind. The contrast lies in Valentine's present
lovesick condition, when 'he speaks puling, like a beggar at Hallowmas,' with his
former manly estate, when he was wont to crow like a cock when he laughed.—ED.]

32. **Chanticleere**] SKEAT, *s. v. chant : Chant-i-cleer, i. e.* clear-singing ; equivalent to Middle English *chaunte-cleer ;* Chaucer, *Nun's Prestes*, T. 1. 29.

33. **deepe contemplatiue**] For other compound adjectives, see Abbott, § 2.

34. **sans**] WRIGHT (Note on *Temp.* I, ii, 97) : This French preposition appears
to have been brought into the language in the fourteenth century, and occurs in the
forms *saun, sanz, sauntz, saunz*, and *saunce*. It may, perhaps, have been employed
at first in purely French phrases, such as 'sans question.'—*Love's Lab. L.* V, i, 91 ;
'sans compliment,' *King John*, V, vi, 16. But Shakespeare uses it with other words,
as here, and in *Ham.* III, iv, 79. Nares quotes instances from Jonson, Beau. & Fl.,
Massinger, and others. So that it appears to have had an existence for a time as an
English word. Cotgrave gives : '*Sans. Sanse*, without, besides' ; and Florio has,
'*Senza*, sans, without, besides.'

36. **Motley**] CALDECOTT : There was a species of mercery known by that name,
'Polymitus. He that maketh motley. Polymitarius.'—Withal's *little Dict.*, 1568.
'Frisadoes, Motleys, bristowe frices' are in the number of articles recommended for
northern traffic in 1580. Hakluyt's *Voyages*, 1582.

Du. Sen. What foole is this?   37

Iaq. O worthie Foole : One that hath bin a Courtier
And fayes, if Ladies be but yong, and faire,
They haue the gift to know it : and in his braiue,   40
Which is as drie as the remainder bisket
After a voyage : He hath ftrange places cram'd   42

---

39. *but*] Om. F_3F_4, Rowe i.   40. *braiue*] F_1.

36, 38. **A worthy . . . O worthie**] An anonymous conjecture recorded in the
CAM. ED. is, I think, an *emendatio certissima ;* it had occurred to me independently.
It is that this 'A' and this 'O' should change places. When the Duke asks Jaques a
direct question, 'What fool is this?' Jaques, according to the text, instead of answering, breaks out into an apostrophe, 'O worthie Foole!' which, however much it may
relieve his feelings, is certainly somewhat discourteous to the Duke. It is this discourtesy and this irrelevancy which first made the phrase suspicious. Change the
'O' into *A*, and at once all is right; we have an answer to the Duke, and the second
half of the line is properly connected with the first : 'A worthie Foole, one that hath
bin,' &c. Thus, too, in line 35, after apostrophising the fool : 'Oh noble foole,' there
is to me something weak in falling to the third person, and adding 'a worthie foole.'
It should be 'Oh worthy foole.'—ED.

41. **drie**] WRIGHT : In the physiology of Shakespeare's time a dry brain accompanied slowness of apprehension and a retentive memory. We read in Batman *vppon
Bartholome*, fol. 37, *b*, 'Good disposition of the braine and euill is knowne by his
deedes, for if the substaunce of the braine be soft, thinne, and cleere : it receiueth
lightly the feeling & printing of shapes, and lykenesses of thinges. He that hath
such a braine is swift, and good of perseueraunce and teaching. When it is con-
trarye, the braine is not softe; eyther if he be troubled, he that hath such a braine
receiueth slowly the feeling and printing of thinges : But neuerthelesse when hee hath
taken and receiued them, he keepeth them long in minde. And that is signe and
token of drinesse, as fluxibility & forgetting is token of moisture, as Haly sayth.' See
Tro. & Cress. I, iii, 329.

41. **bisket**] BOSWELL : So in Jonson's *Every Man Out of his Humour* [Induc-
tion] : 'And, now and then, breaks a dry biscuit jest, Which,' &c.

42. **places**] DELIUS : That is, strange passages from books, remarkable citations.
SCHMIDT (p. 455) : This interpretation of Delius's must be left undecided; no parallel example in Shakespeare occurs to me. WRIGHT : Topics or subjects of discourse.
Compare Bacon, *Advancement of Learning*, ii, 13, § 7 : 'Ancient writers of rhetoric
do give it in precept, that pleaders should have the places, whereof they have most
continual use, ready handled in all the variety that may be.' NEIL : A scholastic
phrase for stock arguments, ideas, topics—*Loci communes.* ROLFE : That is, odd
corners. Wright's explanation as 'topics or subjects of discourse' does not suit so
well with 'cramm'd.' [There can be no doubt, I think, that Bacon uses the word
as Wright has exactly defined it. In § 9, Bacon says : 'The other part of invention,
which I term suggestion, doth assign and direct us to certain marks or places, which
may excite our mind to return and produce such knowledge as it hath formerly collected, to the end we may make use thereof;' which is very nearly in Jaques's exact
phrase a 'place, cramm'd with observation.' Again, 'I do receive particular topics,

With obferuation, the which he vents   43
In mangled formes.   O that I were a foole,
I am ambitious for a motley coat.   45
   Du. Sen.   Thou fhalt haue one.
   Iaq.   It is my onely fuite,   47

---

that is, places or directions of invention and inquiry in every particular knowledge, as things of great use.'—§ 10. DR JOHNSON, in his *Dictionary*, gives as one of the definitions of 'Place,' 'a passage in writing,' but under the definition 'separate room' he cites as an example the present phrase of Jaques.   That Delius's, Wright's, and Neil's interpretation is correct is shown by the rest of the sentence: these strange subjects the fool 'vents in mangled forms.'   It is not easy to see how 'separate rooms' or 'odd corners' could be either vented or mangled.—ED.]

43. obseruation] To be pronounced as five syllables.   This *dissolution*, as it is called, of the *-ion* is almost universal at the end of a line, but it is comparatively rare in the body of the line.   See Walker, *Vers.* p. 230.

45. ambitious] WRIGHT: This word, as would appear from the word 'suit' in the next speech of Jaques, is here used with something of the meaning of the Latin *ambitiosus*, going about as a candidate.

47. suite] JOHNSON: That is, *petition*, I believe, not *dress*.   STEEVENS: It is a quibble, as in IV, i, 85.   STAUNTON: The old, old play on the double meaning of the word.   [No fit opportunity has presented itself thus far to set forth Whiter's theory of the Association of Ideas.   As the present passage fairly unfolds it, it is given here, and repetition hereafter is rendered needless.   It is defined (p. 68) as 'the power of *association* over the genius of the poet, which consists in supplying him with words and with ideas, which have been suggested to the mind by a principle of union unperceived by himself, and independent of the subject to which they are applied.   From this definition it follows: First, that as these words and sentiments were prompted by a cause which is concealed from the poet, so they contain no *intentional* allusion to the source from whence they are derived; and secondly, that as they were forced on the recollection of the writer by some accidental concurrence not necessarily dependent on the sense or spirit of the subject, so they have no necessary resemblance in this secondary application to that train of ideas in which they originally existed.'   On p. 82 we find the following illustration of this theory as thus defined: 'It is certain that those ideas are apparently very remote from each other which relate to *dress*, to a *noisome plant*, and to that which is expressive of *asking* or *accommodating;* and yet the curious reader will be astonished to discover that the Poet is often led to connect some of these dissimilar objects, because they have been by accident combined under the same sound; and because certain words, by which they are expressed, are sometimes found to be coincident in sense.   The words to which I allude are SUIT and WEED, which from their equivocal senses have strangely operated on the mind of the Poet to produce, without his own knowledge and without confusion of metaphor, the union of words or the connexion of the ideas.'   Among his first examples Whiter quotes the present passage from line 45 to line 50, italicising *coat, suit,* and *weed,* and then continues: 'This the reader must acknowledge to be a singular combination.   I agree with Dr Johnson that "suit" means *petition* and not *dress*, and I think Steevens is mistaken in supposing that the Poet meant a quibble.   Let me observe in this place that there is a species of quibble which may be referred in a certain sense to the prin-

[It is my onely suite,]

ciple which I am discussing; and it is therefore necessary to remind the reader that I mean only to produce those instances of *association* where the author himself was unconscious of its effect. . . . . In the following passage *dress* is united to the *plant :* "they are . . . . preachers to us all; admonishing, That we should *dress* us fairly for our end. Thus may we gather honey from the *weed*, And make a moral of the devil himself."—*Hen. V :* IV, i, 9. The argument, which I am illustrating, will not be affected by the sense in which *dress* is taken; whether it signifies *address*, to prepare, or *dress*, to clothe; as the association arising from the same sound bearing an equivocal sense will be equally remarkable. . . . . In the following passage *dress* is connected with *suit* in its sense of *accommodation*. " Bravery " (as every one knows) is splendour in *dress :* " That says his *bravery* is not on my cost (Thinking that I mean him), but therein *suits*," &c. [ll. 83, 84 of the present Scene]. . . . . In the following passage from *Coriolanus* " weed " in the sense of *dress* is connected with the word " suit " in the sense of *petition ;* and there is likewise a new notion annexed, which relates to a peculiar meaning of the equivocal word " suit " : " forget not With what contempt he wore the humble *weed ;* How in his *suit* he scorn'd you; but your loves, Thinking upon his *services*, took from you The apprehension of his present portance, Which most gibingly, ungravely, he did *fashion* After," &c.—*Cor.* II, iii, 228. In this passage the remarkable words are *weed, suit, services, fashion ;* and the reader, I hope, will not imagine that I refine too much, when I inform him that the word *services* is to be referred to the same association; and that it was suggested to the Poet by another signification which *suit* sometimes bears of *livery*, the peculiar dress by which the servants and retainers of one family were distinguished from those of another. These distinctions were considered matters of great importance; and we accordingly find both in Shakespeare and in all our ancient writers allusions of this sort perpetually occur, and the idea of *service* is often connected with the *badge* or *dress* by which it is accompanied. Thus: " Wear this for me; one out of *suits* with fortune," &c. [I, ii, 242 of the present play, where Steevens's and Malone's notes are quoted by Whiter as confirming his view]. . . . . I could produce numberless passages in which familiar metaphors are directly taken from the distinguishing dress of servants; but those instances only are directed to explain my present argument, in which *words relating* to a certain subject, though not *all applied* to it, have been connected with each other by an involuntary association. To illustrate more fully the passage produced above from *Coriolanus*, take the following, where *service* and *fashion* are likewise again united : " How well in thee appears The constant *service* of the antique world, When *service* sweat for duty, not for meed ! Thou art not for the *fashion* of these times " [II, iii, 58 of the present play]. " Suit " and " service " we know are terms familiar to the language of our Feudal Law. No ideas are more impressed on the mind of our Poet than those that have reference to the Law. In the following passages *suit* and *service* are again united : *Mer. of Ven.* II, ii, 153–156; *Love's Lab. L.* V, ii, 275, 276; *Ib.* V, ii, 849, 850.' [It is not necessary that we should agree with Whiter in order to admire his ingenuity. That his theory is incapable of downright proof must be confessed, and yet who can gainsay it? There is one rather striking instance of what he urges in regard to an association in Shakespeare's mind between *weeds* and *suits* in *Lear*, which strangely escaped Whiter's observation. Cordelia says to Kent: ' Be better *suited ;* These *weeds* are memories of those worser hours; I prithee put them off.'—IV, vii, 6. Here 'weed' is used, as in many another place in these plays, for *garment* (it still survives in ' widow's weeds '), and it

Prouided that you weed your better iudgements   48
Of all opinion that growes ranke in them,
That I am wife. I muſt haue liberty   50
Wiithall, as large a Charter as the winde,
To blow on whom I pleaſe, for ſo fooles haue :
And they that are moſt gauled with my folly,
They moſt muſt laugh : And why ſir muſt they ſo ?
The why is plaine, as way to Pariſh Church :   55
Hee, that a Foole doth very wiſely hit,
Doth very fooliſhly, although he ſmart
Seeme ſenſeleſſe of the bob. If not,   58

---

51. *Wiithall*] F₁.

55. *why*] *way* Rowe ii.

56. *Hee, that*] *He whom* Pope +.

58. *Seeme*] Ff, Rowe, Pope. *But to* Coll. (MS), Wh. i, Coll. ii, iii, Dyce iii, Rlfe. *Not to* Theob. et cet.

---

was because it thus means *garments* that it was associated elsewhere with *suits of clothes*, even when it means a *troublesome plant*, as in this present speech of Jaques. Whiter noted that ' suit ' here in Jaques's mind suggested ' weed ' ; it did not, perhaps, come within the scope of his special association to note that ' weed ' in turn suggested ' rank growth ' in the next line.   And may we not carry on the association and fill out the picture, and see the gaudy blossoms bending in ' the wind ' that ' blows on whom it pleases,' along the summer pathway to the ' Parish Church ' ?—ED.]

51. **Wiithall**] See I, i, 130.

51. **Charter**] STEEVENS : So in *Hen. V :* I, i, 48 : ' The wind, that charter'd libertine, is still.'

53. TIECK (p. 311) infers, from what he considers a resemblance between this and a passage in Jonson's *Every Man Out of his Humour*, that there is more or less reference in this character of Jaques to Jonson himself.   The passage occurs in the Induction (p. 12, ed. Gifford) : ' I'll strip the ragged follies of the time Naked as at their birth—and with a whip of steel Print wounding lashes in their iron ribs,' &c. While the character itself of Jaques may have been intended for Jonson, Tieck thinks that in the rest of this speech, and especially in the Duke's reply, there may be an allusion to Marston, in whose *Scourge of Villainy* Tieck is ' inclined on more than one ground to believe that Shakespeare himself is lashed.'   This fanciful surmise of Tieck's has met with no acceptance.   I have alluded to it again in the Appendix on ' The Date of Composition.'—ED.

53, 54. NEIL : ' The very attempt to disguise embarrassment too often issues in a secondary and more marked embarrassment.'—De Quincey [*Lit. Reminiscences*, i, 25, quoted by Ingleby].

55. **as way**] ABBOTT, § 83 : *A* and *the* are also sometimes omitted after *as, like*, and *than* in comparative sentences.   See ' creeping like snail,' *post* 154.

57, 58. THEOBALD : Besides that [line 58] is defective one whole foot in measure, the tenour of what Jaques continues to say, and the reasoning of the passage, show it no less defective in the sense.   There is no doubt that the two little monosyllables which I have supplied [see Textual Notes] were either by accident wanting in the MS copy, or by inadvertence left out at press.   WHITER (p. 23) : I read and point

[Doth very foolishly, . . . If not,]

the passage thus : ' He, that a fool doth very *wisely* hit, Doth, very *foolishly* although
he smart, Seem senseless of the bob; if not,' &c.   That is, a wise man, whose failings should chance to be well rallied by a simple, unmeaning jester, even though he
should be weak enough really to be hurt by so foolish an attack, appears always
insensible of the stroke.   When the line is smooth it will not be necessary for us to disturb the text on the authority of our fingers.   As the poet did not write with such a
process, so he ought not to be tried by such a test.   CALDECOTT: Olivia in *Twelfth
N.* has much this sentiment : ' To be generous, guiltless, and of free disposition is to
take those things for bird-bolts that you deem cannon-bullets; there is no slander in an
allowed fool, though he do nothing but rail.'—I, v, 100.   COLLIER (*Notes*, &c., p.
131) : Theobald was nearly right, though not entirely so, for the better correction in
the Fol. 1632 is *'But to* seem,' &c.   WHITE (ed. i) : The text of Collier's (MS) better
suits the style of Shakespeare's time.   DYCE (ed. i) : I cannot agree with Singer (*Sh.
Vind.* p. 40) that ' Whiter explains the old text satisfactorily, and neither [Theobald's
nor Collier's] addition is absolutely necessary.'   Whiter's explanation of the old text
here was a little too much even for Caldecott and Knight.   KEIGHTLEY (*Expositor*,
p. 158) : We have the very same omission [as Theobald's *not to*] in ' Yet if it be your
wills *not to* forgive The sin I have committed, let it not fall,' &c.—*Philaster*, II, iv,
where none of the editors have perceived the loss.   [Nor would have accepted ' the
loss ' had it been offered to them.   Keightley's emendation here in *Philaster* is, I
think, utterly wrong.—ED.]   INGLEBY (*Sh. Hermeneutics*, p. 81) disapproves of
Theobald's emendation, and thus attempts the vindication of the original text : Why
does a fool do *wisely* in hitting a wise man ?   Because, through the vantage of his
folly, he puts the wise man ' in a strait betwixt two,' to put up with the smart of the
bob, without dissembling, and the consequential awkwardness of having to do so—
which makes him feel foolish enough—or to put up with the smart, *and dissemble it*,
which entails the secondary awkwardness of the dissimulation, which makes him feel
still more foolish.   Taking the former alternative, *i. e.* ' If not ' (' If *he do* not ') his
' folly is anatomized even by the squandering glances of the fool '; taking the latter
alternative, he makes a fool of himself in the eyes of almost everybody else.   So the
fool gets the advantage both ways. . . . . Observing that [line 58] is too short, we
think it probable that the words *he do* originally formed part of it.   Be that as it may,
' If not ' must mean ' If he do not.'   Perhaps ' very foolishly ' should be in a parenthesis; and ' very wisely ' might be so also.   WRIGHT thus replies to Ingleby : In the
first place, it is not said that the fool doth wisely in hitting a wise man; but if he hits
him wisely, the blow on the part of the fool being struck at random, a squandering
glance, without any wisdom of intention, the wise man will do well to observe a certain line of conduct.   Again, Dr Ingleby's explanation would seem to require ' because
he smarts ' instead of ' although he smarts,' as shewing how it is that the wise man's
dissimulation is foolish or awkward.   If the wise man in his dissimulation very foolishly or awkwardly attempts to seem insensible to the jesting of the fool, his folly is
anatomised or exposed as much as it possibly could be, and the contrast implied in the
' If not ' of the next sentence has no point.   ' If not,' that is, if he do not what is
suggested, ' the wise man's folly is anatomized ' or laid bare even by the extravagant
and random sallies of the fool.   The preceding sentence shows how this is to be
avoided, which is by seeming insensible to the jest and laughing it off; for otherwise,
if the wise man shews that he feels the sting, or even foolishly and awkwardly dis-
guises his feeling, which is the only meaning of which the original text seems capable,

The Wife-mans folly is anathomiz'd
Euen by the fquandring glances of the foole.   60
Inueft me in my motley : Giue me leaue
To fpeake my minde, and I will through and through
Cleanfe the foule bodie of th'infected world,
If they will patiently receiue my medicine.

  Du. Sen. Fie on thee. I can tell what thou wouldft do.   65
  Iaq.   What, for a Counter, would I do, but good ?

59. *Wife-mans*] *wise man's* Rowe et   61. *my*] *the* F_3F_4, Rowe.
seq.   62. *and through*] Om. F_3F_4.
60. *the foole*] *a fool* F_3F_4, Rowe +.

---

his folly is equally exposed. Jaques gives this as the explanation of what he said in line 53 : 'And they that are most galled with my folly, They most must laugh.' The reading of the Folio is not an explanation, but a repetition. [In *Shakespeare the Man*, &c., p. 140, INGLEBY replied to Wright and 'restated' his own argument, but with no essential addition. It seems to me that the original text is capable of being thus paraphrased : He who is hit the hardest by me must laugh the hardest, and that he must do so is plain; because if he is a wise man he must seem perfectly insensible to the hit; no matter how much he smarts, he must still seem foolishly senseless of the bob by laughing it off. Unless he does this, viz.: show his insensibility by laughing it off, any chance hit of the fool will expose every nerve and fibre of his folly. See Dr Johnson's paraphrase below. I really do not see any need of changing the text. —ED.]

58. **bob**] DYCE: A taunt, a scoff. 'A bob, *sanna*,' Coles's *Lat. and Eng. Dict.* WRIGHT: Cotgrave: 'Taloche: A bob, or a rap ouer the fingers ends closed together.'

58. **If not**] JOHNSON: Unless men have the prudence not to appear touched with the sarcasms of a jester, they subject themselves to his power; and the wise man will have his folly 'anatomised,' that is, *dissected* and *laid open*, by the 'squandering glances' or *random shots* of a fool.

60. **squandring**] See the citations in proof that to 'squander' means to *scatter* in *Mer. of Ven.* I, iii, 22 : 'Other ventures hee hath squandred abroad.'

66. **Counter**] STEEVENS: Dr Farmer observes to me that about the time when this play was written the French 'counters' (*i. e.* pieces of false money used as a means of reckoning) were brought into use in England. They are mentioned in *Tro. & Cress.* II, ii, 28 : 'Will you with counters sum The vast proportion of his infinite ?' KNIGHT: The wager proposed by Jaques was not a very heavy one. Jettons or counters, which are small and very thin, are generally of copper or brass, but occasionally of silver, or even of gold; they were commonly used for purposes of calculation in abbeys and other places, where the revenues were complex and of difficult adjustment. From their being found among the ruins of English abbeys they are usually termed abbey-counters. They have been principally coined abroad, particularly at Nürnberg, though some few have been struck in England since the reign of Henry VIII. The most ancient bear on both sides crosses, pellets, and globes; the more modern have portraits and dates and heraldic arms on the reverse. The legends are at times religious, and at others *Gardez vous de mescompter*, and the like.

Du. Sen.   Moſt miſcheeuous foule ſin, in chiding ſin :   67
For thou thy ſelfe haſt bene a Libertine,
As ſenſuall as the brutiſh ſting it ſelfe,
And all th'imboſſed ſores, and headed euils,   70

67. *chiding ſin*] F₁.   69. *ſting*] swine Gould.
68. *bene*] *ben* F₂.   70. *imboſſed*] *embossed* Pope.
69. *brutiſh*] *bruitiſh* F₃F₄.

67, &c. MOBERLY : You would do foul sin in chiding others; for your former profligacy would make you corrupt the world, not amend it, by your experience. To converts like you silence is more suitable than the part of a moral and social reformer. ALLEN (MS) : Jaques understands the sin, which the Duke predicts he will commit, to be false-witness, or calumnious satire, in that he will disgorge upon the world charges ('chidings') of *their* being guilty of such sins as *he* had himself committed.

69. **brutish sting**] JOHNSON : Though 'brutish sting' is capable of a sense not inconvenient in this passage, yet as it is a harsh and unusual mode of speech, I should read the ' brutish *sty*.' STEEVENS : Compare *Oth.* I, iii, 361 : ' our carnal stings, our unbitted lusts.' WRIGHT : The impulse of the animal nature.

70. **imbossed**] DYCE : A hunting term, properly applied to a deer when foaming at the mouth from fatigue. Also, swollen, protuberant. FURNIVALL (*Notes & Qu.* 4th S. vol. xi, 507) shows that the two meanings, scarcely sufficiently distinguished by Dyce, are due to two different derivatives : ' The oldest is a term in hunting from Old French, and, therefore, almost certain to involve some " conceit " or fanciful allusion. When the deer foams at the mouth from fatigue, is covered with bubbles there, he is accordingly said to be " embossed." Cotgrave's " *Embosser :* To swell, or arise in bunches, hulches, knobs; to grow knottie or knurrie." So in *Tam. Shr.* I, i, 17, the " poor cur " Merriman is *emboss'd* or foams at the mouth, and is ill. So again, of Antony foaming with rage against her, Cleopatra says (IV, xiii, 2) " the boar of Thessaly was never so *emboss'd*"; never so foamed with rage. The other *embossed* is from the Old French " *emboser*, emboiter, enchâsser une chose dans une autre. Ducange, v. *imbotare*."—Hippeau. This is Cotgrave's " *Emboister :* To imbox, inclose, insert, fasten, put, or shut up, as within a box," and is Shakespeare's word in *All's Well*, III, vi, " we have almost *embossed* him " (emboxt him), as is clear from the next speech : "*First Lord.* We'll make you some sport with the fox ere we *case* him." ' [Is not ' case,' by the way, in this last speech the ordinary hunting and culinary term, meaning *to skin ?* The distinction, however, between these two meanings, which have caused much discussion, was first, I think, here pointed out by Furnivall, and has been fully confirmed.] SKEAT, *s. v.* '*Emboss* (1), to adorn with bosses or raised work (French). . . . . Lat. *im-* = *in ;* and Old French *bosse*, a boss. *Emboss* (2), to enclose or shelter in a wood (French). . . . . Old French, *embosquer*, to shroud in a wood. . . . . Lat. *im-* = *in ;* and Old French, *bosc* or *bosque*, only used in the diminutive form *bosquet*, a little wood.'

70. **euils**] WALKER (*Crit.* iii, 61) : An old use of ' evil,' still extant in ' king's evil.' [In quoting this line Walker gives it ' *beaded* evils.' Lettsom, in a foot-note, says : ' I follow Walker's manuscript, though, from his silence, *beaded* may be a slip of his pen or memory. I suspect it to be the genuine word, though I believe all editions have " headed." ' It is certainly a good emendation, and follows out the meaning of ' embossed ' even more completely than, probably, Lettsom was aware of.—ED.]

That thou with licenſe of free foot haſt caught,   71
Would'ſt thou diſgorge into the generall world.
 Iaq. Why who cries out on pride,
That can therein taxe any priuate party :
Doth it not flow as hugely as the Sea,   75
Till that the wearie verie meanes do ebbe.

---

74. *taxe*] *be tax'd of* Daniel.
76. *wearie verie meanes*] *weary very means* F_3F_4, Rowe, Knt, Coll. i, Dyce i, iii, Sta. Cam. Clke. *very very means* Pope+, Cap. Steev. Mal. *wearie very*

means Cald. *wearer's very means* Sing. Wh. Dyce ii, Ktly, Coll. iii, Huds. Cla. Rlfe. *very means of wear* Coll. ii. *means, the very means* Jervis. *tributary streams* Lloyd (*ap.* Cam. Ed.).

---

71. **with license**] The definite article is absorbed in the *th* of ' with.'—ED.

73. WALKER (*Crit.* iii, 61) would arrange the lines : ' Why, who cries out on pride, that can therein Tax any private party ?' and begin a new line, ' Doth it not,' &c. [But all such arrangements are merely scansion for the eye, and could not possibly be indicated on the stage.—ED.] KEIGHTLEY (*Expositor*, p. 158) : There is something wanting here; for in this play the speeches never begin with a short line. It is evident also that it is one kind of pride, that of dress, that is spoken of. I therefore read without hesitation 'pride *of bravery*.'

73, &c. MOBERLY : Chide as I will, why should I *offend* them ? Who can say I mean him ? Jaques appears either wilfully or through shallowness to miss the deep wisdom of the Duke's saying and the whole character of his admonition. The Duke had not said that Jaques would *offend* people, but that he would *corrupt* them.

76, 78. **Till that . . . When that**] See I, iii, 44.

76. **wearie verie**] WHITER (p. 24) : The original text is certainly right. The sense is, ' Till that the very means being weary do ebb.' CALDECOTT explains ' wearie ' by *exhausted*. SINGER (*Notes & Qu.* vol. vi, p. 584, Dec. '52) : It is quite obvious we should read ' the *wearer's* very means.' The whole context shows this to be the poet's word, relating as it does to the extravagant cost of finery bestowed by the pride of the wearers on unworthy shoulders, ' until their very means do ebb.' COLLIER (ed. i) : A clear sense can be made out of the passage as it stands in the old text, and we therefore reprint it; but the compositor may have misread ' wearie ' for *wearing*, and transposed ' very ' ; and if we consider Jaques to be railing against pride and excess of apparel, the meaning may be that ' the very *wearing* means,' or means of wearing fine clothes, ' do ebb.' HALLIWELL : The meaning [of the original text] is, does not pride flow as stupendously as the sea, until that its very means, being weary or exhausted, do ebb. The original text is perfectly intelligible, and similar transpositions of adjectives are met with in other places. It may be observed, however, that Rosalind, in the Fourth Act, terms herself ' your *very, very* Rosalind.' COLLIER (ed. ii) : Our reading is that of the (MS), ' the very means of wear ' being the money spent upon the apparel of pride to which Jaques is referring. STAUNTON : The reading of the old text is not very clear; neither are the emendations of it which have been adopted or proposed. . . . . The disputed words should, perhaps, be printed with a hyphen, *weary-very* or *very-weary*. DYCE (ed. i) : Though I believe the line to be corrupted, I follow the old copy, because none of the changes which have been proposed are quite satisfactory. [Herein Dyce takes me completely with him.—ED.]

What woman in the Citie do I name,   77
When that I fay the City woman beares
The coft of Princes on vnworthy fhoulders?
Who can come in, and fay that I meane her,   80
When fuch a one as fhee, fuch is her neighbor?
Or what is he of bafeft function,
That fayes his brauerie is not on my coft,
Thinking that I meane him, but therein fuites
His folly to the mettle of my fpeech,   85
There then, how then, what then, let me fee wherein
My tongue hath wrong'd him : if it do him right,
Then he hath wrong'd himfelfe : if he be free,
why then my taxing like a wild-goofe flies
Vnclaim'd of any.   man But who come here?   90

Enter Orlando.

Orl.   Forbeare, and eate no more.   92

78. *City woman*] *city-woman* Pope.
83. *on my*] *of my* Cam. (misprint?)
Glo. Cla. Wh. ii.
85. *fpeech,*] *fpeech.* Pope. *fpeech?*
Theob.
86. *There then*] *Where then* Mal.
conj.
   There...what then] Ff, Rowe+.
There then; How, what then? Cap.

Steev.   *There then; how then? what
then?* Theob. et cet.
   86. *There...fee*] *Therethen; how then?
let me then see* Han.
   89. *wild-goofe*] *wild goose* Rowe.
   90. *come*] F$_1$.
   91. Scene VIII. Pope+.
      Enter ... with a sword drawn.
Theob. et seq.

DYCE (ed. ii) : I adopt Singer's correction as being, at least, not so violent as the
other proposed readings. . . . . Mr Lettsom queries, 'Till that your bravery bring
your means to ebb.'   DYCE (ed. iii) silently returns to the original text.

76. **meanes**] In *Notes & Qu.* 5th Ser. vol. v, p. 143, S. T. P. proposes to substitute *mains, i. e.* 'main flood, or springtide.'   On p. 345 of the same volume, J. L.
Walker suggests '*mears, i. e.* boundaries or limits.'

82. **function**] MOBERLY : Suppose I say that mean fellows should not be smart,
and suppose any such person, the lowest of the low, tells me he does not dress at my
expense, he only proves that the cap fits.

86. Walker (*Vers.* 116) among instances of the shifting accent of *wherein, whereof,*
&c. cites this line, but reads '*Thus* then' for 'There then.'   Dyce (ed. iii) says Lettsom conjectures '*Where* [*sic* Malone—ED.] then? how then? what then? *let's* see
wherein.'   [The line is inflexibly, and I believe intentionally, trochaic.—ED.]

88. **free**] DYCE : Free from vicious taint, guiltless.   As in 'Make mad the guilty
and appal the free.'—*Ham.* II, ii, 590.

90. **any.   man But**] Another trifling variation in different copies of the First Folio.
The Reprint of 1807, Staunton's Photo-lithograph, and my copy place the period after
'any.'   Booth's Reprint, and the copy used by the Cambridge Editors, place it after
'man.'—ED.

Iaq. Why I haue eate none yet.   93
Orl. Nor fhalt not, till neceffity be feru'd.
Iaq. Of what kinde fhould this Cocke come of?   95
Du. Sen. Art thou thus bolden'd man by thy diftres?.
Or elfe a rude defpifer of good manners,
That in ciuility thou feem'ft fo emptie?
Orl. You touch'd my veine at firft, the thorny point
Of bare diftreffe, hath tane from me the fhew   100
Of fmooth ciuility : yet am I in-land bred,
And know fome nourture : But forbeare, I fay,   102

94. *not*] *thou* Theob. ii, Warb. Johns.
95. *Of what*] *What* Johns. Cap. (corrected in Errata).
come of] *come* Rowe, Pope, Han.

come of— Ktly. *come of, I marvel* Ktly conj.
100. *hath*] *that hath* Ff, Rowe i.
101. *in-land*] *in land* F_4. *inland* Rowe, Johns.

92, 93. According to Abbott, § 500, a trimeter couplet. For 'eate,' see § 343.

95. **Of . . . of**] ABBOTT, § 407: Where the verb is at some distance from the preposition with which it is connected, the preposition is frequently repeated for the sake of clearness. See line 146 below, 'the Sceane Where*in* we play *in*.' [There is the same idiom in Greek and in Latin.—ED.]

96. **bolden'd**] Richardson, *Dict. s. v.*, gives *bold* in the sense of *audacious, impudent*, as well as in a good sense of *fearless*, &c. There seems to be here this worse meaning of 'bolden'd,' making it parallel with 'a rude despiser of good manners' in the next line. Allen (MS) suggests this.—ED.

97. **else**] WRIGHT: Redundant here, as in *R. of L.* 875: 'Or kills his life or else his quality.'

98. **ciuility**] WRIGHT: Politeness in a higher sense than it is used at present. See III, ii, 127, and *Mer. of Ven.* II, ii, 204: 'Use all the observance of civility.'

100. **tane**] JOHNSON: We might read *torn* with more elegance, but elegance alone will not justify alteration.

101. Abbott's scansion (§ 467) of this line is to me objectionable. Perhaps he is right in saying that an unaccented *i* before *-ty* is sometimes dropped, but I doubt if this be here required ; it gives a line which is to my ear anything but pleasant : 'Of smóoth | *civili* | *ty* yét | am I ín | land bréd.' I prefer to pronounce every syllable, 'Of smooth | civil | ity | yet am | I in | land bred,' and term the line a trimeter couplet, or courageously call it a downright Alexandrine.—ED.

101. **in-land**] HOLT WHITE: The opposite to *outland* or *upland.* Orlando means to say that he had not been bred among clowns. CALDECOTT: *Uplandish* in our early writers and dictionaries is interpreted 'unbred, rude, rustical, clownish' ; 'because,' says Minsheu, 'the people that dwell among mountains are severed from the *civilitie* of cities,' 1617. See III, ii, 334.

102. **nourture**] STEEVENS: That is, education, breeding, manners. 'It is a point of *nurture*, or *good manners*, to salute them you meete. Urbanitas est salutare obvios.'—Baret's *Alvearie*, 1580. WRIGHT: See *Saladyne's Complaint* in Lodge's Novel: 'the faults of thy youth . . . . not onely discovering little *nourture*, but blemishing the excellence of nature.'

He dies that touches any of this fruite,   103
Till I, and my affaires are anſwered.

    Iaq. And you will not be anſwer'd with reaſon,   105
I muſt dye.

    Du. Sen. What would you haue?
Your gentleneſſe ſhall force, more then your force
Moue vs to gentleneſſe.

    Orl. I almoſt die for food, and let me haue it.   110

---

105. *And*] Ff, Rowe, Cald. *If* Pope +.
An Cap. et cet.
    anſwer'd] *answered* Rowe.

105, 106. *be...dye*] Sep. line, Pope +.
Prose, Cap. et seq.

107, 109. Two lines, ending *force...
gentleneſſe* Pope et seq.

---

103. **fruite**] It seems superfluous, if not worse, to call attention to Shakespeare's accuracy even in the most trivial details. *Meat* or *food* would have suited the rhythm here, but 'fruite' recalls the 'banket' which was now before the Duke. Of course, a little further on, when Orlando says he dies for 'food,' he had to use that word then; it would have been laughable to say he died for *fruit.*—ED.

104, 105. **answered . . . answer'd**] Abbott, § 474, refers to this as an instance where *-ed* is sonant and mute, even in words in close proximity. It is certainly thus printed in the Folio, as we see; but I doubt if it be the better way. The scansion of these lines is not easy, and the majority of modern editors, following Capell's lead, have evaded the difficulty by printing lines 105 and 106 as prose, which I cannot but think is wrong. The whole scene is in rhythm, and one solitary prose sentence, thus breaking in, is as certainly discordant as it is suspicious. Pope and his followers down to Capell divided the lines, and printed, thus: 'If you will not Be answered with reason I must die,' which is certainly better than prose, and it makes *-ed* sonant in both examples of 'answered,' but the division of the lines at 'not' is objectionable. Why Capell printed as prose I cannot see; he certainly, in his *Notes*, approves of Pope's division, that is, if I can understand his ragged English. I prefer the arrangement as we have it here, merely changing 'answer'd' to *answered*, in order to avoid throwing the ictus on the last syllable of 'reason;' to accent the last syllable of 'reason' weakens the force of what, I am afraid, Jaques intended for a pun.—ED.

105. **reason**] STAUNTON: We should, possibly, read *reasons.* Here, as in other places, Shakespeare evidently indulged in the perennial pun on *reasons* and *raisins.*

108, 109. **gentlenesse . . . force . . . force . . . gentleness**] Moberly calls attention to what he considers the chiasm here. I think this can hardly be called a perfect chiasm, wherein something more is needed than a mere criss-cross position of the terms; to speak arithmetically, the extremes, as well as the means, should be related. For instance, 'warmed and cooled by the same winter and summer,' (*Mer. of Ven.* III, i, 57) is a complete chiasm. There appears to be no such relation here. —ED.

110. **and**] ABBOTT, § 100: *I pray you* may perhaps be understood after this word, implied in the imperative 'let.' DYCE (ed. iii): Probably (as Mr Lettsom remarks), an error caused by 'and' occurring twice in the next line: qy. *so ?* WRIGHT: For this use of 'and' in the sense of 'and so' or 'and therefore,' see below, line 142, and *Temp.* I, ii, 186: ''Tis a good dulness, And give it way.'

Du. Sen.   Sit downe and feed, & welcom to our table   111
Orl.   Speake you fo gently ? Pardon me I pray you,
I thought that all things had bin fauage heere,
And therefore put I on the countenance
Of fterne command'ment.   But what ere you are   115
That in this defert inacceffible,
Vnder the fhade of melancholly boughes,
Loofe, and neglect the creeping houres of time :
If euer you haue look'd on better dayes :
If euer bcene where bels haue knoll'd to Church :   120
If euer fate at any good mans feaft :
If euer from your eye-lids wip'd a teare,   122

---

112. *gently*] *gentle* Ktly.

113. *bin*] *beene* Ff.

115. *command'ment*] Ff. *commandment* Rowe.

116. *defert*] *defart* F₃F₄, Rowe, Pope,
Theob. Han. Warb.

118. *Loofe, and neglect*] *Neglect and
lose* Gentleman.

120. *bcene*] F₁.

111, &c. FLETCHER (p. 210) : Orlando's eagerness to relieve the pressing necessity
of his aged servant, would not have permitted him to waste his time on even the most
eloquent appeal to the feelings of his stranger host and his companions, but that he
now feels 'gentleness' to be his most effective weapon for securing from these men,
with whom he is so newly acquainted, the means of relief to the subject of his solicitude.   Here, therefore, the speaker is making the best use of his time, even for that
immediate purpose; while the passage itself, so touchingly expressing his own sense
of the sweets of social life, as contrasted with that of the wilderness to which he is
yet uninured, is one of those most intimately disclosing that genial nature which
Shakespeare has so studiously developed in this character.

115. **command'ment**] WALKER (*Vers.* p. 126) notes that in certain words in
-ment the *e* which originally preceded this final syllable was sometimes retained and
sometimes omitted.   DYCE (ed. iii) in a note on *Mer. of Ven.* IV, i, 471, says that
'commandment' is to be there read as a quadrisyllable, as also in *1 Hen. VI:* I,
iii. 'In all the other passages in Shakespeare where it occurs in his blank verse it
is a trisyllable.'   Dyce overlooked the fact in this note on *Mer. of Ven.* that it
is only by following the text of Q₁, as Dyce himself did, that 'commandment' in
that place is a quadrisyllable.   In the Folio it follows the rule and is a trisyllable :
'Be vál | uéd | agáinst | your wíues | commándment.'   The Quarto reads : 'Be
val | ew'd gáinst | your wiues | commánd | emént.'   Hence the instance in *1 Hen.
VI* remains the only one where, in Shakespeare's blank verse, the word is a quadrisyllable.   Wright notes that the quadrisyllabic form is to be found in *Pass. Pil.* 418 :
'If to women he be bent They have at commandement.'—ED.

120. **knoll'd**] Cotgrave translates *Carillonner* by ' to chyme, or knowle, bells ';
and *Carillonneur* by ' a chymer, or knowler, of bells '; under *Carillon*, however, he
gives, 'A chyming of bells; a knell.'   Way, in *Prompt. Parv., s. v. Knyllynge*, cites
Palsgrave : I knolle a belle, *Je frappe du batant.*   Halliwell quotes, ' poor weary souls
that hear the bell knoll.'—*Humourous Lieutenant*, II, iv [p. 457].

And know what 'tis to pittie, and be pittied :   123
Let gentleneſſe my ſtrong enforcement be,
In the which hope, I bluſh, and hide my Sword.   125
 Du. Sen. True is it, that we haue ſeene better dayes,
And haue with holy bell bin knowld to Church,
And ſat at good mens feaſts, and wip'd our eies
Of drops, that ſacred pity hath engendred :
And therefore ſit you downe in gentleneſſe,   130
And take vpon command, what helpe we haue
That to your wanting may be miniſtred.
 Orl. Then but forbeare your food a little while :
Whiles (like a Doe) I go to finde my Fawne,
And giue it food. There is an old poore man,   135
Who after me, hath many a weary ſteppe
Limpt in pure loue : till he be firſt ſuffic'd,
Oppreſt with two weake euils, age, and hunger,   138

---

123. *know*] *known* Han. Johns.   136. *a*] Om. F₄, Rowe i.
125. *bluſh*] *buſh* Ff.

---

125. **the which**] See I, ii, 120.

125. **blush**] If by chance the misprint of the three later Folios had occurred in the First, how loudly Shakespeare's classical knowledge would have been extolled, founded on this clear reference to Harmodius and Aristogeiton !—ED.

131. **vpon command**] JOHNSON : It seems necessary to read *demand*, that is, *ask* for what we can supply and have it. [In the next Variorum Edition published after Johnson's death, this note was withdrawn, and in its place, we have] STEEVENS : 'Upon command,' is *at your own command*. COLLIER [ed. ii, reading with his (MS) *commend*] : Orlando has previously spoken of 'commandment,' which he finds unnecessary ; and here the Duke tells him to ' take upon *commend*' (as opposed to command) what he requires. *Commend* is misprinted ' command' in the Folios, but the small, though important error is set right by the alteration of a letter in the (MS). The verb to *commend* is explained in our dictionaries, ' To give anything into the hands of another.' Orlando was to take what he needed as a free gift, and not as a violent enforcement. DYCE (*Strictures*, &c. p. 69) : If Mr Collier had not been under a sort of spell, thrown over him by the (MS), he never would have tried to expound such a senseless alteration as ' upon *commend*' by referring to what precedes,—he would have dismissed it in silence. The meaning of the old reading, though dark to the (MS), hardly requires a gloss ; most people will see immediately that ' upon command' is equivalent to ' as you may choose to order,—at your will and pleasure.'

134. **Whiles**] For this genitive of *while* see Abbott, § 137.

134. **Doe**] Malone refers to the repetition of this simile in *V. & A*. 875.

138. **weak evils**] CALDECOTT : That is, unhappy weaknesses, or causes of weakness. [See ' thriſtie hire,' II, iii, 41, from which this differs in being a genuine prolepsis or anticipation. Walker (*Crit*. ii, 85, followed by Abbott, § 4) gives the following examples of this figure so familiar to the ancients, whereby a predicate, which prop-

I will not touch a bit.

 Duke Sen. Go finde him out.   140

And we will nothing wafte till you returne.

 Orl. I thanke ye, and be bleft for your good comfort.

 Du Sen. Thou feeft, we are not all alone vnhappie:

This wide and vniuerfall Theater

Prefents more wofull Pageants then the Sceane   145

Wherein we play in.

 Ia. All the world's a ftage,   147

---

142. Exit. Rowe et seq.   146. *Wherein...in*] *Wherein we play*
  Scene IX. Pope+.   Rowe, Pope, Han. *Which we do play*
             in Cap. conj.

---

erly indicates effect, is made to express cause. Heywood, *Silver Age*, Lamb's *Speci-mens*, vol. ii, p. 229 (Ceres is threatening the earth), 'With idle agues I'll consume thy swains; . . . . The rotten showers Shall drown thy seed.' Shakespeare, *Sonnet* xiii, 'the stormy gusts of winter's day, And barren rage of death's eternal cold.' Beau. & Fl., *Mad Lover*, III, iv : 'Live till the mothers find you. . . . . And sow their barren curses on your beauty.' Spenser, *Faerie Queene*, Bk. vi, C. xi, St. xvii (speak-ing of dogs), 'striving each to get The greatest portion of the greedie prey.' Walker professed to give merely a few instances in other poets; in Shakespeare are number-less examples. See 'fair state,' *Ham.* III, i, 152; and instances there cited.—ED.]

146. **Wherein . . . in**] STEEVENS : I believe we should read with Pope, and add a word at the beginning of the next speech, to complete the measure, viz.: *Why,* all the worlds,' &c. MAGINN (p. 72) : Qy : 'Wherein we play *on,*' *i. e.* continue to play. [See line 95 above.]

147. **stage**] STEEVENS : This observation occurs in one of the Fragments [No. X] of Petronius : 'Non duco contentionis funem, dum constet inter nos, quod fere *totus mundus exerceat histrioniam.*' MALONE : This observation had been made in an English drama before the time of Shakespeare. See *Damon & Pythias* [1571, p. 31, ed. Hazlitt] : 'Pythagoras said, that this world was like a stage, Whereon many play their parts.' In *The Legend of Orpheus and Eurydice*, 1597, we find these lines : 'Unhappy man Whose life a sad continual tragedie, Himself the actor, in the world, the stage, While as the acts are measur'd by his age.' DOUCE (i, 299) : Petronius had not been translated in Shakespeare's time. . . . . In Withal's *Short Dictionarie in Latine and English*, 1599, is the following passage : 'This life is a certain enterlude or plaie. The world is a stage full of chang everie way, everie man is a plaier.' Also in Pettie's translation of Guazzo's *Civile conversation*, 1586, one of the parties introduces the saying of some philosopher 'that this world was a stage, we the players which present the comedie.' See also *Mer. of Ven.* I, i, 78 : 'I hold the world but as the world, Gratiano; A stage where every man must play a part.' [One cannot but wonder after reading such notes as these by Steevens, Malone, and Douce, not to mention modern editors who have followed them in all seriousness, that it never seems to have occurred to these editors to ask themselves what is the legitimate inference to be drawn from their adducing such citations, and whether they are not hereby vir-tually claiming for such authors as Petronius, or Edwardes, or for Guazzo (almost the barrenest and jejunest of writers), a fund of originality which they deny to William

And all the men and women, meerely Players;   148
They haue their *Exits* and their Entrances,
And one man in his time playes many parts,   150
His Acts being feuen ages.   At firft the Infant,

151. *At*] *As* Cap. conj. Dyce iii.

Shakespeare.—ED.]   KNIGHT: It is scarcely necessary to inquire whether Shakespeare found the idea in the Greek epigram: Σκηνὴ πᾶς ὁ βίος, καὶ παίγνιον. ἢ
μάθε παίζειν, Τὴν σπουδὴν μεταθείς, ἢ φέρε τὰς ὀδύνας.—[Palladas, in *Anthologia
Græca, X. Protreptika*, No. 72.   The idea had almost passed into a proverb.   Halliwell says that the comparison of life to the stage ' is of constant occurrence in English writers of the sixteenth and seventeenth centuries.'   It is therefore needless to
' shed any more Christian ink ' in compiling what would be merely a bibliography of
the phrase, and of no particle of use in the illustration of Shakespeare.   One other solitary reference it is worth while to note.   In that same collection of items which Oldys
had gathered for a life of Shakespeare from which we get the anecdote about old
Adam, see line 176 of this Scene, there is another extract, given by Steevens (Var.
'21, vol. i, p. 467), as follows: ' Verses by Ben Jonson and Shakespeare, occasioned
by the motto to the Globe.Theatre—*Totus mundus agit histrionem.*

> *Jonson.*—" If, but *stage actors*, all the world displays,
> " Where shall we find *spectators* of their plays ?"
> *Shakespeare.*—" Little, or much, of what we see, we do;
> " We are all both *actors* and *spectators* too."

Poetical Characteristics, 8vo, MS, vol. i, some time in the Harleian Library; which
volume was returned to its owner.'—ED.]

148. meerely] That is, absolutely, purely.

151. His Acts being seuen ages] STEEVENS: Dr Warburton observes that this
was ' *no unusual* division of a play before our author's time '; but forbears to offer any
one example in support of his assertion.   I have carefully perused almost every dramatick piece antecedent to Shakespeare, or contemporary with him; but so far from
being divided into acts, they are almost all printed in an unbroken continuity of
scenes.   I should add, that there is one play of six acts to be met with, and another
of twenty-one; but the second of these is a translation from the Spanish, and never
could have been designed for the stage.   In *God's Promises*, 1577, *A Tragedie or
Enterlude* (or rather a *Mystery*), by John Bale, seven acts may indeed be found.   It
should, however, be observed, that the intervals in the Greek Tragedy are known to
have varied from three acts to seven.   MALONE: One of Chapman's plays, *Two
Wise Men and All the Rest Fools*, is in seven acts.   This, however, is the only dramatic piece that I have found so divided.   But surely it is not necessary to suppose
that our author alluded here to any such precise division of the drama.   His comparisons seldom run on four feet.   It was sufficient for him that a play was distributed
into *several* acts, and that human life long before his time had been divided into
seven periods.   In *The Treasury of Ancient and Modern Times*, 1613, Proclus, a
Greek author, is said to have divided the lifetime of man into *seven ages;* over each
of which, one of the seven planets was supposed to rule: ' The *first age* is called
Infancy, containing the space of foure years.   The *second age* continueth ten yeares
until he attaine to the age of fourteene: this age is called *Childhood*.   The *third age*

[His Acts being seuen ages.]

consisteth of eight yeares, being named by our auncients *Adolescencie* or *Youthhood;* and it lasteth from fourteene till two and twenty yeares be fully compleate. The *fourth age* paceth on, till a man have accomplished two and forty yeares, and is tearmed *Young Manhood*. The *fifth age*, named *Mature Manhood*, hath (according to the said author) fifteene yeares of continuance, and therefore makes his progress so far as six and fifty yeares. Afterwards, in adding twelve to fifty-sixe, you shall make up sixty-eight yeares, which reach to the end of the *sixt age*, and is called *Old Age*. The *seaventh* and last of these seven ages is limited from sixty-eight yeares, so far as four-score and eight, being called weak, declining, and *Decrepite Age*. If any man chance to goe beyond this age (which is more admired than noted in many), you shall evidently perceive that he will returne to his first condition of Infancy againe.' Hippocrates likewise divided the life of man into seven ages, but differs from Proclus in the number of years allotted to each period. See Sir Thomas Brown's *Enquiries into Vulgar and Common Errors*, 1686, p. 173 [Book IV, chap. xii: 'Of the great climacterical year']. So also in *The Diamant of Devotion, Cut and Squared into Six Severall Points*, by Abraham Fleming, 1586, Part I: 'Wee are not placed in this world as continuers; for the scripture saith that we have no abiding citie heere, but as travellers and soiourners, whose custome it is to take up a new inne, and to change their lodging, sometimes here, sometimes there, during the time of their travell. Heere we walke like plaiers uppon a stage, one representing the person of a king, another of a lorde, the third of a plowman, the fourth of an artificer, and so foorth, as the course and order of the enterlude requireth; everie acte whereof beeing plaide, there is no more to doe, but open the gates and dismisse the assemblie. Even so fareth it with us; for what other thing is the compasse of this world, beautified with varietie of creatures, reasonable and unreasonable, but an ample and large theatre, wherein all things are appointed to play their pageants, which when they have done, they die, and their glorie ceaseth.' HENLEY: I have seen, more than once, an old print, entitled, 'The Stage of Man's Life,' divided into seven ages. As emblematical representations of this sort were formerly stuck up, both for ornament and instruction, in the generality of houses, it is more probable that Shakespeare took his hint from thence, than from Hippocrates or Proclus. HUNTER (i, 341): The merit of Shakespeare is not that he invented this distribution, but that he has exhibited it more brilliantly, more impressively, than had ever been done before. The beauty and tenderness of the thought that life is a kind of drama with intermingling scenes of joy and sorrow, together with the justness of the sentiment, would have kept this forever in the public view: but the multitude would probably by this time have wholly lost sight of the distribution of life into periods, if it had not been embalmed in these never-to-be-forgotten lines. If it be asked how Shakespeare became acquainted with this distribution of human life, since he certainly did not read Proclus or Hippocrates, nor yet Prudentius or Isidore, it might be sufficient to answer that the notion floated in society, that it was part of the traditionary inheritance of all, which was no doubt the case. But if a printed authority likely to have met his eye is wanted [reference is here made by Hunter to Primaudaye's *French Academy*, 1598, and to 'another contemporary with Shakespeare, Sir John Ferne,' and the distribution in each case is given; but as these 'distributions,' and all others which are not the same as Shakespeare's, are pure surplusage here and now, I have not repeated them. Malone's note is given in full because the substance of it has been so often repeated by subsequent editors]. GRANT WHITE (*Shakespeare's Scholar*, p. 247) gives an extract from Eras-

[His Acts being seuen ages.]

mus's *Praise of Folie, Englished by Sir Thomas Chaloner*, 1549, sig. E, iii, in which
'this life of mortall man' is likened to 'a certain kynde of stage plaie' in which sometimes one man 'comes in two or three times with sundry partes.' [This same passage
was afterwards re-discovered by 'G. W. T.' in *Notes & Queries*, 1856, 2d Ser. ii, 44;
again in the same volume, p. 207, J. Doran adduced a similar allusion in Calderon.]
HALLIWELL cites a poem 'clepid the sevene ages' in the Thornton MS of the fifteenth
century in Lincoln Cathedral; also Arnold's *Chronicle* [ed. 1811, p. 157, Wright];
also a lithographic reproduction of 'the Arundel MS, 83,' 'a highly interesting example executed in England in the early part of the fourteenth century, in which the
various stages of life are depicted with an artistic merit reflecting great credit on the
ancient delineator.' He also reproduces a wood-cut from the *Orbis Sensualium Pic-
tus*, 1689, p. 45, in which the figures are placed on no less than eleven steps. STAUN-
TON refers to 'some Greek verses attributed to Solon,' 'introduced by Philo Judæus
into his *Liber de Mundi opificio*'; also to an Italian engraving of the sixteenth century, by Christopher Bertello, where the school-boy is carrying his books, the lover
bears a branch of myrtle, and at his feet is a young Cupid, the soldier is 'bearded like
the pard,' the justice has an aspect of grave serenity, the sixth age is a senile personage in a long furred robe, slippered, and with spectacles on nose, the last scene of all
exhibits the man of eighty, blind and helpless. Staunton also refers to two elaborate
articles, one in the *Archæologia*, vol. xxvii; and the other in *The Gentleman's Magazine* for May, 1853; and also to a Monumental Brass dated 1487 in the Hôpital S.
Marie, Ypres, in Belgium. WRIGHT refers to 'an interesting paper by Mr Winter
Jones which he published in the *Archæologia*, xxxv, 167–189, on a block print of the
fifteenth century,' wherein a 'good deal of the literature of this subject has been collected'; also 'in the Mishna (*Aboth*, v, 24) fourteen periods are given, and a poem
upon the ten stages of life was written by the great Jewish commentator, Ibn Ezra.
The Midrash on Ecclesiastes, i, 2, goes back to the seven divisions. The Jewish
literature is very fully given by Löw in his Treatise *Die Lebensalter in der Jüdischen
Literatur*,' and finally Wright refers to 'the pavement of the Cathedral of Siena, of
which a description is given by Professor Sidney Colvin in *The Fortnightly Review*,
July, 1875, pp. 53, 54.' C. ELLIOT BROWNE in *Notes & Queries*, 5th Ser. vol. v, p.
143, refers to Vaughan's *Directions for Health*, 1602, and Done's *Polydoron*, 'probably published early in the seventeenth century.' [If a picture were in Shakespeare's
mind, as Henley suggests, and which seems more likely than not, we can understand
why the number of ages was seven. There were three steps of ascent, the soldier
stood on the summit, and then followed three steps of descent. Five steps would
have been too few, and nine would have been too many.—ED.]

151. At] Walker (*Crit.* i, 129) conjectured that this should be *as*, and included it
among the instances of *as* used in the sense of *to wit*. He was, however, anticipated
by Capell. I think the emendation is extremely probable.—ED.

151, &c. I have found it wellnigh impossible so to divide many of these lines that
the eye may be guided to the rhythm. It is noteworthy that with the exception of
the 'school-boy' all the 'ages' begin in the latter half of a line, an indication of
the long pause which should precede; so long, that each of these half lines might
not improperly form a line by itself, thus beginning a new paragraph. But this gives
no help rhythmically to the lines that follow, which, in some cases, if the lines are to
be considered pentameters, remain unalterably trochaic. Indeed, I am not sure that
it would not be the simpler way to regard the whole of this speech as metric prose,

Mewling, and puking in the Nurſes armes :　　　152
Then, the whining Schoole-boy with his Satchell
And ſhining morning face, creeping like ſnaile
Vnwillingly to ſchoole.　And then the Louer,　　155
Sighing like Furnace, with a wofull ballad
Made to his Miſtreſſe eye-brow.　Then, a Soldier,
Full of ſtrange oaths, and bearded like the Pard,　　158

---

153. *Then*] *And then* Rowe ii +, Cap.　　157. *a Soldier*] *the soldier* Dyce iii,
Steev. Ktly, Dyce iii, Wh. ii.　　Huds.

---

exquisitely metric prose; until, toward the close, in harmony with the thought, it
glides into the solemn cadence that énds this stránge evéntful hístory.—ED.

154. **like snaile**] ABBOTT, § 83 : *A* is still omitted by us in adverbial compounds,
such as 'snail-like,' 'clerk-like,' &c.　Then it was omitted as being unnecessarily
emphatic in such expressions as : 'creeping like snail,' 'sighing like furnace.'　'Like
snail' is an adverb in process of formation.　It is intermediate between 'like a snail'
and 'snail-like.'

156. **Furnace**] MALONE: So in *Cymb.* I, vi, 64 : 'a Frenchman . . . . that, it
seems, much loves A Gallian girl at home; he furnaces The thick sighs from him.'

157. **a Soldier**] DYCE (ed. iii) : The Folio has '*a* Soldier,' but compare elsewhere
in the present speech; '*the* infant,' '*the* school-boy,' '*the* lover,' '*the* justice,' &c.
This correction was suggested to me by Mr Robson.　HUNTER (i, 343) : It is the
great beauty of Shakespeare that he does not give us cold abstractions, but the living
figures.　The blood circulates through them; it may be quickly or sluggishly, but the
life-blood is there.　They are personations of the abstract idea, borrowed from what
was the actual life of many Englishmen of the better class in his time, who went to
the wars and returned to execute the duties and enjoy the quiet majesty of the country justice.　A nice critic might, however, raise the question, how far it was proper
thus to introduce the characters of Soldier and Justice, which are not common to all,
with those accidents of life which belong to all conditions.　It might be said that
they are but spirited personations of the active and sedate periods of manhood, which
are common to all; but the proper answer is, that Jaques was a courtier addressing
courtiers, and he speaks, therefore, of human life as it appeared in one of their own
class.

158. **strange oaths . . . bearded**] To the following passage in *Hen. V:* III, vi,
78 MALONE refers in illustration of *beards*, and WRIGHT in illustration of *oaths :*
'And this they con perfectly in the phrase of war, which they trick up with new-
tuned oaths; and what a beard of the general's cut, and a horrid suit of the camp will
do . . . . is wonderful to be thought on.'　'Our ancestors,' says Malone, 'were very
curious in the fashion of their beards, and a certain *cut* or form was appropriated to
the soldier, the bishop, the judge, the clown,' &c.　He cites a ballad wherein a soldier's beard is described as matching 'in figure like a spade,' but the date, 1660, is
rather late to be trusted as a correct description of what is as fickle as fashion.　Wright
explains 'bearded like a pard' by 'long pointed mustaches, bristling like a panther's
or leopard's feelers.'　This, I think, is doubtful.　The beard is not the mustaches, or,
as Stubbes calls them, 'the mowchatowes,' showing by the very use of a specific term
that a distinction was made in Shakespeare's day.　Does not the present phrase refer

Ielous in honor, fodaine, and quicke in quarrell,
Seeking the bubble Reputation   160
Euen in the Canons mouth : And then, the Iuftice
In faire round belly, with good Capon lin'd,   162

---

to the general shagginess characteristic of a true soldier on duty in the field, as distinguished from the trim nicety of a carpet knight, ' whose chin new-reap'd shows like a stubble-land at harvest home ?'—ED.

159. **sodaine**] HUNTER (i, 339): A semicolon is necessary here, that we may not suppose the sense of 'sudden' to pass over to the next clause, so as to become 'sudden in quarrel;' while 'sudden' really stands absolutely. It is the same word which we have in *Macb.* IV, iii, 59 : 'I grant him sudden,' and it seems to be nearly equivalent to *vehement,* or *violent,* or *hasty,* or perhaps still more exactly *prompt in executing a resolve.* And this suggests what is a new, but probably the true, sense of the clause ' quick in quarrel,' *adroit in the duello,* not merely quick and spirited in any dispute. HALLIWELL, however, does not acknowledge this distinction, which is to me a good one ; he says : 'Accepting "sudden " in the common sense of rash or precipitate, the phrase " sudden and quick " may be considered as intentionally pleonastic.'

160. **Reputation**] HUNTER (i, 340) prints this with quotation-marks, regarding it as ' a favorite word of soldiers, at which the cynical Jaques means to sneer, speaking it as a quotation in a contemptuous manner. Thus Peacham : " then at their return [as soldiers from the Netherlands], among their companions they must be styled by the name of Captain, they must stand upon that airy title and mere nothing called *Reputation,* undertake every quarrel," &c.—*Truth of our Times,* p. 140. And so in an admirable little work, entitled *Vade Mecum,* of which the third edition was printed in 1638, "The French in a battle before Moncountre, standing upon their *Reputation,* not to dislodge by night, lost their reputation by dislodging by day." This is sufficient to show that there was a military and kind of technical use of the word, such as might provoke a satirist; and in this sense it is that Jaques uses it, meaning to deride it. Shakespeare has, in this play, still more pointed satire on the affected punctilio of the military profession.'

162. **In**] DYCE (ed. iii) : ' Read,' says Mr Lettsom, '*His;* and six lines below, "*In* youthful hose." ' I must confess that I think both these alterations unnecessary.

162. **Capon lin'd**] HALES (p. 219) : There is an allusion that has been missed in the mention of the ' capon,' an allusion which adds to the bitterness of a sufficiently bitter life-sketch. It was the custom to present magistrates with presents, especially, it would seem, with capons, by way of securing their good will and favour. This fact heightens the satire of Jaques's portrait of an Elizabethan J. P. It gives force and meaning to what seems vague and general. Wither, describing the Christmas season, with its burning ' blocks,' its ' pies,' &c., goes on to sing how : ' Now poor men to the justices With capons make their errants; And if they hap to fail of these, They plague them with their warrants.' That is, the capon was a tribute fully expected and as good as exacted; it was ' understood ' it should be duly paid in. Singer cites a member of the House of Commons as saying, in 1601 : 'A Justice of the Peace is a living creature that for half a dozen chickens will dispense with a dozen of penal statutes.' Other illustrations will be found in Davies's *Supplementary English Glossary.* [Hales quotes from a letter received from the author of this *Glossary,* wherein a sermon is mentioned], probably preached very early in the seventeenth century, which speaks of judges that judge for reward and say with shame, ' Bring you ' such

With eyes ſeuere, and beard of formall cut,　　163
Full of wiſe ſawes, and moderne inſtances,
And ſo he playes his part.　The ſixt age ſhifts　　165

---

as the country calls 'capon justices.'　A further illustration of this morally dubious custom is to be found in Massinger's *New Way to Pay Old Debts* [IV, ii, where Mr Justice Greedy, under promise of a yoke of oxen from Wellborn, drives from his presence Tapwell, whose suit, under promise merely of a pair of turkeys, he had at first favoured].

163. **formall cut**] That is, cut with due regard to his dignity.　It is not to be imagined that the nice customs of beards escaped the stern Stubbes.　He is particularly entertaining in his 'anatomie' of the barber shops : 'The barbers,' he says in his *Anatomie of Abuses*, 1583 (Part II, p. 50, New Sh. Soc. Reprint), 'haue one maner of cut called the French cut, another the Spanish cut, one the Dutch cut, another the Italian, one the newe cut, another the olde, one of the brauado fashion, another of the meane fashion.　One a gentleman's cut, another the common cut, one cut of the court, an other of the country, with infinite the like vanities, which I ouerpasse.　They haue also other kinds of cuts innumerable ; and therefore when you come to be trimed, they will aske you whether you will be cut to looke terrible to your enimie or aimiable to your freend, grime & sterne in countenance, or pleasant & demure (for they haue diuers kinds of cuts for all these purposes, or else they lie).　Then, when they haue done al their feats, it is a world to consider, how their mowchatowes must be preserued and laid out, from one cheke to another, yea, almost from one eare to another, and turned vp like two hornes towards the forehead.'　Harrison, too, has his fling at the fashions of beards.　On p. 172, ed. 1587, he says : ' Neither will I meddle with our varietie of beards, of which some are shauen from the chin like those of Turks, not a few cut short like to the beard of marques Otto, some made round like a rubbing brush, other with a *pique de vant* (O fine fashion !) or now and then suffered to grow long, the barbers being growen so cunning in this behalfe as the tailors.　And therefore if a man haue a leane and streight face, a marquesse Ottons cut will make it broad and large ; if it be platter like, a long slender beard will make it seeme the narrower; if he be wesell becked, then much heare left on the cheekes will make the owner looke big like a bowdled hen, and so grim as a goose, if Cornelis of Chelmeresford saie true ; manie old men doo weare no beards at all.'—*Description of England*, prefixed to Holinshed.

164. **moderne**] STEEVENS : That is, *trite, common*.　So in IV, i, 7 of this play. DYCE : That is, trite, ordinary, common.　(' Per modo tutto fuor del *modern*' uso.'—Dante, *Purg.* xvi, 42, where Biagioli remarks, '*Moderno*, s'usa quì in senso di *ordinario*.')　[It is not worth while to load the page with the various misunderstandings of this word, nor with the various passages wherein it occurs.　It suffices to say that it is now understood to bear throughout the meaning of *trite, trivial, commonplace*. —ED.]

164. **instances**] SCHMIDT (p. 456) : The fundamental idea of this word in Shakespeare is 'proof, sign of the truth of anything,' and hence it can naturally mean 'a single example.'　[Schmidt translates ' modern instances ' by 'Allerwelts-Sentenzen.' In his *Lexicon* he gives as the meaning here : 'A sentence, a saw, a proverb, anything alleged to support one's own opinion.'　There are few words in Shakespeare that are used with a greater variety of shades of meaning than this.　Schmidt seems to be correct in his interpretation of it here.—ED.]

Into the leane and flipper'd Pantaloone,   166
With fpectacles on nofe, and pouch on fide,
His youthfull hofe well fau'd, a world too wide,
For his fhrunke fhanke, and his bigge manly voice,
Turning againe toward childifh trebble pipes,   170
And whiftles in his found.   Laft Scene of all,
That ends this ftrange euentfull hiftorie,
Is fecond childifhneffe, and meere obliuion,
Sans teeth, fans eyes, fans tafte, fans euery thing.   174

---

169. *fhanke*] shanks Han.   170. *trebble pipes*] *treble, pipes* Theob.

---

166. **Pantaloone**] CAPELL (p. 60, *a*) : Pantaloon and his mates seem to have
found their way into England about the year 1607; the conjecture is founded upon
an extract from a play of that date intitl'd : *Travels of Three English Brothers.* [This
extract is found in Capell's *School of Shakespeare*, p. 66, wherein there is the following dialogue between Kempe and the 'Harlaken' : '*Kemp.* Now Signior, how manie
are you in companie ? *Harl.* None but my wife and myselfe, sir. *Kemp.* . . . . but
the project come, and then to casting of the parts. *Harl.* Marry sir, first we will
have an old Pantaloune. *Kemp.* Some iealous Coxcombe,' &c.] STEEVENS refers to
a curious 'Plotte of the deade mans fortune' (reprinted Var. '21, vol. iii, p. 356),
wherein 'the panteloun' is one of the characters, and in one place we find : ' to them
the panteloun and pescode with spectakles,' which Steevens cites in illustration of the
next line in the present passage, albeit as far as we can see 'pescode' and not 'panteloun' may have worn the spectacles. The date of this 'plotte' is unknown, but it may
be fairly assumed to be older than Capell's *Travels*, &c. Malone, however, discovered
in Nashe's *Pierce Pennilesse*, &c. 1592 (p. 92, ed. Grosart) the assertion that 'our
Sceane is more stately furnisht, ... and not consisting like [the foreign scene] of a
Pantaloun, a Curtizan, and a Zanie, but of Emperours,' &c., from which it does not follow that the 'Pantaloun' never appeared at all in 'our sceane.' DYCE : *Il Pantalone*
means properly one of the regular characters in the old Italian comedy : 'There are
four standing characters that enter into every piece that comes on the stage, the Doctor, Harlequin, *Pantalone*, and Coviello. . . . . *Pantalone* is generally an old cully.'—
Addison's *Remarks on Several Parts of Italy*, &c. p. 101, ed. 1705. HALLIWELL :
It is possible that the term may here be applied more generally. Howell, 1660,
makes a pantaloon synonymous with a 'Venetian magnifico.' In Calot's series of
plates illustrating the Italian comedy is one in which the ancient pantaloon is represented as wearing slippers. COWDEN-CLARKE : A comic character of the Italian
stage (of Venetian origin, and taken typically of Venice, as *Arlechino* is of Bergamo,
Policinello of Naples, *Stenterello* of Florence, &c.), wearing slippers, spectacles, and
a pouch, and invariably represented as old, lean, and gullible. WRIGHT : Torriano
in his Italian Dictionary, 1659, gives, 'Pantalone, a Pantalone, a covetous and yet
amorous old dotard, properly applyed in Comedies unto a Venetian.'

167. **on nose . . . on side**] For instances of the omission of *the* after prepositions
in adverbial phrases, see Abbott, § 90.

171. **his sound**] For 'its sound;' for the use of *its*, see Abbott, § 228.

174. **Sans**] See line 34, above. HALLIWELL : The present line may have been

Enter Orlando with Adam. 175

Du Sen. Welcome : fet downe your venerable burthen, and let him feede. 177

175. Scene X. Pope+. 177. *and...feede*] Separate line, Rowe
ii et seq.

---

suggested by the following description of the appearance of the ghost of Admiral
Coligny on the night after his murder at the massacre of St. Bartholomew, which
occurs in Garnier's poem, the *Henriade*, 1594: 'Sans pieds, sans mains, sans nez,
sans oreilles, sans yeux, Meurtri de toutes parts.'

176. **venerable burthen**] CAPELL (p. 60, *b*): A traditional story was current
some years ago about Stratford, that a very old man of that place, of weak intellects,
but yet related to Shakespeare, being asked by some of his neighbors what he remembered about him, answer'd, that he saw him once brought on the stage on another
man's back; which answer was apply'd by the hearers to his having seen him perform in this scene the part of Adam. That he should have done so is made not
unlikely by another constant tradition, that he was no extraordinary actor, and therefore took no parts upon him but such as this: for which he might also be peculiarly
fitted by an accidental lameness, which, as he himself tells us twice in his Sonnets,
befell him in some part of life; without saying how, or when, of what sort, or in what
degree; but his expressions seem to indicate latterly. [It is well to mark the source
of this monstrous idea that Shakespeare was lame, because, forsooth, in *Sonnet* 37 he
says: 'So I, made lame by fortune's dearest spite,' and 'Speak of my lameness and
I straight will halt' in *Sonnet* 89. Every now and then, in the revolving years, this
idea is blazoned forth as new and original by some one who discovers the *Sonnets*—by
reading them for the first time. Let the original folly rest with Capell; few of Shakespeare's editors can better afford to bear it. The story (which is a pleasant one, and
one, I think, we should all like to believe) that Shakespeare acted the part of Adam,
Steevens, also, found in 'the manuscript papers of the late Mr Oldys,' and thus tells it,
Var. 1793, vol. i, p. 65:] Mr Oldys had covered several quires of paper with laborious
collections for a regular life of our author. From these I have made the following
extracts: 'One of Shakespeare's younger brothers, who lived to a good old age, even
some years, as I compute, after the restoration of *King Charles II*, would in his younger
days come to London to visit his brother *Will*, as he called him, and be a spectator
of him as an actor in some of his own plays. This custom, as his brother's fame
enlarged, and his dramatick entertainments grew the greatest support of our principal,
if not of all our theatres, he continued it seems so long after his brother's death as
even to the latter end of his own life. The curiosity at this time of the most noted
actors [exciting them—*Steevens*] to learn something from him of his brother, &c., they
justly held him in the highest veneration. And it may be well believed, as there was
besides a kinsman and descendant of the family, who was then a celebrated actor among
them [Charles Hart. See Shakespeare's Will.—*Steevens*], this opportunity made them
greedily inquisitive into every little circumstance, more especially in his dramatick
character, which his brother could relate of him. But he, it seems, was so stricken
in years, and possibly his memory so weakened with infirmities (which might make
him the easier pass for a man of weak intellects), that he could give them but little
light into their inquiries; and all that could be recollected from him of his brother
Will in that station was, the faint, general, and almost lost ideas he had of having

9

Orl.   I thanke you moſt for him.   178
Ad.   So had you neede,
I ſcarce can ſpeake to thanke you for my ſelfe.   180
Du. Sen.   Welcome, fall too : I wil not trouble you,
As yet to queſtion you about your fortunes :
Giue vs ſome Muſicke, and good Cozen, ſing.   183

---

once seen him act a part in one of his own comedies, wherein, being to personate a
decrepit old man, he wore a long beard, and appeared so weak and drooping and
unable to walk, that he was forced to be supported and carried by another person to
a table, at which he was seated among some company, who were eating, and one of
them sung a song.' MALONE discredits this story as far as the brother of Shakespeare
is concerned, and, after a heartsome sneer at poor old Oldys, says : From Shakespeare's not taking notice of any of his brothers or sisters in his Will, except Joan
Hart, I think it highly probable that they were all dead in 1616, except her, at least
all those of the whole blood; though in the Register there is no entry of the burial
of his brother Gilbert, antecedent to the death of Shakespeare, or at any subsequent
period ; but we know that he survived his brother Edmund. The truth is, that this
account of our poet's having performed the part of an old man in one of his own
comedies, came originally from Mr Thomas Jones of Tarbick, in Worcestershire, who
related it from the information, not of one of Shakespeare's *brothers*, but of a *relation*
of our poet, who lived to a good old age, and who had seen him act in his youth.
Mr Jones's informer might have been Mr Richard Quiney, who lived in London, and
died at Stratford in 1656, at the age of 69; or of Mr Thomas Quiney, our poet's son-
in-law, who lived, I believe, till 1663, and was twenty-seven years old when his
father-in-law died; or some one of the family of Hathaway. Mr Thomas Hathaway,
I believe, Shakespeare's brother-in-law, died at Stratford in 1654–5, at the age of 85.—
Var. 1821, ii, 286. HALLIWELL-PHILLIPPS (*Outlines*, p. 160, 5th ed.) gives the foregoing story of Oldys, and adds : This account contains several discrepancies, but there
is reason for believing that it includes a glimmering of truth which is founded on an
earlier tradition. COLLIER (*Seven Lectures, &c. by Coleridge*, 1856, p. xvi) : I have
a separate note of what Coleridge once said on the subject of the acting powers of
Shakespeare, to which I can assign no date; it is in these words : ' It is my persua-
sion, indeed, my firm conviction, so firm that nothing can shake it—the rising of Shakespeare's spirit from the grave, modestly confessing his own deficiencies, could not alter
my opinion—that Shakespeare, in the best sense of the word, was a very great actor;
nothing can exceed the judgement he displays upon that subject. He may not have
had the physical advantages of Burbage or Field; but they would never have become
what they were without his most able and sagacious instructions; and what would
either of them have been without Shakespeare's plays ? Great dramatists make great
actors. But looking at him merely as a performer, I am certain that he was greater
as Adam, in *As You Like It*, than Burbage as Hamlet or Richard the Third. Think
of the scene between him and Orlando; and think again, that the actor of that part
had to carry the author of that play in his arms ! Think of having had Shakespeare
in one's arms ! It is worth having died two hundred years ago to have heard Shakespeare deliver a single line. He must have been a great actor.'

182. **to question**] That is, by questioning. So, too, I, i, 109; III, v, 66 : ' Foule
is most foule, being foule *to be* a scoffer,' *i. e.* in being. See Abbott, § 356.

Song.

Blow, blow, thou winter winde,   185
Thou art not so vnkinde, as mans ingratitude
Thy tooth is not so keene, becaufe thou art not feene,
        although thy breath be rude.   188

184. Amiens sings. Johns.   187. becaufe...feene] *Thou causest not*
186, 187. As four lines, Pope.   *that teen* Han.

186. **vnkinde**] MALONE: That is, thy action is not so contrary to thy *kind*, or to human nature, as the ingratitude of man. So in *Ven. and Ad.* 204: 'O, had thy mother borne so hard a mind, She had not brought forth thee, but died unkind.' DYCE: That is, unnatural. HALLIWELL: But the ordinary meaning of the term makes here a good, perhaps, a finer, sense. WRIGHT: This literal sense of the word [*i. e.* unnatural] appears to be the most prominent here.

187. **seene**] WARBURTON: This song is designed to suit the Duke's exiled condition, who had been ruined by *ungrateful flatterers.* Now the 'winter wind,' the song says, is to be preferred to 'man's ingratitude.' But why? Because it is not *seen.* But this was not only an aggravation of the injury, as it was done in secret, *not seen,* but was the very circumstance that made the keenness of the ingratitude of his faithless courtiers. Without doubt Shakespeare wrote the line thus: 'Because thou art not *sheen,' i. e.* smiling, shining, like an ungrateful court-servant, who flatters while he wounds, which was a very good reason for giving the 'winter wind' the preference. The Oxford editor [*i. e.* Hanmer] who had this emendation communicated to him, takes occasion to alter the whole line thus: 'Thou causest not that teen.' But in his rage of correction [This, from Warburton.—ED.] he forgot to leave the reason, which is now wanting, Why the *winter wind* was to be preferred to *man's ingratitude.* JOHNSON: Warburton's emendation is enforced with more art than truth. That *sheen* signifies *shining* is easily proved, but when or where did it signify *smiling?* For my part, I question whether the original line is not lost, and this substituted merely to fill up the measure and the rhyme. Yet even out of this line, by strong agitation, may sense be elicited, and sense not unsuitable to the occasion. 'Thou winter wind,' says the Duke [*sic*], 'thy rudeness gives the less pain *as thou art not seen,* as thou art an enemy that dost not brave us with thy presence, and whose unkindness is therefore not aggravated by insult.' FARMER: Perhaps it would be as well to read: 'Because *the heart's* not seen,' yᵉ *harts,* according to the ancient mode of writing, was easily corrupted. EDWARDS (p. 106): Shakespeare has equally forgotten, in the next stanza, to leave the reason, why a *freezing sky* is to be preferred to a *forgetful friend;* which, perhaps, may give a reasonable suspicion that the word 'because' in the first stanza may be corrupt. [In quoting this sentence Kenrick (p. 62) suggests that if 'because' is wrong, 'Shakespeare must use the adverb or preposition disjunctive *beside.*'] HEATH (p. 147): What the meaning of the common reading may be, it is extremely difficult to discover, which gives great ground for suspicion that it may be corrupt. Possibly it might be intended to be this: The impressions thou makest on us are not so cutting, because thou art an unseen agent, with whom we have not the least acquaintance or converse, and therefore have the less reason to repine at thy treatment of us. KENRICK (p. 65): The scoliasts seem to blunder in mistaking the sense of the word 'keen,' which they take to signify *sharp, cutting, piercing;* whereas

Heigh ho, fing heigh ho, vnto the greene holly,
Moft frendfhip, is fayning; moft Louing, meere folly: 190
The heigh ho, the holly,
This Life is moft iolly.

Freize, freize, thou bitter skie that doft not bight fo nigh
as benefitts forgot:
Though thou the waters warpe, thy fling is not fo fharpe,   195
as freind remembred not.
Heigh ho, fing, &c.   197

191. The] *Then* Rowe et seq.   193. bight] *bite* F_3F_4.
193. As two lines, Pope et seq.   196. remembred] *rememb'ring* Han.

---

it only means *eager, vehement;* a sense equally common with the former. The poet here speaks only of a keenness of appetite; he does not mention actual biting till he comes to address a more proper and powerful agent. Besides, if 'keen' here means *sharp, piercing,* this line hath the same meaning as [line 195] where the poet is at the last stage of his climax. And I think he would hardly be guilty of such a piece of tautology, in the space of so few lines, or address the less severe and powerful agent exactly in the same manner as he does that which is more so. STEEVENS: Compare *Love's Lab. L.* IV, iii, 105: 'Through the velvet leaves the *wind,* All *unseen,* can passage find.' MALONE: Again, in *Meas. for Meas.* III, i, 124: 'To be imprison'd in the *viewless winds.*' HARNESS: I never perceived any difficulty till it was pointed out by the commentators, but supposed the words to mean that the inclemency of the wind was not so severely felt as the ingratitude of man, because the foe is unseen, *i. e.* unknown, and the sense of injury is not heightened by the recollection of any former kindness. STAUNTON: If change is imperative, one less violent [than Warburton's or Farmer's] will afford a meaning quite in harmony with the sentiment of the song; we might read, 'Because thou art *foreseen.*' But the original text is, perhaps, susceptible of a different interpretation to that it has received. The poet certainly could not intend that the wintry blast was less cutting because invisible; he might mean, however, that the keenness of the wind's tooth was inherent, and not a quality developed (like the malice of a false friend) by the opportunity of inflicting a hurt unseen. REV. JOHN HUNTER: I have not met with any satisfactory explanation of this line. If the text be accurate, I would venture to interpret as follows: 'It is not because thou art invisible, and canst do hurt in secret and with impunity, that thou bitest so keenly as thou dost.' Here I do not regard the expression 'so keen' as meaning 'so keen as the tooth of ingratitude.' [It is highly probable that Harness speaks for us all, and that our first intimation of a difficulty comes from the commentators. Sufficing paraphrases are given, I think, by Dr Johnson, Heath, and Harness.—ED.]

189. **Heigh ho**] WHITE: The manner in which this is said and sung by intelligent people makes it worth noticing that this is '*hey ho!*' and not the 'heigh, ho!' (pronounced *high, ho!*) of a sigh. It should be pronounced *hay-ho.*

189. **holly**] HALLIWELL: Songs of the holly were current long before the time of Shakespeare. It was the emblem of mirth.

195. **warpe**] KENRICK: The surface of such waters as is here meant, so long as they remain unfrozen, is apparently a perfect plane; whereas when they are frozen,

[Though thou the waters warpe]

this surface deviates from its exact flatness, or *warps*. This is peculiarly remarkable in small ponds, the surface of which, when frozen, forms a regular concave, the ice on the sides rising higher than that in the middle. JOHNSON: To *warp* is to *turn*, and to *turn* is to *change :* when milk is *changed* by curdling, we say it is *turned ;* when water is *changed* or *turned* by frost, Shakespeare says it is *curdled*. To be *warp'd* is only to be changed from its natural state. STEEVENS: Dr Farmer supposes *warp'd* to mean the same as *curdled*, and adds that a similar idea occurs in *Coriol*. V, iii, 66: '—the icicle That's curdled by the frost.' HOLT WHITE: Among a collection of Saxon adages in Hickes's *Thesaurus*, vol. i, p. 221, the succeeding appears: 'winter sceal geweorpan weder,' *winter shall warp water*. [See Wright's note, *post*.] So that Shakespeare's expression was anciently proverbial. WHITER: 'Warp' signifies to *contract*, and is so used without any allusion to the precise physical process which takes place in that contraction. Cold and winter have been always described as *contracting ;* heat and summer as *dissolving* or *softening*. The cold is said to 'warp the waters' when it contracts them into the solid substance of ice and suffers them no longer to continue in a *liquid* or *flowing* state. NARES: It appears that to 'warp' sometimes was used poetically in the sense of to *weave*, from the *warp* which is first prepared in weaving cloth. Hence [the present passage] may be explained, 'though thou weave the waters into a firm texture.' CALDECOTT: In III, iii, 80, Jaques says, 'then one of you will prove a shrunk pannel; and, like green timber, warp, warp;' and from the inequalities it makes in the surface of the earth the mold-*warp* (or mole) is so denominated. And see Golding's *Ovid*, II [p. 22 verso. ed. 1567]: 'Hir handes gan warpe and into pawes ylfauordly to grow.' 'Curvarique manus et aduncos crescere in ungues Cœperunt.' [It is proper to repeat the foregoing notes here, erroneous in the main though they be, because some of them, in whole or in part, are found in modern editions. But the note which supersedes all others, and which conclusively determines the meaning, is as follows:] WRIGHT: In the Anglosaxon *weorpan*, or *wyrpan*, from which 'warp' is derived, there are the two ideas of throwing and turning. By the former of these it is connected with the German *werfen*, and by the latter with Anglosaxon *hweorfan* and Gothic *hvairban*. The prominent idea of the English 'warp' is that of turning or changing, from which that of shrinking or contracting, as wood does, is derivative. So in *Meas. for Meas*. I, i, 15, Shakespeare uses it as equivalent to 'swerve,' to which it may be etymologically akin: 'There is our commission From which we would not have you warp.' Hence 'warped,' equivalent to *distorted*, in *Lear*, III, vi, 56: 'And here's another, whose warp'd looks proclaim What store her heart is made on.' With which compare *Wint. Tale*, I, ii, 365: 'This is strange: methinks My favour here begins to warp.' And *All's Well*, V, iii, 49: 'Contempt his scornful perspective did lend me Which warp'd the line of every other favour.' In the present passage Shakespeare seems to have had the same idea in his mind. The effect of the freezing wind is to change the aspect of the water, and we need not go so far as Whiter, who insists that 'warp' here means to contract, and so accurately describes the action of frost upon water. A fragment from a collection of gnomic sayings, preserved in Anglosaxon in the Exeter (MS), has been quoted by Holt White and repeated by subsequent commentators under the impression that it illustrates this passage. This impression is founded on a mistake. [White renders the fragment 'winter shall warp water.'] But, unfortunately, 'water' is not mentioned, and the word so rendered is 'weather,' that is, 'fair weather,' and is moreover the subject of the following and not the object

Duke Sen. If that you were the good Sir *Rowlands* fon,   198
As you haue whifper'd faithfully you were,
And as mine eye doth his effigies witneffe,   200
Moft truly limn'd, and liuing in your face,
Be truly welcome hither : I am the Duke
That lou'd your Father, the refidue of your fortune,
Go to my Caue, and tell mee.   Good old man,
Thou art right welcome, as thy mafters is :   205
Support him by the arme : giue me your hand,
And let me all your fortunes vnderftand.   *Exeunt.*   207

198, 199. *were*] *are* Dyce conj.   205. *mafters*] F₁.

---

of the preceding verb. [In Caldecott's quotation from Golding's *Ovid*] the idea of bending or turning, and so distorting, is again the prominent one. We may, therefore, understand by the warping of the waters either the change produced in them by the action of the frost or the bending and ruffling of their surface caused by the wintry wind.

196. remembred not] CAPELL (p. 61): This is subject to great ambiguity in this place; as signifying who is not remember'd by his friend, as well as who has no remembrance of his friend; which was sometimes its signification of old, and is so here. MALONE: 'Remember'd' for *remembering*. So afterwards, III, v, 136: 'And now I am remembred,' *i. e.* 'and now that I *bethink* me.' WHITER replies to Malone: Certainly not. If ingratitude consists in one friend not *remembering* another, it surely must consist likewise in one friend not *being* remem*ber'd by* another. So in the former line, ' benefits forgot' *by* our friend, or our friend forget*ting* benefits, will prove him equally ungrateful. MOBERLY: As what an unremembered friend feels—compendiary comparison.

199. whisper'd] By the use of this word we are artfully told that the Duke and Orlando had carried on a subdued conversation during the music. How old this practice is, and what vitality it has !—ED.

200. effigies] A trisyllable, with the accent on the second syllable.

203. residue] By considering the unaccented *i* in the middle of this word as dropped, Abbott, § 467, thus scans: ' That lóv'd | your fáther: | the rési | due óf | your fórtune.' [Again, I doubt.—ED.]

205. Thou] Note the change of address to a servant.—ED.

Actus Tertius . Scena Prima.

Enter Duke, Lords, & Oliuer.

Du. Not fee him fince ? Sir , fir, that cannot be :
But were I not the better part made mercie ,
I fhould not feeke an abfent argument·
Of my reuenge, thou prefent : but looke to it,   5
Finde out thy brother wherefoere he is,
Seeke him with Candle : bring him dead, or liuing
Within this tweluemonth, or turne thou no more
To feeke a liuing in our Territorie.
Thy Lands and all things that thou doft call thine,   10
Worth feizure, do we feize into our hands,
Till thou canft quit thee by thy brothers mouth,
Of what we thinke againft thee.

Ol. Oh that your Highneffe knew my heart in this :
I neuer lou'd my brother in my life.   15

*Duke.*More villaine thou. Well pufh him out of dores

---

1. The Palace. Rowe.

   Duke] Duke junior. Cap.   Duke
Frederick Mal.

   2. *fee*] *seen* Coll. (MS) ii, iii, Sing.
Ktly, Huds.

4. *feeke*] *fee* Ff.

7. *with Candle*] *instantly* Cartwright.

8. *tweluemonth*] *tweluemoneth* F_2F_3.

16. *Well pufh*] *Well—Push* Johns.

---

3. the better part] See, for similar omissions of prepositions, Abbott, § 202.   Cf.
'all points,' I, iii, 123.

4. argument] JOHNSON: An argument is used for the *contents* of a book; thence
Shakespeare considered it as meaning the *subject*, and then used it for *subject* in yet
another sense.   [Cf. I, ii, 278.]

5. thou present] ABBOTT, § 381 : The participle is sometimes implied in the case
of a simple word, such as 'being.'

7. Candle] STEEVENS: Probably alluding to St Luke, xv, 8.

11. seize] The usual legal term for taking possession.   It is doubtful, however,
whether 'seizure' be used in a legal sense, although I am not sure that a nice legal
point might not be herein detected by a wild enthusiast for the still wilder theory
that Shakespeare was not the author of these plays.   As there can be in strict law no
'seizure' until after 'forfeiture,' the forfeiture in the case before us is made alternative
upon Oliver's producing the body of Orlando, in which case a 'verbal seizure' will
hold.   Clearly, therefore, it is this seizure *in posse* which is here intended, and not a
seizure which can follow only conviction and forfeiture; the term is thus used in its
strictest, choicest, legal sense, and approves the consummate legal knowledge of Ba—
I should say, Shakespeare.—ED.

And let my officers of fuch a nature   17
Make an extent vpon his houfe and Lands:
Do this expediently, and turne him going.   *Exeunt*   19

18. **extent**] LORD CAMPBELL (p. 49): A deep technical knowledge of law is here displayed, howsoever it may have been acquired. The usurping Duke wishing all the real property of Oliver to be seized, awards a writ of *extent* against him, in the language which would be used by the Lord Chief Baron of the Court of Exchequer, an *extendi facias* applying to house and lands, as a *fieri facias* would apply to goods and chattels, or a *capias ad satisfaciendum* to the person. [I cannot but think that the present is a passage which so far from showing any ' deep technical knowledge of law,' shows not much more than the ordinary knowledge (perhaps even a little vague at that), which must have been almost universal in Shakespeare's day, when statutes merchant and statutes staple were in common use and wont. It may be even possible that there is here an instance of that confusion which follows like a fate dramatists and novelists who invoke the law as a *Deus ex machinâ*. That Shakespeare is wonderfully correct in general is continually manifest. But I doubt if the present be one of the happiest examples. Lord Campbell, when he says that the Duke aims at Oliver's realty by this writ of *extent*, overlooked the fact that the Duke had already ' seized' not only all Oliver's realty, but even all his personalty, by an act of arbitrary power. After this display on the part of the Duke that he should invoke the aid of the sheriff and proceed according to due process of law and apply for a writ of *extendi facias*, which could only issue on due forfeiture of a recognizance or acknowledged debt (under circumstances which had not here occurred), is inconsequential, to say the least, and betokens either a confused knowledge of law (which could be only doubtfully imputed to Shakespeare), or an entire indifference to such trivial details or sharp quillets which only load without helping the progress of the plot. It was dramatically necessary that Oliver should be set adrift, houseless and landless, in order that he and Orlando should hereafter meet; how he was to be rendered houseless and landless was of little moment, the use of a legal term or so would be all-sufficient to create the required impression; officers of the law are ordered to make ' an extent' upon his house and lands, and the end is gained. A ' deep technical knowledge' of the writ of *extendi facias* in Shakespeare's day would know that with the lands and goods of the debtor in cases where the Crown was concerned, as here, the sheriff was commanded to take the body also; but this would never do in the present case; Oliver must not himself be detained; he has to be sent forth, somewhere to meet with Orlando; either the sheriff will have to apply to the Court for instructions or the writ must be radically modified. In short, is it not clear that the law here, as it is in *The Merchant of Venice*, is invoked merely for dramatic purposes, and was neither intended to be shrilly sounded nor technically exact ?—ED.]

19. **expediently**] JOHNSON: That is, expeditiously. [For other instances of ' expedient,' in the sense of *expeditious*, see Schmidt, *s. v.*]

Scena Secunda.

Enter Orlando.

Orl.   Hang there my verſe, in witneſſe of my loue,
And thou thrice crowned Queene of night ſuruey
With thy chaſte eye, from thy pale ſpheare aboue
Thy Huntreſſe name, that my full life doth ſway.   5
O *Roſalind*, theſe Trees ſhall be my Bookes,
And in their barkes my thoughts Ile charraƈter,
That euerie eye, which in this Forreſt lookes,
Shall ſee thy vertue witneſt euery where.
Run, run *Orlando*, carue on euery Tree,   10
The faire, the chaſte, and vnexpreſſiue ſhee.   *Exit*

---

1. The Forrest. Rowe.   3. *thrice crowned*] *thrice - crowned*
   Orlando] with a Paper. Cap.   Theob. et seq.
                                                5. *name*] *fame* Anon.

---

3. **thrice crowned Queene**] JOHNSON: Alluding to the triple character of Proserpine, Cynthia, and Diana, given by some mythologists to the same goddess, and com-
prised in these memorial lines: ' Terret, lustrat, agit; Proserpina, Luna, Diana; Ima,
superna, feras; sceptro, fulgore, sagittis.'   SINGER: Shakespeare was doubtless familiar with Chapman's *Hymns*, and the following from *Hymnus in Cynthiam*, 1594, may
have been in his mind: ' Nature's bright *eye-sight*, and the night's fair soul, That with
thy *triple forehead* dost control Earth, seas, and hell.'   [Although this has been
repeated by four or five subsequent editors, I fail to detect any grounds for the supposition that Shakespeare had ever seen the passage.—ED.]

5. **Thy Huntresse name**] COWDEN-CLARKE: Orlando calls his mistress one of
Diana's huntresses, as being a votaress of her order; a maiden lady, a virgin princess.
Just as Hero is styled the ' virgin knight' of the ' goddess of the night.'

5. **sway**] STEEVENS: So in *Twelfth N.* II, v, 118: ' M, O, A, I, doth sway my
life.'

11. **vnexpressive**] JOHNSON: For inexpressible.   MALONE: Milton also: ' With
unexpressive notes to Heaven's new-born Heir.'—*Hymn to the Nativity*, 116.   CAL-
DECOTT quotes *Lycidas*, 176: 'And hears the unexpressive nuptial song.'   WALKER
(*Crit.* i, 179) gives many instances of adjectives in *-ive* that ' are frequently used by
Shakespeare and his contemporaries, so to speak, in a passive sense.'   On p. 182 he
asks: ' Did this usage originate in the unmanageable length of some of the adjectives
in *able* and *ible*, as *unsuppressible, uncomprehensible ?*'   The corresponding section in
Abbott is § 3.

11. **shee**] For other instances where *he* and *she* are used for *man* and *woman*, see
Abbott, § 224.   See line 378, *post*.

Enter Corin & Clowne.   12

Co. And how like you this ſhepherds life Mr *Touchſtone*?

Clow. Truely Shepheard, in reſpect of it ſelfe, it is a
good life ; but in reſpect that it is a shepheards life, it is   15
naught. In reſpect that it is ſolitary, I like it verie well :
but in reſpect that it is priuate, it is a very vild life. Now
in reſpect it is in the fields, it pleaſeth mee well : but in
reſpect it is not in the Court, it is tedious. As it is a ſpare
life(looke you) it fits my humor well : but as there is no   20
more plentie in it,   it goes much againſt my ſtomacke.
Has't any Philoſophie in thee ſhepheard *?*

Cor. No more, but that I know the more one ſickens,
the worſe at eaſe he is : and that hee that wants money,
meanes, and content, is without three good frends . That   25
the propertie of raine is to wet, and fire to burne : That
pood paſture makes fat ſheepe : and that a great cauſe of
the night, is lacke of the Sunne : That hee that hath learned no wit by Nature, nor Art, may complaine of good
breeding, or comes of a very dull kindred.   30

Clo. Such a one is a naturall Philoſopher :

12. Scene III. Pope+.

13. *Mr*] M. F$_3$F$_4$. *master* Steev. et
seq.

22. *Has't*] *Hast* Pope.

27. *pood*] F$_1$.

29, 30. *good...or*] *bad breeding, and
Han. gross...or* Warb.

31, 32. Prose, Pope et seq.

22, 32. **Has't . . . Was't**] For instances of the omission of the pronoun, see
Abbott, § 401.

29. **complaine of**] JOHNSON : I am in doubt whether the custom of the language
in Shakespeare's time did not authorise this mode of speech, and make ' complain of
good breeding ' the same with ' complain *of the want of* good breeding.'   In the last
line of the *Mer. of Ven.* we find that to ' fear the keeping ' is to ' fear the *not* keeping.'   CAPELL : May complain of it for being no better, or for having taught them no
better.   WHITER : This is a mode of speech common, I believe, to all languages, and
occurred even before the time of Shakespeare : Εἴ τ' ἄρ' ὅγ' εὐχωλῆς ἐπιμέμφεται, εἴθ'
ἑκατόμβης.—*Il.* i, 65—' Whether he complains of *the want of* prayers or of sacrifice.'

31. **naturall**] WARBURTON : The shepherd had said all the philosophy he knew
was the property of things, that ' rain wetted,' ' fire burnt,' &c.   And the Clown's
reply, in a satire on physicks or natural philosophy, though introduced with a quibble,
is extremely just.   For the natural philosopher is indeed as ignorant (notwithstanding
all his parade of knowledge) of the *efficient* cause of things as the rustic.   It appears,
from a thousand instances, that our poet was well acquainted with the physicks of his
time ; and his great penetration enabled him to see this remediless defect of it.
STEEVENS : Shakespeare is responsible for the *quibble* only ; let the commentator
answer for the *refinement*.   MASON : The clown calls Corin a ' natural philosopher,'

Was't euer in Court, Shepheard?   32
   Cor. No truly.
   Clo. Then thou art damn'd.
   Cor. Nay, I hope.   35
   Clo. Truly thou art damn'd, like an ill roafted Egge,
all on one fide.
   Cor. For not being at Court? your reafon.
   Clo. Why, if thou neuer was't at Court, thou neuer
faw'ft good manners : if thou neuer faw'ft good maners,   40

32, 39. *was't*] Ff, Rowe. *wast* Pope.   35. *hope.*] *hope*— Rowe et seq.

---

because he reasons from his observations on nature. MALONE: A *natural* being a
common term for a fool, Touchstone, perhaps, means to quibble on the word. CAL-
DECOTT: So far as reasoning from his observations on nature, in such sort a philosopher; and yet as having been schooled only by nature, so far no better than a fool, a
motley fool. [See I, ii, 51.]

36, 37. **Truly . . . side**] JOHNSON: Of this jest I do not fully comprehend the
meaning. STEEVENS: There is a proverb that 'a fool is the best roaster of an egg,
because he is always turning it.' This will explain how an egg may be 'damn'd
all on one side'; but will not sufficiently show how Touchstone applies his simile
with propriety; unless he means that he who has not been at court is but *half* educated. MALONE: Touchstone only means to say that Corin is completely damn'd; as
irretrievably destroyed as an egg that is utterly spoiled in the roasting, by being done
all on one side only. [It is by no means easy to decide here on the best punctuation.
It is likely, I think, that it was the punctuation of the Folios which misled Dr Johnson and prevented him from seeing that 'all on one side' applies to the egg and not
to the 'damn'd.' An illustration of the perplexity which may attend the placing of
even a comma is to be found in the texts of the Cambridge Edition, of the Globe, and
of the Clarendon. In the first and second the text is punctuated: 'Thou art damned
like an ill-roasted egg, all on one side,' which is not good, and would not have helped
Dr Johnson. In the Clarendon Edition, however, WRIGHT, improving on the Cambridge and Globe texts, thus punctuates: 'Thou art damned, like an ill-roasted egg
all on one side,' which would have made the jest as clear to Dr Johnson as it does to
us all.—ED.]

39, &c. WARBURTON: This reasoning is drawn up in imitation of Friar John's to
Panurge in Rabelais: 'Si tu es cocqu, *Ergo* ta femme sera belle, *Ergo* seras bien
traicté d'elle: *Ergo* tu auras des amys beaucoup; *ergo* tu seras saulué' [Liv. III,
chap. xxviii. Although there is no good ground for supposing that there is any connection here between Shakespeare and Rabelais, yet it is worth while to note all
these parallelisms; they have lately attracted attention at home and in Germany.
—ED.].

40. **maners**] CALDECOTT (*App.* p. 19): *Good* manners (and manners meant
morals, no such term as *morals* being to be found in the dictionaries of these times)
signified urbanity or civility, *i. e.* cultivated, polished manners as opposed to rusticity,
i. e. coarse, unformed, clownish, or *ill-manners*. He, then, that has only good principles and good conduct, without good breeding and civility, is short of perfection by
the *half;* and for want of this other half of that *good*, which is necessary to salvation,

then thy manners muſt be wicked, and wickednes is ſin,   41
and ſinne is damnation: Thou art in a parlous ſtate ſhepheard.

Cor.   Not a whit *Touchſtone*, thoſe that are good maners at the Court, are as ridiculous in the Countrey, as   45
the behauiour of the Countrie is moſt mockeable at the
Court.   You told me, you ſalute not at the Court, but
you kiſſe your hands; that courteſie would be vncleanlie
if Courtiers were ſhepheards.

Clo.   Inſtance, briefly : come, inſtance.   50

Cor.   Why we are ſtill handling our Ewes, and their
Fels you know are greaſie.

Clo.   Why do not your Courtiers hands ſweate ? and
is not the greaſe of a Mutton, as wholeſome as the ſweat   54

---

42. *parlous*] *par'lous* Cap.
44. Touchſtone] *Mr. Touchſtone* Cap.
Maſter Touchſtone Dyce iii, Huds.

44. *are*] *have* F₃F₄, Rowe i.
54. *a*] Om. F₃F₄, Rowe, Pope, Han.

---

or the perfect man, is like a half-roasted egg, damn'd on one side.   The earlier sense
of the word *manners*, as ' *manners* makyth man,' the motto of William of Wykeham
(and familiar to us almost as the Bible translation of the passage in Euripides : ' Evil
communications corrupt good manners '), occurs in the works of an old pedagogue :
' I wyll somewhat speke of the scholer's *maners* or duty : for *maners* (as they say)
maketh man.   De discipulorum *moribus* pauca contexam.   Nam *mores* (ut aiunt)
hominem exornant.'—*Vulgaria*, Roberti Whittintoni, 1521.   As it does in Milton's
Areopagitica : ' That also, which is impious or evil absolutely against faith or *manners*,
no law can possibly permit, that tends not to unlaw itself.'

42. **parlous**] RITSON (p. 133) : A corruption of *perilous*.   DYCE also gives *alarming, amazing, keen, shrewd*.   COLLIER suggests that it may even sometimes mean
talkative, ' as in Day's *Law Tricks*, 1608 : "A parlous youth, sharp and satirical."
Perhaps, being "sharp and satirical," the youth was on that account *perilous* or " parlous." '   WRIGHT : The spelling represents the pronunciation.

44. **Not a whit**] WRIGHT : As ' not ' is itself a contraction of *nâwiht* or *nawhit*,
' not a whit ' is redundant.

44. **Touchstone**] See Textual Notes.   DYCE : Capell is doubtless right.   The
Folio omits *Master*.   But compare Corin's first speech in this scene ; and let us
remember that the word *Master*, being often expressed in MSS by the single letter
M, might easily be omitted.   [How if Shakespeare intended to indicate increasing
familiarity on the part of the shepherd ?—ED.]

47. **but**] ABBOTT, § 125 : That is, without kissing your hands.

51. **still**] That is, constantly.   See Shakespeare, *passim*.

52. **Fels**] A word of common occurrence in this country.   From the fact that
Wright has an explanatory note, and cites Florio, Chapman, and the Wiclifite Version of Job, it is to be inferred that the word is measurably lost in England.—ED.

54. **a Mutton**] Compare 'As flesh of muttons.'—*Mer. of Ven.* I, iii, 172.

of a man? Shallow, ſhallow: A better inſtance I ſay: 55
Come.

Cor.   Beſides, our hands are hard.

Clo.   Your lips wil feele them the ſooner.   Shallow a-
gen : a more ſounder inſtance, come.

Cor.   And they are often tarr'd ouer, with the ſurgery   60
of our ſheepe : and would you haue vs kiſſe Tarre? The
Courtiers hands are perfum'd with Ciuet.

Clo.   Moſt ſhallow man : Thou wormes meate in re-
ſpeᶜt of a good peece of fleſh indeed : learne of the wiſe
and perpend : Ciuet is of a baſer birth then Tarre, the   65
verie vncleanly fluxe of a Cat.   Mend the inſtance Shepheard.

Cor.   You haue too Courtly a wit, for me, Ile reſt.

Clo.   Wilt thou reſt damn'd? God helpe thee ſhallow
man : God make inciſion in thee, thou art raw.   70

Cor.   Sir, I am a true Labourer, I earne that I eate: get
that I weare; owe no man hate, enuie no mans happi-   72

---

59. *more*] Om. Pope, Han.
60. *ouer, with*] *overwith* F₄.
62. *Courtiers*] *Countiers* F₂.
63. *ſhallow man:*] *shallow, man:*
Rowe.   *shallow man!* Theob.

63. *wormes meat*] *worms-meat* Rowe.
64. *fleſh indeed:*] *flesh, indeed!* Theob.
Warb.   *flesh—indeed!*— Johns.   *flesh:
Indeed!*— Steev.
indeed] *ndeed* F₂.

---

59. **more sounder**] For other instances of double comparatives, see Abbott, § 11.

63. **wormes meate**] WRIGHT: It is not impossible that this expression may have
struck Shakespeare in a book which he evidently read, the treatise of Vincentio
Saviolo, in which [*The 2. Booke*, between sig. G g 3 and H] a printer's device is found
with the motto : 'O WORMES MEATE.   O FROATH : O VANITIE.   WHY ART THOV SO
INSOLENT.'

65. **perpend**] SCHMIDT : A word used only by Polonius, Pistol, and the Clowns.

66. **Cat**] Cotgrave : ' Civette : f. Ciuet; also (the beasts that breeds it) a Ciuet
cat.'

70. **incision**] HEATH (p. 147) : That is, God give thee a better understanding;
thou art very raw and simple as yet.   The expression probably alludes to the common
proverbial saying, concerning a very silly fellow, that he ought to be cut for the simples.   CALDECOTT : That is, enlarge, open thy mind.   COLLIER : Heath's explanation seems supported by the next speech of Touchstone, ' That is another *simple* sense
in you.'   GRANT WHITE : The meaning of this phrase, which evidently had a well-
known colloquial significance, has not been satisfactorily explained.   Heath's explanation is the more plausible ; but the meaning has probably been lost.   WRIGHT : The
reference is to the old method of cure for most maladies by blood-letting.

70. **raw**] MALONE : That is, thou art ignorant, inexperienced.   [This word it is
which, to me, throws a doubt on the explanations that have been offered of ' incision.'
—ED.]

neſſe : glad of other mens good content with my harme :   73
and the greateſt of my pride, is to ſee my Ewes graze, &
my Lambes ſucke.   75

   Clo. That is ȧnother ſimple ſinne in you, to bring the
Ewes and the Rammes together, and to offer to get your
liuing, by the copulation of Cattle, to be bawd to a Bel-
weather, and to betray a ſhee-Lambe of a tweluemonth
to a crooked-pated olde Cuckoldly Ramme, out of all   80
reaſonable match. If thou bee'ſt not damn'd for this, the
diuell himſelfe will haue no ſhepherds, I cannot ſee elſe
how thou ſhouldſt ſcape.

   Cor. Heere comeṡ yong M^r*Ganimed*, my new Miſtriſſes Brother.   85

Enter Roſalind.

Roſ. From the eaſt to weſterne Inde,
no iewel is like Roſalinde,
Hir worth being mounted on the winde,
through all the world beares Roſalinde.   90
All the pictures faireſt Linde,
are but blacke to Roſalinde :   92

73. *good*] *good,* Ff et seq.
78. *bawd*] *a bawd* F₃F₄, Rowe+.
79. *tweluemonth*] *twelvemoneth* F₃. *twelve-month old* Han.
82. *elſe*] Om. F₃F₄, Rowe.
84. *yong*] Om. F₃F₄, Rowe.
   Mr] *M.* F₂. *master* Steev. et seq.
84, 85. *Miſtriſſes*] *mistress'* Cald. Knt, Wh. i.
86. Scene IV. Pope+.

86. Enter...] Enter...with a paper. Rowe.
87. *weſterne*] *the western* Pope, Han. Inde] Jude F₄.
89. Hir] F₂.
90. *beares*] beards F₄.
91. Linde] F₂F₃. Lind F₄, Rowe. *limn'd* Johns. Cap. Mal. '90. *lin'd* Pope et cet.

---

   73. **harme**] KNIGHT : Resigned to any evil. ROLFE : 'Patient in tribulation.'

   84. **Mistrisses**] KEIGHTLEY (*Exp.* 159) : Though it stands thus in the Folio, metre and the usage of the time reject the *s.* [*Aliquando dormitat,* &c. There is no metre here to demand a change.—ED.]

   87. **Inde**] WALKER (*Crit.* iii, 62) : This is the old pronunciation of *Ind,* or rather, as in the Folio, *Inde.* Fairfax's *Tasso,* B. v, st. lii, 'And kill their kings from Egypt unto Inde,' rhyming with *mind* and *inclin'd :* and so B. vii, st. lxix, *finde—Inde—binde.* Spenser, *Faerie Queene,* B. i, C. v, st. iv, *Ynd* (*Ind*), rhyming with *bynd* and *assynd.* And so C. v, st. ii, *behind, unkind, find, Ynd.* Drayton, *Poly-olbion,* Song ii, ' ships That from their anchoring bays have travelled to find Large China's wealthy realmes, and view'd the either Inde.' Sylvester's *Dubartas,* ii. ii. ii. ed. 1641, p. 124, ' More golden words, than in his crown there shin'd Pearls, diamonds, and other gems of Inde.' Carew, ed. Clarke, cxxi, p. 164, ' Go I to Holland, France, or furthest Inde, I change but only countries, not my mind.' Did not Milton thus pronounce it, *Par.*

> *Let no face bee kept in mind,*   93
>   *but the faire of Rofalinde.*

Clo.   Ile rime you fo, eight yeares together ; dinners,   95
and fuppers, and fleeping hours excepted : it is the right
Butter-womens ranke to Market.   97

---

94. faire of] moft fair F_3F_4, Rowe i.   Var. '21, Cald. Knt, Sing. Hal. Ktly,
face of Rowe ii+, Cap. Dyce iii, Huds.   Coll. iii.
fair face of Ktly conj.   97. *ranke*] *rate* Han. Johns. Steev.
97. *womens*] *woman's* Johns. Steev.   Mal. *canter* Cartwright.

L, ii, 2?—' High on a throne of royal state, that far Outshone the wealth of Ormus or
of Ind.' WRIGHT: In *Love's Lab. L.* IV, iii, 222, 'Inde' rhymes with 'blind.'

91. **Linde**] STEEVENS: That is, most fairly delineated. WHITER: The most
beautiful *lines* or touches exhibited by art are inferior to the natural traits of beauty
which belong to Rosalind.

93, 94. **face . . . faire**] STEEVENS: 'Fair' is *beauty, complexion.* Compare
Lodge's *Novel:* 'Then muse not nymphes, though I bemone The absence of faire
Rosalynde, Since for her *faire* there is fairer none.' [See Appendix, *Rosalyndes
Description;* in Rosader's *Third Sonnet* 'faire' is four times used in the sense of
beauty. Walker (*Crit.* i, 327) proposed to read *fair* in line 93; Dyce, who followed
Rowe in reading *face* in line 94, objected to it on account of 'fairest' just above. Both
changes, Rowe's and Walker's, are plausible and attractive, but we ought always reso-
lutely to set our fair faces against any change which is not imperatively demanded;
as Dr Johnson says, the compositors who had Shakespeare's text before them are more
likely to have read it right than we who read it only in imagination.—ED.]

96. **right**] True, exact, downright. See line 119, *post,* 'the right vertue of the
Medler.'

97. **ranke**] GREY (i, 180): A friend puts the qu. If 'butter-woman's *rant at
market* ' might not be more proper. CAPELL (p. 61): 'Rank' means the order
observ'd by such women; travelling all in one road, with exact intervals between
horse and horse. STEEVENS: The sense designed might have been, it is such wretched
rhyme as the butter-woman sings as she is *riding to* market. So, in Churchyard's
Charge, 1580, 'And use a kinde of *riding rime.*' Again in his *Farewell from the
Courte:* 'A man maie, says he, use a kinde of *ridyng rime.*' [Steevens also refers
to the Scotch *ratt rime,* which Jamieson, *s. v.,* defines as 'any thing repeated by rote,
especially if of the doggerel kind.'] HENLEY: The clown is here speaking in reference to the ambling pace of the metre, which, after giving a specimen of, to prove
his assertion, he affirms to be 'the very false gallop of verses.' MALONE: A passage
in *All's Well,* IV, i, 44: 'Tongue, I must put you into a butter-woman's mouth, and
buy myself another of Bajazet's mule, if you prattle me into these perils,' once induced
me to think that the volubility of the butter-woman selling her wares at market was
alone in our author's thoughts, and that he wrote '*rate at* market' [which is a modification of the emendation proposed by Grey's 'friend.'—ED.]; but I am now persuaded that Hanmer's emendation is right. The *hobbling* metre of these verses (says
Touchstone) is like the *ambling, shuffling* pace of a butter-woman's horse, going to
market. The same kind of imagery is found in *1 Hen. IV:* III, i, 134: 'mincing
poetry; 'Tis like the forced gait of a shuffling nag.' WHITER (p. 30): If *rate* con-

[Butter-womens ranke to Market]

veys a sense suitable to the occasion, 'rank' will certainly be preferable; as it expresses the same thing with an additional idea; and perhaps the very idea in which the chief force of the comparison is placed. 'The right Butter-women's *rank* to market' means the *jog-trot rate* (as it is vulgarly called) with which Butter-women uniformly travel *one after another* in their road to market; in its application to Orlando's poetry, it means a *set* or *string* of verses in the *same coarse cadence* and *vulgar uniformity of rhythm.* CALDECOTT: In the same sense we have, 'The *rank* of oziers by the murmuring stream.'—IV, iii, 83. [To Steevens's instances of *riding* rhymes Caldecott adds from Puttenham's *Arte of English Poesie*, p. 76, ed. Arber:] 'Chaucer's other verses of the Canterbury Tales be but riding ryme, neuerthelesse very well becomming,' &c. [Guest (*Hist. of Eng. Rhythms*, vol. ii, p. 238) says: 'The metre of five accents with couplet rhyme, may have got its earliest name of 'riding rhyme' from the *mounted* pilgrims of the Canterbury Tales.'—ED.] KNIGHT: We think that Whiter's explanation is right; and that Shakespeare, moreover, had in mind the *pack-horse* roads, where one traveller must follow another in single *rank.* WALKER (*Crit.* iii, 62): Not, I think, 'rhyme' (rime—*ranke*), on account of the repetition. [This I do not understand.—ED.] At any rate, *rank* is wrong. [To this Lettsom adds the following foot-note:] 'Rank,' no doubt, is rank nonsense. . . . . Hanmer's *rate* seems to me the genuine word. Even Whiter pays it an involuntary homage, when he explains *rank* as 'the jog-trot *rate* with which butter-women uniformly travel one after another in their road to market'; [This shows that Lettsom had not looked up Whiter's note in the original, but had taken the final sentence, which alone is given in the Var. of '21.—ED.] 'one after another' is added to save 'rank,' as if *rank* meant *file.* Butter-women, going each from her solitary farm to the nearest market-town, would travel most of their way alone, and the critics, I suspect, would never have dreamt of drawing them up in rank or file, if they had not had a conjecture to attack. [DYCE, after quoting this note, quietly adds: For my own part, I think 'rank' the true reading.] HALLIWELL: The term 'rank' is of constant occurrence in the sense of range, line, file, order; in fact, to [*sic*] any things following each other. Thus Browne, *Britannia's Pastorals*, speaks of trees 'circling in a ranke.' The more common meaning is row. 'Range all thy swannes, faire Thames, together on a rancke.'—Drayton's *Shepherd's Garland*, 1593. 'There be thirty egges laide in a *rancke*, every one three foote from another.'—Hood's *Elements of Arithmeticke*, 1596. 'Short be the rank of pearls circling her tongue.'—Cotgrave's *Wits Interpreter*, 1671. STAUNTON: Whiter's explanation is not satisfactory. From a passage in Drayton's poem, *The Shepherd's Sirena*, it might be inferred that 'rank' was a familiar term for *chorus* or *rhyme:* 'On thy bank, In a rank, Let thy swans sing her.' And 'butter-women's rank' may have been only another term for verse which rhymed in couplets, called of old 'riding ryme.' DYCE (*Gloss.*) quotes this note of Staunton, and adds, 'but by "rank" Drayton assuredly means *row*.' COLLIER (ed. i): 'Rank,' as Whiter observes, means the order in which they go one after another, and therefore Shakespeare says, 'butter-women's,' and not *butter-woman's*, as it has been corrupted of late years. WRIGHT: That is, going one after another, at a jog-trot, like butter-women going to market. This seems to be the meaning, if 'rank' is the true reading. It is open to the rather pedantic objection that it makes 'rank' equivalent to *file.* But it may be used simply in the sense of *order.* I am inclined to consider *rack* to be the proper word, and I would justify this conjecture by the following quotations from Cotgrave's *Fr. Dict.:* 'Amble: f. An amble, pace, racke; an ambling or

Roſ.   Out Foole.   98
Clo.   For a taſte.
    If a Hart doe lacke a Hinde,   100
       Let him ſeeke out Roſalinde :
    If the Cat will after kinde,
       ſo be ſure will Roſalinde :
    Wintred garments muſt be linde,
       ſo muſt ſlender Roſalinde :   105
    They that reap muſt ſheafe and binde,
       then to cart with Roſalinde.
    Sweeteſt nut , hath ſowreſt rinde,
       ſuch a nut is Roſalinde.
    He that ſweeteſt roſe will finde,   110
       must finde Loues pricke, & Roſalinde.

This is the verie falſe gallop of Verſes, why doe you in-
feɔt your ſelfe with them?   113

100–111. In sens. obsc. In re. *kinde*, cf. *M. of V.* I, iii, 88. In re. *linde*, hoc verbo congressus caninus significabatur, *v.* Cotgrave, *s. v. Ligner;* immo hodie verbum sic usum est. In re. *cart*, quære symbolum incontinentiæ? cf. 'rascal beadle,' &c., *Lear*, IV, vi, 158, et *Tam. Shr.* I, i, 55. In ll. 108, 109, vestimentum virile, quo Rosa. induta est, fortasse significatur. —ED.

100. doe] *doth* Rowe+.

104. Wintred] F_2, Cald. Knt, Coll. i, Wh. i, Hal.   Winter F_3F_4 et cet. linde] lin'd F_4.

108. nut] meat F_3F_4, Rowe.

---

racking pace; a smooth or easie gate.' 'Ambler. To amble, pace; racke; to go easily and smoothly away.' In Holme's *Armoury* (B. ii, c. 10, p. 150) 'rack' is thus defined: 'Rack is a pace wherein the horse neither Trots or Ambles, but is between both.' [Since no change free from objections has been proposed, it seems to me safest to retain the original.—ED.]

102. **Cat . . . kinde**] Halliwell gives half a dozen instances of the use of 'this old proverbial phrase,' and more could be added.

104. **Wintred**] WHITE: See the following instance of the use of this participial adjective in a passage quoted from *A Knack to Know a Knave* [circa, 1590] by Collier in his *History of Eng. Dram. Poetry* [ii, 421, ed. 1879]: 'Now shepherds bear their flocks into the folds, And wint'red oxen, fodder'd in their stalls,' &c. WRIGHT: Compare 'azured' in *The Tempest*, V, i, 43, and perhaps 'damask'd' in *Sonnet* cxxx, 5. [While fully agreeing with Grant White's opinion that 'wintred' is to be here preferred, I doubt the parallelism of his example. 'Wintred garments' are exposed to the winter; 'wint'red oxen' are protected from the winter.—ED.]

112. **false gallop**] MALONE: So in Nashe's [*Foure Letters Confuted*, p. 202, ed. Grosart]: 'I would trot a false gallop through the rest of his ragged Verses, but that if I should retort his rime dogrell aright, I must make my verses (as he doth his) run hobling like a Brewers Cart vpon the stones, and obserue no length in their feete.'

10

Ros.   Peace you dull foole, I found them on a tree.
Clo.   Truely the tree yeelds bad fruite.   115
Ros.   Ile graffe it with you, and then I ſhall graffe it
with a Medler : then it will be the earlieſt fruit i'th coun-   117

HUNTER (i, 348) quotes as follows from *Dictionnaire Raisonné d'Hippiatrique*, &c.
par M. Lafosse, 1776, i, 334 : ' Galoper faux, se dit du cheval lorsqu' en galopant il
lève la jambe gauche de devant la première, car il doit lever la droite la première.'
[The phrase is thus understood, and still used, by horsemen at this day.—ED.]

112. **infect**] This is strong language—strong for the occasion and strong for the
speaker.   It is strange that this passage has escaped those who seem to think that
Shakespeare wrote his plays solely for a chance to make local allusions or to poke ſly
fun or worse at his contemporaries.   Indeed, a very pretty case could be made out for
them here, proving beyond a peradventure that Shakespeare is referring to Nashe's quarrel with Gabriel Harvey, and here indicates in terms too plain to be misunderstood that
he sympathised with Nashe.   In this very paragraph in Nashe, quoted in the preceding note by Malone, where the unusual phrase ' false gallop ' occurs (and mark, it is the
ONLY TIME that either Shakespeare or Nashe uses it !)   Nashe does not conclude his
sentence without using the very identical, unusual, strong word that Touchstone uses
here.   After saying, as we have just seen, that his verses would ' obserue no length in
their feet,' he goes on to say, ' which were *absurdum per absurdius*, TO INFECT my
vaine with his imitation.'   Surely the case is clear that Shakespeare, by using ' false
gallop ' and ' infect,' is alluding to Nashe.   Can mortal man desire better proof ?
Here in one and the same paragraph we have these two unusual words !   As
Chief Justice Kenyon, whose classical quotations sometimes lacked the exactest
parallelism, is said to have been wont to say : ' Gentlemen, the case is as clear as the
nose on your face ; *latet anguis in herbâ*.'—ED.

116. **graffe**] SKEAT (*s. v.*) : The form *graft* is corrupt, and due to a confusion
with *graffed*, which was originally the past participle of ' graff.'   Shakespeare has
grafted, Macb. IV, iii, 51 ; but he has rightly also ' graft ' as a past participle, *Rich.
III :* III, vii, 127.   The verb is formed from the substantive *graff*, a scion.   Old
French, *graffe, grafe*, a style for writing with a sort of pencil ; whence French, *greffe*,
' a graff, a slip or young shoot.'—Cotgrave ; so named from the resemblance of the
cut slip to the shape of a pointed pencil.   Similarly, we have Lat. *graphiolum* (1), a
small style ; (2), a small shoot, scion, graff.

117. **Medler**] BEISLY (p. 32) : The *Mespilus germanica*, a tree, the fruit of which
is small, and in shape like an apple, but flat at the top, and only fit to be eaten when
mellow or rotten.   ELLACOMBE (p. 123) : The medlar is a European tree, but not a
native of England ; it has, however, been so long introduced as to be now completely
naturalised, and is admitted into the English flora.   Chaucer gives it a very prominent place in his description of a beautiful garden ; and certainly a fine medlar tree
' ful of blossomes ' is a handsome ornament on any lawn.   Shakespeare only used the
common language of his time when he described the medlar as only fit to be eaten
when rotten.   But, in fact, the medlar when fit to be eaten is no more rotten than a
ripe peach, pear, or strawberry, or any other fruit which we do not eat till it has
reached a certain stage of softness.   There is a vast difference between a ripe and a
rotten medlar, though it would puzzle many of us to say when a fruit (not a medlar
only) is ripe, that is, fit to be eaten.   These things are matters of taste and fashion,
and it is rather surprising to find that we are accused, and by good judges, of eating

try : for you'l be rotten ere you bee halfe ripe, and that's   118
the right vertue of the Medler.

   Clo. You haue faid : but whether wifely or no, let the   120
Forreft iudge.

         Enter Celia with a writing.

  Rof. Peace, here comes my fifter reading, ftand afide.

    Cel. *Why fhould this Defert bee,*

          for it is vnpeopled? *Noë:*   125

  Tonges Ile hang on euerie tree,

         that fhall ciuill fayings fhoe.   127

---

121. Forreſt] *Forester* Warb.
122. Scene V. Pope +.
124. Cel.] Cel. [reads] Dyce, Cam.
Defert] F_3F_4, Knt, Hal. Defart
F_2. *desert silent* Tyrwhitt, Steev. Mal.

a desert Rowe et cet.
  124, 125. bee,...vnpeopled?] *be?...*
unpeopled. Rowe. *be?...unpeopled?* Cap.
126. Tonges] Tongs F_3F_4.
127. fhoe] fhow F_4.

---

peaches when rotten rather than ripe. 'The Japanese always eat their peaches in an unripe state . . . . they regard a ripe peach as rotten.'

  117. **be**] DYCE (ed. iii): 'Read *bear;* for "it" refers to the tree that is to be graffed.'—W. N. LETTSOM.

  117. **earliest**] STEEVENS: Shakespeare seems to have had little knowledge in gardening. The medlar is one of the *latest* fruits, being uneatable till the end of November. DOUCE (i, 302): If a fruit be fit to be eaten when rotten, and before it be ripe, it may in one sense be termed the earliest. COLLIER (ed. ii): If the medlar were graffed with the forwardness of the clown, instead of being one of the latest, it would be 'th' earliest fruit i' the country,' and rotten before it was half ripe.

  124–153. Halliwell prints this in staves of eight, which, in a modernised edition, is, I think, good.—ED.

  124. TYRWHITT: Although the metre may be assisted by reading '*a* desert,' the sense still is defective; for how will the 'hanging of tongues on every tree' make it less a desert? I am persuaded we ought to read, 'Why should this desert *silent* be?' WHITER: The old reading, I believe, is genuine. Surely the same metaphor has power to *people* woods which is able to afford them *speech.* See what Dr Johnson says in the following note on 'civil sayings.' If the metre should be thought defective, 'why' may be read as a dissyllable. Let the reader repeat the line with a gentle pause upon 'why,' and he will find no reason to reject it for deficiency of metre. KNIGHT: The absence of people, says the sonneteer, does not make this place *desert,* for I will hang tongues on every tree, that will speak the language of *civil* life. *Desert* is here an adjective opposed to *civil.* DYCE (ed. i): As if 'Why should this desert be?' could possibly mean anything else than 'Why should this desert *exist?*' [Change seems unavoidable, and Rowe's is less violent than any other. Qu. *deserted?*—ED.]

  125. **for**] For instances of 'for' in the sense of *because,* see Abbott, § 151.

  127. **civill**] JOHNSON: Here used in the same sense as when we say *civil* wisdom or *civil* life, in opposition to a solitary state or to the state of nature. This desert shall not appear *unpeopled,* for every tree shall teach the maxims or incidents of social life. STEEVENS: 'Civil' is not designedly opposed to *solitary.* It means only *grave*

Some, how briefe the Life of man   128
  runs his erring pilgrimage,
That the ſtretching of a ſpan,   130
  buckles in his ſumme of age.
Some of violated vowes,
  twixt the ſoules of friend, and friend :
But vpon the faireſt bowes,
  or at euerie ſentence end;   135
Will I Roſalinda write,
  teaching all that reade, to know
The quinteſſence of euerie ſprite,
  heauen would in little ſhow.   139

---

131. buckles] bucklefs F_4.   138. The] This F_3F_4, Rowe+.
135. or] *And* Ktly.

---

or *ſolemn.* [For this meaning, which, I think, is the right one here, many examples
could be adduced. The only definitions, in fact, which Dyce gives of 'civil' are
'sober, grave, decent, solemn,' a range of meaning unaccountably overlooked by
Schmidt, who gives as the meaning of this passage, 'decent, well-mannered, polite.'
Scarcely enough weight has been given, I think, by recent editors to this shade of
meaning; not that 'civil' does not here also include the idea of civilisation or of
social life as opposed to 'desert'; but that it also involves the lover's melancholy is
shown in the sigh over the shortness of life, man's erring pilgrimage, and the violated
vows of friends. These, we are expressly told, were to be the 'civil sayings' which
would be hung on every tree.—ED.]

129. **erring**] WRIGHT: Wandering; not used here in a moral sense. See *Ham.* I,
i, 154: 'The extravagant and erring spirit.' The word occurs in its literal sense,
though with a figurative reference, in Isaiah xxxv, 8: 'The wayfaring men, though
fools, shall not err therein.' For 'wandering stars' in the Authorised Version of Jude
13, the Wiclifite versions have 'erringe steeres.' [For 'his' we should now use *its.*]

130. **span**] WORDSWORTH (p. 147): As the Psalmist complains, 'Thou hast made
my days as it were a span long.'—xxxix, 6, Prayer Book Version.

135. **sentence end**] ABBOTT, § 217: The possessive inflection in dissyllables ending in a sibilant sound is often unexpressed both in writing and in pronunciation.

138. **quintessence**] 'Quinta essentia est spiritualis et subtilis quædam substantia,
extracta ex rebus, per separationem, à quatuor elementis, differens realiter ab ejus
essentia, ut *aqua vitæ, spiritus vini*,' &c.—Minsheu, *Guide Into Tongues,* 1617.
WRIGHT: The fifth essence, called also by the mediæval philosophers the spirit or
soul of the world, 'whome we tearme the quinticense, because he doth not consist of
the foure Elementes, but is a certaine fifth, a thing aboue them or beside them. . . . .
This spirit doubtlesse is in a manner such in the body of the world, as ours is in mans
body; For as the powers of our soule, are through the spirit giuen to the members;
so the vertue of the soule of ye world is by the quintecense spread ouer all, for nothing is found in all the world which wanteth the sparke of his vertue.'—Batman *vppon
Bartholome,* fol. 173, *a.*

139. **in little**] MALONE: The allusion is to a miniature portrait. The current

Therefore heauen Nature charg'd,　　　　　　　　140
　　that one bodie fhould be fill'd
With all Graces wide enlarg'd,
　　nature prefently diftill'd
Helens cheeke, but not his heart,
　　　　Cleopatra's *Maieftie* :　　　　　　　145
Attalanta's *better part,*
　　　　fad Lucrecia's *Modeftie.*　　　　　　147

140. charg'd] chang'd Ff.	144. cheeke] cheeks F_3F_4, Rowe+.
142. all] *all the* Rowe i.	his] Ff. *her* Rowe.
wide enlarg'd] *wide-enlarged*	heart] heare F_4.
Dyce, Cam.	147. *Lucrecia's*] *Lucretiaes* F_3. *Lu-*
enlarg'd,] *enlarg'd ;* Rowe.	*cretia's* F_4.

phrase in our author's time was 'painted in *little.*' STEEVENS: So in *Ham.* II, ii,
383 : 'give twenty, forty, fifty, a hundred ducats apiece for his picture in little.' [The
train of thought here is so decidedly astrological, beginning with 'quintessence' and
continuing through 'distillation' to a 'heavenly synod,' that it is possible that 'in
little' may here refer to the microcosm, the 'little world of man,' to which the Gentleman refers in *Lear,* III, i, 10. Where 'in little' elsewhere refers to miniatures, I
think Shakespeare generally couples with it the idea of a 'picture' or of 'drawing.'
—ED.]

140, &c. JOHNSON: From the picture of Apelles, or the accomplishments of Pan-
dora: Πανδώρην, ὅτι πάντες 'Ολύμπια δώματ' ἔχοντες Δῶρον ἐδώρησαν.—[Hesiod,
Erga, 70]. So in the *Temp.* III, i, 48 : 'but you, O you, So perfect and so peerless,
are created Of every creature's best !' CALDECOTT cites : 'Of all complexions the
cull'd sovereignty Do meet, as at a fair, in her fair cheek ; Where several worthies
make one dignity.'—*Love's Lab. L.* IV, iii, 234.

142. **wide enlarg'd**] 'Spread through the world' is given by Schmidt as the
equivalent of this phrase, which I doubt. Does it not refer to the magnitude of the
graces with which Heaven had commanded Nature to fill one body ?—ED.

146. **Attalanta's better part**] JOHNSON was the first to start a discussion which
has not, to this hour, subsided. He said : I know not well what could be the 'better
part' of Atalanta here ascribed to Rosalind. Of the Atalanta most celebrated, and
who therefore must be intended here where she has no epithet of discrimination, the
'better part' seems to have been her heels, and the worse part was so bad that Rosalind would not thank her lover for the comparison. There is a more obscure Atalanta, a huntress and a heroine, but of her nothing bad is recorded, and therefore I
know not which was her 'better part.' Shakespeare was no despicable mythologist,
yet he seems here to have mistaken some other character for that of Atalanta. TOL-
LET : Perhaps the poet means her beauty and graceful elegance of shape, which he
would prefer to her swiftness. But cannot Atalanta's 'better part' mean her virtue or
virgin chastity, with which Nature had graced Rosalind ? In Holland's *Plinie,* bk.
xxxv, chap. 3, we find it stated that 'at Lanuvium there remaine yet two pictures of
lady *Atalanta,* and queen *Helena,* close one to the other, painted naked, by one and
the same hand : both of them are for beauty incomparable, and yet a man may dis-
cerne the one of them [Atalanta] to be a maiden, for her modest and chaste counte-

[Attalanta's better part]

nance.' FARMER : I suppose Atalanta's 'better part' is her *wit, i. e.* the swiftness of her mind. MALONE : Dr Farmer's explanation may derive some support from a subsequent passage [lines 269, 270, *post*]. It is observable that the story of Atalanta in Ovid's *Metamorphoses* is interwoven with that of Venus and Adonis, which Shakespeare had undoubtedly read. Thus, Golding's translation [bk. x, p. 132, ed. 1567] : 'And hard it is to tell Thee whither she did in footemanshippe or beawty more excell.' 'And though that shee Did fly as swift as arrow from a Turkye bowe : yit hee More woondred at her beawtye than at swiftnesse of her pace Her ronning greatly did augment her beawtye and her grace.' [In his ed. 1790, Malone suggested that Atalanta's *lips* were her better part, because in Marston's *Insatiate Countess* he found the reference, ' Those lips were hers that won the golden ball ' ; evidently forgetting, as Wright says, that the allusion there was to Venus. This suggestion was withdrawn.— ED.] STEEVENS : It may be observed that Statius also, in his sixth *Thebaid*, has confounded Atalanta, the wife of Hippomanes, with Atalanta, the wife of Pelops. After all, I believe that 'Atalanta's *better part*' means only *the best part about her*, such as was most commended. [Which is not altogether unlike Lincoln's well-known saying, that ' for those who like this kind of thing, this kind of thing is what they would like ' ; what was ' the best part about' Atalanta is exactly what we are trying to find out.—ED.] WHALLEY : I think this stanza was formed on an old tetrastich epitaph which I have read in a country churchyard : ' She who is dead and sleepeth in this tomb, Had Rachel's comely face, aud Leah's fruitful womb : Sarah's obedience, Lydia's open heart, And Martha's care, and Mary's *better part*.' WHITER, to whom this passage offers a notable instance of the truth of his theory as to the association of ideas, devotes nearly nineteen octavo pages to its elucidation, whereof the following is a digest : It has been remarked that Shakespeare has himself borrowed many of his images from *prints, statues, paintings,* and *exhibitions in tapestry ;* and we may observe that some allusions of this sort are to be found in the play before us, and especially in those places which describe the beauty of Rosalind. . . . . I have always been firmly persuaded that the *imagery* which our Poet has selected to discriminate the more prominent perfections of *Helen, Cleopatra, Atalanta,* and *Lucretia* was not derived from the abstract consideration of their general qualities ; but was caught from those *peculiar traits* of beauty and character which are impressed on the mind of him who contemplates their portraits. It is well known that these celebrated heroines of romance were, in the days of our Poet, the favourite subjects of popular representation, and were alike visible in the coarse hangings of the poor and the magnificent arras of the rich. In the portraits of *Helen,* whether they were produced by the skilful artist or his ruder imitator, though her face would certainly be delineated as eminently beautiful, yet she appears not to have been adorned with any of those charms which are allied to *modesty ;* and we accordingly find that she was generally depicted with a loose and insidious countenance, which but too manifestly betrayed the inward wantonness and perfidy of her heart. [Shelton's *Don Quixote*, Part ii, p. 480, is here cited in proof.] With respect to the 'majesty of Cleopatra' it may be observed that this notion is not derived from classical authority, but from the more popular storehouse of legend and romance. . . . . I infer, therefore, that the *familiarity* of this image was impressed both on the Poet and his reader from pictures and representations in tapestry, which were the lively and faithful mirrors of popular romances. *Atalanta,* we know, was considered likewise by our ancient poets as a celebrated beauty ; and we may be assured therefore that her portraits were everywhere to be found. . . . . Since

[Attalanta's better part]

the story of Atalanta represents that heroine as possessed of singular beauty, zealous
to preserve her maidenliness even with the death of her lovers, and accomplishing
her purposes by extraordinary swiftness in running, we may be assured that the skill
of the artist would be employed in displaying the most perfect expressions of *virgin
purity*, and in delineating the *fine proportions and elegant symmetry of her person.*
. . . . Let us suppose, therefore, that the portraits of these celebrated beauties, Helen,
Cleopatra, Atalanta, and Lucretia, were delineated as I have above described, that in
the days of Shakespeare they continued to be the favorite subjects of popular representation, and that consequently they were familiarly impressed on the mind of the
Poet and on the memory of his audience.   Let us now investigate what the bard, or
the lover, under the influence of this impression, would select as the *better parts* of
these celebrated heroines, which he might wish to be transferred to his own mistress
as the perfect model of female excellence.   In contemplating the portrait of *Helen*
he is attracted only by those charms which are at once the most distinguished, and at
the same time are the least employed in expressing the feelings of the heart.   He
wishes therefore for that rich bloom of beauty which glowed upon her *cheek*, but he
rejects those lineaments of her countenance which betrayed the loose inconstancy of
her mind—the insidious smile and the wanton brilliancy of her eye.   Impressed with
the effect, he passes instantly to the cause.   He is enamoured with the *better part* of
the beauty of Helen; but he is shocked at the depravity of that *heart*, which was too
manifestly exhibited by the worse.   To convince the intelligent reader that ' cheek ' is
not applied to *beauty in general*, but that it is here used in its appropriate and original sense, we shall produce a very curious passage from one of our author's *Sonnets*,
by which it will appear that the portraits of Helen were distinguished by the consummate beauty which was displayed upon *her cheek :* ' Describe Adonis, and the
counterfeit (*i. e.* picture) Is poorly imitated after you.   On Helen's *cheek* all art of
beauty set, And you in Grecian tires are *painted* new.'—*Sonnet* 53. . . . . In surveying the portrait of *Atalanta*, and in reflecting on the character which it displayed, the
lover would not find it difficult to select the *better part* both of her mind and of her
form, which he might wish to be transfused into the composition of his mistress.   He
would not be desirous of that perfection in her person which contributed nothing to
the gratification of his passion, and he would reject that principle of her soul which
was adverse to the object of his wishes.   He would be enamoured with the fine proportions and elegant symmetry of her limbs; though his passion would find but little
reason to be delighted with the quality of *swiftness* with which that symmetry was
connected.   He would be captivated with the blushing charms of unsullied virginity;
but he would abhor that unfeeling coldness which resisted the impulse of love, and
that unnatural cruelty which rejoiced in the murder of her lovers.   The Poet lastly
wishes for the modesty of the *sad Lucretia*, that firm and deep-rooted principle of
female chastity which is so visibly depicted in the *sadness* of her countenance, and
which has rendered her through all ages the pride and pattern of conjugal fidelity.
Such then are the wishes of the lover in the formation of his mistress, that the *ripe
and brilliant beauties* of *Helen* should be united to the *elegant symmetry* and *virgin
graces* of *Atalanta*, and that this union of charms should be still dignified and enno-
bled by the *majestic mien* of *Cleopatra* and the *matron modesty* of *Lucretia*.   [Whiter
concludes by pointing out the allusion to a picture, involved in ' little,' line 139, and
the term of painting, in ' touches ' in line 151.]   CALDECOTT: From the use of it in
Quarles's *Argalus and Parthenia*, it has been suggested that this might have been a

[Attalanta's better part]

well-understood phrase for works of high excellence: 'No, no, 'twas neither brow, nor lip, nor eye, Nor any outward excellence urg'd me, why To love Parthenia. 'Twas her better part (Which mischief could not wrong) surpriz'd my heart.' HAL- LIWELL: The expression 'better part' is a very common one in works of the six- teenth and seventeenth centuries, used in the sense of the soul or mind, or sometimes for the head, the seat of the intellect or soul. Its exact meaning in the present line is somewhat obscure, but it probably refers to the chaste mind of the beautiful Ata- lanta. KNIGHT quotes certain paragraphs from Whiter which are included in those given above. COLLIER has no note on the passage. SINGER says nothing new. STAUNTON (in a note on *Macb.* V, viii, 18: 'it hath cow'd my better part of man'): Atalanta's *better part* was not her *modesty*, nor her *heels*, nor her *wit*, but simply her *spiritual part*. The old epitaph quoted by Whalley almost proves, although he was apparently unconscious of the meaning, that 'better part' signified the *immortal*, the *intelligent* part. But the following lines from Overbury's *Wife* places this beyond doubt: 'Or rather let me *Love*, then *be in love;* So let me chuse, as *Wife* and *Friend* to finde, Let me forget her *Sex*, when I *approve; Beasts* likenesse lies in *shape*, but *ours* in *minde;* Our *Soules no Sexes* have, their Love is cleane, No *Sex*, both in the *better part* are *men*.' The Italics are the author's. [Sig. D 2, ed. 1627.] DYCE says the expression is 'common enough,' but offers nothing new in way of explanation. The COWDEN-CLARKES think that Atalanta's beauty, reticence, and agility form her 'better part.' HUDSON: The 'better part' would refer to Atalanta's exquisite sym- metry and proportion of form; and Orlando must of course imagine all formal, as well as all mental and moral graces, in his 'heavenly Rosalind.' WRIGHT: Whiter's opinion that Shakespeare may have had in mind pictures or tapestry may well have been the case, and it is known that cameos representing classical subjects were much in request. [In a letter to me in 1877 the late A. E. BRAE says: 'My own interpre- tation, unpublished except now to you, is that the allusion is Meleager's Atalanta of *epicene loveliness*, half boy, half girl, with whom Meleager fell in love at first sight, just as Orlando did with Rosalind. The "better part" may be either Atalanta's *feminine* beauty as contrasted with her *boyish* beauty, or it may be her loveliness as contrasted with her equipment in huntress fashion. After the description of which, in Ovid's *Meta.* lib. viii, comes: "Talis erat *cultus;* facies quam dicere vere Virgineam in puero, puerilem in virgine posses." Now, had not Rosalind, even before she donned male attire, this double character of beauty? . . . . It may be objected that Orlando did not know when he was versifying that Rosalind was in boy's dress, but Shake- speare knew it, and the audience knew it, and it is but a very slight discrepancy or oversight compared with the suggestion of "agility" which is nowhere even hinted at as attributable to Rosalind. . . . . Should you think the interpretation here suggested as too abstruse, I should substitute this: that Atalanta's subsequent eager susceptibil- ity to love from Hippomanes and Meleager might well be called her *better* part, as opposed to her former insensibility and cruelty in outpacing and then slaughtering her lovers.' To me both of these interpretations are somewhat too refined; the former Brae himself adequately condemns by referring to the anticipation involved in it. Atalanta wished to remain unwedded not from any love of maidenhood, but simply because the oracle had told her that marriage would prove fatal to her, as it did. It was her physical beauty which attracted her lovers and made them prefer death, to life without her. Staunton's explanation is hardly specific enough; her 'immortal part' she shared in common with the other three types. Her 'better part' was, I

Thus Rofalinde *of manie parts,*   148
    by Heauenly Synode was deuis'd,
Of manie faces, eyes, and hearts,   150
    to haue the touches deereſt pris'd.
Heauen would that ſhee theſe gifts ſhould haue,
    and I to liue and die her ſlaue.

Roſ. O moſt gentle Iupiter, what tedious homilie of   154

154. *Iupiter,*] *Jupiter*, F$_3$F$_4$. *Juniper!* Warb. *pulpiter!* Spedding, Cam. Glo. Cla.

think, her physical, personal charms. Nature's distillation resulted in Helen's face, Cleopatra's bearing, Atalanta's form, and Lucretia's modesty.—ED.]

147. **Lucrecia's**] The spelling in F$_3$, 'Lucretiaes,' if it be phonetic, which is not unlikely, exactly reproduces the New England pronunciation of to-day among thoroughbred Yankees. I have heard from college professors *Cubae, stigmae,* &c. for *Cuba, stigma.* See also what White says about 'lectors,' line 336, *post.*—ED.

150. **WRIGHT**: Shakespeare may have remembered the story of Zeuxis as told by Pliny (xxxv, 9, trans. Holland), 'that when hee should make a table with a picture for the Agrigentines, to be set up in the temple of Iuno Lacinia, at the charges of the citie, according to a vow that they had made, hee would needs see all the maidens of the citie, naked; and from all that companie hee chose five of the fairest to take out as from severall patterns, whatsoever hee liked best in any of them; and of all the lovely parts of those five, to make one bodie of incomparable beautie.'

151. **touches**] JOHNSON: The features; les traits. [See V, iv, 31.]

152, 153. **should . . . and I to liue**] WRIGHT: The construction is loose, although the sense is clear. We may regard the words as equivalent to 'And that I should live,' &c.; or supply some verb from 'would' in line 152, as if it were either 'And I would live,' or 'am willing to live,' &c. ABBOTT refers to this passage in § 416, as an instance of where 'construction is changed for clearness.' 'Here "to" might be omitted, or "should" might be inserted instead, but the omission would create ambiguity, and the insertion would be a tedious repetition.' See also a parallel construction in V, iv, 25, 26. For other instances where 'I' is used before an infinitive, see Abbott, § 216.

154. **Iupiter**] Spedding's emendation, *pulpiter,* adopted by the Cambridge Editors and by Dyce in his Second Edition, but abandoned in his Third, is plausible and alluring. It is the word of all words to introduce the train of thought that follows, with which 'Jupiter' has no connection. This addition of an *-er* to a noun in order to change it to an agent, like 'moraler' in *Othello,* 'justicer' in *Lear,* &c., is, as we all know, thoroughly Shakespearian. Moreover 'Iupiter' is not printed in Italics as though it were a proper name, to which Wright calls attention, and as it is printed in the only other place where it is used in this play, II, iv, 3; which adds to the likelihood that it is here a misprint. All these considerations are clamorous for Spedding's *pulpiter*. But, on the other hand the text is clear without it; once before Rosalind has appealed to 'Jupiter,' and to use this mouth-filling oath, which is 'not dangerous,' may have been one of her characteristics, as certainly the use of expletives in general is. Although 'Jupiter' is not elsewhere printed in Roman, yet 'Jove' is, and in this very scene, line 231; and so also is 'Judas' in III, iv, 10. *Pulpiter* can

Loue haue you wearied your parifhioners withall, and   155
neuer cri'de, haue patience good people.

    Cel. How now backe friends : Shepheard, go off a lit-
tle : go with him firrah.

    Clo. Come Shepheard, let vs make an honorable re-
treit, though not with bagge and baggage, yet with   160
fcrip and fcrippage.   *Exit.*

    Cel. Didft thou heare thefe verfes?

    Rof. O yes, I heard them all, and more too, for fome
of them had in them more feete then the Verfes would
beare.   165

    Cel. That's no matter : the feet might beare y̆ verfes.

    Rof. I, but the feet were lame, and could not beare
themfelues without the verfe, and therefore ftood lame-
ly in the verfe.

    Cel. But didft thou heare without wondering, how   170
thy name fhould be hang'd and carued vpon thefe trees?

    Rof. I was feuen of the nine daies out of the wonder,   172

---

156. *cri'de*] *cride, have your parifh-iones withall, and never cri'de,* F₂.
    157. *How now*] *How now!* Ff. *How now?* Coll.
    backe friends :] *back-friends!* Theob. Han. Warb. Johns. *back friends?*

Cap. Steev. Mal. *back, friends.* Coll. *Back, friends!* Wh. Cam.
    162. Scene VI. Pope+.
    172. *the wonder*] *wonder* Ff, Rowe+, Cap.

---

hardly be called an emendation; there is no obscurity which amounts to a defect. It is an improvement, and against verbal improvements, which it is far from impossible to make in Shakespeare's text, we should, I think, acquire and maintain a dogged habit of shutting our eyes and closing our ears. See IV, iii, 19.—ED.

    168. **without**] That is, outside of the verse.

    171. **should**] ABBOTT, § 328: There is no other reason for the use of 'should' in this line than that it denotes a statement not made by the speaker (compare *sollen* in German). *Should* seems to denote a false story in George Fox's *Journal*: 'From this man's words was a slander raised upon us that the Quakers *should* deny Christ,' p. 43 (edition 1765). 'The priest of that church raised many wicked slanders upon me: "That I rode upon a great black horse, and that I *should* give a fellow money to follow me when I was on my black horse."' 'Why should you think that I *should* woo in scorn.'—*Mid. N. D.* III, ii, 122. WRIGHT: 'Should' is frequently used in giving a reported speech. Thus in Jonson, *The Fox*, II, i: '*Sir Politick.* I heard last night a most strange thing reported By some of my lord's followers, and I long To hear how 'twill be seconded. *Peregrine.* What was 't, sir? *Sir. P.* Marry, sir, of a raven that should build In a ship royal of the king's' [p. 202, ed. Gifford].

    172. **seuen . . . nine**] CAPELL (p. 61): It is still a common saying amongst us, that a wonder lasts nine days; seven of which, says Rosalind, are over with me, for I have been wondering a long time at some verses that I have found.

before you came : for looke heere what I found on a   173
Palme tree; I was neuer fo berim d fince *Pythagoras* time
that I was an Irifh Rat, which I can hardly remember.   175

174. Pythagoras] *Pythagoras's* Rowe+.   *Pythagoras'* Cap.

---

174. **Palme tree**] STEEVENS : A 'palm-tree' in the forest of Arden is as much
out of place as the lioness in a subsequent scene.   CALDECOTT : Bulleyn in his *Booke
of Compounds*, 1562, p. 40 [speaks of] 'the kaies or woolly knottes, growing upon
sallowes, commonly called *palmes.*'   BRAND (*Pop. Ant.* i, 127, ed. Bohn) : It is still
customary with our boys, both in the south and north of England, to go out and gather
slips with the willow-flowers or buds at this time [*i. e.* Palm Sunday].   These seem to
have been selected as substitutes for the real palm, because they are generally the
only things, at this season, which can be easily procured in which the power of vege-
tation can be discovered.   It is even yet a common practice in the neighborhood of
London.   The young people go *a-palming ;* and the sallow is sold in London streets
for the whole week preceding Palm Sunday, the purchasers commonly not knowing
the tree which produces it, but imagining it to be the real palm, and wondering that
they never saw it growing !   HALLIWELL (*Archaic Dict. s. v. Palm*) : Properly exotic
trees of the tribe *Palmaceæ ;* but among our rustics it means the catkins of a delicate
species of willow gathered by them on Palm Sunday.   'Palme, the yelowe that grow-
eth on wyllowes, *chatton.*'—Palsgrave, 1530.   WRIGHT : As the forest of Arden is taken
from Lodge's Novel, it is likely that the trees in it came from the same source.   This
is certainly the case with the 'tuft of olives' in III, v, 78.   Lodge's forest was such
as could only exist in the novelist's fancy, for besides pines, beech trees, and cypresses,
there were olives, figs, lemons, and citrons, pomegranates, and myrrh trees.   The
palm is mentioned, but not as a forest tree, and only in figures of speech ; as, for
example : 'Thou art old, Adam, and thy haires waxe white ; the palme tree is alreadie
full of bloomes.'—Lodge's *Novel.*   COLLIER (ed. i) : Shakespeare cared little about
such 'proprieties' ; but possibly he wrote *plane*-tree, which may have been misread
by the transcriber or compositor.   [Collier did not repeat this suggestion in his subsequent editions.   It seems quite clear from both Bulleyn and Palsgrave that the catkins
of the willow were called *palms,* and presumably for the reason that they were used,
as Brand states, on Palm Sunday.   But I can find no proof that the willow was ever
called a 'palm tree.'   Here, in this city, on that day, in lieu of the Oriental branches,
sprigs of box and the long leaves of the *Phormium tenax* are distributed in the
churches, and are called 'palms,' but no one ever thinks of calling the plants themselves 'palm trees.'   Shakespeare's forest was Lodge's forest, and, as Wright truly
says, that forest could exist only in fancy.—ED.]

174, 175. **berim d ... Rat**] GREY (i, 181) : A banter upon Pythagoras's doctrine of the transmigration of souls.   See Spenser's *Faerie Queene*, I, ix ['As he were
charmèd with inchaunted rimes.'—line 437, ed. Grosart].   In Randolph's *Jealous
Lovers*, v, ii, there is an image much like this : '*Azotus.* And my poets Shall with a
satire steep'd in gall and vinegar Rithme 'em to death, as they do rats in Ireland.'
JOHNSON : The power of killing rats with rhymes Donne mentions in his *Satires* and
Temple in his *Treatises*.   [The passage in Donne's *Satires* to which reference is here
made must be, I think, in Pope's version, pointed out by Wright, *Satire* II, line 22 :
'One sings the fair ; but songs no longer move ; No rat is rhymed to death, nor maid
to love.'   I cannot find it in the original.   The passage in Temple is probably that

Cel. Tro you, who hath done this?   176
Rof. Is it a man?
Cel. And a chaine that you once wore about his neck:
change you colour?
Rof. I pre'thee who?   180
Cel. O Lord, Lord, it is a hard matter for friends to

---

176. *Tro*] *Trow* Theob. ii.   178. *wore*] *wore*, Ff, Rowe et seq.
178. *And*] *Ay, and* Cap.   179. *you*] *your* F_3F_4.

---

which is quoted by M. M. (*N. & Qu.* 1st Ser. vol. vi, p. 460) from the *Essay on Poetry:* 'and the proverb of "rhyming rats to death" came, I suppose, from the same root' [*i. e.* the Runic]. In the same volume of *N. & Qu.* p. 591, G. H. Kingsley supplied another allusion from Scot's *Discouerie of Witchcraft:* 'The Irishmen .... terme one sort of their witches eybiters .... yea and they will not sticke to affirme, that they can rime either man or beast to death.'—Book III, chap. xv, p. 64, ed. 1584.—ED.] STEEVENS: So in an address 'To the Reader' at the conclusion of Jonson's *Poetaster:* 'Rhime them to death, as they do Irish rats In drumming tunes.' MALONE: So in Sir Philip Sidney's *Defence of Poesie:* 'I will not wish vnto you the Asses eares of *Midas* .... nor to be rimed to death, as is said to be done in *Irelād.*'—[p. 518, ad fin. ed. 1598]. HALLIWELL gives several references of a later date, and adds that 'the power of the Irish satirist to rhyme men to death is frequently referred to, and is the subject of various ancient legends. According to Mr Currie, "the most ancient story of rhyming rats to death in Ireland is found in an historico-romantic tale, entitled, *The Adventures of the Great Company.*"' Hereupon, Halliwell quotes the 'adventures,' whereof space and relevancy will scarcely permit the reprint here. 'An anonymous critic adds,' says Halliwell in conclusion, 'that in France, at the present day, similar reliance on the power of rhyme is placed by the peasantry. Most provinces contain some man whose sole occupation is to lure insects and reptiles by song to certain spots where they meet with destruction. The superstition belongs to the same order as that of the serpent-charmers of the East.'

174. **Pythagoras**] WALKER (*Crit.* i, 152) cites this allusion to Pythagoras, among many others, to show the influence of Ovid on Shakespeare. The doctrines of that philosopher are set forth at large in *Met.* xv.

175. **that**] ABBOTT, § 284: Since *that* represents different cases of the relative, it may mean 'in *that*,' 'for *that*,' 'because' ('quod'), or 'at *which* time' ('quum').

175. **which**] For other instances where 'which' is used for 'which thing,' often parenthetically, see Abbott, § 271.

178. **And a chaine**] WRIGHT: This irregular and elliptical construction, in which 'and' does yeoman's service for many words, may be illustrated by the following from *Cor.* I, i, 82: 'Suffer us to famish, and their storehouses crammed with grain.' And in *Cym.* V, iv, 179: 'But a man that were to sleep your sleep, and a hangman to help him to bed, I think he would change places with his officer.'

181, 182. **friends ... meete**] STEEVENS: Alluding to the proverb: 'Friends may meet, but mountains never greet.' See Ray's *Collection*. MALONE: So in *Mother Bombie*, by Lily, 1594: 'Then wee foure met, which argued wee were no mountaines.' —[V, iii].

meete ; but Mountaines may bee remoou'd with Earth-   182
quakes, and fo encounter.

   Rof.   Nay, but who is it?

   Cel.   Is it poffible?   185

   Rof.   Nay, I pre'thee now, with moft petitionary ve-
hemence, tell me who it is.

   Cel.   O wonderfull, wonderfull, and moft wonderfull
wonderfull, and yet againe wonderful, and after that out
of all hooping.   190

   Rof.   Good my complection, doft thou think though

186. *pre'thee*] *pray thee* Cap. Steev. *whooping* Theob. et seq.
Var. '21, Cald. Knt, Sta.   191. *Good my*] *Odd's, my* Theob. Han.
187. *tell*] *till* F₂.   *Od's my* Cap.
190. *hooping*] *hoping* F₄, Rowe. *complection*] *companion* Gould.

182. **with**] For other instances of the use of ' with ' in the sense of *by means of*,
see Abbott, § 193.

183. **encounter**] GREY (i, 181): A plain allusion to the following incident mentioned by Pliny, *Hist. Nat.* ii, 83 [or as it stands in Holland's translation, cited by
Tollet, but no credit given to Grey]: ' There hapned once . . . . a great strange wonder of the earth; for two hils encountered together, charging as it were, and with
violence assaulting one another, yea, and retyring againe with a most mighty noise.'
WRIGHT: There is of course no necessity for supposing that Shakespeare had such a
passage in his mind.

190. **hooping**] STEEVENS: That is, out of all measure or reckoning. MALONE:
This appears to have been a phrase of the same import as another formerly in use,
' out of all *cry*.' CALDECOTT: Literally beyond, or out of all call or stretch of the
voice; metaphorically, and as we are to understand it, not to be expressed by any
figure of admiration. DYCE: Akin to this are the phrases *Out of all cry* and *Out of
all ho*. [Of the former of these kindred phrases examples are given by Steevens, Collier, Wright, and many by Halliwell, but of the phrase itself, ' hooping,' there does not
appear to be another instance, nor is any needed: its meaning is clear enough.—ED.]
WRIGHT: The form *whoop* [see Text. Notes] was in early use. Cotgrave gives:
' Hucher. To whoope, or hallow for; to call vnto.' And earlier still, in Palsgrave, 1530,
we find, ' I whoope, I call. *Je huppe*. . . . . Whooppe a lowde, ... *huppe hault*.'

191. **complection**] Theobald in his first edition confessed himself unable to ' reconcile this expression to common sense,' and hence his emendation, which Hanmer
adopted. The emendation is ingenious, because afterwards Rosalind says, ' Odd's,
my little life,' and again, ' Odd's, my will.' He withdrew it, however, in his second
edition, presumably convinced in the interim by his ' most affectionate friend ' Warburton, who wrote to him (Nichols, *Illust.* ii, 646): ' You say you cannot reconcile
this to common sense. Can you reconcile *odds my complexion* to it? The truth is,
" good my complexion " is a fine proverbial expression, and used by way of apology
when one is saying anything for which one ought to blush, and signifies, *hold good,
my complexion, i. e.* may I not be out of countenance!' Very different this, in tone,
from the sneer which Warburton printed in his own edition seven years later. MA-
LONE: That is, my native character, my female inquisitive disposition, canst thou

I am caparifon'd like a man, I haue a doublet and hofe in   192
my difpofition ? One inch of delay more, is a South-fea
of difcouerie.   I pre'thee tell me, who is it quickely, and   194

192. *hofe*] *a hofe* Ff, Rowe, Pope,
Han.
193, 194. *South-fea of*] Ff, Var. '21,
Cald. Knt, Coll. Sing. Wh. Dyce, Sta.
Cam. Glo. Clke, Cla. Ktly, Huds. Rlfe.
South-sea off Theob. Han. Warb. Mal.
south-sea-off Cap. Steev.

194. *difcouerie*] *discourtesy* Gould.
who is it] *who is it*, Rowe, Pope,
Sta. Coll. iii. *who is it;* Theob. Warb.
Johns. *who is it ?* Han. Cap. Steev. Mal.
Cald. Knt, Sing. *who it is* Anon (*ap.*
Cam. Ed.).

endure this ?   RITSON: It is a little unmeaning exclamatory address to her beauty;
in the nature of a small oath.   HEATH (p. 148): The present occasion afforded nothing which might provoke the lady's blushes, unless it were the suddenness of the news
that Orlando was so near her, and that had already produced its effect, either in
blushes or in paleness, as the lady's emotion happened to determine her.   This
appears from the question asked her by Celia some short time before, ' Change you
colour ?'   She had also long before made Celia her confidante, and owned her passion to her, so as to have got the better of her bashfulness in that respect too; and
now nothing remained but those agitations which were excited in her by Celia's tan-
talising her curiosity.   I must profess myself to concur in opinion with Mr Theobald
and Sir Thomas Hanmer, in defiance of that supercilious haughtiness with which they
are treated by Mr Warburton.   I imagine that the poet may possibly have written,
Good my coz perplexer, that is, I pr'ythee, my perplexing coz; and that the last word,
perplexer, was written with the common abbreviation, thus, ' 𝔓plexer', which might
easily mislead the printer to take the whole, ' coz 𝔓plexer,' for ' complexion.'   CAPELL
[who adopted Theobald's emendation, slightly changing the spelling, says that it is
' abundantly justified by the two similar expressions of the same speaker,' and that] it
means, if such phrases as these can be said to have meaning, so God save my complexion.   CALDECOTT: It is of the same character with what the Princess says in
Love's Lab. L. IV, i, 19: ' Here, good my glass.'   SINGER: It is probably only a
little unmeaning exclamation similar to Goodness me ! Good heart ! or Good now !
but her exclamation implies that this delay did not suit that female impatience which
belonged to her sex and disposition.   STAUNTON: Celia is triumphing in Rosalind's
heightened colour, and the latter's petulant expression may be equivalent to ' plague
on my complexion.'   Or ' Good ' may be a misprint for *Hood.*   Thus Juliet, ' Hood
my unmann'd blood bating in my cheeks.'—III, ii.   [But Juliet's expression was a
simile from hawking and used in anticipation of ' bating.']   MOBERLY: In the name
of all my good looks.   REV. JOHN HUNTER: Rosalind means to compliment her complexion for having by its blushes shown her genuine nature as a woman.   HUDSON:
Merely a common inversion for ' my good complection,' like ' good my lord,' &c.   The
phrase here means, no doubt, ' my good wrapper-up of mystery ' ; as Celia has been tan-
talising Rosalind ' with half-told, half-withheld intelligence.'   ' Complection ' for *com-
plicator.*   For this explanation I am indebted to Mr A. E. Brae.   WRIGHT: Rosalind
appeals to her complexion not to betray her by changing colour.   [Since in this case,
in the interpretation of the original text, there is no aid to be gained from the wise, in
Archæology, Etymology, or Syntax, we simple folk may make what meaning we please
for ourselves, or else pick out one from the foregoing, or combine them all.—ED.]

193, 194. **One . . . discouerie**] ' A South-sea of Discovery: This is stark non-

ſpeake apace : I would thou couldſt ſtammer, that thou　195
might'ſt powre this conceal'd man out of thy mouth, as
Wine comes out of a narrow-mouth'd bottle:either too
much at once, or none at all.　I pre'thee take the Corke
out of thy mouth, that I may drinke thy tydings.　　199

---

sense; We must read *off* Discovery, *i. e. from* Discovery. "If you delay me one
inch of time longer, I shall think this secret as far from discovery as the *South-sea*
is."' [The foregoing note appeared in Theobald's edition of 1733, and again in his
edition of 1740; in neither case is it credited to 'Mr Warburton,' a custom which is
elsewhere, when necessary, duly observed. I can find no allusion to it throughout
the voluminous correspondence between Theobald and Warburton. There is a presumption therefore that it is Theobald's. On the other hand, it appears in Warburton's
edition in 1747 as his own, and is not credited to Theobald, a credit which he never
fails to give where there is a chance to sneer. It is attributed to Warburton by Steevens in the Variorums, but then Steevens was not averse to overlooking, where he
could, poor 'Tib and his Toxophilus.' The peremptory phrase, 'stark nonsense,'
sounds very like Warburton, but the moderation of the emendation does not. On
the whole, the credit may be fairly divided between him and Theobald, and no
great harm, nor good, done to either.—ED.] CAPELL [When Theobald altered 'of'
to *off*] he should have gone a step farther and join'd it to 'South-sea'; for the English language admits of such compounds, but not of interpreting *off* by *from*. JOHN-
SON: I read thus: One inch of delay more is a South Sea. *Discover*, I pr'ythee; tell
me who is it quickly! When the transcriber had once made 'discovery' from *dis-*
cover I, he easily put an article after 'South Sea.' But it may be read with still less
change, and with equal probability: Every inch of delay more is a *South ſea discov-*
ery; Every delay, however short, is to me tedious and irksome as the longest voyage,
as a voyage of *discovery* on the *South ſea*. How much voyages to the South Sea, on
which the English had then first ventured, engaged the conversation of that time, may
be easily imagined. FARMER: 'Of' for *off* is frequent in the elder writers. A
'South Sea of discovery' is a discovery a South Sea off—as far as the South Sea.
HENLEY: A 'South Sea *of* discovery' is not a discovery *as far off*, but as *comprehen-*
sive, as the South Sea; which, being the largest in the world, affords the widest scope
for exercising curiosity. KNIGHT: My curiosity can endure no longer. If you perplex me any further I have a space for conjecture as wide as the South Sea. COL-
LIER: The meaning is, that a single 'inch' of delay is more to Rosalind than a whole
continent in the South Sea. STAUNTON: This is painfully obscure, and the efforts of
the commentators have by no means lessened its ambiguity. Does Rosalind mean
that though 'caparisoned like a man,' she has so much of a woman's curiosity in her
disposition that 'one inch of delay more' would cause her to betray her sex? COW-
DEN-CLARKE: That is, one inch of delay more is as tedious to wait for as a discovery
made in the South Seas. INGLEBY (*Sh. Hermeneutics*, p. 80): The more Celia delays
her revelation as to who the man is, the more she will have to reveal about him.
Why? Because Rosalind fills up the delay (increases it, in fact) with fresh inter-
rogatories, whereby Celia becomes lost in a South Sea of questions. WRIGHT: If you
delay the least to satisfy my curiosity I shall ask you in the interval so many more
questions that to answer them will be like embarking on a voyage of discovery over
a wide and unknown ocean.

Cel. So you may put a man in your belly.   200

Rof. Is he of Gods making? What manner of man? Is his head worth a hat? Or his chin worth a beard?

Cel. Nay, he hath but a little beard.

Rof. Why God will fend more, if the man will bee thankful : let me ftay the growth of his beard, if thou   205 delay me not the knowledge of his chin.

Cel. It is yong *Orlando*, that tript vp the Wraftlers heeles, and your heart, both in an inftant.

Rof. Nay, but the diuell take mocking : fpeake fadde brow, and true maid.   210

Cel. I'faith(Coz) tis he.

Rof. *Orlando*?

Cel. *Orlando*.

Rof. Alas the day, what fhall I do with my doublet & hofe? What did he when thou faw'ft him? What fayde   215

---

210. *maid*] *mind* Anon (*ap.* Cam. Ed.).

---

201. **Gods making**] WRIGHT: Or his tailor's? Compare *Lear*, II, ii, 59: 'nature disclaims in thee : a tailor made thee.' Stephens in his *Essayes and Characters* (2d ed. 1615) has one 'My Mistresse,' of whom he says : 'Her body is (I presume) of God's making & yet I cannot tell, for many parts thereof she made her selfe' (p. 391). [Compare too what Viola answers (*Twelfth N.* I, v, 254) when Olivia unveils her face and asks, 'is't not well done?' 'Excellently done,' replies Viola, 'if God did all.'—ED.]

205. **stay**] For many other instances where 'stay' is equivalent to *wait for*, see Schmidt, *s. v.* 2, g.

209, 210. **sadde ... maid**] RITSON: That is, speak with a grave countenance, and as truly as thou art a virgin; speak seriously and honestly. [In connection with the similar phrase 'I answer you right painted cloth,' line 267, Steevens cites the parallel construction : 'He speaks plain cannon fire, and smoke and bounce '—*King John*, II, i, 462. And Malone cites, 'I speak to thee plain soldier '—*Hen. V:* V, ii, 156; 'He speaks nothing but madman '—*Twelfth N.* I, v, 115. For 'sad' in the sense of *grave*, Schmidt will supply many an instance.]

213. **Orlando**] LADY MARTIN (p. 418): Celia answers, and this time gravely, for Rosalind's emotion shows her this is no jesting matter. Oh happiness beyond belief, oh rapture inexpressible! The tears at this point always welled up to my eyes and my whole body trembled. If hitherto Rosalind had any doubt as to the state of her own heart, from this moment she can have none. Finding how she is overcome at the bare idea of his being near, the thought flashes on her : 'Alas, the day! what shall I do with my doublet and hose?' but Celia has seen him, he perhaps has seen Celia, and that perplexing thought is put aside in the eagerness to learn full particulars about her lover.]

he? How look'd he? Wherein went he? What makes hee   216
heere? Did he aske for me? Where remaines he ? How
parted he with thee ? And when ſhalt thou ſee him a-
gaine? Anſwer me in one vvord.

Cel. You muſt borrow me Gargantuas mouth firſt: 220
'tis a Word too great for any mouth of this Ages ſize, to
ſay I and no, to theſe particulars, is more then to anſwer
in a Catechiſme.   223

216. *makes hee*] *makes him* Han.   +, Steev. Mal. Coll. Sing. Ktly.
218. *he*] *me* F₂.   221. *ſize, to*] *size : To* Cap.   *size.   To*
220. *Gargantuas*] *Garagantua's* Pope   Coll.

216. **Wherein went he?**] HEATH (p. 149): That is, in what manner was he
cloathed? How did he go dressed? REV. JOHN HUNTER: This has been supposed
to mean *in what dress;* but surely it is used for *whereinto.* [This latter interpretation
would be conclusive were it not that *to go* bears the meaning, so very frequently, of *to
dress.* Schmidt gives fourteen or fifteen examples, and the list is far from complete.
Furthermore, is not Hunter's interpretation virtually contained in ' Where remains
he ?'—ED.]

218. **with**] ABBOTT, § 194: Though we still say ' I parted *with* a house ' or ' with
a servant (considered as a chattel),' we could not say ' When you parted *with* the
king.'—*Rich. II:* II, ii, 2.

220. **Gargantuas**] GREY (i, 181): Alluding to Garagantua's swallowing five pilgrims, with their pilgrims' staves, in a salad. [Rabelais, Bk. I, chap. xxxviii.] JOHN-
SON: Rosalind requires nine questions to be answered in *one word.* Celia tells her
that a word of such magnitude is too big for any mouth but that of Garagantua, the
giant of Rabelais. STEEVENS: It appears from the *Stationers' Registers* that in 1592
[April 6—Wright; vol. ii, p. 607, ed. Arber] was published ' Gargantua his prophesie.'
And in 1594 [Dec. 4—Wright; vol. ii, p. 667, ed. Arber] 'A booke entituled, the historie of Gargantua,' &c. The book of Gargantua is likewise mentioned by Laneham
in his letter from Kenilworth, 1575. HALLIWELL: Although there had been no
English translation of Rabelais in Shakespeare's time, yet it is evident from several
notices that a chap-book history of Gargantua was very popular in this country in the
sixteenth century. [Hereupon Halliwell gives several of these notices and other
references. See Text. Notes for the misspelling started among the Editors by Pope.
—ED.] WRIGHT: Cotgrave gives: ' Gargantua. Great throat. Rab.'

222. **I and no**] On that puzzling passage in *Lear,* IV, vi, 99, where Lear says
' "Ay" and "no" too was no good divinity,' COWDEN-CLARKE remarks: ' In
proof that " ay " and " no " was used by Shakespeare with some degree of latitude
as a phrase signifying alternate reply, and not merely in strictness " yes " and " no,"
compare [this present passage], where if the questions Rosalind asks be examined, it
will be perceived that neither " ay " nor " no " will do as answers to any of them,
except to " Did he ask for me ?" ' [Celia's words, as Cowden-Clarke intimates, are
not to be taken literally. I think she means that if she were to give even the very
shortest of answers to all of Rosalind's questions, it would be a longer task than to go
through the Catechism.—ED.]

223. **in a**] HEATH (p. 149): We should read ' to answer a catechism.' ' To

II

Rof. But doth he know that I am in this Forreſt, and
in mans apparrell ? Looks he as freſhly, as he did the day   225
he Wraſtled ?

Cel. It is as eaſie to count Atomies as to reſolue the
propoſitions of a Louer : but take a taſte of my finding
him, and relliſh it with good obſeruance. I found him
vnder a tree like a drop'd Acorne.   230

Rof. It may vvel be cal'd Ioues tree, when it droppes
forth fruite.

Cel. Giue me audience, good Madam.

Rof. Proceed.

Cel. There lay hee ſtretch'd along like a Wounded   235
knight.

Rof. Though it be pittie to ſee ſuch a ſight, it vvell
becomes the ground.   238

---

226. *Wraſtled*] *Wraſted* F₂.

227. *Atomies*] *Atomes* F₃F₄. *Atoms*
Rowe+.

229. *good*] *a good* Steev. Var. '21, Cald.

Knt.

230. *a tree*] *an oak-tree* Han.

232. *forth*] *such* Cap. Ktly, Huds.
forth such Ff, Rowe et cet.

---

answer *in* a catechism' implies no more than to answer a single question in it. The
sense requires that the answer should be to every part of it.

227. **Atomies**] MALONE: 'An atomie,' says Bullokar, in his *Expositor*, 1616, 'is
a mote flying in the sunne. Any thing so small that it cannot be made lesse.' [Prob-
ably this was pronounced *atomeis*. In Sylvester's *Du Bartas, Bethulias Rescue*, 1632,
lib. vi, 346: 'Alas! I erre: for all in Atomies Wert thou divided, all would not suffice.' Again, *Ibid.*, *Battail of Yury*, 421: 'Our State (yerst honour'd where the Sun
doth rise) Would fly in sparks or die in atomies.' Also in R. L.'s *Diella*, Sonn. xxx.,
quoted by Caldecott (not, however, in reference to the pronunciation of *atomie*), we
read: 'Hee that can count the candles of the skie Or number nomberlesse small
attomie.'—ED.]

231. **Ioues**] Because the oak was sacred to Jove, and because Orlando was compared to an acorn, Warburton reads 'under *an oak* tree' in the preceding line. 'A
laughing allusion,' says NEIL, 'to Minerva's springing full-grown from Jupiter's head,
seeing that the oak's acorn Celia spoke of was a full-grown lover.'

232. **forth fruite**] See Text. Notes for the omission supplied by the Second Folio.
Capell asserted that no such phrase as 'drops *forth*' is 'acknowledg'd by Englishmen'; but Malone cites it in this very play, IV, iii, 37.

238. **becomes the ground**] CAPELL: The metaphor is taken from colour'd
needlework, whose figures are more or less beautiful, according to the ground they
are lay'd on. HALLIWELL: But the more obvious meaning may be what is intended.
STEEVENS: So in *Ham.* V, ii, 413: 'Such a sight as this Becomes the field.' WRIGHT:
But 'field' in this case means 'battle-field.' STAUNTON: That is, it well *adorns*, or
graces, or *sets off* the ground. To 'become,' in the present day, signifies usually *to
befit, to be suitable;* formerly it meant more than this. Thus, in *Com. of Err.* III, ii,

Cel. Cry holla, to the tongue, I prethee : it curuettes
vnfeafonably. He was furnifh'd like a Hunter.　　　240
Rof. O ominous, he comes to kill my hart.
Cel. I would fing my fong without a burthen, thou
bring'ft me out of tune.　　　243

239. *holla*] *halla* F₄, Rowe.　　　　241. *hart*] Ff, Pope, Cap. Cald. Knt.
　　the] Ff, Cald. Knt.　*thy* Rowe　　*heart* Rowe et cet.
et cet.

Luciana bids Antipholus, '*become* disloyalty; Apparel Vice, like Virtue's harbinger.'
And in *King John*, V, i, Falconbridge exhorts the king to 'glister like the god of
war, When he intendeth to *become* the field.'

239. **holla**] SKEAT: *Holla, Hollo*, stop, wait! (French). Not the same word as
halloo, and somewhat differently used in old authors. The true sense is stop! wait!
and it was at first used as an interjection simply, though early confused with *halloo*,
and thus acquiring the sense of to shout. ' Holla, stand there.'—*Oth.* I, ii, 56. [The
present passage cited.] French *holà*, 'an interjection, hoe there enough; . . . . also,
hear you me, or come hither.'—Cotgrave. French *ho*, interjection, and *là*, there.
The French *là* is an abbreviation from Latin *illac*, that way, there, originally a feminine ablative, from *illic*, pronoun, he yonder, which is a compound of *ille*, he, and the
enclitic *ce*, meaning 'there.'—*Lear*, III, i, 55; *Twelfth N.* I, v, 291. But note that
there is properly a distinction between *holla* (with final *a*), the French form, and *hollo*
(with final *o*), a variant of *halloo*, the English form. Confusion was inevitable; it is
worth noting that the Fr. *là* accounts for the final *a*, just as Ang. Sax. *lá* accounts for
the final *o* or *oo ;* since Ang. Sax. *á* becomes long *o* by rule, as in *bán*, a bone, *stán*, a
stone.

239. **the**] Walker (*Crit.* ii, 231) has a chapter on the confusion of *thy* and *the*,
of which confusion the present word is an instance. Rapid pronunciation will, I
think, account for this apparent confusion in many an instance. The every-day speech
of the Quakers, or 'their Friends' language,' as they call it, furnishes frequent
examples.—ED.

240. **vnseasonably**] Apparently through a mere oversight Steevens in his edition
of 1793 inserted *very* before this word; thereupon the error curvetted unseasonably
through the Variorums of 1803, 1813, 1821, and Singer's first edition, until Knight
cried holla to it.—ED.

241. **hart**] STEEVENS: A quibble between *heart* and *hart*. [See Schmidt, *s. v.*
heart, for the same pun elsewhere.]

242. **I would**] See Abbott, § 329, for other examples of 'would' used for *will*,
wish, require.

242. **burthen**] CHAPPELL (p. 222): The 'burden' of a song, in the old acceptation of the word, was the *base, foot*, or *under-song*. It was sung throughout, and not
merely at the end of the verse. ' Burden ' is derived from *bourdoun*, a drone base
(French, *bourdon*). 'This sompnour bar to him a stif burdoun, Was nevere trompe
of half so gret a soun.'—[*Cant. Tales, Prol.*, line 673, ed. Morris]. We find as early
as 1250 that *Somer is icumen in* was sung with a foot, or burden, in two parts throughout (' Sing cuckoo, sing cuckoo '); and in the preceding century Giraldus had noticed
the peculiarity of the English in singing under-parts to their songs. That 'burden'
still bore the sense of an under-part or base, and not merely of a ditty, see *A Quest*

Rof.   Do you not know I am a woman, when I thinke,
I muſt ſpeake : ſweet, ſay on.   245

Enter Orlando & Iaques.

Cel.   You bring me out.   Soft, comes he not heere?
Rof.   'Tis he, ſlinke by, and note him.   248

---

244. *when*] *what* Han.   247. *heere*] *neere* F$_2$.   *near* F$_3$F$_4$.
246. Scene VII. Pope+.   248. *ſlinke*] *ſling* F$_3$F$_4$.
    Enter...] After line 248, Dyce.   Cel. and Ros. retire. Theob.
247. *out*] *ont* F$_3$.

---

of Inquiry, &c. 1595, where it is compared to the music of a tabor : ' Good people,
beware of wooers' promises, they are like the musique of a tabor and pipe : the pipe
says golde, giftes, and many gay things; but performance is moralised in the tabor,
which bears the burden of " I doubt it, I doubt it." '   So in *Much Ado*, III, iv, 44,
Margaret says, ' Clap's into " Light o' love;" ' that goes without a burden ' [there
being no man or men on the stage to sing one.—Chappell] : ' do you sing it, and I'll
dance it.'   *Light o' Love* was therefore strictly a *ballet*, to be sung and danced. . . . .
Many of these burdens were short proverbial expressions, such as : ' 'Tis merry in hall
when beards wag all.' . . . . Other burdens were mere nonsense, words that went glibly
off the tongue, giving the accent of the music, such as *hey nonny, nonny no : hey derry
down*, &c.   [See IV, ii, 14.]

247. **bring me out**] Almost a repetition of what she had just said; which explains
itself.   WRIGHT cites *Love's Lab. L.* V. ii, 171 : ' They do not mark me, and that
brings me out.'   If the reference in the present instance be not exclusively to music,
our modern idiom has merely substituted *put* for ' bring.'—ED.

248. COWDEN-CLARKE : One of Shakespeare's touches of womanly nature.   Rosalind, so eager to hear of him, so impatient to extract every particle of description of him,
the instant she sees Orlando approach, draws back, and defers the moment of meeting him.   In the first place, she cannot bear to join him while he has another person
with him, and waits till Jaques is gone; in the next place, she wishes to look upon
him before she looks at him face to face; and lastly, she is glad to have an interval
wherein to recover from her first emotion at hearing he is near, ere she accosts him in
person.   Dramatically, also, the poet is skilful in this pause; he gives opportunity for
the dialogue between Jaques and Orlando, showing them together, and making the
latter avow his passion for Rosalind (in her very presence, though unconsciously)
before he brings the lover to his mistress.   LADY MARTIN (p. 405) : It was surely
a strange perversion which assigned Rosalind, as it once assigned Portia, to actresses
whose strength lay only in comedy.   Even the joyous, buoyant side of her nature
could hardly have justice done to it in their hands; for that is so inextricably mingled
with deep womanly tenderness, with an active intellect disciplined by fine culture, as
well as tempered by a certain native distinction, that a mere comedian could not give
the true tone and colouring even to her playfulness and her wit.   These forest scenes
between Orlando and herself are not, as a comedy actress would be apt to make them,
merely pleasant fooling.   At the core of all that Rosalind says and does lies a passionate love as pure and all-absorbing as ever swayed a woman's heart.   Surely it was the
finest and boldest of all devices, one in which only a Shakespeare could have ventured,
to put his heroine into such a position that she could, without revealing her own secret,

Iaq. I thanke you for your company, but good faith
I had as liefe haue beene my felfe alone.   250
   Orl. And fo had I : but yet for fafhion fake
I thanke you too, for your focietie.
   Iaq. God buy you, let's meet as little as we can.
   Orl. I do defire we may be better ftrangers.   254

251, 252. Prose, Pope et seq.
253. *buy*] Ff, Cam. *b'w'* Rowe+.
be w' Cap. Mal. Sta. *bye,* Coll. *b' wi'*

Wh. Dyce. *be wi'* Cla. Rlfe. *be with*
Steev. et cet.

---

probe the heart of her lover to the very bottom, and so assure herself that the love which possessed her own being was as completely the master of his. Neither could any but Shakespeare have so carried out this daring design, that the woman, thus rarely placed for gratifying the impulses of her own heart and testing the sincerity of her lover's, should come triumphantly out of the ordeal, charming us during the time of probation by wit, by fancy, by her pretty womanly waywardness playing like summer lightning over her throbbing tenderness of heart, and never in the gayest sallies of her happiest moods losing one grain of our respect. No one can study this play without seeing that, through the guise of the brilliant-witted boy, Shakespeare meant the charm of the high-hearted woman, strong, tender, delicate, to make itself felt. Hence it is that Orlando finds the spell which 'heavenly Rosalind' had thrown around him drawn hourly closer and closer, he knows not how, while at the same time he has himself been winning his way more and more into his mistress's heart. Thus, when at last Rosalind doffs her doublet and hose and appears arrayed for her bridal, there seems nothing strange or unmeet in this somewhat sudden consummation of what has in truth been a lengthened wooing. The actress will, in my opinion, fail signally in her task who shall not suggest all this, and who shall not leave upon her audience the impression that when Rosalind resumes her state at her father's court she will bring into it as much grace and dignity as by her bright spirits she had brought of sunshine and cheerfulness into the shades of the forest of Arden.

249–254. Both Walker (*Crit.* i, 1) and Abbott (§ 511) suggest that this passage is verse. The arrangement proposed by the former happens, however, to be exactly the division of lines as given here in the Folio. Unless the whole scene were converted into verse, it is not easy to see what gain would accrue from thus converting these few lines. We must not forget how seldom Shakespeare's prose in serious passages is wholly unrhythmical; it is almost always metric.—ED.

250. **my selfe**] ABBOTT, § 20 (foot-note): 'Myself' seems here used for our *by myself.*

253. **God buy you**] WALKER (*Vers.* 227): *God be with you* is in fact *God b' wi' you;* sometimes a trisyllable, sometimes contracted into a dissyllable;—now *Good bye.* (Quere, whether the substitution of *good* for *God* was not the work of the Puritans, who may have considered the familiar use of God's name in the common form of leave-taking as irreverent? I suggest this merely as a *may-be.*) This form is variously written in the Folio and in old editions of our other dramatists; sometimes it is in full, even when the metre requires the contraction; at others *God b' wi' ye, God be wy you, God bwy, God buy,* &c. I have noticed the form *God b' wi' you* as late as Smollett (*Roderick Random,* chap. iii): 'B' wye, old gentleman'; if not later.

Iaq. I pray you marre no more trees vvith Writing   255
Loue-fongs in their barkes.

Orl. I pray you marre no moe of my verfes with reading them ill-fauouredly.

Iaq. *Rofalinde* is your loues name?   *Orl.* Yes, Iuft.

Iaq. I do not like her name.   260

Orl. There was no thought of pleafing you when fhe
was chriften'd.

Iaq. What ftature is fhe of?

Orl. Iuft as high as my heart.

Iaq. You are ful of prety anfwers : haue you not bin ac- 265
quainted with goldfmiths wiues, & cond thẽ out of rings

---

257. *moe*] Cla. Rlfe. *mo* Mal. *more*   266. *cond*] *conn'd* Rowe. *conned*
Ff et cet.   Knt.

261. *no*] *not* F$_2$.

---

257. **moe**] SKEAT: The modern English word *more* does duty for two Middle
English words which were, generally, well distinguished, viz. : *mo* and *more*, the former
relating to number, the latter to size.   1. Middle English *mo*, more in number, additional. '*Mo* than thries ten' = more than thirty in number; Chaucer, *C. T.* 578.—
Ang. Sax. má, both as adj. and adv., Grein, ii, 201. . . . . This A. S. *má* seems to have
been originally an adverbial form; it is cognate with Ger. *mehr*, Goth. *mais*, adv., Lat.
magis. . . . . 2. Mid. Eng. *more*, larger in size, bigger; '*more* and lesse' = greater and
smaller, Chaucer, *C. T.* 6516. (The distinction between *mo* and *more* is not *always*
observed in old authors, but very often it appears clearly enough)—A. S. *mára*, greater,
larger; Grein, ii, 212. . . . . This is really a *double* comparative, with the additional
comp. suffix -*ra*. . . . . It deserves to be noted that some grammarians, perceiving that
mo-re has one comparative suffix more than *mo*, have rushed to the conclusion that
mo is a positive form. This is false; the positive forms are *mickle*, *much*, and (practically) *many*. [A somewhat different ground of distinction is laid down by the
German grammarians, with whom Wright apparently agrees. It was suggested first
by MOMMSEN (I speak subject to correction), in his edition of *Rom. &. Jul.* p. 12
(cited by Mätzner, i, 277, trans. Grece), who, on the authority of an assertion by
Alexander Gil that *mo* is plural in form, said that he 'knew of scarcely a single passage in any poet of that age where *mo* was used with the singular.' The inference is
that he held *mo* to be used with plurals and *more* with singulars. What we merely
infer from Mommsen is laid down with emphasis by KOCH (*Grammatik*, ii, 209—
cited by Wright), who says: 'The difference seems to be firmly fixed that *more* is
used with the singular and *mo* with the plural; whence it comes that the oldest
grammarians, like Gil and Wallis, set forth *mo* as the comparative of *many*, and *more*
the comparative of *much*. Finally, WRIGHT, with a broader knowledge, says that
'the distinction appears to be that "moe" is used only with the plural, "more" both
with singular and plural.' See Wright's 'Additional Note,' V, i, 34.—ED.]

266. **wiues . . . rings**] The shop-keepers wives decked out in fine clothes were
wont to sit before their doors, and had it in their power by their engaging manners
greatly to augment their husbands' custom. Goldsmiths' Row in Cheapside was the

Orl. Not fo : but I anfwer you right painted cloath,   267
from whence you haue ftudied your queftions.

Iaq. You haue a nimble wit ; I thinke 'twas made of
Attalanta's heeles. Will you fitte downe with me, and   270
wee two, will raile againft our Miftris the world, and all
our miferie.   272

---

267. *you*] *your* Mason.   268. *your*] *you* F$_2$.
    right] *right*, Rowe. *right in the*   271. *Miftris*] *mistress*, Pope+, Cap.
style of the Han.   Mal.

---

pride of London for its display of glittering ware, and naturally a resort for young
fops with more money than brains. The sneer at Orlando is not even thinly veiled.
In Arber's *English Garner*, i, 611, is to be found a collection of *Love Posies* for rings,
many hundred in number, from a MS of about 1596. Other specimens of them may
be found in Tusser's *Five Hundred Points of Good Husbandry*, and Wright refers to
Fairholt's *Rambles of an Archæologist*, pp. 142, 143.—ED.

267. **painted cloath**] CAPELL: In the painted cloth style, *i. e.* briefly and pithily.
Tapestries are improperly call'd painted cloths : therefore the cloths here alluded to
seem rather those occasional paintings that were indeed done upon cloth, *i. e.* linnen
or canvas; and hung out by the citizens upon different publick occasions, but chiefly
—entries; the figures on these cloths were sometimes made to converse and ask questions, by labels coming out of their mouths; and these are the speeches that Jaques
is accused of studying. There was also a furniture of painted cloth; the devices and
legends of one of them, the possessors of Sir Thomas More's works may see among
his poems. [STEEVENS was evidently one of these possessors; he quotes from Sir
Thomas More's *Works*, 1557 :] 'Mayster Thomas More in hys youth devysed in hys
father's house in London, a goodly hangyng of fyne *paynted clothe*, with nine
pageauntes and verses over every of those pageauntes; which verses expressed and
declared what the ymages in those pageauntes represented : and also in those
pageauntes were paynted the thynges that the verses over them dyd (in effecte)
declare.' [Theobald having spoken of this 'painted cloth' as 'tapestry,' NARES corrects him, and says 'it was really *cloth* or canvas *painted in oil* with various devices
or mottoes. Tapestry, being both more costly and less durable, was much less used,
except in splendid apartments; nor though coloured could it properly be called
"painted."' [Steevens, Malone, Knight, Halliwell, all give references throughout
Elizabethan literature to this painted cloth, with specimens of the mottoes, but references from Shakespeare himself are all that is needful, and are far more satisfactory.]
THEOBALD : See *R. of L.* 244 : 'Who fears a sentence, or an old mans saw Shall by
a painted cloth be kept in awe.' WRIGHT : The scenes were frequently of Scripture
subjects. Compare *1 Hen. IV:* IV, ii, 28 : 'Slaves as ragged as Lazarus in the
painted cloth.' And *2 Hen. IV:* II, i, 157 : 'And for thy walls, a pretty slight
drollery, or the story of the Prodigal, or the German hunting in water-work, is worth
a thousand of these fly-bitten tapestries.' ROLFE : Compare *Love's Lab. L.* V, ii,
579, and *Tro. & Cress.* V, x, 47. JOHNSON : This may mean, I give you a true
painted cloth answer; as we say, she talks *right Billingsgate;* that is, exactly such
language as is used at Billingsgate. [For the construction see 'speake sadde brow,'
line 209; and for 'right' see 'right Butterwomans rank,' line 96.]

Orl. I wil chide no breather in the world but my felfe   273
againſt whom I know moſt faults.

Iaq. The worſt fault you haue, is to be in loue.   275

Orl. 'Tis a fault I will not change, for your beſt vertue : I am wearie of you.

Iaq. By my troth, I was ſeeking for a Foole, when I
found you.

Orl. He is drown'd in the brooke, looke but in, and   280
you ſhall ſee him.

Iaq. There I ſhal ſee mine owne figure.

Orl. Which I take to be either a foole, or a Cipher.

Iaq. Ile tarrie no longer with you, farewell good ſig-
nior Loue.   285

Orl. I am glad of your departure : Adieu good Monſieur Melancholly.

Roſ. I wil ſpeake to him like a ſawcie Lacky. and vnder that habit play the knaue with him, do you hear For-

Orl. Verie wel, what would you ?   (reſter.   290

---

273. *breather*] *brother* Rowe i.
274. *moſt*] *no* Ff, Rowe, Pope, Han.
275. *you*] *yon* F₂.
285. Exit.] Rowe. After line 287,
Cap.
286. Scene VIII. Pope+.

287. Cel. and Ros. come forward.
Theob.
288. Aside to Cel. Cap.
289. *him*,] *him :* Rowe+.   *him—*
Johns. *him.* Cap. et seq.

---

273. **breather**] MALONE: So in the 81st *Sonnet :* 'When all the breathers of this
world are dead.' Again, in *Ant. & Cleop*, III, iii, 24 : 'She shows a body rather
than a life, A statue than a breather.' HALLIWELL: 'Let a man examine himself;
for if we would judge ourselves, we should not be judged.'—*1 Corinthians*, xi. It is
Law, if I recollect rightly, who observes, not imagining he was nearly quoting Shakespeare, that every man knows something worse of himself than he is sure of with
respect to others. MOBERLY: As Jaques had been routed by the Duke's sound and
vigorous reflections in II, vii, so here Orlando's sound-heartedness, and afterwards
Rosalind's caustic criticisms, make short work with his melancholic view of life.

274. **know most faults**] See Text. Notes. It is to be regretted that neither Pope
nor Hanmer has vouchsafed to us an interpretation of this fine speech, which, by following the later Folios, they have transformed from modest humility to the extreme
of boastful arrogance.—ED.

282. Is it quite in keeping with Jaques's mother-wit that he should thus tamely fall
into the trap set for him by Orlando?—ED.

283. **Cipher**] WHITE (ed. ii): A pun on 'sigh for,' with an allusion to Narcissus.
[Grant White, in his *Preface* (p. xii), says that 'in determining what passages were
sufficiently obscure to justify explanation,' he 'took advice of his washerwoman.' It
is a comfort to know the source of the foregoing note.—ED.]

289. LADY MARTIN (p. 418): At this moment Orlando is seen approaching with

Rof.   I pray you, what i'ft a clocke?   291

Orl.   You fhould aske me what time o'day: there's no
clocke in the Forreft.

Rof.   Then there is no true Louer in the Forreft, elfe
fighing euerie minute. and groaning euerie houre wold   295
detect the lazie foot of time, as wel as a clocke.

Orl.   And why not the fwift foote of time ? Had not
that bin as proper?

Rof.   By no meanes fir ; Time trauels in diuers paces,
with diuers perfons : Ile tel you who Time ambles with-   300
all, who Time trots withal, who Time gallops withal,
and who he ftands ftil withall.   302

---

299. *paces*] *places* F$_3$F$_4$, Rowe i.   300. *diuers*] *diuerfe* F$_2$.

Jaques through the trees. A glance assures Rosalind that it is indeed he ; but now
the woman's natural shyness at being discovered in so strange a suit comes over her.
'Slink by and note him,' she says ; and withdrawing along with Celia to a point
where she may see and not be seen, she listens, with what delight we may conceive,
to the colloquy in which her lover more than holds his own when the misanthrope
Jaques rallies him on being in love and marring the forest trees 'with writing love-
songs in their bark.' On the assurance given by Orlando's answers that she is the
very Rosalind of these songs, her heart leaps with delight. Not for the world would
she have Orlando recognise her in her unmaidenly disguise ; but now a sudden
impulse determines her to risk all, and even to turn it to account as the means of testing his love. Boldness must be her friend, and to avert his suspicion her only course
is to put on a 'swashing and a martial outside,' and to speak to him 'like a saucy
laquey, and under that habit play the knave with him.' He must not be allowed for
an instant to surmise the 'hidden woman's fear' that lies in her heart. Besides, it is
only by resort to a rough and saucy greeting and manner that she could mask and
keep under the trembling of her voice and the womanly tremor of her limbs. I
always gave her 'Do you hear, forester ?' with a defiant air, as much as to say, 'What
are you, a stranger, doing here, intruding in the forest on those who are "natives of
the place"?' With such a swagger, too, that Orlando feels inclined to turn round
sharply upon the boy, as he had just done upon the cynical Jaques.

   295, 296. ABBOTT refers to *Rich. II:* V, v, 50, etc. : 'For now hath time made me
his numbering clock ; My thoughts are minutes ; and with sighs they jar Their watches
on unto mine eyes, the outward watch, Whereto my finger, like a dial's point, Is pointing still, in cleansing them from tears. Now, sir, the sound that tells what hour it is
Are clamorous groans, which strike upon my heart, Which is the bell ; so sighs and
tears and groans Show minutes, times, and hours.'

   296. detect] ALLEN (MS) : To 'detect' rather implies discovery by *indications*
(τεκμήριον). Then, taking the liberty (as Shakespeare does) to use the verb intransi-
tively, it may mean here : A groan once an hour and a sigh once every minute *give
indications* of the progress of time.

   300, &c. who] See Abbott, § 274, for many other examples of this common use of
'who' for *whom*.

Orl.   I prethee, who doth he trot withal?   303

303, 316. *who*] *whom* Ff, Rowe+, Cap.

303–315. MRS GRIFFITH (p. 84, foot-note) says that to 'trot hard' means *to trot high*, 'which is the most fatiguing rate to a traveller.' HUNTER (i, 349): This portion of this very sprightly dialogue appears to have undergone dislocation at a very early period, for the old copies and the new are alike. To *trot hard*, at least in the present use of the phrase, is a rapid motion, only just below the gallop. How, then, can it be said that Time 'trots hard' when a se'ennight seems as long as seven years? A slow motion is intended, such as is meant by the word *ambling*. Again, Time passes swiftly with the easy priest and the luxurious rich man who is free from gout. He 'trots hard' with them.   And that this transposition is required appears from the order in which Rosalind proposed to show the divers paces of Time with divers persons: 1. ambling; 2. trotting; 3. galloping.   I would therefore propose to regulate the passage thus: '*Orl.* I prythee who ambles Time withal?   *Ros.* Marry, he ambles with a young maid, &c.   Time's pace is so ambling, &c.   *Orl.* Who doth he trot withal?   *Ros.* With a priest that lacks Latin, &c.   There Time trots withal.'   If this is not accepted we are driven to the supposition that when Shakespeare speaks of 'trotting hard' a slow motion is intended, and that ambling denotes a swift motion, neither of which can, I think, be maintained.   WHITE: Of all the means of making a short journey seem long, a hard-trotting horse is the surest; while an ambling nag, on the contrary, affords so easy and luxurious a mode of travelling that the rider arrives all too soon at his journey's end.   That Rosalind's comparison is between comfort and discomfort, not speed and slowness, is, beside, conclusively shown by her saying, afterward, that Time gallops with a thief to the gallows, 'for though he go *as softly as foot can fall*, he thinks himself too soon there.'   HALLIWELL: Can this ['He trots hard with a young maid'] be accepted that Time appears so long to her that it increases the necessary pace to enable him to overcome it?   The repetition of the word *hard* shows that it is unlikely there is any misprint, but the term may perhaps here be interpreted, *with difficulty*, *very slowly*.   'Solid bodies foreshow rain, as boxes and pegs of wood when they draw and wind *hard*.'—Bacon.   'Time goes on crutches, till love hath all his rites.'—*Much Ado* [II, i, 372, cited by Malone].   It is perhaps possible that Rosalind is referring to the idea that in matters of ardent desire even rapidity is reckoned a delay.   'In desiderio etiam celeritas mora est—in desyre, in a thing that a man coveteth, even spede is counted a taryaunce.'—Taverner's *Mimi Publiani*, 1539 [cited by Caldecott].   WRIGHT: The following definition from Holme's *Armoury*, B. II, c. 7, p. 150, justifies the original arrangement: 'Trot, or a Trotting Horse, when he sets hard and goes of an uneasy rate.'   The point is not that Time goes fast, but that he goes at an uneasy pace, and therefore seems to be slow.   [I cannot but agree with Hunter, not in any exchange of the phrases, but that, in the case of the young maid it is the rate of the pace, not its quality, to which Rosalind refers.   I think that here 'hard' means *fast*.   The speed of the trot is increased by the shortness of the time.   Invert the order of the sentence: 'If the interim be but a sennight, Time will trot hard.'   Are we not compelled here to interpret 'hard' as *fast?*   What effect can the flight of time have on the quality of a trot other than on its speed?   How can any shortness of the interim make a trot jauncing?   The faster the trot, as every one knows, the easier it is.   That the time seems long because the trot is jauncing is a mere inference; in actual experience the comfort or discomfort of such a trot depends not a little on the use and wont of the rider.

Rof.   Marry he trots hard with a yong maid, between
the contract of her marriage, and the day it is folemnizd: 305
if the interim be but a fennight,   Times pace is fo hard,
that it feemes the length of feuen yeare.

Orl.   Who ambles Time withal?

Rof.   With a Prieft that lacks Latine, and a rich man
that hath not the Gowt : for the one fleepes eafily be-   310
caufe he cannot ftudy, and the other liues merrily, becaufe he feeles no paine : the one lacking the burthen of
leane and wafteful Learning; the other knowing no burthen of heauie tedious penurie. Thefe Time ambles
withal.   315

Orl.   Who doth he gallop withal?

Rof.   With a theefe to the gallowes : for though hee
go as foftly as foot can fall, he thinkes himfelfe too foon
there.

Orl.   Who ftaies it ftil withal?   320

Rof.   With Lawiers in the vacation : for they fleepe
betweene Terme and Terme, and then they perceiue not
how time moues.

Orl.   Where dwel you prettie youth?

Rof. With this Shepheardeffe my fifter : heere in the   325
skirts of the Forreft, like fringe vpon a petticoat.

Orl.   Are you natiue of this place?

Rof.   As the Conie that you fee dwell where fhee is
kindled.   329

307. *yeare*] *years* F₄, Rowe+, Mal.   320. *ftaies it*] *stands he* Coll. (MS)
Steev. Coll. Sing. Ktly.   ii, iii.
   320. *Who*] *Whom* Ff, Rowe+.   329. *kindled*] *kind-led* Pope i.

Unquestionably, 'hard' may be applied to a trot in the sense of *uneasy*, and it is
apparently so used in Wright's citation from Holme's *Armoury*, but I doubt if it can
be restricted to this sense.   Hunter thinks that a 'slow motion' is intended when Rosalind says that 'Time's pace is so hard that a sennight seems the length of seven years.'
To me it implies fast motion, seven years are compressed into a week; the thoughts,
hopes, wishes, prayers of seven years are felt and lived through while 'the happy
planet dips forward under starry light' only seven times.—ED.]

   307. **yeare**] WRIGHT: We still use *pound* and *stone* with plural numerals as did
Hamlet, III, ii, 298: 'I'll take the Ghost's word for a thousand pound.'   Other
instances of this use are in *Tam. of Shr.* Induct. II, 115; *1 Hen. IV:* II, iv, 50; *2
Hen. IV:* III, ii, 224.—Note on *Temp.* I, ii, 53. [See V, ii, 62.]

   327. **natiue**] WRIGHT: 'Native,' as applied to persons, is always an adjective in
Shakespeare.

Orl. Your accent is ſomething finer, then you could   330
purchaſe in ſo remoued a dwelling.

Roſ. I haue bin told ſo of many : but indeed, an olde
religious Vnckle of mine taught me to ſpeake, who was
in his youth an inland man, one that knew Courtſhip too
well : for there he fel in loue. I haue heard him read ma-   335
ny Lectors againſt it, and I thanke God, I am not a Woman to be touch'd with ſo many giddie offences as hee
hath generally tax'd their whole ſex withal.

Orl. Can you remember any of the principall euils,
that he laid to the charge of women?   340

Roſ. There were none principal, they were all like

336. *Lectors*] *Lecturs* F₂. *Lectures*   336. *and*] Om. F₃F₄, Rowe +.
F₃F₄.

---

329. **kindled**] SKEAT : To bring forth young. Middle English, *kindlen, kundlen.*
. . . . Cf. also : '*Kyndlyn*, or brynge forthe yonge kyndelyngis, *Feto, effeto.*'—*Prompt.
Parv.* p. 275. And in Wyclif, *Luke* iii, 7, we find '*kyndlis* of edderis' in the earlier,
and '*kyndlyngis* of eddris' in the later version, where the A. V. has 'generation of
vipers.' . . . . It refers, in general, to a *numerous* progeny, a litter, especially with
regard to rabbits, &c. [It is still in common use in this country, and always, I
believe, restricted to rabbits.—ED.] CAMBRIDGE EDITORS : In F₄ and in Rowe's
two editions the word 'kindled' happens to be in two lines, and therefore divided
by a hyphen. Pope, misled by this, printed it in his first edition as a compound,
'kind-led,' interpreting it probably with reference to the gregarious habits of the animal in question.

331. **purchase**] That is, simply, to acquire. In technical legal language all land,
howsoever acquired, other than by descent, is by purchase.—ED.

331. **remoued**] REED : That is, remote, sequestered.

332. **of many**] See II, i, 54 or Abbott, § 170.

333. **religious**] MOBERLY : An uncle of mine, who is an aged monk or hermit. ABBOTT (p. 456) refers to *Rich. II :* V, i, 23 : 'Cloister thee in some religious
house.'

334. **inland**] See II, vii, 101.

334. **Courtship**] WHITE : That is, court life. SCHMIDT : Used in the double
sense of civility and elegance of manners and of courting or wooing. So also *Rom.
& Jul.* III, iii, 34 : 'more honourable state, more courtship lives in carrion-flies than
Romeo.'

335. **there**] ALLEN (MS) : That is, at the court, implied in 'courtship.'

336. **Lectors**] WHITE : This is one of the many evidences that the English of
Shakespeare's time has been remarkably preserved, even in sound, by the inhabitants
of New England. Throughout the Eastern States, even among a large proportion of
those who are 'inland-bred and know some culture,' *lecture* is pronounced *lectur.*
WRIGHT : In the same way in Bacon's *Advancement of Learning,* 1605, p. 30, '*ver-
dure* is spelt "verdor."'

337. **touch'd**] COWDEN-CLARKE : That is, tainted, infected.

one another, as halfe pence are, euerie one fault feeming   342
monftrous, til his fellow-fault came to match it.

Orl.   I prethee recount some of them.

Rof.   No: I wil not caft away my phyfick, but on thofe   345
that are ficke.   There is a man haunts the Forreft, that a-
bufes our yong plants with caruing *Rofalinde* on their
barkes; hangs Oades vpon Hauthornes, and Elegies on
brambles; all (forfooth) defying the name of *Rofalinde*.
If I could meet that Fancie-monger, I would giue him   350
fome good counfel, for he feemes to haue the Quotidian
of Loue vpon him.

Orl.   I am he that is fo Loue-fhak'd, I pray you tel
me your remedie.   354

---

342. *euerie one*] *every ones* F₃F₄.   348. *barkes*] *borkes* F₂.
Rowe.   349. *defying*] *deifying* Ff.

---

342. **halfe pence**] WRIGHT: No halfpence were coined in Elizabeth's reign till
1582–3.   Bacon refers to 'the late new halfpence' in the Dedication to the first
edition of his *Essays*, which was published in 1597.   They all had the portcullis with
a mint mark, and on the reverse a cross moline with three pellets in each angle, so
that, in comparison with the great variety in coins of other denominations then in cir-
culation, there was a propriety in saying 'as like one another as halfpence are.'   They
were used till 1601.   See Folkes, *Table of Silver Coins*, p. 57.

343. **monstrous**] One of Walker's most valuable chapters is that on ' Omissions
in consequence of Absorption' (*Crit.* ii, 254).   On p. 264 he cites the present passage, and after it, follows, without comment, '*Most* monstrous'; which is, to me, a
decidedly plausible conjecture.   The fault was not made less monstrous by having a
fellow-fault.   It was its pre-eminence, its superlative degree, that was thereby taken
from it.—ED.

344. **recount some of them**] LADY MARTIN (p. 420): What an opening here
for her to put her lover to the test, to hear him say all that a loving woman most longs
to hear from him she loves, and he all the while ignorant that he is laying bare his
heart before her !

350. **Fancie**] Love.

351. **Quotidian**] RUSHTON (*Shakespeare's Euphuism*, p. 90): ' Doubtlesse if euer
she [Liuia] hir selfe haue bene scorched with the flames of desire, she wil be redy to
quench the coales with courtesie in an other; if euer she haue bene attached of loue,
she wil rescue him that is drenched in desire : if euer she haue ben taken with the
feuer of fancie, she will help his ague, who by a *quotidian* fit is conuerted into
phrensie.'   [Lily's *Euphues*, p. 66, ed. Arber,—Wright.   In Greene's *Planeto-
machia*, 1585, we find 'the peculiar affections of those men, in whom she [Venus]
is predomynant,' and on p. 103 (ed. Grosart), *quotidian fevers* are expressly mentioned as a symptom of love; we there read : 'the peculiar diseases to this starre are
Cathars, Coryse Branchy [qu. Coryza ?], Lethargies, Palsies, ... quotidian feuers,
paines in the heade.'—ED.]

Rof.   There is none of my Vnckles markes vpon you: 355
he taught me how to know a man in loue : in which cage
of ruſhes, I am ſure you art not priſoner.

Orl.   What were his markes?

Rof.   A leane cheeke, which you haue not : a blew eie
and ſunken, which you haue not : an vnqueſtionable ſpi-   360
rit, which you haue not : a beard negleＣted, which you
haue not:(but I pardon you for that, for ſimply your hauing in beard, is a yonger brothers reuennew) then your
hoſe ſhould be vngarter'd, your bonnet vnbanded, your   364

357. *art*] F₁.   363. *in*] *no* Ff, Rowe, Pope.

355. **There is . . . markes**] See Abbott, § 335, for other instances of 'the inflection in -s preceding a plural subject.'

356, 357. **cage of rushes**] C. H. HART (*New Sh. Soc. Trans.*, 1877–9, Pt. iii, p.
462): 'Cage' of course means prison here; but if 'cage of rushes' be not taken to
mean a rush ring, or to allude to it, the phrase seems to me meaningless and deprived
of its pith.   [For *rush rings*, used in mock ceremonies of marriage, and much con-
ducing thereby to immorality, see Nares, *s. v.*; Brand's *Pop. Ant.* ii, p. 107; Skeat's
Two Noble Kins. IV, i, 88—all cited by Hart.   I doubt if there be more of an allusion here to a custom, low and vulgar at its best, than might be suggested by the mere
chance use of the word.   It is in keeping with Rosalind's assumed disbelief in the
strength of Orlando's love, that she should refer to the bars of his prison as no more
than rushes.—ED.]

359. **blew eie**] STEEVENS: That is, blueness about the eyes.   WHITE: That is,
hollow-eyed.   'Blue eyes' were called *grey* in Shakespeare's time.   See 'blue-eyed
hag,' *Temp.* I, ii, 270.

360. **vnquestionable**] CHAMIER: Unwilling to be conversed with.   M. MASON:
So in [III, iv, 34] Rosalind says she had 'much question' with the Duke.   And in
V, iv, 165, the Duke was converted after 'some question with an old religious man.'
In both places, 'question' means *discourse* or *conversation*.   [For many more
instances, see Schmidt, *s. v.* 'Question,' the noun and the verb.   White refers to
'Thou com'st in such a questionable shape,'—*Ham.* I, iv, 43, where the word is used
in exactly the same sense; that is, thou com'st in a shape so proper to be questioned,
and yet this line is often quoted as if 'questionable' meant 'suspicious.']

362. **hauing**] STEEVENS: 'Having' is *possession, estate.*   So in *Merry Wives*, III,
ii, 73: 'The gentleman is of no having.'   [For nine or ten other examples see
Schmidt.]

364. **vngarter'd**] MALONE: The established and characteristical marks by which
the votaries of love were denoted in the time of Shakespeare.   Thus, in *The Fair
Maid of the Exchange*, by Heywood, 1637: 'Shall I that have jested at lovers' sighs,
now raise whirlwinds?   Shall I, that have flouted *ah ! me*'s once a quarter, now practise *ah ! me*'s every minute?   Shall I defy hatbands, and tread garters and shoe-strings
under my feet?   Shall I fall to falling-bands and be a ruff-an no longer?   I must; I
am now liege-man to Cupid, and have read all these informations in his book of Statutes.'—[p. 22, ed. Sh. Soc.   Evidently these signs of love were unmistakeable in the

fleeue vnbutton'd, your fhoo vnti'de, and euerie thing   365
about you, demonſtrating a careleſſe defolation : but you
are no fuch man; you are rather point deuice in your accouſtrements, as louing your felfe, then feeming the Louer of any other.   (I Loue.

   Orl.   Faire youth, I would I could make thee beleeue   370
   Roſ.   Me beleeue it ? You may affoone make her that

---

367. *point*] *a point* F₃F₄.   367, 368. *accouſtrements*] Ff. *Accou-*
    point deuice] *point-de-vice* Johns.   *trements* Rowe.
point-devise Dyce.

---

speaker's mind; what he has just said is after he had seen the Fair Maid of the
Exchange; before he had seen her he says (p. 18): 'if ev'ry tale of love, Or love
itself, or fool-bewitching beauty, Make me cross-arm myself, study *ah-me*'s, Defy my
hatband, tread beneath my feet Shoe-strings and garters, practise in my glass Dis-
tressed looks, and dry my liver up, With sighs enough to wind an argosy, If ever I
turn thus fantastical, Love plague me.'] Again, in *How a Man may Choose a Good
Wife from a Bad,* 1602: 'I was once like thee, A sigher, melancholy humorist,
Crosser of arms, a goer without garters, A hatband-hater, and a busk-point wearer.'—
[I, iii, p. 17, ed. Hazlitt. Hamlet's 'ungartered stockings' will occur to every one.—
ED.]

   364. **vnbanded**] The foregoing extracts, cited by Malone, fairly illustrate this
whole passage. Wright quotes from *The Anatomie of Abuses,* 1583, where Stubbes
describes the fashions of hats: 'An other sort have round crownes, sometimes with
one kinde of bande, sometimes with an other; nowe blacke, now white, now russet,
now red, now greene, now yellowe, now this, nowe that, never content with one
colour or fashion two dayes to an ende. . . . . Besides this, of late there is a new
fashion of wearing their Hattes sprung vp amongst them, which they father vpon the
Frenchmen, namely to weare them without bandes; but how vnseemelie (I will not
say how Assy) a fashion that is, let the wise judge.'—(p. 52, Collier's Reprint) [Part
I, pp. 50, 51, ed. New Sh. Soc.]

   367. **point deuice**] STEEVENS: That is, drest with finical nicety. So in *Love's
Lab. L.* V, i, 21: 'I abhor such fanatical phantasimes, such insociable and point-
devise companions.' SKEAT: A shortened form of the older phrase *at point device,*
equivalent to with great nicety or exactitude, as: 'With limmes [limbs] wrought *at
point device ;'—Rom. of the Rose,* l. 830; a translation of Old French, *à point devis,*
according to a point [of exactitude] that is devised or imagined, *i. e.* in the best way
imaginable.

   FLETCHER (p. 216): Who does not see the pleasure with which, under her
affected disbelief, she dwells on the contrast which Orlando's neatness of personal
appearance presents to that of the ordinary but less healthy kind of lover, 'about
whom everything demonstrates a careless desolation.'

   367, 368. **accoustrements**] WRIGHT: The early form of the French word. In
King John, I, i, 211, and in *Tam. Shr.* III, ii, 121, it occurs in the modern spelling.

   371. **Me beleeue it**] KEIGHTLEY's text reads *'Make* me believe it,' and in a note
(*Exp.* 160) he says: 'Surely the passage thus gains not only in metre, but in spirit.'
[This is the second time (see line 84 above) that Keightley in a prose passage appeals

you Loue beleeue it, which I warrant fhe is apter to do,　372
then to confeffe fhe do's: that is one of the points, in the
which women ftil giue the lie to their confciences. But
in good footh, are you he that hangs the verfes on the　375
Trees, wherein *Rofalind* is fo admired?

Orl. I fweare to thee youth, by the white hand of
Rofalind, I am that he, that vnfortunate he.

Ros. But are you fo much in loue, as your rimes fpeak?

Orl. Neither rime nor reafon can expreffe how much.　380

Rof: Loue is meerely a madneffe, and I tel you, deferues as wel a darke houfe, and a whip, as madmen do :
and the reafon why they are not fo punifh'd and cured, is
that the Lunacie is fo ordinarie, that the whippers are in
loue too : yet I profeffe curing it by counfel.　385

Orl. Did you euer cure any fo?

Rof. Yes one, and in this manner. Hee was to imagine me his Loue, his Miftris : and I fet him euerie day
to woe me At which time would I, being but a moonifh
youth, greeue, be effeminate, changeable, longing, and　390
liking, proud, fantaftical, apifh, fhallow, inconftant, ful

---

381. *and*] *and,* Rowe, Theob. et seq.　　389, &c. *woe*] *woo* Rowe.

---

to the needs of *metre*. I suppose that he assumes all of Shakespeare's prose to be
metric prose, and he therein comes near the truth. I dare not say how flat his
present emendation strikes me. ' Me believe it !' is absolute Rosalind; just as, afterwards, she says ' you a lover !'—ED.]

378. **that he**] See line 11, or Abbott, § 224.

380. **expresse how much**] LADY MARTIN (p. 421): Oh, how intently she has
watched for that answer! with what secret rapture heard it! But he must discern
nothing of this, so, turning carelessly away, and smiling inwardly to think she is herself an illustration of what she says, she exclaims: ' Love is merely,' &c.

381. **meerely**] STAUNTON : It may not be impertinent to say, once for all, that
'merely,' from the Latin *merus,* and 'mere' in old language, meant *absolutely, altogether, purely.* See II, vii, 148. In Lodge's *Rosalynde :* 'And forth they pulled
such victuals as they had, and fed as *merely* as if they had been in Paris.'

382. See Malvolio's treatment in *Twelfth Night.*

387. FLETCHER (p. 217): Her answer shows us one of those subtle devices by
which Shakespeare so well knew how to exalt the ideal perfection of a favorite heroine. The exquisite characterisation which she gives us of feminine caprice in the
weaker portion of her sex most beautifully sets off that contrary disposition by which
her every sentence makes us feel that she herself is animated.

389. **moonish**] STEEVENS : That is, variable. HALLIWELL : It is possible that it
may, however, be correctly rendered *foolish, weak;* for Ben Jonson uses the term
moonling in the sense of a fool or a lunatic.

of teares, full of ſmiles ; for euerie paſſion ſomething, and   392
for no paſſion truly any thing, as boyes and women are
for the moſt part, cattle of this colour : would now like
him, now loath him : then entertaine him, then forſwear   395
him : now weepe for him, then ſpit at him ; that I draue
my Sutor from his mad humor of loue, to a liuing humor
of madnes, ẘ was to forſweare the ful ſtream of ẙ world,
and to liue in a nooke meerly Monaſtick : and thus I cur'd   399

397. *my*] *this* Rowe.   397. *liuing*] *loving* Johns. conj. Coll.
    Sutor] *Suter* F₂.   *Suitor* F₃F₄.   i, ii, iii, Dyce, Sta. Huds.
    from] *for* F₄.   398. *ẘ*] *which* Ff.

397. **liuing**] JOHNSON : If this be the true reading, we muſt by 'living' understand *lasting*, or *permanent;* but I cannot forbear to think that some antithesis was
intended which is now lost; perhaps the passage stood thus : I drove my suitor from
a *dying* humour of love to a living humour of madness. Or rather thus : From a
mad humour of love to a *loving* humour of madness, that is, From a *madness* that
was *love*, to a *love* that was *madness*. This seems somewhat harsh and strained, but
such modes of speech are not unusual in our poet; and this harshness was probably
the cause of the corruption. FARMER : Perhaps we should read : to a humour of
loving madness. MALONE : 'A living humour of madness' is, I conceive, a humour
of *living madness*, a mad humour that operates on *the mode of living;* or, in other
words, and more accurately, *a mad humour of life;* '— to forswear the world, and
live in a nook,' &c. WHITER (p. 51) : Compare : 'Give me a *living* reason she's
disloyal.'—*Oth.* III, iii, 470. That is, give me a *direct, absolute*, and *unequivocal*
proof. Why then may not the 'living humor of madness' mean a *confirmed, abso-*
lute, and *direct* state of madness? This signification is easily deduced from the
sense which the original word bears in the phrases of ' Done or expressed to the *life*'
—*ad* vivum *expressum*. COLLIER : The antithesis is complete if, with Johnson, we
read *loving*, which is only the change of a letter; and this reading is supported by
the MS correction of the early possessor of the First Folio in the library of Lord
Francis Egerton. The meaning thus is, that Rosalind drove her suitor from his mad
humour of love into a humour in which he was in love with madness, and forswore
the world. [It is also *loving* in Collier's (MS).] WHITE : *Loving* is plausible, and
the antithetical conceit quite in the manner of Shakespeare's time. WALKER (*Crit.*
iii, 63) : Of course *loving*. [Walker gives five or six instances where unquestionably
'live' has been printed *love*, and 'love' *live*.] WRIGHT : But 'living' in the sense
of real or actual [as Whiter suggests] gives a very good meaning, and its resemblance
in sound is sufficiently near to keep up the jingle. [Wherewith the present editor
entirely agrees.—ED.]

399. **meerly Monastick**] ALLEN (MS) : I wonder whether it should not be written : ' to live in a nook, merely monastic ' ? That is, ' monastic ' as an adjective in
the nominative, ' he becoming merely monastic,' *i. e.* absolutely *religious*.

399. BLACKWOOD'S MAGAZINE (April, 1833) : Who could resist this? Not
Orlando; for, though love-stricken [Qu. *because* love-stricken ?—ED.], he is full of
the power of life; his passion is a joy; his fear is but slight shadow, his hope strong
sunshine. . . . . There is a mysterious spell breathed over his whole being from that

him, and this way wil I take vpon mee to wafh your Li-   400
uer as cleane as a found fheepes heart, that there fhal not
be one fpot of Loue in't.

Orl.   I would not be cured, youth.

Rof.   I would cure you, if you would but call me *Rofa-*
lind, and come euerie day to my Coat, and woe me.   405

Orlan.   Now by the faith of my loue, I will ; Tel me
where it is.

Rof.   Go with me to it, and Ile fhew it you : and by
the way, you fhal tell me, where in the Forreft you liue :
Wil you go ?   410

Orl.   With all my heart, good youth.

Rof.   Nay, you muft call mee *Rofalind*: Come fifter,
will you go ?   *Exeunt.*   413

---

401. *cleane*] *cleare* F$_2$. *cleer* F$_3$. *clear*   408. *Ile*] *I will* Rowe+.
F$_4$, Rowe+, Cap.   412. *Nay*] *Nay, nay* F$_4$, Rowe +.
405. *Coat*] *cote* Rowe.   *cotte* Theob.

---

silver speech.   Near the happy close of the play the Duke says to him : ' I do remember in this shepherd-boy Some lively touches of my daughter's favour.'   And Orlando
answers : ' My lord, the first time that I ever saw him, Methought he was a brother to
your daughter.'   That sweet thought had passed across his mind at their first meeting,
although he did not tell the ' shepherd-boy.' . . . . And is not this shepherd-boy with
' lively touches of my daughter's favour ' a thousand times better than a dead picture ?
It is a living full-length picture even of Rosalind in a fancy-dress ; and 'tis easy as
delightful to imagine it the very original's own self, ' the slender Rosalind,' ' the
heavenly Rosalind,' 'tis ' Love's young dream !'

400, 401. STEEVENS : This is no very delicate comparison, though produced by
Rosalind in her assumed character of a shepherd.   HALLIWELL : The liver was considered the seat of love.   WRIGHT : See *The Temp.* IV, i, 56 : ' The cold white virgin snow upon my heart Abates the ardour of my liver.'   Compare the ' jecur ulcero-
sum ' of Horace, *Od.* I, xxv, 15.   [Forgetfulness of this fact, so familiar to every
student, whether English or Classical, led Dr Bucknill (p. 110) to propose that the
words ' heart ' and ' liver ' should be transposed.   Whereto attention was called by
' Speriend,' *Notes & Qu.* 5th S. vol. iv, p. 182.]

406. I will] NEIL : Francis, ' the dramatic Censor,' suggests the insertion here of
the words, ' The more so as thou hast strong traces of Rosalind's favour,' justified
by V, iv, 32, 33.

413. FLETCHER (p. 218) : We must bear in mind that Orlando cannot be supposed
to lose sight for a moment of the resemblance in feature and in voice which the supposed forest youth bears to his noble and graceful mistress.   Nor does he any more
wish for his own cure than Rosalind herself desires it.   On the contrary, it is because
he feels the lively and delicate charm which he finds in this new acquaintance, opera-
ting, by strong affinity, to nourish and deepen the impression which his real mistress's
perfections have made upon his heart, that he at last accepts the sportive invitation to

[will you go]

visit the cottage of the fictitious Ganymede.   On the other hand, Rosalind has secured to herself the pleasure of hearing under her disguise the continued addresses of her lover; while the fact of her remaining undiscovered is brought within the limits of probability by the exceeding unlikelihood to Orlando's mind of such a metamorphosis on the part of his princess, and yet more by the perfect self-possession and finished address wherewith both she and her cousin are enacting their forest and pastoral parts, as if they were as native to the scene, to borrow Rosalind's expression, 'as the coney that you see dwell where she is kindled.'   But, above all, she is talking herself more deeply into love.   How beautifully does this appear in her subsequent conversation with Celia, when Orlando has failed to keep his wooing appointment: ' Never talk to me, I will weep,' &c., and in her account of how she had avoided recognition by her father, although she and her cousin had set out upon their wanderings on purpose to seek him.   LADY MARTIN (p. 422): I need scarcely say how necessary it is for the actress in this scene, while carrying it through with a vivacity and dash that shall divert from Orlando's mind every suspicion of her sex, to preserve a refinement of tone and manner suitable to a woman of Rosalind's high station and cultured intellect; and by occasional tenderness of accent and sweet persuasiveness of look, to indicate how it is that, even at the outset, she establishes a hold upon Orlando's feelings, which in their future intercourse in the forest deepens, without his being sensibly conscious of it, his love for the Rosalind of his dreams.   I never approached this scene without a sort of pleasing dread, so strongly did I feel the difficulty and the importance of striking the true note in it.   Yet when once engaged in it, I was borne along I knew not how.   The situation in its very strangeness was so delightful to my imagination that from the moment when I took the assurance from Orlando's words to Jaques that his love was as absolute as woman could desire, I seemed to lose myself in a sense of exquisite enjoyment.   A thrill passed through me; I felt my pulse beat quicker; my very feet seemed to dance under me.   That Rosalind should forget her first woman's fears about her ' doublet and hose ' seemed the most natural thing in the world.   Speak to Orlando she must at any hazard.   But oh, the joy of getting him to pour out all his heart, without knowing that it was his own Rosalind to whom he talked,—of proving if he were indeed worthy of her love, and testing, at the same time, the depth and sincerity of her own devotion!   The device to which she resorted seemed to suggest itself irresistibly; and, armed with Shakespeare's words, it was an intense pleasure to try to give expression to the archness, the wit, the quick, ready intellect, the ebullient fancy, with the tenderness underlying all, which give to this scene its transcendent charm.   Of all the scenes of this exquisite play, while this is the most wonderful, it is for the actress certainly the most difficult.   GRANT WHITE (*Studies*, &c., p. 254): Now here most Rosalinds go shyly off with Celia and leave Orlando to come dangling after them; but when I read the passage I see Ganymede jauntily slip his arm into Orlando's, and lead him off, laughingly lecturing him about his name; then turn his head over his shoulder, and say, ' Come, sister !' leaving Celia astounded at the boundless ' cheek ' of her enamored cousin.   [In a foot-note:] I have used the words ' cheek ' and ' chaff ' in connection with Rosalind, because they convey to us of this day the nature of her goings-on as no other words would; and Shakespeare himself, who always treats slang respectfully, although he contemns and despises cant, would be the first to pardon me.

Scæna Tertia.

Enter Clowne, Audrey, & Iaques:

Clo. Come apace good *Audrey*, I wil fetch vp your
Goates, *Audrey* : and how *Audrey* am I the man yet?
Doth my fimple feature content you *?*

Aud. Your features, Lord warrant vs: what features?   5

Scene IX. Pope+.   3. *how*] *now* F_3F_4, Rowe+.
2. Audrey] Audrie F_2.

---

3. **the man**] ABBOTT, § 92: *The* used to denote notoriety.

5. **features**] STEEVENS: *Feat* and *feature*, perhaps, had anciently the same meaning. The Clown asks if the *features* of his face content her; she takes the word in
another sense, *i. e. feats, deeds,* and in her reply seems to mean what *feats, i. e.* what
have we done yet? Or the jest may turn on the Clown's pronunciation. In some
parts, 'features' might be pronounced *faitors,* which signify *rascals, low wretches.*
Pistol uses the word in *2 Hen. IV:* II, iv, 173, and Spenser very frequently. MA-
LONE: In Daniel's *Cleopatra,* 1594: 'I see then artless feature can content, And that
true beauty needs no ornament' [III, ii, line 729, ed. Grosart]. Again, in *The
Spanish Tragedy:* 'My feature is not to content her sight; My words are rude, and
work her no delight' [II, i, p. 37, ed. Hazlitt]. 'Feature' appears to have formerly signified the whole countenance. So, in *1 Hen. VI:* V, v, 68: 'Her peerless
feature, joined to her birth, Approves her fit for none but for a king.' WHITER (p.
51): 'Feature' appears to have three senses. First, The cast and make of the face.
Secondly, Beauty in general. Thirdly, The whole turn of the body. CALDECOTT:
'Feature' strictly is *form* or *figure.* NARES: This passage may as well be explained
by supposing that the word 'feature' is too learned for the comprehension of the simple Audrey. 'Feature' is sometimes used for form or person in general: 'She also
dofft her heavy haberieon, Which the fair feature of her limbs did hide.'—Spenser,
Faerie Queene, III, ix. As a magical appearance: 'Stay, all our charms do nothing
win Upon the night; our labour dies! Our magick feature will not rise.'—Jonson,
Masque of Queens. On the preceding charm Jonson's own note says: 'Here they
speake as if they were creating some new feature, which the devil persuades them to
be able to do often, by the pronouncing of words, and pouring out of liquors on the
earth.' DYCE: 'Feature' is form, person in general. WALKER (*Crit.* ii, 305):
'Feature,' in its earliest form, the Latin *factura,* signifies, in our old writers, the *make*
of a person, his *tout-ensemble.* Jonson, *Poetaster,* II, i, Gifford, vol. ii, p. 416: 'her
fair *features*'*;* surely an error; in the very same scene, p. 418, l. 4, we have, 'No
doubt of that, sweet feature'; as Browne, *B. P.* i, *Song* iv, Clarke, p. 112: 'from the
ruins of this mangled creature Arose so fair and so divine a feature, That envy from
her heart would dote upon her,' &c.; and, I think, Milton, *P. L.* x: 'So scented the
grim feature'; *abstractum pro concreto, ut persæpe in poëtt. vett. Anglicis. Uncertain
Poets,* Chalmers, vol. ii, p. 439, col. 2, *Praise of M.* [*Mistresse*] *M.:* 'I woxe asto-

[Your features . . . what features?]

nied (?) to read the feator [*feature*] of her shape, And wondred that a mortall hart such heavenly beames could scape.' Browne, *B. P.* B. i, *Song* ii, Clarke, p. 67 (of a fountain) : 'Not changing any other work of nature, But doth endow the drinker with a feature More lovely,' &c. Spenser, *F. Q.* B. iv, C. ii, St. xliv : 'And to her service bind each living creature, Through secret understanding of their feature'; *i. e. their construction, their make.* C. ii, *of Mutabilitie*, St. iv: 'And thither also came all other creatures, Whatever life or motion do retaine, According to their sundry kinds of features.' Carew, *Epitaph on the Lady S.*, Clarke, lviii, *init.* p. 76 : 'The harmony of colours, *features*, grace, Resulting airs (the magic of a face) Of musical sweet tones, all which combined, To crown one sovereign beauty, lies confined To this dark vault.' *Drunken Barnaby:* 'Where I sought for George à Green a; But cou'd find not such a creature, Yet on a sign I saw his feature,' &c. [p. 19, ed. 1805]. Dubartas, i, vi, ed. 1641, p. 54, col. 2: 'Can you conceal the feet's rare-skilful feature, The goodly bases of this glorious creature?' Wright: There is possibly some joke intended here, the key to which is lost. 'Feature' in Shakespeare's time signified shape and form generally, and was not confined to the face only. [In the *Transactions*, 1877–9, Part I, p. 100, of *The New Shakspere Soc.*, W. Wilkins 'made Touchstone use "feature" in its etymological sense of "making," that is, the Early English *making* or writing of verses, as we use "composition," &c. now. Ben Jonson,' continues Furnivall, 'seems to use the word in the same sense when he says of his creature or creation, the play of *Volpone*, that two months before it was no *feature:* "think they can flout them, With saying he was a year about them. To this there needs no lie, but this his creature, Which was two months since no *feature.*" —Prologue to *Volpone*, 1607. Mr. W. A. Harrison finds the same sense in Bp. Latimer and Pliny: "Some of them ingendred one, some other such *features*, and euery one in that he was deliuered of was excellent, politike, wise."—*Frvitfvll Sermons*, &c. by Master Hvgh Latimer, &c. 1596, Sig. B 4, p. 12. *Feture* means here "a thing made," "a production." Pliny (Præf. Lib. I) uses *fetura* figuratively of a literary production, and calls his work on Natural History *proxima fetura:* "Libros Naturalis Historiæ . . . . natos apud me proxima fetura."' Nares's citations are also repeated in a foot-note.] Brinsley Nicholson (*Scot's Discovery of Witchcraft*, Reprint, 1886, p. 548) : 'Feature.' An example of its being used for the make of a man, and not merely of the features of his countenance, to which it is now appropriated; but till I can find—and as yet I have found none, though I have looked out for it—an example of feature used for things inanimate, I cannot accept the interpretation of song or sonnet in [the present passage.] Did it refer to verse we should expect *features.* . . . . All Touchstone's reference to verse-making in this passage may readily have arisen from his reference to his new situation as like that of the *honest* poet Ovid among the Goths. Had he been poetical and given her verses, he could not have explained to Audrey that he, being a poet, only feigned to love her. [We know, from Steevens's note, that the jest was lost over a hundred years ago, and it seems vain to hope to find it now. We may have our own little explanations and theories, but it is doubtful that any can be now proposed which will be generally accepted. The latest that has been offered, that of Wilkins and of *The New Shakspere Soc.*, is to me far from satisfactory, and indeed is scarcely a clue to the joke at all, which does not lie in what Touchstone says, but in Audrey's interpretation. It makes but little difference to us what Touchstone's 'feature' is; it may be anything in the world, from a sonnet to the cut of his beard, it may be 'feature' in the sense of composition, or it

Clo.   I am heere with thee, and thy Goats, as the moſt   6
capricious Poet honeſt *Ouid* was among the Gothes.

---

7. *Gothes*] Goths F₄.

may be, which I think extremely probable, that the sentence is merely a repetition by
Touchstone, in different words, of his previous question, 'am I the man yet?' But
what is important, and must be known before our lungs can crow like chanticleer, is
the meaning that Audrey attaches to it which necessitated a 'Lord warrant us' when
she alluded to it. Here lay the jest, and I think it still lies there, not in Touchstone's
meaning, but hidden in his pronunciation of 'feature,' as Steevens suggested. We
need have little doubt that the *ea* in 'feature' was pronounced to rhyme with the *a* in
our pronunciation of *nature*. Ellis (*Early Eng. Pronun.* p. 992) gives 'feature' in
palæotype as 'fee·tyyr,' wherein 'ee' has the sound of a in Mary, and 'yy' the sound
of the German softened ü. By the analogy of 'Lectors,' however, which we had in
the last scene, and of many similar words, I think we have a right to suppose that
Touchstone varied this pronunciation and may have said 'fee-tor.' If so, Audrey
may readily have accepted it as meaning *faitor*, which is exactly what Steevens suggested. *Faitor* means a *cheat*, a *vagabond*, a *villain*. Pistol in *2 Hen. IV:* II, iv,
173, says 'Down, down, dogs! down, faitors!' and in Spenser we have 'The false
faitor Scudamore.' If this be the jest, it is not, it must be confessed, side-splitting,
but it is quite enough to disconcert Touchstone, who was fishing for a compliment,
whether we take 'feature' to mean his manly proportions (as I think he means it) or
his verses, as Wilkins supposes. In support of the latter interpretation it is a little
unfortunate that no other exactly parallel instance of the use of 'feature' in the sense
of *factura* has been cited. In the quotation from Jonson's *Volpone* the allusion is
more physiological than psychological, and, it seems to me, clearly refers to the shape
or outline of his play. If, however, Jonson, with his unquestionable scholarship, here
uses 'feature' in its classical sense, it should be classed, I think, with the *fetura* of
Pliny (cited above by Harrison), which comes from quite a different root, and has
quite a different meaning, from *factura*. There may well have been some peculiarity,
not confined to Touchstone, in the pronunciation of 'feature.' In Willobie's *Avisa*,
1594, on pp. 19, 46, 99 (ed. Grosart), it is spelled *fewture*, and in no other way, as
far as I noticed. This may have been a peculiarity of a Northern dialect, of which
there are other indications in the poem, or it may have arisen from some peculiarity
in the handwriting of 'Hadrian Dorrell,' but at any rate I think it helps to justify us
in looking to Touchstone's pronunciation as the source wherein Audrey's jest lies
perdu.—ED.]

5. FARMER: I doubt not this should be 'Your *feature!* Lord warrant us! *what's
feature?'*

7. **capricious**] CALDECOTT: *Caper, capri,* caperitious, capricious, fantastical,
capering, goatish; and by a similar process are we to smooth 'Goths' into 'goats.'
DYCE quotes LETTSOM: No doubt there is an allusion to *caper* here: but there seems
to be also one to *capere;* at least the word *capricious* may be used in the sense of
'taking.' Compare [Brewer's?—Dyce] *Lingua,* II, ii: 'Carry the conceit I told you
this morning to the party you wot of. In my imagination 'tis capricious; 'twill take,
I warrant thee.'—[p. 368, ed. Hazlitt].

7. **Gothes**] CALDECOTT: In our early printing *Goths* and *Gothic* were spelt *Gotes*
and *Gottishe.* Wylliam Thomas's *Historye of Italye,* 1561, fol. 86: 'against the
gotes'; and fol. 201: 'Attila, kyng of the *Goti.'* So in Chapman's *Homer, passim.*

Iaq.   O knowledge ill inhabited, worſe then Ioue in   8
a thatch'd houſe.

8, 29, 42. Aside. Johns. et seq.

WHITE (Introd. to *Much Ado*, p. 226, ed. i) : This joke of Touchstone's is quite decisive upon the point that the combination *o t h* was sometimes, at least, pronounced *ote*.
If the pronunciation of ' Goths ' was not *gotes*, he might as well have said ' among the
Vandals.' [See also vol. xii, p. 431 of Grant White's first edition, where, in one of
the earliest attempts to fix the pronunciation of Elizabethan English, White argues
rather more strongly perhaps than he would have maintained in his maturer years that
'*d, th,* and *t* were indiscriminately used to express a hardened and perhaps not uniform
modification of the Anglosaxon ð.' Ellis (*Early Eng. Pronunciation*, p. 971) reviews
at length White's conclusions and dissents from them : 'there does not appear,' he
says, p. 972, ' to be any reason for concluding that the genuine English *th* ever had the
sound of *t,* although some final *t*'s have fallen into *th*.' This seems to be stated a little
too broadly, especially with Touchstone's joke before us, which Ellis elsewhere recognises, but refers to the category of Latin, Greek, and Hebrew words in which at that
time there was probably great uncertainty of pronunciation. Again, there is a little
strain in thus classing with Latin, Greek, or Hebrew a word as thoroughly Anglosaxon as ' goat.'

We all know that poor Ovid for an unknown misdeed was banished to the bleak
shores of the Euxine among the Getæ, who are the Goths.—ED.]

8. **inhabited**] STEEVENS : That is, ill-lodged. An unusual sense of the word. A
similar phrase occurs in Reynolds' *God's Revenge against Murder*, book v, hist. 21 :
' Pieria's heart is not so ill-lodged, ... but that she is very sensible of her disgrace.'
Again, in *The Golden Legend*, ed. Wynkyn de Worde, fol. 196 : ' I am ryghtwysnes
that am enhabyted here, and this hous is myne.' [' But,' adds WRIGHT, 'there is no
evidence that in Shakespeare's time " inhabit " was equivalent to " lodge " in the
active sense. *Ill-lodged* must be the meaning, although it is not easy to say why.']
ABBOTT thus explains this curious word, § 294 : Hence [*i. e.* from the license in the
formation of verbs] arose a curious use of passive verbs, mostly found in the participle.
Thus '*famous'd* for fights' (*Sonn.* 25) means ' made famous '; but in ' Who . . . .
would not be so *lover'd ?*'—*L. C.* ' lover'd ' means ' gifted with a lover.' And this is
the general rule : A participle formed from an adjective means ' made (the adjective),'
and derived from a noun means ' endowed with (the noun).' [Hereupon a page and
a half of examples follow, which see ; among them, the present phrase is interpreted
' made to inhabit.' See also ' guiled shore,' *Mer. of Ven.* III, ii, 103.]

9. **thatch'd house**] UPTON : That of Baucis and Philemon ; ' Stipulis et canna
tecta palustri.'—Ovid, *Met.* viii, 630. [' The roofe therof was thatched all with straw
and fennish reede.'—Golding's trans. 1567, p. 106]. KNIGHT : The same allusion is
in *Much Ado*, II, i, 99 : '*Don Pedro.* My visor is Philemon's roof ; within the house
is Jove. *Hero.* Why, then, your visor should be thatched.'

9. CAPELL : Does not this reflection of Jaques upon Touchstone's speech imply a
sort of consciousness in the Poet, that he had made his clown a little too learned ?
for, besides that he has made him acquainted with Ovid's situation in Pontus, and his
complaints upon that subject in his Poems *de Tristibus*, he has put into his mouth a
conundrum that certainly proves him a latinist ; ' Capricious ' . . . . as if it had sprung
directly from *caper*, without the medium either of the French *caprice* or the Italian

Clo. When a mans verſes cannot be vnderſtood, nor   10
a mans good wit ſeconded with the forward childe, vn-
derſtanding: it ſtrikes a man more dead then a great reckoning in a little roome : truly, I would the Gods hadde
made thee poeticall.

Aud. I do not know what Poetical is : is it honeſt in   15
deed and word: is it a true thing?

Clo. No trulie : for the trueſt poetrie is the moſt faining, and Louers are giuen to Poetrie : and what they
ſweare in Poetrie, may be ſaid as Louers, they do feigne.

Aud. Do you wiſh then that the Gods had made me   20
Poeticall ?

Clow. I do truly : for thou ſwear'ſt to me thou art honeſt : Now if thou wert a Poet, I might haue ſome hope
thou didſt feigne.

Aud. Would you not haue me honeſt ?   25

Clo. No truly, vnleſſe thou wert hard fauour'd : for

12, 13. *reckoning*] *reeking* Han.   19. *may*] *it may* Mason, Coll. (MS) ii, iii.

---

capriccio : The Poet has indeed qualify'd his learning a little, by giving him ' Goths ' for *Getes.*

13. **roome**] WARBURTON : Nothing was ever wrote in higher humour than this simile. It implies that the entertainment was mean, and the bill extravagant. MOBERLY : To have one's poetry not understood is worse than the bill of a first-class hotel in a pot-house. REV. JOHN HUNTER : An extensive reckoning to be written out in very small space. [Can this last interpretation possibly be right ? To me Moberly's paraphrase is admirable, and the only one.—ED.]

14. **poeticall**] GILES (p. 193) : Touchstone is the Hamlet of motley. He is bit-ter, but there is often to me something like sadness in his jests. He mocks, but in his mockery we seem to hear echoes from a solitary heart. He is reflective ; and melan-choly, wisdom, and matter aforethought are in his quaintness. He is a thinker out of place, a philosopher in mistaken vesture, a gentleman without benefice, a genius by nature, an outcast by destiny.

15. **honest**] That is, chaste. So in I, ii, 38, and ' dishonest,' V, iii, 5.

17, 18. **the truest . . . faining**] CAPEL LOFFT (p. 285) : This was Waller's courtly apology to Charles II for having praised Cromwell.

19. **feigne**] JOHNSON : This sentence seems perplexed and inconsequent ; perhaps it were better read thus : What they swear as lovers, they may be said to feign as poets. MASON : I would read : *it* may be said as lovers they do feign. WRIGHT : The construction is confused. Shakespeare may have intended to continue the sen-tence ' may be said to be feigned.' [Mason's emendation is so trifling, and yet effective withal, that, if change be necessary, it may well be adopted. But I think change is unnecessary ; confused as the construction is, the sense is quite intelligible. —ED.]

honeſtie coupled to beautie, is to haue Honie a ſawce to   27
Sugar.

Iaq.   A materiall foole.

Aud.   Well, I am not faire, and therefore I pray the   30
Gods make me honeſt.

Clo.   Truly, and to caſt away honeſtie vppon a foule
ſlut, were to put good meate into an vncleane diſh.

Aud.   I am not a ſlut, though I thanke the Goddes I
am foule.   35

---

26. **hard fauour'd**] COWDEN-CLARKE: These words show that Audrey was not
uncomely; although she in her modesty, and Touchstone in his pleasantry, choose to
make her out to be plain.   It is evident that the court-jester had the wit to perceive
something genuinely and intrinsically attractive about the girl, beneath her simple
looks and manner.   Besides, she was an oddity, and that had charms for him.   Moreover, she evidently idolises him; which rivets him to her.

29. **materiall**] JOHNSON: A fool with *matter* in him; a fool stocked with notions.
[Dyce adopts this.] STEEVENS: So in Chapman's version of the 24th Iliad: 'his
speech even charm'd his eares, So order'd, so materiall.' HALLIWELL: The Duke
has said of Jaques that he likes to meet with him when he is 'full of matter.'—II, i,
73.   WHITE (ed. i): Does not the clown's apparent unwillingness to have his wife
both honest and beautiful make it clear that the cynical Jaques means to say that he
is materially = thoroughly, essentially a fool?   [In his second edition White has
grown positive; he no longer asks a question, but asserts that 'a material fool is equivalent to an absolute fool; a fool in what is material or of essential importance.']

32. **foule**] The CAMBRIDGE EDITION notes this as *faule* in the Second Folio.
There is, therefore, a variation in the copies here; mine reads as in the First Folio.
—ED.

35. **foule**] HANMER: By 'foul' is meant *coy* or *frowning*. TYRWHITT: I rather
believe 'foul' to be put for the rustic pronunciation of *full*.   Audrey, supposing the
clown to have spoken of her as 'a foul slut,' says, naturally enough, 'I am not a slut,
though, I thank the gods, I am *foul*, i. e. *full*.' RITSON: Audrey says she is not
fair, i. e. handsome, and therefore prays the gods to make her honest.   The clown
tells her that to 'cast honesty away upon a foul slut' (*i. e. an ill-favoured, dirty creature*) is to put meat in an unclean dish.   She replies, she is no 'slut' (no *dirty drab*),
though in her great simplicity she thanks the gods for her *foulness* (homeliness), *i. e.*
for being as she is.   MASON: By 'foul' Audrey means *not fair*, or what we call
homely.   Audrey is neither coy nor ill-humoured; but she thanks God for her homeliness, as it rendered her less exposed to temptation.   So Rosalind says to Phœbe,
III, v, 66: 'Foul is most foul, being foul, to be a scoffer.' MALONE: I believe
Mason's interpretation to be the true one.   So in *Abraham's Sacrifice*, 1577: 'The
fayre, the fowle, the crooked, and the right.' So also in Gascoigne's *Steele Glasse:*
'those that loue to see themselues How foule or fayre, soeuer they may be' [p. 55,
ed. Arber].   TALBOT: That 'foul' retained the meaning in which it is used here as
low down as Pope, we find by the following lines in *The Wife of Bath:* 'If fair,
though chaste, she cannot long abide, By pressing youth attack'd on every side; If
foul, her wealth the lusty lover lures.' WHITER (p. 55): What can be more mani-

Clo. Well, praifed be the Gods, for thy foulneffe; flut-   36
tifhneffe may come heereafter.   But be it, as it may bee,
I wil marrie thee: and to that end, I haue bin with Sir
Oliuer Mar-text, the Vicar of the next village, who hath
promis'd to meete me in this place of the Forreft, and to   40
couple vs.

Iaq. I would faine fee this meeting.

Aud. Wel, the Gods giue vs ioy.

Clo. Amen.   A man may if he were of a fearful heart,
ftagger in this attempt : for heere wee haue no Temple   45
but the wood, no affembly but horne-beafts.   But what

44. *may*] *might* Coll. (MS).   44. *were*] *weare* F$_2$.

---

fest than that the humour of the passage (such as it is) consists in the equivocal sense
of 'foul,' which in our poet's time not only signified what it does at present, but
means likewise *plain* or *homely*?   CALDECOTT: 'Foul' is used in opposition to *fair :*
' If the maiden be fayre she is sone had, and little money geven with her : if she be
foule, they avaunce hir with a better portion.'—Thomas's *Historie of Italye*, 1561, p.
83.   [Schmidt gives between twenty and thirty instances of the use of 'foul' as
opposed to 'fair,' and possibly his list is not complete.   In the present passage the
jest's prosperity lies not alone in the ear of the hearer, but in the mouth of the
speaker, and in its double meaning.   There is no humour nor thought of laughter
when Rosalind says of Silvius and Phœbe, 'He's fallen in love with her foulness.'
—ED.]

36. **foulnesse**] COWDEN-CLARKE: Judging by these jumbled axioms upon fairness, foulness, and sluttishness, Shakespeare seems to have been looking into the
twelfth chapter of Florio's *Second Frutes*, where are strung together as many of
these trite sayings upon women's various qualities as Sancho Panza's irrelevant proverbs.   We believe that this work of Florio's was often in Shakespeare's hand; for it
is curious to observe how many of the words and phrases therein he has adopted.
For instance, one of the scores of whimsical axioms in the above-mentioned twelfth
chapter is, ' If fayre, she is sluttish; if foule, she is prowd.'

38. **with**] ALLEN (MS) : Equivalent to j'ai été *chez*, I went to the house of.

38. **Sir**] See notes on *Dramatis Personæ*.

43. That more may be meant by this exclamation of Audrey than meets our modern ears may be inferred, I think, from the following passage in Lilly's *Mother Bombie*, where there is a dispute over the marriage of two young people : '*Lucio.* Faith
there was a bargaine during life, and the clocke cried, God give them joy. *Prisius.*
Villaine ! they be married ! *Halfepenie.* Nay, I thinke not so. *Sperantus.* Yes,
yes ! God give you joy is a binder !'—p. 138, ed. Fairholt.   To Audrey, therefore,
this exclamation may have meant the firm conclusion of the match, if not of the marriage itself.—ED.

46. **horne-beasts**] This is one of the very many examples which WALKER cites
(*Crit.* ii, 63) of the confusion, in the Folio, of final *d* and final *e*, a confusion which
arose 'in some instances, perhaps, from the juxtaposition of *d* and *e* in the compositor's case; but far oftener—as is evident from the frequency of the erratum—from

though? Courage. As hornes are odious, they are necef-   47
farie.It is faid, many a man knowes no end of his goods;
right : Many a man has good Hornes, and knows no end
of them.   Well, that is the dowrie of his wife, 'tis none   50
of his owne getting ; hornes, euen fo poore men alone :
No, no, the nobleft Deere hath them as huge as the Raf-   52

51. *hornes,...alone :*] *Horns ? even so*
—poor men alone— Rowe, Pope. *Horns ?*
even so—poor men alone ?— Theob. Han.
Warb. Johns. Steev. Mal. Knt, Sta. Cam.
Ktly, Wh. ii (subs.).   *Are horns given to*
poor men alone ? Coll. (MS) ii, Wh. i,

Rlfe. *Horns ! never for poor men alone ?*
Sing. *Horns ? ever to poor men alone ?*
Dyce. *Horns ! Are horns given to poor*
men alone ? Coll. iii.   *Horns are not for*
poor men alone. Spedding (*ap.* Cam.
Ed.).

something in the old method of writing the final *e* or *d*, and which those who are
versed in Elizabethan MSS may perhaps be able to explain.'   In a foot-note LETTSOM
adds : ' Walker's sagacity, in default of positive knowledge, has led him to the truth.
The *e*, with the last upstroke prolonged and terminated with a loop, might be easily
mistaken for *d*. It is frequently found so written.'   The many instances in which the
sense imperatively demands this correction, and in which the change from *e* to *d* and
from *d* to *e* is made in all modernized editions, ought to embolden us to make the
change here from nonsense to sense, and instead of ' horne-beasts,' write *horn'd*
beasts.—ED.

46, 47. **what though**] JOHNSON : What then ? [Seeing that ' so,' ' originally
meaning *in that way*, is frequently inserted,' according to Abbott, § 63, ' in replies
where we should omit it ' (*e. g.* '*Trib.* Repair to the Capitol.   *People.* We will *so.*'—
Cor. II, iii, 262), so after ' I think,' ' if,' &c. ' so ' is sometimes omitted ; see Abbott,
§ 64.   Thus here the full meaning of the phrase is ' But what though *it may be so.*']

51. **hornes, . . . alone**] COLLIER (*Notes & Emend.* p. 133) : It appears that *are*
had accidentally dropped out, and that for ' euen so ' we ought to read *given to*, and
then Touchstone's question will be perfectly intelligible : '*Are* horns *given to* poor
men alone ?' ' No, no (replies Touchstone to his own interrogatory) : the noblest
deer,' &c. This emendation may have been obtained from some good authority.
SINGER : I prefer, as a less violent innovation [than Theobald's text], to read, instead
of ' euen so,' *never for ;* which makes the passage intelligible and less incoherent.
WHITE (ed. i) : Collier's (MS) furnishes the emendation which is more consistent
with the context than either [Theobald's or Singer's].   DYCE quotes Singer's text,
and adds ' which I hardly understand.'   HALLIWELL : The effect of this ruminating
is impaired by the violent alteration proposed by Collier's (MS).   STAUNTON : We
adopt the ordinary punctuation of this hopeless passage, though with reluctance.
WHITE (ed. ii) : Unsatisfactory as it is, this reading [Theobald's] is perhaps the best
that can be made of the original.

52. **Rascall**] CALDECOTT : 'As one should in reproch say to a poore man, thou
raskall knaue, where *raskall* is properly the hunters terme giuen to young deere, leane
and out of season, and not to people.'—Puttenham's *Arte of English Poesie,* 1589, p.
150. Again, ' The bucks and lusty stags amongst the rascals strew'd As sometimes
gallant spirits amongst the multitude.'—Drayton's *Poly-olbion* [Thirteenth Song, p.
304, ed. 1748].   WAY (foot-note to *Rascalye,—Prompt. Parv.*) : Fabyan, under the
year 1456, speaks of ' a multitude of rascall and poore people of the cytye.'   Certain

call : Is the fingle man therefore bleffed ? No, as a wall'd   53
Towne is more worthier then a village, fo is the forehead of a married man, more honourable then the bare   55
brow of a Batcheller : and by how much defence is better then no skill, by fo much is a horne more precious
then to want.

Enter Sir Oliuer Mar-text.

Heere comes Sir *Oliuer* : Sir *Oliuer Mar-text* you are   60
wel met. Will you difpatch vs heere vnder this tree, or
fhal we go with you to your Chappell ?

    Ol.   Is there none heere to giue the woman ?

    Clo.   I wil not take her on guift of any man.

    Ol.   Truly fhe muft be giuen, or the marriage is not   65
lawfull.

    Iaq.   Proceed, proceede : Ile giue her.

    Clo.   Good euen good Mr what ye cal't : how do you
Sir, you are verie well met : goddild you for your laft
companie, I am verie glad to fee you, euen a toy in hand   70
heere Sir : Nay, pray be couer'd.

    Iaq.   Wil you be married, Motley ?   72

---

54. *more*] Om. Pope.   69. *goddild*] *godild* Ff. *God'ild* Theob.
68. *Mr*] *M.* Ff, Rowe.   *God ild* Dyce.
   cal't], *call* Rowe ii+.

---

animals, not accounted as beasts of chase, were likewise so termed. In the St Albans
Book it is stated that 'there be fiue beasts which we cal beasts of the chace, the buke,
the doe, the foxe, the marterne, and the roe; all other of what kinde soeuer terme
them Rascall.' It appears, however, from the Mayster of Game, that the hart, until
he was six years old, was accounted 'rascayle or foly.'—*Vesp.* B. xii, f. 25. In the
Survey of the Estates of Glastonbury Abbey, taken at the Dissolution, the deer in the
various parks are distinguished as 'deere of anntler' and 'deere of Rascall.'

    53, 54. **wall'd ... village**] ALLEN (MS) : A town has the defence of a wall; a
village has none. Shakespeare has got *fortification* into his head. I wonder, therefore, whether he is not thinking of a 'hornwork' as one work in a system of defences.
How early was the term used ?

    56. **defence**] STEEVENS : 'Defence,' as here opposed to 'no skill,' signifies the
art of fencing. Thus, 'and gave you such a masterly report, for arts and exercise in
your defence.'—*Ham.* IV, vii, 98. CALDECOTT : Any means of defence is better
than a lack of science; in proportion as something is to nothing. [Steevens's is the
better interpretation, I think.—ED.]

    69. **goddild you**] STEEVENS : That is, God yield you, God reward you. So in
Ant. & Cleop. IV, ii, 33 : 'And the gods yield you for 't.' [According to Skeat, the
original meaning of 'yield' is to *pay*.]

Clo. As the Oxe hath his bow fir, the horfe his curb,   73
and the Falcon her bels, fo man hath his defires, and as
Pigeons bill, fo wedlocke would be nibling.   75

Iaq. And wil you (being a man of your breeding)be
married vnder a bufh like a begger ? Get you to church,
and haue a good Prieft that can tel you what marriage is,
this fellow wil but ioyne you together, as they ioyne
Wainfcot, then one of you wil proue a fhrunke pannell,   80
and like greene timber, warpe, warpe.

Clo. I am not in the minde, but I were better to bee
married of him then of another, for he is not like to marrie me wel : and not being wel married, it wil be a good
excufe for me heereafter, to leaue my wife.   85

---

73. *bow*] *bough* Cap.   74. *defires*] *defire* F_3F_4, Rowe+.
74. *her bels*] *his bells* F_3F_4, Rowe+.   82–85. Aside. Cap.

---

73. **bow**] CAPELL: The wooden collar or yoke, that lyes across the neck of draft
oxen, and to which their traces are fastened, is call'd their *bow ;* and this being the
spelling of the word in former editions, it has probably been the sense it was taken
in; but a little attention to the true meaning of the other two similies, and to the
matter they are meant to illustrate, will show that we must seek for another interpretation of *bow :* The faulcon is thought to take delight in her 'bells,' and to bear her
captivity the better for them; 'curbs' and their jingling appendages, add a spirit to
horses; and if we interpret 'bow' to signify *bough* of a tree, the ox becomes a proper
similitude too, who, thus adorn'd, moves with greater legerity : and the same effect
that these things have upon the several animals, 'desires,' and their gratifications,
have upon men; making them bear their burthens the better, and jog on to the end
of life's road. [Can perverted ingenuity further go? Steevens said that the 'bow'
was the *yoke*, and has been followed, I think, by every English editor except Halliwell, who rightly defines it. The fact is, that the *bow*, and the *yoke*, in which the
bow is inserted, being two different things, cannot bear the same name; as well might
we say a horse's *bit* is his *bridle.*—ED.]

74. **Falcon her**] The gender here is properly feminine ; the male hawk was called
a *tiercel*, perhaps from its lesser size. See the notes on 'tassel-gentle' in *Rom. &*
Jul. II, ii, 159. WRIGHT: Shakespeare once makes 'falcon' masculine in *R. of L.*
507, but the gender of the pronoun in that passage may be explained by the fact that
it refers to Tarquin, who is compared to a falcon.

82. **not in the minde, but**] CALDECOTT: That is, I am of no other opinion or
inclination than, *my mind is*, that it were better to be married by him. [The foregoing paraphrase is all the help that is offered to us on this somewhat puzzling construction, which is, I think, intelligible only on the principle of two negations making
an affirmative. Touchstone was not in the mind that it were not better, and therefore
he was in the mind that it was. For the phrase 'I were better,' see Abbott, §§ 352
and 230, where we find that in this and similar expressions, like 'You were best,'
'Thou wert better,' &c., *I, Thou,* and *You* originally datives, were changed to nominatives.—ED.]

Iaq.   Goe thou with mee,   86
And let me counfel thee.

    Ol.   Come fweete *Audrey*,
We muft be married, or we muft liue in baudrey :
Farewel good Mr *Oliuer* : Not O fweet *Oliuer*, O braue   90

86, 87. One line, Pope et seq.

88. Ol.] F₁.

88, 89. Prose, Pope +.

90. *M^r*] *M.* Ff. *Sir* Theob. ii, Warb. Johns.

90, 91. *Not...But*] Included in the verse, Cap. Excluded from the verse, Mal. et seq. (subs.).

90–92. *Not...thee*] Six lines of verse, Cap. et seq.

90, &c. **Not O sweet Oliuer,** &c.] CAPELL : These words have no appearance of a ballad as [Warburton] has fancy'd ; but rather of a line in some play, that perhaps might run thus, ' O my sweet Oliver, leave me not behind thee ' ; which this wag of a clown puts into another sort of metre, to make sport with sir Oliver, telling him : ' I'll not say to you, as the play has it, " O sweet Oliver, | O brave Oliver, | Leave me not behind thee " ; but I say to you, " wind away," ' &c., continuing his speech in the same metre. In this light the passage is truly humorous ; but may be much heighten'd by a certain droleness in speaking the words, and by dancing about sir Oliver with a harlequin gesture and action. [The world cannot afford to lose the flash of histrionic genius with which Capell illumines this passage.—ED.] JOHNSON : Of this speech, as it now appears, I can make nothing, and think nothing can be made. In the same breath he calls his mistress to be married, and sends away the man that should marry them. Warburton has very happily observed that ' O sweet Oliver ' is a quotation from an old song ; I believe there are two quotations put in opposition to each other. For ' wind ' I read *wend*, the old word for *go*. Perhaps the whole passage may be regulated thus : *'Jaques.* Go thou with me, and let me counsel thee. [*They whisper.*] *Clown.* Farewell, good sir Oliver, not *O sweet Oliver, O brave Oliver, leave me not behind thee,*—but—*Wend* away,—Begone, I say,—I will not to wedding with thee to-day.' Of this conjecture the reader may take as much as shall appear necessary to the sense or conducive to the humour. TYRWHITT : The epithet ' sweet ' seems to have been peculiarly appropriated to ' Oliver,' for which, perhaps, he was originally obliged to the old song before us. See Jonson's *Underwoods :* 'All the mad Rolands and sweet Olivers.'—[LXII, p. 417, ed. Gifford.] STEEVENS : ' O brave Oliver, leave me not behind you ' is a quotation at the beginning of one of Breton's Letters in his *Poste with a Packet of Mad Letters,* 1600 [vol. ii, p. 34, ed. Grosart]. In the Stationers' Registers, Aug. 6, 1584, was entered by Richard Jones, the ballad of ' O swete Olyuer, Leave me not behind the.' Again [on the 20th of August], ' The answeare of O sweete Olyuer.' Again [on Aug. 1st] in 1586, ' O swete Olyver, altered to ye scriptures.'—[vol. ii, pp. 434, 435, 451, ed. Arber]. FARMER : I often find a part of this song applied to Cromwell. In a paper called *A Man in the Moon, Discovering a World of Knavery under the Sun,* ' the *juncto* will go near to give us the *baggage,* if *O brave Oliver* come not suddenly to relieve them.' The same allusion is met with in Cleveland. ' Wind away ' and *wind off* are still used *provincially ;* and, I believe, nothing but the *provincial* pronunciation is wanting to join the parts together. I read : ' Leave me not *behi' thee*—But—wind away—Begone, I say,—I will not to wedding *wi' thee.*' STEEVENS : ' Wind ' is used for *wend* in *Cæsar and Pompey,* 1607 : ' Winde we then, Antony, with this royal queen.'

Oliuer leaue me not behind thee : But winde away, bee   91
gone I fay, I wil not to wedding with thee.

Ol. 'Tis no matter ; Ne're a fantaftical knaue of them
all fhal flout me out of my calling.   *Exeunt*   94

Scœna Quarta.

Enter Rofalind & Celia.

Rof. Neuer talke to me, I wil weepe.

Cel. Do I prethee, but yet haue the grace to confider,
that teares do not become a man.

Rof. But haue I not caufe to weepe ?   5

Cel. As good caufe as one would defire,
Therefore weepe.

Rof. His very haire
Is of the diffembling colour.   9

---

91. *behind thee*] *behi' thee* Steev. *be-*
hind thee, pr'ythee! Ktly.
            winde] *wend* Sing. Coll. (MS) ii,
iii, Clke, Huds.
    92. *with thee*] *wi' thee* Steev. *bind*
thee Coll. (MS) ii, iii.

92. Exeunt Jaques, Clown, and Audrey. Cap.
94. Exeunt.] Exit. Cap.
Scene X. Pope +.
A Cottage in the Forest. Theob.
6–16. Prose, Pope et seq.
9. *the*] *a* Rowe ii, Pope, Han.

COLLIER (*Notes*, &c., p. 133): All printed editions have missed the rhyme in the last
line of the fragment of the ballad, ' O sweet Oliver.' Perhaps it was only the extem-
poral invention of Touchstone, but it is thus given by the MS corrector of the Folio,
1632 : ' But *wend* away; begone I say, I will not to wedding *bind* thee.' DYCE :
But there is no reason to suppose that a rhyme in the last line was intended by Shakespeare; for it would seem that Touchstone is citing two distinct portions of the ballad.
Nor can we doubt that ' wind away ' was the reading of the old ditty; compare *The
History of Pyramus and Thisbie :* ' That doone, *away* hee *windes*, as fier of hell or
Vulcan's thunder,' &c.—*The Gorgious Gallery of Gallant Inventions*, 1578, p. 171,
reprint. ' Wind ' is an early form of *wend*. [In both his first and second editions
Collier refers to his Introduction to *Mid. N. D.*, where a stanza of *Robin Goodfellow*
is given, in which ' wind ' is used for *wend*. This particular copy of the ballad, however, was in a MS of the time, and the stanza does not appear in Percy's *Reliques*,
1765, although the word ' wend ' does appear there in line 110.—ED.]

1–16. These lines, with their division into apparent verse, are an indication, I
think, of the piecemeal printing of the Folio. They are the last lines on the page,
at the foot of the column. The compositor to whom this portion was intrusted was
apparently anxious to complete his stint with a full page, and, indeed, was perhaps
forced to do so, that there might be no gap between his share and his neighbor's, and
so spread out the text by thus dividing the lines.—ED.

Cel.   Something browner then Iudaſſes :   10
Marrie his kiſſes are Iudaſſes owne children.
    Roſ.   I'faith his haire is of a good colour.
    Cel.   An excellent colour :
Your Cheſſenut was euer the onely colour :
    Roſ. And his kiſſing is as ful of ſanctitie,   15
As thc touch of holy bread.

10, 11. *Iudaſſes*] F₂.   *Judas's* F₃F₄.   16. *bread*] *beard* Theob. Warb. Johns.
16. *thc*] F₁.   Cap.

---

9. **dissembling colour**] HUNTER (i, 349) : That certain colours of the hair were supposed to indicate particular dispositions was an opinion of the time, as may be seen at large in *The Shepherd's Calendar*, not Spenser's beautiful poem so entitled, but the medley of moral and natural philosophy, of verse and prose, which, under that title, was a favourite book of the common people in the reigns of the Tudors. 'A man that hath black hair,' we are told, 'and a red beard, signifies to be letcherous, disloyal, a vaunter, and one ought not to trust him.' HALLIWELL : 'Hair of the colour of gold denotes a *treacherous* person, having a good understanding, but mischievous ; red hair, enclining to black, signifies a *deceitful* and malicious person.'— Saunders, *Physiognomie and Chiromancie*, 1671, p. 189.

10. **Iudasses**] STEEVENS : Judas was constantly represented in ancient painting or tapestry with red hair and beard. TOLLET : The new edition of Leland's *Collectanea*, vol. v, p. 295, asserts that 'painters constantly represented Judas, the traytor, with a red head.' Dr Plot's *Oxfordshire*, p. 153, says the same : 'This conceit is thought to have arisen in England, from our ancient grudge to the red-haired Danes.' NARES : The current opinion that Judas had red hair arose from no better reason than that the colour was thought ugly. Thiers in his *Histoire des Perruques*, p. 22, gives this as one of the reasons for wearing wigs : 'Les rousseaux portèrent des perruques, pour cacher la couleur de leurs cheveux, qui sont en horreur à tout le monde, parce que Judas, à ce qu'on prètend, etoit rousseau.' Dryden, in *Amboyna*, has, 'there's treachery in that Judas-colour'd beard,' and in a fit of anger he described Jacob Tonson, 'with two left legs, and Judas-coloured hair.' As Tonson is in the same attack described as 'freckled fair,' there can be no doubt that Judas's hair was always supposed to be red. A red beard was considered as an infallible token of a vile disposition.

15. WALKER (*Crit.* iii, 94) would let Celia interrupt this speech, thus : '*Ros.* And his kissing— *Cel.* Is as full of sanctity as,' &c., and it is not to be denied that it is quite in the spirit of the rest of the dialogue, but—it is improving Shakespeare, or rather, it is improving the plain, unsophisticated text, which should not be.—ED.

16. **holy bread**] WARBURTON : We should read *beard*, that is, the kiss of an holy saint or hermit, called the *kiss of charity*. This makes the comparison just and decent ; the other impious and absurd. COLLIER : 'Holy bread,' as the Rev. Mr Barry observes to me, 'is sacramental bread' ; and he adds that 'pax-bread' is rendered by Coles *panis osculandus*. BARRON FIELD (*Sh. Soc. Papers*, vol. iii, p. 133) : It is strange that these reverend gentlemen should have been so ill-read in Church History as not to know what 'holy bread' was. Sacramental bread, in those times, would have been called a great deal more than *holy* bread, and would never have

Cel.   Hee hath bought a paire of caſt lips of *Diana* : a   17
Nun of winters fiſterhood kiſſes not more religiouſlie,
the very yce of chaſtity is in them.   19

17. *caſt*] *chaſt* Ff.   *chaste* Rowe, Pope, Huds.   *casts* Mal. (misprint ?).

been profaned by Shakespeare.   Rosalind is guilty of no impiety.   ' Holy bread ' was
merely one of the ' ceremonies ' which Henry VIIIth's *Articles of Religion* pronounced good and lawful, having mystical significations in them.   ' Such,' he says,
' were the vestments in the worship of God, sprinkling holy water . . . . *giving holy
bread*, in sign of our union to Christ,' &c.   Another of these Articles declared that in
the sacrament at the Altar, under the form of bread and wine, there was truly and
substantially the body of Christ.   WRIGHT : Tyndale in his *Obedience of a Christian
Man* (Doctrinal Treatises, p. 284, Parker Society ed.), says : ' For no man by sprinkling himself with holy water, and with eating holy bread, is more merciful than
before,' &c.   [Do we ever stop to think how either Rosalind or Celia could have
known anything of Orlando's kisses ?   Rosalind, as Rosalind, had met him but once,
after the wrestling, and it is unlikely, indeed scarcely thinkable, that Orlando should
have kissed Ganymede, and yet Celia's allusion to ' the very ice of chastity ' seems to
imply that she spoke either from experience or as a witness.   In a subsequent scene,
where Ganymede and Orlando are talking of kisses, they would surely have kissed
then had they ever kissed before.   Perhaps Rosalind is thinking here only how pure,
of necessity, must be the kisses of such a man as Orlando, and the kisses to which
she now refers are of ' those by hopeless fancy feigned on lips that are for others.'
But, after all, we are in the forest of Arden, and this is but a part of Shakespeare's
glamour, into which it is sacrilege to pry too curiously.—ED.]

   17. **cast**] THEOBALD : That is, a pair *left off* by Diana.   WRIGHT : Compare *Jer.*
xxxviii, 11 : ' old ' cast clouts and rotten rags.'   [Again, 'Tis state . . . . to have an
. . . . usher march before you . . , . in a tuftafata jerkin Made of your old cast gown.'
—*Ram Alley*, IV, i.   We have retained the word to this day, having added merely
off.—ED.]   DOUCE (i, 303) : It is not easy to conceive how the goddess could *leave
off* her lips ; or how, being left off, Orlando could purchase them.   Celia seems rather
to allude to a statue *cast in plaister* or *metal*, the lips of which might well be said to
possess the *ice* of chastity.   [Halliwell adopted this note by Douce, and even added
to it the suggestion by one who prudently remained ' Anonymous,' that ' it would be
more correct to say that it [*sic*] is to a pair of lips cast for a statue, as that kind of
workmanship is commonly executed in detached parts.'   It was a note of Douce's
similar to the above, though not quite so far fet, that elicited from Dyce the assertion
that ' except those explanatory of customs, dress, &c. the notes of Douce are nearly
worthless.'—*Remarks*, p. 96.   And here let me record my respectful, but unflinching, protest against the interpretation of ' cast,' in the sense of *cast off*, as it is given
in modern editions.   The idea that Celia, whose references to Orlando's kisses have
been thus far, to say the least, dainty and refined, should be here represented as saying
that he had bought a pair of worn-out, second-hand, *old-clo'* lips, is to me worse than
absurd ; it is abhorrent.   ' Cast ' is here either the mere phonetic spelling of *chaste*,
which from the Latin *castus* retained, it is not unlikely, the hard sound of *c*, or it is a
downright misprint for *chast* or *chaste*, which the editor of the Second Folio quickly
corrected.   Moreover, an allusion to her chastity is almost inseparable from Diana ;
this, of itself, would almost justify us in making the change.—ED.]

Rofa. But why did hee fweare hee would come this 20
morning, and comes not *?*

Cel. Nay certainly there is no truth in him.

Rof. Doe you thinke fo?

Cel. Yes, I thinke he is not a picke purfe, nor a horfe-
ftealer, but for his verity in loue, I doe thinke him as 25
concaue as a couered goblet, or a Worme-eaten nut.

Rof. Not true in loue?

Cel. Yes, when he is in, but I thinke he is not in.

Rof. You haue heard him fweare downright he was.

Cel. Was, is not is : befides, the oath of Louer is no 30
ftronger then the word of a Tapfter, they are both the
confirmer of falfe reckonings, he attends here in the forreft on the Duke your father. 33

20. *why*] *wy* F₂.

30. *Louer*] *a Lover* Ff, Rowe+, Cap. Steev. Var. '21 et seq.

32. *confirmer*] *confirmers* Pope+, Cap. Mal. Steev. Coll. Sta. Clke, Dyce iii, Huds.

---

18. **winters**] THEOBALD : It seems to me more probable that the Poet wrote : 'a nun of *Winifred's* sisterhood.' Not, indeed, that there was any real religious Order of that Denomination, but the legend of St Winifred [as given in Camden's *Britannia*] tells how she suffered death for her chastity. [Warburton, after a vigorous sneer at Theobald, in the course of which he denied that there was any sisterhood of St Wini-fred, which Theobald had never affirmed, proceeded to apportion the year, to his own satisfaction and without the smallest classical authority, among the heathen goddesses, winding up with the assertion that ' the *sisterhood of winter* were the votaries of Diana.' In his long note there is only one sentence worth heeding or remembering : ' Shake-speare meant an *unfruitful sisterhood* which had devoted itself to chastity.' To this add a remark by DOUCE, which even Dyce adopts, that ' Shakespeare poetically feigns a new order of nuns most appropriate to his subject,' and the passage has received all requisite attention, except, perhaps, that STEEVENS notes ' one circumstance in which [Warburton] is mistaken. *The Golden Legend*, p. ccci, &c., gives a full account of St Winifred and her sisterhood.—Wynkyn de Worde, 1527.'—ED.]

22. COWDEN-CLARKE : Nothing can exceed the sweetness of the touches whereby Shakespeare has painted the character of Celia. In three several scenes she appears comforting her sprightly cousin in the April tears she sheds, and pretty poutings she gives way to, ever petting, humouring, loving, and ministering to Rosalind. Here, her irony of banter, her praising under guise of disparaging, her affecting to blame the man her cousin loves, that her cousin may have an opportunity of defending and eulogising him, are all in the highest taste and most perfect knowledge of womanly nature.

26. **couered**] WARBURTON : A goblet is never kept ' covered ' but when empty. M. MASON : It is the idea of hollowness, not that of emptiness, that Shakespeare wishes to convey; and a goblet is more completely hollow when covered than when it is not.

Rof. I met the Duke yefterday, and had much queftion with him : he askt me of what parentage I was ; I   35
told him of as good as he, fo he laugh'd and let mee goe.
But what talke wee of Fathers, when there is fuch a man
as *Orlando ?*

Cel. O that's a braue man, hee writes braue verfes,
fpeakes braue words, fweares braue oathes, and breakes   40
them brauely, quite trauers athwart the heart of his lo-

---

34. HARTLEY COLERIDGE (ii, 140): Rosalind is not a very dutiful daughter, but
her neglecting so long to make herself known to her father, though not quite proper,
is natural enough. She cannot but be aware that in her disguise she is acting a perilous and not very delicate part, which yet is so delightful that she cannot prevail on
herself to forego it, as her father would certainly have commanded her to do. Nothing is more common than for children to evade the sin of flat disobedience by deception and concealment. Jennie Deans, a stricter moralist than Rosalind, set out on
her pious pilgrimage without consulting her father, because she could expect no blessing if she had incurred his express prohibition. This, to be sure, was a practical
sophism; but no Jesuit's head is so full of sophistry as a woman's heart under the
influence of strong affection. Yet Rosalind might, at any rate, have shown more
interest in her father's fortunes.

34, 35. question] STEEVENS: That is, conversation. See III, ii, 360, or V, iv,
165, or Schmidt.

37. what] For other examples of 'what' used for *why*, see Abbott, § 253.

37, 38. man as Orlando] LADY MARTIN (p. 423): What a world of passionate
emotion is concentrated in that last sentence, and how important it is to bear this in
mind in the subsequent scenes with Orlando!

41. trauers] WARBURTON: As breaking a lance against his adversary's breast, in
a direct line, was honorable, so the breaking it *across* his breast was, as a mark either
of want of courage or address, dishonorable; hence it is that Sidney, describing the
mock combat of Clinias and Dametas, says: 'The wind tooke such hold of his staffe,
that it crost quite ouer his breast [and in that sort gaue a flat bastonado to Dametas.'
—*Arcadia*, III, p. 284, ed. 1598]. To *break across* was the usual phrase, as appears
from some verses of the same author, speaking of an unskilful tilter: 'For when he
most did hit, he ever yet did miss. One said he brake across, full well it so might be.'
[It is to be feared that Warburton did not read his *Arcadia* with needful attention, or
he would have seen that his quotation affords a most meagre illustration of the present
passage, if indeed it afford any at all. Clinias's staff crossed over, not his adversary's
breast, but his own, and, moreover, we are expressly told a few lines further on that
it was not broken. It would not have been worth while to notice this, were it not
that several editors have followed Warburton and adopted his note without verifica-
tion.—ED.] STEEVENS: So in *Northward Ho*, 1607 : 'melancholie like a tilter, that
had broke his staves foul before his mistress.'—[III, i, p. 189, ed. Dyce]. NARES
calls attention to the skilful manner in which the author of *Ivanhoe* has introduced
this circumstance into his tournament. ['The antagonist of Grantmesnil, instead of
bearing his lance-point fair against the crest or shield of his enemy, swerved so much
from the direct line as to break the weapon athwart the person of his opponent, a
circumstance which was accounted more disgraceful than that of being actually

uer, as a puiſny Tilter, y̆ ſpurs his horſe but on one ſide,   42
breakes his ſtaffe like a noble gooſe; but all's braue that
youth mounts, and folly guides : who comes heere?

                         Enter Corin.   45
       Corin.   Miſtreſſe and Maſter, you haue oft enquired

42. *puiſny*] *puny* Cap.   43. *noble*] *nose-quilled* Han.   *notable*
    y̆] *that* Ff.   Sing. Ktly.
    on] Om. Pope, Theob. Warb.   44. *heere*] *heete* F₂.
Johns.

---

unhorsed; because the latter might happen from accident, whereas the former evinced
awkwardness and want of management of the weapon and the horse.'—*Ivanhoe*,
chap. viii.]

41, 42. **louer**] MALONE: That is, of his mistress. 'Lover' was applied to both
men and women. Compare *A Lover's Complaint*, where the 'lover' is a despairing
maiden. So *Meas. for Meas. :* 'Your brother and his lover have embraced,' I, iv, 40.

42. **puisny**] CAM. ED.: Here used not in the modern sense of *diminutive*, but in
the now obsolete sense of *inferior, unskilled.* WRIGHT: Cotgrave has ' Puisné. Punie,
younger, borne after.'

42, 44. **spurs . . . guides**] Again, there is a variation in copies of the Second
Folio (see line 32 of the preceding scene). The CAM. ED. records as the spelling
of these two words in that Folio: *spurnes* and *guider.* In my copy they are *spurres*
and *guides.* Again, a similar variation occurs in 'drops' of line 8 in the next scene,
which in the Cambridge Editors' copy of F₂ is *props ;* in mine it is not misspelled.
Therefore, the proof is conclusive that the copy of the CAM. ED. is an earlier impression than mine, and as all four of these errors, *faule, spurnes, guider,* and *props,* occur on
two pages facing each other, it is likely that they were all corrected at the same time,
and their number was a sufficient cause to stop the work of striking off and to unlock
the forms. *Hæc fabula docet* how remote from Shakespeare's hand the text of the
Folios is, and how careful we should be not to place too much reliance on collation.
—ED.

43. **noble**] For this word Hanmer actually substituted in the text *nose-quilled ;*
'but,' says FARMER, with naïveté, 'no one seems to have regarded the alteration.'
Whereupon he proceeds to 'regard' it seriously, and adds : 'Certainly *nose-quilled* is
an epithet likely to be corrupted; it gives the image wanted, and may in a great
measure be supported by a quotation from Turberville's *Falconrie :* " Take with you a
ducke, and slip one of her *wing-feathers,* and having thrust it through her *nares,*
throw her out unto your hawke." ' STEEVENS too backs up Farmer with a citation
from *Philaster :* 'He shall . . . . be seel'd up With a feather through his nose, that,'
&c.—[V, iv, p. 298, ed. Dyce. However much such a tampering with the text of
Shakespeare, by exsufflicate and blown surmises, invites flippancy and excuses disre-
spect, the temptation must be resisted to couple for the nonce in the same sentence the
name of Sir Thomas Hanmer and a 'noble goose.'—ED.] CALDECOTT: By the
phrase ' noble goose ' is perhaps meant a magnanimous simpleton of an adventurer.
SINGER : I do not hesitate to read 'notable goose ' instead of ' noble.' The epithet
is often used by the poet. KEIGHTLEY: Singer, very unnecessarily and most tamely,
reads *notable.* Printing from his edition, I have heedlessly followed him in mine.

After the Shepheard that complain'd of loue,   47
Who you faw fitting by me on the Turph,
Praifing the proud difdainfull Shepherdeffe
That was his Miftreffe.   50
    Cel.   Well : and what of him ?
    Cor.   If you will fee a pageant truely plaid
Betweene the pale complexion of true Loue,
And the red glowe of fcorne and prowd difdaine,
Goe hence a little, and I fhall conduct you   55
If you will marke it.
    Rof.   O come, let vs remoue,
The fight of Louers feedeth thofe in loue :
Bring vs to this fight, and you fhall fay
Ile proue a bufie actor in their play.   *Exeunt.*   60

Scena Quinta.

Enter Siluius and Phebe.

    Sil.   Sweet *Phebe* doe not fcorne me, do not *Phebe*
Say that you loue me not, but fay not fo
In bitterneffe ; the common executioner   4

48. *Who*] *Whom* Ff, Rowe+, Cap.
Huds.

55. *and*] *as* Allen conj.

59. *Bring vs to*] *Bring us but to*
Pope+. *Come, bring us to* Cap. *Bring
us unto* Mal. Steev. Cald. Ktly. *Bring*

us to see Jervis, Dyce iii, Coll. iii, Huds.
Rlfe.

60. *Ile*] *I* Dyce conj.
Scene XI. Pope+.
[Changes to another part of the
Forest. Theob.

2. *not* Phebe] *not, Phebe,* F₃F₄.

47. **that**] ABBOTT, § 260 : Since *that* introduces an essential characteristic without
which the description is not complete, it follows, that, even where this distinction is
not marked, *that* comes generally nearer to the antecedent than *who* or *which.* [As
to 'who' for *whom* in the next line, see Shakespeare, *passim,* or Abbott, § 274. See
also the same sequence, 'that' followed by 'who,' in lines 14, 15 of the next Scene.]

52. **pageant**] WHITER (p. 56) : The 'pageant' of *love* seems to have been
impressed on the mind of our poet. So in *Mid. N. D.* III, ii, 112, Puck speaks of
'the youth, mistook by me, Pleading for a *lover's* fee. Shall we their fond *pageant*
see ?'

59. **vs to**] JERVIS (p. 12) : Read : 'Bring us to *see*,' &c. Compare 'To see this
sight, it irks my very soul.'—*3 Hen. VI :* II, ii.

4. Even this line Abbott (§ 494) will not countenance as an Alexandrine ; he says

Whofe heart th'accuftom'd fight of death makes hard   5
Falls not the axe vpon the humbled neck,
But firft begs pardon : will you fterner be
Then he that dies and liues by bloody drops?   8

8. *dies and liues by*] *deals and lives*   *by*, Cap. *lives and dies by* Coll. conj.
by Theob. *lives and thrives by* Han.   Ktly. *sheds and lives by* Ktly conj.
deals, and lives by, Warb. *eyes, and lives*   *daily lives by* Heath.

---

that in the last foot one of the two extra syllables is slurred : ' In bft | ternéss. | The
cóm | mon éx | ecútioner.' To my ear the remedy is worse than the disease.—ED.

6. **Falls**] For many instances of the conversion of intransitive into transitive verbs
see Abbott, § 291 ; also the same, § 120, for the use of ' But' in the next line, in the
sense of *except* or *without*. DOUCE (i, 303) : There is no doubt that the expression
' to fall the axe ' may with propriety refer to the usual mode of decapitation ; but if it
could be shown that in the reign of Elizabeth this punishment was inflicted in England by an instrument resembling the French guillotine, the expression would perhaps
seem even more appropriate. Among the cuts to the first edition of Holinshed's
Chronicle such a machine is twice introduced. [Douce hereupon shows that the
so-called ' Halifax Gibbet' and ' the Maiden' in Scotland were quite similar instruments, and from a contemporary MS account in his possession of the execution of
Morton for the murder of Darnley, where it is said he ' layde his head *under the axe*,'
there can be no doubt of the fact that such a mode of beheading was practised.
Haydn (*Dict. of Dates*) says that the ' Halifax Gibbet' was used as late as 1650.]

8. **dies and liues**] WARBURTON : The executioner *lives*, indeed, by bloody drops,
if you will ; but how does he *die* by bloody drops? The poet must certainly have
wrote '*deals* and lives,' &c. JOHNSON : I should rather read : ' he that dyes *his lips*
by bloody drops.' Will you speak with more sternness than the executioner, whose
lips are used to be *sprinkled* with blood? STEEVENS : I am afraid our bard is at his
quibbles again. To *die* means as well as to *dip a thing in a colour foreign to its own*, as
to expire. In this sense, contemptible as it is, the executioner may be said to *die* as
well as *live* by *bloody drops*. Shakespeare is fond of opposing these terms to each
other. TOLLET : That is, he who, to the very end of his life, continues a common
executioner ; as in V, ii : ' *live and die* a shepherd.' MUSGRAVE : To *die and live* by
a thing is to be constant to it, to persevere in it to the end. *Lives*, therefore, does not
signify *is maintained*, but the two verbs taken together mean who is conversant all his
life with bloody drops. CAPELL [see Text. Notes] : That is, is accustomed to look
upon blood, and gets his livelihood by it. That this is the sense of the line, and *eyes*
the true correction of the printer's word ' dies,' will want no proving to him who but
considers it's nearness, and gives another perusal to the third line before it. CAL-
DECOTT : Who by bloodshed makes to die or causes death ; and by such death-doing
makes his living or subsists—who by the means he uses to cut off life, carves out to
himself the means of living. Compare the epitaph on Burton : ' Cui Vitam pariter et
Mortem Dedit Melancholia.' COLLIER (*Notes*, &c., p. 134) : The MS corrector for
' dies' substitutes *kills*. Can *dines* have been the true word? ARROWSMITH (*Notes
& Qu.* 1st Ser. vol. vii, p. 542) : This *hysteron proteron* is by no means uncommon :
its meaning is, of course, the same as live and die, *i. e.* subsist from the cradle to the
grave. All manner of whimsical and farfetched constructions have been put by the
commentators upon this very homely sentence. As long as the question was whether

Enter Rofalind, Celia, and Corin.

Phe.　I would not be thy executioner,　　　　　　10
I flye thee, for I would not iniure thee :
Thou tellft me there is murder in mine eye,
'Tis pretty fure, and very probable,
That eyes that are the frailft, and fofteft things,
Who fhut their coward gates on atomyes,　　　　　15
Should be called tyrants, butchers, murtherers.
Now I doe frowne on thee with all my heart,
And if mine eyes can wound, now let them kill thee:
Now counterfeit to fwound, why now fall downe,　　19

---

9. Enter...] Enter Celia and Rosalind, at a distance, Corin leading them.
Cap. Enter...Corin, behind. Coll.
12. *murder*] *murther* Ff, Rowe, Pope,
Theob. Han. Warb. Wh. i.

12. *eye*] *eyes* Rowe +.
13. *pretty fure,*] Ff, Rowe, Pope.
pretty, sure, Theob. et seq.
19. *fwound*] *swoon* Pope.

---

their wits should have license to go a-woolgathering or no, one could feel no great concern to interfere ; but it appears high time to come to Shakespeare's rescue when Collier's 'clever' old commentator, with some little variation in the letters, and not much
less in the sense, reads *kills* for ' dies.' Compare ' With sorrow they both die and live
That unto richesse her hertes geve.'—*The Romaunt of the Rose,* v. 5789. ' He is a
foole, and so shall he dye and liue, That thinketh him wise, and yet can he nothing.'
—Barclay's *Ship of Fooles,* 1570, fol. 67. ' Behold how ready we are, how willingly
the women of Sparta will die and live with their husbands.'—*The Pilgrimage of
Kings and Princes,* p. 29. [Until this conclusive note appeared, Dyce (*Few Notes,*
p. 68) was inclined to agree with Steevens's 'quibble.' Halliwell repeats Arrowsmith's note, and to the examples there given adds one which, as he says, is somewhat
different : ' I live and die, I die and live, in languor I consume.'—Achelley's *Lamentable and Tragicall Historie,* &c., 1576. Ingleby (*The Still Lion,* p. 59) adopts Dr
Sebastian Evans's paraphrase of the present passage, as meaning ' a man's profession
or calling, by which he lives, and failing which he dies,' where the felicitousness of
the phrase blinds us to the fact that it does not explain the curious inversion of *dying
and living.*—ED.]

11. **for**] That is, because.

13. **pretty sure**] Note the almost comic turn which the omission of the comma
gives this phrase. Of course, as Douce points out, 'sure' is here *surely.*—ED.

14. **That**] See line 47 of the preceding scene ; and for ' who,' in the next line,
see Abbott, § 264, where examples may be found of ' *who* personifying irrational antecedents.'

18. **And if**] This is *an if,* according to Abbott, § 103.

19. **swound**] The pronunciation of this word also was in a transition state when
the Folio was printing. In IV, iii, 166 it is spelled ' swoon, and in V, ii, 29 it appears
in its homely garb ' sound,' which, I think, must have been its common pronunciation
for many a long day. The Nurse in *Rom. & Jul.* III, ii, 56 says : 'All in gore blood :
I *sounded* at the sight ;' where ' sounded ' may possibly have been pronounced *soonded ;*

Or if thou canſt not, oh for ſhame, for ſhame,   20
Lye not, to ſay mine eyes are murtherers :
Now ſhew the wound mine eye hath made in thee,
Scratch thee but with a pin, and there remaines
Some ſcarre of it : Leane vpon a ruſh
The Cicatrice and capable impreſſure   25

22. *eye hath*] *eyes hath* Rowe ii, Steev.   Ktly, Dyce iii, Rlfe, Wh. ii. *Lean thee*
'85. *eyes have* Pope+.   Jervis.
24. *Leane*] *Leane but* Ff, Rowe+,   25. *capable*] *palpable* Sing. Coll. (MS)
Cap. Steev. Mal. Coll. Sing. Cam. Clke,   ii, Ktly.

---

at least, no *w* was pronounced, whatever may have been the sound of the *ou*. Certain it is that 'sound' rhymed with *found* in Scottish poetry, where again the latter word may have been pronounced *foond*. It is simply noteworthy that the sound of the *w* is sometimes present and sometimes lacking, and that, when lacking, it is by no means a mark of vulgarity, as we might, perhaps, infer from its use by Juliet's Nurse; 'sound' from Rosalind's lips could not but be refined. Cf. an old ballad of *The Wofull Death of Queene Jane, wife to King Henry the Eight, and how King Edward was cut out of his mother :* 'She wept and she waild till she fell in a swoond. They opend her two sides, and the baby was found.'—Child's *English and Scottish Popular Ballads*, Part vi, p. 373. We do not now pronounce the *w* in *answer*, nor commonly in *sword*, although my father says that in his childhood, more than eighty years ago, in New England, he was always taught to pronounce the *w* in the latter word, and I have heard Edward Everett pronounce it. Many, very many instances could be given of *sound* in the old dramatists. Malone went so far as to say that it was *always* so written, or else *swound ;* the example 'swoon' in the present play shows that his remark was too general, and that the pronunciation was, as I have said, in a transition state.—ED.

19. **why now**] I think a comma should be placed after 'now,' not after 'why,' where it is generally put.

21. **Lye not, to say**] ALLEN (MS) : That is, lie not to such an extent as to say.

24. **Leane**] As Wright says, *but* is added in the Second Folio 'perhaps unnecessarily, as broken lines are defective in metre '; at the same time, it keeps up the construction, 'scratch thee but with a pin.'—ED.

25. **Cicatrice**] JOHNSON : Here not very properly used; it is the scar of a wound. [Here it is simply, as Dyce defines it, the mark.] STAUNTON : The only difficulty in the line is this word, which certainly appears here to be used in an exceptional sense.

25. **capable impressure**] JOHNSON : That is, hollow mark. MALONE : 'Capable,' I believe, here means *perceptible*. Our author often uses the word for *intelligent*. So in *Ham.* III, iv, 126 : 'His form and cause conjoin'd, preaching to stones, Would make them capable.' SINGER : It is evident we should read *palpable*. For no one can surely be satisfied with the strained explanations offered by Johnson and Malone. COLLIER : *Palpable* is the correction of the (MS). BLACKWOOD'S MAGAZINE : 'Capable impressure' means an indentation in the palm of the hand sufficiently deep to *contain* something within it. WHITE : 'Capable' is used here in a peculiarly and unmistakeably Shakespearian manner for *receivable*. Yet it has been proposed to read *palpable*. The change is one of a kind that commends itself to the approval of

Thy palme ſome moment keepes : but now mine eyes   26
Which I haue darted at thee, hurt thee not,
Nor I am ſure there is no force in eyes
That can doe hurt.

   Sil.   O deere *Phebe*,   30
If euer (as that euer may be neere)
You meet in ſome freſh cheeke the power of fancie,
Then ſhall you know the wouuds inuiſible
That Loues keene arrows make.

   Phe.   But till that time   35
Come not thou neere me : and when that time comes,
Afflict me with thy mockes, pitty me not,
As till that time I ſhall not pitty thee.

   Roſ.   And why I pray you?who might be your mother   39

---

28. *Nor*] *Now* Quincy (MS). *And*
Ktly conj.
  29. *doe hurt*] *do any hurt* Han. *do
hurt to any* Cap. *do hurt to any one*
Ktly.
 · 30. *O*] *O my* Han.

31. *neere*] *near* F₃F₄.
32. *meet*] *met* Ff, Rowe i.
33. *wouuds*] F₁. *wound's* Pope, Han.
39. *why...you ?*] *why ?...you,* Coll.
ii.
   you ?] *you ?* [Advancing] Cap.

---

those who have not fully apprehended the peculiarities of Shakespeare's diction, peculiarities without affectation, and who seize on an emendation of a supposed corruption
to guide them through an obscurity which exists but in their own perception. A complete counterpart to the use of 'capable impressure' here is found in the phrase 'cap-
tious and intenible sieve.'—*All's Well*, I, iii, 208. STAUNTON: 'Capable' means
sensible. [See Abbott, §§ 3, 445, for instances of other adjectives in -*ble*, used both
actively and passively.]

   26. some moment] ROLFE: Compare *Rom. & Jul.* V, iii, 257: 'some minute
ere the time,' &c. 'Some' is still used with singular nouns to express kind or quantity; as in 'some fresh cheek' in line 32 just below, 'some food.'—*Temp.* I, ii, 160, &c.
We can even say 'some half an hour,'—*Love's Lab. L.* V, ii, 90; 'some month or
two.'—*Mer. of Ven.* III, ii, 9, &c. It is doubtful, indeed, whether there is any Shakespearian use of the word which might not be allowed now. In *Temp.* I, ii, 7 ('Who
had no doubt some noble creature in her'), Dyce, Staunton, and others read 'creatures'; but even here the singular would not be clearly an exceptional instance.

   28. Nor . . . no] For double negatives see Shakespeare, *passim*, or Abbott, §§ 406,
408.

   30. deere] MOBERLY: A dissyllable, and the missing syllables are probably filled
up by a laugh of derision.

   32. fancie] JOHNSON: Here used for *love* [and always so used in Shakespeare,
might be added].

   39. mother] JOHNSON: It is common for the poets to express cruelty by saying
of those who commit it that they were born of rocks or suckled by tigresses. COW-
DEN-CLARKE: It seems evident to us that there was in Shakespeare's time some point
in making allusion to a beauty's *mother.* Here there is a scoff implied in this ques-

That you insult, exult, and all at once   40
Ouer the wretched? what though you hau no beauty

40. *insult...once*] insult, and, all at
once, exult Ktly.
    and ... once] and rail, at once
Theob. Warb. Sing. *and domineer* Han.
à l'outrecuidance Forbes (*N. & Qu.* vi,
423) *and tyrannise* Gould.
  41. *what though*] What though ? Sing.

What! though Ktly.
  41. *hau no*] F₁. *have* Theob. Warb.
Johns. Steev. *have some* Han. Dyce iii.
have mo Mal. Var. '21. *have more* Steev.
'93.
  41, 42. *hau no beauty As*] *have more
beauty Yet* Quincy (MS).

---

tion, and in *Cym.* III, iv, there is a passage which has puzzled commentators, but
which we think is readily comprehensible if our theory be correct. 'Some jay of
Italy, whose *mother* was her painting,' appears to us to contain the like contemptuous
reference to a would-be beauty's origin, as in the sentence of the text.

  40. **all at once**] WARBURTON: If the speaker intended to accuse the person
spoken to only for insulting and exulting, then, instead of ' *all* at once,' it ought to
have been '*both* at once.' But, by examining the crime of the person accused, we
shall discover that the [phrase should be] : '*rail* at once.' HEATH (p. 150): Phebe
had in truth both insulted and exulted, but had not said one single word which could
deserve the imputation of *railing*. STEEVENS : I see no need of emendation. The
speaker may mean: 'that you insult, exult, and that, too, *all in a breath*.' Such is,
perhaps, the meaning of 'all at once.' SINGER : It has been asked, 'What "all at
once" can possibly mean here ?' It would not be easy to give a satisfactory answer.
It is certainly a misprint, and we confidently read *rail*, with Warburton. GRANT
WHITE speaks of Warburton's conjecture as 'somewhat plausible.' [On the following passage in *Hen. V:* I, i, 36: 'Never was such a sudden scholar made; Never
came reformation in a flood; With such a heady currance, scouring faults; Nor never
Hydra-headed wilfulness So soon did lose his seat, *and all at once*, As in this king,'
STAUNTON has this note :] This 'and all at once' was a trite phrase in Shakespeare's
day, though not one of his editors has noticed it. [The present passage in *As You
Like It* is then referred to.] It is frequently met with in the old writers. Thus, in
The Fisherman's Tale, 1594, by F. Sabie: 'She wept, she cride, she sob'd, and all at
once.' And in Middleton's *Changeling*, IV, iii: 'Does love turn fool, run mad, and
all at once?' KEIGHTLEY: Read, 'That you insult and exult all at once.' This
transposition removes all necessity for correction. Strange that the critics should not
have thought of it! In my edition the transposition is wrong. SCHMIDT (*s. v. once*,
i): And all the rest, and everything else. WRIGHT, after citing Staunton's illustrations, says: The first of these [from *Hen. V*] is not to the point, and a reference to
the others would not have been necessary had it not been proposed to substitute for
what gives a very plain meaning, either *rail* or *domineer*. [If a paraphrase be really
needed, Steevens's seems to be near enough.—ED.]

  41. **hau no**] THEOBALD: It is very accurately observed to me, by an ingenious
unknown correspondent, who signs himself L. H., that the *negative* ought to be left
out. [The letter of L. H. to Theobald is printed in Nichols's *Illust.* vol. ii, p. 632.]
CAPELL: The gentlemen who have thrown out the negative, and the other who has
chang'd it to *some*, make the Poet a very bad reasoner in the line that comes next to
this sentence; and guilty of self-contradiction in several others, if 'no' be either
alter'd or parted with: besides the injury done to him in robbing him of a lively
expression, and a pleasantry truly comick; for as the sentence now stands, the conse-

[what though you hau no beauty]

quence that should have been from her *beauty* he draws from her 'no beauty,' and extorts a smile by defeating your expectation. This 'no beauty' of Phebe's is the burthen of all Rosalind's speeches, from hence to her exit. MALONE: That 'no' is a misprint appears clearly from the passage in Lodge's *Rosalynde*, which Shakespeare has here imitated: 'Because thou art beautiful, be not so coy; as there is nothing more faire, so there is nothing more fading.' 'No' was, I believe, a misprint for *mo*. So in III, ii, 257: 'mar no moe of my verses.' 'What though I should allow you had *more* beauty than he (says Rosalind), *though* by my faith,' &c. (for such is the force of *As* in the next line), 'must you therefore treat him with disdain?' M. MASON: If *more* is to stand, then we must read '*had* more beauty,' instead of 'have.' TOLLET: I have no doubt that the original reading 'no' is right. It is conformable to the whole tenor of Rosalind's speech, particularly the line: 'Foul is most foul, being foul to be a scoffer.' That *mo* or *more* was not the word used is proved by the passage: 'You are a thousand times a *properer man* Than *she a woman*.' WHITER: Tollet's instance is foreign to the purpose. Take an example in point: '*tho*' there was *no* great matter in the ditty, yet the note was very *un*tunable.'—V, iii. COLLIER: The meaning seems quite clear. Rosalind intends throughout her speech to check the vanity of Phebe, and begins by telling her she has no beauty, and therefore no excuse for being 'proud and pitiless.' The difficulty seems to be to understand the passage when, varying from the old copies, *mo* is substituted for 'no.' *Mo* or *more* indicates comparison, but with whom was Phebe here to be compared in point of beauty? Not with Sylvius, because Rosalind says he was 'a properer man.' SINGER: The negative particle was not intended to be taken literally. *What though?* is an elliptical interrogation, and is again used in *Mid. N. D.*, 'What though he love your Hermia? Lord, what though?' GRANT WHITE: Rosalind's purpose is solely to take the conceit out of Phebe. WALKER (*Crit.* i, 308): 'No' is evidently wrong. *Some*, I think, little as (even when shortened to *som*) it resembles 'no.' [Foot-note by LETTSOM]: In this class of errors there is often little or no resemblance between the ejected and the substituted word. I believe *som* to be right; but we should also read *had* for 'hau,' as the Folio prints the word, confounding *d* with the long *u* or *v*. See Dyce's *Remarks*, p. 21 [where unquestionable instances are given of such confusion]. DYCE (ed. iii): The fact is, 'no' was inserted by a mistake of the transcriber or compositor, whose eye caught it from the next line. WRIGHT: The negative is certainly required, because Rosalind's object is to strike a blow at Phebe's vanity. [Unquestionably, Rosalind's object is 'to strike a blow at Phebe's vanity' and 'to take the conceit out of her.' The question, it seems to me, is: will this end be gained as effectively by denying that the girl has any beauty at all as by granting that she has no more than the ordinary of nature's sale-work. To tell Phebe roundly that she had no beauty whatsoever would be overshooting the mark. The devotion of Silvius disproves that. Phebe knew she was pretty, and though inky brows and black silk hair were not deemed as bewitching, in former times, as those of gold, yet cheeks of cream have never been despised since blushes first mantled them. To have acknowledged that she had *some* beauty, no more than without candle may go dark to bed, is damning with very faint praise, the bitterest of all condemnation; it is a disprizing, the pangs whereof Hamlet teaches us. Furthermore, to be strictly logical, can a maiden with *no* beauty, *therefore*, or on that account, be proud? But if she has only a little beauty it may well be asked whether she is therefore to be proud and pitiless. Accordingly, the text which I should follow would be Hanmer's.—ED.]

As by my faith, I fee no more in you   42
Then without Candle may goe darke to bed :
Muſt you be therefore prowd and pittileſſe ?
Why what meanes this ? why do you looke on me ?   45
I fee no more in you then in the ordinary
Of Natures ſale-worke ? 'ods my little life,
I thinke ſhe meanes to tangle my eies too :
No faith proud Miſtreſſe, hope not after it,
'Tis not your inkie browes, your blacke ſilke haire,   50
Your bugle eye-balls, nor your cheeke of creame
That can entame my ſpirits to your worſhip :
You fooliſh Shepheard, wherefore do you follow her
Like foggy South, puffing with winde and raine,
You are a thouſand times a properer man   55
Then ſhe a woman.   'Tis ſuch fooles as you

---

43. Cf. La nuit, tous les chats sont gris.—ED.

48. *my eies*] *mine eyes* Ff, Rowe+, Cap.

50. *your inkie*] *you inkie* F₃.

50. *blacke ... haire*] *black-silk hair* Cap. Steev. Mal. Coll. Sing. Dyce, Sta. *black silk-hair* Ktly.

52. *entame*] *entraine* Warb. conj.

56. *woman.*] *woman :* Cap.

---

43. darke] MOBERLY : That is, without exciting any particular desire for light to see it by.

46. This line, as line 4 above, Abbott classes among 'Apparent Alexandrines' by a mode of scansion to which I cannot become reconciled : 'I sée | no móre | in yóu | than ín | the órdinary.'   I had rather have the slow dragging of a dozen wounded boa-constrictors than the 'slurring' of syllables which is here recommended.—ED.

47. sale-worke] WARBURTON : The allusion is to the practice of mechanics, whose *work* bespoke is more elaborate than that which is made up for chance-customers, or to sell in quantities to retailers, which is called 'sale-work.'   WRIGHT : The modern phrase is 'ready-made goods.'

51. bugle] MURRAY (*New Eng. Dict.*) : A tube-shaped glass bead, usually black, and to ornament wearing apparel.   [Examples follow from Spenser, 1579, to the present day.   Its colour here, we learn from Phebe ; in line 135 she says : 'He said mine eyes were black.'—ED.]

52. entame] ABBOTT, § 440 : That is, bring *into* a state of tameness.

53. Again Abbott, § 458, thus scans : 'You fool | ish shép | herd, whére | fore dó | you fóllow her.'

54. foggy South, puffing] CALDECOTT : Compare 'Puffs away from thence, Turning his face to the dew-dropping south.'—*Rom. & Jul.* I, iv.

56. 'Tis] Capell was the first to desert the good punctuation of the Folio here, and has been followed by nearly every editor, except White in his first edition, even down to Verity in his edition for Irving.   A full stop in the middle of a line is so unusual in F₁, that it deserves more attention than the punctuation in that edition generally merits.   Frequently it indicates a change of address, as in II, vii, 204 ; III,

That makes the world full of ill-fauourd children :   57
'Tis not her glaffe, but you that flatters her,
And out of you fhe fees her felfe more proper
Then any of her lineaments can fhow her :   60
But Miftris, know your felfe, downe on your knees
And thanke heauen, fafting, for a good mans loue;
For I muft tell you friendly in your eare,
Sell when you can, you are not for all markets :
Cry the man mercy, loue him, take his offer,   65
Foule is moft foule, being foule to be a fcoffer.
So take her to thee Shepheard, fareyouwell.

    Phe. Sweet youth, I pray you chide a yere together,
I had rather here you chide, then this man wooe.

    Ros. Hees falne in loue with your foulneffe, & fhee'll   70

<hr/>

57. *makes*] Ff, Rowe, Cap. Cam. Ktly, Rlfe, Wh. ii. *make* Pope et cet.
  58. *flatters*] *flatter* Rowe ii+.
  64. *when*] *what* Rowe i.
  67. *fareyouwell*] *fare you well* Ff.
  70–73. Dividing lines, *fhee'll...fo,... lookes,...words...me ?* Ktly. As Prose,

Pope et cet.
  70. [Aside.] Johns.
    your] *her* Han. Johns. Cap. Steev. Mal. Dyce iii, Coll. iii, Huds.
    & fhee'll] To Silvius. *And shee'll* Sing.
    fhee'll] *you'll* Ktly.

<hr/>

i, 16, also in line 71 of this present scene; and such a change, I think, is indicated here. It is to Phebe, not to Silvius, that Rosalind says, ''Tis such fools as you,' &c. The words are another stab at Phebe's personal vanity. It is she, with her folly, that is to be the mother of ill-favoured children. Rosalind is espousing Silvius's part, and although she has just called him ' foolish,' that is not the same as calling him a ' fool.' After having compared him with Phebe on the score of physical beauty, and pronounced him a thousand times a properer man, it is not exactly in keeping to say that he is to be the father of ugly children. Of course, the text shows clearly enough that lines 58–60 are addressed to Silvius, but it is the punctuation here in line 56 which, I think, was intended to be our guide.—ED.

  57. **That makes**] WRIGHT: The verb is singular because the nominative is the idea contained in what precedes, as if it had been, '' 'tis the fact of there being such fools as you that makes,' &c. [See Abbott, § 247.]

  66. WARBURTON: The only sense of this is: An ill-favoured person is most ill-favoured when, if he be ill-favoured, he is a scoffer. Which is a deal too absurd to come from Shakespeare; who, without question, wrote : ' being *found* to be a scoffer '; *i. e.* where an ill-favoured person ridicules the defects of others, it makes his own appear excessive. HEATH : Mr Warburton first of all gives us a very false and absurd interpretation of this passage, and then on the foundation of that very absurdity, which is wholly his own, and not to be found in the text, he rejects the authentic reading, to make room for his own very flat emendation. JOHNSON : The sense is, The ugly seem most ugly, when, *though* ugly, they are scoffers. ABBOTT, § 356 : This seems to mean : foulness is most foul when its foulness consists *in being* scornful. [For this use of the infinitive see I, i, 109; II, vii, 182.]

Fall in loue with my anger. If it be fo, as faft   71
As fhe anfweres thee with frowning lookes, ile fauce
Her with bitter words : why looke you fo vpon me?
   Phe. For no ill will I beare you.
   Rof. I pray you do not fall in loue with mee,   75
For I am falfer then vowes made in wine :
Befides, I like you not : if you will know my houfe,
'Tis at the tufft of Oliues, here hard by :
Will you goe Sifter ? Shepheard ply her hard :
Come Sifter : Shepheardeffe, looke on him better   80
And be not proud, though all the world could fee,
None could be fo abus'd in fight as hee.
Come, to our flocke,   *Exit.*
   Phe. Dead Shepheard, now I find thy faw of might,
Who euer lov'd, that lou'd not at firft fight ?   85

---

80. *Sifter :*] *Sifter*, F$_3$. *Sifter* F$_4$.   84. *Dead*] *Deed* Ff, Rowe, Warb.
81. *fee*] *see ye* Han.   *'Deed*, Han.
83. *Come,*] *Come* F$_3$F$_4$, Rowe i.

---

70. **your**] If Hanmer's change to *her* be adopted, Johnson's marking of this speech as an *Aside* seems proper enough. And yet it seems necessary that Silvius should hear it in order that he may understand why Rosalind should sauce Phebe with bitter words. Again, note the break in the line, which may give emphasis, as in line 56, to the change of address; yet it will not do to build too much on this, or on any punctuation in the Folio. Surely, if anywhere, a full stop as an indication of the change of address is needed in line 73.—ED.

72. **sauce**] ROLFE: Cf. our vulgarism of 'sassing' a person. From meaning to give zest or piquancy to language, the word came to be used ironically in the sense of making it hot and sharp; or, in other words, from meaning to *spice*, it came to mean to *pepper*.

77. Again, according to Abbott, § 499, this is only an 'apparent Alexandrine.' But this time it is not the final syllables which are slurred over, but the single foot ' Besides ' which precedes the line and creates the false show.

82. **abus'd**] JOHNSON : Though all mankind could look on you, none could be so *deceived* as to think you beautiful but he.

84. **Dead Shepheard**] DYCE (Marlowe's *Works*, i, xlviii) : These words sound not unlike an expression of pity for Marlowe's sad and untimely end.

85. Capell was the first to discover that this 'saw' is from Marlowe's *Hero and Leander*, the paraphrase of a poem by the Pseudo-Musæus, first printed in 1598, although the edition which Capell used was that of 1637. The line is in the First Sestiad (p. 12, ed. Dyce) : 'Where both deliberate, the love is slight : Who ever lov'd, that lov'd not at first sight ?' It is also given in *England's Parnassus*, 1600, p. 308, Collier's Reprint, and on p. 423 of Capell's *School.*—ED. MALONE : This poem of Marlowe's was so popular (as appears from many contemporary writers) that

Sil. Sweet *Phebe.*   86
Phe. Hah: what faift thou *Siluius?*
Sil. Sweet *Phebe* pitty me.
Phe. Why I am forry for thee gentle *Siluius.*
Sil. Where euer forrow is, reliefe would be :   90
If you doe forrow at my griefe in loue,
By giuing loue your forrow, and my griefe
Were both extermin'd·
Phe. Thou haft my loue, is not that neighbourly?
Sil. I would haue you.   95
Phe. Why that were couetoufneffe :
Siluius; the time was, that I hated thee ;
And yet it is not, that I beare thee loue,
But fince that thou canft talke of loue fo well,
Thy company, which erft was irkefome to me   100
I will endure ; and Ile employ thee too :
But doe not looke for further recompence
Then thine owne gladneffe, that thou art employd
Sil. So holy, and fo perfeſt is my loue,
And I in fuch a pouerty of grace,   105
That I fhall thinke it a moft plenteous crop
To gleane the broken eares after the man
That the maine harueft reapes: loofe now and then   108

---

86. Phebe.] *Phebe,*— Cap. et seq.
87. Siluius] *Silvia* Johns. (misprint?).
92. *loue your forrow,*] *love, your sor-*
row Rowe et seq.
105. *And I in*] *And in* F$_2$. *And* F$_3$F$_4$,

Rowe, Pope, Han.
105. *grace*] *grace attends it* Rowe,
Pope, Han.
106. *plenteous*] *plentious* Ff.
108. *loofe*] *lofe* F$_4$, Rowe.

---

a quotation from it must have been known at once, at least by the more enlightened
part of the audience. Shakespeare again alluded to it in *The Two Gent.* [This
'allusion' is merely a reference to the story of Hero and Leander. The only twist
whereby Malone can there make it refer to Marlowe's Poem, which is of a later date
than *The Two Gent.*, is to suppose that Shakespeare read the poem in MS before its
publication.—ED.]

93. **extermin'd**] Exterminated. WRIGHT: Compare *extirp* and *extirpated.*
ROLFE: Used by Shakespeare only here. Its equivalent, *exterminate*, he does not
use at all.

94. **neighbourly**] HALLIWELL: These words seem scarcely natural to the
speaker, unless it be presumed there is here an allusion to the injunction to 'love
thy neighbour as thyself.'

98. **yet it is not**] REV. JOHN HUNTER: The time is not yet.
99. **since that**] See I, iii, 44, or Abbott, § 287.

A ſcattred ſmile,and that Ile liue vpon. (while?

 Phe. Knowſt thou the youth that ſpoke to mee yere- 110
 Sil. Not very well,but I haue met him oft,
And he hath bought the Cottage and the bounds
That the old *Carlot* once was Maſter of.
 Phe. Thinke not I loue him,though I ask for him,
'Tis but a peeuiſh boy,yet he talkes well, 115
But what care I for words? yet words do well
When he that ſpeakes them pleaſes thoſe that heare:
It is a pretty youth,not very prettie,
But ſure hee's proud,and yet his pride becomes him;
Hee'll make a proper man: the beſt thing in him 120
Is his complexion : and faſter then his tongue
Did make offence,his eye did heale it vp :
He is not very tall,yet for his yeeres hee's tall :
His leg is but ſo ſo,and yet 'tis well : 124

---

109. *ſcattred*] *ſcattered* Ff, Rowe.
scatter'd Pope et seq.
 110. *yerewhile*] F₂F₃.
 113. Carlot] Roman, first by Steev.

123. *very*] Om. Han. Cap. Steev. '93,
Dyce iii.
124. *ſo ſo*] *so* Johns.

---

110. yerewhile] WRIGHT calls attention to this spelling in the first three Folios, and adds: 'So in the Authorised Version of 1611 'ere' is spelt 'yer' in *Numbers* xi, 33; xiv, 11.'

113. Carlot] DOUCE: That is, *peasant*, from *carle* or *churl;* probably a word of Shakespeare's coinage. DYCE: It is evidently the diminutive of *carl*—churl (compare 'My master is of *churlish* disposition,'—II, iv, 84, where the same person is alluded to). And see Richardson's *Dict.* in v. *Carle.* COLLIER (ed. ii): Richardson, under *Carl,* quotes Shakespeare's 'Carlot,' and says Drayton has *Carlet* in his *Barons' Wars,* B. v. He has *Carlel* in B. iv, but by *Carlel* he means Herckley, Constable of *Carlisle.* Shakespeare alone uses 'Carlot.' KEIGHTLEY: It is printed as a proper name, and it may be the Spanish *Carloto.* No such substantive as 'carlot' is known.

114. CALDECOTT: Trinculo does not more naturally betray himself when he says: 'By this good light, a very shallow monster: *I afeard of him?* a very shallow monster.'—*Temp.* II, ii. FLETCHER (p. 203): Of Phebe, in name and character no less an ideal shepherdess than Rosalind is an ideal princess, it may be said that we might have been grateful for her creation, even had she been introduced for no other purpose than to give us the enamoured lines which convey so exquisite a portrait of this terrestrial Ganymede.

115. peeuish] Cotgrave has: *Hargneux.* Peeuish, wrangling, diuerous, ouerthwart, crosse, waiward, froward; ill to please, euer complayning, neuer quiet.

123. very] WALKER (*Crit.* i, 269) agrees with Hanmer in erasing this 'very'; which is, I think, justifiable, seeing how frequently this word is interpolated. To avoid the baleful name Alexandrine, Abbott, § 501, calls the line a trimeter couplet, and thus divides it: 'He ís | not vé | ry táll: ‖ yet fór | his yéars | he's táll.'—ED.

There was a pretty redneſſe in his lip,   125
A little riper, and more luſtie red
Then that mixt in his cheeke: 'twas iuſt the difference
Betwixt the conſtant red, and mingled Damaske.
There be ſome women *Siluius,* had they markt him
In parcells as I did, would haue gone neere   130
To fall in loue with him : but for my part
I loue him not, nor hate him not : and yet
Haue more cauſe to hate him then to loue him,
For what had he to doe to chide at me?
He ſaid mine eyes were black, and my haire blacke,   135
And now I am remembred, ſcorn'd at me :
I maruell why I anſwer'd not againe,
But that's all one : omittance is no quittance :
Ile write to him a very tanting Letter,
And thou ſhalt beare it, wilt thou *Siluius?*   140
      Sil.   Phebe, with all my heart.
      Phe.   Ile write it ſtrait :
The matter's in my head, and in my heart,
I will be bitter with him, and paſſing ſhort ;
Goe with me *Siluius.*   *Exeunt.*   145

---

133. *Haue*] Dyce i, Sta. Clke.   *I have* Ff, Rowe et cet.   *Have much* Sta. conj.

139. *tanting*] *taunting* F₄.
Letter] *Lettler* F₂.
144. *and*] Om. Cap.

---

127. Abbott, § 494, tells us to slur the extra syllables in ' difference.'

128. **Damaske**] STEEVENS : ' Constant red ' is *uniform* red.   *'Mingled* damask ' is the silk of that name, in which, by a various direction of the threads, many lighter shades of the same colour are exhibited, KNIGHT : We doubt this.   The *damask rose* was of a more varied hue than the *constant red* of other species of rose. WRIGHT : Red and white, like the colour of the damask roses.   Compare *Sonn.* cxxx, 5 : ' I have seen roses damask'd, red and white, But no such roses see I in her cheeks.'   [' Mingled damask ' is of course a colour, and a colour well known, but what the colour was, it is doubtful if we can by any means tell at present.   It is even possible that ' damask ' may refer to some kind of material, and not to roses. Cotgrave tells us distinctly that damask roses are white.   At the present day and in this country there is no variation, such as Knight speaks of, in the hue of the old-fashioned damask rose, other than in the paler hue which accompanies its fading ; otherwise its tint of light pink is quite as ' constant ' as that of any of its redder sisters.   Until we can gain more information we must rest content with imagining Ganymede's cheek to be of the fairest earthly tint and finest earthly texture.   But where is the umber?—ED.]

138. **omittance is no quittance**] WALKER (*Crit.* iii, 64) : A proverb of course. Milton, *P. L.* x, 53, man ' soon shall find Forbearance is no quittance ere day end.'

14

Actus Quartus . Scena Prima.

Enter Rofalind, and Celia, and Iaques.

Iaq.   I prethee, pretty youth, let me better acquainted with thee.

Rof   They fay you are a melancholly fellow.

Iaq.   I am fo : I doe loue it better then laughing.

Rof.   Thofe that are in extremity of either, are abhominable fellowes, and betray themfelues to euery moderne cenfure, worfe then drunkards.   8

The Forest. Rowe.   6, 7. *abhominable*] *abominable* F₄.
2. *me*] *me be* Ff et seq.

---

5. **I do loue it**] MOBERLY: 'You are always complaining of melancholy,' says Johnson to Boswell (iv, 301), 'and I conclude from those complaints that you are fond of it.   Do not pretend to deny it; *manifestum habemus furem.*   Make it an invariable and obligatory law on yourself never to mention your own mental diseases.   If you are never to speak of them you will think of them but little; and if you think little of them they will molest you rarely.'

7, 8. **moderne . . . drunkards**] The drift of Rosalind's whole speech appears to be that both classes of men, those who are profound in their melancholy and those who are boisterous in their mirth, expose themselves even more openly than drunkards to every commonplace, hackneyed criticism.   She had taken down Phebe's conceit by asserting that her beauty was no more than a fair average of Nature's ready-made goods; she is now about to do the same to Jaques by saying that he was no more interesting in his sentimental melancholy than a common drunkard.   But MOBERLY interprets it somewhat differently; and as his interpretation of the whole comedy, with which I cannot altogether agree, is charming and attractive, every word he utters in support of it deserves to be well weighed.   To Moberly, this encounter between Jaques and Rosalind is one of the passages where the great moral lesson of cheerfulness is conveyed, a lesson which Shakespeare happened to need in his own life at that time, and the need whereof he saw in the anxious thought of eminent men around him: 'Thus,' says Moberly, 'Sir H. Sidney writes to his son Sir Philip, "Let your first action be the lifting up of your mind to Almighty God by hearty prayer; . . . . then give yourself to be merry; for you degenerate from your father, if you find not yourself most able in wit and body to do anything when you are most merry."'   This present speech of Rosalind is one of the happy hits, and is thus paraphrased by Moberly (*Introd.* p. 9) : 'And what iṣ this melancholy of which Jaques boasts? [asks Rosalind sarcastically].   Something as bad or worse than the most giddy merriment : something that incapacitates him from action as completely and more permanently than drunkenness.'   Again, his note *ad loc.* is : '*Worse than drunkards.*   For both alike are as incapable of action as drunkards, and their state is more permanent.'

Iaq.   Why, 'tis good to be fad and fay nothing.

Rof.   Why then 'tis good to be a pofte.   10

Iaq.   I haue neither the Schollers melancholy, which
is emulation : nor the Mufitians, which is fantafticall ;
nor the Courtiers, which is proud : nor the Souldiers,
which is ambitious : nor the Lawiers, which is politick :
nor the Ladies, which is nice : nor the Louers, which   15
is all thefe : but it is a melancholy of mine owne, compounded of many fimples, extracted from many obiects,
and indeed the fundrie contemplation of my trauells, in   18

14. *politick*] *political* Rowe i.   *tions of* F$_3$F$_4$, Rowe i.
18. *fundrie*] *fundty* F$_4$.   18, 19. *in which*] *which* Var. '21. *on
contemplation of my] *contempla-*   *which* Seymour.

Here Moberly seems to take 'worse' as qualifying the subject; I think it qualifies
the verb 'betray.'—ED.

11–20. MAGINN: This is printed as prose, but assuredly it is blank verse. The
alteration of a syllable or two, which in the corrupt state of the text of these plays is
the slightest of all possible critical licenses, would make it run perfectly smooth. At
all events, 'emulation' should be *emulative*, to make it agree with the other clauses of
the sentence. The courtier's melancholy is not *pride*, nor the soldier's *ambition*, &c.
The adjective is used throughout : 'fantastical,' 'proud,' 'ambitious,' 'politic,' 'nice.'
[Maginn thus divides the lines : 'Neither the scholar's melancholy, which ‖ Is emulation ; nor the musician's, which is ‖ Fantastical ; nor the courtier's, which is proud ; ‖
Nor the soldier's, ‖ Which is ambitious ; nor the lawyer's, which ‖ Is politic ; nor the
lady's, which is nice ; ‖ Nor the lover's, which is all these ; but it is ‖ A melancholy
of mine own, compounded ‖ Of many simples, extracted from many objects ‖ And
indeed ‖ The sundry contemplation of my travels, ‖ In which my often rumination
wraps me ‖ In a most humorous sadness.'.   [Rather ragged verse, it must be owned.
I should prefer to call it metric prose, or measurably like the semi-metric prose of
Walt Whitman at the present day.   There would be a lack of harmony in giving
Jaques a single speech in regular blank verse in a scene where every other speech is
in prose.—ED.]

14. MOBERLY: The scholar's melancholy springs from envy of other men's superior mental powers, which his diligence may be unable to cope with ; the courtier's is
from pride, which puts him out of sympathy with his kind ; the lady's is from fastid-
iousness ; the soldier's from disappointed ambition ; the lawyer's from professionally
assumed or half-real sympathy with his client.   [To understand the musician's melancholy, I think we must take 'fantastical' as referring to love-sick music ; and may we
not take both 'politic' and 'lawyer' in a somewhat wider sense than that just given ?
May not 'lawyers' be lawgivers, and 'politic' denote that which is connected with
the science of government ?—ED.]

15. nice] STEEVENS: Silly, trifling.   CALDECOTT: Affected, over-curious in trifles.
NARES: Foolish, trifling.   HALLIWELL: Delicate, affected, effeminate.   DYCE:
Scrupulous, precise, squeamish.   HUDSON: Fastidious, dainty, or squeamish.   VERITY:
Squeamish, super-subtle, finicking.   [An object-lesson, to teach the student to make
his own definitions,—especially where none is required.—ED.]

which by often rumination, wraps me in a moſt humo-
rous ſadneſſe.   20

Roſ. A Traueller : by my faith you haue great reaſon to be ſad : I feare you haue ſold your owne Lands,
to ſee other mens ; then to haue ſeene much, and to haue
nothing, is to haue rich eyes and poore hands.

Iaq. Yes, I haue gain'd my experience.   25

Enter Orlando.

Roſ. And your experience makes you ſad : I had rather haue a foole to make me merrie, then experience to
make me ſad, and to trauaile for it too.

Orl. Good day, and happineſſe, deere *Roſalind*.   30

Iaq. Nay then God buy you, and you talke in blanke
verſe.   32

---

19. *by*] Var. '21, Coll. Sing. Sta. Ktly,
Dyce iii. *my* Ff, Rowe et cet.
 rumination,] *rumination* Rowe et
seq.
 in] *is* Steev. '93.
 25. *my*] Om. Rowe, Pope, Han. *me*
Theob. ii, Warb. Johns.
 29. *trauaile*] *travel* F_3F_4.

31. Iaq.] Orl. F_2.
 buy] Ff, Cam. *b'w'y* Rowe +.
b' wi' Wh. Dyce. *be wi'* Cap. et cet.
 and] Ff, Rowe, Cald. *an* Pope
et cet.
 32. *verſe*] *verſe*. Exit. Ff, Rowe et
seq.
 Scene II. Pope, Han. Warb.

18–20. in . . . sadnesse] MALONE, reading 'by often,' omitted the first 'in,' in
line 18; STEEVENS, reading 'my often,' changed the second 'in,' in line 19, to *is*,
adding : 'Jaques first informs Rosalind what his melancholy was *not;* and naturally
concluded by telling her what the quality of it *is*.' CALDECOTT, reading 'my often,'
thus paraphrases : It is the diversified consideration or view of my travels, in which
process my frequent reflection, and continued interest that I take, wraps me in a
whimsical sadness. KNIGHT, reading *my :* His melancholy is the contemplation of
his travels, the rumination upon which wraps him in a most humorous sadness.
WHITE : 'By' is clearly a corruption, as it leaves 'wraps' without a nominative
expressed or understood. The point of the speech is that the satirical Jaques finds in
the contemplation of his travels his cause for melancholy. He means to sneer, *more
suo*, at the whole world ; and this he is made to do by the substitution of *my* for 'by,'
and of a semicolon for a comma after 'travels.' The pleonastic use of 'in' is quite
in conformity to the custom of the time.

 19. humorous] CALDECOTT : In his *Apology for Smectymnus*, Milton says of his
own ear for numbers, that it was 'rather nice and humorous in what was tolerable
than patient to read every drawling versifier.'—Warton's *Milton*, p. 207. [See
'humorous.'—I, ii, 265.]

 31. and] That is, *an*. See Abbott, § 101, if necessary. WRIGHT : In this form
it occurs where it is little suspected in the Authorised Version of *Genesis*, xliv, 30 :
'Now therefore when I come to thy servant my father, and the lad be not with
us.'

 31, 32. blanke verse] What are we to understand by this ? It is Orlando who

Rof. Farewell Mounſieur Trauellor : looke you   33
liſpe, and weare ſtrange ſuites ; diſable all the benefits

---

has just uttered the only line of blank verse. Jaques, therefore, hears Orlando, even
if Rosalind does not, or pretends that she does not; see Grant White's interpretation,
in the next note.—ED.

32. Nearly every modern edition follows the Ff in putting *Exit* at the end of this
line. Dyce placed it after ' gondola' in line 38, and is followed by Cowden-Clarke,
Hudson, and the Irving. DYCE (*Remarks*, p. 63) quotes Rosalind's speech from line
33 down to her address to Orlando in line 38, and asks : ' Does Rosalind say all this
to Jaques *after he has left the stage ?*' He then goes on to say, in regard to the *Exit*
of the Ff, that '*Exits* as well as *Entrances* were very frequently marked much earlier
than they were really intended to take place ; and nothing can be more evident than
that here the *exit* of Jaques ought to follow " gondola."' WHITE (ed. i) : The question has been raised, whether Jaques should go out when he takes leave, or just before
Rosalind addresses Orlando. It seems plain that in the latter case a charming and
characteristic incident would be lost. Rosalind is a little vexed with Orlando for not
keeping tryst. She sees him when he comes in, but purposely does not look at him,
no woman needs be told why. He speaks, but she, with her little heart thumping at
her breast all the while, refuses to notice her lover, and pretends to be absorbed in
Jaques ; and as he retires, driven off by the coming scene of sentiment, the approach
of which he detects, she still ignores the presence of the poor delinquent, and continues to talk to Jaques till a curve in the path takes him out of sight; then turning,
she seems to see Orlando for the first time, and breaks upon him with, ' Why, how
now ?' &c. Well might the old printer in *Promos and Cassandra* say that there are
some speeches ' which in reading wil seeme hard, and in action appeare plaine.'
DYCE quotes this note of White's, and adds : 'All this is, no doubt, very ingenious ;
but I cannot help thinking that it shows little knowledge of stage-business. The
modern acting-copies of *As You Like It* do not allow Jaques to take any part in the
present scene.' WHITE, however, did not lay to heart this criticism and improve his
' knowledge of stage-business.' In his second edition he says : ' Rosalind's speech,
until she chooses to notice the tardy Orlando, is addressed to the retiring Jaques.'
[I cannot avoid thinking that Dyce is entirely right. There is something humiliating
in the idea of Rosalind talking to Jaques's back, and if he walked away at even a
leisurely pace Rosalind's final words must have been pitched, if he is to hear them,
almost in the scream of a virago. We must note the effect on Jaques of these final
thrusts, we must count the wounds, or else Rosalind's victory is small. If Jaques's
back is turned, his ears are deaf, and the victory is his rather than Rosalind's. At
the same time that I give in my adhesion to Dyce, I must confess that he does not
explain Orlando's address to Rosalind, nor her disregard of it. It may be that
he would accept that much of Grant White's interpretation which attributes her
silence to a punishment for his tardiness, but then one of Dyce's strong points
is that the *entrances* are marked (for stage purposes) many lines in advance. Here
the *entrance* is marked, and Orlando speaks, many lines before he is addressed by
Rosalind.—ED.]

34. liſpe] See Mercutio's invective against Tybalt.—*Rom. & Jul.* II, iv, 26.
WRIGHT : See Overbury's *Characters* (*Works*, p. 58, ed. Fairholt), where 'An Affec-
tate Traueller' is described : ' He censures all things by countenances, and shrugs,
and speakes his owne language with shame and lisping.' [Sig. F, ed. 1627. Over-

of your owne Countrie: be out of loue with your   35
natiuitie, and almoſt chide God for making you that
countenance you are; or I will ſcarce thinke you haue
ſwam in a Gundello. Why how now *Orlando,* where
haue you bin all this while? you a louer? and you
ſerue me ſuch another tricke, neuer come in my ſight   40
more.

Orl. My faire *Roſalind,* I come within an houre of my
promiſe.

Roſ. Breake an houres promiſe in loue? hee that
will diuide a minute into a thouſand parts, and breake   45
but a part of the thouſand part of a minute in the affairs

---

38. *Gundello*] *Gondallo* Rowe. *Gon-*
dola Pope. *gondola.* [Exit Jaques] Dyce.
39, 50. *and*] Ff, Rowe, Cald. *an* Pope

et cet.
   46. *thouſand*] *thousandth* Rowe et
seq.

---

bury's *Characters* were published in 1614; after his death.] MOBERLY quotes a
passage from *The Scholemaster* [p. 75, ed. Arber] where Ascham says: 'I know
diverse, that went out of England, men of innocent life, men of excellent learnyng,
who returned out of *Italie,* not onely with worse manners, but also with lesse learnyng; neither so willing to liue orderly, nor yet so hable [Lat. *habilis*] to speake
learnedlie, as they were at home, before they went abroad.' But this is only one sentence where whole paragraphs might be quoted from these closing ten pages of
Ascham's *First booke.* His denunciation of the life led by Englishmen in Italy, and
of their manners when they return, is unmeasured. 'And so,' he says, 'beyng Mules
and Horses before they went, returned verie Swyne and Asses home agayne'; and
further on, 'they should carie at once in one bodie, the belie of a Swyne, the head
of an Asse, the brayne of a Foxe, and the wombe of wolfe'; and that even the
Italians have a proverb which says: 'Englese Italianato, e vn diabolo incarnato.'
It is from these pages that in the *Mer. of Ven.* p. 297, I quoted Ascham's indignation at the translations of Italian novels then 'sold in euery shop in London.'
—ED.]

   34. **disable**] That is, undervalue, disparage. See V, iv, 79.

   38. **Gundello**] JOHNSON: That is, been at Venice, the seat at that time of all licen-
tiousness, where the young English gentlemen wasted their fortunes, debased their
morals, and sometimes lost their religion. MRS GRIFFITH (p. 87): Venice was then
the polite *goal,* as Paris is now: so that to 'swim in a Gondola' is as if we should say,
'ride in a vis-à-vis,' at present. [A Mrs Griffith to date is needed to give us a note
on a 'vis-à-vis.—ED.] WHITE (ed. i): Ladies say that their shoes are 'as big as a
gundalow' (what lady's shoes are ever otherwise?), without any notion that they are
comparing them to the coaches of Venice. But it is so. [For the spelling see 'Gun-
delier.'—*Oth.* I, i, 138. Walker (*Vers.* 218) gives 'gondelay,' from Spenser, *F. Q.*
II, c. vi, st. ii; and '"gundelet," *i. e.* a gondoletta,' from Marston's *Ant. & Mellida,*
III, ii.]

   46. **thousand**] This is merely phonetic spelling, like 'sixt'' for *sixth.*—ED.

of loue, it may be faid of him that *Cupid* hath clapt　　47
him oth' fhoulder, but Ile warrant him heart hole.

Orl.　Pardon me deere *Rofalind*.

Rof.　Nay, and you be fo tardie, come no more in my　　50
fight, I had as liefe be woo'd of a Snaile.

Orl.　Of a Snaile?

Rof.　I, of a Snaile: for though he comes flowly, hee
carries his houfe on his head; a better ioynĉture I thinke
then you make a woman: befides, he brings his deftinie　　55
with him.

Orl.　What's that?

Rof.　Why hornes: ẘ fuch as you are faine to be beholding to your wiues for: but he comes armed in his
fortune, and preuents the flander of his wife.　　　　60

---

48. *heart hole*] *heart whole* F$_4$. *heart-
whole* Rowe.

55. *you make*] *you can make* Han.
Johns. Steev. Mal. Wh. i, Dyce iii, Coll.
iii.

58. *be*] Om. Rowe i.

58, 59. *beholding*] Ff, Rowe, Cap.
Cam. Coll. iii, Wh. ii. *beholden* Pope
et cet.

59. *comes*] *come* F$_2$F$_3$.

---

47. **clapt**] It is not easy to decide whether this means a clap by way of friendly
encouragement, as it is used in *Much Ado*, I, i, 261: 'He that hits me, let him be
clapped on the shoulder, and called Adam'; and again, *Love's Lab. L.* V, ii, 107:
'With that, all laugh'd and clapp'd him on the shoulder, Making the bold wag by
their praises bolder'; and again in *Tro. & Cress.* III, iii, 138: 'even already They
clap the lubber Ajax on the shoulder, As if his foot were on brave Hector's breast';
or a clap by way of arrest from a court officer, as in *Cym.* V, iii, 78: 'fight I will no
more, But yield me to the veriest hind that shall Once touch my shoulder.' Wright
prefers the latter interpretation, as does also Schmidt, whom Rolfe follows, and there
is colour for the preference in the use of the word 'warrant' immediately following.
But, on the whole, the former interpretation seems preferable.—ED.

51. **of**] If necessary, see Abbott, § 170.

55. **you make**] Hanmer's change, 'than you *can* make,' is upheld by WHITE
(ed. i) on the score that 'Rosalind is speaking not of Orlando's acts, but of his abilities.' To me, however, the change is not only needless, but erroneous. 'You' does
not refer to Orlando personally, any more than 'your wives,' in line 59, accuses him
of polygamy. It is the French 'on.' I suppose the meaning of the sentence is that
a snail is better off than a woman because he enjoys all the time the possession of his
house, whereas a woman cannot possibly possess her jointure until she becomes a
widow, and if she dies before her husband will never have it at all.—ED.

59. **beholding**] The almost universal form, among the dramatists, of the present
beholden.

60. **fortune**] ALLEN (MS): That is, come armed in that which it is his fortune to
come to.

60. **prevents**] Anticipates, in its Latin derivative sense. For examples, see
Schmidt.

Orl. Vertue is no horne-maker : and my *Rofalind* is   61
vertuous.

Rof. And I am your *Rofalind.*

Cel. It pleafes him to call you fo : but he hath a *Rofa-*
lind of a better leere then you.   65

Rof. Come, wooe me, wooe mee : for now I am in a
holy-day humor, and like enough to confent : What
would you fay to me now, and I were your verie, verie
Rofalind ?

Orl. I would kiffe before I fpoke.   70

Rof. Nay, you were better fpeake firft, and when you
were grauel'd, for lacke of matter, you might take occafion to kiffe : verie good Orators when they are out,
they will fpit, and for louers, lacking (God warne vs)
matter, the cleanlieft fhift is to kiffe.   75

66. *me, wooe*] *me, wooe*, F_3.   71. Rof.] Orl. F_2.
68. *and*] Ff, Rowe, Cald.   *an* Pope   74. *warne*] *warr'nt* Anon. (*ap.* Cam.
et cet.   Ed.).

---

65. **leere**] TOLLET : That is, of a better feature, complexion, or colour than you.
SKEAT : The Mid. Eng. *lere* means the cheek, also the face, complexion, mien, look.
'A loveli lady of *lere*' = a lady of lovely mien.—*P. Plowman,* B. i, 3. It was originally almost always used in a good sense, and with adjectives expressive of beauty,
but in Skelton we find it otherwise in two passages : 'Her lothely *lere* Is nothynge
clere, But vgly of chere' = her loathsome look is not at all clear, but ugly of aspect.
—*Elynour Rummynge,* l. 12 ; 'Your lothesum *lere* to loke on.'—2d *Poem against*
Garnesche, l. 5.   Shakespeare has it in two senses : (1) the complexion, aspect [the
present passage], *Tit. And.* IV, ii, 119 ; (2) a winning look, *Merry Wives,* I, iii,
50.   At a later period it is generally used in a sinister sense.   From Ang. Sax. *hleór,*
the cheek ; hence the face, look.   The original sense may have been 'slope,' from the
Teut. base HLI, to lean.   [Does not this refer to the umber with which Ganymede's
face was smirched ?—ED.]

72. **grauel'd**] Cotgrave has : '*Assablé :* Grauelled ; filled with sand ; also, stucke
in, or run on, the sand.' WRIGHT : Compare Bacon, *Advancement of Learning* (ed.
Wright), i, 7, § 8, p. 57 : 'But when Marcus Philosophus came in, Silenus was gravelled and out of countenance.' [See also Richardson's *Dict.* for several other examples of the verb.]

73. **kisse**] STEEVENS : Thus also in Burton's *Anatomy of Melancholy :* 'and when
he [Stratocles] hath pumped his wits dry, can say no more, kissing and colling are
never out of season.'—[p. 506, ed. 1651].

74. **warne**] STEEVENS : If this exclamation (which occurs again in the Qq. of
Mid. N. D.) is not a corruption of 'God *ward* us,' *i. e. defend* us, it must mean '*sum-*
mon us to himself.' So in *Rich. III :* I, iii, 39 : 'And sent to warn them to his royal
presence.' SCHMIDT interprets it : 'God guard us,' 'God forbid,' which has a meaning, like *Dii avertite omen,* but in ' God summon us ' here, there seems to be none.—ED.

Orl.   How if the kiffe be denide ?   76

Rof.   Then fhe puts you to entreatie, and there begins
new matter.

Orl.   Who could be out, being before his beloued
Miftris ?   80

Rof.   Marrie that fhould you if I were your Miftris,
or I fhould thinke my honeftie ranker then my wit.

Orl.   What, of my fuite ?

Rof.   Not out of your apparrell, and yet out of your
fuite :   85 ·
Am not I your *Rofalind ?*

Orl.   I take fome ioy to fay you are, becaufe I would
be talking of her.

Rof.   Well, in her perfon, I fay I will not haue you.

Orl.   Then in mine owne perfon, I die.   90

Rof.   No faith, die by Attorney : the poore world is
almoft fix thoufand yeeres old, and in all this time there
was not anie man died in his owne perfon (*videlicet*) in
a loue caufe : *Troilous* had his braines dafh'd out with a
Grecian club, yet he did what hee could to die before,   95
and he is one of the patternes of loue. *Leander,* he would
haue liu'd manie a faire yeere though *Hero* had turn'd   97

81–85. In sens. obs.   84, 86. Prose, Pope et seq.
  82. *thinke...ranker]   thank...rather*   90. *die]* doe F_2F_3.   *dye* F_4.
Coll. (MS) ii, iii.   94. Troilous] F_1.
  83. *of] out of* Coll. (MS).   *braines] braine* Ff.

---

82. thinke . . . ranker] COLLIER (referring to the MS corrector's change to *thank
. . . . rather*) : This is said in answer to the question of Orlando how he could possibly be out ? and Rosalind replies that if he were not out, but continued his suit, he
would be more indebted to her honesty, which allowed him to proceed, than to her
wit in disconcerting him.   The two misprints were easily made, and the restoration is
exactly to the point.   WHITE (ed. i) : Strange to say, Collier's reading has found
some favour.   For in the alternative supposed by Rosalind, she would have no honesty to thank ! and therefore it is that she says that in that case she should think her
honesty ranker than her wit.   DYCE (ed. ii) : Mr Collier understands the passage no
more than his corrector.

95. club] WRIGHT : Troilus, in the story of his death as told by Dictys Cretensis,
Dares Phrygius, Tzetzes, and Guido Colonna, was slain by Achilles ('impar congressus Achilli.'—Verg. *Æn.* I, 474), either with sword or spear, and the Grecian club is
as much an invention of Rosalind's as Leander's cramp.

96. Leander, he] Those who wish to find other examples of this insertion of the
pronoun may find them in Abbott, § 243.

Nun; if it had not bin for a hot Midſomer-night, for   98
(good youth)he went but forth to waſh him in the Hel-
leſpont, and being taken with the crampe, was droun'd,   100
and the fooliſh Chronoclers of that age, found it was
Hero of Ceſtos. But theſe are all lies, men haue died
from time to time, and wormes haue eaten them, but not
for loue.   104

98. *had*] *bad* F$_2$.   *ners* Han. Sing. Coll. (MS) ii, iii, Ktly,
99. *him*] Om. Ff, Rowe+.   Glo. Wh. ii.
101. *Chronoclers*] *chroniclers* Ff. *coro-*   101. *it was*] *it* Han.
                                           102. *Ceſtos*] *Seſtos* Ff.

---

101. Chronoclers] CAPELL: If to make his author more witty than there is reason to think he deſign'd to be, was an editor's business, he of Oxford [*i. e.* Hanmer,
see Text. Notes] may *seem* to have demean'd himself rightly, ... but the judicious
will hardly allow this. . . . . ' Chroniclers ' could never be a mistake, nor ' was ' a meer
insertion of printers; *coroners*, and the phrase recommended, being too well known
to them to suspect an alteration of either for what was certainly not so familiar. It
follows then, if the above observation be just, that they were true to their copy in this
place; and the Poet will stand acquitted for writing so, if it be consider'd that too
much wit, or wit too much pointed, is not a beauty in comedy; especially in such
comedy as this, which is simple and of the pastoral kind. M. MASON: I am surprised that Hanmer's just and ingenious amendment should not be adopted as soon as
suggested. . . . . ' Found ' is the legal term on such occasions. EDWARDS refers to
Ham. V, i, 5 : ' The crowner hath sat on her, and finds it Christian burial.' CALDE-
COTT: In the language of a coroner's jury, the chroniclers of that age, who record
and transmit facts to posterity, *found* (*i. e.* stated) it to be Hero. KNIGHT: We are
unwilling to alter the text, but there can be little doubt that Hanmer's change, perhaps *crowners*, gives the true word. The technical use of ' found ' decides this. We
must accept ' chroniclers ' in the sense of *coroners*. WHITE (ed. i) denounces Hanmer's change on the same ground as Capell, and as earnestly: ' If we can at will
reduce a perfectly appropriate and uncorrupted word of ten letters to one of eight,
and strike out such marked letters as *h, l,* and *e,* we may re-write Shakespeare at our
pleasure.' [And yet after these brave words Grant White in his second edition follows Hanmer. The reason is, I think, that he printed from the Globe Edition, where
the Cambridge Editors in a temporary aberration of mind deserted the sound text of
the Cambridge Edition. The printed text before our eyes always exercises a strong
influence, and from this influence, in the present case, that excellent editor Grant
White did not free himself.—ED.] HALLIWELL: " Found ' here merely means *found
out, discovered, stated.* . . . . The alteration made by Hanmer will not even make good
sense, for though the coroner's jury might *find* a verdict of ' drowning,' they could
not have ' found it was Hero of Sestos.' The passage in *Hamlet* is written in intentional error, and cannot fairly be appealed to in the present discussion. Dyce (ed.
iii) quotes LETTSOM: ' The word " found " makes for *coroners;* but the plural number and the phrase " of that age " tell the other way.' WRIGHT: I have left the old
reading, for there would be only one coroner, and the ' chroniclers ' might be considered to be the jurymen.

Orl. I would not haue my right *Rofalind* of this mind,   105
for I proteft her frowne might kill me.

Rof. By this hand, it will not kill a flie : but come,
now I will be your *Rofalind* in a more comming-on difpofition : and aske me what you will, I will grant it.

Orl. Then loue me *Rofalind*.   110

Rof. Yes faith will I, fridaies and faterdaies, and all.

Orl. And wilt thou haue me?

Rof. I, and twentie fuch.

Orl. What faieft thou ?

Rof. Are you not good?   115

Orl. I hope fo.

Rofalind. Why then, can one defire too much of a
good thing : Come fifter, you fhall be the Prieft, and
marrie vs : giue me your hand *Orlando* : What doe you
fay fifter *?*   120

Orl. Pray thee marrie vs.

Cel. I cannot fay the words.

Rof. You muft begin, will you *Orlando*.

Cel. Goe too *:* wil you *Orlando,* haue to wife this *Ro-*
falind?   125

Orl. I will.

Rof. I, but when ?

Orl. Why now, as faft as fhe can marrie vs.

Rof. Then you muft fay, I take thee *Rofalind* for
wife.   130

Orl. I take thee *Rofalind* for wife.

---

109. *aske me*] *ask* Rowe.   129. Rof.] Cel. Anon. (*ap.* Cam.
127. *I*] Om. F₃F₄, Rowe i.   Ed.).

---

107. **kill a flie**] LADY MARTIN (p. 427) : This rejoinder should, I think, be given
with a marked change of intonation, sufficient to indicate that, notwithstanding all
the wild raillery of her former speech, there is in herself a vein of tenderness that
would make it impossible for her to inflict pain deliberately. We should be made to
feel the woman just for the moment,—before she passes on to her next words, which,
playful as they are, lead her on unawares to what I believe was regarded by her as a
very real climax to this sportive wooing.

126–131. **I will . . . for wife**] LADY MARTIN (p. 428) : It is not merely in pastime,
I feel assured, that Rosalind has been made by Shakespeare to put these words into
Orlando's mouth. This is for her a marriage, though no priestly formality goes with
it; and it seems to me that the actress must show this by a certain tender earnestness
of look and voice, as she replies, ' I do take thee, Orlando, for my husband.' I could

Rof. I might aske you for your Commiffion,   132
But I doe take thee *Orlando* for my husband : there's a
girle goes before the Priest, and certainely a Womans
thought runs before her actions.   135

Orl. So do all thoughts, they are wing'd.

Rof. Now tell me how long you would haue her, after you haue poffeft her ?

Orl. For euer, and a day.

Rof. Say a day, without the euer: no, no *Orlando*, men   140
are Aprill when they woe, December when they wed :
Maides are May when they are maides, but the sky changes when they are wiues : I will bee more iealous of
thee, then a Barbary cocke-pidgeon ouer his hen, more   144

132–135. Prose, Pope et seq.   Var. '21.   *Thus* Lloyd (*ap.* Cam.
133. *But I*] Ff, Rowe+. *but, I* Cap.   Ed.).
Cam. Wh. ii.   *but—I* Mal. et cet.   137. *haue*] *love* Han.
    there's] *There* Farmer, Steev. '95,   141. *they wed*] *they're wed* Daniel.

never speak these words without a trembling of the voice, and the involuntary rushing
of happy tears to the eyes, which made it necessary for me to turn my head away
from Orlando. But, for fear of discovery, this momentary emotion had to be overcome and turned off by carrying his thoughts into a different channel. Still, Rosalind's gravity of look and intonation will not have quite passed away—for has she not
taken the most solemn step a woman can take ?—as she continues : ' Now tell me how
long,' &c.

133, 134. there's . . . goes] COLLIER: Alluding to her anticipating what Celia
ought to have said: There's a girl who goes faster than the priest. WRIGHT:
Farmer's change is unnecessary, for the relative is only omitted. [For omission of
the relative, see Abbott, § 244.]

140, &c. FLETCHER (p. 220): Rosalind's heart is now at leisure to gratify itself
with another of those conscious contrasts between the imputed capriciousness of her
sex and the steady affectionateness of her own character. We have heard already
her description of feminine weakness and perverseness as exhibited in the season of
courtship; she now gives us a still more lively one of the same failings as they show
themselves after marriage.

144. Barbary cocke-pidgeon] FULTON (*Book of Pigeons*, p. 7): Shakespeare
was evidently a close observer, if not an actual student, of pigeons. It is difficult to
avoid the conclusion that he was at heart, if not in practice, a fancier, his intimate
knowledge of them comes out in so many different ways. Thus he alludes to the
mode in which they feed their young [in I. ii, 90, *supra ;* and again in the present
line we may find a proof], collateral, if not strictly historical, of the great antiquity of
the Barb. Such allusions as these, it is true, only prove a general acquaintance with
the birds; but when the great poet makes Hamlet say : ' But I am pigeon-livered, and
lack gall To make oppression bitter,' he shows a knowledge, however acquired, of the
singular physiological fact that the pigeon, like the horse, has no gall-bladder. Again,
one of his inimitable comparisons is, 'As patient as a female dove, When that her

clamorous then a Parrat againſt raine, more new-fang-   145
led then an ape, more giddy in my defires, then a mon-
key : I will weepe for nothing, like *Diana* in the Foun-   147

---

golden couplets are disclosed.' Now pigeons, unlike poultry, will readily leave their eggs
before hatching, if disturbed; but very rarely when once the beautiful little ' golden '
young claim their care; then, as the same close observer elsewhere says, even ' doves
will peck in safeguard of their brood.' (P. 225) There can be very little doubt that this
pigeon [the Barb] did, as the name implies, come to us originally from the north of
Africa, and was first known as the Barbary pigeon. [I have searched for any intimation that the Barb is of a pre-eminently jealous disposition, but have found none.
Nor is any needed. ' Barbary ' of itself implies Oriental watchfulness and jealousy.
Is there left in the world any human trade, profession, or pursuit wherein Shakespeare
is not claimed as a fellow-craftsman? Did any of us ever think that we should live
to see him hailed as a ' pigeon-fancier ' ?—ED.]

   145, 146. **new-fangled**] SKEAT: Fond of what is new, novel. The old sense is
' fond of what is new '; see *Love's Lab. L.* I, i, 106 [and the present passage], and
in Palsgrave. The final *-d* is a late addition to the word, due to a loss of a sense of
the old force of *-le* (see below); the Mid. Eng. form is *newefangel* (4 syllables), fond
of novelty, Chaucer, *C. T.* 10932. So also Gower, *C. A.* ii, 273: ' But euery newe
loue quemeth To him, that *newefangel* is ' = but every new love pleases him who is
fond of what is new. Compounded of *newe*, new; and *fangel*, ready to seize, snatching at, not found in Ang. Sax., but formed with perfect regularity from the base *fang-*,
to take (occurring in Ang. Sax. *fang-en*, pp. of *fôn*, contracted form of *fangan*, to
take), with the suffix *-el* (= Ang. Sax. *-ol*), used to form adjectives descriptive of an
agent. This suffix is preserved in modern Eng. *witt-ol* = one who knows, sarcastically
used to mean an idiot; cf. A. S. *sprec-ol*, fond of talking, talkative; *wac-ol*, vigilant.
So also *fangel* = fond of taking, readily adopting, and *new-fangle* = fond of taking
up what is new; whence *new-fangle-d*, by later addition of *d*. The suffix *-ol*, by the
usual interchange of *l* and *r*, is nothing but another form of the familiar suffix *-er*,
expressive of the agent. Thus *newfangle = new-fang-er*.

   147. **Diana**] MALONE conjectured that Shakespeare must have had in mind somè
well-known conduit, and WHALLEY discovered what has been generally accepted as
the allusion in Stowe's *Survey*, where [p. 484, ed. 1618], in giving a history of the
' Elianor Cross,' or ' the great Crosse in West Cheape,' Stowe says: ' in the yeer next
following [*i. e.* 1596] was then set vp a curious wrought Tabernacle of gray Marble,
and in the same an Alablaster Image of Diana, and water conuayed from the Thames,
prilling from her naked brest for a time, but now decayed.' ' Statues,' continues
Whalley, ' and particularly that of Diana, with water conveyed through them to give
them the appearance of weeping figures, were anciently a frequent ornament of foun-
tains. So in *The City Match*, III, iii: " Now could I cry like any image in a fountain, which Runs lamentations."—[p. 263, ed. Dodsley; first printed 1639]. Again,
in Rosamond's Epistle to Henry II, by Drayton: " Here in the garden, wrought by
curious hands, Naked Diana in the fountain stands." '—[p. 80, ed. 1748]. HALLI-
WELL (p. 69): It should be remembered that the image of a fountain-figure weeping
was an exceedingly common one, and that Diana was a favorite subject with the
sculptors for such an object. WRIGHT: If Shakespeare had this image of Diana
[mentioned by Stowe] in his mind, his recollection of it was not strictly accurate.
[It seems to me most unlikely that there is any reference here to the Diana on the

taine, & I wil do that when you are difpos'd to be merry: 148
I will laugh like a Hyen, and that when thou art inclin'd
to fleepe.   150

Orl. But will my *Rofalind* doe fo ?

Rof. By my life, fhe will doe as I doe.

Orl. O but fhe is wife.

Ros. Or elfe fhee could not haue the wit to doe this :
the wifer, the waywarder : make the doores vpon a wo-   155
mans wit, and it will out at the cafement : fhut that, and
'twill out at the key-hole : ftop that, 'twill flie with the
fmoake out at the chimney.

Orl. A man that had a wife with fuch a wit, he might
fay, wit whether wil't ?   160

149. *thou art*] *you are* Rowe ii +.
150. *fleepe*] *weep* Theob. conj. Warb.
Coll. iii.
155. *doores*] *doors fast* Rowe ii +, Cap.
Quincy (MS).

157. *'twill flie*] *it will flye* F₄, Rowe +,
Steev. '85.
160. *whether*] *whither* Rowe.
wil't] F₂. *wilt* F₃F₄ et seq.

Eleanor Cross.   And I think Malone in his secret heart thought so too.   In his
Second Appendix and in his own edition he was inclined to claim the credit of discovering the allusion, but he afterwards silently resigned it to Whalley.   For aught
we can tell, this 'prilling' Diana may not have been a symbol of sorrow; it was evidently an excrescence, and had no connection with the other Biblical figures around
the Cross.   See Appendix, 'Date of Composition.'—ED.]

149. **Hyen**] KENRICK (p. 69) could discover no 'propriety in this allusion'; he
knew of 'no animal in nature possessed of the streperous part of risibility' vigorous
enough 'to prevent a drowsy man's going to sleep,' 'except man.'   Wherefore he
proposes a change, and, like a true-born Briton, offers 'to lay a good bet, if it could be
determined,' that Shakespeare wrote ' "laugh like a *Hyad*." '   To be sure, 'a Hyad'
is not a man, but a *woman*, and to 'laugh' must be interpreted to *cry*.   But apart
from these trifles the simile is assured, because the Hyads 'wept so vehemently' that
they were translated as constellations to the sky.   BARCLAY, in his vindication of
Johnson from Kenrick's attack, proposed (p. 49), as a sarcastic jest, that the text be :
'laugh like a *Hoyden*, or *Hyden*,' as he had seen it spelt.   STEEVENS : The bark of
the hyena was anciently supposed to resemble a loud laugh.   So in Webster's *Duchess
of Malfy*, 1623: 'Methinks I see her laughing, Excellent hyena !'—[II, v, p. 223,
ed. Dyce].

150. **sleepe**] JOHNSON : I know not why we should read to *weep* [as in Warburton's text].   I believe most men would be more angry to have their *sleep* hindered
than their *grief* interrupted.   [Theobald's conjecture, *weep* is to be found in Nichols's
Illust. ii, 331.]

155. **make the doores**] STEEVENS : This is an expression used in several midland counties, instead of *bar the doors*.   So in *Com. of Err.* III, i, 93 : 'The doors
are made against you.'

160. **wit whether wil't**] JOHNSON : This must be some allusion to a story well

Rof. Nay, you might keepe that checke for it, till you 161
met your wiues wit going to your neighbours bed.

Orl. And what wit could wit haue, to excufe that?

Rofa. Marry to fay, fhe came to feeke you there : you
fhall neuer take her without her anfwer, vnleffe you take 165
her without her tongue : ô that woman that cannot
make her fault her hufbands occafion, let her neuer nurfe
her childe her felfe, for fhe will breed it like a foole. 168

167. *occafion*] *accusation* Han. Sing.   168. *fhe will...it like a*] *she'll...it a*
Ktly. *accusing* Coll. (MS) ii, iii.   Cap. conj.

known at that time, though now perhaps irretrievable. STEEVENS: This was an
exclamation much in use when any one was either talking nonsense or usurping a
greater share in conversation than justly belonged to him. So in Decker's *Satiro-
mastix*, 1602: ' My sweet *wit, whither wilt thou ?* my delicate poetical fury,' &c. [p.
166, ed. Hawkins]. Again, in Heywood's *Royal King: 'Captain.* I since came to
purchase that Which all the wealth you have will never win you. *Bonville.* And
what's that, I pray? *Capt.* Wit. Is the word strange to you? Wit. *Bon.* Whither
wilt thou? *Capt.* True; Wit will to many ere it come to you' [I, i, p. 18, ed. Sh.
Soc. Steevens quoted, of the above, only the phrases containing the proverb. But I
think the Captain's answer throws some light on the obscure meaning of the phrase; it
seems as though it were equivalent to saying: ' Wit, whither wilt thou go? Thou art
clearly leaving the present company.' Halliwell adds several other authorities for
the use of the phrase, to which more could be added without increasing our knowledge of the meaning. Malone believed the phrase to be the first words of an old
madrigal. See I, ii, 55.—ED.]

165. **answer**] TYRWHITT: See Chaucer, *Marchaundes Tale* [line 1020, ed. Mor-
ris, where Proserpine assures Pluto that May shall have an answer ready to excuse
any escapade:] ' Now by my modres *Ceres* soule I swere, That I schal yive hir suffi-
saunt answere, And alle wommen after for hir sake; That though thay be in any gult
i-take, With face bold thay schul hemself excuse, And bere hem doun that wolde hem
accuse. For lak of answer, noon of hem schal dyen. Al had a man seyn a thing
with bothe his yen, Yit schul we wymmen visage it hardily, And wepe, and swere,
and chide subtilly, So that ye men schul ben as lewed as gees.'

166. **ô**] What rule, if any, guided the compositor in the use of this circumflexed *ô*
it seems almost impossible to discover. Perhaps, as it does not begin a sentence, the
lower case *o* seemed too insignificant without some distinction, or perhaps it was that,
unlike Othello, its demerits could not speak unbonneted. Walker (*Crit.* i, 104) says
that '*O*' in the forms *o' my truth, o' my life*, &c. is frequently expressed by *ô*.' As
we see here, in the present instance, the same type is used in the mere exclamation.
It is, however, purely a matter of typography, and very remotely, if at all, connected
with Shakespeare.—ED.

167. **occasion**] JOHNSON: That is, represent her fault as occasioned by her husband. CAPELL: That cannot make her husband the cause of it. CALDECOTT: That
is, an act done upon his occasions, in prosecution of his concerns. STAUNTON:
If any deviation is required, we might perhaps, and without departing far from the
text, read, ' her husband's *confusion*.' KEIGHTLEY: I find I have followed Hanmer,

Orl. For thefe two houres *Rofalinde,* I wil leaue thee.

Rof. Alas, deere loue, I cannot lacke thee two houres.   170

Orl. I muft attend the Duke at dinner, by two a clock
I will be with thee againe.

Rof. I, goe your waies, goe your waies : I knew what
you would proue, my friends told mee as much, and I
thought no leffe : that flattering tongue of yours wonne   175
me : 'tis but one caft away, and fo come death : two o'
clocke is your howre.

Orl. I, fweet *Rofalind.*

Rof. By my troth, and in good earneft, and fo God
mend mee, and by all pretty oathes that are not dange-   180
rous, if you breake one iot of your promife, or come one
minute behinde your houre, I will thinke you the moft
patheticall breake-promife, and the moft hollow louer,   183

---

176. *o'*] *o' th'* Rowe +.   *o' the* Steev.   183. *patheticall*] *atheistical* Warb.
'85.   *jesuitical* Grey.

---

but doubt if I was justified in so doing. WRIGHT: That is, an occasion against her
husband; an opportunity for taking advantage of him.

168. In Kemble's Acting Copy Rosalind here sings the song from *Love's Labour
Lost :* 'When daisies pied,' &c.

170. FLETCHER (p. 221): How deliciously after all this *acted* levity and mischiev-
ousness, comes immediately this fond exclamation!

171, 176. **two a . . . two o'**] Let us note this variation in spelling, a compositor's
mere vagary, within half a dozen lines, and let our souls be instructed.—ED.

176. **come death**] It is not impossible that there is here just an allusion to that
popular song of Anne Bullen's : ' Death, rock me asleep. Bring me to quiet rest,'
&c. It sounds to me like some quotation or allusion, whose popularity excuses, or at
least lightens, the charming exaggeration.—ED.

177. **your howre**] LADY MARTIN (p. 429): This is to be ' full of tears;' and
when she has put a pang into her lover's heart by this semblance of reproachful grief,
she suddenly floods it with delight by turning to him her face radiant with smiles,
and saying, ' Two o'clock's your hour!' This is to be ' full of smiles,' and the charm
so works upon him that we see he has lost the consciousness that it is the boy Ganymede, and not his own Rosalind, that is before him, as he answers, 'Ay, sweet Rosalind.' And she, too, in her parting adjuration to him, comes nearer than she has ever
done before to letting him see what is in her heart.

183. **patheticall**] HEATH: The meaning is, That of all break-promises he best
counterfeits a real passion. I suppose the old salvo of faithless lovers : ' perjuria ridet
amantum,' maintained its ground even in Shakespeare's time. TALBOT: We now use
pitiful in a like sense. WHITER (p. 57): ' Pathetical,' in its first sense, means *full
of passion* and *sentiment.* In a ludicrous sense, a ' pathetical break-promise' is a
whining, canting, promise-breaking swain. Shakespeare, perhaps, caught this word
from Lodge's *Novel,* where Phœbe's indifference to Montanus is described : ' But she,

and the moſt vnworthy of her you call *Roſalinde*, that
may bee choſen out of the groſſe band of the vnfaith-   185
full : therefore beware my cenſure, and keep your promiſe.

Orl. With no leſſe religion, then if thou wert indeed
my *Roſalind* : ſo adieu.

Roſ. Well, Time is the olde Iuſtice that examines all   190
ſuch offenders, and let time try : adieu.   *Exit.*

Cel. You haue ſimply miſus'd our ſexe in your loue-
prate : we muſt haue your doublet and hoſe pluckt ouer
your head, and ſhew the world what the bird hath done
to her owne neaſt.   195

Roſ. O coz, coz, coz : my pretty little coz, that thou
didſt know how many fathome deepe I am in loue : but
it cannot bee founded : my affeċtion hath an vnknowne
bottome, like the Bay of Portugall.   199

---

191. *try*] *try you* Coll. (MS).   191. Scene III. Pope, Han. Warb.

---

measuring all his passions with a coy disdaine, and triumphing in the poore shepheard's patheticall humours.' &c. WRIGHT: Cotgrave explains ' Pathetique' as
Patheticall, passionate; persuasiue, affection-moving. ALLEN (MS): Rosalind
merely misplaces the epithet (by a kind of hypallage); ' pathetical' properly belongs
to ' lover,' as if she had said : ' I will think you the most passionate—not *lover* as now
—but break-promise.'

183. **breake-promise**] ' At lovers' *perjuries* They say Jove laughs.'—*Rom. &
Jul.* II, ii, 93.

190. **olde Iustice**] STEEVENS: So in *Tro. & Cress.* IV, v, 225 : ' that old common arbitrator, Time, Will one day end it.'

192. **misus'd**] MOBERLY: Completely libelled our sex. WRIGHT: That is,
abused. On the other hand, *abuse* in Shakespeare's time was equivalent to the modern ' misuse.'

195. **neast**] STEEVENS: So in Lodge's *Rosalynde:* ' I pray (quoth Aliena) if
your robes were off, what mettal are you made of that you are so satyrical against
women? is it not a foule bird that defiles his own nest?'

199. **Portugall**] WRIGHT: In a letter to the Lord Treasurer and Lord High
Admiral, Ralegh gives an account of the capture of a ship of Bayonne by his man
Captain Floyer in ' the bay of Portugal' (Edwards, *Life of Ralegh,* ii, 56). This is
the only instance in which I have met with the phrase, which is not recognised, so far
as I am aware, in maps and treatises on geography. It is, however, I am informed,
still used by sailors to denote that portion of the sea off the coast of Portugal from
Oporto to the headland of Cintra. The water there is excessively deep, and within a
distance of forty miles from the shore it attains a depth of upwards of 1400 fathoms,
which in Shakespeare's time would be practically unfathomable. NEIL: Perhaps this
simile ought to be taken as a time-mark of the production of the play. The history
of Portugal engaged a good deal of attention between 1578 and 1602. On the 4th

Cel. Or rather bottomleffe, that as faft as you poure   200
affeƈtion in, in runs out.

Rof. No, that fame wicked Baftard of *Venus*, that was
begot of thought, conceiu'd of fpleene, and borne of
madneffe, that blinde rafcally boy, that abufes euery
ones eyes, becaufe his owne are out, let him bee iudge,   205
how deepe I am in loue : ile tell thee *Aliena*, I cannot be
out of the fight of *Orlando* : Ile goe finde a fhadow, and
figh till he come.

Cel. And Ile fleepe.   *Exeunt.*   209

---

201. *in, in*] *in, it* F₂ et seq.   207. Orlando] Orland F₂. Orlanda F₄.
206. *ile tell*] *I tell* Cam. Edd. conj.   209. *Ile*] *I'll go* Ktly.

---

of August, 1578, the destructive battle of Alcazar, on which George Peele composed
a play published in 1594, was fought, and Don Sebastian, the king, was lost on the
field. . . . . In 1589, before the public exultation at the defeat of the Spanish Armada
had subsided, a band of adventurers, 21,000 in 180 vessels, engaged in an expedition
into Portugal, under the command of Sir Francis Drake and Sir John Norris, in which
the Earl of Essex also had a share.   Instead of returning with the bays of victory,
11,000 persons perished; of the 1100 gentlemen volunteers, only 350 returned to their ·
native country.   They were embayed in its [*sic*] unknown bottom.   In *Der Bestrafte
Brudermord*, founded, it is believed, about 1598, on an early draught of Shakespeare's
Hamlet, the Prince of Denmark suggests ironically to his uncle-father, ' Send me off
to Portugal, so *that I may never come back again.*'   In 1602 there appeared at London *The true History of the late and lamentable Adventures of Don Sebastian, King
of Portugal*, on which Massinger founded his play, *Believe as you List*, a drama only
recently discovered and printed, whose title is a sort of echo of the play before us.
A *Portingal Voyage* is noticed also as a memorable thing in Webster's *Northward-
Ho!* published in 1607, but acted some time before that date.

203. **thought**] This is *melancholy*, according to Steevens, Malone, Caldecott, and
Dyce.   It is also *moody reflection*, according to Halliwell.   Or with Schmidt we can
take it as applied to *love*, ' a passion bred and nourished in the mind.'   It is hardly
to be taken as *care, anxiety*, the sense in which Hamlet uses it in ' sicklied o'er with
the pale cast of thought,' or as in ' take no thought of the morrow.'—ED.

203. **spleene**] SCHMIDT : That is, caprice ; a disposition acting by fits and starts.
WRIGHT : A sudden impulse of passion, whether of love or hatred.

206. **ile tell thee**] DYCE (ed. iii) : ' Qu. " I *tell thee* " ?   This blunder, if it be
one, is not uncommon.'—LETTSOM.   It is not a blunder.   [See Text. Notes, where
Lettsom is anticipated.]

207. **shadow**] STEEVENS : So in *Macb.* IV, iii, 1 : ' Let us seek out some desolate
shade, and there Weep our sad bosoms empty.'

Scena Secunda.

Enter Iaques and Lords, Forreſlers.

Iaq. Which is he that killed the Deare?

Lord. Sir, it was I.

Iaq. Let's preſent him to the Duke like a Romane
Conquerour, and it would doe well to ſet the Deares   5
horns vpon his head, for a branch of victory; haue you
no ſong Forreſter for this purpoſe?

Lord. Yes Sir.

Iaq. Sing it : 'tis no matter how it bee in tune, ſo it
make noyſe enough.   10

Muſicke, Song.

What ſhall he haue that kild the Deare?
His Leather skin, and hornes to weare :
Then ſing him home, the reſt ſhall beare this burthen;   14

Scene IV. Pope, Han. Warb. Johns.   8. Lord.] For. Rowe+, Cam. 2. F.
Scene continued, Theob.   Cap. 2 Lord. Mal.
3. Lord.] 1. F. Cap. 1 Lord. Mal.   14. For Text. Notes, see p. 231.
A Lord. Cam.

1. JOHNSON : This noisy scene was introduced to fill up an interval which is to represent two hours. [See note on Rosalind's first speech in next Scene.] GERVINUS
(p. 388) : This is characteristic of idle rural life, where nothing of more importance
happens than a slaughtered deer and a song about it. [Gervinus presumes also to
call this scene 'a stop-gap.' It is all very well for Dr Johnson to say that this scene
is merely to fill up an interval : from him, we accept all notes and rate them as they
deserve, but the learned German should have remembered that 'That in the captain's
but a cholerick word, Which in the soldier is flat blasphemy.'—ED.]

2. FLOWER (*Memorial Theatre Edition*) : On the occasion of the first representation of *As You Like It* in the Memorial Theatre, April 30th, 1879, a fallow deer was
carried on the stage by the foresters [in this scene] which had been that morning shot
by H. S. Lucy, Esq., of Charlecote Park, out of the herd descended from that upon
which Shakespeare is credited with having made a raid in his youth. The deer is
now stuffed, and carried on whenever the play is acted in Stratford.

4–7. NEIL : Sir Thomas Elyot, in *The Governour*, 1531, says, regarding the hunting of red deer and fallow : ' To them which in this huntynge do showe moste prowess
and actyvyty, a garlande or some other lyke token to be given in sign of victory, and
with a joyful manner to be broughte in the presence of hym that is chiefe of the company there, to receive condigne prayse for their good endeavour.'—Bk. I, chap. xviii.

12, 13. MALONE : Shakespeare seems to have formed this song on a hint afforded

[the rest shall beare this burthen]

by Lodge's *Rosalynde :* 'What newes, forrester? hast thou wounded some deere, and
lost him in the fall? Care not, man, for so small a losse; thy fees was but the skinne,
the shoulder, and the horns.'

14. In the arrangement of this Song, Rowe and Pope followed the Folio, and
their 'sagacity' in so doing was sarcastically pronounced by Theobald 'admirable.'
'One would expect,' he continues, in a tone which was intended to be very bitter,
'when they were *Poets*, they would at least have taken care of the *Rhymes*, and not
foisted in what has Nothing to answer it. Now where is the Rhyme to "the rest
shall bear this Burthen"? Or, to ask another Question, where is the sense of it?
Does the Poet mean that He, that kill'd the Deer, shall be sung home, and the Rest
shall bear the Deer on their Backs? This is laying a Burthen on the Poet, which
We must help him to throw off. In short, the Mystery of the Whole is, that a Marginal Note is wisely thrust into the Text; the Song being design'd to be sung by a
single Voice, and the Stanza's to close with a Burthen to be sung by the whole Company.' And so Theobald printed it. 'The rest shall bear this burthen' was placed
as a stage-direction in the margin; and then to show that he too was a Poet he thus
patched and pieced out the lines: 'Then sing him home: take thou no scorn ‖ To
wear the horn, the horn, the horn.' Hanmer, Warburton, and Johnson followed him,
except that Hanmer, in line 18, read: 'And thy *own* father bore it.' JOHNSON reprinted Theobald's note 'as a specimen,' he said, 'of Mr Theobald's jocularity, and
of the eloquence with which he recommends his emendations;' but Johnson adopted
Theobald's text nevertheless. CAPELL remodelled the whole Song thus, wherein '1.
V.' and '2. V.' stand for First and Second Voice respectively, and 'both' means both
voices:

> 1. V. *What shall he have, that kill'd the deer?*
> 2. V. *His leather skin, and horns to wear.*
> 1. V. *Then sing him home :—*
> > both.
> > *Take thou no scorn*
> > *to wear the horn, the lusty horn*
> > *it was a crest ere thou wast born :—*
> > > 1. V. *Thy father's father wore it;*
> > > 2. V. *And thy father bore it :—*
> > cho.
> > *The horn, the horn, the lusty horn,*
> > *is not a thing to laugh to scorn.*

Capell suggested that if line 18 'should be perfected' we might read: 'Ay and thy
father,' &c., or 'Ay and *his* father bore it,' 'meaning his father's father's father; which
makes the satire the keener, by extending the blot to another generation.' 'Cho.'
means the whole band of foresters, 'Jaques and all.' However much Steevens might
laugh at Capell and his crabbed English, and Dr Johnson say of him, 'Sir, if he had
come to me, I'd have endowed his purposes with words,' there can be no doubt that
Capell's text had deservedly great influence with both of these two editors in their
Variorum editions. (Indeed, it is scarcely too much to say that to Theobald and to Capell, more than to any other two editors, is due the largest share of the purity of Shakespeare's text to-day.) Accordingly, in the Variorum of 1773 the lines of the Song were
numbered 1 and 2, as Capell had numbered them, but the imitation was not carried so

[the rest shall beare this burthen]

far as to add 1. V. or 2. V., and 'The rest shall bear this burthen' was retained in the margin, whereas, as we have seen, Capell omitted it altogether. In the next Variorum, 1778, Capell's reading was silently adopted in line 15 : 'To wear the horn, the lusty horn.' This, however, was rejected by Malone in 1790, and the text of the Folio substantially retained, except that 'The rest,' &c. was inserted as a stage-direction, 1. and 2. as given by Capell were adopted, and before the last two lines was prefixed '*All.*' This arrangement Steevens followed in his own edition of 1793; and Boswell also in Malone's Variorum of 1821. In the latter edition BOSWELL has the following : 'In Playford's *Musical Companion*, 1673, where this is to be found set to music, the words " Then sing him home " are omitted. From this we may suppose that they were not then supposed to form any part of the song itself, but spoken by one of the persons as a direction to the rest to commence the chorus. It should be observed, that in the old copy the words in question, and those which the modern editors have regarded as a stage-direction, are given as one line.' KNIGHT, the next critical editor (Caldecott confessedly followed the Folio), omitted this line (line 14) altogether, lines 12 and 17 were numbered 1, and lines 13 and 18 were numbered 2, and to line 19 was prefixed 'All.' Knight's note is as follows : 'The music to this " song " ' [which is here reprinted from Knight at the end of this note] ' is from a curious and very rare work, entitled *Catch that Catch can ; or a Choice Collection of Catches, Rounds, &c.*, *collected and published by John Hilton, Batch. in Musicke*, 1652; and is there called a *catch*, though, as in the case of many other compositions of the kind so denominated, it is a *round*, having no *catch* or play upon the words, to give it any claim to the former designation. It is written for four bases, but by transposition for other voices would be rather improved than damaged. John Hilton, one of the best and most active composers of his day, was organist of St Margaret's, Westminster. His name is affixed to one of the madrigals in *The Triumphs of Oriana*, 1601, previously to which he was admitted, by the University of Cambridge, as a Bachelor in Music. Hence he was of Shakespeare's time, and it is as reasonable to presume as agreeable to believe that a piece of vocal harmony so good and so pleasing, its age considered, formed a part of one of the most delightful of the great poet's dramas. In Hilton's round the brief line, " Then sing him home," is rejected. The omission was unavoidable in a round for four voices, because in a composition of such limit, and so arranged, it was necessary to give one couplet, and neither more nor less, to each part. But it is doubtful whether that line really forms part of the original text, [where it is] printed as *one* line without any variation of type. Is the whole of the line a stage-direction? " Then sing him home " may be a direction for a stage procession. Mr Oliphant, in his useful and entertaining *Musa Madrigalesca*, 1837, doubts whether the John Hilton, the author of the *Oriana* madrigal, could have been the same that subsequently published *Catch that Catch can*, as well as another work which he names. This is a question into which we shall not enter, our only object being to give such music, as part of Shakespeare's plays, as is supposed to have been originally sung in them, or that may have been introduced in them shortly after their production.' COLLIER agrees with Knight that the whole of line 14 is clearly only a stage-direction, printed by error as a part of the song in the old copies, but instead of omitting it he places it in the margin, and has the following note : ' " Then sing him home " has reference to the carrying of the lord, who killed the deer, to the Duke; and we are to suppose that the foresters sang as they quitted the stage for their " home " in the wood. " The rest shall bear this burden " alludes to the last six

[the rest shall beare this burthen]

lines, which are the burden of the song.' DYCE in his first edition says : ' Much discussion has arisen whether these words [line 14] are a portion of the song or of the
stage-direction. It is a question on which I do not feel myself competent to speak
with any positiveness.' Accordingly, Dyce prints the line in the margin, in smaller
type merely. In his two later editions he has no note, except the remark that Grant
White altered ' Then' to *They.* GRANT WHITE divided the song into two stanzas
of four lines each, and marked them I and II; line 14 appears as a stage-direction
with ' Then,' as has just been noted, changed to *They.* At the end, instead of ' Exeunt,'
he reads : [' *They bear off the deer, singing.*'] In his first edition, after giving his
reasons for believing line 14 to be a stage-direction, which are the same as those
advanced by preceding editors, he says : ' " Then sing him home " has reference to
Jaques's suggestion to present the successful hunter to the Duke " like a Roman con-
queror "; for the song was " for this purpose." That there is an alternation of two
lines of solo with two of chorus or burthen, the latter being in both cases lusty lines
about the lusty horn, no musician or glee-singer, and it would seem no reader with an
ear for rhythm, can entertain a doubt. " Then " in the original stage-direction seems
plainly a misprint for *they.*' STAUNTON prints only ' The rest,' &c. in the margin as
a stage-direction. ' We rather take,' he says, ' " Then sing him home " to form the
burden, and conjecture it ought to be repeated after each couplet.' HALLIWELL says :
' There can be little doubt that the greater part of this song, in fact, the last six lines,
was originally intended to be sung in chorus, Jaques being indifferent to the tune, " so
it make noise enough," ' wherefore Halliwell divides line 14 after ' beare,' thus keeping up the rhyme to ' weare'; places ' This burthen' in a line by itself; and assigns
the rest to be sung by the whole company. He claims for this arrangement that it
' seems on the whole more likely to be correct than considering any portion of the line
as a stage-direction.' BARRON FIELD (*Sh. Soc. Papers,* 1847, iii, 135) was the first,
I think, to suggest that ' This burthen' should be printed by itself, but then he said it
should be in a marginal note, wherein his treatment is slightly different from Halliwell's. He also suggested '*Men* sing him home,' instead of ' They.'

I have thus given all, I think, of the diverse textual arrangements of this song.
Subsequent editors have ranged themselves under one or the other leader as best
suited their fancy. The majority, however, agree in holding ' Then sing him home '
as part of the song, and ' The rest shall beare this burthen' as a stage-direction; which
is also the belief of Roffe (p. 12) and of the present ED.

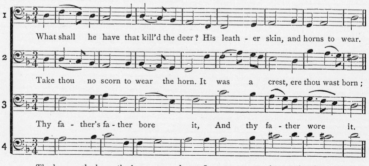

Take thou no ſcorne to weare the horne,   15
It was a creſt ere thou waſt borne,
Thy fathers father wore it,
And thy father bore it,
The horne, the horne, the luſty horne,
Is not a thing to laugh to ſcorne.   *Exeunt.*   20

14. Om. Knt. In margin, Coll. Wh. Dyce, Huds.

the…burthen] In margin, Theob. +, Steev. Mal. Sing. Sta. Clke, Ktly, Rlfe.

14, 15. Then…ſcorne] As one line, Theob. Han. Warb. Johns. As two lines, Steev. '85.

15. to…horne] One line, reading *To wear the horn, the horn, the horn* Theob. Han. Warb. Johns. One line, reading *To wear the horn, the lusty horn* Steev. '85.

18. thy] *thy own* Han.

19. The] All. *The* Mal. Steev. '93.

19, 20. Marked as 'Burthen,' Wh. ii.

19. luſty] luſtly F_2.

14. **burthen**] See III, ii, 242.

15. **horne**] COLERIDGE (p. 108): I question whether there exists a parallel instance of a phrase that, like this of 'horns,' is universal in all languages, and yet for which no one has discovered even a plausible origin.

Scœna Tertia.

Enter Rosalind and Celia.

Rof. How say you now, is it not past two a clock?
And heere much *Orlando*.

Cel. I warrant you, with pure loue, & troubled brain,

Enter Siluius.   5

He hath t'ane his bow and arrowes, and is gone forth

Scene V. Pope, Han. Warb. Johns.   *much Orlando!* Steev. '85. *and here's*
Scene continued, Theob.   *no Orlando.* Ritson, Quincy (MS). *And*
   2. *a clock*] *o'clock* Theob.   *here—much, Orlando!* John Hunter.
   3. *And...*Orlando] *I wonder much*   4–7. Prose, Pope et seq. (except Coll.).
Orlando is not here. Pope+. *and how*   6. *t'ane*] *ta'ne* F_4. *ta'en* Rowe.
much Orlando comes? Cap. *and here's*   6, 7. *forth To*] *forth—to* Cap. et seq.

   1. After the remark upon the 'noisy scene,' which has just passed (see the first note in preceding scene), and which was introduced to fill up the interval of two hours, JOHNSON continues: This contraction of time we might impute to poor Rosalind's impatience but that a few minutes after we find Orlando sending his excuse. I do not see that by any probable division of the Acts this absurdity can be obviated. [This remark, if I understand it, and I am not sure that I do, is an undeserved slur on Shakespeare's dramatic art. To defend any dramatist, let alone Shakespeare, against the charge of absurdity in representing the passage of time by the shifting of scenes, is in itself an absurdity which no one, I think, would consciously commit. As this comedy is performed now-a-days, the 'noisy scene' is frequently omitted altogether, and this present scene opens in 'another part of the Forest;' this of itself is sufficient to indicate a flight of time, and no spectator notes an 'absurdity.' How much more pronounced is this flight when a whole scene intervenes, with new characters and wholly new action. It is to be feared that, in very truth, this Song penetrated to Dr Johnson's deaf ears only as 'noise,' and that, furthermore, Shakespeare's art in dramatic construction was in general so exquisitely concealed that when once it stood revealed with unmistakable plainness, Dr Johnson resented the attempt to sway his mood as a personal affront.—ED.]

   3. **heere much**] WHALLEY: We have still this use of 'much,' as when we say, speaking of a person who we suspect will not keep his appointment, 'Ay, you will be sure to see him *much !*' MALONE: So the vulgar yet say, 'I shall get *much* by that, no doubt,' meaning that they shall get nothing. HOLT WHITE: It is spoken ironically. GIFFORD, in a note on 'Much wench, or much son !'—*Every Man in his Humour*, IV, iv, p. 117, says 'Much !' is an ironical exclamation for *little* or *none*, in which sense it frequently occurs in our old dramatists. Thus in Heywood's *Edward IV :* '*Much* duchess! and *much* queen, I trow !' [On p. 40 of *Edward IV*, ed. Sh. Soc. there is 'Much queen, I trow !' but I cannot find the line as given by Gifford, who is usually accurate.—ED.]

   4–7. WALKER (*Crit.* i, 16): These lines are printed as verse in the Folio; which,

To fleepe : looke who comes heere.   7

   Sil.   My errand is to you, faire youth,
My gentle *Phebe,* did bid me giue you this :
I know not the contents, but as I gueffe   10
By the fterne brow, and wafpifh action
Which fhe did vfe, as fhe was writing of it,
It beares an angry tenure ; pardon me,
I am but as a guiltleffe meffenger.

   Rof.   Patience her felfe would ftartle at this letter,   15
And play the fwaggerer, beare this, beare all :
Shee faies I am not faire, that I lacke manners,
She calls me proud, and that fhe could not loue me
Were man as rare as Phenix : 'od's my will,   19

---

9. *did*] Mal. Cald. Knt, Coll. i, Wh.   13. *tenure*] *tenour* Theob. et seq.
i, Dyce i.   Om. Ff et cet.   16. After reading the letter. Han.
   10. *know*] *knew* Ff.

---

coupled with their being followed by a dialogue, also in verse, inclines me to think
Shakespeare meant them as such.   [Walker makes no new division of the lines,
but aids the rhythm by reading 'warrant' as *warr'nt,* and contracting 'and is' to
and's.]   COLLIER (ed. ii) : [Lines 4 and 6] are underscored in the Folio (MS) as
if they were a quotation, and they read like it.   Celia applied them to Orlando, who
had nothing to do with 'bows and arrows' that we are anywhere informed.   [In line
6] 'is' was erased by the old annotator.   [Capell introduced a dash after 'forth,' in
line 6, and has been followed in every subsequent edition, I think, except the Cambridge, the Globe, Wright's, and White's second edition.]

   8. **faire youth**] Abbott (§ 510), considers an interjectional line, and thus scans :
'Look, whó | comes hére ? | My ér | rand ís | to yóu ‖ Fair yóuth, ‖ My gént | le
Phé | be bíd | me gíve | you thís.'

   9. **did bid**] KEIGHTLEY : Editors, myself included, follow F$_2$, and omit 'did.'   I
think we are wrong.   [We are, therefore, to infer that Keightley would here pronounce 'Phebe' as a monosyllable, wherein he has Collier for company.   It is not
impossible that it may have been the lover's pet-name, but where it occurs further on,
in V, iv, 25, it seems wholly out of place from Rosalind.   I think it should be pronounced uniformly as a dissyllable.—ED.]

   12. **writing of it**] For other instances of this construction of verbal nouns, see, if
need be, Abbott, § 178.

   14. **as**] ABBOTT, § 115 : *As* was used almost, but not quite, redundantly after
'seem' (as it is still after 'regard,' 'represent') : 'To prey on nothing that doth seem
as dead,'—[line 123, below], and even after 'am' [as here, where it means] : 'I am
here *in the character of,*' &c.

   18. **calls . . . and that**] ABBOTT, § 382 : As in Latin, a verb of speaking can be
omitted where it is implied by some other word, as here : 'She *calls* me proud, and
(says) that,' &c.

   19. **man . . . Phenix**] WALKER in his Article (LI, *Vers.* p. 243) on the plural of
Substantives ending in a plural sound which are found without the usual addition of *s*

Her loue is not the Hare that I doe hunt,   20
Why writes ſhe ſo to me ? well Shepheard, well,
This is a Letter of your owne deuice.

    Sil.   No, I proteſt, I know not the contents,
Phebe did write it.

    Roſ.   Come, come, you are a foole,   25
And turn'd into the extremity of loue.

---

20. *doe*] *did* Ff, Rowe.
25. *you are*] *you're* Pope+, Dyce iii, Huds.

26. *turn'd into the*] *turned in the* or *turn'd so in the* Cap. conj.
    the extremity] *th' extremity* Pope +, Dyce iii, Huds.

---

or *es*, instances (p. 266) 'words ending in *x*,' and cites the present line thus : 'Were men as rare as Phœnix,' which last word he evidently thinks should be thus printed : Phœnix' as an indication of the plural. LETTSOM'S foot-note is as follows : 'Walker does not say from what edition he took the reading *men*. I find it in a small edition published by Tilt in 1836, professedly "from the text of the corrected copies of Steevens and Malone," and therefore I suppose it is the reading of what used to be called the received text. The Four Folios, Pope, Hanmer, Theobald, Capell, Var. 1821, Knight, and Collier all read "man," but the sense seems to demand *men*.' Lettsom might have added, as reading 'man,' Rowe i, ii, Warburton, Johnson, the Var. 1773, 1778, 1785, Steevens, 1793, Malone, 1790, Rann, Var. 1803, 1813, Harness, Singer's First Edition, Chalmers, Campbell,—all except Hazlitt, 1851, who reads *men*. In Hazlitt I am inclined to think that the reading is by no means accidental.—ED.

    19. **Phenix**] HALLIWELL : 'That there is but one Phœnix in the World, which after many hundred years burneth it self, and from the ashes thereof ariseth up another, is a conceit not new or altogether popular, but of great Antiquity.'—Brown's *Vulgar Errors* [Book III, chap. xii, p. 144, ed. 1672].

    19. **'od's my will**] Are not all these oaths, in which Rosalind indulges with marked freedom, her attempts to assume a swashing and a martial outside ? Before she donned doublet and hose she uttered none. 'Faith' was then her strongest affirmation, but from the hour she entered Arden we hear these charming little oaths from Ganymede. This, among others, is a reason, I think, why we should not adopt Spedding's *pulpiter* in place of 'Jupiter' in III, ii, 154; or Collier's 'Love, love' in lieu of 'Jove, Jove' in II, iv, 60.—ED.

    24. **write it**] MASON (p. 87) : The metre of this line is imperfect, and the sense of the whole ; for why should Rosalind dwell so much upon Phebe's hands unless Silvius had said something about them ? I have no doubt but the line originally ran thus : 'Phebe did write it *with her own fair hand.*' And then Rosalind's reply will naturally follow. COWDEN-CLARKE : Mason's conjecture is very plausible. Some allusion to the whiteness and delicacy of Phebe's hand seems requisite to account for Rosalind's abuse of its colour and texture.

    26. **turn'd into**] CAPELL : Had Silvius been at firſt a cool lover, as now a hot one, the word 'turn'd' had been proper; but as this was never the case, we must either put a sense upon 'turn'd' that is not common, to wit, got or fall'n; or else suspect a corruption, and look out for amendment : [See Text. Notes] both [of these are]

I faw her hand, fhe has a leatherne hand   27
A freeftone coloured hand : I verily did thinke
That her old gloues were on, but twas her hands:
She has a hufwiues hand, but that's no matter :   30
I fay fhe neuer did inuent this letter,
This is a mans inuention, and his hand.
   Sil.   Sure it is hers.
   Rof.   Why, tis a boyfterous and a cruell ftile,
A ftile for challengers : why, fhe defies me,   35
Like Turke to Chriftian : vvomens gentle braine
Could not drop forth fuch giant rude inuention,
Such Ethiop vvords, blacker in their effect
Then in their countenance : vvill you heare the letter ?
   Sil.   So pleafe you, for I neuer heard it yet :   40
Yet heard too much of *Phebes* crueltie.
   Rof.   She *Phebes* me : marke how the tyrant vvrites.   42

---

29. *on*] *one* F₂F₃.   et cet.
36. *vvomens*] Ff, Cam. *woman's* Rowe   37. *giant rude*] *giant-rude* Var. '21.

---

within the bounds of probability, but the first of them seems the most eligible : for 'turned' will signify—head-turned ; and then Rosalind's meaning will be,—Come, come, you're a simpleton, and the violence of your love has turn'd your head. WRIGHT : That is, brought into. Compare, for this sense of 'turn,' *Two Gent.* IV, iv, 67 : 'A slave, that still an end turns me to shame.' *The Temp.* I, ii, 64 : 'O, my heart bleeds To think o' the teen that I have turn'd you to.' *Twelfth N.* II, v, 224 : 'It cannot but turn him into a notable contempt.' *Cor.* III, i, 284 : 'The which shall turn you to no further harm.' Hence Capell's emendations are unnecessary.

28. **freestone coloured**] WRIGHT : Of the colour of Bath brick. NEIL : Stratford-on-Avon is situated on the Oolite strata, which are much used in building because they are able to be worked freely or easily by the mason. This, therefore, is a glover's-son-like descriptive phrase for a somewhat brownish-yellow hand, readily suggested to a Warwickshire man.

32. **his hand**] Is the key to the masculine character of Phebe's handwriting, which evidently surprises Rosalind, to be found in the emphatic 'waspish action' with which Silvius says she wrote the letter ? Like Hamlet's nervous gesture when he writes : 'So, uncle, there you are !'—ED.

34, &c. Phebe's letter, apart from the deception which is practised on Silvius, is, I think, charming, *pace* Hartley Coleridge ; Rosalind is therefore forced into this furious, exaggerated abuse of it, and into fictitious quotations from it, in order to arouse in Silvius a proper degree of manly indignation against Phebe, and to make him, poor tame snake, believe in her cruelty.—ED.

37. **giant rude**] For many more such compounds see Abbott, § 430.

39. **countenance**] For the sake of exactest rhythm this is to be pronounced as a dissyllable. See Abbott, § 468,

Read. *Art thou god, to Shepherd turn'd?*   43
That a maidens heart hath burn'd.
Can a vvoman raile thus?   45
     Sil. Call you this railing?
     Rof. Read. *Why, thy godhead laid a part,*
War'ft thou with a womans heart?
Did you euer heare fuch railing?
Whiles the eye of man did wooe me,   50
That could do no vengeance to me.
Meaning me a beaft.
If the fcorne of your bright eine
Haue power to raife fuch loue in mine,
Alacke, in me, what ftrange effect   55
Would they worke in milde afpect?
Whiles you chid me, I did loue,
How then might your praiers moue?
He that brings this loue to thee,

43, 47. Read.] Reads. Rowe et seq.   47. a part] apart Ff.
43. god] *a god* Ktly.   48. War'ft] Waft F₄.
     Shepherd] fheapheard F₂.   52. *me*] *me*, Theob. Warb.
43, 44. turn'd?...burn'd.] *turn'd,...*   53. eine] *Eyne* Rowe.
burn'd? Rowe et seq.   57. chid] *chide* Rowe.

43, 47. **Read**] This imperative mood here betrays the stage copy.—ED.

43. HARTLEY COLERIDGE (ii, 144): Phebe is no great poetess. It may be remarked in general that the poetry, introduced as such by Shakespeare, is seldom better than doggerel. A poem in a poem, a play in a play, a picture in a picture, the imitation of flageolet or trumpet in pianoforte music, are all departures from legitimate art; and yet how frequent in our old drama was the introduction of play within play! Sometimes, as in *Bartholomew Fair*, *The Knight of the Burning Pestle*, *The Taming of the Shrew*, and others, the main performance is as it were double-dramatised; an expedient which Moore, in his *Lalla Rookh*, has transferred to narrative. But more frequently the episodic drama is more or less subservient to the plot, as in *Hamlet*, *The Roman Actor*, &c.; or purely burlesque, as in *Midsummer Night's Dream*.

51. **vengeance**] JOHNSON: Here used for *mischief*.

52. That is, of course, meaning that I am a beast. Theobald, by his comma after 'me,' made it possible to suppose that Rosalind calls Phebe a beast.—ED.

54. **Haue**] ABBOTT, § 412: The subjunctive is not required, and therefore 'have' is probably plural here.

56. **aspect**] SCHMIDT paraphrases this as *look, air, countenance*, but WRIGHT is clearly more correct in interpreting it as 'an astrological term used to denote the favourable or unfavourable appearance of the planets,' for which interpretation Schmidt furnishes many examples. 'The accent,' adds Wright, 'is always on the last syllable.'

59. **loue**] WALKER (*Crit.* i, 295) marks this word as suspicious, but does not suggest any in its room; he merely says: '*Love* occurs three other times in the course

Little knowes this Loue in me :   60
And by him feale vp thy minde,
Whether that thy youth and kinde
Will the faithfull offer take
Of me, and all that I can make,
Or elfe by him my loue denie,   65
And then Ile ftudie how to die.

   Sil. Call you this chiding?

   Cel· Alas poore Shepheard.

   Rof. Doe you pitty him? No, he deferues no pitty :
wilt thou loue fuch a woman? what to make thee an in-   70
ftrument, and play falfe ftraines vpon thee *?* not to be endur'd. Well, goe your way to her ; (for I fee Loue hath
made thee a tame fnake) and fay this to her ; That if fhe
loue me, I charge her to loue thee : if fhe will not, I will
neuer haue her, vnleffe thou intreat for her : if you bee a   75
true louer hence, and not a word ; for here comes more
company.   *Exit. Sil.*

           Enter Oliuer.   know)
  Oliu. Good morrow, faire ones : pray you, (if you   79

---

60. this] *that* Rowe ii.   78. Scene VI. Pope, Han. Warb.
71. *ftraines] strings* Ff, Rowe.   Johns.
76. *louer hence,] lover, hence,* Rowe.

---

of these fourteen lines.' If repetition is in itself suspicious, and it often is, I cannot
think that this is the 'love' on which suspicion should light; it is connected indissolubly with the preceding 'love,' that flourished even under chiding. It is this very
love which is now sent by Silvius, so it seems to me.—ED.

62. kinde] JOHNSON: The old word for *nature*. CALDECOTT: Natural and
kindly affections.

64. make] STEEVENS: That is, raise as profit from anything. So in *Meas. for
Meas.* IV, iii, 5 : 'He's in for a commodity of brown paper, ... of which he made
five marks.' CALDECOTT: That is, make up, all that shall be my utmost amount.
HALLIWELL: Probably used in its ordinary acceptation, make by my labour or skill.

70. instrument] That is, use thee as a messenger while deceiving thee; as
WRIGHT says, it is here used in two senses, as a tool and as a musical instrument.

73. snake] MALONE: This term was frequently used to express a poor, contemptible fellow. So in *Sir John Oldcastle*, 1600: 'Priest. —and you, poor snakes, come
seldom to a booty.'—[p. 253, *a*, F₄]. Again, in *Lord Cromwell*, 1602: '*Hales.* —and
the poorest Snake, that feeds on Lemmons, Pilchers.'—[p. 234, *b*, F₄. Cotgrave
(always a good authority) gives: '*Haire.* m. A leane, or ill-fauoured curtall; a carrion
iade; (hence) also, a wretched or miserable fellow; a poore snake.'—ED.]

79. faire ones] WRIGHT: Shakespeare seems to have forgotten that Celia was

Where in the Purlews of this Forreſt, ſtands   80
A ſheep-coat, fenc'd about with Oliue-trees.

  Cel. Weſt of this place, down in the neighbor bottom
The ranke of Oziers, by the murmuring ſtreame
Left on your right hand, brings you to the place :
But at this howre, the houſe doth keepe it ſelfe,   85
There's none within.

  Oli. If that an eye may profit by a tongue,
Then ſhould I know you by deſcription,
Such garments, and ſuch yeeres : the boy is faire,
Of femall fauour, and beſtowes himſelfe   90

---

80. *Where in*] *Wherein* F$_3$F$_4$.
84. *brings*] *bring* Ff, Rowe i.
85. *howre*] F$_1$.

89–92. *the boy...brother*] As a quotation, Theob. et seq.
90. *femall*] F$_2$. *female* F$_3$F$_4$.

---

apparently the only woman present. Perhaps we should read 'fair *one.*' [Decidedly. It is the very last oversight which Shakespeare would be likely to commit. It is Celia who replies, which increases the likelihood that it is she alone who is addressed.—ED.]

79. **(if you know)**] ROWE exchanged these parentheses of the Folios for commas. JOHNSON was the first to drop the second comma and read : ' Pray you, if you know Where in the,' &c., and was followed, except by Capell, in all editions down to and including Knight. Collier restored the second comma, which has been since retained. It is a trifling matter, but it involves a shade of meaning which an editor cannot disregard.—ED.

80. **Purlews**] MALONE: Bullokar, *Expositor*, has : '*Purlue.* A place neere ioining to a Forrest, where it is lawfull for the owner to the ground to hunt, if hee can dispend fortie shillings by the yeere of free land.' REED : *Purlieu*, says Manwood's *Treatise on the Forest Laws*, c. xx, ' is a certaine territorie of ground adjoyning unto the forest, meared and bounded with unmoveable marks, meeres, and boundaries : which territories of ground was also forest, and afterwards disaforested againe by the perambulations made for the severing of the new forest from the old.'

82. **bottom**] CAPELL: This word should have a fuller stop after it, a semicolon ; for the meaning of these lines, whose construction is a little perplex'd, is as follows : It stands to the *west of this place*, and *down in the neighbour bottom ;* if you leave *the rank of osiers*, that grows by the brook-side, *on your right hand*, it will bring *you to the place.* [For many examples of noun compounds, see Abbott, § 430.]

83. **ranke**] See III, ii, 97.

84. **Left**] See Capell's foregoing note.

90. **fauour**] MOBERLY : *To favour* is *to resemble* in Yorkshire even now [and here in this country also.—ED.]. Hence it might be argued that ' favour ' means *resemblance*, and therefore *countenance.* It would, however, be more accurate to derive the verb from the substantive, as in the parallel phrase of the same dialect, ' you breed o' me,' for *you are like me.* In that case ' favour ' may perhaps be a corruption (by proximity) of ' feature ' (faiture), which is similarly used as a verb (' a glass that featur'd them '). Compare, for the vanishing of the *t*, ' vetulus ' with ' vieil,' and ' em-

Like a ripe fifter : the woman low   91

91. *ripe fifter*] *right forester* Lettsom,   Steev. Mal. Sing. Clke, Ktly, Dyce iii,
Huds.   Coll. iii.

   the] *But the* Ff, Rowe+, Cap.

---

phyteusis' with '(en)fief.' WRIGHT : ' Favour' is aspect, look; used generally of the face. Compare *Macb.* I, v, 73 : ' To alter favour ever is to fear.' And *Hamlet*, V, i, 214 : ' Let her paint an inch thick, to this favour she must come.'

90. **bestowes**] STEEVENS : Compare *2 Hen. IV :* II, ii, 186 : ' How might we see Falstaff bestow himself to-night in his true colours, and not ourselves be seen ?' REV. JOHN HUNTER : I apprehend the meaning here to be, that by stuffing out his bosom, he gives himself the appearance of a girl of ripe age. [Schmidt supplies many examples where ' bestow,' used reflectively, means *to deport one's self.*]

91. **ripe sister**] WALKER (*Vers.* 209): 'A ripe sister' seems an odd expression. LETTSOM [in a foot-note to Walker] : Odd, no doubt, and it is not less odd that nobody, as far as I know, made this remark before. ' Ripe sister' seems corrupted from *right forester.* This last word was often written *forster* and *foster.* Perhaps, too, the first ' and' has usurped the place of *but.* The F$_2$ reads : ' Like a ripe sister : *But* the woman low,' &c. So in *Macb.* I, vii, the same edition has : 'And dasht the Branes out, had I *but* so sworne,' &c. *But,* in both these passages, is a crutch furnished by the compassionate editor to assist the lameness of the metre. In *Macbeth* the idiom of our language, as well as the harmony of the verse, seems to require us to read : 'And dash'd the brains *on't* out, had I so sworn,' &c. DYCE (ed. iii) pronounces this emendation of Lettsom's ' most ingenious,' a commendation by no means too strong. 'A ripe sister,' not only as a phrase by itself, but as applied to a young man or even to a ' boy,' seems to be not merely ' odd,' but almost unintelligible, and until something better is proposed Lettsom's *right forester* holds, for me, pre-eminent rank. But, on the other hand, WRIGHT, our highest Shakespearian authority now living, accepts the present text, and says : ' The meaning must be that Rosalind, though in male attire and acting the part of a brother, was in her behaviour to Celia more like an elder sister.' See also Hunter's explanation in the preceding note.—ED.

91. **sister**] Of course it is manifest that the scansion of this line halts if we read it in the right butterwoman's rank to market. To smooth it out Walker (*Vers.* 209) suggested that ' sister' be pronounced as he says *daughter* is sometimes pronounced ; that is, as a trisyllable. Oxen and wainropes will never draw me to the belief that either word was ever so pronounced, or at least ever should be so pronounced. Almost invariably where the rhythm halts over these two words there is a pause in the sense ; and this pause it is which takes the place of the extra syllable. How Walker missed seeing this, it is difficult to comprehend. He himself even calls attention to this pause, and notes that in at least half of the instances of his trisyllabic *daughter* there is not only a pause, but a full stop after the word. And yet he speculated on the original form of the word as a source of its prolonged pronunciation, and Lettsom suggested that it might lie in the original guttural sound. Abbott, too, is scarcely better; for he suggests (§ 478) that the *-er* final may have been ' sometimes pronounced with a kind of " burr," which produced the effect of an additional syllable,' and thus scans the present line : ' Líke a | ripe sís | tér : | the wóm | an lów.' ' Trisyllables' and ' burrs' may make lines rhythmical on paper, but let them remain on the paper, and never leave it. Or let them be set to the music which is asked for in Othello, ' that may not be heard.'—ED.

And browner then her brother : are not you   92
The owner of the houſe I did enquire for?
 Cel. It is no boaſt, being ask'd, to ſay we are.
 Oli. *Orlando* doth commend him to you both,   95
And to that youth hee calls his *Roſalind,*
He ſends this bloudy napkin; are you he?
 Roſ. I am : what muſt we vnderſtand by this?
 Oli. Some of my ſhame, if you will know of me
What man I am, and how, and why, and where   100
This handkercher was ſtain'd.
 Cel. I pray you tell it.
 Oli. When laſt the yong *Orlando* parted from you,
He left a promiſe to returne againe
Within an houre, and pacing through the Forreſt,   105
Chewing the food of ſweet and bitter fancie,

---

93. *owner*] *owners* Cap. conj. Hal. Dyce iii, Huds.
97. *this*] *his* Warb. (misprint?).
101. *handkercher*] Ff, Dyce, Cam.

Huds. Rlfe. *handkerchief* Rowe et cet.
105. *an houre*] *two hours* Han.
106. *food*] *cud* Sta. Dyce ii, iii, Coll. iii, Huds.

---

92. **browner**] COWDEN-CLARKE: It must be remembered that when Celia proposed to disguise herself as a shepherdess, she says that she will 'with a kind of umber smirch' her 'face'; and this browner complexion, mentioned here, shows that she has fulfilled her idea.

93. **owner**] Capell's conjecture is harmless; but COWDEN-CLARKE thus vindicates the original text in a note on Celia's reply 'we are': 'In this little touch there is a manifestation of Shakespeare's subtlety and true taste. Oliver, wholly occupied with Celia, asks her if she be the "owner of the house" he inquires for; but she, with the uſual delicacy, modesty, and generosity which characterise her, especially where sharing all things equally with her cousin is concerned, answers by a word that comprehends them both as joint-owners.'

97. **napkin**] STEEVENS: That is, handkerchief [as it is called within five lines.— ED.]. Ray says that a pocket-handkerchief is so called about Sheffield in Yorkshire. BOSWELL: Napkin is still a handkerchief in Scotland, and probably in all the northern English counties. ['Oft did she heave her napkin to her eyne.'—*Lover's Complaint*, 21. See *Oth.* III, iii, 335, where the fatal 'handkerchief spotted with strawberries' is also called a 'napkin.'—ED.]

101. **handkercher**] This is the uniform spelling in the First Quarto of *Othello;* and once the Third Folio (IV, i, 167) spells it 'Hankerchiffe.' In the First Folio in *Othello* the spelling is uniformly 'handkerchiefe.'

105. **an houre**] 'We must read,' says JOHNSON, 'within *two* hours,' and then did not so read in his text. As Tyrwhitt asks, 'may not "within an hour" signify *within a certain* time?' It does not mean *one;* it is simply the indefinite article.—ED.

106. **food**] STAUNTON: Undoubtedly a misprint. 'To chew the cud,' metaphorically, to *ruminate,* to *resolve in the mind,* is an expression of frequent occurrence in

Loe vvhat befell : he threw his eye afide,   107
And marke vvhat obieƈt did prefent it felfe
Vnder an old Oake, whofe bows were mofs'd with age
And high top, bald with drie antiquitie :   110
A wretched ragged man, ore-growne with haire
Lay fleeping on his back ; about his necke   112

---

109. *old*] Om. Pope+, Cap. Steev.   110. *with*] *of* Rowe ii, Pope, Han.
Wh. Cam. Dyce iii, Huds. Rlfe.

---

our old authors. DYCE (ed. ii): In the Introduction to *Quentin Durward* the imaginary Marquis de Hautlieu is made to quote the present line thus : '*Shewing* the *code*
of sweet and bitter fancy'; which is followed by the remark : 'Against this various
reading of a well-known passage in Shakespeare I took care to offer no protest; for I
suspect Shakespeare would have suffered in the opinion of so delicate a judge as the
Marquis, had I proved his having written " *chewing* the *cud*," according to all other
authorities.'—p. xxxvi, ed. 1823. Sir Walter Scott, therefore, was not aware that 'all
authorities' agreed in 'chewing the *food* of,' &c.; and to him, in fact, we owe the
correction of the line. EREM (*Notes & Qu.* 5th ser. iv, 4): The *cud* is identically
the *chewed*. There is, then, a chewing that is not the cud, but of fresh food, which,
become so a cud, is laid by for re-chewing. Orlando chews no cud, but the food,
ever springing afresh, of sweet and bitter love-thoughts, a crop in repute for quick
and thick growth. . . . . How at home the metaphor is in the English mind is shown
in the curious fact that the oral tradition of our educated society has usurped possession of the verse, turning ' food ' into *cud*. Engage ten persons of literary cultivation
with the elder brother's revelation of the younger's reverie, and, if the world is as it
was, nine will, I expect, pledge their scholarship to that reading of this text which,
on the page of Shakespeare, they have not read. With a step back into the world
as it was you have wonderfully Sir Walter Scott in example, [who] deliberately
alleges *cud* for the universal reading, more than a generation before [a single text]
had it.

106. **bitter fancy**] CAPELL: The epithets given to ' Fancy ' look'd so like a translation of the Greek γλυκύπικρον, that the editor thought for some time, the Poet must,
somehow or other, have been fishing in those waters; but turning again to his novelist, he found a passage he had not reflected on, and thus it runs : 'Wherein I have
noted the variable disposition of fancy, ... being as it should seeme a combat mixt
with disquiet, and a bitter pleasure wrapt in a sweet prejudice '; the words are
address'd to Rosalind by this identical speaker. [See Appendix.] MALONE: *Love*
is always thus described by our old poets, as composed by contraries. See notes on
Rom. & Jul. I, i, 169. FARMER: Watson begins one of his canzonets: ' Love is a
sowre delight, a sugred griefe, A living death, an ever-dying life,' &c.

109. **old**] STEEVENS: As this epithet hurts the measure without improvement of
the sense (for we are told in the same line that its ' boughs were moss'd with *age*,'
and, afterwards, that its top was bald with dry *antiquity*), I have omitted it, as an
unquestionable interpolation. WHITE : I cannot believe that in an otherwise deftly
wrought and perfectly rhythmical passage, Shakespeare would load a line with a
heavy monosyllable, entirely superfluous to any purpose other than that of marring
the description and making the verse halt.

16

A greene and guilded fnake had wreath'd it felfe,   113
Who with her head, nimble in threats approach'd
The opening of his mouth : but fodainly   115
Seeing *Orlando*, it vnlink'd it felfe,
And with indented glides, did flip away
Into a bufh, vnder which bufhes fhade
A Lyonneffe, with vdders all drawne drie,
Lay cowching head on ground, with catlike watch   120
When that the fleeping man fhould ftirre ; for 'tis
The royall difpofition of that beaft
To prey on nothing, that doth feeme as dead :   123

---

114. *threats*] *threats*, Rowe.   118. *which*] *whofe* Ff, Rowe.

---

113. **guilded**] ROLFE cites Schmidt as 'noting that Shakespeare uses "gilded" twenty times and "gilt" only six times.'

113. **snake**] MAGINN (p. 91) : Some sage critics have discovered as a great geographical fault in Shakespeare that he introduces the tropical lion and serpent into Arden, which, it appears, they have ascertained to lie in some temperate zone. I wish them joy of their sagacity. Monsters more wonderful are to be found in that forest; for never yet, since water ran and tall tree bloomed, were there gathered together such a company as those who compose the *dramatis personæ* of *As You Like It*. All the prodigies spawned by Africa, *leonum arida nutrix*, might well have teemed in a forest, wherever situate, that was inhabited by such creatures as Rosalind, Touchstone, and Jaques. [Maginn refers to certain 'sage critics' who have severely criticised Shakespeare's geography. Other commentators refer to 'wiseacres,' or to 'would-be critics,' who sneer at Shakespeare's 'lions' and scoff at his 'palm trees' here in the forest of Arden, but nowhere that I can find are these 'sage critics' or 'wiseacres' mentioned by name. I would gladly know who they are. My reading has been tolerably extensive in what has been written about this play, and yet I have never come across these sneerers and scoffers. Allusion to them is abundant, and illimitable ridicule is heaped on them, and no end of indignation is stirred in defence of poor dear Shakespeare against their inanities, but the cowards skulk, and dodge, and hide, and show never a face. Exist somewhere they must. It cannot be that we are all turned Don Quixotes. At last, in my search for these wretches, I have concluded, in my despair, that it is absolutely necessary to take a hint from the Law, and to adopt, for the nonce, into our circle of commentators a 'John Doe' and a 'Richard Roe,' whom we may here load with obloquy, cover with ridicule, and wither with indignation, to our own immense relief, and with the heartsome reflection that no breather in the world will be, for it all, one atom the worse.—ED.]

114. **Who**] See III, v, 15, and again, line 137 below, or Abbott, § 264, for instances of 'who' personifying irrational antecedents.

119. **drie**] STEEVENS : So in *Arden of Feversham*, 1592 : 'the staruen Lyones, When she is dry suckt of her eager young.'—[II, ii, p. 37, ed. Bullen. Compare *Lear*, III, i, 12 : 'This night wherein the cub-drawn bear would couch.']

121. **that . . . should**] For 'that,' see I, iii, 44; for 'should,' see Abbott, § 326.

123. **dead**] The belief in this disposition is probably as old as Aristotle; it is men-

This feene, *Orlando* did approach the man,
And found it was his brother, his elder brother.   125
     Cel.   O I haue heard him fpeake of that fame brother,
And he did render him the moft vnnaturall
That liu'd amongft men.
     Oli.   And well he might fo doe,
For well I know he was vnnaturall.   130
     Rof.   But to *Orlando* : did he leaue him there
Food to the fuck'd and hungry Lyonneffe ?
     Oli.   Twice did he turne his backe, and purpos'd fo :
But kindneffe, nobler euer then reuenge,
And Nature ftronger then his iuft occafion,   135
Made him giue battell to the Lyonneffe :
Who quickly fell before him, in which hurtling   137

---

128. *amongft*] Ff, Rowe i, Cam. Wh. ii.   *among* Rlfe.   '*mongst* Rowe ii et cet.

---

tioned by Pliny in his chapter on Lions, which he says he derived in the main from
the Greek. GREY (i, 185) called attention to this passage in Pliny, which thus appears
in Holland's translation (Book VIII, chap. xvi) : 'The Lion alone of all wilde beasts,
is gentle to those that humble themselues vnto him, and will not touch any such vpon
their submission, but spareth what creature soeuer lieth prostrate before him.'   Naturally, in the case of a belief so old and so popular, allusions to it abound.   'The rag-
ing Lyon neuer rendes The yielding pray, that prostrate lyes,' it stands written in
Willobie's *Avisa*, p. 99, ed. Grosart; and DOUCE (i, 308) cites Bartholomæus, *De
Propriet. Rerum :* 'their mercie is known by many and oft ensamples : for they spare
them that lye on the ground.'   Shakespeare refers to the nobleness of the lion in
Twelfth N. and in *Tro. & Cress.*   Moreover, this delay of the lion in devouring
Oliver is mentioned in Lodge's *Novel* (see Appendix), although it is there stated as
due not to a royal disposition, but to a disrelish of 'dead carkasses.'—ED.

     123. as] See line 14, above.
     127. render him] MALONE: That is, describe him.   [This line is another furtive
Alexandrine which Abbott would unmask by 'slurring' the last two syllables of
'unna*tural*.'   To say *unnat'ral* would come nat'ral to Hosea Bigelow, but, I think,
to no one else.—ED.]
     131, &c. FLETCHER (p. 222) : How finely is this scene contrived so as to show us
the dignity of Rosalind's affection ever keeping pace with its increasing warmth.
Her first solicitude, on this occasion, is not about her lover's personal safety, but as to
the worthiness of his conduct under this new and extraordinary trial of his generosity.
     135. occasion] CALDECOTT : That is, such reasonable ground as might have amply
justified, or given just occasion for abandoning him.   See IV, i, 167.
     137. Who] See line 114, above.
     137. hurtling] STEEVENS : To *hurtle* is to move with impetuosity and tumult.   So
in *Jul. Cæs.* II, i, 22 : 'The noise of battle hurtled in the air.'   SKEAT : To come
into collision with, to dash against, to rattle.   Nearly obsolete, but used in Gray's
Fatal Sisters, st. i; imitated from Shakespeare's *Jul. Cæs.*   Middle English, *hurtlen*,

From miſerable ſlumber I awaked.   138
   Cel. Are you his brother?
   Roſ. Was't you he reſcu'd?   140
   Cel. Was't yòu that did ſo oft contriue to kill him?
   Oli. 'Twas I : but 'tis not I : I doe not ſhame
To tell you what I was, ſince my conuerſion
So ſweeetly taſtes, being the thing I am.
   Roſ. But for the bloody napkin?   145
   Oli. By and by:
When from the firſt to laſt betwixt vs two,
Teares our recountments had moſt kindely bath'd,
As how I came into that Deſert place.
I briefe, he led me to the gentle Duke,   150
Who gaue me freſh aray, and entertainment,

---

140. *Was't*] Ff, Rowe, Pope, Han. Theob. i, Sing. Wh. Sta. Cam. Rlfe. *Was it* Theob. ii et cet.

   reſcu'd] *rescued* Knt, Cam. Ktly, Coll. iii, Huds. Rlfe.

141. *Was't*] *Was it* Theob. ii, Warb.

144. *ſweeetly*] F₁.

149. *As how*] *As, how* Steev. '93 et seq. (subs.).

   Deſert] *Deſart* F₂, Rowe, Pope, Theob. Han. Warb.

150. *I*] *In* Ff.

---

to jostle against, dash against, push. 'And he him *hurtleth* with his hors adoun.'—Chaucer, *C. T.* 2618, in the Ellesmere MS, where most other MSS have *hurteth*. In fact, *hurt-le* is merely the frequentative of *hurt*, in the sense of 'to dash.' And this *hurt* is the Mid. Eng. *hurten*, to dash, to dash one's foot against a thing, to stumble. 'If ony man wandre in the dai, he *hirtith* not,' *i. e.* stumbles not.—Wyclif, *John*, xi, 9. *Hurten*, to dash, is the same with the modern English word.

147, &c. CAPELL: No heedful peruser of this line, and the three it is follow'd by, can think we have the passage entire; other heads of these brothers' 'recountments' are apparently necessary to make the Poet's 'in brief' right and sensible. What the accident was, or whose the negligence, that has depriv'd us of these heads, the editor does not take upon him to say; this only he is bold to assert, that there is a *lacuna*, and (perhaps) of two lines : if the public thinks well to admit of them, here are two that may serve to fill up with : ' How, in that habit; what my state, what his; ‖ And whose the service he was now engag'd in;— ‖ In brief,' &c. MALONE: I believe a line has been lost after line 149. STEEVENS: I suspect no omission. KEIGHTLEY: There may have been a line lost, but I rather think it is an aposiopesis. [The omission of a line is so serious a defect that we might diminish the chances of its having occurred by converting ' recountments ' into the singular. That final *s* is an unruly letter, which has given so much trouble that Walker even goes so far as to suggest, as I have already noted many times, that its presence may have been due to some peculiarity in Shakespeare's handwriting. At any rate, its omission here is certainly less violent than the insertion of a whole line, or, worse still, of two whole lines. Keightley's ' aposiopesis ' is not without its dramatic effect, as though emotion choked the speaker.—ED.]

149. **As**] STEEVENS: 'As,' in this place, signifies—as for instance. [See II, i, 8.]

Committing me vnto my brothers loue,   152
Who led me inftantly vnto his Caue,
There ftript himfelfe, and heere vpon his arme
The Lyonneffe had torne fome flefh away,   155
Which all this while had bled ; and now he fainted,
And cride in fainting vpon *Rofalinde*.
Briefe, I recouer'd him, bound vp his wound,
And after fome fmall fpace, being ftrong at heart,
He fent me hither, ftranger as I am   160
To tell this ftory, that you might excufe
His broken promife, and to giue this napkin
Died in this bloud, vnto the Shepheard youth,
That he in fport doth call his *Rofalind*.

 Cel. Why how now *Ganimed*, fweet *Ganimed*.   165
 Oli. Many will fwoon when they do look on bloud.
 Cel. There is more in it ; Cofen *Ganimed*.
 Oli. Looke, he recouers.
 Rof. I would I were at home.
 Cel. Wee'll lead you thither :   170

---

161. *ftory*] Om. F$_3$F$_4$.

163. *this*] Mal. Steev. '93, Cald. Knt. *his* Ff, Rowe+, Cap. Coll. Wh. Dyce, Sta. Cam. Ktly.

164. [Ros. faints. Pope et seq. (subs.).

165. Ganimed, *fweet* Ganimed.] *Ganymed!—Sweet !—Ganymed !* Johns.

167. *more in it*] *no more in it* F$_3$F$_4$, Rowe. *no more in't* Pope, Han.

Cofen Ganimed] *Cousin Ganimed!* Rowe. *Cousin—Ganymed!* Johns. Steev. Mal. Wh. i.

168. [Raising her. Coll. ii (MS).

169. *I would*] *Would* Pope+.

---

158. **Briefe**] In Schmidt will be found other instances of 'brief' thus used.

163. **this**] MALONE: The change to *his* of F$_2$ is unnecessary. Oliver points to the handkerchief when he presents it; and Rosalind could not doubt whose blood it was after the account that had been before given. STEEVENS: Either reading may serve; and certainly *his* is not the worst, because it prevents the disgusting repetition of the pronoun 'this,' with which the present speech is infested. [This is one of the examples in Walker's chapter on 'the Substitution of Words' (*Crit.* i, 317), and on it he remarks: ' Here the proneness of *this* and *his* to supplant each other might facilitate the error.' '*This* blood' is weak compared with '*his* blood.' That it is *his* blood, Orlando's very blood, makes Rosalind faint.—ED.]

167. JOHNSON: Celia, in her first fright, forgets Rosalind's character and disguise, and calls out 'cousin,' then recollects herself, and says, 'Ganymede.' DYCE: But 'cousin' is used here merely as a term of familiar address. CAPELL: Celia's fright makes her almost forget herself; begin, with telling more than she should do; and end, with calling Ganimed 'cousin,' whom her hearer has call'd 'brother,' and believes him to be so. The incident that gives birth to this fright, 'the bloody napkin,' has no existence in the Novel that furnish'd most of the others.

I pray you will you take him by the arme.   171
   Oli.   Be of good cheere youth : you a man?
You lacke a mans heart.
   Rof.   I doe fo, I confeffe it :
Ah, firra, a body would thinke this was well counterfei-   175
ted, I pray you tell your brother how well I counterfei-
ted : heigh-ho.   '   177

---

171. *will you*] Om. F₃F₄, Rowe.
172–175. Prose, Pope et seq.
175. *firra*] *Sir* Pope+, Cap. Steev.

Mal. [*Sic* F₂, *ap.* Mal. '90, but corrected
in Var. '21.]

---

171. COWDEN-CLARKE: Here is another of Shakespeare's subtly characteristic
touches. Celia, like a true woman for the first time in love, and in love at first sight,
eagerly takes the opportunity of retaining near her the man she loves, and as gladly
enlists his services of manly support and kindness on behalf of one dear to her. But
while indicating this womanly trait in Celia, he at the same time marks her generosity
of nature, by making her, even in the first moment of awakened interest in Oliver, still
most mindful of her cousin Rosalind, whom, when she sees likely to betray her secret,
she recalls to herself by the words : ' Come, you look paler and paler ; pray you, draw
homewards.'

174. **I doe so**] LADY MARTIN (p. 432) : The rest of the scene, with the struggle
between actual physical faintness and the effort to make light of it, touched in by the
poet with exquisite skill, calls for the most delicate and discriminating treatment in the
actress. The audience, who are in her secret, must be made to feel the tender, loving nature of the woman through the simulated gaiety by which it is veiled ; and yet
the character of the boy Ganymede must be sustained. This is another of the many
passages to which the actress of comedy only will never give adequate expression.
How beautiful it is !

175. **Ah, sirra**] CALDECOTT : Yet scarce more than half in possession of herself,
in her flutter and tremulous articulation she adds to one word the first letter, or
article, of the succeeding one. DYCE : ' Sirrah ' was sometimes nothing more than a
sort of playful familiar address. In *1 Hen. IV :* I, ii, Poins says to the Prince :
'*Sirrah,* I have some cases of buckram for the nonce,' &c., compare, too, *Rom. &*
Jul. I, v : '*Ah, sirrah,* this unlook'd-for sport comes well.'   '*Ah, sirrah,* by my fay,
it waxes late.'   [Dyce, in his first edition, added, what he subsequently omitted, Caldecott's note, with the remark that it ' could not well be surpassed in absurdity.']
WHITE : On recovering herself, Rosalind immediately resumes her boyish sauciness,
and a little overdoes it. The printing of *sir* for ' sirrah ' by some editors, and the comments, laboriously from the purpose, of others, who give the original word, must serve
as the excuse for this note. MOBERLY : A similar form seems still in use in America
(without any notion of upbraiding). ROLFE : Moberly apparently refers to the vulgar
sirree, which is of very recent origin, and of course has no connection with ' sirrah.'

175. **a body**] HALLIWELL : It may be worth notice that the term ' body ' was formerly used in the way it is here in the text in serious composition. WRIGHT : It is
common enough in Scotch and provincial dialects, and was once more common still.
Compare *Psalm* liii, 1 (Prayer Book Version) : ' The foolish body hath said in his
heart.' So in *Meas. for Meas.* IV, iv, 25 : ' an eminent body.'

Oli. This was not counterfeit, there is too great te-   178
ſtimony in your complexion, that it was a paſſion of ear-
neſt.   180

Roſ. Counterfeit, I aſſure you.

Oli. Well then, take a good heart, and counterfeit to
be a man.

Roſ. So I doe : but yfaith, I ſhould haue beene a woman by right.   185

Cel. Come, you looke paler and paler : pray you draw
homewards : good ſir, goe with vs.

Oli. That will I : for I muſt beare anſwere backe
How you excuſe my brother, *Roſalind.*

Roſ. I ſhall deuiſe ſomething : but I pray you com-   190
mend my counterfeiting to him : will you goe?

                                        Exeunt.   192

---

179. *a paſſion*] *paſſion* Ff, Rowe.

---

181. WHITE (*Studies*, &c., p. 256): When is it that we have seen a stage Rosalind
that showed us what the Rosalind of our imagination felt at the sight of the bloody
handkerchief? I never saw but one : Mrs Charles Kean. The last that I saw
behaved much as if Oliver had shown her a beetle, which she feared might fly upon
her; and in the end she turned and clung to Celia's shoulder. But as Oliver tells his
story the blood of the real Rosalind runs curdling from her brain to her heart, and she
swoons away,—falls like one dead, to be caught by the wondering Oliver. Few words
are spoken, because few are needed; but this swoon is no brief incident; and Rosalind recovers only to be led off by the aid of Celia and Oliver. And here the girl
again makes an attempt to assert her manhood. She insists that she counterfeited,
and repeats her assertion. Then here, again, the stage Rosalinds all fail to present her
as she is. They say 'counterfeit' with at least some trace of a sly smile, and as if
they did not quite expect or wholly desire Oliver to believe them. But Rosalind was
in sad and grievous earnest. Never word that she uttered was more sober and serious
than her 'counterfeit, I assure you.' And the fun of the situation, which is never
absent in *As You Like It*, consists in the complex of incongruity,—the absurdity of a
young swashbuckler's fainting at the sight of a bloody handkerchief, the absurdity
of Rosalind's protest that her swoon and deadly horror were counterfeit, combining
with our knowledge of the truth of the whole matter.

Actus Quintus.   Scena Prima.

Enter Clowne and Awdrie.

Clow. We ſhall finde a time *Awdrie*, patience gentle *Awdrie*.

Awd. Faith the Prieſt was good enough, for all the
olde gentlemans ſaying.   5

Clow. A moſt wicked Sir *Oliuer*, *Awdrie*, a moſt vile
Mar-text. But *Awdrie*, there is a youth heere in the
Forreſt layes claime to you.

Awd. I, I know who 'tis : he hath no intereſt in mee
in the world : here comes the man you meane.   10

Enter William.

Clo. It is meat and drinke to me to ſee a Clowne, by
my troth, we that haue good wits, haue much to anſwer
for : we ſhall be flouting : we cannot hold.

Will. Good eu'n *Audrey*.   15

Aud. God ye good eu'n *William*.

Will. And good eu'n to you Sir.

Clo. Good eu'n gentle friend. Couer thy head, couer
thy head : Nay prethee bee eouer'd. How olde are you
Friend ?   20

Will. Fiue and twentie Sir.

Clo. A ripe age : Is thy name *William* ?   22

---

9. *in mee*] Om. Pope, Han.
11. Enter...] After line 14, Dyce, Sta.
Cam.

15, &c. *eu'n*] F$_2$. *ev'n* F$_3$F$_4$. *even*
Coll. Dyce, Sta. Cam.
16. *ye*] *give* Johns.
19. *eouer'd*] F$_1$.

---

5. **olde gentlemans**] There is nothing disrespectful here in thus speaking of
Jaques; it merely gives us a hint of his age. Yet Dingelstedt translates it 'der alte
Murrkopf.'—ED.

12. **meat and drinke**] Of this common old proverbial phrase Halliwell gives many
examples, and Wright refers to its repetition in *Merry Wives*, I, i, 306.

14. **shall**] See I, i, 126.

14. **flouting**] MOBERLY: We must needs be jeering people. WRIGHT: We must
have our joke.

15, 16. These two appear as 'Godden' and 'Godgigoden' in the Qq and Folios
of *Rom. & Jul.* I, ii, 55, 56.

Will. *William*, ſir.   23
Clo. A faire name. Was't borne i'th Forreſt heere?
Will. I ſir, I thanke God.   25
Clo. Thanke God : A good anſwer :
Art rich?
Will. 'Faith ſir, ſo, ſo
Cle. So, ſo, is good, very good, very excellent good:
and yet it is not, it is but ſo, ſo :   30
Art thou wiſe?
Will. I ſir, I haue a prettie wit.
Clo. Why, thou ſaiſt well. I do now remember a ſay-
ing: The Foole doth thinke he is wiſe, but the wiſeman
knowes himſelfe to be a Foole. The Heathen Philoſo-   35
pher, when he had a deſire to eate a Grape, would open
his lips when he put it into his mouth, meaning there-
by, that Grapes were made to eate, and lippes to open.
You do loue this maid?
Will. I do ſit.   40

26, 27, and throughout, Prose, Pope.   36. *deſire*] *design* (so quoted in foot-
34. *wiſeman*] *wise man* Rowe et   note) Theob.
seq.   40. *ſit*] *ſir* Ff.

---

34. **The Foole**, &c.] MOBERLY: The marrow of the *Apologia Socratis* condensed
into a few words. See *Prov.* xii, 15. WORDSWORTH (p. 340) asks, 'Is the "saying" here quoted derived from *1 Corinthians*, iii, 18?'

34. **wiseman**] CAMBRIDGE EDITORS: There can be no doubt that the words *wise
man*, printed as two, in obedience to modern usage, were frequently in Shakespeare's
time written and pronounced as one word, with the accent on the first syllable, as
'madman' is still. See Walker (*Crit.* ii, 1391). [See I, ii, 83, where this note
should have also appeared, but was unaccountably omitted. See also *Mer. of Ven.* I,
i, 116. Here, too, be another omission supplied, which was discovered only when it
was too late to change the stereotyped page, and space could be found on that page
only to refer to this present penitential expiation of the oversight. On p. xxxvi of the
'Clarendon Edition,' WRIGHT, none of whose words can we afford to lose, has the
following 'Additional Note' on 'moe,' III, ii, 257: 'The statement that "moe" is
used *only* with the plural requires a slight modification. So far as I am aware, there is
but one instance in Shakespeare where it is not immediately followed by a plural, and
that is in *The Tempest*, V, i, 234 (First Folio) : "And mo diversitie of sounds." But in
this case also the phrase "diversity of sounds" contains the idea of plurality.'—ED.]

38. **open**] CAPELL: What he says of the 'heathen philosopher' is occasion'd by
seeing his hearer stand gaping (as well he might), sometimes looking at him, sometimes the maid; who, says he, is not a grape for your lips. . . . . When the Poet was
writing this speech his remembrance was certainly visited by some other expressions
in *Euphues*. [See Appendix. 'Phœbe is no lettice for your lippes, and her grapes
hang so high, that gaze at them you may, but touch them you cannot.']

Clo. Giue me your hand : Art thou Learned ?   41
Will. No fir.
Clo. Then learne this of me, To haue, is to haue. For
it is a figure in Rhetoricke, that drink being powr'd out
of a cup into a glaffe, by filling the one, doth empty the   45
other. For all your Writers do confent, that *ipfe* is hee :
now you are not *ipfe*, for I am he.
Will. Which he fir ?
Clo. He fir, that muft marrie this woman : Therefore
you Clowne, abandon : which is in the vulgar, leaue the   50
focietie : which in the boorifh, is companie, of this female : which in the common, is woman : which together, is, abandon the fociety of this Female, or Clowne
thou perifheft : or to thy better vnderftanding, dyeft; or
(to wit) I kill thee, make thee away, tranflate thy life in-   55
to death, thy libertie into bondage : I will deale in poyfon with thee, or in baftinado, or in fteele : I will bandy
with thee in faction, I will ore-run thee with police : I   58

43, 49. Clo.] Col. F$_2$.   Steev.'93, Dyce iii.
54, 55. *or* (*to wit*)] *to wit* Farmer,   58. *police*] *policy* Ff et cet.

---

56. **poyson**] WARBURTON'S far-fetched idea, that ' all this seems an allusion to Sir
Thomas Overbury's affair,' was properly refuted by HEATH, who recalled the date of
Sir Thomas Overbury's ' affair,' which ' did not break out till 1615, long after Shake-
speare had quitted the stage and within a year or a little more of his death.'

57. **bastinado**] WRIGHT : This spelling has been adopted in modern times. But
Cotgrave gives : ' Bastonnade : f. A bastonadoe; a banging or beating with a cudgell.'
Florio (*Ital. Dict.*) has : ' Bastonata, a bastonado, or cudgell blow.'

57. **bandy**] SKEAT : To beat to and fro, to contend. Shakespeare has *bandy*, to
contend, *Tit. And.* I, 312, but the older sense is to beat to and fro, as in *Rom. & Jul.*
II, v, 14. It was a term used at tennis, and was formerly also spelt *band*, as in ' To
band the ball.'—Turberville. The only difficulty is to account for the final -*y ;* I suspect it to be a corruption of the Fr. *bander* (or *bandé*), the Fr. word being taken *as a
whole*, instead of being shortened by dropping -*er* in the usual manner; Fr. ' *bander*, to
bind, fasten with strings; also to *bandie*, at tennis.'—Cotgrave. He also gives : ' Jouer
à *bander* et à racler contre, to *bandy* against, at tennis; and (by metaphor) to pursue
with all insolencie, rigour, extremitie.' Also : ' Se *bander* contre, to *bandie* or oppose
himselfe against, with his whole power; or to ioyne in league with others against.'
Also : ' Ils *se bandent* à faire un entreprise, they are ploting a conspiracie together.'
The word is therefore the same as that which appears as *band*, in the phrase 'to *band*
together.' The Fr. *bander* is derived from the Ger. *band*, a band, a tie, and also
includes the sense of Ger. *bande*, a crew, a gang.

58. **police**] This is one of the many examples in Walker's chapter (*Crit.* ii, 48)
on the confusion of *e* and *ie* final.

will kill thee a hundred and fifty wayes, therefore tremble and depart.   60

   Aud. Do good *William.*

   Will. God reſt you merry ſir.   *Exit*

Enter Corin.

   Cor. Our Maſter and Miſtreſſe ſeekes you : come a-
way, away.   65

   Clo. Trip *Audry*, trip *Audry*, I attend,

I attend.   *Exeunt*   67

Scœna Secunda.

Enter Orlando & Oliuer.

   Orl. Is't poſſible, that on ſo little acquaintance you   2

61. *Do*] *Do*, Rowe.   64. *ſeekes*] F$_2$. *ſeeks* F$_3$F$_4$, Knt, Dyce
62. *you merry*] *you merry,* Rowe et   i, Sta. Cam. Wh. ii. *seek* Rowe et cet.
seq.   66. Audry] F$_2$. Audrey F$_3$F$_4$.

---

   64. seekes] Again that obtrusive *s* to which our attention is so often directed in
the Folio. Whatever it be, a compositor's oversight or a flourish in Shakespeare's
handwriting, it is not, as far as Shakespeare is concerned, 'that figment of the grammarians,' so says Wright in happy phrase, the old Northern plural in *s.* See I, ii, 101.
ABBOTT ingeniously suggests that 'being indicated by a mere line at the end of a
word in MS, it was often confused with the comma, full stop, dash, or hyphen.'—
§ 338. Sometimes, of course, the rhyme shows that it is genuinely present.—ED.

   1. DYCE: Here, perhaps, the Scene ought to be marked: 'Another part of the
Forest. Before a Cottage.'

   2. possible] STEEVENS: Shakespeare, by putting this question into the mouth of
Orlando, seems to have been aware of the impropriety he had been guilty of by deserting his original. In Lodge's *Novel* the elder brother is instrumental in saving Aliena
from a band of ruffians. Without the intervention of this circumstance, the passion
of Aliena appears to be very hasty indeed. BLACKWOOD'S MAGAZINE (April, 1833,
p. 558): Dr Johnson saith: 'I know not how the ladies will approve the facility with
which both Rosalind and Celia give away their hearts. To Celia much may be forgiven for the heroism of her friendship.' The ladies, we are sure, have forgiven
Rosalind. What say they to Celia? They look down, blush, shake head, smile, and
say, ' Celia knew Oliver was Orlando's brother, and in her friendship for Rosalind she
felt how delightful it would be for them two to be sisters-in-law as well as cousins.
Secondly, Oliver had made a narrow escape of being stung by a serpent and devoured
by a lionness, and " pity is akin to love." Thirdly, he had truly repented him of his
former wickedness. Fourthly, 'twas religiously done by him, that settlement of all
the revenue that was old Sir Rowland's upon Orlando. Fifthly, what but true love,

ſhould like her? that, but ſeeing, you ſhould loue her?   3
And louing woo? and wooing, ſhe ſhould graunt? And
will you perſeuer to enioy her?   5

   Ol.   Neither call the giddineſſe of it in queſtion; the
pouertie of her, the ſmall acquaintance, my ſodaine wo-   7

---

5. *perſeuer*] F₂, Cap. Steev. Var. Cald.   Ktly, Huds. Rlfe.   *perſevere* F₃F₄, Rowe
Knt, Coll. i, Sing. Wh. Dyce, Sta. Cam.   +, Mal. Coll. iii.

---

following true contrition, could have impelled him thus to give all up to his younger
brother, and desire to marry Aliena, " who, with a kind of umber, had smirched her
face," a woman low and browner than her brother? Sixthly, " tell me where is fancy
bred?" At the eyes.' Thank thee, *ma douce philosophe.* There is a kiss for thee,
flung off the rainbow of our Flamingo! HARTLEY COLERIDGE (ii, p. 144): I confess I know nothing in Shakespeare so improbable, or, truth to say, so unnatural, as
the sudden conversion of Oliver from a worse than Cain, a coward fratricide in will,
to a generous brother and a romantic lover. Neither gratitude nor love works such
wonders with the Olivers of real life. . . . . Romance is all very well in the Forest of
Arden, but Oliver is made too bad in the first scenes ever to be worthy of Celia, or
capable of inspiring a kindly interest in his reformation. Celia . . . . should at least
have put his repentance on a twelvemonth's trial. But in the Fifth Act ladies have no
time for discretion. SWINBURNE (*A Study*, &c., p. 151): Nor can it well be worth
any man's while to say or to hear for the thousandth time that *As You Like It* would
be one of those works which prove, as Landor said long since, the falsehood of the
stale axiom that no work of man's can be perfect, were it not for that one unlucky slip
of the brush which has left so ugly a little smear on one corner of the canvas as the
betrothal of Oliver to Celia; though with all reverence for a great name and a noble
memory, I can hardly think that matters were much mended in George Sand's adaptation of the play by the transference of her hand to Jaques. Once elsewhere, or
twice only at the most, is any other such sacrifice of moral beauty or spiritual harmony
to the necessities and traditions of the stage discernible in all the world-wide work
of Shakespeare. In the one case it is unhappily undeniable; no man's conscience,
no conceivable sense of right and wrong, but must more or less feel as did Coleridge's
the double violence done it in the upshot of *Meas. for Meas.* Even in the much more
nearly spotless work which we have next to glance at [*Much Ado*], some readers
have perhaps not unreasonably found a similar objection to the final good fortune of
such a pitiful fellow as Count Claudio. It will be observed that in each case the sacrifice is made to comedy. The actual or hypothetical necessity of pairing off all the
couples after such a fashion as to secure a nominally happy and undeniably matrimonial ending is the theatrical idol whose tyranny exacts this holocaust of higher and
better feelings than the more liquorish desire to leave the board of fancy with a palat-
able morsel of cheap sugar on the tongue.

   5. **perseuer**] WRIGHT: The common spelling in Shakespeare's time, the accent
being on the second syllable. The only exception to the uniformity of this spelling,
given by Schmidt (*Lexicon*), is in *Lear*, III, v, 23, where the Qq have *persevere* and
the Ff *persever.* [As is seen by the Text. Notes, this spelling did not last down to
1664.]

   7. **of her**] For other instances of the use of the pronoun for the pronominal adjective, see Abbott, § 225.

ing, nor ſodaine conſenting : but ſay with mee, I loue   8
Aliena : ſay with her, that ſhe loues mee; conſent with
both, that we may enioy each other : it ſhall be to your   10
good : for my fathers houſe, and all the reuennew, that
was old Sir *Rowlands* will I eſtate vpon you, and heere
liue and die a Shepherd.

Enter Roſalind.

Orl.   You haue my conſent.   15
Let your Wedding be to morrow : thither will I
Inuite the Duke, and all's contented followers :
Go you, and prepare *Aliena*; for looke you,
Heere comes my *Roſalinde*.
Roſ.   God ſaue you brother.   20
Ol.   And you faire ſiſter.

---

8. *nor*] Ff, Knt. *nor her* Rowe et cet.
14. Enter...] After line 17, Coll.
After line 19, Dyce.
15–19. As verse, Ff, Rowe, Coll. As
prose, Pope et cet.

17. *all's*] Ff, Rowe, Coll. Wh. Dyce,
Cam. *all his* Pope et cet.
19. [Exit Oliver. Hal.
21. Ol.] Orl. F₃F₄, Rowe i, Hal.
[Exit Oliver. Cap.

---

8. **nor sodaine**] Knight is the solitary editor who retains this reading, which cannot but be a misprint; even with Knight it is apparently an oversight; he has no note
on it, and he rarely fails to plead his loyalty to the Folio. Caldecott, who is a greater
stickler for the Folio than even Knight, here falls into line and prints 'nor *her* sudden.'—ED.

12. **estate**] For other instances of the use of this verb in the sense of *bestow, settle*,
see Schmidt.

21. **faire sister**] JOHNSON: I know not why Oliver should call Rosalind 'sister.'
He takes her yet to be a man. I suppose we should read: 'And you, *and your* fair
sister.' CHAMIER: Oliver speaks to her in the character she had assumed, of a
woman courted by Orlando, his brother. WHITE: Much wonder is expressed as to
how the knowledge of Rosalind's sex, which this reply evinces, was obtained; and
forgetfulness is attributed to Shakespeare. But those who wonder must themselves
forget that since the end of the last Act Oliver has wooed and won Celia; for to suppose that she kept Rosalind's secret from him one moment longer than was necessary
to give her own due precedence, would be to exhibit an ignorance in such matters
quite deplorable. DYCE: To me none of these notes is satisfactory. HALLIWELL:
The words in the text seem, under any explanation, improperly assigned to Oliver,
who had probably taken his departure just previously. All difficulty is obviated by
giving them to Orlando. [But would Rosalind address Orlando as 'brother'?—ED.]
COWDEN-CLARKE: Oliver has a double reason for calling Rosalind 'sister': he calls
her so, because she is the girlish-looking brother of the woman he hopes to marry,
and because she is the youth whom his own brother courts under the name of a
woman. It should be remembered, that in the very first scene where they meet,

Rof. Oh my deere *Orlando*, how it greeues me to fee   22
thee weare thy heart in a fcarfe.

Orl. It is my arme.

Rof. I thought thy heart had beene wounded with   25
the clawes of a Lion.

Orl. Wounded it is, but with the eyes of a Lady

Rof. Did your brother tell you how I counterfeyted
to found, when he fhew'd me your handkercher?

Orl. I, and greater wonders then that.   30

Rof. O, I know where you are: nay, tis true: there
was neuer any thing fo fodaine, but the fight of two
Rammes, and *Cefars* Thrafonicall bragge of I came, faw,
and ouercome. For your brother, and my fifter, no fooner met, but they look'd: no fooner look'd, but they   35
lou'd; no fooner lou'd, but they figh'd: no fooner figh'd

---

29. *found*] F₂F₃, Cald. Knt. *fwound*   32. *fight*] *fight* F₄.
F₄, Rowe. *swoon* Pope et cet.   34. *ouercome*] *ouercame* Ff, Rowe et
          handkercher] F₂F₃, Dyce, Cam.   seq.
handkerchief F₄, Rowe et cet.

Oliver thus addresses her: ' I must bear answer back how you excuse my brother,
Rosalind.' He at once acknowledges the assumed character, humours its assumption
by giving her the name she is supposed to assume, and now follows up this playful
make-believe by giving her the title and relationship she has a claim to, as the feigned
Rosalind. WRIGHT: Oliver enters into Orlando's humour in regarding the apparent
Ganymede as Rosalind. [The explanation of the Cowden-Clarkes and of Wright carry
conviction. Gervinus has here one of those disheartening remarks (in which it must
be sadly confessed he abounds) which reveal his incapacity, partly owing to his
nationality, thoroughly to appreciate Shakespeare. He says (i, 492, ed. 1872), ' Nothing prevents us from so interpreting the action as to see that Orlando, at Oliver's suggestion, after the fainting fit, has detected the disguise of the fair Ganymede, and
suffers him to play the game through to the end only that his joy may not be marred;
if this can be made clear in the performance, the exquisite delicacy (*Feinheit*) of the
play will be extraordinarily increased.'—ED.]

    29. **sound**] See III, v, 19.

    31. **where you are**] WRIGHT: I know what you mean, what you are hinting at.
[Hamlet uses the same phrase, I think, when he says, 'Ah, ha, boy! say'st thou so?
art thou there, true-penny?'—I, v, 150. He does not refer to his father's being in the
' cellarage,' but rather ' is that your meaning? there is need of secresy?'—ED.]

    33. **Thrasonicall**] FARMER (note on *Love's Lab. L.* V, i, 14): The use of this
word is no argument that our author had read [the *Eunuchus* of] Terence. It was
introduced to our language long before Shakespeare's time. MALONE: It is found in
Bullokar's *Expositor*, 1616. HALLIWELL: Stanyhurst, 1582, writes: ' Linckt was in
wedlock a loftye Thrasonical huf snuffe '—[p. 143, ed. Arber]. Compare, also,
Orlando Furioso, 1594: ' Knowing him to be a Thrasonical madcap,' &c.

but they ask'd one another the reaſon : no ſooner knew   37
the reaſon, but they ſought the remedie : and in theſe
degrees, haue they made a paire of ſtaires to marriage,
which they will climbe incontinent, or elſe bee inconti-   40
nent before marriage; they are in the verie wrath of
loue, and they will together. Clubbes cannot part
them.

Orl. They ſhall be married to morrow : and I will
bid the Duke to the Nuptiall. But O, how bitter a thing   45
it is, to looke into happines through another mans eies :
by ſo much the more ſhall I to morrow be at the height
of heart heauineſſe. by how much I ſhal thinke my brother happie, in hauing what he wiſhes for.   49

46, 47. *eies : by*] *eyes ! By* Cap. et seq.

---

39. **degrees**] COWDEN-CLARKE: Used here in its original sense as derived from the Latin *gradus*, and French *degrè*, a step; which affords the pun with the word 'stairs' immediately after.

39. **paire of staires**] H. C. HART (*New Sh. Soc. Trans.* 1877–9, Pt. iii, p. 471) believes that in this phrase there lurks an allusion to wedlock which time has lost; it reappears in the phrase 'below stairs' (*Much Ado*, V, ii, 10), in which, Hart says, 'there is always some hidden meaning'; in proof whereof he brings forward several examples from Jonson and Chapman. It is more than likely that he is right in regard to the phrase 'below stairs,' which cannot always be explained by reference to the servants' hall. But in the present passage the simile is so clear, that though some allusion may be hid in it, we scarcely feel the lack of our knowledge of it.—ED.

40. **incontinent**] CALDECOTT: Without restraint or delay, immediately.

42. **Clubbes**] MALONE: It appears from many of our old dramas that it was a common custom, on the breaking out of a fray, to call out 'Clubs ! clubs !' to *part* the combatants. So in *Tit. And.* II, i, 37 : 'Clubs, clubs ! these lovers will not keep the peace.' The words 'they are in the very *wrath* of love' show that our author had this in contemplation. MASON: So in *Henry VIII:* V, iv, 53 : 'I missed the meteor once, and hit that woman; who cried out "Clubs !" when I might see from far some forty truncheoners draw to her succour.' KNIGHT (Note on *Rom. & Jul.* I, i, 66) : Scott has made the cry familiar to us in *The Fortunes of Nigel.* 'The great long club,' as described by Stow, on the necks of the London apprentices, was as characteristic as the flat cap of the same quarrelsome body in the days of Elizabeth and James. DYCE: 'Clubs' was originally the popular cry to call forth the London apprentices, who employed their clubs for the preservation of the public peace; sometimes, however, they used these weapons to raise a disturbance, as they are described as doing [in the foregoing example from *Henry VIII.*].

45. **Nuptiall**] WRIGHT: The plural form, which is now the prevailing one, is used only twice by Shakespeare : in *Per.* V, iii, 80 and in *Oth.* II, ii, 9. In the latter passage the Ff have the singular, while the Qq read *nuptialls.* [In *Mid. N. D.* V, i, 75, the First Folio has the singular, while the three later Ff have the plural, as noted by Schmidt.]

Rof. Why then to morrow, I cannot ferue your turne   50
for *Rofalind?*

Orl. I can liue no longer by thinking.

Rof. I will wearie you then no longer with idle talking. Know of me then (for now I fpeake to fome purpofe) that I know you are a Gentleman of good conceit: 55
I fpeake not this, that you fhould beare a good opinion
of my knowledge : infomuch (I fay) I know you arc:nei-
ther do I labor for a greater efteeme then may in fome
little meafure draw a beleefe from you, to do your felfe
good, and not to grace me. Beleeue then, if you pleafe,   60
that I can do ftrange things : I haue fince I was three
yeare olde conuerft with a Magitian, moft profound in   62

57. *I know you*] *I know what you*   62. *yeare*] F_2. years F_4, Rowe+,
Rowe+.   Steev. Mal. Coll. Sing. Ktly. *year* F_3,
    arc] F_1.   Cap. et cet.

54–57. **Know . . . arc**] WHITER (p. 58): This thought we find in *Ham.* V, ii,
134: '*Osric.* You are not ignorant of what excellence Laertes is. *Ham.* I dare not
confess that, lest I should compare with him in excellence; but, to know a man well,
were to know himself.'

55. **conceit**] SCHMIDT: Rosalind says this to Orlando in order to convince him
of her pretended knowledge of mysteries. It cannot therefore be equivalent to a
gentleman of good parts, of wit; for there 'needs no magician to tell her this.'
[Schmidt's definition, therefore, of "conceit' in this passage (and his note in his
translation (p. 461) is substantially the same) is 'extraction, birth,' but he indicates
his doubt of its correctness by placing after 'birth' an interrogation-mark. In this
instance, as elsewhere, there are indications, I think, that Schmidt held, and deservedly held, Heath in high regard; but here, however, I am afraid Heath led him
slightly astray. Heath's definition of 'conceit' here is, 'of good estimation and
rank.'—ED.] CRAIK (*Jul. Cæs.* I, iii, 142): To *conceit* is another form of our still
familiar *conceive.* And the noun 'conceit,' which survives with a limited meaning (the conception of a man by himself, which is so apt to be one of over-estima-
tion), is also frequent in Shakespeare, with the sense, nearly, of what we now call
conception, in general. Sometimes it is used in a sense which might almost be said
to be the opposite of what it now means; as when Juliet employs it as the term to
denote her all-absorbing affection for Romeo, II, v, 30. Or as Gratiano uses it in
Mer. of Ven. I, i, 102, that is, in the sense of *deep thought.* So, again, when Rosaline, in *Love's Lab. L.* II, i, speaking of Biron, describes his 'fair tongue' as 'conceit's expositor,' all that she means is that speech is the expounder of thought. The
scriptural expression, still in familiar use, 'wise in his own conceit,' means merely
wise in his own thought or in his own eyes, as we are told in the margin the Hebrew
literally signifies. WRIGHT: Of good intelligence or mental capacity. Shakespeare
never uses the word in its modern sense.

62. **yeare**] WRIGHT: F_4 had already 'years,' or the change would have been
made by Pope, on the ground that the singular was vulgar. See III, ii, 307.

his Art, and yet not damnable. If you do loue *Rofalinde*   63
fo neere the hart, as your gefture cries it out: when your
brother marries *Aliena*, fhall you marrie her. I know in-   65
to what ftraights of Fortune fhe is driuen, and it is not
impoffible to me, if it appeare not inconuenient to you,
to fet her before your eyes to morrow, humane as fhe is,
and without any danger.

   Orl.   Speak'ft thou in fober meanings?   70
   Rof.   By my life I do, which I tender deerly, though

---

63. *Art*] *heart* F₄.   65. *fhall you*] F₂. *you fhall* F₃F₄,
64. *cries it*] *cryeth* Cap. conj.   Rowe+, Steev.
                                   70. *meanings*] *meaning* Dyce iii.

---

   64. **gesture**] Bearing.

   68. **humane**] JOHNSON: That is, not a phantom, but the real Rosalind, without
any of the danger generally conceived to attend the rites of incantation.

   FLETCHER (p. 224) [on ll. 53–69]: Here we have another of those exquisite passages which no masculine hand but Shakespeare's could ever write, and which so
charmingly betray to the auditor the delicate woman under her masculine garb. It is
pretty to contrast the rapid, pointed volubility of Rosalind, so long as Orlando's courtship
is carried on in seeming jest, with the circumlocutory manner in which, speaking now,
as she says, 'to some purpose,' she announces to him that he shall so soon be married
if he will. . . . . Every female reader, and especially every female auditor, if the
actress's own instinct lead her aright, will well understand this delicately-rendered
coyness of the speaker in approaching seriously so decisive a declaration to her lover,
even under the mask of her fictitious personation.

   70. **meanings**] Again the superfluous *s* which Walker (*Crit.* i, 248) detected, and
Dyce (ed. iii) at once erased.

   71. **deerly**] STEEVENS: It was natural for one who called herself a magician to
allude to the danger [to her life from the Acts of Parliament] in which her avowal,
had it been a serious one, would have involved her. [Warburton inferred from this
allusion that this play 'was written in James's time, when there was a severe inquisi-
tion after witches and magicians.' But Malone, having shown that the play was
entered on the Stationers' Registers as early as 1600, it followed that there could be
here no allusion to the Act of James, but if there be an allusion at all, it must be to
the Act then in force, which was passed under Elizabeth; this Act is thus cited, with
an abstract, by] WRIGHT: By 5 Eliza. cap. 16, 'An Act agaynst Conjuracons,
Inchantmentes, and Witchecraftes,' it was enacted that all persons using witchcraft,
&c., whereby death ensued, should be put to death without benefit of clergy. If the
object of the witchcraft were to cause bodily harm, the punishment was, for the first
offence, one year's imprisonment and pillory; and for the second, death. To use
witchcraft for the purpose of discovering treasure or to provoke unlawful love was an
offence punishable upon the first conviction with a year's imprisonment and pillory,
and upon the second with imprisonment for life and forfeiture of goods. This Act
was repealed by another, 1 Jac. I, cap. 12, which was even more severe. By this any
one invoking or consulting with evil spirits and practising witchcraft was to be put to
death; and for attempting by means of conjurations to discover hidden treasure or to

   17

I fay I am a Magitian : Therefore put you in your beft a-   72
ray, bid your friends : for if you will be married to morrow, you fhall : and to *Rofalind* if you will.

Enter Siluius & Phebe.   75

Looke, here comes a Louer of mine, and a louer of hers.

Phe.   Youth, you haue done me much vngentleneffe,
To fhew the letter that I writ to you.

Rof.   I care not if I haue : it is my ftudie
To feeme defpightfull and vngentle to you :   80
you are there followed by a faithful fhepheard,
Looke vpon him, loue him : he worfhips you.

Phe. Good fhepheard, tell this youth what 'tis to loue

Sil.   It is to be all made of fighes and teares,
And fo am I for *Phebe.*   85

Phe.   And I for *Ganimed.*

Orl.   And I for *Rofalind.*

Rof.   And I for no woman.

Sil.   It is to be all made of faith and feruice,
And fo am I for *Phebe.*   90

Phe.   And I for *Ganimed.*

Orl.   And I for *Rofalind.*

Rof.   And I for no woman.

Sil.   It is to be all made of fantafie,
All made of paffion, and all made of wifhes,   95
All adoration, dutie, and obferuance,

---

72. *put you in*] *put you on* Rowe +, Steev. '85.

75. Scene III. Pope, Han. Warb. Johns.
    Enter...] After line 76, Cap. Dyce, Sta.

84. *all made*] F_2.   *made all* F_3F_4, Rowe +, Steev. '85.

89. *all made*] *made all* Rowe +, Steev. '85.

96. *obferuance*] *obferbance* F_2. *obedience* Coll. (MS) ii, iii, Wh. i, Dyce, Rlfe.

---

procure unlawful love the punishment was one year's imprisonment and pillory for the first offence, and for the second, death.

73. **bid**] More than one editor has thought it best to explain the meaning of this word here and in line 45. But surely the New Testament has made us all familiar with it.—ED.

76. **comes**] See I, ii, 113.

82. **vpon him**] Abbott, § 483, calls attention to the emphasis thrown by the rhythm on this 'him.'

94. **fantafie**] CRAIK (*Jul. Cæs.* p. 167): That is, fancy or imagination, with its unaccountable anticipations and apprehensions, as opposed to the calculations of reason. [See II, iv, 32.]

All humbleneſſe, all patience, and impatience,   97
All puritie, all triall, all obſeruance:
And ſo am I for *Phebe*.

   Phe. And ſo am I for *Ganimed*.   100
   Orl. And ſo am I for *Roſalind*.
   Roſ. And ſo am I for no woman.
   Phe. If this be ſo, why blame you me to loue you?
   Sil. If this be ſo, why blame you me to loue you?   104

98. *obſeruance*] *obedience* Mal. conj.   103. [To Ros.] Pope et seq.
Rann. *endurance* Harness conj. Sing.   104. [To Phe.] Pope et seq.
Ktly, Huds.

98. **all obſeruance**] RITSON: Read *obeisance*. HEATH (p. 153): As the word
'observance' had been already employed but two lines before, might not the poet possibly have written in this place 'all *perseverance*,' which follows very aptly after 'trial'?
CAPELL approves of this emendation of Heath's, and calls attention to the accent,
which is persévérance; RANN adopted it. MALONE: I suspect our author wrote:
'all *obedience*.' HARNESS: Perhaps *endurance* might be more in harmony with the
context; SINGER adopted it; and of it COLLIER (ed. ii) says: 'It may be a very
good word, but it is not Shakespeare's; he uses it only twice in his thirty-seven plays,
and then not as applied to the sufferings of a lover; whereas he has "obedience" in
fifty places.' According to Collier's 'old corrector' it is the preceding 'observance'
in line 96 that is wrong, and that 'observance' was changed by him into *obedience*,
'which,' adds Collier, 'more properly follows "duty" than "trial."' This *obedience*
WHITE also adopted, because: 'Obedience to the wishes of the beloved is one of the
first fruits and surest indices of love, one which in such an enumeration could not be
passed over; and yet according to the text of the Folio it is not mentioned, while
"observance" is specified twice in three lines. Such a repetition is not in Shakespeare's manner, for although he had peculiarities, senseless iteration was not one of
them.' In his second edition White returns to the Folio with the remark that although
'the word is corrupt, no acceptable substitute has been suggested.' WALKER (*Crit.*
i, 280) thinks Ritson's conjecture preferable. [The CAMBRIDGE EDITION records
'*deservance*, Nicholson conj.' Whether or not this conjecture is elsewhere in print, I
do not know, nor who is the Nicholson. If it be Dr Brinsley Nicholson, the conjecture is worthy of all respect, as any conjecture from that source always is. We
shall all agree, I think, that one of these two 'observances' must be wrong; for two
reasons it is more likely to be the second than the first: where it occurs in line 96 it
is 'appropriately associated,' WRIGHT says, 'with adoration and duty;' to 'observe'
meant to 'regard with respectful attention,' as where Hamlet is spoken of as 'the
observed of all observers'; this usage lasted even to Milton's time; in *Par. Lost*
(xi, 817) Noah is spoken of as 'the one just man of God *observed*.' Secondly,
there is the compositor's common error of repetition. Of the substitutes that have
been proposed, I think the weight of probability lies with *obedience*, not alone on the
score of propriety, but on account of the *ductus literarum*, wherein it much resembles
'observance.'—ED.]

103, &c. **to loue**] The infinitive is here used as we have had it several times before
in this play. We should now use the participle with *for* or *in*. See I, i, 109.

Orl.   If this be fo, why blame you me to loue you?   105
Rof.   Why do you fpeake too, Why blame you mee
to loue you.

Orl.   To her, that is not heere, nor doth not heare.

Rof.   Pray you no more of this, 'tis like the howling
of Irifh Wolues againft the Moone : I will helpe you   110
if I can : I would loue you if I could : To morrow meet
me altogether : I wil marrie you, if euer I marrie Woman, and Ile be married to morrow : I will fatisfie you,
if euer I fatisfi'd man, and you fhall bee married to morrow.   I wil content you, if what pleafes you contents   115
you, and you fhal be married to morrow : As you loue
Rofalind meet, as you loue *Phebe* meet, and as I loue no   117

106. *Why...too*] Ff, Cald. Coll. i, Dyce, Wright, Rlfe. *Whom...to* Sing. *Who... to*, Rowe et cet.

111. *can*] *can* [To Orl.] Johns. *can* [To Sil.] Cap. et seq.
could] *could* [To Phe.] Johns. et seq.

112. *altogether*] *all together* Rowe et seq.

113. *to morrow*] *tomorrow* [To Phe.] Pope et seq.

114. *to morrow*] *tomorrow* [To Orl.] Pope et seq.
fatisfi'd] *satisfy* Douce, Dyce iii, Huds.

116. *to morrow*] *tomorrow* [To Sil.] Pope et seq.

117. Rofalind] *Rosalind* [To Orl.] Johns. et seq.
Phebe *meet*] *Phebe meet* [To Sil.] Johns. et seq.

106. **Why . . . too**] COLLIER (ed. i) : This reading is perfectly intelligible when addressed to Orlando, who replies that he speaks *too*, notwithstanding the absence of his mistress.   If altered, it need not be altered, as by the modern editors, to bad English : '*Who* do you speak to?'   COLLIER (ed. ii) : Here again we follow the (MS), the old text being : 'Why do you speak too?'   The grammar is defective, according to the strictness of modern rules, but perfectly intelligible, and no doubt what Shake-peare wrote : '*Whom* do you,' &c. is a modern colloquial refinement.   [I cannot see the trace of a sufficient reason for deserting the Folio.—ED.]

110. **Irish Wolues**] MALONE : This is borrowed from Lodge's *Novel :* 'I tell thee, Montanus, in courting Phœbe, thou barkest with the wolves of Syria against the moone.' [See Appendix.]   CALDECOTT : That is, the same monotonous chime weari-somely and sickeningly repeated.   In the passage to which Malone refers it imports an aim at impossibilities, a sense, which, whatever may be Rosalind's meaning, can-not very well be attached to it here.   WRIGHT : In Ireland wolves existed as late as the beginning of the last century.   Spenser, in his *View of the Present State of Ire-land* (p. 634, Globe ed.), mentions some of the Irish superstitions connected with the wolf.   [The clue to this allusion is probably lost.   There were wolves in England which presumably howled against the moon quite as monotonously or dismally as in Ireland.   We know well that a wolf 'behowled the moon' on one certain Midsum-mer's Night.   But these are Irish wolves—can there be an adumbration of the Irish wailings?   The loan from Lodge, which Malone alleges, is not so manifest.   It is a far cry, or, rather, a far 'bark,' from Syria to Ireland, and, as Caldecott says, the two phrases are dissimilar in meaning.—ED.]

woman, Ile meet : ſo fare you wel : I haue left you com-   118
mands.

Sil.   Ile not faile, if I liue.   120

Phe.   Nor I.

Orl.   Nor I.   *Exeunt.*   122

Scœna Tertia.

Enter Clowne and Audrey.

Clo.   To morrow is the ioyfull day *Audrey*, to morrow
will we be married.

Aud.   I do deſire it with all my heart: and I hope it is
no diſhoneſt deſire, to deſire to be a woman of y̐ world?   5
Heere come two of the baniſh'd Dukes Pages.

Enter two Pages.

1. *Pa.*   Wel met honeſt Gentleman.

Clo.   By my troth well met : come, ſit, ſit, and a ſong.

2. *Pa.*   We are for you, ſit i'th middle.   10

1. *Pa.*   Shal we clap into't roundly, without hauking,

Scene IV. Pope, Han. Warb. Johns.   5. *world ?*] F₂F₃. *world.* F₄ et seq.
1, &c. Clowne] Touchstone Mal. et   10. *you, ſit*] *you.* *Sit* Johns. et seq.
seq.   (subs.).

---

118. **you commands**] ALLEN (MS) : I suspect that the compositor has left out
your here as a repetition : ' I have left you your commands,' just as an officer would
now say : ' I have given you your orders.'

5. **dishonest**] As we have had ' honest ' in the sense of *chaste* in I, ii, 38 ; III, ii,
15, so here ' dishonest ' means *unchaste*. WRIGHT : In ' the character of the persons '
prefixed to Ben Jonson's *Every Man out of his Humour*, Fallace is described : ' She
dotes as perfectly upon the courtier, as her husband doth on her, and only wants the
face to be dishonest.'

5. **world**] STEEVENS : To go to the world is *to be married.* So in *Much Ado*, II,
i, 331 : ' Thus goes every one to the world but I. . . . . I may sit in a corner and cry
heigh-ho for a husband !' WHITER : So also in *All's Well*, I, iii, 20 : ' If I may
have your Ladyship's good will to go to the world.' [Dyce defines it ' to commence
housekeeper,' which is good as a hint of what, it may be presumed, is the origin of the
phrase : when a young couple married and set up for themselves, they really entered
the world and its ways for the first time.—ED.]

10. **sit i'th middle**] DINGELSTEDT (p. 234) : This is clearly a reference to an
old English proverb [*Sprichwort*] : ' hey diddle diddle, fool in the middle.' [See
Roffe's note below, on line 16.]

11. **clap into't**] SCHMIDT : To enter upon, to begin with alacrity and briskness.
Thus, *Meas. for Meas.* IV, iii, 43 : ' I would desire you to clap into your prayers ; for,

or ſpitting, or ſaying we are hoarſe, which are the onely   12
prologues to a bad voice.

 2. *Pa.*   I faith, y'faith, and both in a tune like two
gipſies on a horſe.   15

Song.

It was a Louer, and his laſſe,
*   With a hey, and a ho, and a hey nonino,*
*   That o're the greene corne feild did paſſe,*   19

---

12. *the onely*] *only the* Cap. conj.   18, 20, 21. As two lines each, Cap.
Huds.   *your only* Wh. i.   19. *feild*] F₂.

---

look you, the warrant's come'; *Much Ado*, III, iv, 44 : ' Clap's into " Light o' Love,"
that goes without a burden.'

   12. **the onely**] WHITE (ed. i) : Hawking and spitting are often only the prologues
to a bad voice ; but no one . . . . can consider them the *only* premonitory symptoms
of that inflection, and it does not appear that ' the only ' was an old idiom for *only
the.*   *Your only*, meaning the chief, the principal, was, however, an idiom in common
use ; and it seems plain that it is here intended, the printer having mistaken yʳ for yᵉ.
WHITE (ed. ii) : ' The only,' as if without ' the ' ; only prologues.   [See I, ii, 185.]

   14, 15. **a tune . . . a horse**] That is, one.   Compare ' Doth not rosemary and
Romeo both begin with a letter.'—*Rom. & Jul.* II, iv, 188.

   16. **Song**] The music, with the words, which is here reprinted is taken from Chappell's *Popular Music of the Olden Time*, p. 205.   The transposition of the stanzas
which we find here was also independently made by Dr JOHNSON, who says that it
had been also ' made by Dr Thirlby in a copy containing some notes on the margin '
which Dr Johnson had ' perused by the favour of Sir Edward Walpole.'   Malone's
slighting remark (in reference to Steevens's conjecture), that ' the passage does not
deserve much consideration,' is expanded by Tieck into a very positive sneer.   ' It is
not impossible,' says TIECK (p. 212), ' that the arrangement of the stanzas of this
utterly silly ditty may have been intentionally adopted in the Folio to produce this
confused effect.'—ED.   CHAPPELL : [This Song is taken] from a Qto MS, which
has successively passed through the hands of Mr Cranston, Dr John Leyden, and Mr
Heber ; and is now in the Advocates' Library, Edinburgh.   It contains about thirty-
four songs with words (among them the ' Farewell, dear love,' quoted in *Twelfth
Night*), and sixteen song and dance tunes without.   The latter part of the MS, which
bears the name of a former proprietor, William Stirling, and the date of May, 1639,
consists of Psalm Tunes, evidently in the same handwriting, and written about the
same time as the earlier portion. . . . . The words used here are printed from the MS
in the Advocates' Library.

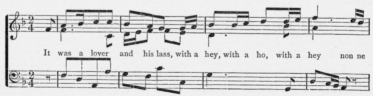

It was a lover   and his lass, with a hey, with a ho, with a hey   non ne

[Song]

no, And a hey . . . non ne no ni no. That o'er the green corn-field did pass In

spring time, in spring time, in spring time; The only pretty ring time, When birds do sing, Hey

ding a ding a ding, Hey ding a ding a ding, Hey ding a ding a ding, Sweet lovers love the spring.

[In the words which accompany the music, as given by Chappell, the chiefest variations are '*ring* tune' instead of '*rang* tune'; line 23 reads: 'Then, *pretty lovers*,
take the time'; line 29 is: 'These pretty country *fools did* lie'; and line 33: 'How
that life was but a flower.'] KNIGHT: It seems quite clear that this manuscript cannot have been written later than sixteen years after the publication of the present play,
and may have existed at a much earlier period; it is, therefore, not straining probability too hard to suppose that this air was, in some form,—most likely as a duet, unless
the two Pages sang in unison,—performed in the play, either as it was originally acted
or not long after its production. ROFFE (p. 16): Mr Linley has set this poem as a
duet for the two Pages; it occurs to me as being very possible that Shakespeare con-
templated a trio between the Pages and Touchstone, who, it may be observed, is the
first to ask for a song, and upon the Pages making ready to comply, Touchstone is
requested to 'sit i' the middle.' It might also strike many that, granting Touchstone
and the Pages personated by competent vocalists, the dramatic effect of a trio would
be very superior to that of a duett. Should an objection be raised to this view,
grounded upon the Pages' ideas as to 'clapping into it roundly,' '*both* in a tune,' that
objection, even if allowed, would not necessarily shut Touchstone out from joining in *the
three lines common to every verse*, and beginning at ' In the pretty spring-time.' It would
be most highly natural, as well as dramatically effective, that Touchstone should do so.

18. WRIGHT: In the Preface to his *Ghostly Psalms*, Coverdale (*Remains*, p. 537,
Parker Soc.) refers to these meaningless burdens of songs: 'And if women, sitting
at their rocks, or spinning at the wheels, had none other songs to pass their time
withal, than such as Moses' sister, Glehana's [Elkanah's] wife, Debora, and Mary the
mother of Christ, have sung before them, they should be better occupied than with
hey nony, nony, hey troly loly and such like phantasies.' [In serious poetry, Sir
Philip Sidney reached, I think, the extreme limit in the use of 'such like phantasies,'
when he bequeathed to us the following stanza: 'Fa la la leridan, dan dan dan deridan: ‖ Dan dan dan deridan deridan dei: ‖ While to my mind the outside stood ‖
For messenger of inward good.'—*Arcadia*, p. 486, ed. 1598.—ED.]

In the ſpring time, the onely pretty rang time. 20
When Birds do ſing, hey ding a ding, ding.
Sweet Louers loue the ſpring,
And therefore take the preſent time,
With a hey, & a ho, and a hey nonino,
For loue is crowned with the prime. 25
In ſpring time, &c.

Betweene the acres of the Rie,
With a hey, and a ho, & a hey nonino :
Theſe prettie Country folks would lie.
In ſpring time, &c. 30

This Carroll they began that houre,
With a hey and a ho, & a hey nonino :
How that a life was but a Flower,
In ſpring time, &c.

Clo. Truly yong Gentlemen, though there vvas no 35
great matter in the dittie, yet ẙ note was very vntunable

20. onely] Om. Rowe ii+, Cap. Steev. '85.

rang] Ff, Rowe i, Cald. *Spring* Rowe ii+, Cap. *rank* Steev. Mal. Var. *ring* Steev. conj. Knt et cet.

23–26. Transposed to follow line 34, Johns. et seq. (except Cald. Knt).

26. In] Ff. *In the* Rowe+, Cap. Steev. Dyce i, Clke.

30, 34. In] *In the* F_3F_4, Rowe+, Cap. Steev. Dyce i, Clke.

31. This] F_2. *The* F_3F_4, Rowe+, Cap. Steev.

32. With a hey] With a hoy F_2.

33. a life] *our life* Han. Coll. ii. *life* Steev. '85.

36. *vntunable*] *untimeable* Theob. Warb. Sing. Wh. Coll. ii, iii, Dyce iii, Huds.

19. W. RIDGEWAY (*The Academy*, 20 Oct. 1883): Is there not here a reference to the ancient system of open-field cultivation? The corn-field being in the singular implies that it is the special one of the common fields which is under corn for the year. The common field being divided into acre-strips by balks of unploughed turf, doubtless on one of these green balks, 'Between the acres of the rye These pretty country folks would lie.'

20. **rang**] STEEVENS: I think we should read '*ring* time,' *i. e.* the aptest season for marriage. WHITER (p. 60): Why may not 'rang time' be written for '*range* time,' the only pleasant time for *straying* or *ranging* about? [The MS in the Advocates' Library confirmed Steevens's conjecture.]

36. **vntunable**] THEOBALD: It is evident, from the sequel of the dialogue, that the poet wrote *untimeable*. *Time* and 'tune' are frequently misprinted for one another in the old editions. [It may be remarked, too, that *time* and *tune* were formerly synonymous.—DYCE, *Strictures*, &c., p. 70.] JOHNSON: This emendation is received, I

1. *Pa.*   you are deceiu'd Sir, we kept time, we loſt not   37
our time.

Clo.   By my troth yes : I count it but time loſt to heare
ſuch a fooliſh ſong.   God buy you, and God mend your   40
voices.   Come *Audrie.*   *Exeunt.*

---

37. *kept*] *keep* F$_3$F$_4$.

40. *buy you*] Ff, Cam.   *b'w'y you*
Rowe +.   *be wi' you* Cap. Mal. Coll. Sta.

be with you Steev. Var. Cald. Knt, Sing.
Ktly.   *b' wi' you* Wh. Dyce, Huds.

---

think very undeservedly, by Dr Warburton.   M. MASON : The reply of the Page
proves to me, beyond any possibility of doubt, that we ought to read *untimeable.*
STEEVENS : The sense seems to be : 'Though the words of the song were trifling, the
music was not (as might have been expected) good enough to compensate their defect.'
CALDECOTT : Though there was so little meaning in the words, yet the music fully
matched it ; the note was as little tuneable.   COLLIER (ed. i) : Touchstone would
hardly say that 'the note' of the song was very *untimeable.*   The Page might mistake the nature of Touchstone's remark, and apply to the time what was meant of
the tune : the clown subsequently hopes that their voices may be mended, in order
that they may sing more tunably.   COLLIER (ed. ii) : Here the (MS) comes materially to our aid ; the printed reading is amended to *untimeable*, which entirely accords
with what follows.   WALKER (*Crit.* i, 295) would retain 'vntunable,' but change
'time' in the Page's reply to *tune.*   WHITE : Shakespeare was a good musician ; and
the answer of the Page and the reply of Touchstone make it plain that [the word is]
untimeable ; otherwise the Page's answer is no reply at all.   In the manuscript of any
period it is very difficult to tell *time* from *tune*, except by the dot of the *i*, so frequently omitted ; and as most people think that to be in tune or out of tune is the
principal success or the principal failure of a musical performance, it is by no means
strange that the word written in the old hand, with the *i* undotted, should be taken
for 'untunable.'   I can speak from experience that in ninety-nine cases out of a hundred in which *time* is written, it will be first put in type as *tune.*   One curious instance
occurs in *King John*, III, iii : 'I had a thing to say, But I will fit it with some better
time.'   The original has 'some better *tune.*'   WRIGHT : Theobald forgot that Touchstone is the speaker.   The Page misunderstands him in order to give him an opening
for another joke.   COWDEN-CLARKE : 'Untunable' was sometimes used in Shakespeare's day for 'out of time' as well as 'out of tune,' and it is probable that pert
Master Touchstone wished to insinuate both defects in the Pages' singing ; while the
First Page defends himself and his fellow-chorister from the more pardonable musical
error of the two.   This may be the better comprehended if it be imagined (as we
always do when we read this amusing little scene, so pointed in satire as it is upon the
affectations of musical amateurs, both performers and listeners) that Touchstone, with
the air of a connoisseur, beats time to the music while the song is proceeding ; which
accounts for the Page's words in answer to the action that preceded the word 'untunable,' and gave it the meaning then often attached to the term.   Be it observed that
the Second Page's words immediately before the song '*both in a tune*,' &c. tend to
show that 'in a *tune*' was sometimes used for 'in *time*' ; as the simile of two fellows
jogging along on the same horse implies measure, rhythm, uniform pace.

Scena Quarta.

*Enter Duke Senior, Amyens, Iaques, Orlan-
do, Oliuer, Celia.*

Du. Sen. Doſt thou beleeue *Orlando*, that the boy
Can do all this that he hath promiſed ?

Orl. I ſometimes do beleeue, and ſomtimes do not,   5
As thoſe that feare they hope, and know they feare.

Scene V. Pope, Han. Warb. Johns.

6. *feare ... feare*] Ff, Rowe, Pope,
Theob. Steev. Var. Rann, Cald. Harness, Coll. i, Sing. Wh. Dyce, Hal.
Sta. Cam. Clke, Neil, Mob. Rlfe. *think
they hope, and know they fear* Han.
fear, they hope, and know they fear
Johns. Mal. *fear their hope, and know
their fear* Heath, Cap. *fear,—they
hope and know they fear* Knt. *fear
to hope, and know they fear* Coll. (MS)
ii, iii, Huds. *fear their hope and hope
their fear* Lettsom, Ktly. *fear with hope,*
and hope with fear or *fear, they hope,
and now they fear* Johns. conj. *feign
they hope, and know they fear* Blackstone. *fear, then hope ; and know, then
fear* Musgrave. *who fearing hope, and
hoping fear* M. Mason. *fear ; they hope,
and know they fear* Henley, J. Hunter.
fear thee, hope, and know thee, fear
Rann. conj. *fear may hope and know
they fear* Harness conj. *fear that they
hope, and know they fear* Jervis. *fain
would hope and know they fear* Cartwright.

1. DYCE: This ought, perhaps, to be marked 'Another part of the Forest. Before
a Cottage.'

6. **As . . . feare**] WARBURTON: This strange nonsense should be read thus: 'As
those that fear *their hap*, and know *their* fear,' *i. e.* As those that fear the issue of a
thing when they know their fear to be well grounded. HEATH (p. 153): I think it
may be better corrected with less alteration, thus: 'As those that fear *their* hope, and
know *their* fear,' *i. e.* As those that fear a disappointment of their hope, whose hope
is dashed and rendered doubtful by their fear, but who are most undoubtedly certain
they fear. MALONE: *As those who fear,—they*, even those very persons, entertain
hopes that their fears will not be realized; *and yet* at the same time they well *know*
that there is reason for *their fears.* CALDECOTT: As those, that under a sad misgiv-
ing entertain a trembling hope, at the same time that they feel real apprehension and
fears. A man might, with propriety, say, I fear I entertain so much hope, as teaches
me I cannot be without fear of disappointment. Orlando says he is like that man.
KNIGHT: That is, those who fear, they, even they, hope, while they know they fear.
COLLIER: Orlando dares not hope that Rosalind will perform her promise, yet hopes
that she will, and knows that he fears she will not. SINGER: As those who are
alarmed at their own tendency to be sanguine (fear that they are harbouring secret
hopes which will lead to disappointment), and are quite aware that they fear. Hope
and Fear alternating, they are not quite certain whether they hope, but *fear* they do.
They fear, because to hope is imprudent :—they are quite certain that they fear. DYCE
(ed. i): I believe that the line now stands as Shakespeare wrote it. WHITE: As

Enter Rosalinde, Siluius, & Phebe.   7

Rof. Patience once more, whiles our cõpact is vrg'd:
You fay, if I bring in your *Rofalinde*,
You wil beftow her on *Orlando* heere?   10

  Du. Se. That would I, had I kingdoms to giue with hir.
  Rof. And you fay you wil haue her, when I bring hir?
  Orl. That would I, were I of all kingdomes King.
  Rof. You fay, you'l marrie me, if I be willing.
  Phe. That will I, fhould I die the houre after.   15
  Rof. But if you do refufe to marrie me,
You'l giue your felfe to this moft faithfull Shepheard.
  Phe. So is the bargaine.
  Rof. You fay that you'l haue *Phebe* if fhe will.   19

8. cõpact] *compact* Ff.
  vrg'd] *heard* Coll. (MS).
9. [To the Duke] Rowe et seq. (except Cap. Cam. Wh. ii, Rlfe).
11, 12. hir] F₂. *her* F₃F₄.

12. [To Orl.] Rowe et seq. (except Cap. Cam. Wh. ii, Rlfe).
14. [To Phe.] Rowe et seq. (except Cap. Cam. Wh. ii, Rlfe).
19. [To Sil.] Rowe et seq. (except Cap. Cam. Wh. ii, Rlfe).

those who are apprehensive that they are deceiving themselves by indulging a secret hope, although they know they fear the issue,—a state of mind in which few readers of Shakespeare can have failed to be at some time. Apology is surely necessary for offering even a paraphrastic explanation of so simple a passage. HALLIWELL: As those that fear what they hope, and know very well they fear a disappointment. STAUNTON: This line, not without reason, has been suspected of corruption. . . . . A somewhat similar form of expression is found in *All's Well*, II, ii: 'But know I think, and think I know most sure.' KEIGHTLEY: Coleridge thus expresses the same thought: 'And Fears self-willed, that shunned the eye of Hope; And Hope that scarce would know itself from Fear.' COWDEN-CLARKE: Those who dread that they may be hoping without foundation, knowing that they really fear. MOBERLY: Of the many conjectures for the emendation of this passage the most likely is Johnson's [qu. Heath's?]: 'As they who fear their hope and know their fear.' HUDSON: As those that fear lest they may believe a thing because they wish it true, and at the same time know that this fear is no better ground of action than their hope. Who has not sometime caught himself in a similar perplexity of hope and fear? WRIGHT: Who are so diffident that they even hope fearfully, and are only certain that they fear. ROLFE: Whose hopes are mingled with fear, and only their fears certain. [In the preceding notes, it is pleasing to observe, in the general interpretation of the meaning, such a remarkable unanimity.—ED.]

8. cõpact] See Abbott, § 490, for a long list of words, chiefly derived from the Latin, where the accent is nearer the end than with us.

8. vrg'd] COLLIER: The (MS) has *heard* for 'urg'd,' and the ear may have misled the scribe or the printer; but as 'urg'd' sufficiently well answers the purpose, we refrain from making any change. DYCE: *Heard* is unnecessary, not to say, foolish.

Sil. Though to haue her and death, were both one   20
thing.

Roſ. I haue promis'd to make all this matter euen :
Keepe you your word, O Duke, to giue your daughter,
You yours *Orlando*, to receiue his daughter :
Keepe you your word *Phebe*, that you'l marrie me,   25
Or elſe refuſing me to wed this ſhepheard :
Keepe your word *Siluius*, that you'l marrie her
If ſhe refuſe me, and from hence I go
To make theſe doubts all euen.   *Exit Roſ. and Celia.*   29

---

22. *I haue*] *I've* Pope+, Dyce iii,
Huds.

25. *you*] Om. Rowe+, Cap. Steev.

Mal. Sing. Cam. Ktly, Dyce iii, Huds.
Rlfe, Wh. ii.

29. *euen*] *even—even so* Coll. (MS) ii,
iii.

---

22. **euen**] SCHMIDT : That is, plain, smooth. Compare what the Doctor says of Lear, ''tis danger to make him even o'er the time he has lost.' So, too, the last line of this speech of Rosalind's, where Steevens cites : 'yet death we fear That makes these odds all even.'—*Meas. for Meas.* III, i, 41.

25. **Phebe**] Is 'Phebe' a monosyllable or a dissyllable ? A momentous question. If a dissyllable, then we must follow Pope and read : 'Keep your word,' wherein the ictus falls excellently on 'your.' If the present text is to stand, then is 'Phebe' a monosyllable ; as an affectionate abbreviation it seems utterly out of place in Rosalind's mouth. See IV, iii, 9.—ED.

25, 26. **that you'l . . . to wed**] ABBOTT, § 416 : Just as *that* is sometimes omitted and then inserted to connect a distant clause with a first part of a sentence, so sometimes 'to' is inserted apparently for the same reason. Here 'to' might be omitted, or ['you'll'] might be inserted instead, but the omission would create ambiguity, and the insertion be a tedious repetition. See III, ii, 152, 153.

29. COLLIER : The line is deficient, and we may be confident, from the rhyme, if from nothing else, that the speech of the heroine was originally thus concluded : ' To make these doubts all even—even so.' [This is one of the class of changes in Shakespeare's text which, I am sure, aroused the sharpest antagonism to Collier's old corrector's emendations,—an antagonism which, when once started, quickly spread to all the other emendations from the same source. It is one thing to change the words we have before us, but it is another, and a very different thing, to add words entirely new. In the one case we are groping after Shakespeare's genuine words which we know stood there. But in the other case we are asked to accept words, and phrases, and even whole lines, which could not possibly have been written on the margin of Collier's Second Folio until after Shakespeare had been sixteen years in his grave. Before giving these additions place in Shakespeare's text we must have some plainer plea for them than mere propriety. The gulf which separates this class and Shakespeare's hand is impassable. All other changes may be tried on their merits ; the question of ' forgery ' (a most disagreeable word, even to write) has nothing to do with them. On many grounds I have faith in Collier : first, there is in all of his pleadings that I have read on the subject the quiet breast of truth ; he is never violent,

Du. Sen.   I do remember in this ſhepheard boy,   30
Some liuely touches of my daughters fauour.

Orl.   My Lord, the firſt time that I euer ſaw him,
Me thought he was a brother to your daughrer:
But my good Lord, this Boy is Forreſt borne,
And hath bin tutor'd in the rudiments   35
Of many deſperate ſtudies, by his vnckle,
Whom he reports to be a great Magitian.
          Enter Clowne and Audrey.
Obſcured in the circle of this Forreſt.

Iaq.   There is ſure another flood toward, and theſe   40
couples are comming to the Arke.   Here comes a payre

30. *ſhepheard*] *ſhepherds* F₄.	38. Enter…] After line 43, Dyce.
33. *daughrer*] F₁.	Clowne] Touchstone Mal.
37. *Whom*] *Who* F₃F₄, Rowe i.	40. Scene VI. Pope, Han. Warb.
Magitian.] Ff.	Johns.

---

nor, when severe, abusive; secondly, he had not the ability, the natural gifts, as he himself urged, to devise so vast a number of corrections; in none of his previous editings, and they are voluminous, did he give promise of that fertility of conjecture or of emendation which the old corrector displays on every page; and thirdly, and mainly (a ground any criminal lawyer will immediately appreciate), there is an entire absence of motive.   Dishonesty would have copied out all these emendations, flames would have consumed the original, and the fame fearlessly claimed (and as surely bestowed) as the keenest editor Shakespeare had ever had.   With such a chance before him of being deemed the author, would a dishonest man be content with the reputation of a mere transcriber?   Does a man 'forge' for the benefit of another who can make him no return?   Does the fame of a mere scribe equal the fame of an author?   Had Collier been dishonest he would have seized the latter.   He openly assumed the former. —ED.]

31. **touches**] CALDECOTT: That is, traits.   See 'the touches dearest priz'd.'— III, ii, 151.   WRIGHT: As Orlando does not recognise Rosalind in her disguise, it is not surprising that her father fails to do so.   But his curiosity is excited, and the inquiries which must certainly have followed upon Orlando's speech are checked by the entry of Touchstone and Audrey.

36. **desperate**] ALLEN (MS): Magical studies (sorcery, &c.) were supposed to be pursued by men who had made a league with the Devil, and who had, therefore, already *despaired of,* or renounced, their salvation; that is, they would not, unless they had already come to despair of their salvation, have made a league with the Enemy of mankind.   Cf. *Friar* Bacon, for the union of 'religion' and magic.   Observe, too, this is Orlando's statement; Rosalind says the 'magician was most profound in his art, and *yet not damnable.*'—V, ii, 62.   [Prospero, in the Epilogue to *The Tempest,* says, as a magician, that his 'ending is despair.'   Schmidt interprets it as 'forbidden by law,' which is, I think, far afield.—ED.]

40. **toward**] Compare ' O proud Death, What feast is toward in thine eternal cell.' —*Ham.* V, ii, 375.

of verie ſtrange beaſts, which in all tongues, are call'd   42
Fooles.

   Clo. Salutation and greeting to you all.

   Iaq. Good my Lord, bid him welcome : This is the   45
Motley-minded Gentleman, that I haue ſo often met in
the Forreſt: he hath bin a Courtier he ſweares.

   Clo. If any man doubt that, let him put mee to my
purgation, I haue trod a meaſure, I haue flattred a Lady,
I haue bin politicke with my friend, ſmooth with mine   50
enemie, I haue vndone three Tailors, I haue had foure
quarrels, and like to haue fought one.

   Iaq. And how was that tane vp?

   Clo. 'Faith we met, and found the quarrel was vpon
the ſeuenth cauſe.   55

---

  42. *verie ſtrange*] *unclean* Han.   53. *tane*] *ta'en* Rowe.
Warb.

---

  42. verie strange] WARBURTON: What 'strange beasts'! and yet such as have a name in all languages! Noah's ark is here alluded to; into which the *clean* beasts entered by *sevens*, and the *unclean* by *two*, male and female. It is plain then that Shakespeare wrote 'a pair of *unclean* beasts,' which is highly humorous. JOHNSON: 'Strange beasts' are only what we call *odd* animals. WHITE: There were female jesters as well as male, and it is possible that there may be here an allusion to that custom,—Audrey being whimsically supposed by Jaques to have assumed the profession as well as the station of her husband. Else why does he call them a pair of Fools?

  49. measure] MALONE: Touchstone, to prove that he has been a courtier, particularly mentions a 'measure,' because it was a very stately, solemn dance. REED: 'Measures' were performed at court, and at public entertainments of the societies of law and equity at their halls, on particular occasions. It was formerly not deemed inconsistent with propriety even for the gravest persons to join in them; and accordingly at the revels which were celebrated at the Inns of Court it has not been unusual for the first characters in the law to become performers in treading the measures. See Dugdale's *Origines Juridiciales.* Sir John Davies, in his poem called *Orchestra,* 1622, describes them [concluding with]: 'Yet all the feet wherein these measures go, Are only spondees, solemn, grave, and slow.' CHAPPELL (p. 626): The 'measure' was a grave and solemn dance, with slow and measured steps, like the minuet. To *tread* a measure was the usual term, like to *walk* a minuet. [Young Lord Lochinvar has made us familiar enough with the phrase.—ED.]

  52. like] CRAIK (note on 'is like.'—*Jul. Cæs.* I, ii, 175): This form of expression is not quite, but nearly, gone out. ROLFE: It is still vulgarly used, at least in New England.

  53. tane] CALDECOTT: That is, made up. Touchstone presently says, an *if* did it once, 'when seven justices could not *take up* a quarrel.'

  54. was vpon] JOHNSON: It is apparent from the sequel that we must read, 'the quarrel was *not* upon the seventh cause.' MALONE: By 'the seventh cause' Touch-

Iaq.   How feuenth caufe?   Good my Lord, like this   56
fellow.

Du. Se.   I like him very well.

Clo.   God'ild you fir, I defire you of the like : I preffe
in heere fir, amongft the reft of the Country copulatiues   60
to fweare, and to forfweare, according as mariage binds
and blood breakes : a poore virgin fir, an il-fauor'd thing
fir, but mine owne, a poore humour of mine fir, to take
that that no man elfe will : rich honeftie dwels like à mi-
fer fir, in a poore houfe, as your Pearle in your foule oy-   65
fter.

Du. Se.   By my faith, he is very fwift, and fententious.

Clo.   According to the fooles bolt fir, and fuch dulcet
difeafes.   69

---

56. *feuenth*] *the feuenth* F_3F_4, Rowe
+, Coll. i, Dyce iii, Huds.

59. *you of*] *of you* Han. Warb.

61, 62. *binds…breakes*] *bids and blood
bids break* Warb. conj.

65. *foule*] Om. F_3F_4, Rowe i.

---

stone, I apprehend, means the lie seven times removed; *i. e.* ' the retort courteous,'
which is *removed* seven times (counted backwards) from the *lie direct*, the last and
most aggravated species of lie.   See the subsequent note on line 72.

59. **God'ild you**] See III, iii, 69.

59. **desire you of the like**] See I, ii, 53.

60. **copulatiues**] WRIGHT : Who desire to be joined in marriage.   For the force
of the termination *-ive* in Shakespeare see III, ii. 11.

61, 62. **sweare . . . breakes**] HENLEY : A man, by the marriage ceremony,
swears that he will keep only to his wife ; when, therefore, he leaves her for another,
blood breaks his matrimonial obligation, and he is *forsworn*.   [It is a case of respect-
ive construction ; ' to swear ' refers to ' *marriage*,' and ' to forswear ' refers to ' blood.'
Dyce or Schmidt will furnish many examples where ' blood ' means temperament,
passion.—ED.]

62. WEISS (p. 116) : We see Touchstone's good sense, too, in the scene where he
brings his wife into the Duke's company, with such an air of self-possession mixed
with a pleased sense that she is his best joke at the punctilio of fashionable life.

64. **honestie**] Again used as Celia and Audrey have used it before.

67. **swift, and sententious**] CALDECOTT : Prompt and pithy.

68. **fooles**] Another variation in the old copies.   The CAM. ED. here records *foles*
in F_2.   In my copy it is *fooles*.—ED.

68, 69. **dulcet diseases**] JOHNSON : This I do not understand.   For ' diseases '
it is easy to read *discourses ;* but perhaps the fault may lie deeper.   CAPELL : ' Dulcet diseases ' mean wits or witty people ; so call'd because the times were infested
with them ; they and fools—that is, such fools as the speaker—being all their delight.
STEEVENS : Perhaps he calls a proverb a *disease*.   Proverbial sayings may appear to
him the *surfeiting diseases* of conversation.   They are often the plague of commentators.   Dr Farmer would read : ' *in* such dulcet diseases,' *i. e.* in the sweet uneasiness
of love, a time when people usually talk nonsense.   MALONE : Without staying to

Iaq. But for the ſeuenth cauſe. How did you finde   70
the quarrell on the ſeuenth cauſe?

Clo. Vpon a lye, ſeuen times remoued : (beare your   72

---

examine how far the position last advanced is founded on truth, I shall only add that
I believe the text is right, and that this word is *capriciously* used for *sayings*, though
neither in its primary nor figurative sense has it any relation to that word. In *The
Mer. of Ven.* the Clown talks in the same style, but more intelligibly. M. MASON:
For 'diseases' we should probably read *phrases*, unless we suppose that Shakespeare
intended that the Clown should blunder; and Touchstone is not one of his blundering clowns. WRIGHT: The Clown only shares the fate of those, even in modern
times, who use fine phrases without understanding them, and 'for a tricksy word defy
the matter.' WALKER (*Crit.* iii, 64): He is resuming his former speech; point, if
the names be rightly prefixed to the characters: 'as your pearl in your foul oyster;—
Duke Sen. By my faith, he is very swift and sententious. *Touchstone.* According to
the fool's bolt, sir;—and such dulcet diseases— *Jaques.* But, for the seventh cause;
how did you find,' &c. But I have scarcely any doubt that the parts ought to be disposed thus: '—and sententious. *Jaques.* According to the fool's bolt, sir. *Touchstone.* And such dulcet diseases,' &c. [TIESSIN (*Englische Studien*, II, ii, p. 454)
conjectures that possibly Touchstone means to say 'dulcet *diesises*.' It is such fantastic tricks as this which, now and then, Germans will insist upon playing before
high Shakespeare, that make the judicious English critic grieve, and stone his heart
against all foreign meddling with the language of these plays. Schlegel omitted the
phrase, having detected in it,—what no English commentator has detected,—something which, so he says, had better remain untranslated.—ED.]

72. **seuen times remoued**] MALONE: Touchstone here enumerates seven kinds
of lies, from the 'Retort courteous' to the *seventh* and most aggravated species of lie,
which he calls the 'lie direct.' The courtier's answer to his intended affront he
expressly tells us was 'the Retort courteous,' the *first* species of lie. When, therefore, he says that they *found the quarrel* was on 'the lie seven times *removed*,' we
must understand by the latter word, the lie removed seven times, counting backwards,
(as the word *removed* seems to intimate,) from the last and most aggravated species
of lie,—namely, 'the lie direct.' So, in *All's Well:* 'Who hath some four or five
removes come short To tender it herself.' Again, in the play before us: 'Your accent
is something finer than you could purchase in so removed a dwelling,' *i. e.* so *distant*
from the haunts of men. When Touchstone and the courtier met, they found their
quarrel *originated* in the *seventh cause, i. e.* on the *Retort courteous* or the lie *seven
times removed.* In the course of their altercation *after* their meeting, Touchstone did
not dare go further than the sixth species, (counting in regular progression from the
first to the last,) the *lie circumstantial;* and the courtier was afraid to give him the
lie direct; so they parted. In a subsequent enumeration of the degrees of a lie,
Touchstone expressly names the *Retort courteous* as the *first;* calling it, therefore,
here 'the *seventh* cause,' and 'the lie *seven* times removed,' he must mean *distant*
seven times from the most offensive lie, the *lie direct.* There is certainly, therefore,
no need of reading with Dr Johnson in a former passage : 'the quarrel was *not* in the
seventh cause.' [It is, I am afraid, a waste of time to attempt to reconcile any discrepancy in Touchstone's category of lies and causes. There can be no doubt that
his 'Lie circumstantial' was not the seventh cause, although the lie may have been
seven times removed. One single, simple question will, I think, show Malone's fal-

bodie more feeming *Audry*) as thus fir : I did diflike the   73
cut of a certaine Courtiers beard : he fent me word, if I
faid his beard was not cut well, hee was in the minde it   75
was : this is call'd the retort courteous.   If I fent him
word againe, it was not well cut, he wold fend me word   77

---

77. *not*] Om. F₃F₄, Rowe i.

---

lacy. If the Retort courteous be the seventh cause, as he says it is, what was the
eighth cause or the ninth cause, for Touchstone had not exhausted the tale? We may
count the 'lies' backwards, but the 'causes' forwards. And in that case Touchstone's computation of causes is wrong. Halliwell, however, makes him out to be
right.—ED.]   HALLIWELL: In Touchstone's calculation the quarrel really was, or
rather depended upon, the *lie direct*, or the seventh cause. Six previous causes had
passed without a duel; there were six modes of giving the lie, none of which had
been considered sufficient to authorise a combat; but the seventh, the *lie direct*, would
have been the subject of the quarrel, and this is also what is to be understood by a
'lie seven times removed.' The absurdity of the dispute just terminating before the
necessity of fighting had arrived, and of there being two lies of higher intensity than
the *countercheck quarrelsome* 'I lie,' is evidently intentional.

   73. **seeming**] STEEVENS: That is, seemly. 'Seeming' is often used by Shakespeare for *becoming*, or *fairness of appearance*. [But 'seeming' is here used adverbially, and is not 'often' so found.—ED.]   DANIEL (p. 38): No editor, I presume,
would venture to alter 'seeming' in this phrase; but the following passages may suggest a doubt whether we have the right word : 'she, with pretty and with *swimming*
gait.'—*Mid. N. D.* II, ii. 'Where be your ribbands, maids? *Swim* with your
bodies, And carry it sweetly and deliverly.'—Beau. & Fl. *Two Noble Kins.* III, v.
'Carry your body *swimming*.'—Massinger, *The Bondman*, III, iii. 'Come hither,
ladies, carry your bodies *swimming*.'—Massinger, *A Very Woman*, III, v. The following passage from Steele's *Tender Husband*, III, i, may be interesting as showing
the sense in which the phrase was understood at a later period : 'Your arms do but
hang on, and you move upon joints, not with a *swim* of the whole person.' ELZE
(*Sh. Jahrbuch*, xi, 284): To the passages which Daniel has brought forward in support of his brilliant conjecture, another may be added which shows unmistakably
that a 'swimming gait' was a fashion of the day. It is as follows : 'Carry your body
in the *swimming fashion*.'—Chapman, *The Ball*, II, p. 494, ed. Shepherd.

   73. **dislike**] STAUNTON: 'Dislike' here imports not merely the entertaining an
aversion, but the expressing it; so in *Meas. for Meas.* I, ii, 18 : 'I never *heard* any
soldier *dislike* it.' Also in [the passage from] Beau. & Fl. *Queen of Corinth*, IV, i
[quoted by Warburton] : 'has he familiarly Dislik'd your yellow starch? or said your
doublet Was not exactly Frenchified?' [Dyce also gives this especial meaning of
'dislike' here. It escaped Schmidt. The rest of Warburton's quotation from *The
Queen of Corinth*, p. 457, ed. Dyce, which was cited to illustrate, not this word 'dislike,' but Touchstone's degrees of a lie, is as follows : 'has he given the lie In circle,
or oblique, or semi-circle, Or direct parallel? you must challenge him.' See also
Jonson's *Alchemist*, p. 107, ed. Gifford, where the safety that lies in quarrels is estimated in half-circles, acute and blunt angles, &c., &c., and the whole subject is ridi-
culed.—ED.]
18

he cut it to pleafe himfelfe:this is call'd the quip modeſt.   78
If againe, it was not well cut, he difabled my iudgment:
this is called, the reply churlifh. If againe it was not well   80
cut, he would anfwer I fpake not true : this is call'd the
reproofe valiant.   If againe, it was not well cut, he wold
fay, I lie : this is call'd the counter-checke quarrelfome :
and fo ro lye circumftantiall, and the lye direct.

Iaq.   And how oft did you fay his beard was not well   85
cut ?

Clo.   I durſt go no further then the lye circumftantial:
nor he durſt not giue me the lye direct : and fo wee mea-
fur'd fwords, and parted.

Iaq.   Can you nominate in order now, the degrees of   90
the lye.

Clo.   O fir, we quarrel in print, by the booke : as you   92

83. *I lie*] *I lied* Han. Cap. Glo. Dyce   84. *fo ro*] *fo the* Rowe +.   *fo to the*
iii, Coll. iii, Huds. Wright, Rlfe, Wh. ii.   Ff, Cap. et cet.

---

78. **quip**] WRIGHT: Cotgrave explains ' Sobriquet ' as 'A surname; also, a nick-
name, or byword ; and a quip or cut giuen, a mocke or flowt bestowed, a ieast broken
on a man.' . . . . Another form of the word is *quib*, which is found in Coles's *Dict.*,
and in Webster it is given on the authority of Tennyson in a quotation from *The
Death of the Old Year*, l. 29.   I have, however, been unable to find it in any English edition.   [And I in any American.—ED.]

79. **disabled**] See IV, i, 34: ' disable all the benefits,' &c.

83. **lie**] Hanmer's change is as good as it is trifling.

92. **booke**] THEOBALD : The boisterous Gallants in Queen Elizabeth's reign did
not content themselves with practising at the Sword in the Schools, but they studied
the Theory of the Art, the Grounding of Quarrels, and the Process of Challenging,
from Lewis de Caranza's *Treatise of Fencing*, Vincentio Saviola's *Practise of the
Rapier and Dagger*, and Giacomo di Grassi's *Art of Defence*.   WARBURTON : The
particular book here alluded to is a very ridiculous treatise of one Vincentio Saviolo,
1594.   [Only the Second Book is dated 1595; the First is 1595, but as, in *The Epistle Dedicatorie*, the Earl of Essex is requested to accept this book as ' a new yeeres
gifte,' both books were probably struck off in 1594, and the latest possible date given
only to the First.   It is from the First Book that we learn the use of the terms that
Mercutio ridicules, ' the immortal passado! the punto reverso!' &c.   The Second
Book treats ' Of Honor and Honorable Quarrels,' and these are the ' quarrels in
print' to which it is supposed Touchstone alludes; in especial there is 'A Discourse
most necessarie for all Gentlemen that haue in regarde their honors touching the giuing and receiuing of the Lie, wherevpon the Duello & the Combats in diuers sortes
doth insue, & many other inconueniences, for lack only of the true knowledge of
honor, and the contrarie : & the right vnderstanding of wordes, which heere is plainly
set downe.'   Whereupon, to guard us from these ' inconueniences ' and impart to us
' a right understanding of wordes,' Saviolo proceeds to discourse ' Of the manner

[we quarrel in print, by the booke]

and diuersitie of Lies.' First comes 'Of lies certaine'; this was supposed by Warburton to correspond to Touchstone's 'lie direct,' but erroneously, I think. For a 'lie
certain' it is requisite 'that the cause whereupon it is giuen, be particularlye specified
and declared.' It is the quality of the lie, not the terms of the answer, which must
be 'certaine.' Then comes 'Of conditionall Lyes.' Here Warburton was nearer right
in finding a correspondence to Touchstone's 'lie circumstantial.' 'Conditionall lyes,'
says Saviolo, 'be such as are giuen conditionally: as if a man should saie or write
these woordes, If thou hast saide that I haue offered my Lord abuse, thou lyest: or if
thou saiest so heerafter, thou shalt lye. And as often as thou hast or shalt so say, so
oft do I and will I say that thou doest lye. Of these kinde of lyes giuen in this manner, often arise much contention in words, and diuers intricate worthy [*sic*] battailes,
multiplying wordes vpon wordes whereof no sure conclusion can arise.' 'By which
he means,' says Warburton, 'they cannot proceed to cut one another's throats, while
there is an IF between. Which is the reason of Shakespeare's making the Clown
say "I know seven justices," &c.' Saviolo, however, utterly disapproved of conditionall lies, of which the issue is always doubtful. 'Therefore,' he pluckily concludes,
'not to fall into any error, all such as haue any regarde of their honor or credit, ought
by all meanes possible to shunne all conditionall lyes, neuer geuing anie other but cer-
tayne Lyes: the which in like manner they ought to haue great regarde, that they
giue them not, vnless they be by some sure means infallibly assured, that they giue
them rightly, to the ende that the parties vnto whome they be giuen, may be forced
without further Ifs and Ands, either to deny or iustifie, that which they haue spoken.'
Then follow short chapters, 'Of the Lye in generall,' 'Of the Lye in particular,' 'Of
foolish Lyes,' and finally, 'A Conclusion touching the Challenger and the Defender,
and of the wresting and returning back of the lye, or Dementie.' Warburton cites
this last chapter thus: 'A conclusion touching the wresting or returning back of the
lye,' and thereupon interprets it, 'or the countercheck quarrelsome,'—a quotation as
unfairly stated as its interpretation is unwarranted; the contents of the chapter are
clearly defined by its title, and have nothing whatever to do with 'quarrelsome counter-
checks.' (It is not needless thus to criticise Warburton; he has been blindly followed
by more than one editor.) Who will refuse a sympathetic response to Saviolo's pious
sigh of relief as he concludes the whole matter? 'And so (God be thanked) we finde
that almost we haue dispatched this matter, no lesse vneasie (as it is sayd before) to be
handled & vnderstood, than necessary to be knowen of all caualiers and Gentlemen.'
It is doubtful if too much importance has not been attached to this book of Saviolo.
Its connection with Touchstone's speech is really very slight; there is in it nothing of
the enumeration of causes, and there can be scarcely a doubt that the names for the
'degrees' are wholly Shakespeare's own. There is, however, another book wherein
the 'causes' of quarrels, to judge by its title, are expressly mentioned, and it, rather
than Saviolo, would seem to be the 'booke' referred to by Touchstone, if he referred
to any special book at all. Its title runs: *The Booke of Honor and Armes, wherein
is discoursed the Causes of Quarrell, and the nature of Iniuries, with their Repulses,*
&c. 4to, 1590. In all likelihood this volume was well sifted by Malone, and the following is apparently the only extract which he found germane to Touchstone's speech:
'Another way to procure satisfaction is, that hee who gave the lie, shall say or write
vnto the partie belied to this effect: I pray you advertise me by this bearer, with what
intent you spake those words of injurie whereupon I gave you the lie. The other
will answere, I spake them in choller, or with no meaning to offend you. Thereunto

haue bookes for good manners : I will name you the de-   93
grees.   The firft, the Retort courteous : the fecond, the
Quip-modeft : the third, the reply Churlifh : the fourth,   95
the Reproofe valiant : the fift, the Counterchecke quarrelfome : the fixt, the Lye with circumftance : the fea-
uenth, the Lye direct : all thefe you may auoyd, but the
Lye direct : and you may auoide that too, with an If.   I
knew when feuen Iuftices could not take vp a Quarrell,   100
but when the parties were met themfelues, one of them
thought but of an If; as if you faide fo, then I faide fo :
and they fhooke hands, and fwore brothers.   Your If, is
the onely peace-maker : much vertue in if.

Iaq.   Is not this a rare fellow my Lord ? He's as good   105
at any thing, and yet a foole.

Du. Se. He vfes his folly like a ftalking-horfe, and vnder the prefentation of that he fhoots his wit.   108

96, 97. *fift...fixt*] F₂. *fifth...fixth*   105. *as*] Om. Rowe+, Steev. '85.
F₃F₄.   108. Scene VII. Pope+.
    100. *take*] *make* Quincy (MS).

may be answered by him again that gave the lie thus : If your words were said onlie
in anger and no intent to challenge me, then I do assure you that my lie given shall
not burthen you, for I acknowledge you to be a true speaker and a gentleman of good
reputation : wherefore my desire is that the speech passed between us may be forgotten.   This mode of pacification may serve in many cases, and at sundrie occasions.'
Sorry enough, as far as yielding hints for Touchstone's speech is concerned; it is not
even as fruitful as Saviolo's *Practise*, for all the promise of its title.   Wherefore I do
greatly doubt if any particular book was hinted at by Shakespeare, or that there was
any one book in that day which was so widely known that Shakespeare's promiscuous
audience would have instantly recognised the allusion.   The very essence of a popular allusion is that what is alluded to, should be popular.—ED.]

    93. **bookes for good manners**] FURNIVALL has edited for the *Early English Text
Society*, 1868, many of these 'books of manners,' including Hugh Rhodes's *Boke of
Nurture*, mentioned by Steevens.   It is an invaluable compilation, enriched with
exhaustive Prefaces.   Again, for the same *Society* in the same year the same Editor
reprinted Caxton's *Book of Curtesye*.—ED.   WRIGHT: These 'books' are like 'the
card or calendar of gentry' to which Osric compares Laertes, evidently in allusion to
the title of some such book.

    102. **as**] WALKER (*Crit.* i, 129) cites this as an instance of the use of *as* in the
sense of *to wit*.   Compare Jaques's Seven Ages : '*As* first, the infant,' &c.

    103. **swore brothers**] ROLFE: Like the *fratres jurati*, who took an oath to share
each other's fortunes.

    107. **stalking-horse**] STEEVENS (note on *Much Ado*, II, iii, 95) : A horse, either
real or fictitious, by which the fowler anciently sheltered himself from the sight of the
game.   So in the 25th Song of Drayton's *Poly-olbion :* 'One underneath his horse to

Enter Hymen, Rofalind, and Celia.

Still Muficke.   110

Hymen.   *Then is there mirth in heauen,*
When earthly things made eauen
attone together.   113

109. Rofalind] Rosalind in Woman's   their proper Dress. Ros. led by a Per-
Cloths. Rowe. Rosalind and Celia in   son presenting Hymen. Cap.
                                        113. attone] *atone* Rowe.

---

get a shoot doth stalk.' REED: Again in *New Shreds of the Old Snare*, 1624, by
John Gee: 'Methinks I behold the cunning fowler, such as I have knowne in the
fenne countries and els-where, that doe shoot at woodcockes, snipes, and wilde fowle,
by sneaking behind a painted cloth which they carrey before them, having pictured in
it the shape of a horse; which while the silly fowle gazeth on, it is knockt down with
hale shot, and so put in the fowler's budget.'

108. **presentation**] SCHMIDT: Show (deceptions), semblance.

109. **Hymen**] JOHNSON: Rosalind is imagined by the rest of the company to be
brought by enchantment, and is therefore introduced by a supposed aërial being in
the character of Hymen. CAPELL: The following masque-like eclarcissement, which
is wholly of the Poet's invention, may pass for another small mark of the time of this
play's writing: for precisely in those years that have been mentioned in former notes
[1604 and 1607] the foolery of masques was predominant; and the torrent of fashion
bore down Shakespeare, in this play and the *Tempest*, and a little in *Timon* and *Cymbeline*. But he is not answerable for one absurdity in the conduct of this masque, that
must lye at his editor's doors; who, by bringing in Hymen in *propriâ personâ*, make
Rosalind a magician indeed; whereas all her conjuration consisted—in fitting up one of
the foresters to personate that deity, and in putting proper words in his mouth. [See
Text. Notes.] If, in representing this masque, Hymen had some Loves in his train,
the performance would seem the more rational; they are certainly wanted for what is
intitl'd the *Song;* and the other musical business, beginning: 'Then is there mirth,'
&c. would come with greater propriety from them, though editions bestow it on
Hymen. STEEVENS: In all the allegorical shows exhibited at ancient weddings,
Hymen was a constant personage. Ben Jonson, in his *Hymenæi, or the Solemnities
of Masque and Barriers*, has left instructions how to dress this favorite character:
'On the other hand, entered *Hymen*, the god of marriage, in a saffron coloured robe,
his under vestures white, his sockes yellow, a yellow veile of silke on his left arme,
his head crowned with roses and marjoram, in his right hand a torch of pine-tree.'

110. **Still Musicke**] STAUNTON: That is, *soft, low, gentle* music: 'then calling
softly to the gentlemen who were witnesses about him, he bade them that they should
command some *still* musicke to sound.'—*A Patterne of the painefull Adventures of
Pericles, prince of Tyre*, 1608. Again: 'After which ensued a *still* noyse of recorders
and flutes.'—*A true reportarie . . of the Baptisme of . . Prince Frederik Henry*, &c.,
1594.

113. **attone**] SKEAT: To set at one; to reconcile. Made up of the two words *at*
and *one;* so that *atone* means to 'set at one.' This was a clumsy expedient, so much
so as to make the etymology look doubtful; but it can be clearly traced, and there need
be no hesitation about it. The interesting point is that the old pronunciation of Middle English *oon* (now written *one*, and corrupted in pronunciation to *wun*) is here

Good Duke receiue thy daughter,
Hymen from Heauen brought her,   115
Yea brought her hether.
That thou mightſt ioyne his hand with his,
Whoſe heart within his boſome is.   118

---

116. hether] F₂. hither F₃F₄.   118. his boſome] *her bosom* Mal. Steev.
117. his hand] F₂, Cald. Hal. her   '93, Knt, Coll. Sing. Wh. i, Dyce, Ktly,
hand F₃F₄ et cet.   Huds. Rlfe.

---

exactly preserved; and there are at least two other similar instances, viz. in *alone* (from Mid. Eng. *al*, all, and *one*), and *only* (Mid. Eng. *oonly*), etymologically *one-ly* [frequently spelled *onely* in the Folio.—ED.], but never pronounced *wunly* in the standard speech. In *anon*, lit. ' on one,' the *-on* is pronounced as the preposition ' on,' never as *anwun*. The use of *atone* arose from the frequent use of Mid. Engl. *at oon* (also written *at on*) in the phrases ' to be at oon ' = to agree, and ' set at oon,' *i. e.* to set at one, to make to agree, to reconcile. [Hereupon Skeat traces the phrase from Robert of Gloucester to Dryden.] WRIGHT: The verb 'atone' does not occur in the Authorised Version, but we have there, in *Acts* vii, 26; *2 Macc.* i, 5, the phrases ' to set at one ' in the sense of ' to reconcile,' and ' to be at one ' in the sense of ' to be reconciled,' from which both are derived. . . . . The spelling of the Folio has given occasion to the conjectural emendation *attune*.

117, 118. **his hand . . . his bosome**] MALONE reads ' *her* hand ' and ' *her* bosom ' ; he followed the Third and Fourth Folios in reading ' *her* hand ' ; but in reading ' *her* bosom ' the change was his own. Of the text (which is his, and not Shakespeare's) he gives the following paraphrase : ' " That thou might'st join her hand with the hand of him whose heart is lodged in her bosom," *i. e.* whose affection she already possesses.' COLLIER (adopting Malone's text) says ' his ' is evidently wrong in both instances; ' the error was, no doubt, produced by the not infrequent custom at that date of spelling " her," *hir*, which misled the compositor.' *Her* is also the correction of Collier's (MS). WALKER (if I understand him aright) also (*Crit.* i, 317) approves of Malone's text.

On the other hand, CALDECOTT adheres to the Folio, reading ' his ' in both places, with the following note : Before our attention had been directed to the variance between the old copies and modern editions, we had conceived that our author had repeatedly used the masculine pronoun in reference to the previously assumed character, and ' doublet and hose ' dress of Rosalind ; but it seems now, from this as well as other considerations, that her dress could not have been altered. The Duke, her father, who did not now know or suspect who she was (although he had just before said ' he remembered some lively touches of his daughter in this shepherd-boy '), must, one would think, have at once recognised her in a female dress ; and she must also have delivered the epilogue in a male habit, or she could hardly have used the expression ' if I were a woman.' That the text is correct there may be much doubt. The introduction of the words ' in women's clothes ' in the modern editions, was probably in consequence of stage practice. [It is not easy to see what leads Caldecott to suppose that the Duke fails to recognise his daughter; he quite forgets, too, that when Rosalind in the Epilogue says ' if I were a woman,' it was the boy-actor who spoke. There can be no doubt that from Rowe's times to the present Rosalind here appears ' in woman's clothes '; and it is clear, I think, that Phebe would not at once have

Rof.   To you I giue my felfe, for I am yours.

To you I giue my felfe, for I am yours.   120

  Du. Se . If there be truth in fight, you are my daughter.

  Orl.   If there be truth in fight, you are my *Rofalind.*

  Phe . If fight & fhape be true, why then my loue adieu

  Rof.   Ile haue no Father, if you be not he :

Ile haue no Husband, if you be not he :   125

Nor ne're wed woman, if you be not fhee.

  Hy.   Peace hoa : I barre confufion,

'Tis I muft make conclufion

Of thefe moft ftrange euents :

Here's eight that muft take hands,   130

To ioyne in *Hymens* bands,

---

119. [To the Duke] Rowe et seq.
120. *To you*] Or. *To you* F₃F₄.
    [To Orl.] Rowe et seq.
122. *fight*] *shape* Johns. conj. Dyce
iii, Coll. iii, Huds.

123. Two lines, Pope et seq.
124. [To the Duke] Johns. et seq.
125. [To Orl.] Johns. et seq.
126. [To Phe.] Johns. et seq.

---

renounced her if she had not.   The stage-directions in Rowe are to be accepted with the respect due to the directions which most probably governed the stage of Shakespeare himself.   At the same time it may be permitted to doubt whether the change to woman's dress has anything to do with a change of 'his' to *her*.   It is by no means certain that when we adopt '*her* hand' and '*her* bosom' we are following Shakespeare; but our leader may be the admirable, though prosaic, Malone.   It is conceivable that the text as we have it is just as it should be.   First, on that sound, healthy principle, too often neglected now-a-days, of *durior lectio*, &c.; and, secondly, since Orlando had wooed his love as a boy, nay, even been married to her as a boy, and had even in very truth once 'joined his hand to his,' it is not, I think, over-refinement to suppose that the 'mirth in heaven' here prompts this allusion to the past, and by the use of 'his' we are reminded that though we have Rosalind before us, we are not to forget Ganymede.—ED.]

  122. sight] JOHNSON: The answer of Phebe makes it probable that Orlando says : 'If there be truth in *shape*,' that is, 'if a form may be trusted'; if one cannot usurp the form of another.   WALKER (*Crit.* i, 306): Read *shape*, to which Phebe evidently refers.   *Shape* is *dress;* see Gifford's Massinger [*The Emperor of the East*, III, iv, p. 294, where the word unquestionably means, as Gifford says, *dress*.   Pulcheria says to Eudocia, whom she had previously caused to be gorgeously clad in order to win her brother's heart : 'When, ... The garments of thy sorrows cast aside, I put thee in *a shape* as would have forced Envy from Cleopatra, had she seen thee.'   It was the dress, and the dress alone, that made the difference to Orlando between his Rosalind and his Ganymede.   I yield to Johnson and to Walker as did the conservative Dyce in his last edition.   WRIGHT, however, does not accept *shape* in this sense : he adheres to the Folio.   'Rosalind's woman's shape,' he explains, 'was more fatal to Phebe's hopes than the mere fact of her identity, whereas her identity was everything to Orlando.'—ED.].

If truth holds true contents.   132

You and you, no croſſe ſhall part;

You and you, are hart in hart:

You, to his loue muſt accord,   135

Or haue a Woman to your Lord.

You and you, are ſure together,

As the Winter to fowle Weather:

Whiles a Wedlocke Hymne we ſing,

Feede your ſelues with queſtioning: 140

That reaſon, wonder may diminiſh

How thus we met, and theſe things finiſh.

Song.

Wedding is great Iunos crowne,

   O bleſſed bond of boord and bed: 145

'Tis Hymen peoples euerie towne,

High wedlock then be honored:

   Honor, high honor and renowne

   To Hymen, God of euerie Towne.

Du. Se.   O my deere Neece, welcome thou art to me,   150

---

133. *and you*] *and and you* F₃.
   [To Orl. and Ros.] Johns. et
seq.
134. [To Oli. and Cel.] Johns.

136. [To Phe.] Johns.
138. [To the Clo. and Aud.] Johns.
142. *theſe things*] *thus we* Coll. (MS).
149. of *euerie*] *in every* Coll. (MS).

---

132. **contents**] JOHNSON: That is, if there be *truth in truth*, unless truth fails of veracity. WRIGHT: This appears to be the only sense of which the poor phrase is capable. [It is merely a strong asseveration, stronger, perhaps (since there is no contradiction), than the occasion demands; but then, what of that? Hymen is *always* a little incomprehensible. Isabel, in *Meas. for Meas.*, says: 'truth is truth to the end of reckoning.'—ED.]

136. **to your Lord**] Compare *Matthew*, iii, 9: 'We have Abraham to our father.'

137. **sure**] SCHMIDT: That is, indissolubly united, betrothed.

140. **questioning**] STEEVENS: Though Shakespeare frequently uses 'question' for *conversation*, in the present instance 'questioning' may have its common and obvious signification. [See III, ii, 360.]

143. **Song**] WHITE: Both the thought and the form of the thought in this 'Song' seem to me as unlike Shakespeare's as they could well be, and no less unworthy of his genius; and for the same reasons I think it not improbable that the whole of Hymen's part is from another pen than his. ROLFE: We are inclined to agree with White; and it may be noted also that lines 127–149 make an awkward break in the dialogue, which would run along very naturally without them.

147. This should be punctuated, I think, if necessary, 'High, wedlock then, be honored,' to indicate, at a glance, the word which 'High' qualifies.—ED.

Euen daughter welcome, in no leſſe degree.   151
   Phe. I wil not eate my word, now thou art mine,
Thy faith, my fancie to thee doth combine.

             Enter Second Brother.

   2. Bro. Let me haue audience for a word or two: 155
I am the ſecond ſonne of old *Sir Rowland*,
That bring theſe tidings to this faire aſſembly.
Duke Frederick hearing how that euerie day
Men of great worth reſorted to this forreſt,
Addreſt a mightie power, which were on foote   160
In his owne conduĉt, purpoſely to take
His brother heere, and put him to the ſword :
And to the skirts of this wilde Wood he came ;
Where, meeting with an old Religious man,   164

---

151. *daughter welcome,*] F₂F₃. *daugh-*
ter, welcome, F₄, Rowe, Pope, Cam. Rlfe,
Wh. ii. *daughter-welcome,* Theob. Warb.
Johns. Dyce iii, Huds. *daughter, wel-*
come Han. Cap. Steev. Mal. Cald. Knt,
Coll. i, ii, Sing. Wh. i, Dyce i, Sta. Ktly.
daughter,—welcome, Coll. iii. *as a*
daughter Cartwright.
   152. [To Sil.] Coll.
   154. Scene VIII. Pope+.
     Enter...] Enter Jaques de Boyes.
Rowe.
   155. 2. Bro.] Jaq. de B. Rowe. de B.
Cap.

---

   151. daughter welcome] WALKER (*Crit.* iii, 64): Read ' daughter-welcome ';
as welcome as a daughter. [Anticipated by Theobald. See Text. Notes.] DOWDEN
(*The Academy*, 19 Jan. 1884): Is not Shakespeare at his old trick of blundering
about *no less*, and does he not mean ' Even a daughter is welcome in no higher
degree than you, my niece ?' LITTLEDALE (*The Academy*, 26 Jan. 1884): Surely
there is no need to explain ' no less ' as a mere blunder for *no higher*. A comma
after ' daughter ' (and even so much is not essential) yields the natural sense : ' O my
dear niece . . . . nay, my daughter, welcome, in no less (or lower) degree *than that of*
daughter, not in the more distant relation of niece.' ALLEN (MS): That is, I address
you, not as *niece* merely, but as *daughter*, since thou art welcome in no less degree
than daughter.

   153. combine] STEEVENS: That is, to bind; as in *Meas. for Meas.* IV, iii, 149 :
' I am combined by a sacred vow.'

   154. Second Brother] COLLIER: He is thus called to avoid confusion with the
' melancholy Jaques.' [The ' confusion ' could arise only in print, and could not last
long even there; he says at once that he is old Sir Rowland's second son.—ED.]

   160. Addrest] CALDECOTT: Prepared. WHITE: At this day and in this country
it is perhaps necessary to point out that Jaques de Bois means that Duke Frederick
made ready a mighty power, not that he made a speech to them.

   164. old Religious man] FRANÇOIS-VICTOR HUGO (p. 58): Sous le froc véné-
rable du solitaire, c'est la nature elle-même qui s'est révélée à Frédéric. C'est la
nature qui l'a arrêté au passage et qui, par cette voix sainte, lui a crié : Tyran, tyran,
pourquoi me persécutes-tu ? Le duc est entré dans la forêt par la route de Damas.

After fome queftion with him, was conuerted   165
Both from his enterprize, and from the world :
His crowne bequeathing to his banifh'd Brother,
And all their Lands reftor'd to him againe
That were with him exil'd.   This to be true,
I do engage my life.   170
   Du. Se.   Welcome yong man :
Thou offer'ft fairely to thy brothers wedding :
To one his lands with-held, and to the other
A land it felfe at large, a potent Dukedome.
Firft, in this Forreft, let vs do thofe ends   175
That heere vvete well begun, and wel begot :
And after, euery of this happie number
That haue endur'd fhrew'd daies, and nights with vs,   178

---

168. *to him*] Ff, Coll. i. *to them* Rowe
et cet.
   169. *to be*] *to prove* Abbott, so quoted,
§ 354.
   172. *brothers*] F₂F₃, Rowe i, Han.

Cald. *brother's* F₄, Rowe ii, Pope, Theob.
Warb. Johns. Mal. Coll. iii, Wh. ii.
brothers' Cap. et cet.
   176. *vvete*] *were* Ff.

Un rayon d'en haut a percé la nue, et, éclairé par cette clarté divine, le despote a
reconnu toute l'horreur de son despotisme.   Le bourreau du droit en est devenu
l'apôtre.   Il s'est prosterné devant les vérités qu'il venait combattre.   Usurpateur, il
a renié l'usurpation : porte-sceptre, il s'est défait de la couronne ; homme de guerre,
il a mis bas les armes ; porte-glaive, il a rendu son épée à la nature anachorète et il
s'est constitué prisonnier du désert.

   168. to him] COLLIER in his first edition retained this obvious misprint, on the
ground that the converted Duke restores to the banished Duke all the lands of those
who were exiles with him, in order that the latter might afterwards restore these lands
to their former owners.   ' The Duke,' he says, ' afterwards tells his nobles [line 180]
that he will give them back their estates.'   DYCE, however, points out (*Remarks*, p.
64) that Collier mistook the meaning of line 180, where ' states ' does not mean
estates, but that the line means, ' all my faithful followers shall receive such rewards
as suit their various stations.'   Collier afterwards followed his (MS) corrector, who
followed Rowe.   WHITE thinks it conclusive that ' him ' is a misprint because of the
verb ' were ' in the next line.   It is not impossible to suppose that the nominative to
' were ' is contained in ' their.'—ED.

   168. all . . . restored] WRIGHT : This may be grammatically explained either by
regarding it as a continuation of the sentence in line 165, ' was converted,' the intervening line being parenthetical ; or by supposing an ellipsis of *were*, ' all their lands
were restored ' ; or, which seems best, as an independent participial clause, ' all their
lands *being* restored.'

   169. This to be true] See Abbott, § 354, for instances of a ' noun and infinitive
used as subject or object.'

   177. euery] For other examples of ' every ' used as a pronoun, see Abbott, § 12.

   178. shrew'd] ' The air,' Hamlet says, ' bites shrewdly, it is very cold.'   This

Shal fharc the good of our returned fortune,
According to the meafure of their ftates.   180
Meane time, forget this new-falne dignitie,
And fall into our Rufticke Reuelrie :
Play Muficke, and you Brides and Bride-groomes all,
With meafure heap'd in ioy, to'th Meafures fall.

 Iaq. Sir, by your patience : if I heard you rightly,   185
The Duke hath put on a Religious life,
And throwne into negleft the pompous Court.

 2. *Bro.* He hath.

 Iaq. To him will I : out of thefe conuertites,
There is much matter to be heard, and learn'd :   190
you to your former Honor, I bequeath

---

179. *fharc*] F₁. *have* Walker, so quoted, *Vers.* 40.
 180. *ftates*] *'states* Coll.

191. [To the Duke] Rowe.
 bequeath] *bequeath ;* F₂. *bequeath,* Rowe.

---

allusion to 'shrewd days and nights,' here in the last words of the Duke, recalls
to us the first, when he could smile at the churlish chiding of the winter's wind.—ED.

 180. states] WHITE: That is, of course, their *estates.* Dyce would read 'states,'
i. e. conditions. DYCE (ed. iii) : I certainly do read 'states,' but as certainly I understand that reading to mean *estates.* Can Grant White for a moment suppose that
when Theobald, Hanmer, Capell, Malone, Staunton, &c. printed (and rightly), as I
do, 'states,' without a mark of elision, they understood it to mean *conditions ?* [See
line 168.]

 185. Sir] CAPELL: To the duke; putting himself, without ceremony, between
him and de Boys, and then addressing the latter : and the subject of this address is
the most admirable expedient for Jaques to make his exit in character that ever human
wit could have hit upon; nor can the drama afford an example in which Horace's
servetur ad imum has been better observ'd than in this instance.

 187. pompous] Of course, in its original true meaning, full of pomp.

 189. conuertites] Cotgrave : Covers [a misprint for Conuers] : vn con. A con-
uertite ; one that hath turned to the Faith; or is woon vnto religious profession; or
hath abandoned a loose, to follow a godlie, a vicious to lead a vertuous, life.

 191. you to your . . . Honor] That this apparent inversion, whereby the Duke
is bequeathed to his crown, puzzled the compositors, is clear from the punctuation,
revealing, as it does, their attempts to grapple with the meaning. The compositor of
the Second Folio was more successful, and has been universally followed. Schmidt,
in the closing pages of his *Lexicon* (p. 1424), has given a list of passages, of which
the present is one, where he says 'the whole relation of ideas is inverted.' It is likely
that he is correct in thus interpreting the present passage. It is, however, not impossible that the inversion is here intentional. There may be a covert, cynical intimation
to the Duke that his crown is more substantial than he, that he is a mere chattel to be
passed by bequest; and, therefore, Jaques so phrases it that instead of bequeathing a
legacy to a legatee he bequeaths a legatee to a legacy.—ED.

 191. bequeath] WRIGHT : Loosely used in the sense of 'leave,' as above, line

your patience, and your vertue, well deſerues it.   192
you to a loue, that your true faith doth merit :
you to your land, and loue, and great allies :
you to a long, and well-deſerued bed :   195
And you to wrangling, for thy louing voyage
Is but for two moneths victuall'd : So to your pleaſures,
I am for other, then for dancing meazures.

    Du. Se. Stay, *Iaques*, ſtay.

    Iaq. To ſee no paſtime, I : what you would haue,   200
Ile ſtay to know, at your abandon'd caue.   *Exit.*

192. *deſerues*] *deserve* Pope+, Coll.
Dyce iii, Huds.
193. [To Orl.] Rowe.
194. [To Oli.] Rowe.

195. [To Sil.] Rowe.
196. [To the Clown] Rowe.
197. *moneths*] *months* F₄.

---

167. Properly, like the A. S. becwœþan, it signifies only to give by will, and is applied to personal property. This passage is not quoted by those who insist upon Shakespeare's intimate technical knowledge of law. [But we must remember that Jaques was about to join the Duke, who by 'putting on a religious life' became dead to the world. By the use of this very word 'bequeath' Jaques intimates to us that he too will become the same.—ED.]

192. **deserues**] For this singular after two nominatives, see Abbott, § 336, if necessary; or Shakespeare, *passim.*

201. STEEVENS : Amid this general festivity, the reader may be sorry to take his leave of Jaques, who appears to have no share in it, and remains behind unreconciled to society. He has, however, filled with a gloomy sensibility the space allotted to him in the play, and to the last preserves that respect which is due to him as a consistent character and an amiable, though solitary, moralist. It may be observed, with scarce less concern, that Shakespeare has, on this occasion, forgot old Adam, the servant of Orlando, whose fidelity should have entitled him to notice at the end of the piece, as well as to that happiness which he would naturally have found, in the return of fortune to his master. FARMER : It is the more remarkable that old Adam is forgotten; since, at the end of the novel, Lodge makes him 'captaine of the king's guard.' [Or, in other words, William Shakespeare was not Thomas Lodge.—ED.] MAGINN (p. 90): Whether he would or not, Jaques departs from the stage with the grace and easy elegance of a gentleman in heart and manners. He joins his old antagonist, the usurping Duke, in his fallen fortunes; he had spurned him in his prosperity; his restored friend he bequeaths to his former honour, deserved by his patience and his virtue,—he compliments Oliver on his restoration to his land, and love, and great allies,—wishes Silvius joy of his long-sought and well-earned marriage,—cracks upon Touchstone one of those good-humoured jests to which men of the world on the eve of marriage must laughingly submit,—and makes his bow. MOBERLY : It is remarkable that Jaques himself had been convicted by the Duke of being a 'convertite,' whose new-born morality was not likely to do much good to the world. Thus, therefore, he ends as he began; learning from profligacy, and cherishing as if it were wisdom, that contempt of mankind and their affairs which came to Hamlet only through misery, and was hated by him as a fresh misery. He has failed to learn the

Du. Se. Proceed, proceed : wee'l begin thefe rights,   202
As we do truft, they'l end in true delights.   *Exit*

Rof. It is not the fafhion to fee the Ladie the Epilogue : but it is no more vnhandfome, then to fee the   205
Lord the Prologue.   If it be true, that good wine needs
no bufh, 'tis true, that a good play needes no Epilogue.   207

---

202. *wee'l*] Wh. i.   *we will* Ff et cet.   203. *truft, they'l end*] *trust they'll*
   rights] Ff.   *rites* Rowe.   *end,* Pope.
203. *As*] *And* Var. '03, '13, '21, Cald.   Exit.] Om. Ff et seq. A Dance.
Knt.   Cap.
    203. Epilogue. Theob. ii.

---

lessons either of prosperity or of adversity; has, to the last, eyes for nothing but the
meanness of human nature; and is, to the last, the type of the man characterised in
Bacon's striking sentence : ' He that is prudent may seek to have a desire ; for he who
does not strive after something with eagerness finds everything burdensome and
tedious.'

203. **As**] In Reed's Variorum of 1803 this appears as *And*.   It is probably a mere
misprint, but its vitality is surprising.—ED.

203. **Exit**] COLLIER : The universal modern stage-direction here [see Text. Notes]
is ' a dance,' which probably followed the Duke's speech. . . . There seems no sufficient reason why the Duke should go out before the conclusion of the Epilogue—
nevertheless, according to the custom of our old stage, he may have done so. [Appa-
rently, he did not do it in 1632. See Text. Notes.—ED.] WHITE : It appears that
this ' Exit ' is an accidental repetition of that intended for Jaques just above.

204. **not the fashion**] G. S. B. (*The Prologue and Epilogue*, &c. p. 13) : The
dramatists of the early age of our drama did not begin (habitually, at least) to assign
their Prologues and Epilogues to the characters of the play so soon as we should suppose from the instances of such a practice which we find in *As You Like It, The
Tempest*, and in several other plays of Shakespeare.   Some contemporaries of Shakespeare, no doubt, adopted the practice ; but, though by the time of Congreve and
Wycherley, and even of Dryden, it had become usual, it was rather the exception
than the rule in the sixteenth century. . . . . The next decided novelty, as regards
the character of the person deputed to speak the Prologue, was introduced in 1609,
when a female character (not a woman, of course, as women had not begun to act at
this time, but a boy-actor personating a female) spoke the Prologue to *Every Woman
in her Humour*.   The stage-directions are : ' Enter Flavia, as a Prologue ' ; and, having entèred, she says, ' Gentles of both sexes, and of all sorts, I am sent to bid ye
welcome.   I am but instead of a Prologue, for a she-Prologue is as rare as a usurer's
alms.'   So also Rosalind feels bound to justify what was not yet an established usage.
. . . Not long after the introduction of Killigrew's and D'Avenant's actresses at the
Restoration, we find women, instead of boys, in female characters, speaking both Prologues and Epilogues.   Nell Gwynne, Mrs Mountford, and Mrs Bracegirdle became
particularly noted for their art in this respect, and one or other of them was often
selected for the purpose by Dryden and his fellow-dramatists.

207. **bush**] STEEVENS : It appears formerly to have been the custom to hang a
tuft of ivy at the door of a vintner.   I suppose ivy was chosen rather than any other
plant, as it has relation to Bacchus.   So in Gascoigne's *Glass of Government*, 1575 :

Yet to good wine they do vſe good buſhes : and good   208
playes proue the better by the helpe of good Epilogues:
What a caſe am I in then, that am neither a good Epi-   210

' Now a days the good wyne needeth none ivye garland.'   Again in *Summer's Last Will and Testament,* 1600 : Green ivy-bushes at the vintners' doors.'   RITSON : The practice is still observed in Warwickshire and the adjoining counties at statute-hirings, wakes, &c. by people who sell ale at no other time.   HALLIWELL : Chaucer alludes to the bush, and its customary position appended to an ale-stake or sign-post, when he speaks of 'A garland hadde he sette upon his hede As gret as it were for an alestake.' —*Prologue,* 668. [The allusions to this custom are endless.—ED.]   H. C. HART (*Sh. Soc. Trans.* 1877-9, Part iii, p. 461) : Holly and ivy would no doubt, from their freshness and greenness, have been used from the earliest period as symbols of rejoicing ; but in reference to wine, ivy bears a further meaning, without a knowledge of which the real force of the proverb is, I believe, lost.   This may be proved from abundant sources, but the following will suffice : ' In their feasting, they would sometimes separate the water from the wine that was therewith mixed, as Cato teacheth " de re rustica " (c. 3), and Pliny (l. 16, c. 35) with an ivie cup would wash the wine in a bason full of water, then take it out again with a funnel pure as ever.'—*Rabelais,* Bk. i, ch. 24, Ozell's Trans.   And again, ' after that ; how would you part the water from the wine and purify them both in that case ?   I understand you well enough, your meaning is that I must do it with an Ivy Funnel.'—*Ib.* Bk. iii, ch. 52.   And Gervase Markham : ' If it came to pass that wine have water in it, and that we find it to be so, ... cause a vessel of ivie wood to be made, and put therein such quantitie of wine as it will hold, the water will come forth presently, and the wine will abide pure and neate.'—*The Countrie Farme,* Bk. vi, ch. 16.   Hence the meaning of the proverb would appear to be that good (that is to say, pure or neat) wine would not, like diluted wine, require ivy to make it drinkable ; otherwise the saying means no more than that humanity has wit enough to find its way to a good thing without being directed, which is neither a very pointed, nor yet a very true, remark.   But that this was the meaning of the proverb we are not without actual proof, thus : ' The common saying is, that an ivie bush is hanged at the Taverne-dore to declare the wine within ; But the nice searchers of curious questions affirme this the secret cause, for that that tree by his native property fashioned into a drinking vessel plainly describeth unto the eye the subtile art of the vintner in mingling licors, which else would lightly deceive the thirsty drinker's taste.'—*Accedens of Armorie,* Gerard Leigh, 1591 : Richard Argol to the Reader. . . . . In Ray's *Proverbs* may be found its Italian, French, Latin, and Spanish equivalents.

210. then] JOHNSON : Here seems to be a chasm, or some other depravation, which destroys the sentiment here intended.   The reasoning probably stood thus : ' Good wine needs no bush, good plays need no Epilogue' ; but bad wine requires a good bush, and a bad play a good Epilogue.   ' What case am I in, then ?'   To restore the words is impossible ; all that can be done, without copies, is to note the fault. M. MASON : Johnson mistakes the meaning of this passage.   Rosalind says, that good plays need no Epilogue ; yet even good plays do prove the better for a good one.   What a case, then, was she in, who had neither presented them with a good play, nor had a good Epilogue to prejudice them in favor of a bad one !   KENRICK (*Rev. of Johnson,* p. 71) : It can hardly be called a *supposition* that Shakespeare wrote *tho'* instead of ' then.'   It is obvious he must, as he plays on the word ' good'

logue, nor cannot infinuate with you in the behalfe of a   211
good play?   I am not furnifh'd like a Begger, therefore
to begge will not become mee.   My way is to coniure
you, and Ile begin with the Women.   I charge you (O
women) for the loue you beare to men, to like as much   215
of this Play, as pleafe you: And I charge you (O men)
for the loue you beare to women (as I perceiue by your
fimpring, none of you hates them) that betweene you,   218

211. *nor cannot*] *nor can* Pope+,   *them* Steev. '93.
Steev. '85.   216. *And I*] *and so I* Steev. '93.
216. *pleafe you*] *pleafes you* F_3F_4,   218. *hates*] *hate* Pope+, Steev. Mal.
Rowe, Pope, Theob. Johns. Mal. *pleases*   *them) that*] *them) to like as much*
them Han. Warb. Cap. Steev. '85. *please*   *as pleases them, that* Han. Warb. Cap.

all through the passage, not once introducing the epithet *bad*, made use of by Dr
Johnson, nor hinting at the antithesis which the editor conceives so necessary to the
sense.   *Tho'*, at the end of a sentence, is commonly used in discourse for *however*,
and has the same meaning as *but* at the beginning of it.   Thus it is the same thing
as if the speaker had said, '*But* what a case,' &c.

211. **insinuate with**] Schmidt supplies other instances of this use in the sense of
ingratiating one's self.

212. **furnish'd**] JOHNSON: That is, dressed; so before [III, ii, 240] he was furnished like a huntsman.

216. **please**] ABBOTT, § 367, gives this as an example of the 'subjunctive used
indefinitely after the Relative.'   WRIGHT gives as a parallel instance: 'Yes, faith, it
is my cousin's duty to make curtsy and say, " Father, as it please you." '—*Much Ado*,
II, i, 56, where it is used impersonally.   But WALKER (*Crit.* i, 206) well suggests
that there may be 'a double meaning here: *as may be acceptable to you;*' and so,
indeed, it seems to have been interpreted by the older editors down to Steevens.

216, 218. **please you: . . . that betweene**] WARBURTON: This passage should
be read thus, 'to like as much of this play as pleases *them:* and I charge you, O
men, for the love you bear to women (as I perceive, &c.), *to like as much as pleases
them*, that between you,' &c.   Without the alteration of 'you' into *them* the invocation is nonsense; and without the addition of the words *to like as much as pleases
them*, the inference of, 'that between you and the women the play may pass' [*sic*],
would be unsupported by any precedent premises.   The words seem to have been
struck out by some senseless Player, as a vicious redundancy.   HEATH (p. 155): As
[Warburton] hath managed his cards, the poet is just between two stools.   The men
are to like only just as much as pleased the women; and women only just as much
as pleased the men; neither are to like anything from their own taste; and if both
of them disliked the whole, they would each of them equally fulfil what the poet
desires of them. . . . . But Shakespeare did not write so nonsensically; he desires the
women to like as much as pleased the men, and the men to set the ladies a good
example; which exhortation to the men is evidently enough implied in these words,
'that between you and the women, the play may please.'   [Although CAPELL must
have seen Heath's criticism (he refers more than once to Heath with commendation,
as well he might), he was nevertheless borne down by Warburton's confidence, and

and the women, the play may pleafe.   If I were a Wo-   219

---

not only 'subscribes to his reasoning very heartily,' but actually inserted Warburton's words in the text. JOHNSON did not follow Warburton in his text, but of the change of 'please you' into *pleases them*, he says]: The words *you* and *y^m*, written as was the custom in that time, were in manuscript scarcely distinguishable.   The emendation is very judicious and probable.   MALONE: The text is sufficiently clear without any alteration.   Rosalind's address appears to me simply this: 'I charge you, O women, for the love you bear to men, to approve as much of this play as affords you entertainment; and I charge you, O men, for the love you bear to women [not to *set an example to*, but] to *follow* or *agree in opinion* with the ladies; that between you both the play may be successful.'   The words 'to follow, or agree in opinion with, the ladies,' are not, indeed, expressed, but plainly implied in those subsequent: 'that, between you and the women, the play may please.'   In the Epilogue to *2 Henry IV* the address to the audience proceeds in the same order: 'All the gentlewomen here have forgiven [*i. e.* are favourable to] me; if the gentlemen will not, then the gentlemen do not *agree with* the gentlewomen, which was never seen before in such an assembly.'   GRANT WHITE: Warburton's suggestion would be plausible, were not the whole speech a bit of badinage.   [Heath seems to have disposed of Warburton's suggestion once and for ever.—ED.]

219. **If I were a Woman**] HANMER: Note that in this author's time the parts of women were always performed by men or boys.   [There can be no doubt that Hanmer is right.   There is, however, one unfortunate little phrase in Tom Coryat's *Crudities* which has never been explained, except by conjecture.   Coryat was in Venice in August, 1608, and writes as follows (p. 247, ed. 1611; vol. ii, p. 16, ed. 1776): 'I was at one of their play-houses where I saw a Comedie acted.   The house is very beggarly and base in comparison of our stately Play-houses in England: neyther can their Actors compare with vs for apparell, shewes, and musick.   Here I obserued certaine things that I neuer saw before.   For I saw women acte, a thing that I neuer saw before, though *I haue heard that it hath beene sometimes vsed in London*, and they performed it with as good a grace, action, gesture, and whatsoeuer convenient for a Player, as euer I saw any masculine Actor.'   Collier explains this allusion to actresses in London by supposing that Coryat refers to companies of foreign actors. But were this so, Coryat's contrast between the English stage and the Venetian stage would lose its point.   Still, for lack of any better, this explanation of Collier's must suffice.   We know that some years after this, foreign actors did perform in London. COLLIER (*Annals of the Stage*, vol. i, p. 451, ed. 1879) says substantially as follows: The year 1629 is to be especially marked as the first date at which any attempt was made in this country to introduce female performers upon our public stage.   The experiment was tried, though without success, by a company of French comedians at the Blackfriars' Theatre.   On the 4th of November, 1629, Sir H. Herbert received 2*l.* as his fee 'for the allowing of a French company to play a farce at Blackfriars'.' In Prynne's *Histriomastix* (1633, p. 414) is inserted a marginal note in these words: 'Some French-women, or monsters rather, in Michaelmas term, 1629, attempted to act a French play at the playhouse in Blackfriars, an impudent, shameful, unwomanish, graceless attempt.'   [From a private letter written by one Thomas Brande, which Collier discovered among some miscellaneous papers in the library of the Archbishop of Canterbury at Lambeth, bearing date the 8th of November, the following extract is given:] 'Furthermore you should know, that last daye certaine vagrant French

[If I were a Woman]

players, who had beene expelled from their owne countrey, *and those women*, did attempt, thereby giving just offence to all vertuous and well-disposed persons in this town, to act a certain lascivious and unchaste comedye, in the French tonge at the Blackfryers. Glad I am to saye they were hissed, hooted, and pippin-pelted from the stage, so as I do not thinke they will soone be ready to trie the same againe.' Brande was mistaken in supposing that their failure would deter them from renewing their attempt. A fortnight later they again appeared 'for a daye' at the Red Bull. More than three weeks elapsed before they ventured once more to face an English audience, when they chose the Fortune playhouse. But failure attended them here as elsewhere, and the Master of the Revels remitted half his fee on a representation of the unprofitableness of the speculation. 'Some stress,' adds Collier, in a foot-note, 'has been recently laid upon a MS in the British Museum, dated 1582, as showing that, even then, an actress had appeared in London; but it only means that a boy " without a voice " had unsuccessfully played the part of a " virgin " at the theatre in that year.' PECK (*Memoirs of Milton*, p. 233) suggests that the ladies may have acted at Court before women appeared in public, and hence may have arisen any allusions which precede in date the year when we know with certainty that women first took part in public performances. WARD (ii, 422) says that 'in the masks at Court ladies constantly took part as performers; so that when in Christmas, 1632–3, the Queen with her ladies acted in a Pastoral at Somerset House, there was no real novelty in the proceeding.' LANGBAINE (p. 117), speaking of *King John and Matilda*, a Tragedy, 'printed in quarto, *Lond.* 1655,' says that it was published by '*Andrew Penny-cuicke*, who acted the part of *Matilda*, Women in those times not having appear'd on the stage.' It seems not unlikely that in this, as in other things, the change was gradual, and it is extremely probable that it arose from necessity. During the eighteen years, from 1642 to 1660, while the theatres were suppressed, the young boys who had been trained to act as women had grown to man's estate, with valanced faces. The incongruity, therefore, between the actor and his part must have been monstrous. As Jordan, in 1662, said :

> ' For to speak truth, men act, that are between
> Forty and fifty, wenches of fifteen;
> With bone so large, and nerve so incompliant,
> When you call Desdemona—enter Giant.'

Of course, reform was necessary, and what innovation could be more natural than that women should assume the roles of women ? Accordingly, very soon after the re-opening of the theatres, possibly at the very re-opening, or within a few months at least, we find Pepys (as noted by Wright) thus recording: 'January 3, 1660. To the Theatre, where was acted " Beggar's Bush," it being very well done; and here the first time that ever I saw women come upon the stage.' Again, 'Feb. 12, 1660–1. By water to Salsbury Court play-house, where not liking to sit, we went out again, and by coach to the Theatre, and there saw " The Scornful Lady," now done by a woman, which makes the play appear much better than ever it did to me.' It needs no great penetration to see that a change which made a 'play please much better than ever it did' before was likely to become permanent. It is, I believe, generally conceded that the first play in which it was openly announced that women would take part is *Othello*, for which a Prologue heralding the fact was printed in 1662,

19

man, I would kiſſe as many of you as had beards that   220
pleas'd me, complexions that lik'd me, and breaths that
I defi'de not : And I am ſure, as many as haue good
beards, or good faces, or ſweet breaths, will for my kind
offer, when I make curt'ſie, bid me farewell.   *Exit.*   224

FINIS.

---

224. *curt'ſie*] *my curtesy* Ktly.   224. Exit.] Exeunt. Ff. Exeunt Om-
                                                         nes. Pope.

---

and from which some lines have just been quoted. Who was the first performer of
Desdemona remains in doubt. Dyce (Shirley's *Works*, v, 353) found evidence,
though he does not give it, which satisfied him that it was Mrs Hughs. Malone
(*Var.* '21, iii, 126) says that it is 'the received tradition that Mrs Saunderson was
the first English actress.' (See *Othello*, p. 397, of this edition, where the subject is
more fully discussed.)—ED.

221. **lik'd me**] See Schmidt, s. v. 2, for many other instances of this use in the
sense of *to please.*

222. **defi'de**] NARES: To reject, refuse, renounce.

224. **farewell**] BLACKWOOD'S MAGAZINE (April, 1833): But Rosalind,—she is
the Star, the Evening and the Morning Star,—setting and rising in that visionary,
sylvan world,—and we leave her,—unobscured,—but from our eyes hidden,—in that
immortal umbrage.

APPENDIX

APPENDIX

THE TEXT

THE TEXT of this play is derived from the First Folio of 1623; no copy of it in a separate form, or Quarto in shape, is known to exist. That its publication in such a form was at one time intended, we learn from *The Stationers' Registers*.

The early volumes of these *Registers* are designated by the letters of the alphabet. The volume **C**, containing entries of books from 1595 to 1620, has in the beginning a couple of leaves containing sundry somewhat promiscuous notes, the earliest dated August, 1595, and the last, May, 1615; in all about sixteen or seventeen in number. With two or three exceptions all these notes, when they refer to the entries of books, contain a *caveat*, or warning that permission to print is not accorded unless upon better proof of ownership than the printer offers at the time the note is made. In the mean time the printer is restrained or 'staied' from issuing the book. These two leaves look, in fact, like a 'Blotter,' or a rough 'Check-list' to help the clerk's or the Master Warden's memory in the granting of future entries; and, moreover, it looks as if the clerk had begun this especial list at the top of the third page, and after two or three entries had gone back to the first. With the exception of the very first note of all, at the top of the first page, which is dated 1596, and does not refer to the printing of books, but is merely a memorandum of a business detail of the Stationers' Company, every item on the first and second pages is of a date subsequent to that at the top of the third page. This detail, trivial though it be, is not unimportant if we learn from it with what carelessness all these items were set down, and consequently how much uncertainty in the matter of chronology must attend every entry on these leaves where the exact date is not explicitly set forth—a misfortune which happens to be true of the item containing the title of the present play. It is among these irregular items on this fly-leaf, as it were, of the *Register* that the memorandum containing the title of *As You Like It* is to be found, and it is dateless.

The last entry at the foot of the second page (Arber's *Transcript*, iii, 36) is of a ballad, 'to be stayed,' of the 'Erle of Essex going to Cales'; its date is 'vltimo maij [1603].' The top of the third page begins, and continues as follows: [Be it observed that the entry to Thomas Thorp and william Aspley, which follows the *As You Like It* item, and is here reprinted merely to show the way in which that item falls in with the others on the page, is quoted by Malone as of the 23 *January*, an error (that is, if Arber's Reprint is correct) quite insignificant, it is true, but which has been followed by Halliwell, Stokes, and all other later editors who have referred to the item]:

'my lord chamberlens menns plaies Entred
                              viz

27 may 1600
To master   A moral of clothe breches and velvet hose
   Robertes
27 May   Allarum to London/
To hym

4 Augusti

As you like yt/a booke   ⎫
Henry the Ffift/a booke   ⎪
Euery man in his humour/a booke   ⎬ to be staied
The commedie of muche A doo about nothing   ⎪
   a booke/   ⎭

23 Junij/1603

Thomas Thorp
william Aspley   This is to be their copy gettinge aucthority for it,' &c.

It is to be noticed that there is, as I have already mentioned, no date in the margin opposite this *As You Like It* item, nor any date following 'August.' Malone (*Var.* '*21*, vol. ii, p. 367) says that 'it is extremely probable that this " 4 of August" was of 'the year 1600; which, standing a little higher on the paper, the clerk of the Sta-'tioners' Company might have thought unnecessary to be repeated,' especially, too, if, as I have suggested, these leaves were a mere rough check-list for his own use and behoof. But the Registers themselves, further on, supply us with evidence which is abundantly satisfactory that this is the August of the year 1600. On the 14th of August in the '42 Regine' (*i. e.* 1600) we find that certain books were entered to Thomas Pavyer (Arber, iii, 169), and among them is ' The historye of Henry the Vth with the 'battell of Agencourt.' 'These Copyes followinge,' says the entry, 'beinge thinges 'formerlye printed and sett over to the sayd Thomas Pavyer.' On the same day in this month of August Master Burby and Walter Burre entered 'a booke called Euery man in his humour.' And nine days later, on the 23d, there was ' entred' to Andrewe Wyse and William Aspley 'Two bookes. the one called Muche a Doo about nothinge. ' The other the second parte of the history of king Henry iiijth with the humours of ' Sir John Ffallstaff: Wrytten by master Shakespere.'

Unfortunately, no mention can elsewhere be found of *As You Like It*. But the appearance in 1600 of the other plays settles the date of the August item in 'the check-list,' and we may be sure that in that year the present comedy existed, in some shape or other.

There still remains to be considered in the *As You Like It* item that mysterious little sentence 'to be staied.' On this we may exercise our ingenuity to our heart's content; the field of our conjectures need be neither a desert nor unpeopled.

COLLIER (*Introduction to Much Ado about Nothing*) supposes that 'the object of ' the "stay" probably was to prevent the publication of *Henry V, Every Man in his* ' *Humour,* and *Much Ado* by any other stationers than Wise and Aspley.'

With this supposition STAUNTON agrees, and adds that 'as the three other "books"

' were issued by them in a quarto form, probabilities are in favour of the fourth having
' been so published also. At all events, there are sufficient grounds for hope that a
' quarto edition may some day come to light.'

WRIGHT: 'We can only conjecture that *As You Like It* was not subsequently
' entered, because the announcement of its publication may have been premature and
' the play may not have been ready. [To this conjecture Wright is led, because]
' even in the form in which it has come down to us there are marks of hasty work,
' which seem to indicate that it was hurriedly finished. For instance, the name of
' Jaques is given to the second son of Sir Rowland de Boys at the beginning of the
' play, and then when he really appears in the last scene he is called in the Folios
' " second Brother," to avoid confounding him with the melancholy Jaques. Again,
' in the First Act there is a certain confusion between Celia and Rosalind which is
' not at all due to the printer, and gives me the impression that Shakespeare himself,
' writing in haste, may not have clearly distinguished between the daughter and niece
' of the usurping Duke. I refer especially to I, ii, 78, 79: "*Clo.* One that old *Fred-*
' "*ericke* your Father loues. *Ros.* My Fathers loue is enough to honor him," &c.
' Theobald was the first to see that the last speaker must be Celia and not Rosalind,
' while Capell proposed to substitute *Ferdinand* for ' Frederick' in the Clown's
' speech, supposing the former to be the name of Rosalind's father. It may be said,
' of course, that this is a mere printer's blunder, and I cannot assert that it may not
' have been. But it would be too hard upon the printer to attribute to him the slip in
' Le Beau's answer (I, ii, 271) to Orlando's inquiry, which of the two was daughter
' of the Duke: " But yet indeede the taller is his daughter," when it is evident from
' the next scene (I, iii, 121) that Rosalind is the taller. Again, Orlando's rapturous
' exclamation, " O heavenly Rosalind !" comes in rather oddly. His familiarity with
' her name, which has not been mentioned in his presence, is certainly not quite con-
' sistent with his making inquiry of Le Beau, which shewed that up to that time he
' had known nothing about her. Nor is Touchstone, the motley-minded gentleman,
' one that had been a courtier, whose dry humour had a piquancy even for the worn-
' out Jaques, at all what we are prepared to expect from the early description of him
' as " the clownish fool" or " the roynish clown." I scarcely know whether to attrib-
' ute to the printer or to the author's rapidity of composition the substitution of "Juno "
' for *Venus* in I, iii, 78. But it must be admitted that in the last scene of all there is
' a good deal which, to say the least of it, is not in Shakespeare's best manner, and
' conveys the impression that the play was finished without much care.'

FLEAY, in his *Introduction to Shakespearian Study*, 1877 (p. 24), says that this
' "staying" was probably carried out, because the play was still acting at the Globe ';
and in his *Life and Work of Shakespeare*, 1886, he somewhat modifies this opinion.
On p. 40, speaking of the ' staying' of the plays mentioned in the *As You Like It*
item, he says: ' They were probably suspected of being libellous, and reserved for
' further examination. Since the " war of the theatres" was at its height, they may
' have been restrained as not having obtained the consent of the Chamberlain, on
' behalf of his company, to their publication. . . . . *As You Like It* was not allowed
' to appear, the company probably objecting that it had only been on the stage for one
' year.' And again on p. 140: ' I think [the staying] likely to have been caused by
' the supposed satirical nature of the plays.'

Wright's conjecture would carry conviction, if, in the course of time, after the ' staying,' a Quarto had actually appeared bearing all these marks of haste which Wright
detects in the play as we now have it; then all these oversights would make assur-

ance double sure, and from this proven haste we might be not unreasonably certain that it was to gain time and thwart injurious stealth that the booke had been 'staied.' But no Quarto appeared at all, complete or incomplete; and for twenty-three years the play carried these marks which Wright, and with much probability, attributes to haste. Rapid, miraculously rapid, the composition of *As You Like It* must have been, but the connection is not so obvious between this rapidity of execution on Shakespeare's part and a refusal to permit the play to be printed on the Warden's part. If the play could be acted, an unscrupulous printer might suppose it could be printed, and make the attempt to enter it at Stationers' Hall; and if the author or legitimate owner had power enough to 'stay' the printing of this play and the others for a time, he would have, one would think, enough power to stay their printing altogether. But, as we see, the 'stay' was of the shortest in the case of *Henry V.* The prohibition lasted only ten days; on 14th of August, Thomas Pavyer received permission to print that play; and nine days after that, Andrew Wyse received permission to print *Much Ado.*

It is this same expeditious removal of the caveat which is also fatal, it seems to me, to Fleay's conjecture that the plays were 'staied' because they were satirical or libellous. However libellous *Every Man in his Humour* or *Henry V* might be, I cannot recall a single accusation of libel or of even keen satire in *As You Like It*, except the one or two accusations of satire against Jonson, which Tieck urges; and these charges were born and died in the learned German's brain. Certainly, Fleay himself specifies no libel in this play. And yet this is the very play of all where the 'stay' is permanent. The libellous or satirical character ceased to be operative in the case of all the others within the month.

Of course, in cases like the present, where all our speculations must be, necessarily, of the vaguest and most shadowy character, it is easy to criticise and pick flaws. All the influences at work in connection with the printing of Shakespeare's plays we do not know and probably never shall know. Accordingly, in this realm of pure speculation a critic is a chartered libertine, and he may take up with any theory he may chance to meet. Wherefore, in the exercise of this right, I scarcely shrink from suggesting that one of the causes of all this 'staying' (I have hinted at another one in 'The Source of the Plot'), and at the bottom of all this entanglement over the printing of *As You Like It*, was James Roberts. If we look back at the entries in the *Stationers' Registers*, we shall see that his is the last name before the *As You Like It* item set down as an applicant for an entry; and the same needlessness which deterred the clerk from repeating, on this informal sheet, the date of the year, deterred him from repeating in the margin opposite the titles of these new 'bookes' the name of the applicant; who was (is it not probable?) this very same James Roberts. Now, this James Roberts was far from being one of the best of the Stationers, at least if we can judge from the fact that he came more than once under the ban of the Wardens and was fined by them. Perhaps it was that he violated the professional etiquette of the Stationers, which forbade a trespass on a neighbour's manor even when that neighbour had merely a prescriptive right to his manor and did not hold it by Letters Patent. The right to print certain books and certain classes of books was secured by Letters Patent to certain printers; thus Letters Patent secured to Richard Tottell the exclusive right to print Law books, and to Tallis to print Music, and to Bowes to print Playing Cards, &c., &c., and to James Roberts, this same James Roberts, the right to print 'Almanackes and Pronostycacyons.' But there were no Letters Patent guarding the right to print 'plaie bookes'; only prescription could confer that, and courtesy guard it, especially as this branch of the trade may not have been in the best repute. Now, it looks much as if James Roberts felt at times that his horizon of Almanackes and Pronostycacyons was too restricted. (He held the privilege for only twenty-one years, and the term had more than half expired in 1600.) He once made an attempt on the Queen's Printer's realm of Catechisms, and was promptly repressed by the Master Wardens of the Stationers' Company, and fined. Next he seems to have turned his attention to the stage, and clasped itching palms with some of my Lord Chamberlain's men. In a mysterious way he gained possession of a copy of *The Merchant of Venice*, and would have incontinently printed it, had not the Wardens 'staied' it, and staied it for two years too, at the end of which time James sold his copy to young 'Thomas haies,' and at once proceeded to print a second and better copy for himself. Clearly, James Roberts was what the Yankees would call 'smart,' or rather, in the true Yankee pronunciation, which gives a more admiring tone to it, 'smah't.' I believe he had made some friends with the mammon of unrighteousness among my Lord Chamberlain's men, and by underhand dealings obtained possession of stage copies of sundry plays of Shakespeare which happened to be unusually popular. His name does not appear often in the *Registers* in these years. After he was foiled in his attempt to print *The Merchant of Venice* in 1598, he made one other entry towards the close of that year, and succeeded in getting permission to print Marston's *Satires*. Then in March of the next year he tried to enter a translation of Stephan's *Herodotus*, but was 'staied.' Again in the following October he was permitted to print a *History of Don Frederigo*, but with the permission was coupled the very unusual condition that he should print 'only one impression and pay six pence in the pound to the use of the poore'; manifestly, James Roberts was in ill repute. His next venture was in May, when he tried to enter 'A morall of Clothe breches and velvet hose, As yt is Acted by my lord Chamberlens servantes,' but there follows the proviso 'that he is not to putt it in prynte Without further and better Aucthority.' Two days later, on the 29th of May, he again tried to enter a book : 'the Allarum to London,' and again there follows the inevitable caveat 'that yt be not printed without further Aucthoritie.' These two items, which appear in their proper order in the main body of the *Registers*, the clerk, as I suppose, briefly jotted down on the blank page at the beginning of the book, as a reminder to keep his eye on James Roberts. When, therefore, on the 4th of August, James Roberts brought forward four more plays that were performed by 'my lord chamberlen's menn,' the clerk noted them down on his fly-leaf under the others, and did not take the trouble to repeat James Roberts's name, which was already there in the margin opposite the 'Clothe breches and velvet hose,' but added (what was almost the synonym of James Roberts) 'to be staied.'

This it was, the bad reputation of James Roberts, which caused the printing of these plays when first offered to be forbidden. Be it remembered that all this, on my part, is merely conjecture. What the circumstances were which, within the month, gave to Thomas Pavyer and Andrew Wyse and others the privilege of printing these very plays, we do not know, and cannot know unless some new sources of information are discovered. We must remember that Heminge and Condell, when they issued the First Folio, denounced every one of these printers as 'injurious imposters,' who had abused the public with 'stolne and surreptitious copies.' Where the line was among the printers, which the Master Wardens of the Stationers drew, blessing some and banning others, we cannot know. Only it looks as though where all were bad James Roberts was somehow among the worst, and that to his unsavory reputation is due the fact that we have no Quarto edition of *As You Like It.*

Staunton expressed the hope that a Quarto might yet be discovered. But I fear the hope is groundless. When Master Blounte and Isaak Jaggard received permission in 1623 to print the First Folio, a list of plays was made of such as 'are not formerly entred to other men,' that is, of such of which there were no Quarto copies. In this list stands *As You Like It.*

The conclusion, therefore, is safe that the only Text we shall ever have for this play is that of the First Folio, and we may well congratulate ourselves that it is, on the whole, unusually good.

The only voice dissenting from this opinion in regard to the excellence of the First Folio is that of JOSEPH HUNTER, and his voice is very dissenting indeed. 'The text 'has come down to us,' he says (i, 331), 'in a state of very gross corruption. Some-'times speeches are assigned to the wrong characters. Sometimes the corruptions 'are in particular passages. There are within the compass of this play at least twenty 'passages in which the corruption is so decided that no one would for a moment think 'of defending the reading: and there are about fifteen where the probability of cor-'ruption is so great that the most scrupulous editor would think it his duty, if not to 'substitute a better text, yet to remark in his notes the text as delivered to us and the 'text as it probably should be.' I am afraid that the excellent Hunter has here said more in a minute than he could stand to in a month. We might reasonably expect that after this prologue, which roars so loud of gross corruption and thunders in the index, he would help us bravely to a purer text in the fifteen or twenty passages which he had in mind. But, omitting his notes purely illustrative, in which he is always happy, bringing forth for us, from the stores of his great learning, things new and old,—omitting these, his notes on the text, as such, amount to four in number, and of these four, two sustain and uphold the Folio.

KNIGHT's opinion is that 'the text of the original Folio is, upon the whole, a very 'correct one;' and GRANT WHITE, much more emphatic in his praise, says that 'the 'text of *As You Like It* exists in great purity in the original Folio. Few of its cor-'ruptions are due to any other cause than the lack of proof-reading; and those few 'it is not beyond the power of conjectural criticism to rectify.' Of the two extremes, I think, Grant White is nearer the truth than Hunter. Every student, however, with the Textual Notes in the present edition before him, can solve the question for himself, and with decidedly more profit than if it were solved for him. Those who can find any pleasure in such a task will make the examination for themselves; and for those who do not care for it, it would be a waste of time to prepare it.

HALLIWELL (p. 261) notes the somewhat singular fact that 'a copy of the First 'Folio many years in the possession of the late James Baker of King's Arms Yard, con-'tains two cancelled leaves of *As You Like It* in sheet R, or rather two leaves, each 'of which has been cancelled on account of one of the pages being wrongly printed. 'The first is a cancel of sig. R, comprising pp. 193, 194, the first page being erron-'eously given as 203, and the signature as R 2. The second is the last leaf of the 'sheet, pp. 203, 204, the second page of which is misprinted 194. There do not 'appear to be any textual variations in consequence of these cancels, which are chiefly 'curious as showing that the work received some corrections while in the process of 'being passed through the press. In another copy of the First Folio, at p. 204, col. 'I, the Clown's speech, "a ripe age," is given to Orlando, and William's speech, 'immediately following it, is assigned to the Clown.' I am inclined to think that what Halliwell has here attributed to two copies is true of only one. The 'Baker copy' to which he refers is now in the *Lenox Library* in New York; it is the celebrated copy which is supposed to be dated 1622 instead of 1623; and it is on the cancelled page 204, misprinted 194, of this copy that the Clown's speech, 'A ripe age,' &c. is given to Orlando, and William's speech given to the Clown; so that to this extent there were textual variations in consequence of these cancels, and they are the only ones, in this play, mentioned by Lenox (p. 36) in his printed collation.

In all copies, I believe, p. 189 is misprinted 187; and on p. 197 the running title is *As Yoa Like It.*

Practically, the text of the Four Folios is one and the same. The discrepancies between the First and the Fourth are mainly such as we might expect in the changes of the language within the dates of publication. In the last century Steevens professed to give to the Second Folio a preference over the First. But I doubt if this preference sprang from any very deep conviction; I am not sure that Steevens did not profess it mainly for the sake of annoying Malone, whose 'learning and perspicacity' Steevens extolled chiefly for the purpose, I am afraid, of calling him in the same sentence his 'Hibernian coadjutor,' a cruel little stab at one who had tried to obliterate his nationality, it is said, by dropping, with the letter *y*, the accent on the final vowel of his name. In the present play there are two or three instances where unquestionably the Second Folio corrects the First. For instance, Oliver says (IV, iii, 150) : 'I briefe, he led me to the gentle Duke'; this trifling typographical error is corrected in the Second Folio to '*In* brief he,' &c. Again, in line 163 of the same speech, Oliver says 'this napkin died in this blood,' where the Second Folio reads 'died in *his* blood.' But these are insignificant, and not beyond the chance corrections of a good compositor, who, however, overshot the mark when he changed Rosalind's words (IV, iii, 71) from 'false strains' to 'false *strings*,' and did even worse for Orlando, when one of the finest sentences in the whole play was converted into limitless bombast. 'I will chide no breather in the world,' says Orlando in the Second Folio, 'but myself, against whom I know *no* faults.' It is a little singular that what is always in the First Folio 'Monsieur' is in the Second and following Folios, *Mounsieur*. Whether this indicates a change in general pronunciation from Elizabeth's time to Charles the First's, or is merely peculiar to one compositor, I do not know.

The evidences of haste in this play, which Wright points out, such as the same name for two characters, the use of 'Juno' for *Venus*, and the like, are chargeable, I am afraid, to the author rather than to the printer. The conclusion then remains unshaken that in the First Folio we have an unusually pure text, and that in this, as in everything else about this delightful comedy, it is exactly As You Like It.

DATE OF COMPOSITION

The Date of the Composition of a Play may be approximated by External and by Internal evidence. External evidence, which is generally documentary, gives us a date *before* which a play must have existed in some shape or other, and Internal evidence, which consists of allusions, in the play itself, direct or indirect, to contemporary events, gives us a date *after* which the play must have been written.

First, the External evidence in the case of *As You Like It* is the provisional entry in the *Stationers' Registers*, which was discovered by Steevens. Although no publication of the play followed this entry on the 4th of August, 1600, yet this record has been accepted, not unnaturally, as sufficient proof that the play in some shape or other was in existence at that date. Wright thinks that 'the play was probably written 'in the course of the same year,' and conjectures that the reason why it was not afterward entered for publication, in due form, is that 'the announcement of its publi-'cation may have been premature and the play may not have been ready.' With the exception of Capell (who knew nothing of this entry in the *Stationers' Registers*), and, perhaps, of Knight, no editor oversteps the date of this year, but all concede that the latest limit for the Date of Composition is 1600. Other External evidence, than this in the *Stationers' Registers*, there is none.

For the earliest limit we must look to Internal evidence, with which the Play itself must supply us. From this source, however, we gain nothing either satisfactory or decisive, at least so decisive as to carry instant conviction. Before Steevens had discovered the memorandum in the *Stationers' Registers*, Capell conjectured that the Date of Composition was about 1607, and on two grounds: first, because at about that date 'the foolery of masques was predominant;' and secondly, because in Jaques's 'lean and slippered Pantaloon' he found an allusion to an obscure play of that date, called *The Travels of Three English Brothers*, wherein Will Kempe proposes to act the part of 'an old Pantaloune.' This is a good illustration of the small reliance which is in general to be placed on this Internal evidence. Had not the entry in the *Stationers' Registers* been subsequently discovered, probably no arguments could have conclusively disproved this far-fetched conjecture of Capell's.

In another piece of Internal evidence Capell was more successful. He discovered the 'dead Shepherd' to be Marlowe, whose saw: 'Who ever loved that loved not at 'first sight,' Phebe found to be of might. (Capell has not received the credit of this discovery; it is always accorded to Malone. Capell gives, on p. 66 of his 'School,' the extract containing this line from *Hero and Leander*.) Marlowe's poem was published in 1598. It was entered in the *Stationers' Registers* on the second of March, in that year. This seems to afford the earliest date *after* which the play was written, thus narrowing down the range to the years 1598, 1599, and 1600. Some slight doubt, however, can be cast on 1598 as the very earliest date. Marlowe died in 1593; and in the five years that passed before his *Hero and Leander*, with Chapman's conclusion, was printed, it is not impossible that Shakespeare may have read the line before it was published,—nay, even before Marlowe's death, while the poem was still in manuscript in Marlowe's hands. It is generally conceded that Lodge must have read the *Tale of Gamelyn* in some manuscript. Why may not Shakespeare, as Malone surmises, have thus read *Hero and Leander*, or, as Halliwell suggests, have heard it recited? I cannot say that I think either supposition likely. The mere fact that the quotation is put in the mouth of Phebe implies that the poem, at that time, was well known and popular, and would be recognised by the audience. Still, these are suppositions which all have a right to make, and that we can make them, or others like them, in regard to allusions thus detected in this play, helps to reveal the unsure, shifting character of Internal evidence.

Again in Orlando's verses: ' From the *East to farthest Ind*, No jewel is like Rosalind; Her worth being mounted on the wind Through *all the World* bears Rosalind.' CHALMERS (p. 382) sees ' obvious allusions to the frequent voyages for distant dis-'covery, which seem to have ended, for a time, in 1596.' Again, on p. 383, Chalmers continues: ' It seems to be more than probable that the intrigues at Court, which 'became apparent to every eye, after the return of Essex from Ireland, on the 28th 'of September, 1599, may have extorted the sarcasm of the Duke's question: "Are '" not these woods *More free* from *peril* than the *envious Court?*" ' ' If there be any 'allusion,' Chalmers goes on to say, ' in these reflections, to the fall of Essex; who ' was sequestered from Court soon after his arrival, the epoch of *As You Like It* must ' be fixed in the winter of 1599. There can be no doubt that it was imitated by ' Drayton in his *Owl*, which was first published in 1604.'

Again, the negative proof is adduced that if the play had been acted before 1598, FRANCIS MERES would have enumerated it, with the others which he mentions, in his well-known reference to Shakespeare. Cuthbert Burbie entered the *Palladis Tamia* on the 7th of September, 1598; of course Meres must have written it before that date, and although it does seem highly improbable that Meres should have mentioned such a play as *The Comedy of Errors* or *Titus Andronicus*, and omitted *As You Like It*, yet we must remember that Meres did not undertake to give a complete list; it is to be presumed that only the most popular plays are there given, and if the play had only just then been brought out, its popularity could hardly have been sufficiently tested. Moreover, Meres's list of the plays of Shakespeare is longer than his list of any other poet, and he may not have cared to swell it.

Again, in Rosalind's words, ' I will weep for nothing like Diana in the fountain,' WHALLEY detected an allusion to a statue of Diana set up on the Eleanor Cross in Cheapside, 'with water prilling from her naked breast' (see notes on IV, i, 147). According to HALLIWELL, Stowe, in his edition of 1598, described this statue as perfect and in use; but in his edition of 1603 Stowe says that the statue is ' now decayed.' ' It is evident, therefore,' says Halliwell, ' that if Shakespeare alludes to the Cheap-'side fountain, the words of Rosalind must have been penned somewhere between ' the year 1596, when it was erected, and 1603, when it had been allowed to go to ' ruin. At the same time, it should be remembered that the image of a fountain-'figure weeping was an exceedingly common one, and that Diana was a favorite ' subject with the sculptors for such an object.'

I think Shakespeare is entitled to more respect, to say the very least, than to suppose that in Rosalind's words he made any allusion to the Cheapside Diana. If that statue was perfectly familiar to his audience, and in running order, it is almost inconceivable that any hearer in that audience could ever have associated, for one single instant, this statue with Rosalind's *weeping*, or that any amount of poetic license can so ludicrously defy the laws of physiology.

Again, WRIGHT says (p. vi), ' there may possibly be a reference in V, ii, 71 (" By '" my life, I do; which I tender dearly, though I say I am a magician ") to the ' severe statute against witchcraft which was passed in the first year of James the ' First's reign [1603]. Again, in IV, i, 180 (" by all pretty oaths that are not danger-'" ous ") we might imagine the Act to Restrain the Abuses of Players (3 Jac. I, chap. ' 21, 1605) to be pointed at. But both these would give dates too late, and they may

'easily have been added at some subsequent representation of the play, which was
'mainly composed, as I think, in the year 1600, and after the other plays which are
'mentioned with it in the entry at Stationers' Hall.'

TIECK is positive in his date of the composition. In his *Notes* (p. 308) he speaks
of this comedy as 'the most daring and defiant of all Shakespeare's comedies; here
'Shakespeare, with his palms and lions and snakes, laughs at time and place, and
'derides all rules of composition; nay, the very rules which he himself devised and
'elsewhere practises he here parodies, and wends his wild and wanton way to make a
'pure, free, joyous Comedy, which was assuredly first performed in the summer of
'1599. Therefore shortly after *Twelfth Night*.' Even if Tieck be correct in his
conclusion, and other critics have adopted the same year, 1599, yet the reasons which
have led him to it are, to say the least, fanciful. Tieck's knowledge of our early
drama was remarkable, very remarkable for a foreigner and at that early date, in the
first quarter of this century, but he can scarcely be accepted as a safe guide now. He
had no drama nor early literature at home to study, and so was driven, as his coun-
trymen ever since have been driven, to study those of other nations. In the present
case he discovered that 'B. Jonson, in *Every Man Out of his Humour*, ridicules
'the freedom from all rules which Shakespeare displayed in *As You Like It*.' This
ridicule was infused not only into the *Prologue*, where it is pointedly said that 'Art
hath an enemy called Ignorance,' but throughout the running commentary in the play
itself the rules which ought to govern comedy are pedantically laid down. 'The play
'was a failure,' says Tieck, 'and so in the year 1600 Jonson brought out another com-
'edy, *Cynthia's Revels*, wherein he spoke even more offensively of himself as the great
'reformer of the stage,' and throughout, so says Tieck, referred to Shakespeare; but
pre-eminently in the Epilogue, where Jonson vaunts himself, and, in contemptuous disregard of his audience, says of his own work: 'By —— 'tis good, and if you like 't
you may.' 'The title of his play,' says Tieck, 'which was not perhaps, at first, *As
'You Like It*, Shakespeare intended as a jest on Jonson's boastfulness and braggart
'treatment of his audiences. In effect, Shakespeare says: " If you like it, and as you
'" like it, it is a comedy. It is not so in itself, but only after you, the spectators, have
'" so pronounced it by your applause." ' It is almost needless to call attention to the
visionary supposition to which Tieck is forced to resort in order to support his theory,
—viz. : that this comedy bore originally a different name; without some such postulate
his dates will not fadge. Tieck asserts that *Every Man Out of his Humour* was 'a
'failure, which greatly irritated its author'; a sequence entirely credible when 'B.
'Jonson's' temperament is remembered; but that the play was a failure escaped the
research of Gifford, who says of it: 'its merits are unquestionable; but I know not
'its success.'

W. W. LLOYD suspects that 'Shakespeare's creation of Rosalind followed that of
'Portia, and pretty closely'; it undoubtedly followed Portia, but if the date of *The
Merchant of Venice* be about 1596, and if the line from Marlowe be taken from the
volume published in 1598, then at least two very busy years must have separated the
Forest of Arden from the Garden of Belmont.

MOBERLY says: 'This charming comedy was probably represented in 1599, the
'year when Essex was Lord Lieutenant in Ireland, and when a new Spanish Armada
'was expected. . . . . A period which may be called that of Shakespeare's highest
'genius. He was then thirty-five years old; his powers of thought were maturing,
'and his language was pure, manly, and simple in the highest degree.'

FLEAY also adopts this year, 1599, as that wherein this comedy was written. The

Globe Theatre was opened in the spring of that year, and among the plays produced after the opening was *Henry V*, ' and soon after in this year *As You Like It.'—Shakespeare's Life and Work*, p. 138. Again, on p. 208, Fleay says, ' The date may, I ' think, be still more exactly fixed from I, ii, 84, " the little wit that fools have was ' " silenced," which alludes probably to the burning of satirical books by public ' authority 1st of June, 1599. Every indication points to the latter part of 1599 as ' the date of production. . . . . The comparison of the world to a stage in II, vii, sug- ' gests a date subsequent to the building of The Globe, with its motto, *Totus mundus* ' *agit histrionem ;* and the introduction of a fool proper, in place of a comic clown, ' such as is found in all the anterior comedies, confirms this : the " fools " only occur ' in plays subsequent to Kempe's leaving the company.' I have no great faith in the allusion to the burning of the satirical books, but that the change from ' clowns ' to ' fools ' should follow the retirement from my lord Chamberlain's men of Will Kempe, the pre-eminent ' clown,' is one of those shrewd, happy inferences which Fleay's through and through familiarity with the stage-history of Shakespeare's day enables him at times to make, with so much force.

To the two kinds of evidence, External and Internal, concerning the Date of Composition there may be added a third,—viz. : that derived from a close scrutiny and comparison of the metre of the different plays. It is assumed that certain peculiarities of style or methods of poetic treatment will mark the growth of the dramatist, and that, in general, the Seven Ages will prove true of the inner as of the outer man. This idea had been floating dimly in men's minds ever since it was first put forth by Edwards in his criticism of Warburton, in the last century. But it attracted little attention, despite the pleas put forth in its behalf by such fine minds as Spedding in England and Herzberg in Germany, until the *New Shakspere Society* arose and Fleay came to the fore with his laborious results of years of silent study. Since then a fierce light has beat on ' weak endings ' and ' light endings,' on ' end-stopped lines ' and ' pauses,' until now we have all of Shakespeare's plays as elaborately, if not as accurately, tabulated and calculated as the Ephemerides of the *Nautical Almanac.* If the results have not been quite commensurate with the outlay, it is not for a moment to be thought that the time for all the workers has been lost. Like the magic book of the physician Douban in the Arabian Tale, by merely turning the leaves of Shakespeare a subtle charm is imparted and absorbed. If in the first flush of accomplished work the advocates of this new test somewhat exaggerated their claims for its accuracy, surely with Burke, who could ' pardon some things to the spirit of Liberty,' we may pardon some things to the zeal for Shakespeare. And we should surely remember such temperate words as these of Dr INGRAM's, which we may accept as a summary of the best thought on the subject : ' I quite recognise the necessity of subordi- ' nating verse-tests in general to the ripe conclusions of the higher criticism, if these ' two sorts of evidence should ever be found at variance. But I believe that the more ' thoroughly the former are understood, and the more scientifically they are used, the ' more they will be found in accordance with the best æsthetic judgements. What ' appears to me surprising is, not that the verse-tests should sometimes appear to ' sanction wrong conclusions, but that they should, to such a remarkable extent, agree ' amongst themselves, and harmonize with every other mode of investigation which ' can be applied to the same questions.'

BATHURST, who was the first, I believe, to apply systematically to all the plays the test of metre as a means of determining their chronology, says (p. 76) : '*As You Like*

'*It* is in a more advanced style of metre than *Much Ado* [which was printed in
'1600]; see, particularly, the speech of Jaques about the Fool, Orlando's speech, ' If
' you have,' &c. Double endings not unusual. Rhymes at the end of speeches occur.
' One speech is in alternate rhymes, III, i. The " Seven Ages " are well known.
' The verse there broken, though it is an enumerative passage. Weak endings :
' " Swearing that we ‖ Are mere usurpers." " For 'tis ‖ The royal disposition of that
' " beast." The speeches often end on a half-line, which is, I believe, always regu-
' larly taken up. This is perfectly the reverse of an historical or political play. I
' would put it as early as possible. So say 1598 or 1599.'

INGRAM, however, places it, according to its proportion of ' Light and Weak End-
ings,' after *Much Ado*. In his List (*New Shakspere Society's Transactions*, 1874,
Series I, p. 450) *Much Ado* is No. 14, *As You Like It*, No 15, and *Twelfth Night*,
No. 16. *The Merchant of Venice* is No. 9. This would put the date of *As You Like
It* well into 1600, and to that extent confirms Wright's conjecture.

FURNIVALL divides all the plays into ' Periods,' and the ' Periods ' into ' Groups.'
This play is placed in 'the Second Period,' and in a Group of ' Three Sunny- or
' Sweet-Time Comedies : *Much Ado* (1599–1600); *As You Like It* (1600); *Twelfth
' Night* (1601).'

DOWDEN divides the Histories, Comedies, and Tragedies into Early, Middle, and
Later each, and subdivides into Groups. The same three plays, just enumerated, he
places in a Group of ' Musical Sadness,' with Jaques as a link to the next Group of
' Discordant Sadness.'

To recapitulate :

The Date of Composition of *As You Like It* is assigned by

COLLIER to ' summer of '	1598
DYCE	? 1598
NEIL	1598
BATHURST, GRANT WHITE	1598 or 1599
HUDSON ' between '	1598 and 1599
MALONE, SKOTTOWE, STAUNTON, HALLIWELL, COWDEN-CLARKE, MOBERLY, ROLFE, FLEAY	1599
REV. JOHN HUNTER	1599 or 1600
CHALMERS, DRAKE, WRIGHT, FURNIVALL	1600
KNIGHT	1600 or 1601
CAPELL	1607

In conclusion, there is on this Date of the Composition a happy unanimity, which
centres about the close of the year 1599; if a few months carry it back into 1598, or
carry it forward almost to 1601, surely we need not be more clamorous than a parrot
against rain over such trifles. As I have said before, and shall repeat until I change
my opinion, the whole subject is one which to my temperament has absolutely no
relation whatsoever to the play itself or to the enjoyment thereof. An exact knowledge, to the very day of the week, or of the month, when Shakespeare wrote it, can
no more heighten the charm of Rósalind's loveliness and wit than would the knowledge of the cost per yard of her doublet and hose. Does ever a question concerning
the Date of Composition arise in our thoughts when we are sitting at the play ? Still,
it would be a very grey, sombre world if we all thought alike, and undoubtedly to

many minds of far higher reach than mine the Date of the Composition has charms: for such as seek information about it, in the foregoing pages a full and, I trust, impartial account of what has been written thereon will be found.

SOURCE OF THE PLOT

IN 1754 DR ZACHARY GREY (*Critical, Historical, and Explanatory Notes on Shakespeare,* vol. i, p. 156) wrote: 'Several passages in this play were certainly bor-'rowed from the *Coke's Tale of Gamelyn* in Chaucer,' and thereupon proceeded to give an abstract of this *Tale of Gamelyn,* reciting the passages wherein Shakespeare had followed Chaucer, as Grey supposed.

Some time after, both CAPELL and FARMER, in the same year, 1767, announced what was more nearly the truth, that *As You Like It* was founded, not on the *Tale of Gamelyn,* but on a novel by Lodge.

CAPELL, in the *Introduction* to his edition (p. 50), writes as follows: 'A novel or '(rather) pastoral romance, intitl'd " Euphues' *Golden Legacy*," written in a very fan-'tastical style by Dr *Thomas* LODGE, and by him first publish'd in the year 1590, in 'quarto, is the foundation of *As you like it.* Besides the fable, which is pretty exactly 'follow'd, the out-lines of certain principal characters may be observ'd in the novel; 'and some expressions of the novelist (few, indeed, and of no great moment) seem 'to have taken possession of Shakespeare's memory, and thence crept into the play.'

Dr FARMER'S note is to be found in his Essay *On the Learning of Shakespeare* (one cannot but think, from the style and contents of this Essay, that a more exact title would have been *On the Learning of Richard Farmer, and the Ignorance of William Shakespeare*). On p. 15 the essayist says: '*As You Like It* was " certainly '" borrowed," if we believe Dr Grey and Mr Upton, from the *Coke's Tale of Game-'lyn,* which, by the way, was not printed till a century afterwards; when, in truth, 'the old Bard, who was no hunter of M.S.S., contented himself with Dr Lodge's '*Rosalynd* or *Euphues' Golden Legacye.*'

STEEVENS supplemented Farmer's remark with: 'Shakespeare has followed 'Lodge's *Novel* more exactly than is his general custom when he is indebted to such 'worthless originals; and has sketched some of his principal characters and borrowed 'a few expressions from it. His imitations, &c., however, are in general too insig-'nificant to merit transcription. It should be observed that the characters of Jaques, 'the Clown, and Audrey are entirely of the poet's own formation.'

This judgement of Steevens stirred COLLIER'S indignation; in the *Poetical Decameron* (vol. ii, p. 176, ed. 1820) Collier exclaims, in reference to it, 'Steevens 'was a tasteless pedant, and nothing better could be expected from him.'

KNIGHT, too, was no less angered, and after quoting the remark of Steevens, which I have just given, bursts forth: 'All this is very unscrupulous, ignorant, and 'tasteless. Lodge's *Rosalynd* is *not* a worthless original; Shakspere's imitations of 'it are *not* insignificant. Lodge's *Novel* is, in many respects, however quaint and 'pedantic, informed with a bright poetical spirit, and possesses a pastoral charm 'which may occasionally be compared with the best parts of Sidney's *Arcadia.*'

When COLLIER reprinted *Rosalynde* in his *Shakespeare Library,* he again replies to Steevens: 'Comparing *Rosalynde* with *As You Like It,* the former may indeed be

20

'termed "worthless," inasmuch as Shakespeare's play is so immeasurably superior to
'it; . . . but placing Lodge's *Novel* by the side of other productions of the same class,
'we cannot hesitate to declare it a very amusing and varied composition, full of agree-
'able and graceful invention (for we are aware of no foreign authority for any of the
'incidents) [Does "foreign authority" exclude the *Tale of Gamelyn ?*—ED.], and
'with much natural force and simplicity in the style of the narrative. That it is here
'and there disfigured by the faults of the time, by forced conceits, by lowness of allu-
'sion and expression, and sometimes by inconsistency and want of decorum in the
'characters, cannot be denied. There are errors which the judgement and genius of
'Shakespeare taught him to avoid; but the admitted extent and nature of his general
'obligations to Lodge afford a high tribute to the excellence of that "original," which
'Steevens pronounced "worthless." It may be almost doubted whether he had even
'taken the trouble to read carefully that performance upon which he delivered so
'dogmatical and definitive a condemnation.'

GRANT WHITE rates Lodge's *Novel* differently. 'Although,' he says (ed. i),
'there is this identity in the plots of the tale and the comedy, Shakespeare's creative
'power appears none the less remarkably in the latter. The personages in the two
'works have nothing in common but their names and the functions which they per-
'form. In the tale they are without character, and exist but to go through certain
'motions and utter certain formally constructed Complaints and Passions. The ladies
'quote Latin in a style and with a copiousness which would delight a Women's Rights
'Convention, and quench, in any man of flesh and blood the ardor of that love which
'is the right most prized of woman. Rosalind, for instance, musing upon her dawn-
'ing passion for Rosader and his poverty, says: " Doth not Horace tell thee what
'"methode is to be used in love ? *Querenda pecunia primum, post nummos virtus.*"
'There was a model for the traits and language of Shakespeare's Rosalind !'

Nor did age mellow White's judgement. In his second edition he reiterates:
'The comedy is, in fact, a mere dramatization of the tale—an adaptation it would
'now be called—the personages, the incidents, most of the names, and even some of
'the language, being found in Lodge's *Novel*. The chief difference between the two
'—more remarkable, even, than that one is a tale and the other a drama—is that the
'ambitious tale is one of the dullest and dreariest of all the obscure literary perform-
'ances that have come down to us from past ages, and the comedy, written as journey-
'work by a playwright to please a miscellaneous audience, is the one bright, immortal
'woodland poem of the world.'

DYCE (ed. iii): 'If Steevens somewhat undervalues [Lodge's *Rosalynde*], Mr
'Collier greatly overrates it.'

W. C. HAZLITT, on the other hand, in his reprint of Collier's *Shakespeare Library*,
says: 'It appears to me that Mr Collier states the matter fairly enough.'

'Never,' says CAMPBELL, 'was the prolixity and pedantry of a prosaic narrative
'transmuted by genius into such magical poetry. In the days of James I, George
'Heriot, the Edinburgh merchant, who built a hospital still bearing his name, is said
'to have made his fortune by purchasing for a trifle a quantity of sand that had been
'brought as ballast by a ship from Africa. As it was dry, he suspected from its
'weight that it contained gold, and he succeeded in filtering a treasure from it.
'Shakespeare, like Heriot, took the dry and heavy sand of Lodge and made gold
'out of it.'

As we have seen, Steevens, by his supercilious reference to Lodge, stirred Knight's
anger, and Dr Farmer was equally unfortunate when he said that 'the old bard was

'no hunter of MSS.' 'Thus,' exclaims KNIGHT, '"the old bard," meaning Shake-
'speare, did not take the trouble of doing, or was incapable of doing, what another
'old bard (first a player and afterwards a naval surgeon) did with great care—consult
'the manuscript copy' of the *Tale of Gamelyn*. Thereupon, Knight undertakes to
show that both Shakespeare and Lodge made use of the *Tale of Gamelyn*. That
Lodge was indebted to *Gamelyn* will be, I think, conceded by all, but Shakespeare's
indebtedness to that source is founded by Knight on three incidents wherein Lodge
and Shakespeare do not agree, and wherein Shakespeare took the hint, so Knight
thinks, from *Gamelyn :* First, Lodge represents Rosader (pronounced, by the way,
with the accent on the first syllable : Rósader) as having had bequeathed to him the
largest share of his father's estate. That to Orlando should have been devised the
smallest, Knight maintains is due to the hint which Shakespeare took from the delib-
erations of the old Knight's friends in *Gamelyn*. To this difference in treatment
Knight thinks is due the entirely different conception of the two characters, Rosader
and Orlando. Secondly, in *Gamelyn*, the old man, whose sons are fatally injured by
the Wrestler, 'bigan bitterly his hondes for to wrynge.' In Lodge's *Novel* the father
'never changed his countenance.' Wherefore, when Shakespeare represents the old
father as making 'pitiful dole' over his boys, Knight detects therein the direct traces
of *Gamelyn*. Thirdly, in Lodge, when the Champion approaches Rosader, he simply gives him 'a shake by the shoulder'; in *As You Like It* he mocks Orlando with
taunting speeches; and so in *Gamelyn* he starts towards the youth, 'and sayde "who
'" is thy fader, and who is thy sire? For sothe thou art a gret fool, that thou come
'" hire."'

    The force of these proofs is, I think, weakened by the following considerations :
Had the largest share of the father's estate been bequeathed, contrary to English
custom, to the youngest son, Orlando, Oliver's jealousy and envy would not have
been motiveless; it would have been scarcely unnatural. Secondly, the bitter lamentations of a father over the violent deaths of his sons, or, thirdly, the mocking jeers
of a braggart, are none of them of so unusual or of so extraordinary a character that
Shakespeare need have hunted round for authority or suggestion.

    In *The New Shakspere Society's Transactions* (Part ii, p. 277, 1882) W. G. STONE
compares *As You Like It* and *Rosalynde*. In addition to Knight's three points of
resemblance between Gamelyn and Orlando, Stone, in this good essay, detects 'five
'other parallelisms, more or less clear,' as follows : 'After his father's death, Johan,
'Gamelyn's eldest brother, "clothed him [Gamelyn] and *fed him yvel* and eek wrothe "
'[see l. 73, *post*]. Orlando complains to Adam that Oliver's "horses . . . . are faire
'" with their *feeding*, ... hee lets mee *feede* with his Hindes." Lodge only says,
'generally, that Saladym made "Rosader his foote boy for the space of two or three
'" yeares, keeping him in such servile subjection, as if he had been the sonne of any
'" country vassal." When Oliver called Orlando a "villaine," the latter replied : "I
'" am no villaine : I am the yongest sonne of Sir Rowland de Boys, he was my father,
'" and he is thrice a villaine that saies such a father begot villaines." Gamelyn
'answered the epithet "gadelyng," thus : "I am no worse gadelyng ne no worse
'" wight, But born of a lady and geten of a knight" (ll. 107, 108). As Gamelyn
'rode away to the wrestling-match, Johan [hoped] "He mighte *breke his nekke* in
'" that wrastlyng" (l. 194). In commending Orlando to Charles's "discretion,"
'Oliver said : "I had as liefe thou didst *breake his necke* as his finger." The wrestler
'thus taunted Gamelyn : "Come thou ones in myn hond, schalt thou never the " (l.
'234). Duke Frederick said : "You shall trie but one fall." Charles answered :

' " No, I warrant your Grace, you shall not entreat him to a second." Lastly, the
' forest of Arden and that to which Gamelyn and Adam betook themselves are
' described by the same adjective. Adam remarked : " That lever me were keyes for
' " to bere, Then walken in this *wilde woode* my clothes for to tere." [See *post*.]
' Compare "And to the skirts of this *wilde Wood* he [Duke Frederick] came." '

I cannot say that I think these five additional instances carry much weight. The
phrases common to the Tale and the Drama are in no respect either unusual or striking. It is only fair to add that the author of the paper by no means insists on their
parallelism, and that they are given only incidentally to the main purpose of his Essay,
which, as I have stated, is a comparison between Shakespeare and Lodge.

W. W. LLOYD, whose *Critical Essays* form by far the most valuable portion of
Singer's second edition, shares to some extent Knight's belief that Shakespeare had
at least read *Gamelyn*. On p. 114 he says : ' There can be no doubt that [Lodge's
' *Novel*] was carefully gone through by the poet, and it is not improbable that he had
' also in his hands the *Tale of Gamelyn*. Still, in this case, as in others, we must not
' rashly conclude that we possess all the sources. We have only negative proof that
' Shakespeare was the first to dramatise *Rosalynde*, and in those days of originality
' we shall make a great mistake if in eagerness to elevate Shakespeare we disable the
' inventive resources of his predecessors and contemporaries. Hence we tread but on
' uncertain ground when in comparing novel and play we too broadly assume that the
' improvements in the latter are necessarily more than adoptions from another source,
' an intermediate mind. Still, duly guarded, the value of comparison remains ; the
' glory of Shakespeare rests in any case not on the taste or judgement of particular
' alterations, but on the completeness with which, among multitudes of alternatives, he
' has gone right where he might so easily have been tempted wrong ; and in the com-
' parison of the finished work with the remoter rudiment, however many links of inter-
' mediate developement are lost, the attention is invariably guided to the spirit in which
' irregularities were corrected, relief supplied, and crudity or coarseness refined or
' suppressed.'

There is no evidence in *As You Like It* which is to me at all conclusive that
Shakespeare drew any the smallest inspiration from *The Tale of Gamelyn*. The
atmospheres of the two works are heavenwide apart, and as for mere verbal repetitions,
it is not impossible that a number of phrases might be found common to *As You
Like It* and the *Book of Job*. As between Lodge and Shakespeare, however, the
case is different ; there can be no doubt that the *Novel* is interwoven in the drama,
but whether by Shakespeare's hand, or, as Lloyd suggests, by another's, who can tell ?
Whether Shakespeare went directly to the *Novel* itself, or gilded with his heavenly
alchemy some pale, colorless drama which had been tried and failed, but whose
dramatic capabilities Shakespeare's keen eye detected, I find it impossible to decide.
The trivial blemishes in *As You Like It* which have been ascribed with probability,
by Wright and others, to haste on Shakespeare's part, may be attributed, it seems to
me, quite as plausibly to the outcroppings of the original play, which Shakespeare
remodelled, and their presence would still be due, more or less, to haste. Among these,
there is one, however, for which, I think, haste is hardly a sufficient explanation, and
this is, the character of Touchstone. If there is one quality in which Shakespeare is
forever Shakespeare, it is in the unity of his characters, in their thorough individuality,
in their absolute truth to themselves. A hundred and fifty years ago Pope said that
to prefix names to the speeches in Shakespeare's plays was almost superfluous ; the

speeches themselves unerringly proclaimed the speakers. We also know that either before the entrance of an important character, or very soon after, Shakespeare is wont to give either a prelude or a keynote, as it were, of that character, and with this keynote we all know how absolutely every subsequent trait or utterance is in harmony. If, then, this test be applied to Touchstone (or, why not say, this touchstone to Touchstone), will his character from first to last stand it? Is the 'clownish fool' and the 'roynish clown' of the First Act, with his bald jests of knights and pancakes, the Touchstone of the Fifth Act, who had trod a measure, flattered a lady, been politic with his friend and smooth with his enemy? Is the simpleton of the First Act, 'Nature's natural' as he is in truth, the same with the Touchstone who can cite Ovid and quarrel in print, by the book? Are there not here two separate characters? These two clowns cannot be one and the same. The true Touchstone we meet for the first time in the Forest of Arden, and although when Jaques speaks of him we have already seen him and heard him, yet it is Jaques who gives us the keynote of his character; and in the Touchstone of the last Act we recognise our old acquaintance, who solemnly pondered that 'from hour to hour we ripe and ripe, and then from hour to 'hour we rot and rot, and thereby hangs a tale.'

However rapid may have been Shakespeare's composition, I cannot suppose—it is to me unthinkable—that from the very first instant each character was not present before him in perfect symmetry and absolute completeness. For any discrepancy, therefore, any distortion in the character of Touchstone, haste in composition is hardly, I think, an adequate explanation, and I humbly suggest one of two courses as a possible solution: First, either we have, in the Clown of the Second Scene of the play, the genuine roynish fool of the original old play which Shakespeare rewrote, and who here crops out, perhaps through an oversight (here, at least, due to haste), or perhaps purposely retained to please the groundlings; or else, secondly, that the Clown who cracks his joke about beards and mustard was not Touchstone, but a separate and very different character, and who should never have been called Touchstone. Theobald, be it observed, was the first (and this, too, not till his second edition) to call this Clown Touchstone. He is our sole authority for it. This Clown Rosalind threatens with the whip—would she ever have thus menaced Touchstone?

Although this latter suggestion will relieve Touchstone's character from inconsistency,—an inconsistency which all must have felt, and to which Wright expressly calls attention,—yet the other trifling blemishes remain, such as styling Rosalind at one time the 'shorter,' and at another time the 'taller,' or speaking of 'Juno's swans,' &c. For these, I think, we must fall back on the explanation that they are the survivals of the older play. Theobald's error in nomenclature (that is, in calling the Clown of the Second Scene Touchstone) may account for the most serious of all; but for the others, I think, we can account by supposing that there was an older drama, which was intermediate between our *As You Like It* and Lodge's *Novel*.

Moreover, the weakness which we all feel here and there in the last scene, in passages which, as Wright fitly says, 'are not, to say the least, in Shakespeare's best 'manner,'—all these imperfections will be readily accounted for if we suppose them to be remnants of the old play, which Shakespeare was either too hurried, or too indifferent, to erase. The chiefest objection to this lies in the uncritical method which is herein implied, whereby we attribute, as a rule, whatever is good to Shakespeare, and whatever is less good to some one else. Still, I think, the rule may be, for the nonce, applied with due propriety to the close of this play.

Furthermore, is there not a mystery hanging over the staying of *As You Like It* by the Wardens of the Stationers' Company? It is not utterly beyond the pale of possibility that a clue to the mystery might be found in a clashing of pecuniary interests between the owners of the old play and of the new, and which was never set at rest until the ownership of both passed into the same hands before the First Folio was entered on the *Stationers' Registers* and permitted to be printed.

The student will find elaborate comparisons between Lodge's *Novel* and this play in the *Shakespeare Jahrbuch*, vol. vi, pp. 226–249, by DELIUS; also an extremely valuable analysis of the *Tale of Gamelyn*, in the *Shakespeare Jahrbuch*, vol. xxi, pp. 69–148, by ZUPITZA; and again in the *New Shakspere Society's Transactions*, Part ii, pp. 277–293, 1882, by W. G. STONE, wherein the writer ' examines Shakspere's treat-' ment of Lodge's *Rosalynde* from a negative point of view; and instead of showing ' his agreement therewith, dwells upon his divergence therefrom in varying the plot ' and in modifying the characters.' All these valuable Essays are designed for the benefit of those who have no access to the originals, and it is needful here merely to give their titles. In reprinting on the following pages both *The Tale of Gamelyn* and Lodge's *Rosalynde*, the original material is supplied from which the student, with best profit to himself, can make his own deductions and comparisons.

THE TALE OF GAMELYN

The Tale of Gamelyn is here reprinted from SKEAT's admirable edition (*Clarendon Press Series*, Oxford, 1884). The following few facts, all that are germane to this play, are wholly derived from that editor's excellent *Introduction*, and as much as possible in his very words: We may roughly date the *Tale of Gamelyn* near the middle of the fourteenth century. It so happens that all the copies of it which have been preserved occur in MSS of the *Canterbury Tales;* in three of the best MSS, however, it does not appear; but when it does appear it is always in the same place, *i. e.* in the gap left in Chaucer's work by his omission to finish the composition (or, more probably, the revision) of the *Cook's Tale*. There is, in fact, no connection between *Gamelyn* and any work of Chaucer, and no reason for connecting it with the *Cook's Tale* in particular, beyond the mere accident that the gap here found in Chaucer's work gave an opportunity for introducing it. ' I cannot but protest,' says Skeat, ' against the stupidity of the botcher whose hand wrote above it " The Cokes ' Tale of Gamelyn." That was done because it happened to be found *next after* ' the Cook's Tale, which, instead of being about Gamelyn, is about Perkin the reveller, ' an idle apprentice.'

It so happens that none of the black-letter editions of Chaucer contain the *Tale*, which was, in fact, never printed till 1721, but MSS of Chaucer circulated among readers, and in this way Thomas Lodge became acquainted with it. He certainly made use of a MS, which gave the name of the old Knight as Sir John of Burdeux; a Cambridge MS is the only one known to Skeat which has the spelling *burdeuxs*. Whence Lodge obtained the latter part of his *Rosalynde* does not appear, but it is not improbable that he had it from some Italian novel. *Gamelyn* is remarkable as being a story without a heroine; no female name is even mentioned in it, and it is only in the fifth line from the end that we are told that the hero ' wedded a wife both good and fair.' Hence it is not surprising that Lodge thought it necessary to expand the story, and to provide a Rosalind for his Rosader.

The footnotes are wholly taken from Skeat's *Notes* and *Glossary*. In reprinting, the only liberty I have taken is to change the character ȝ into *y* at the beginning, and into *gh* in the middle, of a word.

L ITHETH, and lesteneth · and herkeneth aright,   1
   And *ye* schulle here a talkyng · of a doughty knight;
Sire Iohan of Boundys · was his righte name,   3
He cowde of norture ynough · and mochil of game.   4
Thre sones the knight hadde · that with his body he wan;
The eldest was a moche schrewe · and sone he bygan.   6
His bretheren loued wel here fader · and of him were agast,   7
The eldest deserued his fadres curs · and had it at the last.
The goode knight his fader · lyuede so yore,   9
That deth was comen him to · and handled him ful sore.

But his chief anxiety was for his children's future. He, therefore, sent for some wise knights to come and help him dispose of his property; and charged them to divide his land evenly, and not to forget Gamelyn, his young son. The knights having learned his wishes,

Tho lete they the knight lyen · that was nought in hele,   41
And wenten in-to counseil · his landes for to dele;   42
For to delen hem alle · to oon, that was her thought   43
And for Gamelyn was *y*ongest · he schulde haue nought.
Al the lond that ther was · they dalten it in two,   45
And leten Gamelyn the *y*onge · withoute londe go,
And ech of hem seyde · to other full lowde,
His bretheren might *y*eve him lond · whan he good cowde.   48

When they reported this division to the knight, he liked it right nought, and told them to keep still, and he would deal out his land at his own will, as follows:

Johan, myn eldeste sone · schal haue plowes fyue   57
That was my fadres heritage · whil he was on lyue   58
And my myddeleste sone · fyue plowes of lond;
That I halp for to gete · with my righte hond;
And al myn other purchas · of londes and of leedes,   61
That I byquethe to Gamelyn · and alle my goode steedes.

1. *Litheth*, Hearken ye. The imperative plural.——3. *Boundys.* It is not clear what is meant by 'Boundys,' nor is there any clear indication of the supposed locality of the story. 'Boundys,' a place-name, is perhaps = bounds, marches, border-land; or possibly Bons, near Falaise in Normandy.——4. 'He was sufficiently instructed in right bringing up, and knew much about sport.' ——6. *schrewe*, wicked man.——6. *sone he bygan*, viz. to make good his reputation.——7. *agast*, afraid (in a good sense).——9. *yore*, a long time.——41. 'Then they left the knight lying there, who was not in health.'——42. *dele*, divide.——43. 'To apportion them all to one, that was their plan.'——44. *And for*, And because.——45. *dalten*, divided.——48. *whan he good cowde*, when he knew what was good, *i. e.* when he was old enough to know right from wrong; or, as we now say, when he came to years of discretion. Observe that the division of land here proposed was not final; the good knight, being still alive, altered it.——57. *plowes*, plough-lands. 'A *plough* of land was as much as could be ploughed with one plough.'—Wright, *ap.* Skeat.——58. *on lyue*, in life; alive.——61. *purchas*, i. e. purchases. Still applied, in law, to all property obtained otherwise than by descent.

Having thus disposed of his land, he lay stone still and died when his time came.
When he was buried under the grass,

> Sone the elder brother · gyled the *y*onge knaue;   70
> He took into his hond · his lond and his leede,   71
> And Gamelyn himselfe · to clothen and to feede.
> He clothed him and fedde him · yuel and eek wrothe,   73
> And leet his londes for-fare · and his houses bothe,   74
> His parkes and his woodes · and dede nothing wel;
> And seththen he it aboughte · on his faire fel.   76

Now Gamelyn waxed strong, so that neither man nor boy dared vex him.

> Gamelyn stood on a day · in his brotheres *y*erde,   81
> And bygan with his hond · to handlen his berde;
> He thoughte on his londes · that layen vnsawe,   83
> And his faire okes · that down were i-drawe;   84
> His parkes were i-broken · and his deer byreued.   85

Not a single good steed did he have left. Soon after his brother came up, and
asked Gamelyn if the meat was ready, which enraged Gamelyn, who 'swore by
goddes book Thou shalt go bake thyself; I will not be thy cook.' His brother is
astonished at such language, and Gamelyn rehearses his grievances, *thou*-ing his
brother instead of using the respectful *you*, and winds up with cursing him. Whereupon his quick-tempered brother replied:

> 'Stond stille, gadelyng · and hold right thy pees;   102
> Thou schalt be fayn for to haue · thy mete and thy wede; 103
> What spekest thou, Gamelyn · of lond other of leede?'   104
> Thanne seyde Gamelyn · the child that was ying,   105
> 'Cristes curs mot he haue · that clepeth me gadelyng!
> I am no worse gadelyng · ne no worse wight,   107
> But born of a lady · and geten of a knight.'

The brother dared not approach Gamelyn, but bade his men get staves to beat the
boy, who, when he saw them, all thus armed, draw near, looked round for some means
of defence, and his eye lit on a large pestle standing up against a wall; this he seized,
and looking like a wild lion he laid round him lustily, and soon had all the men lying
in a heap. His brother, not relishing this turn of affairs, fled up into a loft and shut
the door fast. Gamelyn looked everywhere for his brother, and finally espied him
looking out at a window. Then began a parley which ended in the brother's coming
down and making his peace, and promising that all of Gamelyn's inheritance should
be restored, and more too if he wanted it. 'But the knight thoughte on tresown and
Gamelyn on none, And wente and kiste his brother when they were at oon,' *i. e.* at
one, *i. e.* reconciled. Alas, young Gamelyn, nothing he wist with what a false treason
his brother him kissed!

---

70. *gyled*, beguiled the young boy.——71. *leede*, people, serfs.——73. *yuel and eek wrothe*,
badly, nay abominably.——74. *leet his londes for-fare*, let his lands go to ruin.——76. 'And
afterwards he paid for it in his fair skin.' We should now say, his recompense fell upon his own
head.——81. *yerde*, yard, courtyard.——83. *vnsawe*, unsown.——84. *i-drawe*, pulled down
to the ground.——85. *byreued*, stolen.——102. *gadelyng*, fellow; a term of reproach. But
observe that the sarcasm lies in the similarity of the sound of the word to Gamelyn. Hence Gamelyn's indignant reply.——103. 'Thou shalt be glad to get mere food and clothing.'——104. *other*,
either.——105. *ying*, young.——107. *wight*, man.

Litheth and lesteneth · and holdeth your tonge 169
And ye schul heere talkyng · of Gamelyn the yonge.
Ther was ther bysiden · cryed a wrastlyng, 171
And therfor ther was set vp · a ram and a ring;
And Gamelyn was in wille · to wende therto
For to preuen his might · what he cowthe do. 174
' Brother,' seyde Gamelyn · ' by seynt Richer, 175
Thou most lene me to-nyght · a litel courser 176
That is freisch to the spores · on for to ryde; 177
I most on an erande · a litel her byside.' 178
' By god !' seyde his brother · ' of steedes in my stalle
Go and chese the the best · and spare non of alle 180
Of steedes or of coursers · that stonden hem bisyde;
And tel me, goode brother · whider thou wolt ryde.'
   ' Her byside, brother · is cryed a wrastlyng,
And therfor schal be set vp · a ram and a ryng;
Moche worschip it were · brother, to vs alle, 185
Might I the ram and the ryng · bring home to this halle.'
A steede ther was sadeled · smertely and skeet; 187
Gamelyn did a paire spores · fast on his feet.
He sette his foot in the styrop · the steede he bystrood,
And toward the wrastelyng · the *y*onge child rood.
Tho Gamelyn the yonge · was riden out at gat, 191
The false kni*gh*t his brother · lokked it after that,
And bysoughte Iesu Crist · that is heuen kyng,
He mighte breke his nekke · in that wrastelyng.
As sone as Gamelyn com · ther the place was, 195
He lighte doun of his steede · and stood on the gras,
And ther he herd a frankeleyn · wayloway synge, 197
And bigan bitterly · his hondes for to wrynge.
' Goode man,' seyde Gamelyn · ' why makestow this fare ? 199
Is ther no man that may · *y*ou helpe out of this care ?'
' Allas !' seyde this frankeleyn · ' that euer ◄was I bore !
For tweye stalworthe sones · I wene that I haue lore ; 202
A champioun is in the place · that hath i-wrou*gh*t me sorwe, 203
For he hath slayn my two sones · but-if god hem borwe, 204
I would *y*eue ten pound · by Iesu Crist ! and more,
With the nones I fand a man · to handelen him sore.' 206
' Goode man,' sayde Gamelyn · ' wilt theu wel doon, 207
Hold myn hors, whil my man · draweth of my schoon,

---

171. *bysiden*, close by.————171. *cryed*, proclaimed.————174. *preuen*, test, shew.————174. *cowthe*, could.————175. *Richer*, Richard.　His name still appears in our Prayer-books.———— 176. *lene*, loan.————177. *spores*, spurs.————178. *her byside*, close by here.————180. *chese*, choose.————185. *worschip*, honour.————187. *smertely and skeet*, quickly and swiftly.————191. *Tho*, when.————195. *ther*, where.————197. *wayloway*, wellaway.　For Ang. Sax. *wá lá wá*, lit. ' woe! lo ! woe !'————199. *makestow*, makest thou.————199. *fare*, behaviour.————202. *lore*, lost. ————203. *sorwe*, sorrow.————204. *but-if*, &c., unless God be surety for them, *i. e.* ensure their recovery.　The two are not slain, but greatly disabled.————206. *With the nones*, on the occasion that, provided that.　*For the nones*, for the occasion, stands for *for then ones*, for the once ; so here *with the nones* = with *then ones*, with the once.————207. *wilt thou*, &c., if thou wishest to do a kind deed.

And help my man to kepe · my clothes and my steede, 209
And I wil into place go · to loke if I may speede.'
'By god!' sayde the frankeleyn · 'anon it schal be doon;
I wil my-self be thy man · and drawen of thy schoon,
And wende thou into place · Iesu Crist the speede,
And drede not of thy clothes · nor of thy goode steede.' 214
    Barfoot and vngert · Gamelyn in cam,
Alle that weren in the place · heede of him they nam, 216
How he durste auntre him · of him to doon his might 217
That was so doughty champioun · in wrastlyng and in fight.
Vp sterte the champioun · rapely anoon, 219
Toward *y*onge Gamelyn · he bigan to goon,
And sayde, 'who is thy fader · and who is thy sire?
For sothe thou art a gret fool · that thou come hire!'
Gamelyn answerde · the champioun tho,
'Thou knewe wel my fader · whil he couthe go, 224
Whiles he was on lyue · by seint Martyn!
Sir Iohan of Boundys was his name · and I Gamelyn.'
'Felaw,' seyde the champioun · 'al-so mot I thryue, 227
I knew wel thy fader · whil he was on lyue;
And thiself, Gamelyn · I wil that thou it heere,
Whil thou were a *y*ong boy · a moche schrewe thou were.' 230
Than seyde Gamelyn · and swere by Cristes ore 231
'Now I am older woxe · thou schalt fynde me a more!' 232
'Be god!' sayde the champioun · 'welcome mote thou be!
'Come thou ones in myn hond · schalt thou neuer the.' 234

The time was night and the moon was shining when the wrestling began. Many a trick did the champion try on Gamelyn, but in vain. Then said Gamelyn to the champion: 'I have withstood many tricks of thine, now you must try one or two of mine.' Whereupon, of all his tricks he showed him only one, 'and cast him on the left side, that three ribbes to brak.' And thereto one of his arms that gave a great crack. Then said the Franklin: 'Blessed be thou, Gamelyn, that ever thou wast born,' and being no longer in awe of the champion he scoffed at him for being beaten by so young a man. But the champion answered that Gamelyn was the master of all, and that never in his life had he been so roughly handled. And Gamelyn stood there shirtless, and dared any one to encounter him, satirically remarking that the champion did not appear to want any more. Not a soul came forward. At last two gentlemen, the overseers of the games, told Gamelyn to put on his shoes and stockings, for the fair was over. Then said Gamelyn: 'So mote I well fare, I have not yet sold out the half of my ware.' Whereupon the champion grimly spoke up: 'He is a fool that thereof buyeth, thou sellest so dear.' 'Fellow,' said the Franklin, 'why dost thou blame his ware? what thou boughtest thou hadst too cheap.' Then the wardens that were of that wrestling came and brought Gamelyn the ram and the ring,

---

214. *drede not of*, fear not for.——216. *nam*, took.——217. 'How he dared adventure himself, to prove his strength upon him that was so doughty a champion?'——219. *rapely anoon*, quickly in a minute.——224. *whil he couthe go*, whilst he was able to go about.——227. *Felaw*, fellow (as a term of reproach).——227. *al-so mot I*, as I may.——230. *a moche schrewe*, &c., thou wast a great doer of mischief. Gamelyn retorts that he is now *a more*, i. e. a still greater doer of mischief.——231. *ore*, grace.——232. *woxe*, grown.——234. *the*, thrive.

and he went, with much joy, home in the morning. His brother saw him coming with a great rowte, and bade shut the gate, and hold him without. The porter of his lord was full sore agast, and started at once to the gate, and locked it fast.

[The chief points of resemblance between *As You Like It* and *The Tale of Gamelyn* here cease. In what remains only the name Adam, and Adam's flight with Gamelyn to a forest where they find outlaws feasting, can be at all considered common to both. I have been careful to retain, as far as possible, the phraseology of the original in the following abstract of the remaining six hundred lines of *The Tale*. It is of necessity brief, and gives merely an outline of the story, from which it can be seen that there are no situations, except possibly the forest-scene, wherein young Gamelyn could have served in the least as the direct prototype of Orlando.]

When Gamelyn, flushed with victory, returned home with the ram and the ring and a disorderly crew of friends, he found the gate shut against him. Whereupon he kicked the gate in, caught the porter, broke his neck, and threw him down a well. His friends were cordially invited by him to help themselves to meat, and for drink five tuns of wine were hospitably placed at their disposal. His brother meanwhile lay hid in a 'litel toret' of the castle and saw them 'wasting his good,' but 'durste he not speke.' This carousal lasted for eight days, then the guests took their leave, and when they had 'riden and i-goon, Gamelyn stood allone, friends had he noon.' His brother ventured then from his hiding-place, which he had apparently changed, though we are not told why, from the 'toret' to the 'selleer.' The treacherous knight forgave Gamelyn, and even went so far as to tell him that because 'of my body, brother, heir geten have I noon, I will make thee mine heir, I swear by St Johan.' Gamelyn was, of course, very grateful, but nothing wist of his brother's guile. Under the plea of an oath which he had made when from his hiding-place he had seen Gamelyn throw the porter down the well, the brother persuaded Gamelyn to be bound hand and foot, merely out of formality, that his oath should not be broken. But as soon as he was bound and securely fettered, his brother told everybody that Gamelyn was mad. For two days and two nights, without meat or drink, was the young fellow fastened to a post. Then he appealed privately to Adam, who was the spencer, or officer of the household who dispensed the provisions, to succour him, which Adam, the spencer, did, with food and drink. It was then agreed between them that Adam should unlock Gamelyn's fetters, and when the feasting and revelry was at its height, with all the Abbots and Priors, on Sunday, Gamelyn should make an appeal to all the men of holy Church for help, and if they refused he should break forth, and he with a good staff, and Adam with another, fight for freedom. And it so befell, the men of holy Church banned him instead of blessing him, whereupon he cast away his fetters and began to work, and with such good effect that there was none of them all that with his staff met but he made him overthrow, and quit them his debt. 'Gamelyn,' said Adam, 'do them but good; they are men of holy church, draw of them no blood, take heed of the tonsure, and do them no harms, but break both their legs, and after that their arms.' This provident advice was followed until at last Gamelyn got at his brother; him he struck in the neck, and also a little above the girdle, and bruised his backbone, and set him in the fetters. The sheriff was summoned by those who escaped, and when Gamelyn saw him and his posse approach he fled with Adam, so that when the sheriff got to the castle he found a nest, but no egg; however, he found the brother fettered, and anone sent for a doctor to heal his backbone.

Gamelyn and Adam meanwhile marched steadily into the wood; but the latter

took it ill, and at last said: ' I see now that it is better to be a spencer. It is far
'preferable keys for to bear than to walk in this wild wood my clothes for to tear.'
' Adam,' said Gamelyn, ' dismay thee right nought; many a good man's child into
' care is i-brought.' And as they were walking together they heard talking of men
near by. Then Gamelyn under the wood looked aright, and seven score of young
men he saw well a-dight, that is, accoutred; all sat at meat in a circle about. 'Adam,'
said Gamelyn, ' now have we no doubt, after ill cometh good, through grace of God
' almight; me thinketh of meat and drink that I have a sight.' Adam looked then
under wood-bough, and when he saw meat he was glad enow; for he hoped to God
to have his share or deel, and he was sore alonged after a good meal. The master
outlaw, after finding out who they were, bade them sit there adown for to take rest,
and bade them eat and drink, and that of the best. In the course of time Gamelyn
rose to be king of the outlaws. Meanwhile his false brother had risen to be sheriff,
and caused Gamelyn to be proscribed as an outlaw and summoned to appear at the
next sessions. 'Alas,' said Gamelyn, ' that ever I was so slack As not to break his
' neck, though I did break his back.' However, Gamelyn was thrust in prison. His
brother Ote now appeared, and became surety for Gamelyn's appearance on the next
court day. On that day Gamelyn entered the court with a band of his merry men,
and finding that his false brother had suborned a jury to condemn to death his brother
Ote, as a forfeit for his absence, he seized the Judge, the sheriff (his brother), and
the jury, and hanged them all. This act of summary justice seemed somehow to
strike the king very favourably, for he not only made Ote a Justice, but Gamelyn a
Chief Justice. The latter thus recovered his land and his serfs; brother Ote made
him his heir, and Gamelyn wedded a wife both good and fair. And they lived
together, while that Crist wold, Until Gamelyn was buried under the mold. And so
shall we all; that none may flee: God bring us to the joy, that ever shall be.

LODGE'S ROSALYNDE

The Text of *Rosalynde* here given is from a copy issued by the *Hunterian
Club*, and placed, with alacrity, at my disposal by my kind friend, Mr Alexander
Smith, of Glasgow. In the *Fifth Annual Report*, 1878, of this excellent Club, that
has done, and is still doing, such fine work in its especial field, this issue of Lodge's
Novel is thus spoken of: ' In regard to " Rosalynde," it may be noted that the first
' edition, 1590, has never until now been reprinted. For the use of the unique original
' (unfortunately imperfect) in the Britwell library, the Club is indebted to the kindness
' of Mr S. Christie-Miller. The deficiency (Sig. R, 4 leaves) has been supplied from
' the second edition, 1592, in the collection of Mr Henry Huth.'

Marginal references are placed opposite those passages only which have been
specifically mentioned by critics in the preceding Commentary on the Play.

The *Novel* is so long, and demands so many pages, that I have compressed its
form, not its substance, in all possible ways, running into the text when practicable
lines of poetry, titles of chapters, &c., &c., which in the original stand out in the
page with generous margins. For the same reason I have not followed the original
in printing every name in small capitals. Be it remembered, therefore, that the substance alone is here reproduced; the form is quite disregarded.

Rosalynde. || Euphues golden le- || gacie: found after his death || *in his Cell at Si-* || lexedra. || *Bequeathed to Philautus fonnes* || nourfed vp with their || *father in Eng-* || land. || Fetcht from the Canaries. || *By T. L. Gent.* || London, || Imprinted by *Thomas Orwin* for *T. G.* || and *John Busbie.* || 1590. ||

To the right ho- || nourable and his moſt eſteemed || *Lord the Lord of Hunſdon, Lord* || Chamberlaine of her Maieſties || *houſhold, and Gouernor of her* || Towne of Barwicke : || *T. L.G. wiſheth increaſe* || of all honourable ver- || tues. ||

SVch Romanes (*right Honourable*) *as delighted in martiall exploytes, attempted their actions in the honour of* Auguſtus, *becauſe he was a Patron of ſouldiers : and* Virgil *dignified him with his poems, as a* Mœcenas *of ſchollers; both ioyntly aduauncing his royaltie, as a Prince warlike and learned. Such as ſacrifice to* Pallas, *preſent her with bayes as ſhe is wiſe, and with armour as ſhe is valiant; obſeruing herein that excellent* το πρεπον *which dedicateth honours according to the perfection of the perſon. VVhen J entred (right honourable) with a deep inſight into the conſideration of theſe premiſſes, ſeeing your L. to be a Patron of all martiall men, and a* Mœcenas *of ſuch as applie themſelues to ſtudie; wearing with* Pallas *both the launce and the bay, and ayming with* Auguſtus *at the fauour of all, by the honourable vertues of your minde : being my ſelfe firſt a Student, and after falling from bookes to armes, euen vowed in all my thoughts dutifully to affect your L. Hauing with Capt :* Clarke *made a voyage to the Jlands of* Terceras *&* the Canaries, *to beguile the time with labour, J writ this booke ; rough, as hatcht in the ſtormes of the Ocean, and feathered in the ſurges of many perillous ſeas. But as it is the worke of a ſouldier and a ſcholler, J preſumed to ſhrowde it vnder your Honors patronage, as one that is the fautor and fauourer of all vertuous actions; and whoſe honourable Loues growen from the generall applauſe of the whole Common wealth for your higher deſerts, may keep it frõ the mallice of euery bitter tung. Other reaſons more particular (right Honorable) chalenge in me a ſpeciall affection to your L. as being a ſcholler with your two noble ſonnes, Master* Edmond Carew *&* M. Robert Carew, (*two ſiens worthie of ſo honorable a tree, and a tree glorious in ſuch honourable fruite) as alſo being ſcholler in the Vniuerſitie vnder that learned and vertuous Knight Sir* Edward Hobbie, *when he was Batcheler in Arts, a mã as well lettered as well borne, and after the Etymologie of his name ſoaring as high as the wings of knowledge can mount him, happie euerie way, & the more fortunate, as bleſſed in the honor of ſo vertuous a Ladie. Thus (right honourable) the duetie that J owe to the ſonnes, chargeth me that all my affection be placed on the father; for where the braunches are ſo precious, the tree of force muſt be moſt excellent. Commaunded and emboldened thus with the conſideration of theſe forepaſſed reaſons, to preſent my Booke to your Lordſhip; I humbly intreate, your Honour will vouch of my labours, and fauour a ſouldiers and a ſchollers pen with your gracious acceptance; who anſweres in affection what he wants in eloquence; ſo deuoted to your Honour, as his onely deſire is, to end his life vnder the fauour of ſo martiall and learned a Patron.*

Resting thus in hope of your Lordſhips courteſie, in deyning the Patronage of my worke, J ceaſe : wiſhing you as many honourable fortunes as your Lordſhip can deſire, or I imagine.

Your Honours ſouldier
humbly affectionate :
Thomas Lodge.

To the Gentlemen Readers.

GEntlemen, look not here to find anie fprigs of *Pallas* bay tree, nor to heare the humour of any amorous Lawreate, nor the pleafing vaine of anie eloquent Orator : *Nolo altum fapere,* they be matters aboue my capacitie ; the Coblers checke fhall neuer light on my head, *Ne futor vltra crepidam,* I will goe no further than the latchet, and then all is well. Heere you may perhaps find· fom leaues of *Venus* mir- tle, but heawen down by a fouldier with his curtleaxe, not bought with **I, iii, 124** the allurement of a filed tongue. To be briefe Gentlemen, roome for a fouldier, & a failer, that giues you the fruits of his labors that he wrought in the *Ocean,* when euerie line was wet with a furge, & euerie humorous pafsion counter- checkt with a ftorme. If you like it, fo : and yet I will be yours in duetie, if you bee mine in fauour. But if *Momus* or anie fquint-eied affe that hath mightie eares to con- ceiue with *Midas,* and yet little reafon to iudge ; if hee come aboord our Barke to find fault with the tackling, when he knows not the fhrowdes, Ile downe into the hold, and fetch out a ruftie pollax, that fawe no funne this feauen yeare, and either well be baft him, or heaue the cockfcombe ouer boord to feede cods. But courteous Gentlemen that fauour moft, backbite none, & pardon what is ouerslipt, let fuch come & vvelcome, Ile into the Stevvards roome, & fetch them a kan of our beft beuradge. VVell Gentlemen, you haue *Euphues Legacie.* I fetcht it as farre as the Ilands of *Terceras,* and therefore read it ; cenfure vvith fauour, and farevvell.

Yours T. L.

Rofalynd.

THere dwelled adioyning to the citie of *Bourdeaux* a Knight of moft honorable parentage, whom Fortune had graced with manie fauours, and Nature honored with fundrie exquifite qualities, fo beautified with the excellence of both, as it was a queftion whether Fortune or Nature were more prodigall in deciphering the riches of their bounties. Wife hee was, as holding in his head a fupreme conceipt of policie, reaching with Nestor into the depth of all ciuill gouernment ; and to make his wife- dome more gracious, he had that *falem ingenij* and pleafant eloquence that was fo highlie commended in Vlisses : his valour was no leffe than his wit, nor the ftroake of his Launce no leffe forcible, than the fweetneffe of his tongue was perfwafiue : for he was for his courage chofen the principall of all the Knights of *Malta.* This hardie Knight thus enricht with Vertue and Honour, furnamed Sir Iohn of *Bourdeaux,* hau- ing paffed the prime of his youth in fundrie battailes againft the *Turkes,* at laft (as the date of time hath his courfe) grew aged : his haires were filuer hued, and the map of age was figured on his forehead : Honour fat in the furrowes of his face, and many yeres were pourtraied in his wrinckled liniaments, that all men might perceiue his glaffe was runne, and that Nature of neceffity chalenged her due. Sir Iohn (that with the Phenix knewe the tearme of his life was now expyred, and could with the Swanne difcouer his end by her fongs) hauing three fonnes by his wife Lynida, the verie pride of all his forepaffed yeres, thought now (feeing death by conftraint would compell him to leaue them) to beftowe vpon them fuch a Legacie as might bewray his loue, and increafe their enfuing amitie. Calling therefore thefe yong Gentlemen before him in the prefence of all his fellowe Knights of *Malta,* he refolued to leaue them a memoriall of his fatherlie care, in fetting downe a methode of their brotherlie dueties. Hauing therefore death in his lookes to mooue them to pitie, and teares in his eyes to paint out the depth of his paffions, taking his eldeft fonne by the hand, hee began thus.——Sir Iohn of Bourdeaux Legacie he gaue to his Sonnes.——

Oh my Sonnes, you fee that Fate hath fet a period of my yeares, and Deftinies haue determined the finall ende of my daies: the Palme tree waxeth away ward, for he ftoopeth in his height, and my plumes are full of ficke feathers touched with age. I muft to my graue that difchargeth all cares, and leaue you to the world that encreafeth many forowes: my filuer haires conteineth great experience, and in the number of my yeares are pend downe the fubtilties of Fortune. Therefore as I leaue you fome fading pelfe to counterchecke pouertie, fo I will bequeath you infallible precepts that fhall leade you vnto vertue. Firft therefore vnto thee Saladyne the eldeft, and therefore the chiefeft piller of my houfe, wherein fhould be ingrauen as well the excellence of thy fathers qualities, as the effentiall forme of his proportion, to thee I giue foureteene ploughlands, with all my Mannor houfes and richeft plate. Next vnto Fernandyne I bequeath twelue ploughlands. But vnto Rofader the yongeft I giue my Horfe, My Armour and my Launce, with fixteene ploughlands: for if the inward thoughts be difcouered by outward fhadowes, Rofader will exceed you all in bountie and honour. Thus (my Sonnes) haue I parted in your portions the fubftance of my wealth, wherein if you bee as prodigall to fpend, as I haue been carefull to get, your friends will grieue to fee you more waftfull than I was bountifull, and your foes fmile that my fall did begin in your exceffe. Let mine honour be the glaffe of your actions, and the fame of my vertues the Loadftarre to direct the courfe of your pilgrimage. Ayme your deedes by my honorable endeuours, and fhewe your felues fiens worthie of fo florifhing a tree: leaft as the birds Halcyones which exceede in whiteneffe, I hatch yong ones that furpaffe in blackneffe. Climbe not my fonnes; afpiring pride is a vapour that afcendeth hie, but foone turneth to a fmoake: they which ftare at the Starres, ftumble vppon ftones; and fuch as gaze at the Sunne (vnleffe they bee Eagle eyed) fall blinde. Soare not with the Hobbie, leaft you fall with the Larke; nor attempt not with Phaeton, leaft you drowne with Icarus. Fortune when fhe wils you to flie, tempers your plumes with waxe, and therefore either fit ftill and make no wing, or els beware the Sunne, and holde Dedalus axiome authenticall (*medium tenere tutiffimum*). Low fhrubbes haue deepe rootes, and poore Cottages great patience. Fortune lookes euer vpward, and enuie afpireth to neftle with dignitie. Take heede my fonnes, the meane is fweeteft melodie; where ftrings high ftretcht, either foone cracke, or quicklie growe out of tune. Let your Countries care be your hearts content, and thinke that you are not borne for your felues, but to leuell your thoughts to be loyall to your Prince, careful for the Common weale, and faithfull to your friends; fo fhall *France* fay, thefe men are as excellent in vertues, as they be exquifite in features. Oh my fonnes, a friend is a precious Iewell, within whofe bofome you may vnloade your forowes and vnfolde your fecretes, and hee either will releeue with counfaile, or perfwade with reafon: but take heede in the choyce, the outward fhew makes not the inward man, nor are the dimples in the face the Calenders of trueth. When the Liquorice leafe looketh moft drie, then it is moft wet. When the fhoares of *Lepanthus* are moft quiet, then they forepoint a ftorme. The Baaran leafe the more faire it lookes, the more infectious it is, and in the fweeteft words is oft hid the moft trecherie. Therefore my fonnes, choofe a friend as the Hiperborei do the mettals, feuer them from the ore with fire, & let them not bide the ftamp before they be currant; fo trie and then truft, let time be touchftone of friendfhip, & then friends faithfull lay them vp for Iewells. Be valiant my fonnes, for cowardife is the enemie to honour; but not too rafh, for that is an extreame. Fortitude is the meane, and that is limitted within bonds, and prefcribed with circumftance. But aboue all, and with that he fetcht a deepe figh, beware of Loue, for it is farre more perilous than pleafant, and yet I tell you it allureth as ill as the Syrens. Oh my fonnes, fancie is a fickle thing, and beauties paintings are trickt vp with times colours, which being fet to drie in the Sunne, perifh with the fame. Venus is a wanton, & though her lawes pretend libertie, yet there is nothing but loffe and gliftering miferie. Cupids wings are plumed with the feathers of vanitie, and his arrowes where they pearce, inforce nothing but deadly defires: a womans eye as it is precious to behold, fo it is preiudiciall to gaze vpon; for as it affoordeth delight, fo it fnareth vnto death. Truft not their fawning fauours, for their loues are like the breath of a man vpon fteele, which no fooner lighteth on but it leapeth of, and their paffions are as momentarie as the colours of a Polipe, which changeth at the fight of euerie obiect. My breath waxeth fhort and mine eyes dimme, the houre is come and I muft away: therefore let this fuffice, women are wantons, and yet men cannot want one: and therefore if you loue, choofe her that hath her eyes of Adamant, that will turne only to one poynt; her heart of a Diamond, that will receiue but one forme; her tongue of a Sethin leafe, that neuer wagges but with a Southeaft winde: and yet my fonnes, if fhe haue all thefe qualities, to be chaft, obedient, and filent; yet for that fhe is a woman, fhalt thou finde in her fufficient vanities to counteruaile her uertues. Oh now my fonnes, euen now take thefe my laft words as my lateft Legacie, for my thrid is fponne, and my foote is in the graue: keepe my precepts as memorialls of your fathers counfailes, and let them bee lodged in the fecrete of your hearts; for wifedome is better than wealth, and a golden fentence worth a world of treafure. In my fall fee & marke my fonnes the follie of man, that being duft climbeth with Biares to reach at the Heauens, and readie euerie minute to dye, yet hopeth for an age of pleafures. Oh mans life is like lightning that is but a flafh, and the longeft date of his yeares but as a bauens blaze. Seeing then man is fo mortall, bee carefull that thy life bee vertuous, that thy death may be full of admirable honours; so fhalt thou challenge fame to bee thy fautor, and put obliuion to exile with thine honorable actions. But my Sonnes, leaft you fhould forget your fathers axiomes, take this fcroule, wherein reade what your father dying, wils you to execute liuing. At this hee fhrunke downe in his bed and gaue vp the ghoft.

Iohn of *Bourdeaux* being thus dead, was greatlie lamented of his Sonnes and bewayled of his friends, efpeciallie of his fellowe Knights of *Malta*, who attended on his Funeralls, which were performed with great folemnitie. His Obfequies done, Saladyne caufed next his Epitaph the contents of the fcroule to be pourtraied out, which were to this effect.

The contents of the fcedule which Sir Iohn of Bourdeaux gaue to his Sonnes.

MY Sonnes, behold what portion J doo giue;
I leaue you goods, but they are quicklie lost;
J leaue aduice, to fchoole you how to liue;
I leaue you wit, but wonne with little cost:
But keepe it well; for counfaile ftill is one,
When Father, friends, and worldlie goods are gone.

In choice of thrift let honour be thy gaine,
Winne it by vertue and by manly might;
In dooing good esteeme thy toyle no paine,
Protect the fatherleffe and widowes right:
Fight for thy faith, thy Countrie and thy King,
For why? this thrift will prooue a blefsed thing.

In choice of wife, preferre the modeſt chaſt,
Lillies are faire in ſhew, but foule in ſmell;
The ſweeteſt lookes by age are ſoone defaſt :
Then chooſe thy wife by wit and liuing well.
Who brings thee wealth and many faults withall,
Preſents thee honie, mixt with bitter gall.

In choice of friends, beware of light beliefe,
A painted tongue may ſhroud a ſubtill heart;
The Syrens *teares doo threaten mickle griefe,*
Foreſee my ſonne, for feare of ſodaine ſmart :
Chuſe in thy wants : and he that friends thee then,
When richer growne, befriend him thou agen.

Learne of the Ant *in ſommer to prouide;*
Driue with the Bee the Droane from out thy hiue;
Builde like the Swallowe in the ſommer tide;
Spare not too much (my ſonne) but ſparing thriue :
Be poore in follie, rich in all but ſinne :
So by thy death thy glorie ſhall beginne.

Saladine hauing thus ſet vp the Scedule, and hangd about his Fathers hearſe many paſſionate Poems, that *France* might ſuppoſe him to be paſſing ſorrowfull, he clad him-ſelfe and his Brothers all in black, & in ſuch ſable ſutes diſcourſed his griefe : but as the Hiena when ſhe mournes is then moſt guilefull, ſo Saladine vnder this ſhew of griefe ſhadowed a heart full of contented thoughtes : the Tyger though hee hide his clawes, will at laſt diſcouer his rapine : the Lions lookes are not the mappes of his meaning, nor a mans phiſnomie is not the diſplay of his ſecrets. Fire cannot bee hid in the ſtraw, nor the nature of man ſo concealed, but at laſt it will haue his courſe : nourture and art may doo much, but that *Natura naturaus* which by propagation is ingrafted in the heart, will be at laſt perforce predominant according to the olde verſe. *Naturam expellas furca licet, tamen vſque recurret.* So fared it with Saladyne, for after a months mourning was paſt, he fell to conſideration of his Fathers teſtament, how he had bequeathed more to his younger brothers than himſelfe, that Rosader was his Fathers darling, but now vnder his tuition, that as yet they were not come to yeres, & he being their gardin, might (if not defraud them of their due) yet make ſuch hauock of their legacies and lands, as they ſhould be a great deale the lighter : whereupon hee began thus to meditate with himſelfe.——Saladynes meditation with himſelfe.——Saladyne, how art thou diſquieted in thy thoughts, & perplexed with a world of reſtleſſe paſſions, hauing thy minde troubled with the tenour of thy Fathers teſtament, and thy heart fiered with the hope of preſent preferment ς by the one, thou art counſaild to content thee with thy fortunes; by the other, perſwaded to aſpire to higher wealth. Riches (Saladyne) is a great royalty, & there is no ſweeter phiſick thã ſtore. Auicen like a foole forgot in his Aphoriſmes to ſay, that golde was the moſt precious reſtoratiue, and that treaſure was the moſt excellent medecine of the minde. Oh Saladyne, what were thy Fathers precepts breathed into the winde ? haſt thou ſo ſoone forgottẽ his principles ? did he not warne thee from coueting without honor, and climing without vertue ς did hee not forbid thee to aime at any action that ſhould not be honourable ς and what will bee more preiudiciall to thy credit, than the careleſſe ruine of thy brothers welfare ς why ſhouldſt not thou bee the piller of thy brothers proſperitie; and wilt thou become the ſubuerſion of their fortunes ς is there

21

any fweeter thing than concord, or a more precious Iewel then amity? are you not fons of one Father, fiens of one tree, birds of one neft ſ and wilt thou become fo vnnaturall as to rob them, whome thou fhouldft relieue ſ No Saladyne, intreate them with fauours, and intertaine them with loue; fo fhalt thou haue thy confcience cleare and thy renowne excellent. Tufh, what words are thefe bafe foole; farre vnfit (if thou be wife) for thy humour. What though thy Father at his death talked of many friuolous matters, as one that doated for age, and raued in his fickneffe: fhal his words be axioms, and his talke be fo authenticall, that thou wilt (to obferue them) preiudice thy felfe ſ No no Saladyne, fick mens wills that are parole, and haue neither hand nor feale, are like the lawes of a Citie written in duft; which are broken with the blaft of euerie winde. What man thy Father is dead, and hee can neither helpe thy fortunes, nor meafure thy actions: therefore burie his words with his carkaffe, and bee wife for thy felfe. What, tis not fo olde as true: *Non fapit, qui fibi non fapit.* Thy Brother is young, keepe him now in awe, make him not check mate with thy felfe: for *Nimia familiarit as contemptum parit.* Let him knowe little, fo fhall he not be able to execute much; fuppreffe his wittes with a bafe eftate, and though hee be a Gentleman by nature yet forme him a new, and make him a peafant by nourture: fo fhalt thou keepe him as a flaue, and raign thy felfe fole Lord ouer al thy Fathers poffeffions. As for Fernandyne thy middle brother he is a fcholer, and hath no minde but on Aristotle, let him reade on Galen while thou rifleft with gold, and pore on his booke til thou dooft purchafe lands: wit is great wealth, if hee haue learning it is enough; and fo let all reft.

In this humour was Saladyne making his brother Rosader his foote boy, for the fpace of two or three yeares, keeping him in fuch feruile fubiection, as if hee had been the fonne of any countrie vaffall. The yong Gentleman bare al with patience, til on a day walking in the gardē by himfelf, he began to confider how he was the fon of Iohn of *Bourdeaux*, a knight renowmed for many victories, & a Gentlemā famozed for his vertues, how contrarie to the teftament of his father, he was not only kept from his land, and intreated as a feruant, but fmothered in fuch fecret flauerie, as he might not attaine to any honourable actions. Ah quoth he to himfelfe (nature working thefe effectuall paffions) why fhould I that am a Gentleman borne, paffe my time in fuch vnnaturall drudgerie? were it not better either in *Paris* to become a fcholler, or in the court a courtier, or in the field a fouldier, than to liue a foote boy to my own brother: nature hath lent me wit to cōceiue, but my brother denied me arte to contemplate: I haue ftrength to performe any honorable exployte, but no libertie to accomplifh my vertuous indeuours: thofe good partes that God hath beftowed vpon me, the enuie of my brother dooth fmother in obfcuritie: the harder is my fortune, and the more his frowardneffe. With that cafting vp his hand he felt haire on his face, and perceiuing his beard to bud, for choler hee began to blufh, and fwore to himfelfe he would bee no more fubiect to fuch flauerie. As thus he was ruminating of his melancholie paffions, in came Saladyne with his men, and feeing his brother in a browne ftudie, and to forget his wonted reuerence, thought to   **I, i, 52** fhake him out of his dumps thus. Sirha (quoth hee) what is your heart on your halfe penie, or are you faying a Dirge for your fathers foule? what is my dinner readie ſ At this queftion Rosader turning his head afcance, and bending his browes as if anger there had ploughed the furrowes of her wrath, with his eyes full of fire, he made this replie. Doeft thou afke me (Saladyne) for thy Cates ſ afke fome of thy Churles who are fit for fuch an office: I am thine equall by nature, though not by birth; and though thou haft more Cardes in the bunch, I haue as many trumps in my hands as thy felfe. Let me queftion with thee, why thou haft feld my Woods, fpoyled my Manner houfes, and made hauock of fuch vtenfals as my father bequeathed vnto me ς I tell thee Saladyne, either anfwere me as a brother, or I will trouble thee as an enemie.

At this replie of Rosaders, Saladyne fmiled as laughing at his prefumption, & frowned as checking his follie: hee therefore tooke him vp thus fhortlie. What firha, well I fee earlie prickes the tree that will prooue a thorne : hath my familiar conuerfing with you made you coy, or my good lookes drawne you to be thus contemptuous ς I can quickly remedie fuch a fault, and I will bende the tree while it is a wand : In faith (fir boy) I haue a fnaffle for fuch a headftrōg colt. You   **I, i, 53** firs lay holde on him and binde him, and then I will giue him a cooling carde for his choller. This made Rosader halfe mad, that ftepping to a great rake that ftood in the garden, he laide fuch loade vpon his brothers men that he hurt fome of them, and made the reft of them run away. Saladyne feeing Rosader fo refolute, and with his refolution fo valiant, thought his heeles his beft fafetie, and tooke him to a loaft adioyning to the garden, whether Rosader purfued him hotlie. Saladyne afraide of his brothers furie, cried out to him thus. Rosader bee not fo rafh, I am thy brother and thine elder, and if I haue done thee wrong Ile make thee amends : reuenge not anger in bloud, for fo fhalt thou ftaine the vertue of olde Sir Iohn of *Bourdeaux :* fay wherein thou art difcontent and thou fhalt be fatiffied. Brothers frownes ought not to be periods of wrath : what man looke not fo fowerlie, I knowe we fhall be friends, and better friends than we haue been. For, *Amantium iræ amoris redint egratio eft.* .

Thefe wordes appeafed the choller of Rosader, (for hee was of a milde and courteous nature) fo that he laide downe his weapons, and vpon the faith of a Gentleman affured his brother he would offer him no preiudice: wherevpon Saladyne came downe, and after a little parley they imbraced each other and became frends, and Saladyne promifing Rosader the reftitution of al his lands, and what fauour els (quoth he) any waies my abilitie or the nature of a brother may performe. Vpon thefe fugred recōciliations they went into the houfe arme in arme together, to the great content of all the old feruants of Sir Iohn of *Bourdeaux.* Thus continued the pad hidden in the ftrawe, till it chaunced that Torismond King of *France* had appoynted for his pleafure a day of Wraftling and of Tournament to bufie his Commons heads, leaft being idle their thoughts fhould runne vpon more ferious matters, and call to remembrance their old banifhed King; a Champion there was to ftand againft all commers a Norman, a man of tall ftature and of great ftrength; fo valiant, that in many fuch conflicts he alwaies bare away the victorie, not onely ouerthrowing them which he incountred, but often with the weight of his bodie killing them outright. Saladyne hearing of this, thinking now not to let the ball fall to the ground, but to take oportunitie by the forehead : firft by fecret meanes conuented with the Norman, and procured him with rich rewards to fweare, that if Rosader came within his clawes he fhould neuer more returne to quarrell with Saladyne for his poffeffions. The Norman defirous of pelfe, as (*Quis nifi mentis inops oblatum refpuit aurum.*) taking great gifts for little Gods, tooke the crownes of Saladyne to performe the ftratagem. Hauing thus the Champion tied to his vilanous determination by oath, he profecuted the intent of his purpofe thus. Hee went to young Rosader, (who in all his thoughts reacht at honour, and gazed no lower than vertue commaunded him) and began to tell him of this Tournament and Wraftling, how the King fhould be there, and all the chiefe Peeres of *France,* with all the beautifull damofels of the

Countrey: now brother (quoth he) for the honor of Sir Iohn of *Bourdeaux* our renowmed father, to famous that houfe that neuer hath been found without men approoued in Cheualrie, fhewe thy refolution to be peremptorie. For my felfe thou knoweft though I am eldeft by birth, yet neuer hauing attempted any deedes of Armes, I am yongeft to performe any Martiall exploytes, knowing better **I, i, 54** how to furuey my lands, than to charge my Launce : my brother Fernandyne he is at *Paris* poring on a fewe papers, hauing more infight into Sophiftrie and principles of Philofophie, than any warlike indeuours : but thou Rosader the youngeft in yeares, but the eldeft in valour, art a man of ftrength and dareft doo what honour allowes thee; take thou my fathers Launce, his Sword, and his Horfe, and hie thee to the Tournament, and either there valiantlie crack a fpeare, or trie with the Norman for the palme of actiuitie. The words of Saladyne were but fpurres to a free horfe; for hee had fcarce vttered them, ere Rosader tooke him in his armes, taking his proffer fo kindly, that he promifed in what he might to requite his courtefie. The next morowe was the day of the Tournament, and Rosader was fo defirous to fhew his heroycall thoughts, that he paft the night with little fleepe : but affoone as Phœbus had vailed the Curteine of the night, and made Aurora blufh with giuing her the *bezoles labres* in her filuer Couch, he gat him vp; and taking his leaue of his brother, mounted himfelfe towards the place appoynted, thinking euery mile ten leagues till he came there. But leauing him fo defirous of the iourney : to Torismond the King of *France*, who hauing by force banifhed Gerismond their lawfull King that liued as an outlaw in the Forreft of *Arden*, fought now by all meanes to keepe the *French* bufied with all fportes that might breed their content. Amongft the reft he had appointed this folemne Tournament, whereunto he in moft folemne manner reforted, accompanied with the twelue Peeres of *France*, who rather for feare than loue graced him with the fhewe of their dutifull fauours : to feede their eyes, and to make the beholders pleafed with the fight of moft rare and gliftring obiects, he had appoynted his owne daughter Alinda to be there, & the faire Rosalynd daughter vnto Gerismond, with all the beautifull damofels that were famous for their features in all *France*. Thus in that place did Loue and Warre triumph in a fimpathie : for fuch as were Martiall, might vfe their Launce to bee renowmed for the excellence of their Cheualrie; and fuch as were amorous, might glut themfelues with gazing on the beauties of moft heauenly creatures. As euerie mans eye had his feuerall furuey, and fancie was partiall in their lookes, yet all in generall applauded the admirable riches that Nature beftowed on the face of Rosalynd : for vppon her cheekes there feemed a battaile betweene the Graces, who fhould beftow moft fauours to make her excellent. The blufh that gloried Luna when fhe kift the fhepheard on the hills of *Latmos* was not tainted with fuch a pleafant dye, as the Vermilion flourifht on the filuer hue of Rosalynds countenance; her eyes were like thofe lampes that make the wealthie couert of the Heauens more gorgeous, fparkling fauour and difdaine; courteous and yet coye, as if in them Venus had placed all her amorets, and Diana all her chaftitie. The tramells of her hayre, foulded in a call of golde, fo farre furpaft the burnifht glifter of the mettall, as the Sunne dooth the meaneft Starre in brightneffe : the treffes that foldes in the browes of Apollo were not halfe fo rich to the fight; for in her haires it feemed loue had laide her felfe in ambufh, to intrappe the proudeft eye that durft gafe vppon their excellence : what fhould I neede to decipher her particular beauties, when by the cenfure of all fhe was the paragon of all earthly perfection. This Rosalynd fat I fay with Alinda as a beholder of thefe fportes, and made the Caualiers crack their lances with more courage : many deeds of Knighthoode that day were performed, and many prizes were giuen according to their feuerall deferts: at laft when the tournament ceafed, the wraftling began; and the Norman prefented himfelfe as a chalenger againft all commers; but he looked like Hercules when he aduaunft himfelfe againft Acheloüs; fo that the furie of his countenance amafed all that durft attempt to incounter with him in any deede of actiuitie: till at laft a luftie Francklin of the Countrie came with two tall men that were his Sonnes of good lyniaments and comely perfonage: the eldeft of thefe dooing his obeyfance to the King entered the lyft, and prefented himfelfe to the Norman, who ftraight coapt with him, and as a man that would triumph in the glorie of his ftrength, roufed himfelfe with fuch furie, that not onely hee gaue him the fall, but killed him with the weight of his corpulent perfonage: which the younger brother feeing, lept prefently into the place, and thirftie after the reuenge, affayled the Norman with fuch valour, that at the firft incounter hee brought him to his knees: which repulft fo the Norman, that recouering himfelfe, feare of difgrace doubling his ftrength, hee ftept fo ftearnely to the young Francklin, that taking him vp in his armes he threw him againft the ground fo violently, that he broake his neck, and fo ended his dayes with his brother. At this vnlookt for maffacre, the people murmured, and were all in a deepe paffion of pittie; but the Francklin, Father vnto thefe, neuer changed his countenance; but as a mã of a couragious refolution, tooke vp the bodies of his Sonnes without any fhew of outward difcontent. All this while ftoode Rosader and fawe this tragedie: who noting the vndoubted vertue of the Francklins minde, alighted of from his horfe, and prefentlie fat downe on the graffe, and commaunded his boy to pull off his bootes, making him readie to trie the ftrength of this Champion; being furnifhed as he would, hee clapt the Francklin on the fhoulder and faide thus. Bolde yeoman whofe fonnes haue ended the tearme of their yeares with honour, for that I fee thou fcorneft fortune with patience, and twharteft the iniurie of fate with content, in brooking the death of thy Sonnes: ftand a while and either fee mee make a third in their tragedie, or elfe reuenge their fall with an honourable triumph; the Francklin feeing fo goodlie a Gentleman to giue him fuch courteous comfort, gaue him hartie thankes, with promife to pray for his happie fucceffe. With that Rosader vailed bonnet to the King, and lightlie lept within the lifts, where noting more the companie than the combatant, hee caft his eye vpon the troupe of Ladies that gliftered there like the ftarres of heauen, but at laft Loue willing to make him as amourous as he was valiant, prefented him with the fight of Rosalynd, whofe admirable beautie fo inueagled the eye of Rosader, that forgetting himfelfe, he ftoode and fed his lookes on the fauour of Rosalynds face, which fhe perceiuing, blufht: which was fuch a doubling of her beauteous excellence, that the bafhfull red of Aurora at the fight of vnacquainted Phaeton was not halfe fo glorious: The Norman feeing this young Gentleman fettered in the lookes of the Ladies, draue him out of his *memento* with a fhake by the fhoulder; Rosader looking back with an angrie frowne, as if he had been wakened from fome pleafant dreame, difcouered to all by the furie of his countenance that he was a man of fome high thoughts: but when they all noted his youth, and the fweeteneffe of his vifage, with a generall applaufe of fauours, they grieued that fo goodly a young man fhould venture in fo bafe an action: but feeing it were to his difhonour to hinder him from his enterprife, they wifht him to be graced with the palme of victorie. After Rosader was thus called out of his *memento* by the Norman, hee roughlie clapt to him with fo fierce an incounter, that they both fell to the ground, and with the violence of the fall were forced to breathe: in which fpace the Norman called to minde by all tokens, that this was hee whom Saladyne had appoynted him to kil; which coniecture made him ftretch euerie limb, & trie euerie finew, that working his death he might recouer the golde, which fo bountifully was promifed him. On the contrarie part, Rosader while he breathed was not idle, but ftill caft his eye vppon Rosalynd, who to incourage him with a fauour, lent him fuch an amorous looke, as might haue made the moft coward defperate: which glance of Rosalynd fo fiered the paffionate defires of Rosader, that turning to the Norman hee ran vpon him and braued him with a ftrong encounter; the Norman receiued him as valiantly, that there was a fore combat, hard to iudge on whofe fide fortune would be prodigall. At laft Rosader calling to minde the beautie of his new Miftreffe, the fame of his Fathers honours, and the difgrace that fhould fall to his houfe by his miffortune, roufed himfelfe and threw the Norman againft the ground, falling vpon his Cheft with fo willing a waight, that the Norman yeelded nature her due, and Rosader the victorie. The death of this Champion; as it highlie contented the Francklin, as a man fatiffied with reuenge, fo it drue the King and all the Peeres into a great admiration, that fo young yeares and fo beautifull a perfonage, fhould containe fuch martiall excellence: but when they knew him to be the yongeft Sonne of Sir Iohn of *Bourdeaux*, the King rofe from his feate and imbraced him, and the Peeres intreated him with al fauourable courtefie, commending both his valour and his vertues, wifhing him to goe forward in fuch haughtie deedes, that he might attaine to the glorie of his Fathers honourable fortunes. As the King and Lordes graced him with embracing, fo the Ladies fauored him with their lookes, efpecially Rofalynd, whome the beautie and valour of Rosader had alreadie touched; but fhe accounted loue a toye, and fancie a momentarie paffion, that as it was **I, ii, 25** taken in with a gaze, might bee fhaken off with a winck; and therefore feared not to dallie in the flame, and to make Rosader knowe fhe affected him; tooke from hir neck a Iewell, and fent it by a Page to the young Gentleman. The Prize that Venus gaue to Paris was not halfe fo pleafing to the Troian, as this Iemme was to Rosader: for if fortune had fworne to make him fole Monark of the world, he would rather haue refufed fuch dignitie, than haue loft the iewell fent him by Rofalynd. To retourne her with the like he was vnfurnifhed, and yet that hee might more- than in his lookes difcouer his affection, he ftept into a tent, and taking pen and paper writ this fancie.

> *Two Sunnes at once from one faire heauen there fhinde,*
> *Ten branches from two boughes tipt all with rofes,*
> *Pure lockes more golden than is golde refinde,*
> *Two pearled rowes that Natures pride inclofes:*
>
> *Two mounts faire marble white, downe-foft and daintie,*
> *A fnow died orbe; where loue increaft by pleafure*
> *Full wofull makes my heart, and bodie faintie:*
> *·Hir faire (my woe) exceedes all thought and meafure.*   **III, ii, 93**
>
> *In lines confufde my luckleffe harme appeereth;*
> *Whom forrow clowdes, whom pleafant fmiling cleereth.*

This fonnet he fent to Rosalynd, which when fhe read, fhe blufht, but with a fweete content in that fhe perceaued loue had alotted her fo amorous a feruant. Leauing her to her new intertayned fancies, againe to Rosader; who triumphing in the glory of this conqueft, accompanied with a troupe of young Gentlemen, that were defirous to be his familiars, went home to his brother Saladynes, who was walking

before the gates, to heare what fucceffe his brother Rosader fhould haue, affuring him
felf of his death, and deuifing how w^t diffimuled forrow, to celebrate his funeralls;
as he was in this thought, hee caft vp his eye, & fawe where Rosader returned with
the garlande on his heade, as hauing won the prize, accompanied with a crew of
boone companions; greeued at this, hee ftepped in and fhut the gate. Rosader feeing this, and not looking for fuch vnkinde intertaynement, blufht at the difgrace, and
yet fmothering his griefe with a fmile, he turned to the Gentlemen, and defired them
to holde his brother excufed, for hee did not this vpon any malicious intent or nig-
gardize, but being brought vp in the countrie, he abfented him felfe, as not finding his
nature fit for fuch youthfull companie. Thus hee fought to fhadow abufes proffred
him by his brother, but in vayne, for he could by no meanes be fuffered to enter:
whereupon hee ran his foote againft the doore, and brake it open; drawing his fworde
and entring bouldly into the Hall, where hee founde none (for all were fled) but one
Adam Spencer an Englifh man, who had been an olde and truftie feruant to Sir Iohn
of *Bourdeaux*: he for the loue he bare to his deceafed Maifter, fauored the part of
Rosader, and gaue him and his fuch intertaynement as he coulde. Rosader gaue him
thankes, and looking about, feeing the hall empty, faide, Gentlemen, you are welcome, frolicke and be merie, you fhall be fure to haue Wine enough, whatfoeuer your
fare be, I tell you Caualiers my brother hath in his houfe, fiue tunne of wine, and as
long as that lafteth, I befhrewe him that fpares his liquor. With that he burft open
the butterie dore, and with the helpe of Adam Spencer, couered the Tables, and fet
downe whatfoeuer he could finde in the houfe, but what they wanted in meate, Rosader fupplied with drinke, yet had they royall cheere, and withall fuch a hartie welcome, as would haue made the courfeft meates, feeme delicates. After they had
feafted and frolickt it twife or thrife with an vpfey freeze, they all tooke their leaues
of Rosader and departed. Affoone as they were gone Rosader growing impatient of
the abufe, drewe his fworde, and fwore to be reuenged on the difcurteous Saladyne:
yet by the meanes of Adam Spencer, who fought to continue friendfhip and amitie
betwixt the brethren, and through the flattering fubmiffion of Saladyne, they were
once agayne reconciled, & put vp all fore paffed iniuries, with a peaceable agreement,
liuing together for a good fpace in fuch brotherly loue, as did not onely reioyce the
feruants, but made all the Gentlemen and bordring neighbours glad of fuch friendlie
concord. Saladyne hiding fire in the ftraw, and concealing a poyfoned hate in a
peaceable countenance, yet deferring the intent of his wrath till fitter opportunitie, he
fhewed him felfe a great fauorer of his brothers vertuous endeuours: where leauing
them in this happie league, let vs returne to Rosalynd.

Rosalynd returning home from the triumph, after fhe waxed folitarie, loue prefented her with the Idea of Rosaders perfection, and taking her at difcouert, ftrooke
her fo deepe, as fhe felt her felfe grow paffing paffionate: fhe began to call to minde
the comelineffe of his perfon, the honor of his parents, and the vertues that excelling
both, made him fo gracious in the eies of euerie one. Sucking in thus the hony of
loue, by imprinting in her thoughtes his rare qualities, fhe began to furfit with the contemplation of his vertuous conditions, but when fhe cald to remembrance her prefent
eftate, and the hardneffe of her fortunes, defire began to fhrink, & fancy to vale bonnet, that betweene a *Chaos* of confufed thoughtes, fhe began to debate with her felfe
in this manner.——R o s a l y n d s p a f s i o n.——Infortunate Rosalynd, whofe miffortunes are more than thy yeeres, and whofe paffions are greater than thy patience.
The bloffomes of thy youth, are mixt with the froftes of enuie, and the hope of thy
enfuing frutes, perifh in the bud. Thy father is by Torifmond banifht from the

crowne, & thou the vnhappie daughter of a King detained captiue, liuing as difquieted in thy thoughts, as thy father difcontēted in his exile. Ah Rosalynd what cares wait vpõ a crown, what griefes are incident to dignitie? what forrowes haunt royal Pallaces ꝙ The greateſt feas haue the foreſt ſtormes, the higheſt birth ſubieƈt to the moſt bale, and of al trees the Cedars ſooneſt ſhake with the winde: ſmall Currents are euer calme, lowe valleyes not ſcorcht in any lightnings, nor baſe men tyed to anye balefull preiudice. Fortune flies, & if ſhe touch pouertie, it is with her heele, rather diſdayning their want with a frowne, than enuying their wealth with diſparagement. Oh Rosalynd, hadſt thou been borne lowe, thou hadſt not fallen ſo high; and yet being great of bloud, thine honour is more, if thou brookeſt misfortune with patience. Suppoſe I contrary fortune with content, yet Fates vnwilling to haue me any way happie, haue forced loue to ſet my thoughts on fire with fancie. Loue Rosalind ꝙ becommeth it women in diſtreſſe to thinke of loue ꝙ Tuſh, deſire hath no reſpeƈt of perſons, Cupid is blinde and ſhooteth at randon, as ſoone hitting a rag, as a robe, and percing aſſoone the boſome of a Captiue, as the breaſt of a Libertine. Thou ſpeakeſt it poore Rosalynd by experience, for being euerie way diſtreſt, furcharged with cares, and ouergrowne with ſorrowes, yet amidſt the heape of all theſe miſhaps, loue hath lodged in thy hart the perfeƈtion of young Rosader, a man euery way abſolute as well for his inward life, as for his outward lyniaments, able to content the eye with beauty, and the eare with the report of his vertue. But conſider Rosalind his fortunes, and thy preſent eſtate, thou art poore and without patrimonie, and yet the daughter of a Prince, he a younger brother, and voide of ſuch poſſeſſions as eyther might maintayne thy dignities, or reuenge thy fathers iniuries. And haſt thou not learned this of other Ladies, that louers cannot liue by lookes; that womens eares are ſooner content with a dram of giue me, than a pound of heare me; that gould is ſweeter than eloquence; that loue is a fire, & wealth is the ſewell; that Venus Coffers ſhould be euer full. Then Rosalynd, ſeeing Rosader is poore, thinke him leſſe beautifull, becauſe he is in want, and account his vertues but qualities of courſe, for that hee is not indued with wealth. Doth not Horace tell thee what methode is to be vſed in loue, *Querenda pecunia primum, post nummos virtus.*

Tuſh Rosalynd, be not ouer raſh; leape not before thou looke; eyther loue ſuch a one as may with his landes purchaſe thy liberty, or els loue not at all. Chooſe not a fayre face with an emptie purſe, but ſay as moſt women vſe to ſay, *Si nihil attuleris, ibis Homere foras.*

Why Rosalynd, can ſuch baſe thoughtes harbour in ſuch high beauties ꝙ Can the degree of a Princes, the daughter of Gerismond harbour ſuch ſeruile conceites, as to prize gold more than honor, or to meaſure a Gentleman by his wealth, not by his vertues. No Rosalynd, bluſh at thy baſe reſolution, and ſay if thou loueſt, either Rosader or none: and why ꝙ becauſe Rosader is both beautifull and vertuous. Smiling to her ſelfe to thinke of her new entertayned paſſions, taking vp her Lute that lay by her, ſhe warbled out this dittie.

Roſalynds Madrigal.

Loue in my boſome like a Bee
doth ſucke his ſweete :
Now with his wings he playes with me,
now with his feete.
Within mine eies he makes his neaſt,
His bed amidst my tender breaſt,

My kiſſes are his daily feast;
And yet he robs me of my rest.
 Ah wanton, will ye?

And if J ſleepe, then pearcheth he
  with pretie flight,
And makes his pillow of my knee
  the liuelong night.
Strike I my lute he tunes the ſtring,
He muſicke playes if ſo I ſing,
He lends me euerie louelie thing;
Yet cruell he my heart doth ſting.
 Whiſt wanton ſtill ye?

Els I with roſes euerie day
  will whip you hence;
And binde you when you long to play,
  for your offence.
Ile ſhut mine eyes to keepe you in,
Ile make you fast it for your ſinne,
Ile count your power not worth a pinne;
Ahlas what hereby ſhall I winne,
 Jf he gainſay me?

What if J beate the wanton boy
  with manie a rod?
He will repay me with annoy,
  becauſe a God.
Then ſit thou ſafely on my knee,
And let thy bowre my boſome be:
Lurke in mine eyes J like of thee:
Oh Cupid ſo thou pitie me.
 Spare not but play thee.

Scarce had Rosalynde ended her Madrigale, before Torismond came in with his daughter Alinda, and manie of the Peeres of *France*, who were enamoured of her beautie: which Torismond perceiuing, fearing leaſt her perfeƈtion might be the beginning of his preiudice, and the hope of his fruite ende in the beginning of her bloſſomes, hee thought to baniſh her from the Court: for quoth he to himſelfe, her face is ſo full of fauour, that it pleades pitie in the eye of euerie man; her beautie is ſo heauenly and deuine, that ſhe will prooue to me as Helen did to Priam: ſome one of the Peeres will ayme at her loue, ende the marriage, and then in his wiues right attempt the kingdome. To preuent therefore had I wiſt in all theſe aƈtions, ſhe tarries not about the Court, but ſhall (as an exile) either wander to her father, or els feeke other fortunes. In this humour, with a ſtearne countenance full of wrath, hee breathed out this cenſure vnto her before the Peeres, that charged her that that night ſhee were not ſeene about the Court: for (quoth he) I haue heard of thy aſpiring ſpeaches, and intended treaſons. This doome was ſtrange vnto Rosalynde, and preſently couered with the ſhield of her innocence, ſhee boldly brake out in reuerend tearmes to haue cleared her ſelfe: but Torismond would admit of no reaſon, nor durſt his Lordes plead for Rosalynde, although her beautie had made ſome of them paffionate, feeing the figure of wrath portraied in his brow. Standing thus all mute, and Rosalynde amazed, Alinda who loued her more than her felfe, with griefe in her heart, & teares in her eyes, falling downe on her knees, began to intreate her father thus:——A l i n d a s   o r a t i o n   t o   h e r   f a t h e r   i n   d e f e n c e   o f   f a i r e   R o f a - l y n d e.——If (mightie Torismond) I offende in pleading for my friend, let the law of amitie craue pardon for my boldnes; for where there is depth of affection, there friendfhip alloweth a priuiledge. Rosalynde and I haue beene foftered vp from our infancies, and nurfed vnder the harbour of our conuerfing together with fuch priuate familiarities, that cuftome had wrought an vnion of our nature, and the fympathie of our affections fuch a fecrete loue, that we haue two bodies, and one foule. Then meruaile not (great Torismond) if feeing my friend diftreft, I finde my felfe perplexed with a thoufand forrowes: for her vertuous and honourable thoughts (which are the glories that maketh women excellent) they be fuch, as may challenge loue, and race out fufpition: her obedience to your Maieftie, I referre to the cenfure of your owne eye, that fince her fathers exile hath fmothered all griefes with patience, and in the abfence of nature, hath honoured you with all dutie, as her owne Father by nouriture: not in word vttering anie difcontent, nor in thought (as farre as coniecture may reach) hammering on reuenge; onely in all her actions feeking to pleafe you, & to winne my fauour. Her wifedome, filence, chaftitie, and other fuch rich qualities, I need not decypher: onely it refts for me to conclude in one word, that fhe is innocent. If then, Fortune who triumphs in varietie of miferies, hath prefented fome enuious per-fon (as minifter of her intended ftratagem) to taint Rosalynde with anie furmife of treafon, let him be brought to her face, and confirme his accufation by witneffes; which prooued, let her die, and Alinda will execute the maffacre. If none can auouch anie confirmed relation of her intent, vfe Iuftice my Lord, it is the glorie of a King, and let her liue in your wonted fauour: for if you banifh her, my felfe as copartner of her hard fortunes, wil participate in exile fome part of her extremities.

Torismond (at this fpeach of Alinda) couered his face with fuch a frowne, as Tyrannie feemed to fit triumphant in his forehead, and checkt her vp with fuch taunts, as made the Lords (that onlie were hearers) to tremble. Proude girle (quoth he) hath my lookes made thee fo light of tung, or my fauours incouraged thee to be fo forward, that thou dareft prefume to preach after thy father? Hath not my yeares more experience than thy youth, and the winter of mine age deeper infight into ciuill policie, than the prime of thy florifhing daies? The olde Eion auoides the toyles where the yong one leapes into the net: the care of age is prouident and forefees much: fufpition is a vertue, where a man holds his enemie in his bofome. Thou fonde girle meafureft all by prefent affection, & as thy heart loues thy thoughts cen-fure: but if thou kneweft that in liking Rosalynd thou hatcheft vp a bird to pecke out thine owne eyes, thou wouldft intreate as much for her   **I, iii, 83** abfence, as now thou delighteft in her prefence. But why do I alleadge policie to thee ᶜ fit you downe hufwife and fall to your needle: if idleneffe make you fo wanton, or libertie fo malipert, I can quicklie tie you to a fharper tafke: and you (maide) this night be packing either into *Arden* to your father, or whether beft it fhall content your humour, but in the Court you fhall not abide. This rigorous replie of Torismond nothing amazed Alinda, for ftill fhe profecuted her plea in the defence of Rosalynd, wifhing her father (if his cenfure might not be reuerft) that he would appoint her partner of her exile; which if he refufed to doo, either fhe would (by fome fecret meanes) fteale out and followe her, or els end her daies with fome def-perate kinde of death. When Torismond heard his daughter fo refolute, his heart

was fo hardened againft her, that he fet downe a definitiue and peremptorie fentence that they fhould both be banifhed : which prefentlie was done. The Tyrant rather choofing to hazard the loffe of his only child, than any waies to put in queftion the ftate of his kingdome : fo fufpicious and feareful is the confcience of an vfurper. Well, although his Lords perfwaded him to retaine his owne daughter, yet his refolution might not bee reuerft, but both of them muft away from the court without either more companie or delay. In he went with great melancholie, and left thefe two Ladies alone. Rosalynd waxed very fad, and fat downe and wept. Alinda fhe fmiled, and fitting by her friende began thus to comfort her.——A l i n d a s   c o m -
f o r t   t o   p e r p l e x e d   R o f a l y n d.——Why how now Rosalynd, difmaide with a frowne of contrarie fortune ς Haue I not oft heard thee fay that high minds were difcouered in fortunes contempt, and heroycall feene in the depth of extremities ς Thou wert wont to tell others that complained of diftreffe, that the fweeteft falue for miferie was patience ; and the onlie medicine for want, that precious implaifter of content : being fuch a good Phifition to others, wilt thou not minifter receipts to thy felfe ς But perchance thou wilt fay : *Confulenti nunquam caput doluit.*

Why, then, if the patients that are ficke of this difeafe can finde in themfelues neither reafon to perfwade, nor arte to cure ; yet (Rosalynd) admit of the counfaile of a friend, and applie the falues that may appeafe thy paffions. If thou grieueft that beeing the daughter of a Prince, and enuie thwarteth thee with fuch hard exigents, thinke that royaltie is a faire marke ; that Crownes haue croffes when mirth is in Cottages ; that the fairer the Rofe is, the fooner it is bitten with Catterpillers ; the more orient the Pearle is, the more apt to take a blemifh ; and the greateft birth, as it hath moft honour, fo it hath much enuie. If then Fortune aimeth at the faireft, be patient Rosalynd ; for firft by thine exile thou goeft to thy father ; nature is higher prifed than wealth, & the loue of ones parents ought to bee more precious than all dignities : why then doth my Rosalynd grieue at the frowne of Torismond, who by offering her a preiudice, proffers her a greater pleafure ς and more (mad laffe) to be melancholie, when thou haft with thee Alinda a frend, who will be a faithfull copartner of al thy miffortunes, who hath left her father to followe thee, and choofeth rather to brooke all extremities than to forfake thy prefence. What Rosalynd : *Solamen miferis focios habuiffe doloris.*

Cheerelie woman, as wee haue been bedfellowes in royaltie, we will be fellowe mates in pouertie : I will euer bee thy Alinda, and thou fhalt euer reft to me Rosalynd : fo fhall the world canonize our friendfhip, and fpeake of Rosalynd and Alinda, as they did of Pilades and Orestes. And if euer Fortune fmile and wee returne to our former honour, then folding our felues in the fweete of our friendfhip, wee fhall merelie fay (calling to minde our forepaffed miferies) ; *Olim hæc meminiffe iuuabit.*

At this Rosalynd began to comfort her ; and after fhee had wept a fewe kind teares in the bofome of her Alinda, fhe gaue her heartie thanks, and then they fat them downe to confult how they fhould trauell. Alinda grieued at nothing but that they might haue no man in their companie : faying, it would be their greateft preiudice in that two women went wandring without either guide or attendant. Tufh (quoth Rosalynd) art thou a woman, and haft not a fodaine fhift to preuent a miffortune ς I (thou feeft) am of a tall ftature, and would very **I, iii, 121**
well become the perfon and apparell of a page, thou fhalt bee my Miftris,
and I will play the man fo properly, that (truft me) in what company fo euer I come I will not be difcouered ; I will buy mee a fuite, and haue my rapier very handfomely at my fide, and if any knaue offer wrong, your page will fhew him the point of his

weapon. At this Alinda fmiled, and vpon this they agreed, and prefentlie gathered vp all their Iewels, which they truffed vp in a Cafket, and Rofalynd in all haft prouided her of roabes, and Alinda (from her royall weedes) put her felfe in more homelie attire. Thus fitted to the purpofe, away goe thefe two friends, hauing now changed their names, Alinda being called Aliena, and Rofalynd I, iii, **131** Ganimede: they trauailed along the Vineyards, and by many by-waies; at laft got to the Forreft fide, where they trauailed by the fpace of two or three daies without feeing anie creature, being often in danger of wild beafts, and payned with many paffionate forrowes. Now the black Oxe began to tread on their feete, and Alinda thought of her wonted royaltie: but when fhe caft her eyes on her Rofalynd, fhe thought euerie danger a ftep to honour. Paffing thus on along, about midday they came to a Fountaine, compaft with a groue of Cipreffe trees, fo cunninglie and curiouflie planted, as if fome Goddeffe had intreated Nature in that place to make her an Arbour. By this Fountaine fat Aliena and her Ganimede, and foorth they pulled fuch victualls as they had, and fed as merilie as if they had been in *Paris* with all the Kings delicates: Aliena onely grieuing that they could not fo much as meete with a fhepheard to difcourfe them the way to fome place where they might make their aboade. At laft Ganimede cafting vp his eye efpied where on a tree was ingrauen certaine verfes: which affoone as he efpied, he cried out; bee of good cheere Miftris, I fpie the figures of men; for here in thefe trees be ingrauen certaine verfes of fhepheards, or fome other fwaines that inhabite here about. With that Aliena ftart vp ioyfull to heare thefe newes; and looked, where they found carued in the barke of a Pine tree this paffion.

Montanus pafsion.

> *Hadft thou been borne whereas perpetuall cold*
> *Makes* Tanais *hard, and mountaines filuer old:*
> *Had I complain'd vnto a marble ftone;*
> *Or to the flouds bewraide my bitter mone,*
>   *I then could beare the burden of my griefe.*
> *But euen the pride of Countries at thy birth,*
> *Whil'ft heauens did fmile did new aray the earth*
>   *with flowers chiefe.*
> *Yet thou the flower of beautie bleffed borne,*
> *Haft pretie lookes, but all attir'd in fcorne.*
>
> *Had J the power to weepe fweet* Mirrhas *teares;*
> *Or by my plaints to pearce repining eares;*
> *Hadft thou the heart to fmile at my complaint;*
> *To fcorne the woes that doth my heart attaint,*
>   *I then could beare the burden of my griefe.*
> *But not my teares, but truth with thee preuailes,*
> *And feeming fowre my forowes thee affailes:*
>   *yet fmall reliefe.*
> *For if thou wilt thou art of marble hard;*
> *And if thou pleafe my fuite fhall foone be heard.*

No doubt (quoth Aliena) this poefie is the paffion of fome perplexed fhepheard, that being enamoured of fome faire and beautifull Shepheardeffe, fuffered fome fharpe repulfe, and therefore complained of the crueltie of his Miftris. You may fee (quoth

Ganimede) what mad cattell you women be, whofe hearts fometimes are made of
Adamant that will touch with no impreffion; and fometime of waxe that is fit for
euerie forme: they delight to be courted, and then they glorie to feeme coy; and
when they are moft defired then they freefe with difdaine: and this fault is fo common to the fex, that you fee it painted out in the fhepheards paffions, who found his
Miftris as froward as he was enamoured. And I pray you (quoth Aliena) if your
roabes were off, what mettall are you made of that you are fo fatyricall
againft women ᛋ   Is it not a foule bird defiles the owne neft ᛋ   Beware   **IV, i, 195**
(Ganimede) that Rosader heare you not; if he doo, perchance you will
make him leape fo far from loue, that he wil anger euery vain in your hart.   Thus
(quoth Ganimede) I keepe decorum, I fpeake now as I am Alienas page, not as I
am Gerismonds daughter: for put me but into a peticoate, and I will ftand in defiance
to the vttermoft that women are courteous, conftant, vertuous, and what not.   Stay
there (quoth Aliena) and no more words; for yonder be Characters grauen vpon the
barke of the tall Beech tree: let vs fee (quoth Ganimede): and with that they read
a fancie written to this effect.

> *Firft fhall the heauens want ftarrie light;*
> *The feas be robbed of their waues;*
> *The day want funne, and funne want bright;*
> *The night want fhade, the dead men graues;*
> > *The Aprill, flowers and leafe and tree,*
> > *Before I falfe my faith to thee.*
>
> *Firft fhall the tops of higheft hills*
> *By humble plaines be ouerpride;*
> *And Poets fcorne the Mufes quills,*
> *And fifh forfake the water glide;*
> > *And Iris loofe her coloured weed,*
> > *Before I faile thee at thy need.*
>
> *Firft direfull hate fhall turne to peace,*
> *And loue relent in deepe difdaine;*
> *And death his fatall ftroake fhall ceafe,*
> *And enuie pitie euery paine;*
> > *And pleafure mourne, aud forowe fmile,*
> > *Before I talke of any guile.*
>
> *Firft time fhall ftay his ftayleffe race,*
> *And winter bleffe his browes with corne;*
> *And fnow bemoyften Julies face;*
> *And winter fpring, and fommer mourne,*
> > *Before my pen by helpe of fame,*
> > *Ceafe to recite thy facred name.*   Montanus.

No doubt (quoth Ganimede) this proteftation grewe from one full of paffions.   I
am of that mind too (quoth Aliena) but fee I pray, when poore women feeke to keepe
themfelues chaft, how men woo them with many fained promifes, alluring with fweet
words as the Syrens, and after proouing as trothleffe as AEneas.   Thus promifed
Demophoon to his Phillis, but who at laft grewe more falfe?   The reafon was (quoth
Ganimede) that they were womens fonnes, and tooke that fault of their mother; for
if man had growen from man, as Adam did from the earth, men had neuer been

troubled with inconftancie.   Leaue off (quoth Aliena) to taunt thus bitterly, or els Ile pul off your pages apparell and whip you (as Venus doth her wantons) with net-tles.   So you will (quoth Ganimede) perfwade me to flattrie, and that needs not : but come (feeing we haue found heere by this Fount the trackt of Shepheards by their Madrigals and Roundelaies) let vs forward; for either we fhall finde fome foldes, fheepcoates, or els fome cottages wherein for a day or two to reft.   Cōtent (quoth Aliena) and with that they rofe vp, and marched forward till towards the euen : and then comming into a faire valley (compaffed with mountaines, whereon grewe many pleafant fhrubbs) they might defcrie where two flocks of fheepe did feede.   Then looking about, they might perceiue where an old fhepheard fat (and with him a yong fwaine) vnder a couert moft pleafantlie fcituated.   The ground where they fat was diapred with Floras riches, as if fhe ment to wrap Tellus in the glorie of her veft-ments : round about in the forme of an Amphitheater were moft curiouflie planted Pine trees, interfeamed with Limons and Citrons, which with the thickneffe of their boughes fo fhadowed the place, that Phœbus could not prie into the fecret of that Arbour; fo vnited were the tops with fo thicke a clofure, that Venus might there in her iollitie haue dallied vnfeene with her deereft paramour.   Faft by (to make the place more gorgeous) was there a Fount fo Chriftalline and cleere, that it feemed Diana with her Driades and Hemadriades had that fpring, as the fecrete of all their bathings.   In this glorious Arbour fat thefe two fhepheards (feeing their fheepe feede) playing on their pipes many pleafant tunes, and from mufick and melodie falling into much amorous chat: drawing more nigh wee might defcrie the countenance of the one to be full of forowe, his face to be the verie pourtraiture of difcontent, and his eyes full of woes, that liuing he feemed to dye : wee (to heare what thefe were) ftole priuilie behind the thicke, where we ouerheard this difcourfe.

A pleafant Eglog betweene Montanus and Coridon.

Coridon.

Say fhepheards boy, what makes thee greet fo fore ?
Why leaues thy pipe his pleafure and delight ?
Yong are thy yeares, thy cheekes with roses dight :
Then fing for ioy (fweet fwaine) and figh no more.

This milke white Poppie and this climbing Pine
Both promife fhade; then fit thee downe and fing,
And make thefe woods with pleafant notes to ring,
Till Phœbus *daine all Westward to decline.*

Montanus.

Ah (Coridon) *vnmeet is melodie*
To him whom proud contempt hath ouerborne :
Slaine are my ioys by Phœbes *bitter fcorne,*
Farre hence my weale and nere my ieopardie.

Loues burning brand is couched in my breft,
Making a Phœnix *of my faintfull hart :*
And though his furie doo inforce my fmart,
Ay blyth am I to honour his beheft.

Preparde to woes fince fo my Phœbe *wills,*
My lookes difmaid fince Phœbe *will difdaine :*
I banifh bliffe and welcome home my paine;
So ftreame my teares as fhowers from Alpine hills.

Jn errours maske I blindfolde iudgements eye,
J fetter reafon in the fnares of lust,
J feeme fecure, yet know not how to trust:
J liue by that, which makes me liuing die.

Deuoyd of rest, companion of distreffe,
Plague to myfelfe, confumed by my thought;
How may my voyce or pipe in tune be brought?
Since I am reft of folace and delight.

Coridon.

Ah Lorrell lad, what makes thee Herry loue?
A fugred harme, a poyfon full of pleafure,
A painted fhrine ful-fild with rotten treafure,
A heauen in fhew, a hell to them that proue.

Againe, in feeming fhadowed still with want,
A broken ftaffe which follie doth vpholde,
A flower that fades with euerie frostie colde,
An orient rofe fprong from a wythred plant.

A minutes ioy to gaine a world of greefe,
A fubtill net to fnare the idle minde,
A feeing Scorpion, yet in feeming blinde,
A poore reioyce, a plague without releefe.

For thy Montanus *follow mine arreede,*
(Whom age hath taught the traynes that fancie vfeth)
Leaue foolifh loue; for beautie wit abufeth,
And drownes (by follie) vertues fpringing feede.

Montanus.

So blames the childe the flame, becaufe it burnes;
And bird the fnare, becaufe it doth intrap;
And fooles true loue, becaufe of forrie hap;
And faylers curffe the fhip that ouerturnes:

But would the childe forbeare to play with flame,
And birdes beware to trust the fowlers ginne,
And fooles forefee before they fall and finne,
And maifters guide their fhips in better frame;

The childe would praife the fire, becaufe it warmes;
The birds reioyce, to fee the fowler faile;
And fooles preuent, before their plagues preuaile;
And faylers bleffe the barke that faues from harmes.

Ah Coridon, *though manie be thy yeares,*
And crooked elde hath fome experience left;
Yet is thy minde of iudgement quite bereft
In view of loue, whofe power in me appeares.

The ploughman little wots to turne the pen,
Or bookeman skills to guide the ploughmans cart,
Nor can the cobler count the tearmes of Art,
Nor bafe men iudge the thoughts of mightie men;

Nor wythered age (vnmeete for beauties guide,
Vncapable of loues impreſſion)
Diſcourſe of that, whoſe choyce poſſeſſion
May neuer to ſo baſe a man be tied.

But I (whom nature makes of tender molde,
And youth most pliant yeeldes to fancies fire)
Doo builde my hauen and heauen on ſweete deſire,
On ſweete deſire more deere to me than golde.

Thinke I of loue, ô how my lines aspire ?
How hast the Muſes to imbrace my browes,
And hem my temples in with lawrell bowes,
And fill my braines with chaſt and holy fire ?

Then leaue my lines their homely equipage,
Mounted beyond the circle of the Sunne ;
Amaz'd I read the ſtile when I haue done,
And Herry Loue that ſent that heauenly rage.

Of Phœbe *then, of* Phœbe *then I ſing,*
Drawing the puritie of all the ſpheares,
The pride of earth, or what in heauen appeares,
Her honoured face and fame to light to bring.

Jn fluent numbers and in pleaſant vaines,
J rob both ſea and earth of all their ſtate,
To praiſe her parts : I charme both time and fate,
To bleſſe the Nymph that yieldes me loue ſicke paines.

My ſheepe are turned to thoughts, whom froward will
Guides in the restleſſe Laborynth of loue,
Feare lends them paſture whereſoere they moue,
And by their death their life renueth ſtill.

Hy ſheephooke is my pen, mine oaten reede
My paper, where my manie woes are written ;
Thus ſilly ſwaine (with loue and fancie bitten)
J trace the plaines of paine in wofull weede.

Yet are my cares, my broken ſleepes, my teares,
My dreames, my doubts, for Phœbe *ſweete to me :*
Who wayteth heauen in ſorrowes vale must be,
And glorie ſhines where danger most appeares.

Then Coridon *although I blythe me not,*
Blame me not man, ſince ſorrow is my ſweete ;
So willeth Loue, and Phœbe *thinkes it meete,*
And kinde Montanus *liketh well his lot.*

Coridon.

Oh ſtayleſſe youth, by errour ſo miſguided ;
Where will preſcribeth lawes to perfeĉt wits,
Where reaſon mournes, and blame in triumph ſits,
And follie poyſoneth all that time prouided.

With wilfull blindneſſe bleard, preparde to ſhame,
Prone to neglect Occaſion when ſhe ſmiles :
Alas that Loue (by fond and froward guiles)
Should make thee tract the path to endleſſe blame.

Ah (my Montanus*) curſed is the charme*
That hath bewitched ſo thy youthfull eyes :
Leaue off in time to like theſe vanities;
Be forward to thy good, and fly thy harme.

As manie bees as Hibla *daily ſhields,*
As manie frie as fleete on Oceans *face,*
As manie heards as on the earth doo trace,
As manie flowres as decke the fragrant fields,

As manie ſtarres as glorious heauen containes,
As manie ſtormes as wayward winter weepes,
As manie plagues as hell incloſed keepes;
So manie greefes in loue, ſo manie paines.

Suſpitions, thoughts, deſires, opinions, praiers,
Miſlikes, miſdeedes, fond ioyes, and fained peace,
Jlluſions, dreames, great paines, and ſmall increaſe,
Vowes, hopes, acceptance, ſcornes, and deepe deſpaires,

Truce, warre, and woe doo waite at beauties gate;
Time loſt, lament, reports, and priuie grudge,
And laſt, fierce Loue is but a partiall Iudge,
Who yeeldes for ſeruice ſhame, for friendſhip hate,

Montanus.

All Adder-like I ſtop mine eares (fond ſwaine)
So charme no more; for I will neuer change.
Call home thy flockes in time that ſtragling range :
For loe, the Sunne declineth hence amaine.

Terentius.

Jn amore hœc omnia inſunt vitia, induciæ, inimicitæ, bellum, pax rurſum : incerta
hœc ſi tu postules, ratione certa fieri nihilo plus agas, quam ſi des operam, vt cum
ratione inſanias.

The ſhepheards hauing thus ended their Eglogue, Aliena ſtept with Ganimede
from behinde the thicket : at whoſe ſodaine ſight the ſhepheards aroſe, and Aliena
ſaluted them thus; Shepheards all haile, (for ſuch wee deeme you by your flockes)
and Louers, good lucke; (for ſuch you ſeeme by your paſſions) our eyes being witneſſe of the one, and our eares of the other. Although not by Loue, yet by Fortune,
I am a diſtreſſed Gentlewoman, as ſorrowful as you are paſſionate, and as full of woes
as you of perplexed thoughts : wandring this way in a forreſt vnknowen, onely I and
my Page, wearied with trauaile would faine haue ſome place of reſt. May you
appoint vs anie place of quiet harbour, (be it neuer ſo meane) I ſhall be thankfull to
you, contented in my ſelfe, and gratefull to whoſoeuer ſhall bee mine hoſte. Coridon
hearing the Gentlewoman ſpeak ſo courteouſly returned her mildly and reuerentlie
this aunſwere.

Faire Miſtres, we returne you as heartie a welcome, as you gaue vs a courteous

22

falute. A fhepheard I am, & this a louer, as watchful to pleafe his wench, as to feed his fheep: full of fancies, and therefore (fay I) full of follies. Exhort him I may, but perfwade him I cannot; for Loue admits neither of counfaile, nor reafon. But leauing him to his paffions, if you be diftreft, I am forrowfull fuch a faire creature is croft w^t calamitie: pray for you I may, but releeue you I cannot: marry, if you want lodging, if you vouch to fhrowd your felues in a fhepheards cotage, my houfe (for this night) fhalbe your harbour. Aliena thankt Coridon greatly, and prefently fate her downe and Ganimede by her. Coridon looking earneftly vppon her, and with a curious furuey viewing all her perfections, applauded (in his thought) her excellence, and pitying her diftreffe, was defirous to heare the caufe of her miffortunes, began to queftion with her thus.

If I fhould not (faire Damofell) occafionate offence, or renue your griefes by rubbing the fcarre, I would faine craue fo much fauour, as to know the caufe of your miffortune: and why, and whether you wander with your page in fo dangerous a forreft. Aliena (that was as courteous as fhe was faire) made this reply; Shepheard, a friendlie demaund ought neuer to be offenfiue, and queftions of courtefie carrie priuiledged pardons in their forheads. Know therfore, to difcouer my fortunes were to renue my forrowes, and I fhould by difcourfing my mifhaps, but rake fier out of the cinders. Therefore let this fuffice (gentle fhepheard) my diftreffe is as great as my trauell is dangerous, and I wander in this forreft, to light on fome cottage where I and my Page may dwell: for I meane to buy fome farme, and a flocke of fheepe, and fo become a fhepheardeffe, meaning to liue low, and content me with a countrey life: for I haue heard the fwaynes fay, that they drunke without fufpition, & flept without care. Marry Miftres (quoth Coridon) if you meane fo you came in a good time, for my landflord intends to fell both the farme I till, and the flocke I keepe, & cheap you may haue them for readie money: and for a fhepheards life (oh Miftreffe) did you but liue a while in their content, you would faye the Court were rather a place of forrowe, than of folace. Here (Miftreffe) fhall not Fortune thwart you, but in meane miffortunes, as the loffe of a few fheepe, which, as it breedes no beggerie, fo it can bee no extreame preiudice: the next yeare may mend al with a frefh increafe. Enuie ftirres not vs, wee couet not to climbe, our defires mount not aboue our degrees, nor our thoughts aboue our fortunes. Care cannot harbour in our cottages, nor doo our homely couches know broken flumbers: as we exceede not in diet, fo we haue inough to fatiffie: and Miftres I haue fo much Latin, *Satis est quod fufficit*.

By my troth fhepheard (quoth Aliena) thou makeft me in loue with your countrey life, and therefore fende for thy Landflord, and I will buy thy farme and thy flockes, & thou fhalt ftill (vnder me) be ouerfeer of them both: onely for pleafurefake I and my Page will ferue you, lead the flocks to the field, and folde them: thus will I liue quiet, vnknowen, and contented. This newes fo gladded the hart of Coridon, that he fhould not be put out of his farme, that (putting off his fhepheards bonnet) he did her all the reuerence that he might. But all this while fate Montanus in a mufe thinking of the crueltie of his Phœbe, whom he woed long, but was in no hope to winne. Ganimede who ftill had the remembrance of Rosader in his thoughts, tooke delight to fee the poore fhepheard paffionate, laughing at loue that in all his actions was fo imperious. At laft when fhee had noted his teares that ftole downe his cheekes, and his fighes that broake from the center of his heart, pittying his lament, fhe demaunded of Coridon why the young fhepheard looked fo forrowfull ⸴ Oh fir (quoth he) the boy is in loue. Why (quoth Ganimede) can fhepheards loue? I (quoth Montanus) and ouerloue, els fhouldft not thou fee me fo penfiue. Loue (I tell thee) is as precious in a ſhepheards eye as in the lookes of a King, and we countrey ſwaynes intertain fancie with as great delight, as the proudeſt courtier doth affection. Opportunitie (that is the ſweeteſt freind to Venus) harboureth in our cottages, and loyaltie (the chiefeſt fealtie that Cupid requires) is found more among ſhepheards than higher degrees. Then aſke not if ſuch ſilly ſwaynes can loue? What is the cause then, quoth Ganimede, that Loue being ſo ſweete to thee, thou lookeſt ſo ſorrowfull? Becauſe, quoth Montanus, the partie beloued is froward: and hauing courteſie in her lookes, holdeth diſdaine in her tongues ende. What hath ſhe then quoth Aliena, in her heart? Deſire (I hope Madame) quoth he: or els my hope loſt, deſpaire in Loue were death. As thus they chatted, the Sunne beiug readie to ſet, and they not hauing folded their ſheepe, Coridon requeſted ſhe would ſit there with her Page, till Montanus and he lodged their ſheepe for that night. You ſhall goe quoth Aliena, but firſt I will intreate Montanus to ſing ſome amorous Sonnet, that hee made when he hath been deeply paſſionate. That I will quoth Montanus: and with that he began thus.

Montanus Sonnet.

Phœbe *ſate*
Sweete ſhe ſate,
> *Sweete ſate* Phœbe *when I ſaw her,*
White her brow,
Coy her eye :
> *Brow and eye how much you pleaſe me ?*
Words J ſpent,
Sighes J ſent,
> *Sighes and words could neuer draw her.*
Oh my loue
Thou art loſt,
> *Since no ſight could euer eaſe thee.*

Phœbe *ſat*
By a fount ;
> *Sitting by a fount J ſpide her :*
Sweet her touch,
Rare her voyce ;
> *Touch and voice what may diſtaine you ?*
As ſhe ſung,
I did ſigh,
> *And by ſighs whilſt that I tride her.*
Oh mine eyes
You did looſe
> *Her firſt ſight whoſe want did paine you.*

Phœbes *flocks*
White as wooll,
> *Yet were* Phœbes *locks more whiter.*
Phœbes *eyes*
Douelike mild,
> *Douelike eyes both mild and cruell.*
Montan *ſweares*
In your lampes
> *He will die for to delight her.*

Phœbe *yeeld*,
Or *I die*;

    Shall true hearts be fancies fuell?

Montanus had no fooner ended his fonnet, but Coridon with a lowe courtefie rofe vp and went with his fellow and fhut their fheepe in the foldes: and after returning to Aliena and Ganimede, conducted them home wearie to his poore Cottage. By the way there was much good chat with Montanus about his loues; he refoluing Aliena that Phœbe was the faireft Shepherdice in all France, and that in his eye her beautie was equall with the Nimphs. But (quoth hee) as of all ftones the Diamond is moft cleereft, and yet moft hard for the Lapidory to cut; as of all flowers the Rofe is the faireft, and yet guarded with the fharpeft prickles: fo of all our Countrey Laffes Phœbe is the brighteft, but the moft coy of all to ftoope vnto defire. But let her take heede quoth he, I haue heard of Narciffus, who for his high difdaine againft Loue, perifhed in the follie of his owne loue. With this they were at Coridons cotage, where Montanus parted from them, and they went in to reft. Alinda and Ganimede glad of fo contented a fhelter, made merrie with the poore fwayne: and though they had but countrey fare and courfe lodging, yet their welcome was fo great, and their cares fo litle, that they counted their diet delicate, and flept as foundly as if they had been in the court of Torifmond. The next morne they lay long in bed, as wearied with the toyle of vnaccuftomed trauaile: but affoone as they got vp,
Aliena refolued there to fet vp her reft, and by the helpe of Coridon **II, iv, 97**
fwept a barga ne with his Landflord, and fo became Miftres of the farme & the flocke: her felfe putting on the attire of a fhepheardeffe, and Ganimede of a yong fwaine: euerie day leading foorth her flocks with fuch delight, that fhe held her exile happie, and thought no content to the bliffe of a Countrey cottage. Leauing her thus famous amongft the fhepheards of *Arden*, againe to Saladyne.

When Saladyne had a long while concealed a fecret refolution of reuenge, and could no longer hide fire in the flax, nor oyle in the flame; (for enuie is like lightning, that will appeare in the darkeft fogge). It chaunced on a morning verie early he calde vp certaine of his feruaunts, and went with them to the chamber of Rosader, which being open, he entred with his crue, and furprifed his brother beeing a fleepe, and bound him in fetters, and in the midft of his hall chained him to a poaft. Rosader amazed at this ftraunge chaunce, began to reafon with his brother about the caufe of this fodaine extremitie, wherein he had wrongd ʃ and what fault he had committed worthie fo fharpe a penaunce. Saladyne anfwered him onely with a looke of difdaine, & went his way, leauing poore Rosader in a deepe perplexitie. Who (thus abufed) fell into fundrie paffions, but no meanes of releefe could be had: wherevpon (for anger) he grew into a difcontented melancholy. In which humour he continued two or three dayes without meate: infomuch, that feeing his brother would giue him no foode, he fell into defpaire of his life. Which *A*dam Spencer the olde feruaunt of Sir Iohn of *Bourdeaux* feeing, touched with the duetie and loue he ought to his olde Mafter, felt a remorfe in his confcience of his fonnes mifhap: and therefore, although Saladyne had giuen a generall charge to his feruaunts, that none of them vppon paine of death fhoulde giue either meate or drinke to Rosader, yet *A*dam Spencer in the night arofe fecretely, and brought him fuch victualls as hee could prouide, and vnlockt him and fet him at libertie. After Rosader had well feafted himfelfe, and felt he was loofe, ftraight his thoughts aymed at reuenge, and now (all being a fleepe) hee woulde haue quit Saladyne with the methode of his owne mifchief. But *A*dam

Spencer perfwaded him to the contrarie, with thefe reafons; Sir quoth he, be content, for this night go againe into your olde fetters, fo fhall you trie the faith of friends, and faue the life of an olde feruant. To morrowe hath your brother inuited al your kindred and allyes to a folempne breakfaft, onely to fee you, telling them all, that you are mad, & faine to be tied to a poaft. Affone as they come, make complaint to them of the abufe profered you by Saladyne. If they redreffe you, why fo: but if they paffe ouer your plaints *ficco pede*, and holde with the violence of your brother before your innocence, then thus: I will leaue you vnlockt that you may breake out at your pleafure, and at the ende of the hall fhall you fee ftand a couple of good pol-laxes, one for you, and another for me. When I giue you a wink, fhake off your chaynes, and let vs play the men, and make hauocke amongft them, driue them out of the houfe and maintaine poffeffion by force of armes, till the King hath made a redreffe of your abufes. Thefe wordes of *A*dam Spencer fo perfwaded Rosader, that he went to the place of his punifhment, and ftood there while the next morning. About the time appoynted, came all the guefts bidden by Saladyne, whom he intreated with courteous and curious intertainment, as they al perceiued their wel-come to be great. The tables in the hal where Rosader was tyed, were couered, and Saladyne bringing in his guefts together, fhewed them where his brother was bound, and was inchainde as a man lunaticke. Rosader made replie, and with fome inuectiues made complaints of the wrongs proffered him by Saladyne, defiring they would in pitie feeke fome meanes for his reliefe. But in vaine, they had ftopt their eares with Vlisses, that were his words neuer fo forceable, he breathed onely his paffions into the winde. They careleffe, fat down with Saladyne to dinner, being verie frolicke and pleafant, wafhing their heads well with wine. At laft, when the fume of the grape had entred peale meale into their braines, they began in fatyrical fpeaches to raile againft Rosader: which Adam Spencer no longer brooking, gaue the figne, and Rosader fhaking off his chaines got a pollax in his hand, and flew amongft them with fuch violence and fury, that he hurt manie, flew fome, and draue his brother and all the reft quite out of the houfe. Seeing the coaft cleare, he fhut the doores, and being fore an hungred, and feeing fuch good victuals, he fate him downe with Adam Spencer and fuch good fellows as he knew were honeft men, and there feafted themfelues with fuch prouifion as Saladyne had prepared for his frieds. After they had taken their repaft, Rosader rampierd vp the houfe, leaft vpon a fodaine his brother fhould raife fome crue of his tenaunts, and furprife them vnawares. But Saladyne tooke a contrarie courfe, and went to the Sheriffe of the fhyre and made complaint of Rosader, who giuing credite to Saladyne, in a determined refolution to reuenge the Gentlemans wrongs, tooke with him fiue and twentie tall men, and made a vowe, either to breake into the houfe and take Rosader, or els to coope him in till he made him yeelde by famine. In this determination, gathering a crue together he went forward to fet Saladyne in his former eftate. Newes of this was brought vnto Rosader, who fmiling at the cowardize of his brother, brookt all the iniuries of For-tune with patience, expecting the comming of the Sheriffe. As he walkt vpon the battlements of the houfe, he defcryed where Saladyne and he drew neare, with a troupe of luftie gallants. At this he fmilde, and calde vp Adam Spencer, and fhewed him the enuious treacherie of his brother, and the folly of the Sheriffe to bee fo credulous: now Adam, quoth he, what fhall I doo ₢ It refts for me, either to yeelde vp the houfe to my brother and feeke a reconcilement, or els iffue out, and breake through the companie with courage, for coopt in like a coward I will not bee. If I fubmit (ah Adam) I difhonour my felfe, and that is worfe than death; for by fuch open difgraces the fame of men growes odious: if I iffue out amongſt them, fortune may fauour me, and I may efcape with life; but fuppofe the worſt: if I be flaine, then my death ſhall be honourable to me, and fo inequall a reuenge infamous to Saladyne. Why then Maſter forward and feare not, out amongſt them, they bee but faint hearted lozells, and for Adam Spencer, if he die not at your foote, fay he is a daſtard. Thefe words cheered vp fo the hart of yong Rosader, that he thought himſelfe fufficient for them all, & therefore prepared weapons for him and Adam Spencer, and were readie to intertaine the Sheriffe: for no fooner came Saladyne and he to the gates, but Rosader vnlookt for leapt out and affailed them, wounded manie of them, and caufed the reſt to giue backe, fo that *A*dam and hee broke through the preafe in defpite of them all, and tooke theyr way towards the forreſt of *Arden*. This repulfe fo fet the Sheriffes heart on fire to reuenge, that he ſtraight rayfed al the countrey, and made Hue and Crie after them. But Rosader and Adam knowing full well the fecrete wayes that led through the vineyards, ſtole away priuely through the prouince of *Bourdeaux*, & efcaped fafe to the forreſt of *Arden*. Being come thether, they were glad they had fo good a harbour: but Fortune (who is like the Camelion) variable with euerie obieét, & conſtant in nothing but inconſtácie, thought to make them myrrours of her mutabilitie, and therefore ſtill croſt them thus contrarily. Thinking ſtill to paſſe on by the bywaies to get to *Lions*, they chaunced on a path that led into the thicke of the forreſt, where they wandred fiue or fixe dayes without meat, that they were almoſt famiſhed, finding neither ſhepheard nor cottage to relieue them: and hunger growing on fo extreame, Adam Spencer (being olde) began firſt to faint, and fitting him downe on a hill, and looking about him, efpied where Rosader laye as feeble and as ill perplexed: which fight made him ſhedde teares, and to fall into thefe bitter tearmes.——A d a m S p e n c e r s f p e a c h.——Oh how the life of man may well be compared to the ſtate of the Ocean feas, that for euerie calme hath a thoufand ſtormes: refembling the Rofe tree, that for a few faire flowers, hath a multitude of ſharpe prickles: all our pleafures ende in paine, and our higheſt delights, are croffed with deepeſt difcontents. The ioyes of man, as they are few, fo are they momentarie, fcarce ripe before they are rotten; and wythering in the bloffome, either parched with the heate of enuie, or fortune. Fortune, oh inconſtant friend, that in all thy deedes are froward and fickle, delighting in the pouertie of the loweſt, and the ouerthrow of the higheſt, to decypher thy inconſtancie. Thou ſtandſt vpon a gloabe, and thy wings are plumed with times feathers, that thou maiſt euer be reſtleffe; thou art double faced like Ianus, carying frownes in the one to threaten, and fmiles in the other to betray; thou proffereſt an Eele, and perfourmeſt a Scorpion; and where thy greateſt fauours be, there is the feare of the extreameſt miffortunes; fo variable are all thy aétions. But why Adam dooſt thou exclaime againſt fortune ς ſhe laughs at the plaints of the diſtreffed; and there is nothing more pleafing vnto her, than to heare fooles boaſt in her fading allurements, or forrowfull men to difcouer the fower of their paſſions. Glut her not Adam then with content, but thwart her with brooking all miſhappes with patience. For there is no greater checke to the pride of fortune, than with a refolute courage to paſſe ouer her croffes without care. Thou art olde Adam, and thy haires wax white, the **III, ii, 174** Palme tree is alreadie full of bloomes, and in the furrowes of thy face appeares the Kalenders of death? Wert thou bleffed by fortune thy yeares could not be manie, nor the date of thy life long: then fith Nature muſt haue her due, what is it for thee to refigne her debt a little before the day. Ah, it is not this which grieueth mee: nor doo I care what miſhaps Fortune can wage againſt me: but the fight of Rosader, that galleth vnto the quicke. When I remember the worfhips of his houfe, the honour of his fathers, and the vertues of himfelfe ; then doo I fay, that fortune and the fates are moft iniurious, to cenfure fo hard extreames, againft a youth of fo great hope. Oh Rosader, thou art in the flower of thine age, and in the pride of thy yeares, buxfome and full of May. Nature hath prodigally inricht thee with her fauours, and vertue made thee the myrrour of her excellence : and now through the decree of the vniuft ftarres, to haue all thefe good partes nipped in the blade, and blemifht by the inconftancie of Fortune. Ah Rosader, could I helpe thee, my griefe were the leffe, and happie fhould my death be, if it might be the beginning of thy reliefe : but feeing we perifh both in one extreame, it is a double forrowe. What fhall I do ᧡ preuent the fight of his further miffortune, with a prefent difpatch of mine owne life. Ah, defpaire is a mercileffe finne.

As he was readie to go forward in his paffion, he looked earneftly on Rosader, and feeing him change colour, he rife vp and went to him, and holding his temples, faide, What cheere mafter ? though all faile, let not the heart faint : the courage of a man is fhewed in the refolution of his death. At thefe words Rosader lifted vp his eye, and looking on Adam Spencer began to weepe. Ah Adam quoth he, I forrowe not to die, but I grieue at the manner of my death. Might I with my launce encounter the enemie, and fo die in the field, it were honour, and content : might I (Adam) combat with fome wilde beaft, and perifh as his pray, I wer fatiffied ; but to die with hunger, O Adam, it is the extreameft of all extreames. Mafter (quoth hee) you fee wee are both in one predicament, and long I cannot liue without meate, feeing therefore we can find no foode, let the death of the one preferue the life of the other. I am olde, and ouerworne with age, you are young, and are the hope of many honours : let me then die, I will prefently cut my veynes, & mafter with the warme bloud relieue your fainting fpirits : fucke on that till I ende, and you be comforted. With that *A*dam Spencer was readie to pull out his knife, when Rosader full of courage (though verie faint) rofe vp, and wifht *A*dam Spencer to fit there till his retourne : for my minde giues me quoth he, I fhall bring thee meate. With that, like a mad man he rofe vp, and ranged vp and downe the woods, feeking to encounter fome wilde beaft with his rapier, that either he might carrie his friend *A*dam food, or els pledge his life in pawne of his loyaltie. It chaunced that day, that Gerismond the lawfull king of *France* banifhed by Torismond, who with a luftie crue of Outlawes liued in that foreft, that day in honour of his Birth made a Feaft to all his bolde yeomen, and frolickt it with ftore of wine and venifon, fitting all at a long table vnder the fhadowe of lymon trees. To that place by chance Fortune conducted Rosader, who feeing fuch a crue of braue men hauing ftore of that, for want of which he and *A*dam perifhed, he ftept boldly to the boords end, and faluted the companie thus.

Whatfoere thou bee that art mafter of thefe luftie fquiers, I falute thee as gracioufly, as a man in extreame diftreffe may ; knowe that I and a fellow friend of mine, are heere famifhed in the forreft for want of foode : perifh we muft vnleffe relieued by thy fauours. Therefore if thou be a Gentleman, giue meate to men, and to fuch men as are euerie way worthie of life ; let the proudeft fquire that fittes at thy table, rife & incounter with me in anie honourable point of actiuitie what foeuer, and if he and thou proue me not a man, fend me a way comfortleffe. If thou refufe this, as a niggard of thy cates, I will haue amongft you with my fword ; for rather will I die valiantly, than perifh with fo cowardly an extreame. Gerismond looking him earneftly in the face, and feeing fo proper a Gentleman in fo bitter a paffion, was mooued with fo great pitie ; that rifing from the table, he tooke him by the hand and bad him welcome, willing him to fit downe in his place, and in his roome not onely to eate his fill, but be Lord of the feaft. Gramercie fir (quoth Rosader) but I haue a feeble friend that lies heereby famifhed almoft for food, aged and therfore leffe able to abide the extremitie of hunger than my felfe, and difhonour it were for me to tafte one crum, before I made him partner of my fortunes : therefore I will runne and fetch him, and then I will gratefully accept of your proffer. Away hies Rosader to *A*dam Spencer, and tells him the newes, who was glad of fo happie fortune, but fo feeble he was that hee could not goe : whereupon Rosader got him vp on his backe, and brought him to the place. Which when Gerismond & his men faw, they greatly applauded their league of friendfhip ; and Rosader hauing Gerismonds place affigned him, would not fit there himfelfe, but fet downe Adam Spencer. Well to be fhort, thofe hungrie fquires fell to their victualls, and feafted themfelues with good delicates, and great ftore of wine. Affoone as they had taken their repaft, Gerismond (defirous to heare what hard fortune draue them into thofe bitter extreames) requefted Rosader to dif-courfe, (if it wer not anie way preiudiciall vnto him) the caufe of his trauell. Rosa-der (defirous anie way to fatiffie the courtefie of his fauourable hoft, (firft beginning his *exordium* with a volley of fighes, and a few luke warme teares) profecuted his difcourfe, & told him frō point to point all his fortunes ; how he was the yongeft Sonne of Sir Iohn of *Bourdeaux*, his name Rosader, how his brother fundrie times had wronged him, and laftly, how for beating the Sheriffe, and hurting his men, he fled ; and this olde man (quoth he) whome I fo much loue and honour, is furnamed Adam Spencer, an old feruant of my fathers, and one (that for his loue) neuer fayled me in all my miffortunes. When Gerismond hearde this, hee fell on the necke of Rosader, and next difcourfing vnto him, how he was Gerismond their lawfull King exiled by Torismond, what familiaritie had euer been betwixt his father Sir Iohn of *Bourdeaux* and him, how faithful a fubiect he liued, and how honourable he died ; promifing (for his fake) to giue both him and his friend fuch courteous intertainment, as his prefent eftate could minifter : and vpon this made him one of his forrefters. Rosader feeing it was the King, craude pardon for his boldneffe, in that he did not doo him due reu-erence, and humbly gaue him thankes for his fauourable courtefie. Gerismond not fatiffied yet with newes, began to enquire if he had been lately in the court of Toris-mond, and whether he had feene his daughter Rosalynde, or no ꝗ At this, Rosader fetcht a deep figh, and fhedding manie teares, could not anfwere : yet at laft, gather-ing his fpirites together, hee reuealed vnto the King, how Rosalynde was banifhed, and how there was fuch a fimpathie of affections betweene Alinda and her, that fhee chofe rather to be partaker of her exile, than to part fellowfhippe : whereupon the vnnaturall King banifhed them both ; and now they are wandred none knowes whether, neither could anie learne fince their departure, the place of their abode. This newes driue the King into a great melancholy, that prefently he arofe from all the companie, and went into his priuie chamber, fo fecret as the harbor of the woods would allow him. The companie was all dafht at thefe tidings, & Rosader and Adam Spencer hauing fuch opportunitie, went to take their reft. Where we leaue them, and returne againe to Torismond.

The flight of Rosader came to the eares of Torismond, who hearing that Saladyne was fole heire of the landes of Sir Iohn of *Bourdeaux*, defirous to poffeffe fuch faire reuenewes, found iuft occafion to quarrell with Saladyne, about the wrongs hee proffred to his brother : and therefore difpatching a Herehault, he fent for Saladyne in all poaft haft. Who meruailing what the matter fhould be, began to examine his owne con-fcience, wherein he had offended his Highneffe : but imboldened with his innocence, hee boldly went with the Herehault vnto the Court. Where affoone as hee came, hee was not admitted into the prefence of the King, but prefently fent to prifon. This greatly amazed Saladyne, chiefly in that the Iayler had a ftraight charge ouer him, to fee that he fhould be clofe prifoner. Manie paffionate thoughts came in his head, till at laft he began to fall into confideration of his former follies, & to meditate with him-felfe. Leaning his head on his hand, and his elbowe on his knee, full of forrow, griefe and difquieted paffions, he refolued into thefe tearmes.——S a l a d y n e s c o m - p l a i n t.——Unhappie Saladyne, whome folly hath led to thefe misfortunes, and wanton defires wrapt within the laborinth of thefe calamities. Are not the heauens doomers of mens deedes ⸮ And holdes not God a ballaunce in his fift, to reward with fauour, and reuenge with iuftice ? Oh Saladyne, the faults of thy youth, as they were fond, fo were they foule; and not onely difcouering little

nourture, but blemifhing the excellence of nature. Whelpes of one **II, vii, 102** lytter are euer moft louing, and brothers that are fonnes of one father,

fhould liue in friendfhip without iarre. Oh Saladyne, fo it fhould bee : but thou haft with the deere fedde againft the winde, with the Crab ftroue againft the ftreame, and fought to peruert Nature by vnkindneffe. Rosaders wrongs, the wrongs of Rosader (Saladyne) cries for reuenge, his youth pleades to God to inflict fome penaunce vpon thee, his vertues are pleas that inforce writs of difpleafure to croffe thee : thou haft highly abufed thy kinde & naturall brother, and the heauens cannot fpare to quite thee with punifhment. There is no fting to the worme of confcience, no hell to a minde toucht with guilt. Euerie wrong I offered him (called now to remembrance) wringeth a drop of bloud from my heart, euerie bad looke, euerie frowne pincheth me at the quicke, and fayes Saladyne thou haft find againft Rosader. Be penitent, and affigne thy felfe fome penaunce to difcouer thy forrow, and pacifie his wrath.

In the depth of his paffion, he was fent for to the King : who with a looke that threatned death entertained him, and demaunded of him where his brother was? Saladyne made aunfwere, that vpon fome ryot made againft the Sheriffe of the fhyre, he was fled from *Bourdeaux*, but he knew not whether. Nay villain (quoth he) I haue heard of the wrongs thou haft proffered thy brother fince the death of thy father, and by thy meanes haue I loft a moft braue and refolute Cheualier. Therefore, in Iuftice to punifh thee, I fpare thy life for thy fathers fake, but banifh thee for euer from the Court and Countrey of *France*, and fee thy departere bee within tenne dayes, els truft me thou fhalt loofe thy head, & with that the King flew away in a rage, and left poore Saladyne greatly perplexed. Who grieuing at his exile, yet determined to beare it with patience, and in penaunce of his former follies to trauell abroade in euerie Coaft, till hee had founde out his Brother Rosader. With whom now I begin.

Rosader beeing thus preferred to the place of a Forefter by Gerismond, rooted out the remembrance of his brothers vnkindnes by continual exercife, trauerfing the groues and wilde Forrefts : partly to heare the melodie of the fweete birdes which recorded, and partly to fhewe his diligent indeauour in his mafters behalfe. Yet whatfoeuer he did, or howfoeuer he walked, the liuely Image of Rosalynde remained in memorie : on her fweete perfections he fedde his thoughts, proouing himfelfe like the Eagle a true borne bird, fince as the one is knowen by beholding the Sunne : fo was he by regarding excellent beautie. One day among the reft, finding a fit opor-tunitie and place conuenient, defirous to difcouer his woes to the woodes, hee engraued with his knife on the barke of a Myrtle tree, this pretie eftimate of his Miftres per-fection.

Sonnetto.

Of all chast birdes the Phœnix doth excell,
Of all ſtrong beasts the Lion beares the bell,
Of all ſweete flowers the Roſe doth ſweetest ſmell,
Of all faire maides my Roſalynde *is fairest.*

Of all pure mettals golde is onely purest,
Of all high trees the Pine hath highest crest,
Of all ſoft ſweetes J like my Mistres brest,
Of all chast thoughts my Mistres thoughts are rarest.

Of all proud birds the Ægle pleaſeth Ioue,
Of pretie fowles kinde Venus *likes the Doue,*
Of trees Minerua *doth the Oliue loue,*
Of all ſweete Nimphes I honour Roſalynde.

Of all her gifts her wiſedome pleaſeth most,
Of all her graces vertue ſhe doth boast :
For all theſe giftes my life and ioy is lost,
If Roſalynde *proue cruell and vnkinde.*

In theſe and ſuch like paſſions, Rosader did euerie daye eternize the name of his Rosalynde : and this day eſpeciallie when Aliena and Ganimede (inforced by the heate of the Sunne to ſeeke for ſhelter) by good fortune arriued in that place, where this amorous forreſter regiſtred his melancholy paſſions ; they ſaw the ſodaine change of his looks, his folded armes, his paſſionate ſighes ; they heard him often abruptly call on Rosalynde : who (poore ſoule) was as hotly burned as himſelfe, but that ſhe ſhrouded her paines in the cinders of honorable modeſtie. Whereupon, (geſſing him to be in loue, and according to the nature of their ſexe, being pitifull in that behalfe) they ſodainly brake off his melancholy by their approach : and Ganimede ſhooke him out of his dumpes thus.

What newes Forreſter ç haſt thou wounded ſome deere, and loſt him
in the fall ç   Care not man for ſo ſmall a loſſe, thy fees was but the ſkinne,   **IV, ii, 12**
the ſhoulder, and the hornes : tis hunters lucke, to ayme faire and miſſe :
and a woodmans fortune to ſtrike and yet goe without the game.

Thou art beyond the marke Ganimede, quoth Aliena, his paſſions are greater, and his ſighs diſcouers more loſſe ; perhaps in trauerſing theſe thickets, he hath ſeen ſome beautifull Nymph, and is growen amorous. It maye bee ſo (quoth Ganimede) for heere he hath newly ingrauen ſome ſonnet : come and ſee the diſcourſe of the Forreſters poems. Reading the ſonnet ouer, and hearing him name Rosalynd, Aliena lookt on Ganimede and laught, and Ganimede looking backe on the Forreſter, and ſeeing it was Rosader bluſht, yet thinking to ſhroud all vnder hir pages apparell, ſhe boldly returned to Rosader, and began thus.

I pray thee tell me Forreſter, what is this Rosalynde, for whom thou pineſt away in ſuch paſſions ? Is ſhee ſome Nymph that waites vpon Dianaes traine, whoſe chaſtitie thou haſt decyphred in ſuch Epethites ç Or is ſhee ſome ſhepheardeſſe, that haunts theſe plaines, whoſe beautie hath ſo bewitched thy fancie, whoſe name thou ſhaddoweſt in couert vnder the figure of Rosalynde, as Ouid did Iulia vnder the name of Corinna ? Or ſay mee for ſooth, is it that Rosalynde, of whome we ſhepheards haue heard talke, ſhee Forreſter, that is the Daughter of Gerismond, that once was King, and now an Outlaw in this Forreſt of *Arden*. At this Rosader fetcht a deepe figh, and faid, It is fhee, O gentle fwayne, it is fhe, that Saint it is whom I ferue, that Goddeffe at whofe fhrine I doo bend all my deuotions : the moft faireft of all faires, the Phenix of all that fexe, and the puritie of all earthly perfection. And why (gentle Forrefter) if fhe bee fo beautifull and thou fo amorous, is there fuch a difagreement in thy thoughts ? Happely fhe refembleth the rofe, that is fweete but full of prickles ? or the ferpent Regius that hath fcales as glorious as the Sunne, & a breath as infectious as the *Aconitum* is deadly? So thy Rosalynde, may be moft amiable, and yet vnkinde; full of fauour, and yet froward : coy without wit, and difdainefull without reafon.

O fhepheard (quoth Rosader) kneweft thou her perfonage graced with the excellence of all perfection, beeing a harbour wherein the Graces fhroude their vertues: thou wouldft not breathe out fuch blafphemie againft the beauteous Rosalynde. She is a Diamond, bright but not hard, yet of moft chaft operation : a pearle fo orient, that it can be ftained with no blemifh : a rofe without prickles, and a Princeffe abfolute afwell in beautie, as in vertue. But I, vnhappie I, haue let mine eye foare with the Eagle againft fo bright a Sunne, that I am quite blinde; I haue with Apollo enamoured my felfe of a Daphne, not (as fhee) difdainfull, but farre more chaft than Daphne; I haue with Ixion laide my loue on Iuno, and fhall (I feare) embrace nought but a clowde. Ah fhepheard, I haue reacht at a ftar, my defires haue mounted aboue my degree, & my thoughts aboue my fortunes. I being a peafant haue ventred to gaze on a Princeffe, whofe honors are too high to vouchfafe fuch bafe loues.

Why Forrefter (quoth Ganimede) comfort thy felfe : be blythe and frolicke man, Loue fowfeth as low as fhe foareth high : Cupide fhootes at a ragge affoone as at a roabe, and Venus eye that was fo curious fparkled fauor on pole footed Vulcan. Feare not man, womens lookes are not tied to dignities feathers, nor make they curious efteeme, where the ftone is found, but what is the vertue. Feare not Forrefter, faint heart neuer wonne faire Ladie. But where liues Rosalynde now, at the Court ?

Oh no (quoth Rosader) fhe liues I knowe not where, and that is my forrow; banifht by Torismond, and that is my hell : for might I but find her facred perfonage, & plead before the barre of her pitie the plaint of my paffions, hope tells mee fhee would grace me with fome fauour; and that woulde fuffice as a recompence of all my former miferies. Much haue I heard of thy Miftres excellence, and I know Forrefter thou canft defcribe her at the full, as one that haft furuayd all her parts with a curious eye : then doo me that fauour, to tell mee what her perfections bee. That I will (quoth Rosader) for I glorie to make all eares wonder at my Miftres excellence. And with that he pulde a paper forth his bofome, wherein he read this.

Rofalyndes defcription.

Like to the cleere in highest fpheare
Where all imperiall glorie fhines,
Of felfe fame colour is her haire
Whether vnfolded or in twines :
    Heigh ho faire Rofalynde.
Her eyes are Saphires fet in fnow,
Refining heauen by euerie winke;
The Gods doo feare when as they glow,
And I doo tremble when I thinke.
    Heigh ho, would fhe were mine.

Her cheekes are like the bluſhing clowde
That beautefies Auroraes *face,*
Or like the ſiluer crimſon ſhrowde
That Phœbus *ſmiling lookes doth grace :*
   Heigh ho, faire Roſalynde.
Her lippes are like two budded roſes,
Whom rankes of lillies neighbour nie,   III, ii, 97
Within which bounds ſhe balme incloſes,
Apt to intice a Deitie :
   Heigh ho, would ſhe were mine.

Her necke like to a ſtately towre,
Where Loue himſelfe impriſoned lies,
To watch for glaunces euerie howre,
From her deuine and ſacred eyes,
   Heigh ho, faire Roſalynde.
Her pappes are centers of delight,
Her pappes are orbes of heauenlie frame,
Where Nature moldes the deaw of light,
To feede perfection with the ſame :
   Heigh ho, would ſhe were mine.

With orient pearle, with rubie red,
With marble white, with ſaphire blew,
Her bodie euerie way is fed ;
Yet ſoft in touch, and ſweete in view :
   Heigh ho, faire Roſalynde.
Nature her ſelfe her ſhape admires,
The Gods are wounded in her ſight,
And Loue forſakes his heauenly fires,
And at her eyes his brand doth light :
   Heigh ho, would ſhe were mine.

Then muſe not Nymphes though I bemoane
The abſence of faire Roſalynde :
Since for her faire there is fairer none,   III, ii, 93
Nor for her vertues ſo deuine.
  Heigh ho faire Roſalynde :
  Heigh ho my heart, would God that ſhe were mine.
       Perijt, quia deperibat.

 Beleeue me (quoth Ganimede) either the Forreſter is an exquiſite painter, or Roſalynde faire aboue wonder : ſo it makes me bluſh, to heare how women ſhould be ſo
excellent, and pages ſo vnperfect.

 Rosader beholding her earneſtly, anſwered thus. Truly (gentle page) thou haſt
cauſe to complaine thee, wert thou the ſubſtance : but reſembling the ſhadow, content
thy ſelfe : for it is excellence inough to be like the excellence of Nature. He hath
aunſwered you Ganimede (quoth Aliena) it is inough for pages to waite on beautifull
Ladies, & not to be beautifull themſelues. Oh Miſtres (quoth Ganimede) holde you
your peace, for you are partiall : Who knowes not, but that all women haue deſire to
tie ſouereinto their peticoats, and aſcribe beautie to themſelues, where if boyes might

put on their garments, perhaps they would prooue as comely; if not as comely, it may be more curteous. But tell mee Forreſter, (and with that ſhee turnde to Rosader) vnder whom maintaineſt thou thy walke ς Gentle ſwaine vnder the King of Outlawes ſaid he, the vnfortunate Gerismond: who hauing loſt his kingdome, crowneth his thoughts with content, accompting it better to gouern among poore men in peace, than great men in daunger. But haſt thou not ſaid ſhe, (hauing ſo melancholie opportunities as this Forreſt affoordeth thee) written more Sonnets in commendations of thy Miſtres? I haue gentle Swayne quoth he, but they be not about me: to morrow by dawne of daye, if your flockes feede in theſe paſtures, I will bring them you: wherein you ſhall reade my paſſions, whileſt I feele them; iudge my patience when you read it: till when I bid farewell. So giuing both Ganimede and Aliena a gentle good night, he reſorted to his lodge: leauing Aliena and Ganimede to their prittle prattle. So Ganimede (ſaid Aliena, the Forreſter beeing gone) you are mightely beloued, men make ditties in your praiſe, ſpend ſighes for your ſake, make an Idoll of your beautie: beleeue me it greeues mee not a little, to ſee the poore man ſo penſiue, and you ſo pittileſſe.

Ah Aliena (quoth ſhe) be not peremptorie in your iudgments, I heare Rosalynde praiſde as I am Ganimede, but were I Rosalynde, I could anſwere the Forreſter: If hee mourne for loue, there are medicines for loue: Rosalynde cannot be faire and vnkinde. And ſo Madame you ſee it is time to folde our flockes, or els Coridon will frowne, and ſay you will neuer prooue good hufwife. With that they put their Sheepe into the coates, and went home to her friend Coridons cottage, Aliena as merrie as might be, that ſhe was thus in the companie of her Rosalynde: but ſhee poore ſoule, that had Loue her load ſtarre, and her thoughts ſet on fire with the flame of fancie, coulde take no reſt, but being alone beganne to conſider what paſſionate penaunce poore Rosader was enioyned to by loue and fortune: that at laſt ſhe fell into this humour with her ſelfe.——Roſalynde paſsionate alone.——Ah Rosalynde, how the Fates haue ſet downe in their Synode to make thee vnhappie: for when Fortune hath done her worſt, then Loue comes in to begin a new tragedie; ſhee ſeekes to lodge her ſonne in thine eyes, and to kindle her fires in thy boſome. Beware fonde girle, he is an vnruly gueſt to harbour; for cutting in by intreats he will not be thruſt out by force, and her fires are fed with ſuch fuell, as no water is able to quench. Seeſt thou not how Venus ſeekes to wrap thee in her Laborynth, wherein is pleaſure at the entrance, but within, ſorrowes, cares, and diſcontent: ſhe is a Syren, ſtop thine eares at her melodie; and a Baſiliſcke, ſhut thine eyes, and gaze not at her leaſt thou periſh. Thou art nowe placed in the Countrey content, where are heauenly thoughts, and meane deſires: in thoſe Lawnes where thy flockes feede Diana haunts: bee as her Nymphes, chaſte, and enemie to Loue: for there is no greater honour to a Maide, than to accompt of fancie, as a mortall foe to their ſexe. Daphne that bonny wench was not tourned into a Bay tree, as the Poets faine: but for her chaſtitie her fame was immortall, reſembling the Lawrell that is euer greene. Follow thou her ſteps Rosalynde, and the rather, for that thou art an exile, and baniſhed from the Court: whoſe diſtreſſe, as it is appeaſed with patience, ſo it woulde bee renewed with amorous paſſions. Haue minde on thy forepaſſed fortunes, feare the worſt, and intangle not thy ſelfe with preſent fancies: leaſt louing in haſt thou repent thee at leaſure. Ah but yet Rosalynde, it is Rosader that courts thee; one, who as hee is beautifull, ſo he is vertuous, and harboureth in his minde as manie good qualities, as his face is ſhadowed with gracious fauours: and therefore Rosalynde ſtoope to Loue, leaſt beeing either too coy, or too cruell, Venus waxe wrothe, and plague thee with the reward of diſdaine.

Rosalynde thus paſſionate, was wakened from her dumpes by Aliena, who ſaide it was time to goe to bedde. Coridon fwore that was true, for Charles Wayne was rifen in the North. Whereuppon each taking leaue of other, went to their reft all, but the poore Rosalynde: who was fo full of paffions, that fhee coulde not poffeffe anie content. Well, leauing her to her broken flumbers, expect what was perfourmed by them the nexte morning.

The Sunne was no fooner ftept from the bed of Aurora, but Aliena was wakened by Ganimede: who reftleffe all night had toffed in her paffions: faying it was then time to goe to the field to vnfold their fheepe. Aliena (that fpied where the hare was by the hounds, and could fee day at a little hole) thought to be pleafant with her Ganimede, & therfore replied thus; What wanton? the Sun is but new vp, & as yet Iris riches lies folded in the bofome of Flora, Phœbus hath not dried vp the pearled deaw, & fo long Coridon hath taught me, it is not fit to lead the fheepe abroad: leaft the deaw being vnwholefome, they get the rot: but now fee I the old prouerbe true, he is in haft whom the diuel driues, & where loue prickes forward, there is no worfe death than delay. Ah my good page, is there fancie in thine eie, and paffions in thy heart ¶ What, haft thou wrapt loue in thy looks ¶ and fet all thy thoughts on fire by affection ¶ I tell thee, it is a flame as hard to be quencht as that of ætna. But nature muft haue her courfe, womens eyes haue facultie attractiue like the ieat, and retentiue like the diamond: they dallie in the delight of faire obiects, til gazing on the Panthers beautifull fkinne, repenting experience tell them hee hath a deuouring paunch. Come on (quoth Ganimede) this fermon of yours is but a fubtiltie to lie ftill a bed, becaufe either you thinke the morning colde, or els I being gone, you would fteale a nappe: this fhifte carries no paulme, and therefore vp and away. And for Loue let me alone, Ile whip him away with nettles, and fet difdaine as a charme to withftand his forces: and therefore looke you to your felfe, be not too bolde, for Venus can make you bend; nor too coy, for Cupid hath a piercing dart, that will make you crie *Peccaui*. And that is it (quoth Aliena) that hath rayfed you fo early this morning. And with that fhe flipt on her peticoate, and ftart vp: and affoone as fhe had made her readie, and taken her breakfaft, away goe thefe two with their bagge and bottles to the field, in more pleafant content of mind, than euer they were in the Court of Torismond. They came no fooner nigh the foldes, but they might fee where their difcontented Forrefter was walking in his melancholy. Affoone as Aliena faw him, fhe fmiled, and fayd to Ganimede; wipe your eyes fweeting: for yonder is your fweet hart this morning in deepe praiers no doubt to Venus, that fhe may make you as pitifull as hee is paffionate. Come on Ganimede, I pray thee lets haue a little fport with him. Content (quoth Ganimede) and with that, to waken him out of his deepe *memento*, he began thus.

Forrefter, good fortune to thy thoughts, and eafe to thy paffions, what makes you fo early abroad this morne, in cōtemplation, no doubt of your Rosalynde. Take heede Forefter, ftep not too farre, the foord may be deepe, and you flip ouer the fhooes; I tell thee, flies haue their fpleene, the ants choller, the leaft haires fhadowes, & the fmalleft loues great defires. Tis good (Forrefter) to loue, but not to ouerloue: leaft in louing her that likes not thee, thou folde thy felfe in an endleffe Laborynth. Rosader feeing the fayre fhepheardeffe and her pretie fwayne, in whofe companie he hee felt the greateft eafe of his care, he returned them a falute on this manner.

Gentle fhepheards, all haile, and as healthfull bee your flockes, as you happie in content. Loue is reftleffe, and my bedde is but the cell of my bane, in that there I finde bufie thoughtes and broken flumbers: heere (although euerie where paffionate) yet I brooke loue with more patience, in that euerie obiect feedes mine eye with varietie of fancies; when I looke on Floraes beauteous tapeſtrie, checkered with the pride of all her treaſure, I call to minde the fayre face of Rosalynde, whoſe heauenly hiew exceedes the Roſe and the Lilly in their higheſt excellence; the brightneſſe of Phœbus ſhine, puts me in minde to thinke of the ſparkling flames that flew from her eies, and ſet my heart firſt on fire; the ſweet harmonie of the birds, puts me in remembrance of the rare melodie of her voyce, which like thę Syren enchaunteth the eares of the hearer. Thus in contemplation I ſalue my ſorrowes, with applying the perfection of euerie obiect to the excellence of her qualities.

She is much beholding vnto you (quoth Aliena) and ſo much, that I haue oft wiſht with my ſelfe, that if I ſhould euer prooue as amorous as Oenone, I might finde as faithfull a Paris as your ſelfe.

How ſay you by this *Item* Foreſter, (quoth Ganimede) the faire ſhepheardeſſe fauours you, who is miſtreſſe of ſo manie flockes. Leaue of man the ſuppoſition of Rosalynds loue, when as watching at her, you roue beyond the Moone; and caſt your lookes vpon my Miſtres, who no doubt is as faire though not ſo royall; one birde in the hande is woorth two in the wood; better poſſeſſe the loue of Aliena, than catch friuououſly at the ſhadow of Rosalynde.

Ile tell thee boy (quoth Ganimede) ſo is my fancie fixed on my Rosalynde, that were thy Miſtres as faire as Læda or Danae, whome Ioue courted in tranſformed ſhapes, mine eyes would not vouch to intertaine their beauties: and ſo hath Loue lockt mee in her perfections, that I had rather onely contemplate in her beauties, than abſolutely poſſeſſe the excellence of anie other. Venus is too blame (Forreſter) if hauing ſo true a ſeruant of you, ſhe reward you not with Rosalynde, if Rosalynde were more fairer than her ſelfe. But leauing this prattle, nowe Ile put you in minde of your promiſe, about thoſe ſonnets which you ſaide were at home in your lodge. I haue them about me (quoth Rosader) let vs ſit downe, and then you ſhall heare what a Poeticall furie Loue will infuſe into a man: with that they ſate downe vpon a greene bank, ſhadowed with figge trees, and Rosader, fetching a deepe ſigh read them this Sonnet.

Roſaders Sonnet.

In ſorrowes cell I laid me downe to ſleepe :
But waking woes were iealous of mine eyes,
They made them watch, and bend themſelues to weepe :
But weeping teares their want could not ſuffice :
    Yet ſince for her they wept who guides my hart,
    They weeping ſmile, and triumph in their ſmart.

II, iv, 53

Of theſe my teares a fountaine fiercely ſprings,
Where Venus *baynes her ſelfe incenſt with loue ;*
Where Cupid *bowſeth his faire feathred wings .*
But I behold what paines I muſt approue.
    Care drinkes it drie : but when on her J thinke,
    Loue makes me weepe it full vnto the brinke.

Meane while my ſighes yeeld truce vnto my teares,
By them the windeṣ increaſt and fiercely blow :
Yet when J ſigh the flame more plaine appeares,
And by their force with greater power doth glow :
    Amids theſe paines, all Phœnix like I thriue,
    Since Loue that yeelds me death, may life reuiue.

Roſader en eſperance.

Now furely Forrester (quoth Aliena) when thou madeft this fonnet, thou wert in fome amorous quandarie, neither too fearfull, as defpairing of thy Miftres fauours : nor too gleefome, as hoping in thy fortunes.   I can fmile (quoth Ganimede) at the Sonettoes, Canzones, Madrigales, rounds and roundelayes, that thefe penfiue patients powre out, when their eyes are more ful of wantonneffe, than their hearts of paffions. Then, as the fifhers put the fweeteft baite to the faireft fifh : fo thefe Ouidians (holding *Amo* in their tongues, when their thoughtes come at hap hazarde, write that they be wrapt in an endleffe laborynth of forrow, when walking in the large leas of libertie, they onely haue their humours in their inckpot.   If they finde women fo fond, that they will with fuch painted lures come to theyr luft, then they triumph till they be full gorgde with pleafures : and then fly they away (like ramage kytes) to their owne content, leauing the tame foole their Miftres full of fancie, yet without euer a feather.   If they miffe (as dealing with fome wary wanton, that wats not fuch a one as themfelues, but fpies their fubtiltie) they ende their amors with a few fained fighes : and fo there excufe is, their Miftres is cruell, and they fmoother paffions with patience. Such gentle Forrefter we may deeme you to bee, that rather paffe away the time heere in thefe Woods with writing amorets, than to bee deepely enamoured (as you faye) of your Rosalynde.   If you bee fuch a one, then I pray God, when you thinke your fortunes at the higheft, and your defires to bee moft excellent, then that you may with Ixion embrace Iuno in a clowde, and haue nothing but a marble Miftres to releafe your martyrdome : but if you be true and truftie, eypaind and hart ficke, then accurfed bee Rosalynde if fhee prooue cruell : for Forrefter (I flatter not) thou art woorthie of as faire as fhee.   Aliena fpying the ftorme by the winde, fmiled to fee how Ganimede flew to the fift without anie call : but Rofader who tooke him flat for a fhepheards Swayne made him this anfwere.

Truft me Swayne (quoth Rofader) but my Canzon was written in no fuch humour : for mine eye & my heart are relatiues, the one drawing fancie by fight, the other entertaining her by forrowe.   If thou faweft my Rosalynde, with what beauties Nature hath fauoured her, with what perfection the heauens hath graced her, with what qualities the Gods haue endued her; then wouldft thou fay, there is none fo fickle that could be fleeting vnto her.   If fhe had ben Aeneas Dido, had Venus and Iuno both fcolded him from *Carthage*, yet her excellence defpite of them, woulde haue detained him at *Tyre*.   If Phillis had been as beauteous, or Ariadne as vertuous, or both as honourable and excellent as fhe; neither had the Philbert tree forrowed in the death of defpairing Phillis, nor the ftarres haue been graced with Ariadne : but Demophoon and Theseus had been truftie to their Paragons.   I will tell thee Swaine, if with a deepe infight thou couldft pearce into the fecrete of my loues, and fee what deepe impreffions of her Idea affection hath made in my heart : then wouldft thou confeffe I were paffing paffionate, and no leffe indued with admirable patience.   Why (quoth Aliena) needes there patience in Loue?   Or els in nothing (quoth Rofader) for it is a reftleffe foare, that hath no eafe, a cankar that ftill frets, a difeafe that taketh awaie all hope of fleepe.   If then fo manie forrowes, fodain ioies, momentarie pleafures, continuall feares, daylie griefes, and nightly woes be found in Loue, then is not he to be accompted patient, that fmoothers all thefe paffions with filence?   Thou fpeakeft by experience (quoth Ganimede) and therefore wee holde all thy words for Axiomes : but is Loue fuch a lingring maladie?   It is (quoth he) either extreame or meane, according to the minde of the partie that entertaines it : for as the weedes growe longer vntouchte than the pretie flowers, and the flint lies fafe in the quarrie, when the Emeraulde is fuffering the Lapidaries toole : fo meane men are freeed from Venus iniuries, when kings are enuyroned with a laborynth of her cares. The whiter the Lawne is, the deeper is the moale, the more purer the chryfolite the fooner ftained; and fuch as haue their hearts ful of honour, haue their loues full of the greateft forrowes. But in whomfoeuer (quoth Rosader) he fixeth his dart, hee neuer leaueth to affault him, till either hee hath wonne him to follie or fancie: for as the Moone neuer goes without the ftarre Lunifequa, fo a Louer neuer goeth without the vnreft of his thoughts. For proofe you fhall heare another fancie of my making. Now doo gentle Forrefter (quoth Ganimede) and with that he read ouer this *Sonetto*.

Rofaders fecond Sonetto.

Turne I my lookes vnto the Skies,
Loue with his arrowes wounds mine eies:
Jf fo I gaze vpon the ground,
Loue then in euerie flower is found.
Search J the fhade to flie my paine,
He meetes me in the fhade againe:
Wend J to walke in fecrete groue,
Euen there I meete with facred Loue.
Jf fo I bayne me in the fpring,
Euen on the brinke I heare him fing:
Jf fo I meditate alone,
He will be partner of my moane.
Jf fo I mourne, he weepes with mee,
And where I am, there will he bee.
When as I talke of Rofalynde,
The God from coyneffe waxeth kinde,
And feemes in felfe fame flames to frie,
Becaufe he loues as well as I.
Sweete Rofalynde *for pitie rue,*
For why, then Loue I am more true:
He if he fpeede will quicklie flie,
But in thy loue I liue and die.

How like you this Sonnet, quoth Rosader? Marrie quoth Ganimede, for the penne well, for the paffion ill: for as I praife the one; I pitie the other, in that thou fhould-eft hunt after a clowde, and loue either without rewarde or regarde. Tis not her frowardneffe, quoth Rosader, but my hard fortunes, whofe Deftenies haue croft me with her abfence: for did fhee feele my loues, fhe would not let me linger in thefe forrowes. Women, as they are faire, fo they refpect faith, and eftimate more (if they be honourable) the wil than the wealth, hauing loyaltie the obiect whereat they ayme their fancies. But leauing off thefe interparleyes, you fhall heare my laft *Sonnetto*, and then you haue heard all my Poetrie: and with that he fight out this.

Rofaders third Sonnet.

Of vertuous Loue my felfe may boast alone,
Since no fufpect my feruice may attaint:
For perfect faire fhee is the onely one,   III, ii, 93
Whom I esteeme for my beloued Saint:
   Thus for my faith J onely beare the bell,
   And for her faire fhe onely doth excell.

Then let fond Petrarch *fhrowde his* Lawraes *praife,*
And Taffo *ceafe to publifh his affect;*
Since mine the faith confirmde at all affaies,
And hers the faire, which all men doo refpect :   **III, ii, 93**
   My lines her faire, her faire my faith affures;
   Thus J by Loue, and Loue by me endures.

Thus quoth Rofader, heere is an ende of my Poems, but for all this no releafe of my paffions : fo that I refemble him, that in the deapth of his diftreffe hath none but the Eccho to aunfwere him.   Ganimede pittying her Rofader, thinking to driue him out of this amorous melancholie, faid, that now the Sunne was in his Meridionall heat, and that it was high noone, therefore we fhepheards fay, tis time to goe to dinner : for the Sunne and our ftomackes, are Shepheards dialls.   Therefore Forrefter, if thou wilt take fuch fare as comes out of our homely fcrippes, **III, ii, 161**
welcome fhall aunfwere whatfoeuer thou wahtft in delicates.   Aliena
tooke the entertainment by the ende, and told Rofader he fhould be her gueft.   He thankt them heartely, and fate with them downe to dinner : where they had fuch cates as Countrey ftate did allow them, fawft with fuch content, and fuch fweete prattle, as it feemed farre more fweete, than all their Courtly iunckets.

Affoone as they had taken their repaft, Rofader giuing them thankes for his good cheere, would haue been gone : but Ganimede, that was loath to let him paffe out of her prefence, began thus; Nay Forrefter quoth he, if thy bufines be not the greater, feeing thou faift thou art fo deeply in loue, let me fee how thou canft wooe : I will reprefent Rofalynde, and thou fhalt bee as thou art Rofader; fee in fome amorous Eglogue, how if Rofalynde were prefent, how thou couldft court her : and while we fing of Loue, Aliena fhall tune her pipe, and playe vs melodie.   Content, quoth Rofa-der.   And Aliena, fhee to fhew her willingneffe, drewe foorth a recorder, and began to winde it.   Then the louing Forrefter began thus.

The wooing Eglogue betwixt Rofalynde and Rofader.
Rofader.
J pray thee Nymph by all the working words,
By all the teares and fighes that Louers know,
Or what or thoughts or faltring tongue affords,
J craue for mine in ripping vp my woe.
Sweete Rofalynde *my loue (would God my loue)*
My life (would God my life) ay pitie me ;
Thy lips are kinde, and humble like the doue,
And but with beautie pitie will not be.
Looke on mine eyes made red with rufull teares,
From whence the raine of true remorfe defcendeth,
All pale in lookes, and J though young in yeares,
And nought but loue or death my daies befrendeth.
Oh let no ftormie rigour knit thy browes,
Which Loue appointed for his mercie feate :
The tallest tree by Boreas *breath it bowes,*
The yron yeelds with hammer, and to heate.
   Oh Rofalynde *then be thou pittifull,*
   For Rofalynde *is onely beautifull.*

Roſalynde.

Loues wantons arme their traitrous ſutes with teares,
With vowes, with oathes, with lookes, with ſhowers of golde :
But when the fruite of their affects appeares,
The ſimple heart by ſubtill ſleights is ſolde.
Thus ſuckes the yeelding eare the poyſoned bait,
Thus feedes the hart vpon his endleſſe harmes,
Thus glut the thoughts themſelues on ſelfe deceipt,
Thus blinde the eyes their ſight by ſubtill charmes.
The louely lookes, the ſighs that ſtorme ſo ſore,
The deaw of deepe diſſembled doubleneſſe :
Theſe may attempt, but are of power no more,
Where beautie leanes to wit and ſoothfaſtneſſe.
  Oh Roſader *then be thou wittifull,*
  For Roſalynde *ſcornes fooliſh pitifull.*

Roſader.

J pray thee Roſalynde *by thoſe ſweete eyes*
That ſtaine the Sunne in ſhine, the morne in cleare ;
By thoſe ſweete cheekes where Loue incamped lies
To kiſſe the roſes of the ſpringing yeare.
J tempt thee Roſalynde *by ruthfull plaints,*
Not ſeaſoned with deceipt or fraudfull guile,
But firme in paine, farre more than tongue depaints,
Sweete Nymph be kinde, and grace me with a ſmile.
So may the heauens preſerue from hurtfull food
Thy harmeleſſe ſlockes, ſo may the Summer yeeld
The pride of all her riches and her good,
To fat thy ſheepe (the Citizens of field).
Oh leaue to arme thy louely browes with ſcorne :
The birds their beake, the Lion hath his taile,
And Louers nought but ſighes and bitter mourne,
The ſpotleſſe fort of fancie to aſſaile.
  Oh Roſalynde *then be thou pitifull :*
  For Roſalynde *is onely beautifull.*

Roſalynde.

The hardned ſteele by fire is brought in frame :

Roſader.

And Roſalynde *my loue than anie wooll more ſofter* ;
And ſhall not ſighes her tender heart inflame ?

Roſalynde.

Were Louers true, maides would beleeue them ofter.

Roſader.

Truth and regard, and honour guide my loue.

Roſalynde.

Faine would I trust, but yet I dare not trie.

Roſader.

Oh pitie me ſweete Nymph, and doo but prove.

Rofalynde.

I would refist, but yet I know not why.

Rofader.

Oh Rofalynde *be kinde, for times will change,*
Thy lookes ay nill be faire as now they be,
Thine age from beautie may thy lookes eftrange :
Ah yeelde in time fweete Nymph, and pitie me.

Rofalynde.

Oh Rofalynde *thou must be pitifull.*
For Rofader *is yong and beautifull.*

Rofader.

Oh gaine more great than kingdomes, or a crowne.

Rofalynde.

Oh trust betraid if Rofader *abufe me.*

Rofader.

First let the heauens conspire to pull me downe,
And heauen and earth as abieɛt quite refufe me.
Let forrowes ftreame about my hatefull bower,
And restleffe horror hatch within my breast,
Let beauties eye afflicɛt me with a lowre,
Let deepe despaire purfue me without rest;
Ere Rofalynde *my loyaltie disproue,*
Ere Rofalynde *accufe me for vnkinde.*

Rofalynde.

Then Rofalynde *will grace thee with her loue,*
Then Rofalynde *will haue thee ftill in minde.*

Rofader.

Then let me triumph more than Tithons *deere,*
Since Rofalynde *will* Rofader *respecɛt :*
Then let my face exile his forrie cheere,
And frolicke in the comfort of affecɛt :
And fay that Rofalynde *is onely pitifull,*
Since Rofalynde *is onely beautifull.*

When thus they had finifhed their courting Eglogue in fuch a familiar claufe, Ganimede as Augure of fome good fortunes to light vpon their affeɛctions, beganne to be thus pleafant; How now Forrefter, haue I not fitted your turn ꞅ haue I not plaide the woman handfomely, and fhewed my felfe as coy in graunts, as courteous in defires, and been as full of fufpition, as men of flatterie ꞅ And yet to falue all, iumpt I not all vp with the fweete vnion of loue? Did not Rosalynde content her Rosader? The Forrefter at this fmiling, fhooke his head, and folding his armes made this merrie replie.

Truth gentle Swaine, Rosader hath his Rosalynde : but as Ixion had Iuno, who thinking to poffeffe a goddeffe, onely imbraced a clowde : in thefe imaginarie fruitions of fancie, I refemble the birds that fed themfelues with Zeuxis painted grapes; but they grewe fo leane with pecking at fhaddowes, that they were glad with Aesops Cocke to fcrape for a barley cornell : fo fareth it with me, who to feede my felfe with the hope of my Miftres fauours, footh my felf in thy futes, and onely in conceipt reape a wifhed for content: but if my food be no better than fuch amorous dreames, Venus at the yeares ende, fhall finde mee but a leane louer. Yet doo I take thefe follies for high fortunes, and hope thefe fained affections doo deuine fome unfained ende of enfuing fancies. And thereupon (quoth Aliena) Ile play the prieft, from this day forth Ganimede fhall call thee hufband, and thou fhalt call Ganimede wife, and fo weele haue a marriage. Content (quoth Rosader) and laught. Content (quoth Ganimede) and changed as redde as a rofe: and fo with a fmile and a blufh, they made vp this iefting match, that after prooude to a marriage in earneft; Rosader full little thinking he had wooed and wonne his Rosalynde. But all was well, hope is a fweete ftring to harpe on: and therefore let the Forrefter a while fhape himfelfe to his fhaddow, and tarrie Fortunes leafure, till fhe may make a Metamorphofis fit for his purpofe. I digreffe, and therefore to Aliena: who faid, the wedding was not worth a pinne, vnless there were fome cheere, nor that bargaine well made that was not ftriken vp with a cuppe of wine: and therefore fhe wild Ganimede to fet out fuch cates as they had, and to drawe out her bottle, charging the Forrefter as hee had imagined his loues, fo to conceipt thefe cates to be a moft fumptuous banquet, and to take a Mazer of wine and to drinke to his Rosalynde: which Rosader did; and fo they paffed awaye the day in manie pleafant deuices. Till at laft Aliena perceiued time would tarrie no man, and that the Sunne waxed verie lowe, readie to fet: which made her fhorten their amorous prattle, and ende the Banquet with a frefh Carrowfe; which done, they all three rofe, and Aliena broke off thus.

Now Forrefter, Phœbus that all this while hath been partaker of our fports; feeing euerie Woodman more fortunate in his loues, than hee in his fancies; feeing thou haft wonne Rosalynde, when he could not wooe Daphne, hides his head for fhame, and bids vs adiew in a clowde; our fheep they poore wantons wander towards their foldes, as taught by Nature their due times of reft: which tells vs Forrefter, we muft depart. Marrie, though there were a marriage, yet I muft carrie (this night) the Bryde with me, and to morrow morning if you meete vs heere, Ile promife to deliuer her as good a maide as I finde her. Content quoth Rosader, tis enough for me in the night to dreame on loue, that in the day am fo fond to doate on loue: and fo till to morrow you to your Foldes, and I will to my Lodge; and thus the Forrefter and they parted. He was no fooner gone, but Aliena and Ganimede went and folded their flockes, and taking vp their hookes, their bagges, and their bottles, hied homeward. By the waye, Aliena to make the time feeme fhort, began to prattle with Ganimede thus; I haue heard them fay, that what the Fates forepoint, that Fortune pricketh downe with a period, that the ftarres are fticklers in Venus Court, and defire hangs at the heele of Deftenie; if it be fo, then by all probable coniectures, this match will be a marriage: for if Augurifme be authenticall, or the deuines doomes principles, it cannot bee but fuch a fhaddowe portends the iffue of a fubftaunce, for to that ende did the Gods force the conceipt of this Eglogue, that they might difcouer the enfuing confent of your affections: fo that eare it bee long, I hope (in earneft) to daunce at your Wedding.

Tufh (quoth Ganimede) al is not malte that is caft on the kill, there goes more words to a bargaine than one, loue feeles no footing in the aire, and fancie holdes it flipperie harbour to neftle in the tongue: the match is not yet fo furely made but he may miffe of his market; but if Fortune be his friend, I will not be his foe: and fo I pray you (gentle Miftreffe Aliena) take it. I take all things well (quoth fhee) that is your content, and am glad Rosader is yours: for now I hope your thoughts will be at quiet; your eye that euer looked at Loue, will nowe lende a glaunce on your Lambes: and then they will proue more buxfome and you more blythe, for the eyes of the Mafter feedes the Cattle. As thus they were in chat, they fpied olde Coridon where hee came plodding to meete them: who tolde them fupper was readie: which newes made them fpeede them home. Where we leaue them to the next morrow, and returne to Saladyne.

All this while did poore Saladyne (banifhed from *Bourdeaux* and the Court of *France* by Torifmond) wander vp and downe in the Forreft of *Arden*, thinking to get to *Lions*, and fo trauell through *Germanie* into *Italy:* but the Forreft being full of by-pathes, and he vnfkilfull of the Countrey coaft, flipt out of the way, and chaunced vp into the Defart, not farre from the place where Gerifmond was, and his brother Rosader. Saladyne wearie with wandring vp and   **IV, iii, 109** downe, and hungrie with long fafting; finding a little caue by the fide of a thicket, eating fuch frute as the Forreft did affoord, and contenting himfelfe with fuch drinke as Nature had prouided, and thirft made delicate, after his repaft he fell in a dead fleepe. As thus he lay, a hungrie Lion came hunting downe the edge of the groue for pray, and efpying Saladyne began to ceaze vpon him: but feeing he lay ftill without anie motion, he left to touch him, for that Lions hate to pray on dead carkaffes: and yet defirous to haue fome foode, the Lion   **IV, iii, 123** lay downe and watcht to fee if hee would ftirre. While thus Saladyne flept fecure, fortune that was careful ouer her champion, began to fmile, and brought it fo to paffe, that Rosader (hauing ftriken a Deere that but lightly hurt fled through the thicket) came pacing downe by the groue with a Boare fpeare in his hand in great haft, he fpied where a man lay a fleepe, and a Lion faft by him: amazed at this fight, as hee ftood gazing, his nofe on the fodaine bled; which made him coniecture it was fome friend of his. Whereuppon drawing more nigh, hee might eafely difcerne his vifage, and perceiued by his phifnomie that it was his brother Saladyne: which draue Rosader into a deepe paffion, as a man perplexed at the fight of fo vnex-pected a chaunce, maruelling what fhoulde driue his brother to trauerfe thofe fecrete Defarts without anie companie in fuch diftreffe and forlorne fort. But the prefent time craued no fuch doubting ambages: for either he muft refolue to hazard his life for his reliefe, or els fteale awaye, and leaue him to the crueltie of the Lion. In which doubt, he thus briefly debated with himfelfe.——R o f a d e r s m e d i t a t i o n.

——Now Rosader, Fortune that long hath whipt thee with nettles, meanes to falue thee with rofes; and hauing croft thee with manie frownes, now fhe prefents thee with the brightneffe of her fauours. Thou that didft count thy felfe the moft dif-treffed of all men, maift accompt thy felfe now the moft fortunate amongft men; if fortune can make men happie, or fweete reuenge be wrapt in a pleafing content. Thou feeft Saladyne thine enemie, the worker of thy miffortunes, and the efficient caufe of thine exile, fubiect to the crueltie of a mercileffe Lion: brought into this miferie by the Gods, that they might feeme iuft in reuenging his rigour, and thy iniuries. Seeft thou not how the ftarres are in a fauourable afpect, the plannets in fome pleafing coniunction, the fates agreeable to thy thoughts, and the deftenies per-fourmers of thy defires, in that Saladyne fhall die, and thou free of his bloud; he receiue meede for his amiffe, and thou erect his Tombe with innocent hands. Now Rosader fhalt thou returne to *Bourdeaux*, and enioye thy poffeffions by birth, and his reuenewes by inheritaunce: now maift thou triumph in loue, and hang Fortunes Altares with garlandes. For when Rosalynde heares of thy wealth, it will make her loue thee more willingly: for womens eyes are made of Chrifecoll, that is euer vnper-fect vnleffe tempred with golde: and Iupiter fooneft enioyed Danae, becaufe he came to her in fo rich a fhower. Thus fhall this Lion (Rosader) end the life of a miferable man, and from diſtreſſe raiſe thee to bee moſt fortunate. And with that caſting his Boare ſpeare on his neck, away he began to trudge. But hee had not ſtept backe two or three paces, but a new motion ſtroke him to the very hart, that reſting his Boare ſpeare againſt his breaſt, hee fell into this paſſionate humour.

Ah Roſader, wert thou the ſonne of Sir Iohn of *Bourdeaux*, whoſe vertues exceeded his valour, and yet the moſt hardieſt Knight in all *Europe?* Should the honour of the father ſhine in the actions of the ſonne ᛭ and wilt thou diſhonour thy parentage, in forgetting the nature of a Gentleman? Did not thy father at his laſt gaſpe breathe out this golden principle; Brothers amitie is like the drops of *Balſamum*, that ſalueth the moſt dangerous ſores ᛭ Did hee make a large exhort vnto concord, and wilt thou ſhewe thy ſelfe careleſſe? Oh Roſader, what though Saladyne hath wronged thee, and made thee liue an exile in the Forreſt? ſhall thy nature be ſo cruell, or thy nurture ſo crooked, or thy thoughts ſo ſauage, as to ſuffer ſo diſmall a reuenge ᛭ what, to let him be deuoured by wilde beaſts ᛭ *Non ſapit, qui non ſibi ſapit* is fondly ſpoken in ſuch bitter extreames. Looſe not his life Roſader to winne a world of treaſure: for in hauing him thou haſt a brother, and by hazarding for his life, thou getteſt a friend, and reconcileſt an enemie: and more honour ſhalt thou purchaſe by pleaſuring a foe, than reuenging a thouſand iniuries.

With that his Brother began to ſtirre, and the Lion to rowſe himſelfe: whereupon Roſader ſodainely charged him with the Boare ſpeare, and wounded the Lion verie ſore at the firſt ſtroake. The beaſt feeling himſelfe to haue a mortall hurt, leapt at Roſader, and with his pawes gaue him a ſore pinch on the breaſt that he had almoſt faln: yet as a man moſt valiant, in whom the ſparkes of Sir Iohn of *Bourdeaux* remained, he recouered himſelfe, and in ſhort combat flew the Lion: who at his death roared ſo lowde, that Saladyne awaked, and ſtarting vp was amazed at the ſodayne ſight of ſo monſtrous a beaſt lie ſlaine by him, and ſo ſweete a Gentleman wounded. He preſently (as hee was of a ripe conceipt) began to coniecture, that the Gentleman had ſlain him in his defence. Whereuppon (as a man in a traunce) he ſtood ſtaring on them both a good while, not knowing his Brother beeing in that diſguiſe: at laſt hee burſt into theſe tearmes.

Sir whatſoeuer thou bee, (as full of honour thou muſt needs be, by the view of thy preſent valure) I perceiue thou haſt redreſt my fortunes by thy courage, and ſaued my life with thine owne loſſe: which ties me to be thine in all humble ſeruice. Thankes thou ſhalt haue as thy due, and more thou canſt not haue: for my abilitie denies to performe a deeper debt. But if anie wayes it pleaſe thee to commaund me, vſe me as farre as the power of a poore Gentleman may ſtretch.

Roſader ſeeing hee was vnknowen to his brother, wondred to heare ſuch courteous words come from his crabbed nature; but glad of ſuch reformed nourture, hee made this aunſwere. I am ſir (whatſoeuer thou art) a Forreſter and Ranger of theſe walkes: who following my Deere to the fall, was conducted hether by ſome aſſenting Fate, that I might ſaue thee, and diſparage my ſelfe. For comming into this place, I ſawe thee a ſleepe, and the Lion watching thy awake, that at thy riſing hee might prey vppon thy carkaſſe. At the firſt ſight, I coniectured thee a Gentleman, (for all mens thoughts ought to be fauourable in imagination) and I counted it the hart of a reſolute man to purchaſe a ſtrangers reliefe, though with the loſſe of his owne bloud: which I haue performed (thou ſeeſt) to mine owne preiudice. If therefore thou be a man of ſuch worth as I valew thee by thy exteriour liniaments, make diſcourſe vnto mee what is the cauſe of thy preſent fortunes. For by the furrowes in thy face thou ſeemeſt to be croſt with her frowns: but whatſoeuer or howſoeuer, let me craue that fauour, to heare the tragicke caufe of thy eftate. Saladyne fitting downe, and fetching a deepe figh, began thus.——Saladynes difcourfe to Rofader vnknowen.——Although the difcourfe of my fortunes, be the renewing of my forrowes, and the rubbing of the fcar, will open a frefh wound; yet that I may not prooue ingratefull to fo courteous a Gentleman, I will rather fitte downe and figh out my eftate, than giue anie offence by fmoothering my griefe with filence. Know therefore (fir) that I am of *Bourdeaux*, and the fonne and heire of Syr Iohn of *Bourdeaux*, a man for his vertues and valour fo famous, that I cannot thinke, but the fame of his honours, hath reacht farther than the knowledge of his Perfonage. The infortunate fonne of fo fortunate a Knight am I, my name Saladyne: Who fucceeding my Father in poffeffions but not in qualities, hauing two Brethren committed by my Father at his death to my charge, with fuch golden principles of brotherly concord, as might haue pierft like the Syrens melodie into anie humane eare. But I (with Vlyffes became deafe againft his Philofophicall harmony, and made more value of profite than of vertue, efteeming golde fufficient honour, and wealth the fitteft title for a gentlemans dignitie: I fet my middle brother to the Vniuerfitie to be a Scholler, counting it enough if he might pore on a booke, while I fed vpon his reuenewes: and for the yongeft (which was my fathers ioye) yong Rofader. And with that, naming of Rofader, Saladyne fate him downe and wept.

Nay forward man (quoth the Forrefter) teares are the vnfitteft falue that anie man can applie for to cure forowes, and therefore ceafe from fuch feminine follies, as fhoulde droppe out of a Womans eye to deceiue, not out of a Gentlemans looke to difcouer, his thoughts, and forward with thy difcourfe.

Oh fir (quoth Saladyne) this Rofader that wringes teares from mine eyes, and bloud from my heart, was like my father in exteriour perfonage and in inward qualities: for in the prime of his yeares he aimed all his acts at honor, and coueted rather to die, than to brooke anie iniurie vnworthie a Gentlemans credite. I, whom enuie had made blinde, and couetoufneffe mafked with the vaile of felfe loue, feeing the Palme tree grow ftraight, thought to fuppreffe it being a twig: but Nature will haue her courfe, the Cedar will be tall, the Diamond bright, the Carbuncle gliftering, and vertue will fhine though it be neuer fo much obfcured. For I kept Rofader as a flane, and vfed him as one of my feruile hindes, vntil age grew on, and a fecrete infight of my abufe entred into his minde: infomuch, that hee could not brooke it, but coueted to haue what his father left him, and to liue of himfelfe. To be fhort fir, I repined at his fortunes, and he countercheckt me not with abilitie but valour, vntill at laft by my friends and aid of fuch as followed golde more than right or vertue, I banifht him from *Bourdeaux*, and he pore Gentleman liues no man knowes where in fome diftreffed difcontent. The Gods not able to fuffer fuch impietie vnreuenged, fo wrought, that the King pickt a caufeles quarrell againft me, in hope to haue my lands, and fo hath exiled me out of *France* for euer. Thus, thus fir, am I the moft miferable of all men, as hauing a blemifh in my thoughts for the wrongs I proffered Rofader, and a touche in my ftate to be throwen from my proper poffeffions by iniuftice. Paffionate thus with manie griefes, in penaunce of my former follies, I goe thus pilgrime like to feeke out my Brother, that I may reconcile my felfe to him in all fubmiffion, and afterward wend to the holy Land, to ende my yeares in as manie vertues, as I haue fpent my youth in wicked vanities.

Rofader hearing the refolution of his brother Saladyne began to compaffionate his forrowes, and not able to fmother the fparkes of Nature with fained fecrecie, he burft into thefe louing fpeaches. Then know Saladyne (quoth he) that thou haft met with

Rosader; who grieues as much to fee thy diftreffe, as thy felfe to feele the burden of thy miferie. Saladyne cafting vp his eye, and noting well the phifnomie of the Forrefter, knew that it was his brother Rosader: which made him fo bafh and blufh at the firft meeting, that Rosader was faine to recomfort him. Which he did in fuch fort, y^t he fhewed how highly he held reuenge in fcorne. Much a doo there was betweene thefe two Brethren, Saladyne in crauing pardon, and Rosader in forgiuing and forgetting all former iniuries; the one fubmiffe, the other curteous; Saladyne penitent and paffionate, Rosader kinde & louing; that at length Nature working an vnion of theyr thoughts, they earneftly embraced, and fell from matters of vnkindneffe, to talke of the Countrey life, which Rosader fo highly commended, that his brother began to haue a defire to tafte of that homely content. In this humour Rosader conducted him to Gerismonds Lodge, and prefented his brother to the King; difcourfing the whole matter how all had happened betwixt them. The King looking vppon Saladyne, found him a man of a moft beautifull perfonage, and faw in his face fufficient fparkes of enfuing honours, gaue him great entertainment, and glad of their friendly reconcilement, promifed fuch fauour as the pouertie of his eftate might affoord: which Saladyne gratefully accepted. And fo Gerismond fell to queftion of Torismonds life? Saladyne briefly difcourft vnto him his iniuftice and tyrannies: with fuch modeftie (although hee had wronged him) that Gerismond greatly praifed the fparing fpeach of the yong Gentleman.

Manie queftions paft, but at laft Gerismond began with a deepe figh, to inquire if there were anie newes of the welfare of Alinda or his daughter Rosalynde? None fir quoth Saladyne, for fince their departure they were neuer heard of. Iniurious Fortune (quoth the King) that to double the Fathers miferie, wrongft the Daughter with misfortunes. And with that (furcharged with forrowes) he went into his Cel, & left Saladyne and Rosader, whom Rosader ftreight conducted to the fight of Adam Spencer. Who feeing Saladyne in that eftate, was in a browne ftudie: but when hee heard the whole matter, although he grieued for the exile of his Mafter, yet hee ioyed that banifhment had fo reformed him, that from a lafciuious youth hee was prooued a vertuous Gentleman. Looking a longer while, and feeing what familiaritie paft betweene them, and what fauours were interchanged with brotherly affection, he faid thus; I marrie, thus fhould it be, this was the concord that olde Sir Iohn of *Bourdeaux* wifht betwixt you. Now fulfill you thofe precepts he breathed out at his death, and in obferuing them, looke to liue fortunate, and die honourable. Wel faid Adam Spencer quoth Rosader, but haft anie victualls in ftore for vs ꝗ A peece of a red Deere (quoth he) and a bottle of wine. Tis Forrefters fare brother, quoth Rosader: and fo they fate downe and fell to their cates. Affoone as they had taken their repaft, and had well dined, Rosader tooke his brother Saladyne by the hand, and fhewed him the pleafures of the Forreft, and what content they enioyed in that meane eftate. Thus for two or three dayes he walked vp and down with his brother, to fhewe him all the commodities that belonged to his Walke. In which time hee was mift of his Ganimede, who mufed greatly (with Aliena) what fhould become of their Forefter. Some while they thought he had taken fome word vnkindly, and had taken the pet: then they imagined fome new loue had withdrawen his fancie, or happely that he was ficke, or detained by fome great bufineffe of Gerismonds, or that he had made a reconcilement with his brother, and fo returned to *Bourdeaux*. Thefe coniectures did they caft in their heads, but efpecially Ganimede: who hauing Loue in her heart prooued reftleffe, and halfe without patience, that Rosader wronged hir with fo long abfence: for Loue meafures euerie minute, and thinkes howers to be

dayes, and dayes to be months, till they feed their eyes with the fight of their defired obiect. Thus perplexed liued poore Ganimede: while on a day fitting with Aliena in a great dumpe, fhe caft vp her eye, and faw where Rosader came
pacing towards them with his forreft bill on his necke. At that fight her   **I, ii, 117**
colour chaungde, and fhe faid to Aliena; See Miftreffe where our iolly
Forrefter comes. And you are not a little glad thereof (quoth Aliena) your nofe bewrayes what porredge you loue, the winde can not bee tied within his quarter, the Sunne fhaddowed with a vaile, Oyle hidden in water, nor Loue kept out of a Womans lookes: but no more of that, *Lupus est in fabula.* As foone as Rosader was come within the reach of her tungs ende, Aliena began thus: Why how now gentle Forrefter, what winde hath kept you from hence? that beeing fo newly married, you haue no more care of your Rosalynde, but to abfent your felfe fo manie dayes ʕ Are thefe the paffions you painted out fo in your Sonnets and roundelaies? I fee well hote loue is foone colde, and that the fancie of men, is like to a loofe feather that wandreth in the aire with the blaft of euerie winde. You are deceiued Miftres quoth Rosader, twas a coppie of vnkindneffe that kept me hence, in that I being married, you carried away the Bryde: but if I haue giuen anie occafion of offence by abfenting my felfe thefe three dayes, I humblie fue for pardon: which you muft graunt of courfe, in that the fault is fo friendly confeft with penaunce. But to tell you the truth (faire Miftreffe, and my good Rosalynde) my eldeft Brother by the iniurie of Torismond is banifhed from *Bourdeaux*, and by chaunce hee and I met in the Forreft. And heere Rosader difcourft vnto them what had hapned betwixt them: which reconcilement made them gladde, efpecially Ganimede. But Aliena hearing of the tyrannie of her Father, grieued inwardly, and yet fmothred all things with fuch fecrecie, that the concealing was more forrow than the conceipt: yet that her eftate might be hid ftill, fhee made faire weather of it, and fo let all paffe.

Fortune, that fawe how thefe parties valued not her Deitie, but helde her power in fcorne, thought to haue about with them, and brought the matter to paffe thus. Certaine Rafcalls that liued by prowling in the Forreft, who for feare of the Prouoft Marfhall had caues in the groues and thickets, to fhrowde themfelues from his traines; hearing of the beautie of this faire Shepheardeffe Aliena, thought to fteale her away, and to giue her to the King for a prefent; hoping, becaufe the King was a great lechour, by fuch a gift to purchafe all their pardons: and therfore came to take her and her Page away. Thus refolued, while Aliena and Ganimede were in this fad talk, they came rufhing in, and laid violent hands vpon Aliena and her Page, which made them crie out to Rosader: who hauing the valour of his father ftamped in his heart, thought rather to die in defence of his friends, than anie way be toucht with the leaft blemifh of difhonour; and therfore dealt fuch blowes amongft them with his weapon, as he did witneffe well vpon their carcaffes, that he was no coward. But as *Ne Hercules quidem contra duos,* fo Rosader could not refift a multitude, hauing none to backe him; fo that hee was not onely rebatted, but fore wounded, and Aliena and Ganimede had been quite carried away by thefe Rafcalls, had not Fortune (that ment to turne her frowne into a fauour) brought Saladyne that way by chaunce; who wandring to finde out his Brothers Walke, encountred this crue: and feeing not onely a fhepheardeffe and her boy forced, but his brother wounded, hee heaued vp a forreft bill he had on his necke, and the firft hee ftroke had neuer after more neede of the Phifition: redoubling his blowes with fuch courage, that the flaues were amazed at his valour.

Rosader efpying his brother fo fortunately arriued, and feeing how valiantly he behaued himfelfe, though fore woūded, rufhed amongſt them, and laid on fuch load, that fome of the crue were flaine, and the reſt fled, leauing Aliena and Ganimede in the poſſeſſion of Rosader and Saladyne.

Aliena after ſhe had breathed a while and was come to her felfe from this feare, lookt about her, and faw where Ganimede was bufie dreſſing vp the wounds of the Forreſter: but ſhe caſt her eye vpon this courteous champion that had made fo hote a refcue, and that with fuch affection, that ſhee began to meafure euerie part of him with fauour, and in her felfe to commend his perfonage and his vertue, holding him for a refolute man, that durſt aſſaile fuch a troupe of vnbridled villaines. At laſt gathering her fpirites together, ſhe returned him thefe thankes.

Gentle fir, whatfoeuer you be that haue aduentured your fleſh to relieue our fortunes, as we holde you valiant, fo we eſteeme you courteous, and to haue as manie hidden vertues, as you haue manifeſt refolutions. Wee poore Shepheards haue no wealth but our flockes, and therefore can we not make requitall with anie great treaſures: but our recompence is thankes, and our rewardes to our friendes without faining. For ranfome therefore of this our refcue, you muſt content your felfe to take fuch a kinde gramercie, as a poore Shepheardeſſe and her Page may giue: with promife (in what wee may) neuer to prooue ingratefull. For this Gentleman that is hurt, yong Rosader, he is our good neighbour and familiar acquaintance, weele pay him with fmiles, and feede him with loue-lookes: and though he bee neuer the fatter at the yeares ende, yet wele fo hamper him that he ſhall holde himfelfe fatiſfied.

Saladyne hearing this Shepheardeſſe fpeake fo wifely began more narrowly to prie into her perfection, and to furuey all her liniaments with a curious infight; fo long dallying in the flame of her beautie, that to his coſt he found her to be moſt excellent: for Loue that lurked in all thefe broiles to haue a blowe or two, feeing the parties at the gaze, encountred them both with fuch a venie, that the ſtroke pierſt to the heart fo deepe, as it could neuer after be raced out. At laſt after he had looked fo long, till Aliena waxt red, he returned her this anfwere.

Faire Shepheardeſſe, if Fortune graced mee with fuch good hap, as to doo you anie fauour, I holde my felfe as contented, as if I had gotten a great conqueſt: for the reliefe of diſtreſſed women is the fpeciall point, that Gentlemen are tied vnto by honour: feeing then my hazarde to refcue your harmes, was rather dutie than curtefie, thāks is more than belongs to the requitall of fuch a fauour. But leaſt I might feeme either too coye or too careleſſe of a Gentlewomans proffer, I wil take your kinde gramercie for a recompence. All this while that he fpake, Ganimede lookt earneſtly vpon him, and faid; Trulie Rosader, this Gentleman fauours you much in the feature of your face. No meruaile (quoth hee, gentle Swaine) for tis my eldeſt brother Saladyne. Your brother quoth Aliena? (& with that ſhe bluſht) he is the more welcome, and I holde myfelfe the more his debter: and for that he hath in my behalfe done fuch a peece of feruice, if it pleafe him to doo me that honour, I will call him feruant, and he ſhall call me Miſtreſſe. Content fweet Miſtreſſe quoth Saladyne, and when I forget to call you fo, I will be vnmindfull of mine owne felfe. Away with thefe quirkes and quiddities of loue quoth Rosader, and giue me fome drinke, for I am paſſing thirſtie, and then wil I home for my wounds bleede fore, and I will haue them dreſt. Ganimede had teares in her eyes, and paſſions in her heart to fee her Rosader fo pained, and therefore ſtept haſtely to the bottle, and filling out fome wine in a Mazer, ſhee fpiced it with fuch comfortable drugs as ſhe had about her, and gaue it him; which did comfort Rosader: that riſing (with the helpe of his brother) he tooke his leauē of them, and went to his Lodge. Ganimede aſſoone as they were out of fight ledde his flockes downe to a vale, and there vnder the fhaddow of a Beech tree fate downe, and began to mourne the miffortunes of her fweete heart.

And Aliena (as a woman paffing difcontent) feuering her felfe from her Ganimede, fitting vnder a Lymon tree, began to figh out the paffions of her newe Loue, and to meditate with her felfe on this manner.——A l i e n a e s m e d i t a t i o n.——Ay me, now I fee, and forrowing figh to fee that Dianaes Lawrells are harbours for Venus Doues, that there trace as well through the Lawnes, wantons as chaft ones; that Califto be fhe neuer fo charie, will caft one amorous eye at courting Ioue: that Diana her felf will change her fhape, but fhee will honour Loue in a fhaddow: that maidens eyes be they as hard as Diamonds, yet Cupide hath drugs to make them more pliable than waxe. See Alinda, howe Fortune and Loue haue interleagued themfelues to be thy foes: and to make thee their fubieçt or els an abieçt, haue inueigled thy fight with a moft beautiful obieçt. Alate thou didft holde Venus for a giglot, not a god-deffe; and now thou fhalt be forft to fue fuppliant to her Deitie. Cupide was a boy and blinde, but alas his eye had aime inough to pierce thee to the heart. While I liued in the Court, I helde Loue in contempt, and in high feates I had fmall defires. I knewe not affeçtion while I liued in dignitie, nor could Venus counterchecke me, as long as my fortuue was maieftie, and my thoughtes honour: and fhall I nowe bee high in defires, when I am made lowe by Deftenie ς

I haue hearde them faye, that Loue lookes not at low cottages, that Venus iettes in Roabes not in ragges, that Cupide flyes fo high, that hee fcornes to touche pouertie with his heele. Tufh Alinda, thefe are but olde wiues tales, and neither authenticall precepts, nor infallible principles: for Experience tells thee, that Peafaunts haue theyr paffions, as well as Princes, that Swaynes as they haue their labours, fo they haue theyr amours, and Loue lurkes affoone about a Sheepcoate, as a Pallaice.

Ah Alinda, this day in auoiding a preiudice thou art fallen into a deeper mif-chiefe; being refcued from the robbers, thou art become captiue to Saladyne: and what then ς Women muft loue, or they muft ceafe to liue: and therefore did Nature frame them faire, that they might be fubieçts to fancie. But perhaps Saladynes eye is leuelde vpon a more feemelier Saint. If it be fo, beare thy paffions with patience, fay Loue hath wrongd thee, that hath not wroong him; and if he be proud in con-tempt, bee thou rich in content; and rather die than difcouer anie defire: for there is nothing more precious in a woman, than to conceale Loue, and to die modeft. He is the fonne and heire of Sir Iohn of *Bourdeaux*, a youth comely enough: oh Alinda, too comely, els hadft not thou been thus difcontent; valiant, and that fettered thine eye; wife, els hadft thou not been nowe wonne: but for all thefe vertues, banifhed by thy father; and therefore if hee know thy parentage, he will hate the fruite for the tree, and condempne the yong fien for the olde ftocke. Well, howfoeuer, I muft loue: and whomfoeuer, I will: and whatfoeuer betide, Aliena will thinke well of Saladyne: fuppofe he of me as he pleafe. And with that fetching a deepe figh, fhe rife vp, and went to Ganimede: who all this while fate in a great dumpe, fearing the imminent danger of her friend Rosader; but now Aliena began to comfort her, her felfe beeing ouer growen with forrowes, and to recall her from her melancholie with manie pleafaunt perfwafions. Ganimede tooke all in the beft part, and fo they went home together after they had folded their flockes, fupping with olde Coridon, who had prouided there cates. He after fupper, to paffe away the night while bedde time, began a long difcourfe, how Montanus the yong Shepheard that was in loue with Phœbe, could by no meanes obtaine anie fauour at her hands : but ftill pained in reftleffe paffions, remained a hopeleffe and perplexed Louer. I would I might (quoth Aliena) once fee that Phœbe, is fhee fo faire, that fhe thinkes no fhepheard worthie of her beautie : or fo froward that no loue nor loyaltie will content hir : or fo coye, that fhe requires a long time to be wooed : or fo foolifh that fhe forgets, that like a fop fhe muft haue a large harueft for a little corne ᶜ

I cannot diftinguifh (quoth Coridon) of thefe nice qualities : but one of thefe dayes Ile bring Montanus and her downe, that you may both fee their perfons, and note theyr paffions : and then where the blame is, there let it reft. But this I am fure quoth Coridon, if all maidens were of her minde, the world would growe to a madde paffe ; for there would be great ftore of wooing, and little wedding, manie words and little worfhip, much follie and no faith. At this fad fentence of Coridon fo folempnlie brought foorth, Aliena fmiled : and becaufe it waxt late, fhe and her page went to bed, both of them hauing fleas in their eares to keep thē awake, Ganimede for the hurt of her Rosader, and Aliena for the affeftion fhe bore to Saladyne. In this dif-contented humor they paft away the time, til falling on fleep, their fenfes at reft, Loue left them to their quiet flumbers : which were not long. For affoone as Phœbus rofe from his Aurora, and began to mount him in the Skie, fummoning the Plough-fwaines to their handie labour, Aliena arofe ; and going to the couche where Ganimede laye, awakened her page, and faid the morning was farre fpent, the deaw fmal, and time called them awaye to their foldes. Ah, ah, (quoth Ganimede) is the winde in that doore ᶜ then in faith I perceiue that there is no Diamond fo harde but will yeelde to the file, no Cedar fo ftrong but the winde will fhake, nor anie minde fo chafte but Loue will change. Well Aliena, muft Saladyne be the man, and will it be a match ᶜ Truft me he is faire and valiant, the fonne of a worthie Knight ; whome if hee imi-tate in perfeftion as hee reprefents him in proportion, he is worthie of no leffe than Aliena. But he is an exile : what then ? I hope my Miftres refpefts the vertues not the wealth, and meafures the qualities not the fubftance. Thofe dames that are like Danae, that like loue in no fhape but in a fhower of golde ; I wifh them hufbandes with much wealth and little wit ; that the want of the one may blemifh the abun-dance of the other. It fhould (my Aliena) ftaine the honour of a Shepheardes life to fet the end of paffions vpon pelfe. Loues eyes looks not fo low as gold, there is no fees to be paid in Cupids Courtes : and in elder time (as Coridon hath tolde me) the Shepheards Loue-gifts were apples and cheftnuts, & then their defires were loyall and their thoughts conftant. But now *Quærenda pecunia primum, post nummos vir-tus*. And the time is growen to that which Horace in his Satyres wrote on :

> *omnis enim res*
> *Virtus-fama decus diuina humanaque pulchris*
> *Diuitijs parent : quas qui-constrinxerit ille*
> *Clarus erit, fortis, iustus, fapiens, etiam & rex*
> *Et quic quid volet—*

But Aliena let it not be fo with thee in thy fancies, but refpeft his faith, and there an ende. Aliena hearing Ganimede thus forward to further Saladyne in his affeftions, thought fhe kift the childe for the nurfes fake, and wooed for him that fhe might pleafe Rosader, made this replie ; Why Ganimede, whereof growes this per-fwafion ? Haft thou feene Loue in my lookes ? Or are mine eyes growen fo amorous, that they difcouer fome new entertained fancies ? If thou meafureft my thoughtes by my countenance, thou maift prooue as ill a Phifiognomer as the Lapidarie, that aymes at the fecrete vertues of the Topace, by the exterior fhadow of the ftone. The operation of the Agate is not knowen by the ftrakes, nor the Diamond prized by his brightneffe, but by his hardneffe. The Carbuncle that fhineth moft, is not euer the moft precious : and the Apothecaries choofe not flowers for their coulours, but for their vertues. Womens faces are not alwaies Kalenders of fancie, nor doo their thoughtes and their lookes euer agree : for when their eyes are fulleft of fauors, then they are oft moft emptie of defire : and when they feeme to frown at difdaine, then are they moft forwarde to affection. If I bee melancholie, then Ganimede tis not a confequence that I am entangled with the perfection of Saladyne. But feeing fire cannot be hid in the ftraw, nor Loue kept fo couert but it will bee fpied, what fhould friends conceale fancies ς Know my Ganimede, the beautie and valour, the wit and proweffe of Saladyne hath fettered Aliena fo farre, as there is no obiect pleafing to her eyes, but the fight of Saladyne : and if loue haue done me iuftice, to wrap his thoughts in the foldes of my fare, and that he be as deeply enamoured as I am paffionate ; I tell thee Ganimede, there fhall not be much wooing, for fhe is alreadie wonne, and what needes a longer batterie. I am glad quoth Ganimede that it fhall be thus proportioned, you to match with Saladyne, and I with Rosader : thus haue the Deftenies fauoured vs with fome pleafing afpect, that haue made vs as priuate in our loues, as familiar in our fortunes.

With this Ganimede ftart vp, made her readie, & went into the fields with Aliena : where vnfolding their flockes, they fate them downe vnder an Oliue tree, both of them amorous, and yet diuerflie affected ; Aliena ioying in the excellence of Saladyne, and Ganimede forrowing for the wounds of her Rosader, not quiet in thought till fhe might heare of his health. As thus both of them fate in theyr dumpes, they might efpie where Coridon came running towards them (almoft out of breath with his haft). What newes with you (quoth Aliena) that you come in fuch poft ς Oh Miftres (quoth Coridon) you haue a long time defired to fee Phœbe the faire Shepheardeffe whom Montanus loues : fo nowe if it pleafe you and Ganimede but to walke with me to yonder thicket, there fhall you fee Montanus and her fitting by a Fountaine ; he courting with his Countrey ditties, and fhe as coye as if fhe helde Loue in difdaine.

The newes were fo welcome to the two Louers, that vp they rofe, and went with Coridon. Affoone as they drew nigh the thicket, they might efpie where Phœbe fate, (the faireft Shepheardeffe in all *Arden*, and he the frolickft Swaine in the whole Forreft) fhe in a peticoate of fcarlet, couered with a greene mantle ; and to fhrowde her from the Sunne, a chaplet of rofes : from vnder which appeared a face full of Natures excellence, and two fuch eyes as might haue amated a greater man than Montanus. At gaze vppon this gorgeous Nymph fat the Shepheard, feeding his eyes with her fauours, wooing with fuch piteous lookes, & courting with fuch deep ftraind fighs, as would haue made Diana her felfe to haue been compaffionate. At laft, fixing his lookes on the riches of her face, his head on his hande, and his elbow on his knee, he fung this mournefull Dittie.

Montanus Sonnet.

A Turtle fate vpon a leaueleffe tree,
Mourning her abfent pheare
With fad and forrie cheare :
About her wondring ftood
The citizens of Wood,

II, i, 25

And whileſt her plumes ſhe rents
And for her loue laments,
The ſtately trees complaine them,
The birdes with ſorrow paine them :
Each one that doth her view
Her paine and ſorrowes rue.
But were the ſorrowes knowen
That me hath ouerthrowen,
Oh how would Phœbe *ſigh, if ſhe did looke on me ?*

The loue ſicke Polypheme *that could not ſee,*
Who on the barraine ſhore
His fortunes doth deplore,
And melteth all in mone
For Galatea *gone :*
And with his piteous cries
Afflicts both earth and Skies :
And to his woe betooke
Doth breake both pipe and hooke ;
For whome complaines the Morne,
For whom the Sea Nymphs mourne.
Alas his paine is nought :
For were my woe but thought,
Oh how would Phœbe *ſigh, if ſhe did looke on mee ?*

Beyond compare my paine
yet glad am I,
Jf gentle Phœbe *daine*
to ſee her Montan *die.*

After this, Montanus felt his paſſions ſo extreame, that he fell into this exclamation againſt the iniuſtice of Loue.

Helas Tirant plein de rigueur,
Modere vn peu ta violence :
Que te ſert ſi grande deſpenſe ?
C'eſt trop de flammes pour vn cueur.
Eſparguez en vne eſtin celle,
Puis fay ton effort d'eſmoûoir,
La fiere qui ne veut point voir,
En quel fu je bruſle pour elle.
Execute Amour ce deſſein,
Et rabaiſſe vn peu ſon audace,
Son cuer ne doit eſtre de glace.
Bien que elle ait de Niege le ſein.

Montanus ended his Sonet with ſuch a volley of ſighs, and ſuch a ſtreame of teares, as might haue mooued any but Phœbe to haue graunted him fauour. But ſhe meaſuring all his paſſions with a coye diſdaine, and triumphing in the poore Shepheardes patheticall humours, ſmiling at his martyrdome, as **IV, i, 183** though loue had been no maladie, ſcornefully warbled out this Sonnet.

Phœbes Sonnet a replie to Montanus pafsion.

Downe a downe.

Thus Phillis *fung*
by fancie once distreffed :
Who fo by foolifh Loue are ftung,
are worthely oppreffed.
And fo fing I. With a downe, downe, &c.

When Loue was first begot,
And by the moouers will
Did fall to humane lot
His folace to fulfill.
Deuoid of all deceipt,
A chast and holy fire
Did quicken mans conceipt,
And womens breast inspire.
The Gods that faw the good
That mortalls did approue,
With kinde and holy mood
Began to talke of Loue.
　　　Downe a downe,
　　Thus Phillis *fung*
　　　by fancie once distreffed, &c.

But during this accord,
A wonder ftrange to heare :
Whilest Loue in deed and word
Most faithfull did appeare.
Falfe femblance came in place
By iealozie attended,
And with a doubleface
Both loue and fancie blended.
Which made the Gods forfake,
And men from fancie flie,
And maidens fcorne a make;
Forfooth and fo will I.
　　　Downe a downe.
　　Thus Phillis *fung*
　　　by fancie once distreffed;
Who fo by foolifh Loue are ftung
　　are worthely oppreffed.
And fo fing I.
　　with downe a downe, adowne downe, adowne a,

　　Montanus hearing the cruel refolution of Phœbe, was fo ouergrowen with paffions, that from amorous Ditties he fell flat into thefe tearmes; Ah Phœbe quoth he, whereof art thou made, that thou regardeft not my maladie ? Am I fo hatefull an obiect, that thine eyes condempne me for an abiect ? or fo bafe, that thy defires cannot ftoope fo lowe as to lende mee a gracious looke ς My paffions are manie, my loues more, my thoughts loyaltie, and my fancie faith : all deuoted in humble deuoire to the feruice of Phœbe: & fhal I reape no reward for fuch fealties. The Swaines daylie labours is quit with the euenings hire, the Ploughmans toyle is eafed with the hope of corne, what the Oxe fweates out at the plough he fatneth at the cribbe: but infortu-nate Montanus hath no falue for his forrowes, nor anie hope of recōpence for the hazard of his perplexed paffions. If Phœbe, time may plead the proofe of my truth, twice feuen winters haue I loued faire Phœbe: if conftancie bee a caufe to farther my fute, Montanus thoughtes haue beene fealed in the fweete of Phœbes excellence, as farre from chaunge as fhe from loue: if outward paffions may difcouer inward affeétions, the furrowes in my face may decypher the forrowes of my heart, and the mappe of my lookes the griefes of my minde. Thou feeft (Phœbe) the teares of def-payre haue made my cheekes full of wrinkles, and my fcalding fighes haue made the aire Eccho her pitie conceiued in my plaints: Philomele hearing my paffions, hath left her mournfull tunes to liften to the difcourfe of my miferies. I haue pourtraied in euerie tree the beautie of my Miftreffe, & the defpaire of my loues. What is it in the woods cannot witnes my woes? and who is it would not pitie my plaints ç Onely Phœbe. And why? Becaufe I am Montanus, and fhe Phœbe; I a worthleffe Swaine and fhee the moft excellent of all faires. Beautifull Phœbe, oh might I fay pitifull, then happie were I though I tafted but one minute of that good hap. Meafure Mon-tanus not by his fortunes but by his loues; and ballaunce not his wealthe, but his defires, and lend but one gracious looke to cure a heape of difquieted cares: if not, ah if Phœbe can not loue, let a ftorme of frownes ende the difcontent of my thoughts, and fo let me perifh in my defires, becaufe they are aboue my deferts: onely at my death this fauour cannot be denied me, that all fhall fay, Montanus died for loue of harde hearted Phœbe. At thefe words fhe fild her face full of frownes, and made him this fhort and fharpe replie.

Importunate Shepheard, whofe loues are lawleffe, becaufe reftleffe: are thy paf-fions fo extreame that thou canft not conceale them with patience ç Or art thou fo folly-fick, that thou muft needes be fancie-ficke ç and in thy affeétion tied to fuch an exigent, as none ferues but Phœbe. Well fir, if your market may be made no where els, home again, for your Mart is at the faireft. Phœbe is no lettice for your lippes, and her grapes hangs fo high, that gaze at them you may, but **V, i, 38** touch them you cannot. Yet Montanus I fpeake not this in pride, but in difdaine; not that I fcorne thee, but that I hate Loue: for I count it as great honour to triumph ouer Fancie, as ouer Fortune. Reft thee content therefore Montanus, ceafe from thy loues, and bridle thy lookes; quench the fparkles before they grow to a further flame: for in louing me thou fhalt liue by loffe, & what thou vttereft in words, are all written in the winde. Wert thou (Montanus) as faire as Paris, as hardie as Hector, as conftant as Troylus, as louing as Leander; Phœbe could not loue, becaufe fhe cannot loue at all: and therefore if thou purfue me with Phœbus, I muft flie with Daphne.

Ganimede ouer-hearing all thefe paffions of Montanus, could not brooke the cruel-tie of Phœbe, but ftarting from behinde the bufh faid; And if Damzell you fled from me, I would tranfforme you as Daphne to a bay, and then in contempt trample your branches vnder my feete. Phœbe at this fodaine replie was amazed, efpecially when fhe faw fo faire a Swaine as Ganimede; blufhing therefore, fhee would haue been gone: but that he held her by the hand, and profecuted his replie thus. What Shep-heardeffe, fo fayre and fo cruell ç Difdaine befeemes not cottages, nor coynes maides: for either they be condempned to bee too proude, or too froward. Take heede (faire Nymph) that in defpifing Loue, you be not ouer-reacht with Loue, and in fhaking off

24

all, fhape your felfe to your own fhaddow: and fo with Narciffus prooue paffionate & yet vnpitied. Oft haue I heard, and fometimes haue I feene, high difdaine turnd to hot defires. Becaufe thou art beautifull, be not fo coye: as there is nothing more faire, fo there is nothing more fading, as momentary as the fhadowes which growes from a clowdie Sunne. Such (my faire Shepheardeffe) as difdaine in youth defire in age, and then are they hated in the winter, that might haue been loued in the prime. A wrinkled maide is like to a parched Rofe, that is caft vp in coffers to pleafe the fmell, not worne in the hand to content the eye. There is no follie in Loue to had I wift: and therefore be rulde by me, Loue while thou art young, leaft thou be difdained when thou art olde. Beautie nor time cannot bee recalde, and if thou loue, like of Montauns: for as his defires are manie, fo his deferts are great.

. Phœbe all this while gazed on the perfection af Ganimede, as deeplie enamoured on his perfection, as Montanus inueigled with hers: for her eye made furuey of his excellent feature, which fhe found fo rare, that fhe thought the ghoft of Adonis had been leapt from Elizium in the fhape of a Swaine. When fhe blufht at her owne follie to looke fo long on a ftranger, fhe mildlie made aunfwere to Ganimede thus. I cannot denie fir but I haue heard of Loue, though I neuer felt Loue; and haue read of fuch a Goddeffe as Venus, though I neuer faw anie but her picture: & perhaps, and with that fhe waxed red and bafhful, and with all filent: which Ganimede perceiuing, commended in her felfe the bafhfulneffe of the maide, and defired her to goe forward. And perhaps fir (quoth fhe) mine eye hath ben more prodigall to day than euer before: and with that fhe ftaid againe, as one greatly paffionate and perplexed. Aliena feeing the hare through the maze, bade her forwarde with her prattle: but in vaine, for at this abrupt periode fhe broke off, and with her eyes full of teares, and her face couered with a vermillion die, fhe fate downe and fightht. Whereuppon, Aliena and Ganimede feeing the Shepheardeffe in fuch a ftrange plight, left Phœbe with her Montanus, wifhing her friendly that fhee would be more pliant to Loue, leaft in penaunce Venus ioyned her to fome fharpe repentaunce. Phœbe made no replie, but fetcht fuch a figh, that Eccho made relation of her plaint: giuing Ganimede fuch an adieu with a piercing glaunce, that the amorous Girle-boye perceiued Phœbe was pincht by the heele.

But leauing Phœbe to the follies of her new fancie, and Montanus to attend vpon her; to Saladyne, who all this laft night could not reft for the remembrance of Aliena: infomuch that he framed afweete conceipted fonnet to content his humour, which he put in his bofome: being requefted by his brother Rosader to go to Aliena and Ganimede, to fignifie vnto them that his wounds were not daungerous. A more happie meffage could not happen to Saladyne, that taking his Forreft bil on his necke, he trudgeth in all haft towards the plaines, where Alienaes flockes did feede: comming iuft to the place when they returned from Montanus and Phœbe. Fortune fo conducted this iollie Forrefter, that he encountred them and Coridon, whom he prefently faluted in this manner.

Faire Shepheardeffe, and too faire, vnleffe your beautie be tempred with courtefie, & the liniaments of the face graced with the lowlineffe of minde: as manie good fortunes to you and your Page, as your felues can defire, or I imagine. My brother Rosader (in the griefe of his greene wounds) ftill mindfull of his friends, hath fent me to you with a kind falute, to fhew that he brookes his paines with the more patience, in that he holds the parties precious in whofe defence he receiued the preiudice. The report of your welfare, will bee a great comfort to his diftempered bodie and diftreffed thoughts, and therefore he fent mee with a ftrict charge to vifite you.

And you (quoth Aliena) are the more welcome in that you are meſſenger from ſo
kind a Gentleman, whoſe paines we compaſſionate with as great ſorrowe, as hee
brookes them with griefe; and his wounds breedes in vs as manie paſſions, as in him
extremities: ſo that what diſquiet hee feeles in bodie, wee partake in heart. Wiſhing
(if wee might) that our miſhap might ſalue his maladie. But ſeeing our wills yeelds
him little eaſe, our orizons are neuer idle to the Gods for his recouerie. I pray youth
(quoth Ganimede with teares in his eies) when the Surgeon ſearcht him, helde he his
wounds dangerous ꞇ Dangerous (quoth Saladyne) but not mortall: and the ſooner
to be cured, in that his patient is not impatient of anie paines: whereuppon my
brother hopes within theſe ten dayes to walke abroad and viſite you himſelfe. In the
meane time (quoth Ganimede) ſay his Rosalynde commends her to him and bids him
be of good cheere. I know not (quoth Saladyne) who that Rosalynde is, but whatſoeuer ſhe is, her name is neuer out of his mouth: but amidſt the deepeſt of his paſſions he vſeth Rosalynde as a charme to appeaſe all ſorrows with patience. Inſomuch
that I coniecture my brother is in loue, and ſhe ſome Paragon that holdes his hart
perplexed: whoſe name he oft records with ſighs, ſometimes with teares, ſtraight with
ioy, then with ſmiles; as if in one perſon Loue had lodged a Chaos of confuſed paſſions. Wherein I haue noted the variable diſpoſition of fancie, that like
the Polype in colours, ſo it changeth into ſundrie humours: being as it
ſhould ſeeme a combate mixt with diſquiet, and a bitter pleaſure wrapt **IV, iii, 106**
in a ſweete preiudice, like to the Sinople tree, whoſe bloſſomes delight
the ſmell, and whoſe fruite infects the taſt. By my faith (quoth Aliena)
ſir, you are deepe read in loue, or growes your inſight into affection by experience?
Howſoeuer, you are a great Philoſopher in Venus principles, els could you not diſcouer her ſecrete aphoriſmes. But ſir our countrey amours are not like your courtly
fancies, nor is our wooing like your ſuing: for poore ſhepheards neuer plaine them
till Loue paine them, where the Courtiers eyes is full of paſſions when his heart is
moſt free from affection: they court to diſcouer their eloquence, we wooe to eaſe our
ſorrowes: euerie faire face with them muſt haue a new fancie ſealed with a forefinger
kiſſe and a farre fetcht ſigh; we heere loue one, and liue to that one ſo lōg as life can
maintain loue, vſing few ceremonies becauſe we know fewe ſubtilties, and little eloquence for that wee lightly accompt of flatterie: only faith and troth thats ſhepſheards
wooing, and ſir howe like you of this? So (quoth Saladyne) as I could tie my ſelfe
to ſuch loue. What, and looke ſo low as a Shepheardeſſe, being the Sonne of Sir
Iohn of *Bourdeaux*: ſuch deſires were a diſgrace to your honours. And with that
ſurueying exquiſitely euerie part of him, as vttering all theſe words in a deepe paſſion, ſhe eſpied the paper in his boſome: whereupon growing iealous that it was ſome
amorous Sonnet, ſhee ſodainly ſnatcht it out of his boſome, and aſked if it were any
ſecret ꞇ She was baſhfull, and Saladyne bluſht: which ſhe perceiuing ſayd; Nay
then ſir, if you waxe redde, my life for yours tis ſome Loue matter: I will ſee your
Miſtreſſe name, her praiſes, and your paſſions. And with that ſhe lookt on it: which
was written to this effect.

Saladynes Sonnet.

*Jf it be true that heauens eternall courſe
With reſtleſſe ſway and ceaſeleſſe turning glides,
If aire inconſtant be, and ſwelling ſourſe
Turne and returnes with many fluent tides,
If earth in winter ſummers pride eſtrange,
And Nature ſeemeth onely faire in change.*

Jf it be true that our immortall fpright
Deriude from heauenly pure, in wandring ftill
In noueltie and ftrangeneffe doth delight,
And by difcouerent power difcerneth ill,
    And if the bodie for to worke his best
    Doth with the feafons change his place of rest:

Whence comes it that (inforst by furious Skies)
I change both place and foyle, but not my hart?
Yet falue not in this change my maladies?
Whence growes it that each obiect workes my fmart?
    Alas J fee my faith procures my mifse,
    And change in loue against my nature is.

                    Et florida pungunt.

Aliena hauing read ouer his fonnet, began thus pleafantly to defcant vpon it. I fee Saladyne (quoth fhee) that as the Sunne is no Sunne without his brightneffe, nor the diamond accounted for precious vnleffe it be hard: fo men are not men vnleffe they be in loue; and their honours are meafured by their amours not their labours, counting it more commendable for a Gentleman to be full of fancie, than full of ver- tue. I had thought *Otia fi tollas periere Cupidinis arcus,* || *Contemptæq iacent, & fine luce faces:* But I fee Ouids axiome is not authenticall, for euen labor hath her loues, and extremitie is no pumice ftone to race out fancie. Your felfe exiled from your wealth, friends & countrey by Torismond, (forrowes enough to fuppreffe affections) yet amidft the depth of thefe extreamities, Loue will be Lord, and fhew his power to bee more predominant than Fortune. But I pray you fir (if without offence I maye craue it) are they fome new thoughts, or fome olde defires? Saladyne (that now faw opportunitie pleafaunt) thought to ftrike while the yron was hote, and therefore taking Aliena by the hand fate downe by her; and Ganimede to giue them leaue to their Loues, founde her felfe bufie about the foldes, whileft Saladyne fell into this prattle with Aliena.

Faire Miftres, if I bee blunt in difcouering my affections, and vfe little eloquence in leuelling out my loues: I appeale for pardon to your owne principles that fay, Shepheards vfe few ceremonies, for that they acquaint thefelues with fewe fubtilties: to frame my felfe therefore to your countrey fafhion with much faith and little flatterie, knowe beautifull Shepheardeffe, that whileft I liued in the court I knew not Loues cumber, but I held affection as a toy, not as a maladie; vfing fancie as the Hiperborei do their flowers, which they weare in their bofome all day, and caft them in the fire for fuell all night. I liked al becaufe I loued none, and who was moft faire on her I fed mine eye: but as charely as the Bee, that affoone as fhe hath fuckt honnie from the rofe, flies ftraight to the next Marigold. Liuing thus at mine owne lift, I wondred at fuch as were in loue, & when I read their paffions, I tooke them only for poems that flowed from the quickneffe of the wit not the forrowes of the heart. But nowe (faire Nymph) fince I became a Forrefter, Loue hath taught me fuch a leffon that I muft confeffe his deitie and dignitie, and faye as there is nothing fo precious as beautie, fo there is nothing more piercing than fancie. For fince firft I arriued in this place, and mine eie tooke a curious furuey of your excellence, I haue been fo fettered with your beautie and vertue, as (fweet Aliena) Saladyne without further circumftance loues Aliena. I coulde paint out my defires with long ambages, but feeing in manie words lies miftruft, and that trueth is euer naked; let this fuffice for a countrey wooing, Sala- dyne loues Aliena, and none but Aliena.

Although thefe words were moft heauenly harmonie in the eares of the Shep-heardeffe: yet to feeme coye at the firft courting, and to difdaine Loue howfoeuer fhee defired Loue, fhe made this replie.

Ah Saladyne, though I feeme fimple, yet I am more fubtile than to fwallow the hook becaufe it hath a painted bait: as men are wilie fo women are warie, efpecially if they haue that wit by others harmes to beware. Doo wee not knowe Saladyne, that mens tongues are like Mercuries pipe, that can inchaunt Argus with an hundred eies; and their words as preiudiciall as the charmes of Circes, that tranffourme men into monfters. If fuch Syrens fing, wee poore Women had neede ftoppe our eares, leaft in hearing we proue fo foolifh hardie as to beleeue them, and fo perrifh in truft-ing much, and fufpecting little. Saladyne, *Pifcator ictus fapit*, he that hath been once poyfoned & afterwards feares not to bowfe of euerie potion, is woorthie to fuffer double pennaunce. Giue me leaue then to miftruft, though I doo not condempne. Saladyne is now in loue with Aliena, he a Gentleman of great Parentage, fhe a Shep-heardeffe of meane Parents; he honourable, and fhee poore? Can Loue confift of contrarieties? Will the Fawlcon pearch with the Kiftreffe, the Lion harbour with the Woolfe? Will Venus ioyne roabes and rags together? Or can there be a fim-pathie betweene a King and a begger. Then Saladyne how can I beleeue thee that loue fhould vnite our thoughts, when Fortune hath fet fuch a difference betweene our degrees? But fuppofe thou likeft of Alienaes beautie, men in their fancie refemble the wafpe, which fcornes that flower from which fhe hath fetcht her waxe; playing like the inhabitants of the Ilande *Tenerifa*, who when they haue gathered the fweete fpices, vfe the trees for fuel: fo men when they haue glutted themfelues with the faire of womens faces, holde them for neceffarie euills; and wearied with that which they feemed fo much to loue, caft away fancie as children doo their rattles; and loathing that which fo deepelie before they likte, efpecially fuch as take loue in a minute, & haue their eyes attractiue like ieate apt to entertaine anie obiect, are as readie to let it flip againe. Saladyne hearing howe Aliena harpt ftill vppon one ftring, which was the doubt of mens conftancie, hee broke off her fharp inuectiue thus.

I graunt Aliena (quoth hee) manie men haue doone amiffe in proouing foone ripe and foone rotten, but particular inftances inferre no generall conclufions: and there-fore I hope what others haue faulted in fhall not preiudice my fauours. I will not vfe fophiftrie to confirme my loue, for that is fubtiltie; nor long difcourfes, leaft my words might bee thought more than my faith: but if this will fuffice, that by the honour of a Gentleman I loue Aliena, and wooe Aliena not to crop the bloffomes and reiect the tree, but to confummate my faithfull defires, in the honourable ende of marriage.

At this word marriage: Aliena ftood in a maze what to anfwere: fearing that if fhe were too coye to driue him away with her difdaine; and if fhe were too cour-teous to difcouer the heate of her defires. In a dilemma thus what to doo, at laft this fhe faid. Saladyne euer fince I faw thee, I fauoured thee, I cannot diffemble my defires, becaufe I fee thou dooft faithfully manifeft thy thoughtes, and in liking thee I loue thee fo farre as mine honour holdes fancie ftill in fufpence: but if I knew thee as vertuous as thy father, or as well qualified as thy brother Rofader, the doubt fhoulde be quicklie decided: but for this time to giue thee an anfwere, affure thy felfe this, I will either marrie with Saladyne, or ftill liue a virgine: and with this they ftrained one anothers hand. Which Ganimede efpying, thinking he had had his Miftres long enough at fhrift, faid; what, a match or no? A match (quoth Aliena) or els it were an ill market. I am glad (quoth Ganimede) I would Rofader

18

were well here to make vp a meſſe. Well remembred (quoth Saladyne) I forgot I left my brother Rosader alone: and therefore leaſt being ſolitarie he ſhould increaſe his ſorrowes I will haſt me to him. May it pleaſe you then to commaund me anie ſeruice to him, I am readie to be a duetifull meſſenger. Onely at this time commend me to him (quoth Aliena) & tell him, though wee cannot pleaſure him we pray for him. And forget not (quoth Ganimede) my commendations: but ſay to him that Rosalynde ſheds as manie teares from her heart, as he drops of bloud from his wounds, for the ſorrow of his miſfortunes; feathering all her thoughtes with diſquiet, till his welfare procure her content: ſay thus (good Saladyne) and ſo farewell. He hauing his meſſage, gaue a courteous adieu to them both, eſpecially to Aliena: and ſo playing loath to depart, went to his brother. But Aliena, ſhe perplexed and yet ioyfull, paſt away the day pleaſauntly ſtill praiſing the perfection of Saladyne, not ceaſing to chat of her new Loue, till euening drew on; and then they folding their ſheepe, went home to bed. Where we leaue them and returne to Phœbe.

Phœbe ſiered with the vncouth flame of loue, returned to her fathers houſe; ſo galled with reſtleſſe paſſions, as now ſhe began to acknowledge, that as there was no flower ſo freſh but might bee parched with the Sunne, no tree ſo ſtrong but might bee ſhaken with a ſtorme; ſo there was no thought ſo chaſt, but Time armde with Loue could make amorous: for ſhee that helde Diana for the Goddeſſe of her deuotion, was now faine to flie to the Altare of Venus; as ſuppliant now with prayers, as ſhe was froward afore with diſdaine. As ſhe lay in her bed, ſhe called to minde the ſeuerall beauties of yong Ganimed, firſt his locks, which being amber hued, paſſeth the wreathe that Phœbus puts on to make his front glorious; his browe of yuorie, was like the ſeate where Loue and Maieſtie ſits inthronde to enchayne Fancie; his eyes as bright as the burniſhing of the heauen, darting foorth frownes with diſdaine, and ſmiles with fauor, lightning ſuch lookes as would enflame deſire, were ſhee wrapt in the Circle of the frozen Zoane; in his cheekes the vermilion teinture of the Roſe flouriſhed vpon naturall Alabaſter, the bluſh of the Morne and Lunaes ſiluer ſhowe were ſo liuely portrayed, that the Troyan that fils out wine to Iupiter was not halfe ſo beautifull; his face was full of pleaſance, and all the reſt of his liniaments propor-tioned with ſuch excellence, as Phœbe was fettred in the ſweetnes of his feature. The Idea of theſe perfections tumbling in her minde, made the poore Shepheardſſe ſo perplexed, as feeling a pleaſure tempred with intollerable paines, and yet a diſ-quiet mixed with a content, ſhe rather wiſhed to die, than to liue in this amorous anguiſh. But wiſhing is little worth in ſuch extreames, and therefore was ſhe forſt to pine in her maladie, without anie ſalue for her ſorrowes. Reueale it ſhe durſt not, as daring in ſuch matters to make none her ſecretarie; and to conceale it, why it doubled her griefe: for as fire ſuppreſt growes to the greater flame, and the Current ſtopt to the more violent ſtreame; ſo Loue ſmothred wrings the heart with the deeper paſſions.

Perplexed thus with ſundrie agonies, her foode began to faile, and the diſquiet of her minde began to worke a diſtemperature of her bodie, that to be ſhort Phœbe fell extreame ſicke, and ſo ſicke, as there was almoſt left no recouerie of health. Her father ſeeing his faire Phœbe thus diſtreſt, ſent for his friends, who ſought by medi-cine to cure, and by counſaile to pacifie, but all in vaine: for although her bodie was feeble through long faſting, yet ſhe did *magis agrotare animo quam corpore.* Which her friends perceiued and ſorrowed at, but ſalue it they could not.

The newes of her ſickneſſe was bruted abroad thorough all the Forreſt: which no fooner came to Montanus eare, but he like a madde man came to vifite Phœbe. Where fitting by her bedde fide, he began his Exordium with fo manie teares and fighes, that fhe perceiuing the extremitie of his forrowes, began now as a louer to pitie them, although Ganimede helde her from redreffing them. Montanus craued to knowe the caufe of her ficknefſe, tempred with fecrete plaints : but fhe aunfwered him (as the reft) with filence, hauing ftill the forme of Ganimede in her minde, & coniecturing how fhee might reueale her loues. To vtter it in words fhe found herfelfe too bafh-full, to difcourfe by anie friend fhee would not truft anie in her amours, to remayne thus perplexed ftill and conceale all, it was a double death. Whereuppon for her laft refuge fhe refolued to write vnto Ganimede : and therefore defired Montanus to abfent him felfe a while, but not to depart : for fhe would fee if fhe could fteale a nappe. He was no fooner gone out of the chamber, but reaching to her ftandifh, fhe tooke penne and paper, and wrote a letter to this effect.——Phœbe to Ganimede wifheth what fhe wants her felfe.——Faire Shepheard (and therefore is Phœbe infortunate becaufe thou art fo faire) although hetherto mine eies were ada-mants to refift Loue, yet I no fooner faw thy face but they became amorous to inter-taine Loue : more deuoted to fancie than before they were repugnant to affection, addicted to the one by Nature, and drawn to the other by beautie ; which being rare, and made the more excellent by manie vertues, hath fo fnared the freedome of Phœbe, as fhe refts at thy mercie, either to bee made the moft fortunate of all Maidens, or the moft miferable of all Women. Meafure not Ganimede my loues by my wealth, nor my defires by my degrees : but thinke my thoughts are as full of faith, as thy face of amiable fauours. Then as thou knoweft thy felfe moft beautifull, fuppofe me moft conftant. If thou deemeft me hardhearted becaufe I hated Montanus, thinke I was forft to it by Fate : if thou faift I am kinde hearted becaufe fo lightly I loue thee at the firft looke, thinke I was driuen to it by Deftenie, whofe influence as it is mightie, fo it is not to be refifted. If my fortunes were anie thing but infortunate Loue, I woulde ftriue with Fortune : but he that wrefts againft the will of Venus, feekes to quench fire with oyle, and to thruft out one thorne by putting in another. If then Ganimede, Loue enters at the eie, harbours in the heart, and will neither bee driuen out with Phificke nor reafon : pitie me, as one whofe maladie hath no falue but from thy fweete felfe, whofe griefe hath no eafe but through thy graunt, and thinke I am a Virgine, who is deepely wrongd, when I am forft to wooe : and coniecture Loue to bee ftrong, that is more forceable than Nature.

Thus diftreffed vnleffe by thee eafed, I expect either to liue fortunate by thy fauour, or die miferable by thy deniall. Liuing in hope. Farewell.

She that muft be thine, or not be at all.

Phœbe.

To this Letter fhe annexed this Sonnet.

Sonnetto.

My boate doth paffe the ftraights
 of feas incenft with fire,
Filde with forgetfulneffe :
 amidft the winters night,
A blinde and careleffe boy
 (brought vp by fonde defire)
Doth guide me in the fea
 of forrow and defpight.

For euerie oare, he fets
  a ranke of foolifh thoughts,
And cuts (in ftead of waue)
  a hope without diftreffe;
The windes of my deepe fighs
  (that thunder ftill for noughts)
Haue fplit my fayles with feare,
  with care, with heauineffe.

A mightie ftorme of teares,
  a blacke and hideous cloude,
A thoufand fierce difdaines
  dooo flacke the haleyards oft:
Till ignorance doo pull
  and errour hale the fhrowdes
Nor ftarre for fafetie fhines,
  no Phœbe *from aloft.*
    Time hath fubdued arte,
    and ioy is flaue to woe:
    Alas (Loues guide) be kinde;
    what fhall I perifh fo?

This Letter and the Sonnet being ended, fhe could find no fitte meffenger to fende it by; and therefore fhe called in Montanus, and intreated him to carrie it to Ganimede. Although poore Montanus faw day at a little hole, and did perceiue what paffion pincht her: yet (that he might feeme dutifull to his Miftres in all feruice) he diffembled the matter, and became a willing meffenger of his owne Martyrdome. And fo (taking the letter) went the next morne verie early to the Plaines where Aliena fed her flockes, and there hee found Ganimede fitting vnder a Pomegranade tree forrowing for the hard fortunes of her Rofader. Montanus faluted him, and according to his charge deliuered Ganimede the letters, which (he faid) came from Phœbe. At this the wanton blufht, as beeing abafht to thinke what newes fhould come from an vnknowen Shepheardeffe, but taking the letters vuript the feales, and read ouer the difcourfe of Phœbes fancies. When fhee had read and ouerread them, Ganimede began to fmile, & looking on Montanns fell into a great laughter: and with that called Aliena, to whom fhe fhewed the writings. Who hauing perufed them, conceipted them verie pleafantly, and fmiled to fee how Loue had yoakt her, who before difdained to ftoupe to the lure, Aliena whifpering Ganimede in the eare, and faying; Knewe Phœbe what want there were in thee to perfourme her will, and how vnfit thy kinde is to bee kinde to her, fhe would be more wife and leffe enamoured: but leauing that, I pray thee let vs fport with this Swaine. At that worde, Ganimede tourning to Montanus, began to glaunce at him thus.

I pray thee tell me Shepheard, by thofe fweet thoughts and pleafing fighes that grow from my Miftreffe fauours, art thou in loue with Phœbe? Oh my Youth, quoth Montanus, were Phœbe fo farre in loue with me, my Flockes would be more fat and their Mafter more quiet: for through the forrowes of my difcontent growes the leanneffe of my fheepe. Alas poore Swaine quoth Ganimede, are thy paffions fo extreame or thy fancie fo refolute, that no reafon will blemifh the pride of thy affection, and race out that which thou ftriueft for without hope? Nothing can make me forget Phœbe, while Montanus forget himfelfe: for thofe characters which true Loue hath ftamped, neither the enuie of Time nor Fortune can wipe awaye. Why but Montanus qnoth Ganimede, enter with a deepe infight into the defpaire of thy fancies, and thou fhalt fee the depth of thine owne follies: for (poore man) thy progreffe in loue is a regreffe to loffe, fwimming againft the ftreame with the Crab, and flying with Apis Indica againft winde and weather. Thou feekeft with Phœbus to winne Daphne, and fhee flies fafter than thou canft followe: thy defires foare with the Hobbie, but her difdaine reacheth higher than thou canft make wing.

I tell thee Montanus, in courting Phœbe thou barkeft with the Wolues   **V, ii, 110** of *Syria* againft the Moone, and roaueft at fuch a marke with thy thoughtes, as is beyond the pitch of thy bow, praying to Loue when Loue is pitileffe, and thy maladie remedileffe. For proofe Montanus read thefe letters, wherein thou fhalt fee thy great follies and little hope.

With that Montanus tooke them and perufed them, but with fuch forrow in his lookes, as they bewrayed a fourfe of confufed paffions, in his heart: at euerie line his coulour changed, and euerie fentence was ended with a periode of fighes.

At laft, noting Phœbes extreame defire toward Ganimede, and her difdaine towards him, giuing Ganimede the letter, the Shepheard ftoode as though hee had neither wonne nor loft. Which Ganimede perceiuing, wakened him out his dreame thus; Now Montanus, dooft thou fee thou voweft great feruice, and obteineft but little reward: but in lieu of thy loyaltie, fhe maketh thee as Bellephoron carrie thine owne bane. Then drinke not willinglie of that potion wherein thou knoweft is poyfon, creepe not to her that cares not for thee. What Montanus, there are manie as faire as Phœbe, but moft of all more courteous than Phœbe. I tell thee Shepheard, fauour is Loues fuell: then fince thou canft not get that, let the flame vanifh into fmoake, and rather forrow for a while than repent thee for euer.

I tell thee Ganimede (quoth Montanus) as they which are ftung with the Scorpion, cannot be recouered but by the Scorpion, nor hee that was wounded with Achilles lance be cured but with the fame trunchion: fo Apollo was faine to crie out, that Loue was onely eafed with Loue, and fancie healed by no medecin but fauor. Phœbus had hearbs to heale all hurts but this paffion, Cyrces had charmes for all chaunces but for affeaction, and Mercurie fubtill reafons to refell all griefes but Loue. Perfwafions are bootleffe, Reafon lendes no remedie, Counfaile no comfort, to fuch whome Fancie hath made refolute: and therefore though Phœbe loues Ganimede, yet Montanus muft honor none but Phœbe.

Then quoth Ganimede, may I rightly tearme thee a defpayring Louer, that liueft without ioy, & loueft without hope: but what fhall I doo Montanus to pleafure thee ς Shall I defpife Phœbe as fhe difdaines thee ς Oh (quoth Montanus) that were to renew my griefes, and double my forrowes: for the fight of her difcontent were the cenfure of my death. Alas Ganimede, though I perifh in my thoughtes, let not her die in her defires. Of all paffions, Loue is moft impatient: then let not fo faire a creature as Phœbe finke vnder the burden of fo deepe a diftreffe. Being loue ficke fhe is prooued heart ficke, and all for the beautie of Ganimede. Thy proportion hath entangled her affeaction, and fhe is fnared in the beautie of thy excellence. Then fith fhe loues thee fo deere, miflike not her deadly. Bee thou paramour to fuch a paragon: fhee hath beautie to content thine eye, and flockes to enrich thy ftore. Thou canft not wifh for more than thou fhalt winne by her: for fhe is beautifull, vertuous and wealthie, three deepe perfwafions to make loue frolicke. Aliena feeing Montanus cut it againft the haire, and plead that Ganimede ought to loue Phœbe, when his onely life was the loue of Phœbe: anfwered him thus. Why Montanus dooft thou further this motion ℭ feeing if Ganimede marrie Phœbe thy market is clean mard. Ah Miftres (quoth he) fo hath Loue taught mee to honour Phœbe, that I would preiudice my life to pleafure her, and die in defpaire rather than fhe fhould perifh for want. It fhal fuffice me to fee him contented, and to feed mine eye on her fauour. If fhe marrie though it be my Martyrdome: yet if fhee bee pleafed I will brooke it with patience, and triumph in mine owne ftarres to fee her defires fatiffied. Therefore if Ganimede bee as courteous as hee is beautifull, let him fhew his vertues, in redreffing Phœbes miferies. And this Montanus pronounft with fuch an affured countenance, that it amazed both Aliena and Ganimede to fee the refolution of his loues: fo that they pitied his paffions and commended his patience; deuifing how they might by anie fubtiltie, get Montanus the fauour of Phœbe. Straight (as Womens heads are full of wyles) Ganimede had a fetch to force Phœbe to fancie the Shepheard Malgrado the refolution of her minde hee profecuted his policie thus. Montanus (quoth he) feeing Phœbe is fo forlorne leaft I might bee couuted vnkinde, in not faluing fo faire a creature, I will goe with thee to Phœbe, and there heare her felfe in worde vtter that which fhe hath difcourft with her penne, and then as Loue wills me, I will fet downe my cenfure. I will home by our houfe, and fend Coridon to accompanie Aliena. Montanus feemed glad of this determination, and away they goe towards the houfe of Phœbe. When they drew nigh to the Cottage, Montanus ranne afore, & went in and tolde Phœbe that Ganimede was at the dore. This word Ganimede founding in the eares of Phœbe, draue her into fuch an extafie for joy, that rifing vp in her bed fhe was halfe reuiued, and her wan colour began to waxe red: and with that came Ganimede in, who faluted Phœbe with fuch a curteous looke, that it was halfe a falue to her forrowes. Sitting him downe by her bed fide, hee queftioned about her difeafe, and where the paine chiefly helde her? Phœbe looking as louely as Venus in her night geere, tainting her face with as ruddie a blufh as Clitia did when when fhee bewrayed her Loues to Phœbus: taking Ganimede by the hand began thus. Faire fhepheard, if loue were not more ftrong then nature, or fancie the fharpeft extreame; my immodefty were the more, and my vertues the leffe: for nature hath framed womens eyes bafhfull, their hearts full of feare, and their tongues full of filence: But Loue, that imperious Loue, where his power is predominant, then he peruerts all and wrefteth the wealth of nature to his owne will: an Inftance in my felfe fayre Ganimede, for fuch afire hath he kindled in my thoughts, that to finde eafe for the flame, I was forced to paffe the bounds of modeftie and feeke a falue at thy handes for my fecret harmes, blame mee not if I bee ouer bolde for it is thy beautie, and if I be too forward it is fancie, & the deepe infight into thy vertues that makes me thus fond. For let me fay in a word, what may be contayned in a volume, Phœbe loues Ganimede: at this fhe held downe her head and wept, and Ganimede rofe as one that would fuffer no fifh to hang on his fingers made this replie. Water not thy plants Phœbe, for I doe pitie thy plaintes, nor feeke not to difcouer thy Loues in teares: for I coniecture thy trueth by thy paffions: forrow is no falue for loues, nor fighes no remedie for affection. Therefore frolick Phœbe, for if Ganimede can cure thee, doubt not of recouerie. Yet this let me fay without offence, that it greeues me to thwart Montanus in his fancies, feeing his defires haue ben fo refolute, and his thoughts fo loyall: But thou alleadgeft that thou art forft from him by fate; fo I tell thee Phœbe either fome ftarre or elfe fome deftinie fits my minde rather with Adonis to die in chafe, than be counted a wanton in Venus knee. Although I pittie thy martyrdome, yet I can grant no mariage; for though I held thee faire, yet mine eye is not fettered, Loue growes not like the hearb Spattanna to his perfection in one night but

creepes with the fnaile, and yet at laft attaines to the top *Feftina Lente* efpecially in
Loue: for momentarie fancies are oft times the fruites of follies: If Phœbe I fhould
like thee as the Hiperborei do their Dates, which banquet with them in the morning
and throw them awaie at night, my folly fhould be great, and thy repentance more,
Therefore I will haue time to turne my thoughts, and my Loues fhall growe vp as the
water *Creffes*, flowly but with a deepe roote. Thus Phœbe thou maift fee I difdaine
not though I defire not, remaining indifferent till time and loue makes me refolute.
Therefore Phœbe feeke not to fuppreffe affection, and with the Loue of Montanus
quench the remembrance of Ganimede, ftriue thou to hate me as I feeke to like of
thee, and euer haue the duties of Montanus in thy minde, for I promife thee thou
mayft haue one more welthie but not more loyall. Thefe wordes were corafiues to
the perplexed Phœbe, that fobbing out fighes and ftrayning out teares fhee blubbered
out thefe wordes.

And fhall I then haue no falue of Ganimede, but fufpence, no hope but a doubt-
full hazard, no comfort, but bee pofted off to the will of time ʓ iuftly haue the Gods
ballanft my fortunes, who beeing cruell to Montanus found Ganimede, as vnkinde to
my felfe: fo in forcing him perifh for loue, I fhall die my felfe with ouermuch loue.
I am glad (quoth Ganimede) you looke into your owne faults, and fee where your
fhooe wrings you, meafuring now the paines of Montanns by your owne paffions.
Truth quoth Phœbe, and fo deeply I repent me of my frowardneffe toward the Shepheard, that could I ceafe to loue Ganimede, I would refolue to like Montanus. What
if I can with reafon perfwade Phœbe to miflike of Ganimede, will fhe then fauour
Montanus? When reafon (quoth fhe) doth quench that loue that I owe to thee, then
will I fancie him: conditionallie, that if my loue can bee fuppreft with no reafon, as
beeing without reafon, Ganimede wil onely wed himfelfe to Phœbe. I graunt it faire
Shepheardeffe quoth he: and to feede thee with the fweetneffe of hope, this refolue
on: I will neuer marrie my felfe to woman but vnto thy felfe: and with that Ganimede gaue Phœbe a fruiteleffe kiffe & fuch words of comfort, that before Ganimede
departed fhe arofe out of her bed, and made him and Montanus fuch cheere, as could
be found in fuch a Countrey cottage. Ganimede in the midft of their banquet re-
hearfing the promifes of either in Montanus fauour, which highly pleafed the Shep-
hearde. Thus all three content, and foothed vp in hope, Ganimede tooke his leaue
of his Phœbe & departed, leauing her a contented woman, and Montanus highly
pleafed. But poore Ganimede, who had her thoughtes on her Rofader, when fhe
calde to remembrance his wounds, filde her eyes full of teares, and her heart full of
forrowes, plodded to finde Aliena at the Foldes, thinking with her prefence to driue
away her paffions. As fhe came on the Plaines, fhe might efpie where Rofader and
Saladyne fate with Aliena vnder the fhade: which fight was a falue to her griefe, and
fuch a cordiall vnto her heart, that fhe tript alongft the Lawnes full of ioy.

At laft Coridon who was with them fpied Ganimede, and with that the Clowne
rofe, and running to meete him cried, Oh firha, a match, a match, our Miftres fhall
be maried on Sunday. Thus the poore peafant frolickt it before Ganimede, who
comming to the crue faluted them all, and efpecially Rofader, faying that hee was
glad to fee him fo well recouered of his wounds. I had not gone abroade fo foone
quoth Rofader, but that I am bidden to a marriage, which on Sunday next muft bee
folempnized betweene my brother and Aliena. I fee well where Loue leades delay
is loathfome, and that fmall wooing ferues, where both the parties are willing. Truth
quoth Ganimede: but a happie day fhould it be, if Rofader that day might be married to Rofalynde. Ah good Ganimede (quoth he) by naming Rofalynde renue not

my forrowes : for the thought of her perfections, is the thrall of my miferies. Tufh, bee of good cheere man quoth Ganimede, I haue a friend that is deeply experienft in Negromancie and Magicke, what arte can doo fhall bee acted for thine aduantage : I will caufe him to bring in Rofalynde, if either *France* or anie bordering Nation harbour her; and vppon that take the faith of a young Shepheard. Aliena fmilde to fee how Rofader frownde, thinking that Ganimede had iefted with him. But breaking off from thofe matters, the Page (fomewhat pleafant) began to difcourfe vnto them what had paft betweene him and Phœbe : which as they laught, fo they wondred at; /all confeffing, that there is none fo chaft but Loue will change./ Thus they paft away the day in chat, and when the Sunne began to fet, they tooke their leaues and departed : Aliena prouiding for their marriage day fuch folempne cheere and handfome roabes as fitted their countrey eftate, & yet fomewhat the better, in that Rofader had promifed to bring Gerifmond thether as a gueft. Ganimede (who then meant to difcouer her felfe before her father, had made her a gowne of greene, and a kirtle of the fineft fendall, in fuch fort that fhe feemed fome heauenly Nymph harboured in Countrey attire.

Saladyne was not behind in care to fet out the nuptials, nor Rofader vnmindfull to bid guefts, who inuited Gerifmond and all his Followers to the Feaft : who willinglye graunted; fo that there was nothing but the daye wanting to this marriage. In the meaue while, Phœbe being a bidden gueft, made her felfe as gorgeous as might be to pleafe the eye of Ganimede; and Montanus futed himfelfe with the coft of many of his flocks to be gallant againft that day; for then was Ganimede to giue Phœbe an anfwere of her loues, and Montanus either to heare the doome of his miferie, or the cenfure of his happineffe. But while this geare was a bruing, Phœbe paft not one day without vifiting hir Ganimede, fo farre was fhee wrapt in the beauties of this louely Swaine. Much prattle they had, and the difcourfe of manie paffions, Phœbe wifhing for the daye (as fhee thought) of her welfare, and Ganimede fmiling to thinke what vnexpected euents would fall out at the wedding. In thefe humours the weeke went away, that at laft Sundaye came.

No fooner did Phœbus Hench man appeare in the Skie, to giue warning that his mafters horfes fhoulde bee trapt in his glorious couch, but Coridon in his holiday fute meruailous feemely, in a ruffet iacket welted with the fame, and faced with red worfted, hauing a paire of blew chamlet fleeues, bound at the wrefts with foure yeolow laces, clofed afore verie richly with a doffen of pewter buttons : his hofe was of gray karfie, with a large flop bard ouerthwart the pocket holes with three fair gards, ftitcht of either fide with red thred, his ftock was of the own fewed clofe to his breech, and for to beautefie his hofe, he had truft himfelf round with a dofen of new thredden points of medley coulour : his bonnet was greene whereon ftood a copper brooch with the picture of Saint Denis : and to want nothing that might make him amorous in his olde dayes, he had a fayre fhyrt band of fine lockram, whipt ouer with Couentrey blew, of no fmall coft.

Thus attired, Coridon beftird himfelfe as chiefe ftickler in thefe actions, and had ftrowed all the houfe with flowers, that it feemed rather fome of Floraes choyce bowers, than anie Countrey cottage.

Thether repaired Phœbe with all the maides of the forreft to fet out the bride in the moft feemelieft fort that might be : but howfoeuer fhe helpt to pranke out Aliena, yet her eye was ftill on Ganimede, who was fo neate in a fute of gray, that he feemed Endymion when hee won Luna with his lookes, or Paris when he plaide the Swaine to get the beautie of the Nymph Oenone. Ganimede like a prettie Page waited on

his Miſtreſſe Aliena, and ouerlookt that al was in a readineſſe againſt the Bridegroome
ſhoulde come. Who attired in a Forreſters ſute came accompanied with Gerismond
and his brother Rosader early in the morning; where arriued, they were ſolempnlie
entertained by Aliena and the reſt of the Countrey Swaines, Gerismond verie highly commending the fortunate choyce of Saladyne, in that had choſen a Shepheardeſſe, whoſe
vertues appeared in her outward beauties, being no leſſe faire than ſeeming modeſt.

Ganimede comming in and ſeeing her Father began to bluſh, Nature working
affects by her ſecret effects: ſcarce could ſhe abſtaine from teares to ſee her Father in
ſo lowe fortunes: he that was wont to ſit in his royall Pallaice, attended on by twelue
noble peeres, now to be contented with a ſimple Cottage, and a troupe of reuelling
Woodmen for his traine. The conſideration of his fall, made Ganimede full of ſorrowes: yet that ſhee might triumph ouer Fortune with patience, and not anie way
daſh that merrie day with her dumpes, ſhee ſmothered her melancholy with a ſhaddow of mirth: and verie reuerently welcommed the King, not according to his former
degree, but to his preſent eſtate, with ſuch diligence, as Gerismond began to commend the Page for his exquiſite perſon, and excellent qualities.

As thus the King with his Forreſters frolickt it among the ſhepheards, Coridon
came in with a faire mazer full of Sidar, and preſented it to Gerismond with ſuch a
clowniſh ſalute, that he began to ſmile, and tooke it of the old ſhepheard verie kindly,
drinking to Aliena and the reſt of her faire maides, amongſt whom Phœbe was the
formoſt. Aliena pledged the King, and drunke to Rosader: ſo the carrowſe went
round from him to Phœbe, &c. As they were thus drinking and readie to goe to
Church, came in Montanus apparailed all in tawney, to ſignifie that he was forſaken; on
his head he wore a garland of willowe, his bottle hanged by his ſide whereon was painted
deſpaire, and on his ſheephooke hung two ſonnets as labels of his loues & fortunes.

Thus attired came Montanus in, with his face as full of griefe, as his heart was of
ſorrowes, ſhewing in his countenance the map of extremities. Aſſoone as the Shepheards ſaw him, they did him all the honour they could, as being the flower of all the
Swaines in *Arden*: for a bonnier boy was there not ſeene ſince the wanton Wag of
Troy that kept ſheep in *Ida*. He ſeeing the king, and geſſing it to be Gerismond,
did him all the reuerence his countery curteſie could affoord. Infomuch that the
King wondring at his attire, began to queſtion what he was. Montanus ouerhearing
him made this replie.

I am ſir quoth he Loues Swaine, as full of inward diſcontents as I ſeeme fraught
with outward follies. Mine eyes like Bees delight in ſweete flowers, but ſucking
their full on the faire of beautie, they carrie home to the Hiue of my heart farre more
gall than honnie, and for one droppe of pure deaw, a tunne full of deadly *Aconiton*.
I hunt with the Flie to purſue the Eagle, that flying too nigh the Sunne, I periſh with
the Sunne: my thoughts are aboue my reach, and my deſires more than my fortunes;
yet neither greater than my Loues. But daring with Phaeton, I fall with Irarus, and
ſeeking to paſſe the meane, I dye [for being ſo mean, my night ſleeps are waking
ſlombers, as full of ſorrowes as they be far from reſt, & my dayes labors are fruitleſſe
amors, ſtaring at a ſtar and ſtombling at a ſtraw, leauing reaſon to follow after repentance: yet euery paſſion is a pleaſure thogh it pinch, becauſe loue hides his worme-
ſeed in figs, his poyſons in ſweet potions, & ſhadows preiudize with the maſke of
pleaſure. The wiſeſt counſellers are my deep diſcontents, and I hate that which
ſhould ſalue my harm, like the patient which ſtung with the *Tarantula* loaths muſick,
and yet the diſeaſe incurable but by melody. Thus (Sir) reſtleſſe I hold my ſelfe
remediles, as louing without either reward or regard, and yet louing, bicauſe there is

none worthy to be loued, but the miſtreſſe of my thoughts.   And that I am as full of paſſions as I haue diſcourſt in my plaintes, Sir if you pleaſe ſee my Sonnets, and by them cenſure of my ſorrowes.

Theſe wordes of Montanus brought the king into a great wonder, amazed as much at his wit as his attire : inſomuch that he tooke the papers off his hooke, and read them to this effeƈt.

Montanus firſt Sonnet.

Alas how wander I *amidſt theſe woods,*
Whereas no day bright ſhine doth finde acceſſe :
But where the melancholy fleeting floods
(Darke as the night) my night of woes expreſſe,
Diſarmde of reaſon, ſpoilde of natures goods,
Without redreſſe to ſalue my heauineſſe
    I *walke, whilest thought (too cruell to my harmes)*
    With endles grief my heedles iudgement charmes.

My ſilent tongue aſſailde by ſecret feare,
My traitrous eyes impriſoned in their ioy,
My fatall peace deuourd in fained cheare,
My heart inforſt to harbour in annoy,
My reaſon robde of power by yeelding eare,
My fond opinions ſlaue to euery toy.
    Oh Loue thou guide in my vncertaine way,
    Woe to thy bow, thy fire, the cauſe of my decay.

                                    Et florida pungunt.

When the King had read this Sonnet, he highly commended the deuice of the ſhepheard, that could ſo wittily wrap his paſſions in a ſhaddow, and ſo couertly conceale that which bred his chiefeſt diſcontent : affirming, that as the leaſt ſhrubs haue their tops, the ſmalleſt haires their ſhadowes : ſo the meaneſt ſwaines had their fancies, and in their kynde were as charie of Loue as a King.   Whetted on with this deuice, he tooke the ſecond and read it : the effeƈts were theſe.

Montanus ſecond Sonnet.

When the Dog
Full of rage,
        With his irefull eyes
        Frownes amidſt the ſkies
The Shepheard to aſſwage
        The fury of the heat,
        Himſelfe doth ſafely ſeat
By a fount
Full of faire,
        Where a gentle breath
        (Mounting from beneath)
Tempreth the aire.
There his flocks
Drinke their fill,
        And with eaſe repoſe
        Whilest ſweet ſleep doth cloſe
Eyes from toylſome ill.

But I burne
Without reft,
  No defenfiue power
  Shields from Phoebes *lower :*
Sorrow is my best.
Gentle Loue
Lowre no more,
  If thou wilt inuade,
  In the fecret fhade,
Labour not fo fore.
I *my felfe*
And my flocks
  They their loue to pleafe,
  I my felfe to eafe,
Both leaue the fhadie oakes :
  Content to burne in fire
  Saith Loue doth fo defire.

          Et florida pungunt.

Gerifmond feeing the pithy vaine of thofe Sonets, began to make further enquiry what hee was ⸿ Whereupon *R*ofader difcourft vnto him the loue of Montanus to Phoebe, his great loialtie & her deep crueltie : and how in reuenge the Gods had made the curious Nymph amorous of yoong Ganimede. Vpon this difcourfe, yᵉ king was defirous to fee Phoebe *:* who being broght before Gerifmond by Rofader, fhad-owed the beauty of her face with fuch a vermilion teinture, that the Kings eyes began to dazle at the puritie of her excellence. After Gerifmond had fed his lookes a while vpon her faire, he queftioned with her, why fhe rewarded Montanus loue with fo little regard, feeing his defertes were many, and his paffions extreame. Phoebe to make reply to the Kings demaund, anfwered thus : Loue (fir) is charitie in his lawes, and whatfoeuer hee fets downe for iuftice (bee it neuer fo vniuft) the fentence cannot be reuerft *:* womens fancies lende fauours not euer by defert, but as they are inforft by their defires : for fancy is tied to the wings of Fate, and what the ftarres decree, ftands for an infallible doome. I know Montanus is wife, & womens ears are greatly delighted with wit, as hardly efcaping the charme of a pleafant toong, as Vliffes the melody of the Syrens. Montanus is bewtifull, and womens eyes are fnared in the excellence of obiects, as defirous to feede their lookes with a faire face, as the Bee to fuck on a fweet floure. Montanus is welthy, and an ounce of giue me perfwades a woman more than a pound of heare me. Danae was won with a golden fhower, when fhe could not be gotten with all the intreaties of Iupiter *:* I tell you fir, the ftring of a womans heart reacheth to the pulfe of her hand, and let a man rub that with gold, & tis hard but fhe wil prooue his hearts gold. Montanus is yoong, a great claufe in fancies court : Montanus is vertuous, the richeft argument that Loue yeelds : & yet knowing all thefe perfections I praife them, and wonder at them, louing the qualities, but not affecting the perfon, becaufe the Deftenies haue fet downe a con-trary cenfure. Yet Venus to ad reuenge, hath giuē me wine of yᵉ fame grape, a fip of the fame fauce, & firing me with the like paffiõ, hath croft me with as il a penance : for I am in loue with a fhepheards fwaine, as coy to mee as I am cruel to Montanus, as peremptory in difdain as I was peruerfe in defire, & that is (quoth fhe) Alienaes page, yong Ganimede.

Gerismond defirous to profecute the ende of thefe paffions, called in Ganimede : who knowing the cafe, came in graced with fuch a blufh, as beautified the Chriftall of his face with a ruddie brightneffe.   The King noting well the phifnomy of Gani-mede, began by his fauours to cal to mind the face of his Rosalynd, and with that fetcht a deepe figh.   *R*osader that was paffing familiar with Gerismond, demanded of him why he fighed fo fore ⸫   Becaufe *R*osader (quoth hee) the fauour of Gani-mede puts mee in minde of Rosalynde.   At this word, Rosader fight fo deepely as though his heart would haue burft.   And whats the matter (quoth Gerismond) that you quite mee with fuch a figh ⸫   Pardon mee fir (quoth Rosader) becaufe I loue none but *R*osalynd. And vpon that condition (quoth Gerismond) that *R*osalynd were here, I would this day make vp a marriage betwixt her and thee.   At this Aliena turnd her head and fmilde vpon Ganimede, and fhee could fcarce keep countenance. Yet fhee falued all with fecrecie, and Gerismond to driue away fuch dumpes, quef-tioned with Ganimede, what the reafon was he regarded not Phœbes loue, feeing fhe was as faire as the wantō that brought *Troy* to ruine.   Ganimede mildly anfwered, If I fhuld affeᴄt the fair Phoebe, I fhould offer poore Montanus great wrong to winne that from him in a moment, that hee hath labored for fo many monthes.   Yet haue I promifed to the bewtiful fhepheardeffe, to wed my felf neuer to woman except vnto her : but with this promife, yᵗ if I can by reafon fuppreffe Phoebes loue towards me, fhe fhall like of none but of Montanus.   To yᵗ q. Phoebe I ftand, for my loue is fo far beyond reafon, as it wil admit no perfuafion of reafon.   For iuftice q. he, I appeale to Gerismond : and to his cenfure wil I ftand q. Phoebe.   And in your viᴄtory q. Montanus ftands the hazard of my fortunes : for if Ganymede go away with conqueft, Montanus is in conceit loues Monarch, if Phoebe winne, then am I in effeᴄt moft mif-erable.   We wil fee this controuerfie q. Gerismōd, & then we will to church : there-fore Ganimede let vs heare your argument.   Nay, pardon my abfence a while (quoth fhee) and you fhall fee one in ftore.   In went Ganimede, and dreft her felf in womans attire, hauing on a gowne of greene, with kirtle of rich fandall, fo quaint, that fhe feemed Diana triumphing in the Forreft : vpon her head fhe wore a chaplet of Rofes, which gaue her fuch a grace, yᵗ fhe looked like Flora pearkt in the pride of all hir floures.   Thus attired came *R*osalind in, & prefented her felf at her fathers feete, with her eyes full of teares, crauing his bleffing, & difcourfing vnto him all her for-tunes, how fhee was banifhed by Torismond, and how euer fince fhe liued in that country difguifed.

Gerismond feeing his daughter, rofe from his feat & fel vpon her necke, vttering the paffions of his ioy in watry plaints driuen into fuch an extafie of content, that hee could not vtter one word.   At this fight, if *R*osader was both amazed & ioyfull, I refer my felfe to the iudgement of fuch as haue experience in loue, feeing his Rosa-lynd before his face whom fo long and deeply he had affeᴄted.   At laft Gerismond recouered his fpirites, and in moft fatherly tearmes entertained his daughter *R*osa-lynd, after many queftions demanding of her what had paft betweene her and *R*osa-der.   So much fir (quoth fhe) as there wants nothing but your Grace to make vp the marriage.   Why then (quoth Gerismond) *R*osader take her, fhee is thine, and let this day folemnize both thχ brothers and thy nuptials, *R*osader beyond meafure cōtent, humbly thanked the king, & imbraced his Rosalynde, who turning to Phoebe, de-manded if fhe had fhewen fufficient reafon to fuppreffe the force of her loues.   Yea quoth Phœbe, & fo great a perfwafiue, that if it pleafe you Madame and Aliena to giue vs leaue, Montanus and I will make this day the thirde couple in marriage.   She had no fooner fpake this word, but Montanus, threw away his garland of willow, his bottle, where was painted difpaire, & caſt his fonnets in the fire, ſhewing himfelfe as frolicke as Paris when he hanfeled his loue with Helena. At this Gerifmond and the reſt fmiled, and concluded that Montanus and Phoebe ſhould keepe their wedding with the two brethren. Aliena feeing Saladyne ſtand in a dumpe, to wake him from his dreame began thus. Why how now my Saladyne, all a mort, what melancholy man at the day of marriage ç perchaunce thou art forrowfull to thinke on thy brothers high fortunes, and thyne owne bafe defires to chufe fo meane a ſhepheardize. Cheare vp thy hart man, for this day thou ſhalt bee married to the daughter of a King: for know Saladyne, I am not Aliena, but Alinda the daughter of thy mortal enemie Torismond. At this all the company was amazed, efpecially Gerifmond, who rifing vp, tooke Alinda in his armes, and faid to *R*ofalynd: is this that faire Alinda famous for fo many vertues, that forfoke her fathers court to liue with thee exilde in the country? The fame q. *R*ofalynde. Then quoth Gerifmond, turning to Saladine, iolly Forreſter be frolick, for thy fortunes are great, & thy defires excellent, thou haſt got a princeffe as famous for her perfection, as exceeding in proportion. And ſhe hath with her beauty won (quoth Saladyne) an humble feruant, as full of faith, as ſhe of amiable fauour. While euery one was amazed with thefe Comicall euentes, Coridon came ſkipping in, & told them that the Prieſt was at Church and tarried for their comming. With that Gerifmond led the way, & the reſt followed, where to the admiration of all the countrey fwains in *Arden*, their mariages were folemnly folemnized. As foone as the Prieſt had finiſhed, home they went with Alinda, where Coridon had made all things in readines. Dinner was prouided, & the tables being fpread, and the Brides fet downe by Gerifmond, Rosader, Saladyne, & Montanus that day were feruitors: homely cheare thay had, fuch as their country could affoord: but to mend their fare they had mickle good chat, and many difcourfes of their loues and fortunes. About mid dinner, to make them mery Coridon came in with an old crowd, and plaid them a fit of mirth, to which he fung this pleafant fong.

Coridons Song.

A blyth and bonny country Laffe,
heigh ho the bonny Laffe :
Sate fighing on the tender graffe,
and weeping faid, will none come woo me?
A fmicker boy, a lyther Swaine,
heigh ho a fmicker Swaine :
That in his Loue was wanton faine,
with fmiling looks ftraight came vnto her.

When as the wanton wench efpide,
heigh ho when fhe efpide
The meanes to make her felfe a bride,
fhe fimpred fmooth like bonny bell :
The Swaine that faw her fquint eied kind
heigh ho fquint eyed kind,
His armes about her body twind,
and faire Laffe, how fare ye, well?

The country kit faid well forfooth,
heigh ho well forfooth,
But that I haue a longing tooth,
a longing tooth that makes me crie :

25

Alas said he what garres thy griefe ?
　　heigh ho what garres thy griefe ?
A wound quoth she without reliefe,
　　I feare a maid that I shall die.

If that be all the shepheard said
　　heigh ho the shepheard said,
Ile make thee wiue it gentle maide,
　　and so recure thy maladie.
Hereon they kist with manie a oath,
　　heigh ho with manie a oath,
And fore God Pan *did plight their troath,*
　　and to the Church they hied them fast.

And God send euerie pretie peate
　　heigh ho the pretie peate
That feares to die of this conceate,
　　so kinde a friend to helpe at last.

Coridon hauing thus made them merrie: as they were in the midst of all their iollitie, word was brought in to Saladyne and Rosader, that a brother of theirs, one Fernandyne was arriued, and desired to speake with them. Gerismond ouer hearing this newes, demaunded who it was? It is sir (quoth Rosader) our middle brother, that lyues a Scholler in *Paris*: but what fortune hath driuen him to seek vs out I know not. With that Saladyne went and met his brother, whom he welcommed with all curtesie, and Rosader gaue him no lesse friendly entertainment: brought hee was by his two brothers into the parlour where they al sate at dinner. Fernandyne as one that knewe as manie manners as he could points of sophistrie, & was aswell brought vp as well lettered, saluted them all. But when hee espied Gerismond, kneeling on his knee he did him what reuerence belonged to his estate: and with that burst foorth into these speaches. Although (right mightie Prince) this day of my brothers mariage be a day of mirth, yet time craues another courfe: and therefore from daintie cates rife to sharpe weapons. And you the sonnes of Sir Iohn of *Bourdeaux*, leaue off your amors & fall to armes, change your loues into lances, and now this day shewe your selues as valiant, as hethertoo you haue been passionate. For know Gerismond, that hard by at the edge of this forrest the twelue Peeres of *France* are vp in Armes to recouer thy right; and Torismond troupt with a crue of desperate runnagates is ready to bid them battaile. The Armies are readie to ioyne: therfore shew thy selfe in the field to encourage thy subiects; and you Saladyne & Rosader mount you, and shewe your selues as hardie souldiers as you haue been heartie louers: so shall you for the benefite of your Countrey, discouer the Idea of your fathers vertues to bee stamped in your thoughts, and proue children worthie of so honourable a parent. At this alarum giuen by Fernandyne, Gerismond leapt from the boord, and Saladyne and Rosader betook themselues to their weapons. Nay quoth Gerismond, goe with me I haue horse and armour for vs all, and then being well mounted, let vs shew that we carrie reuenge and honour at our fawchions points. Thus they leaue the Brides full of sorrow, especially Alinda, who desired Gerismond to be good to her father: he not returning a word becaufe his hast was great, hied him home to his Lodge, where he deliuered Saladyne and Rosader horse and armour, and himselfe armed royally led the way: not hauing ridden two leagues before they discouered where in a Valley both the battailes were ioyned. Gerismond feeing the wing wherein the Peeres fought, thruft in there, and cried Saint Denis, Gerismond laying on fuch loade vppon his enemies, that hee fhewed how highly he did eftimate of a Crowne. When the Peeres perceiued that their lawfull King was there, they grewe more eager: and Saladyne and Rosader fo behaued themfelues that none durft ftand in their way, nor abide the furie of their weapons. To be fhort, the Peeres were conquerours, Torismonds armie put to flight, and himfelfe flaine in battaile. The Peeres then gathered themfelues together, and faluting their king, conducted him royallie into *Paris*, where he was receiued with great ioy of all the citizens. Affoone as all was quiet and he had receiued againe the Crowne, hee fent for Alinda and Rosalynde to the Court, Alinda being verie paffionate for the death of her father: yet brooking it with the more patience, in that fhe was contented with the welfare of her Saladyne. Well, affoone as they were come to *Paris*, Gerismond made a royall Feaft for the Peeres and Lords of his Lande, which continued thirtie dayes, in which time fummoning a Parliament, by the consent of his Nobles he created Rosader heire apparant to the kingdom he reftored Saladyne to all his fathers lande, and gaue him the Dukedome of *Nameurs*, he made Fernandyne principall Secretarie to himfelfe; and that Fortune might euerie way feeme frolicke, he made Montanus Lord ouer all the Forreft of *Arden*: Adam Spencer Captaine of the Kings Gard, and Coridon Master of Alindas Flocks.

HERE Gentlemen may you fee in *Euphues golden Legacie,* that fuch as neglect their fathers precepts, incurre much preiudice; that diuifion in Nature as it is a blemish in nurture, so tis a breach of good fortunes; that vertue is not measured by birth but by action; that yonger bretheren though inferiour in yeares, yet may be superiour to honours: that concord is the fweeteft conclufion, and amitie betwixt brothers more forceable than fortune. If you gather any frutes by this Legacie, fpeake well of Euphues for writing it, and me for fetching it. If you grace me with that fauour, you encourage me to be more forward: and affoone as I haue ouerlookt my labours, expect the *Sailers Kalender*.

T. LODGE.

DURATION OF THE ACTION

IN *Othello* and in *The Merchant of Venice* of this edition, Shakespeare's remarkable, artistic management of Time in *The Duration of the Action* is duly noted and set forth. In *Othello* the requirements of the Tragedy demand the utmost haste; there must be given to the Moor and to Desdemona not a chance for mutual explanations, the blow must fall swift as lightning in the collied night, and yet before our eyes the show of a slow and reluctant growth of jealousy must gradually pass, and every faint unfolding of the passion be presented. Accordingly, when Desdemona is murdered within thirty-six hours after her arrival in Cyprus, Shakespeare's art has induced the belief that her ill-starred career has been watched by us for weeks and months.

Again, in *The Merchant of Venice* I endeavored to show that the term of a Bond for three months is made to run its full course within twenty-four hours after it is signed and sealed, and yet so consummate and so potent is Shakespeare's art that this monstrous absurdity is enacted before our very eyes without our being aware of it; on the contrary, it all seems as natural as if we had watched month by month the slow flight of time, and marked the smug Anthonio slowly change into the haggard bankrupt. This is no chance effect, no happy accident, in these two plays alone, but this same legerdemain deals with the time, or the duration of the action, in *As You Like It* also. (I noticed it cursorily in the *Preface* to *Hamlet*, as also true of that play.) That it is pure, genuine, cunningly devised and constructed art, and not hap-hazard chance, we know, because we can by close examination detect the steps whereby the end is gained, we can trace out and spell the syllables of the charm by which the mighty Magician sways our moods and makes us think we count the hours we do not. It is, however, by careful scrutiny alone that we can wring the secret from these plays; we need not hope to do it while they are acted before us on the stage. Then it is, as Christopher North says, that 'a good-natured Juggler has 'cheated our eyes. We ask him to show us how he did it. He does the trick 'slowly,—and we see. "Now, good Conjurer, *do it slowly and cheat us.*" " I ' " can't. I cheat you by doing it quickly. To be cheated you must not see what ' " I do; but you must *think* that you see." When we inspect the Play in our ' closets, the Juggler does his trick slowly. We sit at the Play, and he does it ' quick.'

This 'trick' is Shakespeare's art in dealing with Time. By one series of allusions to time we are either hurried forward with that speed which is an essential element of dramatic action, or else the past is brought vividly before us as the present; by another series we are thrust back, Time's foot is made inaudible and noiseless, the present recedes and we hear only echoes from the past; and then before us slowly and deliberately unfolds the gradual growth of character.

Although from the very nature of the plot this dual treatment of time does not enter as largely into *As You Like It* as in the other plays which I have mentioned, yet Shakespeare's artistic dealing with it may be traced as distinctly here as elsewhere. But in order to appreciate the need in this play of any such use of dual time, let me first very briefly note the dramatic treatment of the plot and mark the development of an idea, which I shall not call 'central,' lest I be understood as intimating that this delightful comedy is that thing of shreds and patches, a 'tendenz-'drama,' a drama with a purpose,—and yet this idea comes in as a motive for much of the action. Other motives there are which modify the action, but in order to see the need of this dual time I wish to regard as one of the main springs Marlowe's 'saw of might: "Who ever loved that loved not at first sight?"'

Let us suppose, then, that this 'love at first sight' is to be treated dramatically. We must see its first flash, then mark its slow and steady confirmation, and, finally, its triumph. This love is to be pure, absolute, boundless both in the man and in the woman. Orlando is to fall in love with Rosalind's 'heavenly' beauty, and Rosalind is to fall in love with Orlando's manly strength and physical prowess. This strength and this prowess can be shown best by contrast. Hence a wrestling match with the professional champion of the land. But wrestling with a professional champion is hardly the sport for a gentleman. Hence Orlando is to be of gentle birth, but temporarily abased. A father's authority carries with it so much respect that were Orlando thus degraded by his father, he could not but fall somewhat in our estimation. Hence Orlando, who has been decidedly a favorite of his father's, is now degraded unjustly, and only for a time, by a cruel elder brother. If this play were to be a tragedy, this is the point where the circumstances must be devised which are to make the loves of the young couple ill-starred, and raise an almost insurmountable barrier between the lovers; but as it is to be a comedy, a sufficient obstruction will be found in the degradation of the lover,—a degradation which had to be, but which while it lasts will effectually debar Orlando from wooing the high-born Rosalind. Hence they must both be made to meet where the distinctions of rank are obliterated. It is not a difficult problem to drive off Orlando to the Forest of Arden. But how to get Rosalind there? It is no easy matter to drive from court an innocent, guileless young girl so that not the faintest stain shall attach to her name. Of course it cannot be for any actual misdeed, but only on suspicion,—suspicion absolutely groundless, but fostered by one who is powerful enough to drive her forth. Here, again, for the same reason as in Orlando's case, it must not be a father who banishes her; this would partake of tragedy. Hence it is an uncle who exiles her, and the only suspicion, absolutely groundless, under which an artless, innocent young girl could fall would be that of treachery against the throne. This could be aroused only in the breast of one who felt his claim to the throne to be unjust, and whose usurped position he imagined to be so insecure that a slight, frail girl could disseat him. Hence the peremptory sentence of banishment pronounced on Rosalind by a most suspicious usurping uncle. The flight of Ganymede and Aliena follows, and as naturally follows the flight of Orlando from his ruthless elder brother, and in the Forest of Arden the course of love can flow on without a ripple. The most difficult problem of the dramatist is now solved. A knot which seemed too intrinse to unloose has been untied. And be it observed most especially that the suspicion felt by the usurping Duke is, in that solution, a most important, a most vital, indeed, a most indispensable, element. Without it Rosalind could never have been sent to Arden in doublet and hose. It is comparatively easy for a dramatist to send a man, disguised or undisguised, to the ends of the earth, but for a lovely young girl to be sent forth disguised in man's apparel, without the faintest forfeiture of our respect, this is the labor, this the toil. And her uncle's suspicion is, of all others, *the* potent factor to effect this.

However stirring may have been the action before we reach the Forest of Arden, as soon as we have entered within that 'immortal umbrage' where no care comes, there must be a calm,—the calm of a long settled repose.

Of course we all know that Shakespeare found the leading features of this story made to his hand in Lodge's Novel, if not (which I think quite likely) in some weakling drama that he remodelled. But then he it was who discerned the dramatic capabilities of the Novel or of the play, and how fold on fold the drama must disclose probabilities in a natural sequence. It is in his dealing with this sequence that we can mark his treatment of Time, and, perchance, discover why the necessity was imposed on him of offering us here a ' fair enchanted cup.'

It is to help in the discovery of Shakespeare's 'two clocks' that I have just exposed, in rude, rough style, the framework of the play, wherein it now remains to note the allusions to time past, or to time present, which are interwoven.

When the play opens it is necessary that the senior Duke's banishment should be recent, so recent that the usurping Duke feels his grasp of the sceptre most insecure. Time can have given to the traitor no prescriptive right. ' What is the new news at the new court ?' asks Oliver. ' There's no news,' answers Charles, ' but the old news : that is, the old Duke is banished by his younger brother, the new Duke, and three or four loving lords have put themselves into voluntary exile with him.' The impression here conveyed is clear enough. The banishment is spoken of almost in the present tense. And if the news is called ' old,' it may be so called on the assumption that its limit of life is nine days. At any rate, it is not so ' old ' but that the ' younger brother ' is called the ' new Duke,' and the report of the banishment has not yet had time (and such news travels fast) to reach Oliver in all its details. Oliver's residence cannot be far removed from the ducal court, the wrestling match was quite in his neighborhood, and yet Oliver neither knows where the banished Duke has gone, nor whether Rosalind has accompanied her father. ' She is at the court,' Charles informs him, ' and no less beloved of her uncle than his own daughter.' ' Where will the old Duke live ?' asks Oliver. ' *They say*,' replies Charles, ' he is already in the Forest of Arden,—*they say*, many young gentlemen flock to him every day.' There can be no shadow of a doubt that the Duke's banishment is most recent. Sufficient time has not elapsed wherein to obtain exact information of his whereabouts. Had the Duke's banishment lasted many months, or even many weeks, some authentic reports would have come back from him, and the public would be fully aware whether he were acquiescing in his exile or gathering forces to resist. The vagueness of the information concerning his movements or his habitation proves conclusively that he had only just been driven from his throne. The ' new court ' cannot be many weeks old. It is so ' new ' that the only news in it is the event which created it. There had been no time for even another piece of gossip to be started. That Charles's ignorance was shared by the public, and was not due to his exclusion from the inner court circle, is clear from the fact that in regard to Rosalind and her position in the ' new court ' he was fully informed ; on any point that could be positively known his information is positive.

It is impossible, it seems to me, to evade the impression which is conveyed in this opening scene, that the old Duke has only just been banished. Since we are studying the conjurer's trick in our closets and making him do it slowly, it is of great importance not only to mark well this first deep impression regarding the recent banishment of the Duke, but also to discern clearly why it is important, and then after we have seen it serve its purpose we must watch the cunning conjurer waive it back into the past, and the colors, now bright and fresh as from the dyer's hand, become before our very eyes worn and faded with the ' seasons' difference.'

Accepting then, as Shakespeare intended we should, the Duke's banishment to be recent, it will be manifest that sufficient time has not elapsed to allow the social upheaval to subside, and there will be no need to tell us that the treacherous usurper eats his meal in fear and sleeps in the affliction of terrible dreams that shake him nightly. This follows as of course, and gives us the clue to understand why the mere mention to the usurping Duke by Orlando of Sir Rowland de Boys's name is sufficient to kindle the spark which blazes into a fury of suspicion against Rosalind. How essential to the plot this suspicion against Rosalind is, we have seen. It is an indispensable element. It is one of the main springs. This suspicion against a gentle girl can be accounted for only by the usurper's extreme terror. This extreme terror is accounted for by his feeling of insecurity. His insecurity arises from the newness of his position. And the newness of his position is due solely to the fact that his elder brother has only just been banished. This recent banishment supplies the motive which drives Rosalind from court to the Forest of Arden. It is vital to the movement of the First Act. But how long are its effects to last? Clearly, not long. Social upheavals are dangerous to meddle with, on or off the stage. 'Abysmal inversions of the centre of gravity,' as Carlyle terms them, belong to tragedy, if anywhere; and if their memories were kept up here, the turbulence of the times would show its effects on the exiled Duke, and we should find him in the Forest of Arden still distraught and dishevelled after his compulsory banishment. The peaceful quiet of a woodland comedy cannot breathe amid such scenes. Therefore after the explosion of wrath and suspicion from the usurper which drives forth both Rosalind and Oliver, there is no longer need of this present impression of the recent civil strife; indeed, it would be destructive of the comedy; and so, having woven its spell around us and solved dramatic difficulties, it is gently effaced by vague, misty allusions to the past; and that which happened but yesterday begins to recede into the dark backward of time; days take the place of hours, and months of days, and we count the time by the chimes of another clock which the cunning conjurer, before our very eyes but without our seeing it, has substituted for the old one.

Perhaps the first faint intimation of the lapse of time—and it is very faint but still marked enough to create an impression—is after the wrestling, when the usurping Duke says to Orlando, ' The world esteemed thy father honourable, But I did find him still mine enemy.' This must refer to old Sir Rowland's loyalty to the senior Duke and his hostility to the usurper during the recent crisis, the only time as far as we know when any proofs of enmity could have been evoked. But the first impression concerning old Sir Rowland which we receive, in the very opening of the play, is that he has been dead several years, at least long enough to account for Orlando's neglected education. This passing reference, then, to Sir Rowland's enmity during his lifetime to the usurping Duke weakens the impression that the *coup d'état* is so very recent, and for one second carries that event with it back into the past, and there is a fleeting vision of unflinching loyalty long years ago to the exiled Duke in the stress that then drove him from his throne.

This allusion, which has swiftly come and swiftly gone, is closely followed by another allusion to time long past, more marked, as it ought to be, than the former, and which can scarcely fail to leave a still more decided impression. Le Beau says to Orlando immediately after the wrestling: ' But I can tell you that *of late* this duke Hath ta'en displeasure 'gainst his gentle niece, Grounded upon no other argument But that *the people praise her for her virtues.*' Charles, the Wrestler, told us that Rosalind was ' no less beloved of her uncle than his own daughter.' To turn love thus deep into ' displeasure' time will be required; and visions arise before us of a blameless life lived by Rosalind in the sight of all men, week by week, and month by month, full of patient submission and deeds of gentle kindness, and not alone winning all hearts, but winning them so strongly that the murmurs of applause swell till at last they reach the throne.

Deep as this impression is of the slow flight of time, and remote as the banishment of the Duke is beginning to grow, this impression is followed up by another still deeper. When the usurping Duke, half crazed by suspicion, wrathfully banishes Rosalind, Celia intercedes for her cousin, and recalls to her cruel father that when he 'stay'd Rosalind,' and she had not 'with her father ranged along,' he had done it out of pity and of love for his own daughter, but, pleads Celia, 'I was TOO YOUNG THAT TIME to value her; But NOW I know her,' and then she goes on to picture *the years that have passed* since that time in her unconscious childhood when the Duke was banished, and how since then she and Rosalind have grown up together, how they had learned their lessons together, played together, slept together, rose at an instant, ate together, and wherever we went 'like Juno's swans still we went coupled and inseparable.' It is necessary only to cite this passage; comment on it is impertinent; no one can evade the impression of years, passing and passed, which it conveys.

But to one fact attention must be called, and this is, the extreme importance, dramatically, of making, just at this point, the time of the Duke's banishment recede into the past. As a present active force its power is spent. It was of vital importance to quicken the usurper's suspicion and to cause him to drive Rosalind forth. It is now equally important that it should recede into the past and, for two reasons, grow dim through a vista of years. First, the next Act is to open in the Forest of Arden; there for the first time we see the banished Duke. No chill air of tragedy can be suffered to disturb the repose of that 'immortal umbrage,' and all traces of a brother's perfidy and treachery must be obliterated; in things evil we must discern the soul of goodness, and recognize it in that philosophic calm which years of exile have brought to the Duke; all thoughts of recent turbulence or of recent violence, so necessary in the first Act, must here, when we first see the exiled Duke, give place to that imperturbable serenity and acquiescence with fate which is the benison of time. Hence it is that the Second Act opens with the immortal lines:

> ' Now, my co-mates and brothers in exile,
> Hath not *old custom* made this life more sweet
> Than that of painted pomp? Are not these woods
> More free from peril than the envious court?
> Here feel we not the penalty of Adam,
> The *seasons' difference.*'

Are not 'old custom' and 'the seasons' difference' 'the very lime-twigs' of Shakespeare's spell? Why else are they here mentioned, if not to catch us with memories of years gone by? Can it be doubted for a moment that Shakespeare did not here intend us to believe that the Duke had lived through many a seasons' difference, or that custom to him had not grown old? Indeed, I think it may be truthfully said that BATHURST speaks for us all when he says (p. 76): 'The elder Duke has long been banished, and is quite contented with his situation.'

The gentle conjurer's legerdemain is over, and the 'trick' is done. The deep impression of the First Act has been effaced in preparation for the Second. The bells, on which the hours in the First Act were struck close to our ears, have been dextrously muffled, and we hear them now only faintly as from the dim distance.

Henceforth there is but little need of any allusion either to fast or to slow movement of time, other than to make us believe that Orlando has been long enough in the Forest of Arden to write love-songs in the bark of the trees, and that he goes wooing every day to Rosalind's sheep-cote.

I have just said that there are two reasons why, dramatically, it is necessary for us to suppose that the Duke has been long an exile in Arden; the reason which has just been given is, I think, of itself quite sufficient. But there is yet another, which renders a long sojourn there by the Duke, at least of many, many months, if not of years, almost, if not absolutely, imperative. Unless the impressions are obliterated that the Duke's exile is 'new news,' and that Jaques and Amiens and the rest have only just fled from the court and flocked to Arden,—unless, I say, these impressions are obliterated, how can we possibly understand why Jaques or the Duke, when they met Touchstone in the Forest, did not instantly recognise him, familiar to them as he must have been in and about the court. A fool of Touchstone's stamp could not be overlooked under any circumstances, and if once seen and heard at any court, be it at the lawful Duke's or at the usurper's, he could not afterwards be readily forgotten. Yet Jaques had apparently never before seen him, and the Duke certainly had not. That this incongruity never occurs to us when sitting at the play shows how powerless we have been all along in fencing our ears against Shakespeare's sorcery, and how completely he has overmastered us in his treatment of dramatic time. If Jaques fails to recognise Touchstone as a court fool, Touchstone fails to recognise Jaques as a courtier. Yet when Touchstone is about to be married by the hedge-priest and Jaques interferes, Touchstone at once recognises and salutes Jaques as his former companion, when he moralised the time. So that their failure to recognise each other at that first meeting could have been due to no lack of observation, and would have been impossible, does it not seem, if Jaques and the rest had only just left the 'envious court' a few weeks before, or as short a time before as we were convinced that they had left it, in the First Act? The conclusion, therefore, is to me inevitable, that the impression which Shakespeare wished to make on us is that the Duke and Jaques and the rest had been so long fleeting the time carelessly in the Forest of Arden that a new set of courtiers had arisen in their old court at home, almost a new generation since their exile had begun.

The student will find the passages indicating 'Long Time' and 'Short Time' gathered together in THE COWDEN-CLARKE'S *Shakespeare Key*, the second great debt which all of us owe to one of the sharers of that honoured union. DANIEL (*New Shakspere Society*, Series I, Part ii) has made a 'Time-Analysis' of this play, wherein, however, by counting, in the right butter woman's rank to market, the mornings, noons, and nights mentioned in the play, and by dividing them up into days, he finds that there are 'ten days represented on the stage, with such sufficient intervals as the reader may imagine for himself as requisite for the probability of the plot.' He is not blind (p. 156) to the difficulties of reconciling to the onward flow of the plot, the Duke's 'old custom' or Celia's pleadings with her father, but attempts no solution.

ENGLISH CRITICISMS

DR JOHNSON: Of this play the fable is wild and pleasing. I know not how the ladies will approve the facility with which both Rosalind and Celia give up their hearts. To Celia much may be forgiven for the heroism of her friendship. The character of Jaques is natural and well preserved. The comic dialogue is very sprightly, with less mixture of low buffoonery than in some other plays; and the graver part is elegant and harmonious. By hastening to the end of this work, Shakespeare suppressed the dialogue between the usurper and the hermit, and lost an opportunity of exhibiting a moral lesson in which he might have found matter worthy of his highest powers.

FRANCIS GENTLEMAN (*Dramatic Censor*, i, 478, 1770): We make no scruple to affirm that *As You Like It* will afford considerable instruction from attentive perusal, with great addition of pleasure from adequate representation.

MRS INCHBALD (1808): This comedy has high reputation among Shakespeare's works, and yet, on the stage, it is never attractive, except when some actress of very superior skill performs the part of Rosalind. This character requires peculiar talents in representation, because it has so large a share of the dialogue to deliver; and the dialogue, though excellently written and interspersed with various points of wit, has still no forcible repartee or trait of humour, which in themselves would excite mirth, independent of an art in giving them utterance. Such is the general cast of all the other personages in the play that each requires a most skilful actor to give them their proper degree of importance. But, with every advantage to *As You Like It* in the performance, it is a more pleasing drama than one which gives delight. The reader will, in general, be more charmed than the auditor; for he gains all the poet, which neither the scene nor the action much adorn, except under particular circumstances. Shakespeare has made the inhabitants of the Forest of Arden appear so happy in their banishment, that when they are called back to the cares of the world, it seems more like a punishment than a reward. Jaques has too much prudence to leave his retirement; and yet, when his associates are departed, his state can no longer be enviable, as refined society was the charm which seemed here to bestow on country life its more than usual enjoyments. Kemble's Jaques is in the highest estimation with the public; it is one of those characters in which he gives certain bold testimonies of genius, which no spectator can controvert, yet the mimic art has very little share in this grand exhibition. Mrs Jordan is the Rosalind both of art and of nature; each supplies its treasures in her performance of the character, and render it a perfect exhibition.

HAZLITT (p. 305, 1817): It is the most ideal of any of this author's plays. It is a pastoral drama in which the interest arises more out of the sentiments and characters than out of the actions or situations. It is not what is done, but what is said, that claims our attention. Nursed in solitude, 'under the shade of melancholy boughs,' the imagination grows soft and delicate, and the wit runs riot in idleness, like a spoiled child that is never sent to school. Caprice and fancy reign and revel here, and stern necessity is banished to the court. The mild sentiments of humanity are strengthened with thought and leisure; the echo of the cares and noise of the world strikes upon the ear of those 'who have felt them knowingly,' softened by time and distance. ' They hear the tumult, and are still.' The very air of the place seems to breathe a spirit of philosophical poetry; to stir the thoughts, to touch the heart with pity, as the drowsy forest rustles to the sighing gale. Never was there such beautiful moralising, equally free from pedantry or petulance. . . . . Within the sequestered and romantic glades of the Forest of Arden, they find leisure to be good and wise or to play the fool and fall in love. Rosalind's character is made up of sportive gayety and natural tenderness; her tongue runs the faster to conceal the pressure at her heart. She talks herself out of breath, only to get deeper in love. The coquetry with which she plays with her lover in the double character which she has to support is managed with the nicest address. . . . . The silent and retired character of Celia is a necessary relief to the provoking loquacity of Rosalind. . . . . The unrequited love of Silvius for Phœbe shows the perversity of this passion in the commonest scenes of life, and the rubs and stops which Nature throws in its way where fortune has placed none.

BLACKWOOD'S MAGAZINE (April, 1833, p. 559) : We call *As You Like It* the only true ' Romance of the Forest.' Touching as it is, and sometimes even pathetic, 'tis all but beautiful holiday amusement, and a quiet melancholy alternates with various mirth. The contrivance of the whole is at once simple and skilful,—art and nature are at one. We are removed just so far out of our customary world as to feel willing to submit to any spell, however strange, without losing any of our sympathies with all life's best realities. Orlando, the outlaw, calls Arden ' a desert inaccessible'; and it is so; yet, at the same time, Charles the King's wrestler's account of it was correct, ' They say he is already in the Forest of Arden, ... where they fleet the time carelessly as they did in the golden world.' The wide woods are full of deer, and in open places are feeding sheep. Yet in the brakes 'hiss green and gilded snakes,' whose bite is mortal, and ' under the bush's shade a lioness lies couching.' Some may think ' they have no business there.' Yet give they not something of an imaginative ' salvage ' character,—a dimness of peril and fear to the depths of the forest ?

CAMPBELL (1838) : Before I say more of this dramatic treasure, I must absolve myself by a confession as to some of its improbabilities. Rosalind asks her cousin Celia, ' Whither shall we go ?' and Celia answers, ' To seek my uncle in the Forest of Arden;' but arrived there, and having purchased a cottage and sheep-farm, neither the daughter nor niece of the banished Duke seem to trouble themselves much to inquire about either father or uncle. The lively and natural-hearted Rosalind discovers no impatience to embrace her sire until she has finished her masked courtship with Orlando. But Rosalind was in love, as I have been with the comedy these forty years; and love is blind; for until a late period my eyes were never couched so as to see this objection. The truth, however, is love is *wilfully* blind, and now that my eyes are opened, I shut them against the fault. Away with your best-proved improbabilities when the heart has been touched and the fancy fascinated ! When I think of the lovely Mrs Jordan in this part, I have no more desire for proofs of probability on this subject, though ' proofs pellucid as the morning dews,' than for ' the cogent logic of a bailiff's writ.' In fact, though there is no rule without exceptions, and no general truth without limitation, it may be pronounced, that if you delight us in fiction you may make our sense of probability slumber as deeply as you please.

But it may be asked whether nature and truth are to be sacrificed at the altar of fiction ? No ! in the main effect of fiction on the fancy they never are nor can be sacrificed. The improbabilities of fiction are only its exceptions, whilst the truth of nature is its general law; and unless the truth of nature were in the main observed, the fictionist could not lull our vigilance as to particular improbabilities. Apply this maxim to Shakespeare's *As You Like It*, and our Poet will be found to make us forget what is eccentric from nature in a limited view, by showing it more beautifully probable in a larger contemplation. In this drama he snatches us out of the busy world into a woodland solitude; he makes us breathe its fresh air, partake its pastoral peace, feast on its venison, admire its bounding wild deer, and sympathise with its banished men and simple rustics. But he contrives to break its monotony by the intrusion of courtly manners and characters. He has a fool and a philosopher, who might have hated each other at court, but who like each other in the forest. He has a shepherdess and her wooing shepherd, as natural as Arcadians; yet when the banished court comes to the country and beats it in wit, the courtiers seem as much naturalised to the forest as its natives, and the general truth of nature is equally preserved.

The events of the play are not numerous, and its interest is preserved by characters more than incidents. But what a tablet of characters! the witty and impassioned Rosalind, the love-devoted Orlando, the friendship-devoted Celia, the duty-devoted old Adam, the humorous Clown and the melancholy Jaques; all these, together with the dignified and banished Duke, make the Forest of Arden an Elysium to our imagination; and our hearts are so stricken by these benevolent beings that we easily forgive the other once culpable but at last repentant characters.

HALLAM (*Literature of Europe*, ii, 396, 1839): The sweet and sportive temper of Shakespeare, though it never deserted him, gave way to advancing years and to the mastering force of serious thought. What we read we know but very imperfectly; yet, in the last years of this century, when five and thirty summers had ripened his genius, it seems that he must have transfused much of the wisdom of past ages into his own all-combining mind. In several of the historical plays, in *The Merchant of Venice*, and especially in *As You Like It*, the philosophic eye, turned inward on the mysteries of human nature, is more and more characteristic; and we might apply to the last comedy the bold figure that Coleridge has less appropriately employed as to the early poems, that 'the creative power and the intellectual energy wrestle as in a war embrace.' In no other play, at least, do we find the bright imagination and fascinating grace of Shakespeare's youth so mingled with the thoughtfulness of his maturer age. This play is referred with reasonable probability to the year 1600. Few comedies of Shakespeare are more generally pleasing, and its manifold improbabilities do not much affect us in perusal. The brave injured Orlando, the sprightly but modest Rosalind, the faithful Adam, the reflecting Jaques, the serene and magnanimous Duke, interest us by turns, though the play is not so well managed as to condense our sympathy, and direct it to the conclusion.

W. W. LLOYD (Singer's Edition, 1856, p. 120): The usurper pays the penalties of a falsely-assumed position; his very lords characterise him justly when they speak in an undertone, and warn away from the range of his passion those whom he is fitfully incensed against. His very daughter disowns the ill-bought advancement he would provide for her, and slips from his side to accompany in peril and privation a victim of his jealousy. Thus in every form of loyalty, compassion, duty, and affection, whether spirited, tender, sentimental, or grotesque, the better spirits fly by natural attraction to a more congenial centre, and in all happy companionship. The lords, Amiens, Jaques, and the pages, tender free duty to an exiled master; Celia proffers companionship to her banished cousin without ostentation, and it is accepted without set acknowledgement, because in the same sympathetic spirit in which it was made; old Adam with limping gait, but with the best heart he may, goes on with his young master; while Touchstone follows his mistress as devotedly as the best, perhaps the most devotedly of all, for he is the only one of them all who, as he is carried along by the current of his attachment, has still the faculty of contemplating his wanderings philosophically, of appreciating his sacrifices, whether in friendship or marriage, correctly, without making them one whit less willingly. Perhaps Jaques, in his parody of Amiens' song, approaches the critical vein of Touchstone pretty closely, but he is inferior in that mixed vein of self-observation and self-knowledge, which approximates Touchstone at one time to Mr Pepys, and at another to Michel de Montaigne.

HALLIWELL (*Introduction*, p. 71): Though said to be oftener read than any other of Shakespeare's plays, *As You Like It* is certainly less fascinating than several of his other comedies. The dramatist has presented us with a pastoral comedy, the characters of which, instead of belonging to an ideal pastoral age, are true copies of what Nature would produce under similar conditions. . . . . The poet has relieved the development of a melancholy subject and an insignificant story by the introduction of a more than usual number of really individual subordinate characters. Even Rosalind, that beautiful but wilful representation of woman's passion, is not an important accessory to the moral purpose of the comedy; and the other characters, however gracefully delineated, are not amalgamated into an artistic action with that full power which overwhelms us with astonishment in the grander efforts of Shakespeare's genius.

BATHURST (p. 76): It is the very pleasantest and sweetest of plays, sprinkled with a good deal of seriousness; and some unhappiness, but none of it cuts deep. The elder Duke has long been banished, and is quite contented with his situation. The distress of Orlando and Adam is speedily relieved. Rosalind and Celia, happy from the first, in each other's company, are quite gay and cheerful when they get into the forest. Even the bad brother partakes of the general sunshine, and is let off very easily, kindly, and pleasantly, though not with any great probability. The cheerfulness of this play is delicate, however, and gentle. There are not the coarse gayeties (if anything Shakespeare did can be called coarse) of Falstaff and his companions, or of the people in Olivia's house; nor the bad conceits of *Romeo & Juliet*. It is a play of conversation more than action, on the whole, and of character. Some of the characters, as Jaques and Touchstone, are shown in what they say merely; not what they do.

HERAUD (p. 235): The poet, in conceiving this fine work, first generated a lofty ideal. His aim was to set forth the power of patience as the panacea for earth's ills and the injustice of fortune, and self-command as the condition without which the power would be inoperative. Neither this power nor its condition can be easily illustrated in the life of courts; but the sylvan life, such as the banished Duke and his companions live in Arden, is favourable to both. In the contrast between the two states of life lies the charm of the play, and the reconciliation of these formal opposites is the fulfilment of its ideal.

MOBERLY (*Introduction*, p. 6, 1872): In the *Introduction* to *Hamlet* an attempt has been made to show how a tendency to melancholy sprang naturally out of the very circumstances of Shakespeare's time; and how the noble spirits of that day occupied themselves in battling against it. The same truths, which are so strongly impressed on us by Hamlet's losing battle against sadness, over-reflection, and want of practical force, are in this play touched with a light and genial hand. It seems written to show how the most depressing circumstances, even if continued year after year, may utterly fail to sink a generous heart into despondency. Orlando has been ill-treated in every way by his tyrannical elder brother, but his good qualities come out only the more by this perpetual bruising. He never loses the elasticity of mind and generosity of impulse which is to carry him through all. One fortunate stroke of audacity, by enabling him to defeat the professional athlete, seems likely to open to him a path leading to honour and rank such as his birth entitles him to hold. But the hope is dashed, as soon as it is conceived, by the dark jealousy of the usurping Duke against the family beloved by his banished brother. Then Orlando fails for a moment in courage and hopefulness; he considers himself 'a rotten tree' that will yield no fruit for any pruning. Yet the sad words have hardly passed his lips when he is already anticipating some 'settled low content;' and, in the next scenes, when we find him in the company of the banished Duke, he has cast all gloom aside, has nothing to say against 'any breather in the world' except himself, against whom he knows more evil than against any one else; and is contented to proclaim his love for Rosalind to any one who will listen to him, without any desponding thoughts as to the hardness of his destiny. As volatile as one of Alfred de Musset's heroes, he has, in all and through all, a firm ground of healthy English sense and truthfulness, which entitles him to serve as a type of those gallant youths who from so many a creek and inlet of Devonshire and Cornwall went forth in Shakespeare's day to war against the Spaniard.

Orlando's Rosalind is his exact counterpart, shaped for his love by similarity of destiny; but with this difference, that she acquiesced in her former lot of dependence and was only unsettled in her contentment, first, by the Duke's taunt against her father, which her true and bold spirit could not endure, and then by her unjust banishment. After this, in her 'doublet and hose,' with Celia in some degree dependent on her, she blazes into energy and vivacity; she has spirit enough for her own affairs and for half a dozen plots beside, and tact enough to make them all run prosperously up to the time when the fourfold wedding comes to settle all. Her skill in repartee is as great as Beatrice's; but there is none of the malice which has to be got rid of in *Much Ado About Nothing* by such a course of rigorous discipline. Rosalind never stings without strong and good reason, and in the interest of truth and right. When she does, however, she shows a talent for saying truth 'the next way' which any professional moralist might envy.

The third gradation of cheerfulness appears in the banished Duke. He is happy, not by youth and animal spirits, like the two others, but by reflection. His character is such that he is able to maintain his state and dignity in the forest as easily as at the court, controlling his followers without an effort, and correcting their crude reflections in a moment by his superior thought and moral force. His good-humour is all-embracing; he loves to 'cope' with those whose whole tone of mind is opposed to his own, and at once enters into the 'swift and sententious' spirit of Touchstone, when that eminent person is at last introduced to him, and produces the choicest flowers of his wit, which he had reserved till then; and as a matter of course the

Duke has long ago reconciled himself to his life of banishment and deprivation, and learned to find happiness in the very feeling of contact with nature unalloyed.

To furnish a marked contrast to these characters, to assail them one after another with attempts to shake their trust in mankind, to whisper sneers against love and happiness, to suggest that their life, simple though it is, still has the taint of the world upon it, and to patronise enthusiastically such rascalities as accident brings there, is the part assigned to the melancholy Jaques; a character created, with consummate skill, to throw the whole meaning of the play into a clear light and to bring out the moral lesson conveyed by it. He has been most profligate in his youth; has travelled in Italy, the mother of all iniquities, to gain experience there; and has spent his estate in so doing. He is therefore persuaded that the knowledge of human nature which he has thus gained will be of great service to the world, if it can only be induced to listen. But how instantly and how humiliatingly he is put to the rout by the three glad hearts which he tries to sour! Orlando absolutely refuses to rail against the world in his company, and reciprocates with hearty good-will, although jocosely, all Jaques's expressions of antipathy to his ways of thinking. Rosalind sarcastically asks him about his travels. What have they done for him? Has he learned to despise home dress and home manners? sold his own lands to see other people's? learned to chide God for making him the countryman he is? And what is this melancholy of which he boasts? Something as bad or worse than the most giddy merriment; something that incapacitates him for action as completely and more permanently than drunkenness. Above all, the Duke tells him, without the slightest reserve, although with perfect good-humour, that his gifts as a moralist can do nothing for the world; that his former life unfits him to be a reformer; that if he attempts such a task, he will only corrupt the world by his experience; and to all these buffetings, right hand and left, Jaques replies in a way which shows he is incapable of understanding the depth of their meaning. He escapes from Rosalind and Orlando because he does not like the 'blank verse' they talk; and shirks the admonition of the Duke and all its serious wisdom, by arguing that no one would have a right to be offended by satire of a general character, or need apply it to himself,—as if the Duke had been admonishing him to avoid offending others and not to avoid corrupting others.

There are traces of great family troubles which afflicted Shakespeare up to within a few years of the time when this play was written, and probably up to that time. When we read of his own father being 'warned' from Stratford Market, and unable to come to church for fear of arrest, this certainly gives much reality to the sad reflection on the 'poor and broken bankrupt' typified by the wounded stag.

The deep sorrowfulness of the subjects chosen by the poet in the years following 1600 leads us to follow up the hint thus given; for between this time and his death we have not only the four tragedies, *Hamlet, Lear, Macbeth*, and *Othello*, but also the gloomy subject of *Timon of Athens*, and in comedies (if they may be so called) the sterner and severer types of *Measure for Measure* and *The Tempest*. As, therefore, we cannot help seeing that the same struggle against melancholy lasted through Shakespeare's life, we shall not be mistaken in seeing the same indications of his nature in *As You Like It*. This play was, therefore, one of the earlier attempts made by the poet to control the dark spirit of melancholy in himself by a process which a great writer (Dr Johnson) well versed in his subject has described as hopeless, that of 'thinking it away.' With this plan in view, he, as it were, held it up to view in many lights, in order to set up a standard for himself against it,—with what effect on himself we can only partially judge, from our extreme ignorance of the events of his later life. But even if Shakespeare's efforts to free himself from the clinging plague were unavailing (as we must needs suppose), they are still calculated to do for others what they could not do for him. Any one who will may learn from *As You Like It*, that the secret of true cheerfulness is to be found in Horace's words, *Mihi res non me rebus subnectere conor;* who treats the state of things in which he finds himself not as a stern unbending order under which his powers as well as his resistance must be crushed, but an arrangement capable of seconding all his endeavours for a high and cheerful life, and of furnishing instruction, help, and encouragement whenever and wherever they are needed.

HUDSON (*Introduction*, p. 22, 1880): The general drift and temper, or, as some of the German critics would say, the ground-idea of this play is aptly hinted by the title. As for the beginnings of what is here represented, these do not greatly concern us; most of them lie back out of our view, and the rest are soon lost sight of in what grows out of them; but the issues, of which there are many, are all exactly to our mind; we feel them to be just about right, and would not have them otherwise. For example, touching Frederick and Oliver, our wish is that they should repent and repair the wrong they have done; in brief, that they should become good; which is precisely what takes place; and as soon as they do this, they naturally love those who were good before. Jaques, too, is so fitted to moralise the discrepancies of human life, so happy and at home, and withal so agreeable in that exercise, that we would not he should follow the good Duke when in his case those discrepancies are composed. The same might easily be shown in respect of the other issues. Indeed, I dare ask any genial, considerate reader, Does not everything turn out *as you like it?* Moreover, there is an indefinable something about the play that puts us in a receptive frame of mind; that opens the heart, soothes away all querulousness and fault-finding, and makes us easy and apt to be pleased. Thus the Poet here disposes us to like things as they come, and at the same time takes care that they shall come as we like. The whole play, indeed, is *as you like it.*

(P. 24): As far as I can determine the matter, *As You Like It* is, upon the whole, my favourite of Shakespeare's comedies. Yet I should be puzzled to tell why; for my preference springs not so much from any particular points or features, wherein it is surpassed by several others, as from the general toning and effect. The whole is replete with a beauty so delicate, yet so intense, that we feel it everywhere, but can never tell especially where it is or in what it consists. For instance, the descriptions of forest scenery come along so unsought, and in such easy, quiet, natural touches that we take in the impression without once noticing what it is that impresses us. Thus, there is a certain woodland freshness, a glad, free naturalness, that creeps and steals into the heart before we know it. And the spirit of the place is upon its inhabitants, its genius within them; we almost breathe with them the fragrance of the Forest, and listen to 'the melodies of woods, and winds, and waters,' and feel

> The Power, the Beauty, and the Majesty,
> That have their haunts in dale, or piny mountain,
> Or forest by slow stream, or pebbly spring.

Even the court Fool, notwithstanding all the crystallising process that has passed upon him, undergoes a sort of rejuvenescence of his inner man, so that his wit catches at every turn the fresh hues and odours of his new whereabout. I am persuaded, indeed, that Milton had a special eye to this play in the lines,

> And sweetest Shakespeare, Fancy's child,
> Warbles his native wood-notes wild.

To all which add, that the kindlier sentiments here seem playing out in a sort of jubilee. Untied from set purposes and definite aims, the persons come forth with their hearts already tuned, and so have but to let off their redundant music. Envy, jealousy, avarice, revenge, all the passions that afflict and degrade society, they have left in the city behind them. And they have brought the intelligence and refinement of the court without its vanities and vexations; so that the graces of art and the simplicities of nature meet together in joyous, loving sisterhood. A serene and mellow atmosphere of thought encircles and pervades the actors in this drama, as if on purpose to illustrate how

> One impulse from a vernal wood
> May teach you more of man,
> Of moral evil, and of good,
> Than all the sages can.

Nature throws her protecting arms around them; Beauty pitches her tent before them; Heaven rains its riches upon them, with 'no enemy but winter and rough weather'; Peace hath taken up her abode with them; and they have nothing to do but to 'fleet the time carelessly, as they did in the golden world.' But no words of mine, I fear, will justify to others my own sense of this delectable workmanship. I can hardly think of anything else in the whole domain of Poetry so inspiring of the faith that 'every flower enjoys the air it breathes.' The play, indeed, abounds in wild, frolicsome graces which cannot be described; which can only be seen and felt; and which the hoarse voice of criticism seems to scare away, as the crowing of the cocks is said to have scared away the fairy spirits from their nocturnal pastimes.

NEIL (*Introduction*, p. 10): When we read this drama, we see that it recognises Love as the pivot and centre of activity and joy—the very core of life. It has been said that its chief end was to 'dally with the innocence of love.' It surely, however, has a higher aim than that. When we observe that all the evils in the play originate in the neglect of the royal law of life: 'Thou shalt love thy neighbour as thyself,' and that all the good results flow from obedience to that Divine rule; when we see how Selfishness complicates, and Love explicates, the plot,—may it not be that *As You Like It* is a Divine morality as well as a charming play? In these words: 'As ye would that men should do to you, do ye also to them likewise,' the Supreme Parablist states the law of life in its social relations; and may not the great dramatist, seeing the fine moral teaching underlying the heavenly maxim, have resolved to show, as in a magic mirror, a little bit of the Eden possible in the world, were the higher sympathies of its denizens ruled by the love commended to us by the wisdom of the incarnated Lord of Life? On this ground we may regard Shakespeare as indicating his intention by the significance with which he renders into verse the saying: 'There is joy in the presence of God over one sinner that repenteth,' bringing out beautifully the fine *At-one-ment* which the following out of the Redeemer's precept, 'As you like it done to you, so do,' would effect in the lines: 'Then is there mirth in heaven When earthly things made even *At-one* together.'

26

DOWDEN (p. 76): Shakspere, when he had completed his English historical plays, needed rest for his imagination; and in such a mood, craving refreshment and recreation, he wrote his play of *As You Like It.* To understand the spirit of this play, we must bear in mind that it was written immediately after Shakspere's great series of tragedies. Shakspere turned with a sense of relief and a long ease-ful sigh from the oppressive subjects of history, so grave, so real, so massive, and found rest and freedom and pleasure in escape from courts and camps to the Forest of Arden.

(P. 80): Upon the whole, *As You Like It* is the sweetest and happiest of all Shakspere's comedies. No one suffers; no one lives an eager, intense life; there is no tragic interest in it as there is in *The Merchant of Venice,* as there is in *Much Ado about Nothing.* It is mirthful, but the mirth is sprightly, graceful, exquisite; there is none of the rollicking fun of a Sir Toby here; the songs are not 'coziers' catches,' shouted in the night-time, 'without any mitigation or remorse of voice,' but the solos and duets of pages in the wild-wood, or the noisier chorus of foresters. The wit of Touchstone is not mere clownage, nor has it any indirect serious significances; it is a dainty kind of absurdity, worthy to hold comparison with the melancholy of Jaques. And Orlando in the beauty and strength of early manhood, and Rosalind,—'A gallant curtle-axe upon her thigh, A boar spear in her hand,' and the bright, tender, loyal womanhood within,—are figures which quicken and restore our spirits as music does, which is neither noisy nor superficial, and yet which knows little of the deep passion and sorrow of the world.

Shakspere, when he wrote this idyllic play, was himself in his Forest of Arden. He had ended one great ambition,—the historical plays,—and not yet commenced his tragedies. It was a resting-place. He sends his imagination into the woods to find repose. Instead of the court and camps of England and the embattled plains of France, here was this woodland scene where the palm tree, the lioness, and the serpent are to be found; possessed of a flora and fauna that flourish in spite of phys-ical geographers. There is an open-air feeling throughout the play. . . . . After the trumpet tones of *Henry V* comes the sweet pastoral strain, so bright, so tender. Must it not be all in keeping? Shakspere was not trying to control his melancholy. When he needed to do that, Shakspere confronted his melancholy very passionately, and looked it full in the face. Here he needed refreshment, a sunlight tempered by forest-boughs, a breeze upon his forehead, a stream murmuring in his ears.

FURNIVALL (*Introduction to* The Leopold Shakspere, p. lvii): The picture is not painted in the same high key of colour as *Much Ado.* Instead of the hot sun of Beat-rice's and Benedick's sharp wit-combats, with its golden reds and yellows, backed by the dark clouds of Hero's terrible distress, we have a picture of greys and greens and blues lit through a soft haze of silvery light. Rosalind's rippling laugh comes to us from the far-off forest glades, and the wedded couples' sweet content reaches us as a strain of distant melody.

LADY MARTIN (*Blackwood's Magazine*, October, 1884, p. 404): When I resolved to make a thorough study of the play, I little thought how long, yet how fascinating, a task I had imposed upon myself. With every fresh perusal new points of interest and of charm revealed themselves to me; while, as for Rosalind, 'she drew me on to love her' with a warmth of feeling which can only be understood by the artist who has found in the heroine she impersonates that 'something never to be wholly known,' those suggestions of high qualities answerable to all the contingencies or trials of circumstance, by which we are captivated in real life, and which it is her aim and her triumph to bring home to the hearts and imaginations of her audience as they have come home to her own. Often as I have played Rosalind since, I have never done so without a fresh study of the play, nor without finding in it something that had escaped me before. It was ever, therefore, a fresh delight to bring out as best I could in action what had thus flashed upon me in my hours of meditation, and to try to make this exquisite creature as dear and fascinating to my audience as she had become to myself. In the very acting I learned much; for if on the stage you leave your mind open to what is going on around you, even an unskilful actor by your side—and I need not say how much more a gifted one—may, by a gesture or an intonation, open up something fresh to your imagination. So it was I came to love Rosalind with my whole heart; and well did she repay me, for I have often thought that in impersonating her I was able to give full expression to what was best in myself as well as in my art.

(P. 406) : To me *As You Like It* seems to be as much a love-poem as *Romeo & Juliet*, with this difference : that it deals with happy love, while the Veronese story deals with love crossed by misadventure and crowned with death. It is as full of imagination, of the glad rapture of the tender passion, of its impulsiveness, its generosity, its pathos. No ' hearse-like airs,' indeed, come wailing by, as in the tale of those ' star-crossed lovers,' to warn us of their too early ' overthrow.' All is blended into a rich harmonious music which makes the heart throb, but never makes it ache. Still, the love is not less deep, less capable of proving itself strong as death; neither are the natures of Orlando and Rosalind less touched to all the fine issues of that passion than those of ' Juliet and her Romeo.'

Is not love, indeed, the pivot on which the action of the play turns,—love, too, at first sight ? Does it not seem that the text the poet meant to illustrate was that which he puts into Phebe's mouth : ' Who ever loved, that loved not at first sight ?' Love at first sight, like that of Juliet and Romeo, is the love of Rosalind and Orlando, of Celia and Oliver, and of Phebe herself for Ganymede. The two latter pairs of lovers are perhaps but of little account, but is not the might of Marlowe's saw as fully exemplified in Rosalind and Orlando as in the lovers of Verona ?

(P. 435) : No word escapes from Rosalind's lips as we watch her there [in the last Scene, after the entrance of Jaques de Bois], the woman in all her beauty and perfect grace, now calmly happy, beside a father restored to ' a potent dukedom,' and a lover whom she knows to be wholly worthy to wield that dukedom when in due season she will endow him with it as her husband. Happiest of women ! for who else ever had such means of testing that love on which her own happiness depends ? In all the days that are before her, all the largeness of heart, the rich imagination, the bright commanding intellect, which made her the presiding genius of the Forest of Arden, will work with no less beneficent sway in the larger sphere of princely duty. With what delight will she recur with her lover-husband to the strange accidents of fortune which ' forced sweet love on pranks of saucy boyhood,' and to the never-to-be-forgotten hours when he was a second time ' o'erthrown' by the wit, the playful wiles, the inexplicable charm of the young Ganymede ! How, too, in all the grave duties of the high position to which his alliance will raise him, will he not only possess in her an honoured and admired companion, but will also find wise guidance and support in her clear intelligence and courageous will ! It is thus, at least, that I dream of my dear Rosalind and her Orlando.

[In the following extracts there is a rude classification of the judgements passed on the several characters, which is as exact, perhaps, as circumstances permit. In the preceding pages there are, of course, allusions to the different characters, but it has not been deemed possible to detach them from their context without injury.]

ROSALIND

MRS JAMESON (*Characteristics of Women*, 1833, vol. i, p. 141): I come now to Rosalind, whom I should have ranked before Beatrice, inasmuch as the greater degree of her sex's softness and sensibility, united with equal wit and intellect, give her the superiority as a woman; but that as a dramatic character she is inferior in force. The portrait is one of infinitely more delicacy and variety, but of less strength and depth. . . . .

(P. 145): Though Rosalind is a princess, she is a princess of Arcady; and notwithstanding the charming effect produced by her first scenes, we scarcely ever think of her with a reference to them, or associate her with a court and the artificial appendages of her rank. She was not made to 'lord it o'er a fair mansion' and take state upon her like the all-accomplished Portia; but to breathe the free air of heaven and frolic among green leaves. She was not made to stand the siege of daring profligacy, and oppose high action and high passion to the assaults of adverse fortune, like Isabel, but to 'fleet the time carelessly, as they did i' the golden age.' She was not made to bandy wit with lords, and tread courtly measures with plumed and warlike cavaliers, like Beatrice, but to dance on the green sward and 'murmur among living brooks a music sweeter than their own.'

Though sprightliness is the distinguishing characteristic of Rosalind, as of Beatrice, yet we find her much more nearly allied to Portia in temper and intellect. The tone of her mind is, like Portia's, genial and buoyant; she has something too of her softness and sentiment; there is the same confiding abandonment of self in her affections; but the characters are otherwise as distinct as the situations are dissimilar. The age the manners, the circumstances in which Shakespeare has placed his Portia, are not beyond the bounds of probability; nay, have a certain reality and locality. We fancy her a contemporary of the Raffaelles and the Ariostos; the sea-wedded Venice, its merchants and Magnificos,—the Rialto, and the long canals,—rise up before us when we think of her. But Rosalind is surrounded with the purely ideal and imaginative; the reality is in the characters and in the sentiments, not in the circumstances or situation. Portia is dignified, splendid, and romantic; Rosalind is playful, pastoral, and picturesque; both are in the highest degree poetical, but the one is epic and the other lyric.

Everything about Rosalind breathes of 'youth and youth's sweet prime.' She is fresh as the morning, sweet as the dew-awakened blossoms, and light as the breeze that plays among them. She is as witty, as voluble, as sprightly as Beatrice; but in a style altogether distinct. In both, the wit is equally unconscious; but in Beatrice it plays about us like the lightning, dazzling but also alarming; while the wit of Rosalind bubbles up and sparkles like the living fountain, refreshing all around. Her volubility is like the bird's song; it is the outpouring of a heart filled to overflowing with life, love, and joy, and all sweet and affectionate impulses. She has as much tenderness as mirth, and in her most petulant raillery there is a touch of softness: 'By this hand it will not hurt a fly!' As her vivacity never lessens our impression of her sensibility, so she wears her masculine attire without the slightest impugnment of her delicacy. Shakespeare did not make the modesty of his women depend on their dress, as we shall see further when we come to Viola and Imogen. Rosalind has, in truth, 'no doublet and hose in her disposition.' How her heart seems to throb and flutter under her page's vest! What depth of love in her passion for Orlando! whether disguised beneath a saucy playfulness, or breaking forth with a fond impatience, or half betrayed in that beautiful scene where she faints at the sight of the kerchief stained with his blood! Here her recovery of her self-possession, her fears lest she should have revealed her sex, her presence of mind and quick-witted excuse, and the characteristic playfulness which seems to return so naturally with her recovered senses, —are all as amusing as consistent. Then how beautifully is the dialogue managed between herself and Orlando! how well she assumes the airs of a saucy page, without throwing off her feminine sweetness! How her wit flutters free as air over every subject! With what careless grace, yet with what exquisite propriety! . . . .

(P. 149): The impression left upon our hearts and minds by the character of Rosalind—by the mixture of playfulness, sensibility, and what the French (and we for lack of a better expression) call *naïveté*—is like a delicious strain of music. There is a depth of delight, and a subtlety of words to express that delight, which is enchanting. Yet when we call to mind particular speeches and passages, we find that they have a relative beauty and propriety which renders it difficult to separate them from the context without injuring their effect. She says some of the most charming things in the world, and some of the most humorous; but we apply them as phrases rather than as maxims, and remember them rather for their pointed felicity of expression and fanciful application, than for their general truth and depth of meaning. . . . .

(P. 152): Rosalind has not the impressive eloquence of Portia nor the sweet wisdom of Isabella. Her longest speeches are not her best; nor is her taunting address to Phebe, beautiful and celebrated as it is, equal to Phebe's own description of her. The latter, indeed, is more in earnest. . . . .

(P. 154): Phebe is quite an Arcadian coquette; she is a piece of pastoral poetry; Audrey is only rustic. A very amusing effect is produced by the contrast between the frank and free bearing of the two princesses in disguise, and the scornful airs of the real shepherdess. In the speeches of Phebe, and in the dialogue between her and Silvius, Shakespeare has anticipated all the beauties of the Italian pastoral, and surpassed Tasso and Guarini. We find two amongst the most poetical passages of the play appropriated to Phebe, the taunting speech to Silvius, and the description of Rosalind in her page's costume: which last is finer than the portrait of Bathyllus in Anacreon.

FLETCHER (p. 225): We must suppose to be of Rosalind's own device that concluding 'wedlock hymn' which commemorates the principal one of the matters that form the main subject of this drama,—the grand comprehensive moral of which is, the eternal triumph of the genial sympathies and the social relations over every form of individual selfishness and misanthropy. No reader who shall have traced, with us, the course of Rosalind's feelings and deportment, through that first period of her fortunes when her heart is engrossed by sorrow for her father's banishment, and that second period when solicitude for her lover's requital of her affection, for his honour, and his safety, fills her whole soul and prompts her every sentence,—will need any further indication on our part to shew him how foreign to the anxiously active state of our heroine's heart and mind throughout is Mrs Jameson's notion, for instance, about her 'fleeting the time carelessly,' 'dancing on the green sward, and frolicking

among green leaves,' a notion which at once brings down the 'heavenly Rosalind' of
Shakespeare's fancy and Orlando's love to the level of a 'Maid Marian,' or, at most,
to a superior May-day Queen.   The same imperfect view of her character causes this
critic to speak in terms comparatively slighting of the intellectual development in
Rosalind.   She tells us : 'Rosalind has not the impressive eloquence of Portia, nor
the sweet wisdom of Isabella.   Her longest speeches are not her best,' &c.   But the
dramatist has placed her in no circumstances that at all admit, much less demand
from her, anything of that solemn declamation which we hear from Isabella and from
Portia.   Any such declamatory strain, so out of place, from her lips to any of the
individuals with whom she is brought into contact, would have testified, not in favour
of the strength and brightness of her intellect, but against them.   Neither is Rosalind any more inherently loquacious than she is declamatory ; she *never* talks merely
for talking's sake ; strong feeling or earnest purpose dictates her every syllable.

(P. 232) : The fundamental error of Mrs Jameson in appreciating this noble as
well as exquisite creation [Rosalind] seems to result from the mistaken attempt which
she makes to classify the characters of which she is treating as 'characters of intellect,' 'characters of affection,' &c.   Of all characters in fiction, those of Shakespeare
least admit of such classification,—their individuality is so inherent and essential,—
so analogous to that of actual and living persons.   This classifying notion has misled
Mrs Jameson into assigning too small a proportion to affectionate feeling in the character of Rosalind.   Mrs Jameson, indeed, commits too frequently, regarding these
Shakespearian personages, the error so often committed in real life, of taking some
prominent part of a character for the whole, or, at least, for a much larger portion of
it than it actually constitutes.   This too constant habit of estimating a given character
simply through looking at it from the outside, rather than by penetrating to its inmost
spirit, and then, as it were, surveying it from the centre, has been peculiarly fatal to
this pleasing writer's criticism of the more ideal among Shakespeare's female characters.   It would even appear to have made her overlook altogether the distinction
between his ideal women and his women of real life ; so much so, that among those
which she classes as 'characters of intellect,' she actually ranks Rosalind, not only
after Portia and Isabella, but even after Beatrice.

(P. 235) : The fundamental error in the established theatrical treatment of this
play has descended from that *Restoration* period of our dramatic history when, under
the ascendency which the restored court gave to French principles of taste and criticism, it was sought to subject even the great *ideal dramas* of Shakespeare to the commonplace classical circumscriptions of *Tragedy* and *Comedy*.   Here we have a signal
example of the perversion which must ever be effected by an endeavour to make the
principles of art subordinate to the distinctions of criticism.   This great, unique, ideal
play being once definitively set down upon the manager's books as a comedy in the limited sense, it followed, of course, according to theatrical reasoning, that the part of its
heroine was evermore to be sustained by whatever lady should be regarded, by distinction, as the *comic* actress for the time being.   Surely on this principle alone can it
have been (notwithstanding all her genuine comic powers) that either the figure, the
spirit, or the manner of a Mrs Jordan, for instance, was ever, not merely tolerated,
but relished and applauded, in her personation of the 'heavenly Rosalind'!   But the
managers have not stopped here.   When the comic actress of this part, as in the
instance just cited, possessed a singing voice, an occasion was to be furnished her of
displaying it, how much soever it might be to the contempt of Shakespeare and con-
sistency, and to the degradation of his heroine.   And so the 'cuckoo song' was taken

out of the mouth of Armado's page in *Love's Labour's Lost* to be warbled in the ears of her lover by the 'heavenly Rosalind.' This barbarism, however, it is due to Mr Macready to observe, was suppressed in the last Drury-Lane revival of this play. . . . .

(P. 237): The comparatively low popular notions respecting the character of Rosalind can be rapidly and thoroughly rectified only by a true Shakespearian actress, in the highest and most peculiar sense of the term. She must no more be either a tragic or a comic performer, in the limited and exclusive sense, than the *As You Like It* is a comedy, or *Cymbeline*, for instance, is a tragedy, in the narrow signification. Indeed, the power of competently personating Imogen affords of itself a far greater presumption of capacity for enacting Rosalind than is to be inferred from the most perfect performance of all the properly *comic* parts in the world. These are two of the noblest and most exquisitely compounded among the ideal women of Shakespeare, each the ascendant character in the drama to which she belongs. In both we find the same essential tenderness,—the same clear and prompt intelligence, —the same consummate grace and self-possession in enacting those masculine parts which the exigencies of their fortune compel them to assume. The deeper pathos and the graver wisdom which lend a more solemn though scarcely more tender colouring to the character of Imogen, seem hardly more than may be sufficiently accounted for by that maturer development which one and the same original character would receive from the maturer years, the graver position, and more tragic trials of the wife, in which the heroine of *Cymbeline* is set before us,—as compared with that early bloom, and those fond anxieties of youthful courtship, which we behold in Rosalind. Each, too, let us observe, is a princely heiress, bestowing her affections upon 'a poor but worthy gentleman.'

[Fletcher, who in his admirable Essays acknowledges his indebtedness at every step to Miss Helen Faucit (LADY MARTIN) for her living revelations of Shakespeare's heroines, quotes a striking sentence from *The Edinburgh Observer* (20th Feb., 1846) as follows: 'The secret of Miss Helen Faucit's excellence lies in her fine intuitions ' of human character in its most diverse aspects, and knowing that the deepest and ' most delicate sportiveness springs only from an earnest and sensitive nature, to which ' thoughtfulness and the capacity of strong emotion are habitual.']

HUDSON (*Introduction*, p. 19, 1880): It is something uncertain whether Jaques or Rosalind be the greater attraction; there is enough in either to make the play a continual feast; though her charms are less liable to be staled by use, because they result from health of mind and symmetry of character; so that in her presence the head and the heart draw together perfectly. I mean that she never starts any moral or emotional reluctances in our converse with her; all our sympathies go along with her freely, because she never jars upon them or touches them against the grain.

For wit, this strange, queer, lovely being is fully equal to Beatrice, yet nowise resembling her. A soft, subtile, nimble essence, consisting in one knows not what, and springing up one can hardly tell how, her wit neither stings nor burns, but plays briskly and airily over all things within its reach, enriching and adorning them; insomuch that one could ask no greater pleasure than to be the continual theme of it. In its irrepressible vivacity it waits not for occasion, but runs on for ever, and we wish it to run on for ever: we have a sort of faith that her dreams are made up of cunning, quirkish, graceful fancies; her wits being in a frolic even when she is asleep. And her heart seems a perennial spring of affectionate cheerfulness: no trial can break, no sorrow chill, her flow of spirits; even her sighs are breathed forth in a wrappage of innocent mirth; an arch, roguish smile irradiates her saddest tears. No sort of unhappiness can live in her company: it is a joy even to stand her chiding; for, 'faster than her tongue doth make offense, her eye doth heal it up.'

So much for her choice idiom of wit. But I must not pass from this part of the theme without noting also how aptly she illustrates the Poet's peculiar use of humour. For I suppose the difference of wit and humour is too well understood to need any special exposition. But the two often go together; though there is a form of wit, much more common, that burns and dries the juices all out of the mind, and turns it into a kind of sharp, stinging wire. Now Rosalind's sweet establishment is thoroughly saturated with humour, and this too of the freshest and wholesomest quality. And the effect of her humour is, as it were, to *lubricate* all her faculties, and make her thoughts run brisk and glib even when grief has possession of her heart. Through this interfusive power her organs of play are held in perfect concert with her springs of serious thought. Hence she is outwardly merry and inwardly sad at the same time. We may justly say that she laughs out her sadness, or plays out her seriousness: the sorrow that is swelling her breast puts her wits and spirits into a frolic; and in the mirth that overflows through her tongue we have a relish of the grief with which her heart is charged. And our sympathy with her inward state is the more divinely moved, forasmuch as she thus, with indescribable delicacy, touches it through a masquerade of playfulness. Yet, beneath all her frolicsomeness, we feel that there is a firm basis of thought and womanly dignity; so that she never laughs away our respect.

It is quite remarkable how, in respect of her disguise, Rosalind just reverses the conduct of Viola, yet with much the same effect. For though she seems as much at home in her male attire as if she had always worn it, this never strikes us otherwise than as an exercise of skill for the perfecting of her masquerade. And on the same principle her occasional freedoms of speech serve to deepen our sense of her innate delicacy; they being manifestly intended as a part of her disguise, and springing from the feeling that it is far less indelicate to go a little out of her character in order to prevent any suspicion of her sex, than it would be to hazard such a suspicion by keeping strictly within her character. In other words, her free talk bears much the same relation to her character as her dress does to her person, and is therefore becoming to her even on the score of feminine modesty.—Celia appears well worthy of a place beside her whose love she shares and repays. Instinct with the soul of moral beauty and female tenderness, the friendship of these more-than-sisters ' mounts to the seat of grace within the mind.'

JAQUES

HAZLITT (p. 306, 1817): Jaques is the only purely contemplative character in Shakespeare. He thinks, and does nothing. His whole occupation is to amuse his mind, and he is totally regardless of his body and his fortunes. He is the prince of philosophical idlers; his only passion is thought; he sets no value on anything but as it serves as food for reflection. . . . . He resents Orlando's passion for Rosalind as some disparagement of his own passion for abstract truth; and leaves the Duke, as soon as he is restored to his sovereignty, to seek his brother out who has quitted it and turned hermit.

SKOTTOWE (p. 346): Jaques, the melancholy-loving Jaques, is broadly distinguished from the common misanthrope, who, disclaiming the sympathies of humanity, in pride or in revenge, mocks at the misfortunes and rails at the pursuits of his fellow-creatures; for the disposition of Jaques is amiable, gentle, and humane. He regards the world, indeed, with a jaundiced and discontented eye; he depreciates its pleasures and undervalues its occupations, for he deduced the emptiness of both from his experience. He had been, it appears, a libertine, but his powerful and highly-cultivated mind revolted at slavery to his passions; the frivolity and monotony of dissipation disgusted him, and his high-toned moral principles triumphed over the grossness of sensual indulgence. The only legitimate pursuit of life he found to be virtue; and the truth which he deeply felt he studiously inculcates; it is the moral his sententious wisdom teaches; it is the weighty 'matter' of his sullen or melancholy musings; which, whether capriciously intruded, or naturally arising out of the passing incident, are at all times welcome and effective. There is weight and dignity about *As You Like It* altogether unusual in comedy, for which it appears principally indebted to the presence of the moralising Jaques, whose character is not only conceived with felicity, but is, throughout, supported with vigour and managed with inimitable tact. It may be partly accounted for on the principle of contrast, that the sombre reflections of Jaques heighten, rather than detract from, the effect of the high-wrought comedy of the play. But the cause of a result so unexpected, from a combination so unusual, lies somewhat more remote. It is to be found in that perfect harmony which the genius of Shakespeare established between the two distinct features of his subject. Had Jaques taken a saturnine view of the vices and follies of mankind, the spirit of comedy would have been damped by the gloom of his misanthropy. But the better feelings of humanity predominate in his bosom, and he never gives utterance to a sentiment which loses not its asperity in the dry humour or good-natured badinage which accompanies it. Nor is even the romantic character of this beautiful drama injured by the introduction of the sententious sage. With equal taste and judgement it is provided that the deep recesses of the forest, and the 'oak, whose antique root peeps out upon the brook that brawls along the wood,' should be the scenes whence Jaques inculcated his lessons of philosophy and morality.

MAGINN (p. 67): Who or what Jaques was before he makes his appearance in the forest, Shakespeare does not inform us, any further than that he had been a *roué* of considerable note, as the Duke tells him when he proposes to 'cleanse the foul body of the infected world' (II, vii, 67–72). This, and that he was one of the three or four loving lords who put themselves into voluntary exile with the old Duke, is all we know about him, until he is formally announced to us as the melancholy Jaques. The very announcement is a tolerable proof that he is not soul-stricken in any material degree. When Rosalind tells him that he is considered to be a melancholy fellow, he is hard put to it to describe in what his melancholy consists (IV, i, 11–20). He is nothing more than an idle gentleman given to musing and making invectives against the affairs of the world, which are more remarkable for the poetry of their style and expression than the pungency of their satire. His famous description of the Seven Ages is that of a man who has seen but little to complain of in his career through life. The sorrows of his infant are of the slightest kind, and he notes that it is taken care of in a nurse's lap. The griefs of his schoolboy are confined to the necessity of going to school; and he, too, has had an anxious hand to attend to him. His shining morning face reflects the superintendence of one—probably a mother—interested in his welfare. The lover is tortured by no piercing pangs of love, his woes evaporating themselves musically in a ballad of his own composition, written not to his mistress, but fantastically addressed to her eyebrow. The soldier appears in all the pride and swelling hopes of his spirit-stirring trade. The fair round belly of the Justice lined with good capon lets us know how he has passed his life. He is full of ease, magisterial authority, and squirely dignity. The lean and slippered pantaloon, and the dotard sunk into second childishness, have suffered only the common lot of humanity, without any of the calamities that embitter the unavoidable malady of old age. All the characters in Jaques's sketch are well taken care of. The infant is nursed; the boy is educated; the youth, tormented by no greater cares than the necessity of hunting after rhymes to please the ear of a lady, whose love sits so lightly upon him as to set him upon nothing more serious than such a self-amusing task; the man in prime of life is engaged in gallant deeds, brave in action, anxious for character, and ambitious of fame; the man in declining years has won the due honours of his rank, he enjoys the luxuries of the table and dispenses the terrors of the bench; the man of age still more advanced is well-to-do in the world. If his shank be shrunk, it is not without hose and slipper; if his eyes be dim, they are spectacled; if his years have made him lean, they have gathered for him the wherewithal to fatten the pouch by his side. And when this strange, eventful history is closed by the penalties paid by men who live too long, Jaques does not tell us that the helpless being, 'sans teeth, sans eyes, sans taste, sans everything,' is left unprotected in his helplessness.

Such pictures of life do not proceed from a man very heavy at heart. Nor can it be without design that they are introduced into this especial place. The moment before, the famished Orlando has burst in upon the sylvan meal of the Duke, brandishing a naked sword, demanding, with furious threat, food for himself and his helpless companion 'oppressed with two weak evils, age and hunger.' The Duke, struck with his earnest appeal, cannot refrain from comparing the real suffering which he witnesses in Orlando with that which is endured by himself and his 'co-mates.' Addressing Jaques, he says: 'Thou seest we are not all alone unhappy,' &c. But the spectacle and the comment upon it lightly touch Jaques, and he starts off at once into a witty and poetic comparison of the real drama of the world with the mimic drama of the stage, in which, with the sight of a well-nurtured youth driven to the savage desperation of perilling his own life and assailing that of others,—and of weakly old age lying down in the feeble but equally resolved desperation of dying by the wayside, driven to this extremity by sore fatigue and hunger,—he diverts himself and his audience, whether in the forest or theatre, on the stage or in the closet, with graphic descriptions of human life; not one of them, proceeding as they do from the lips of the *melancholy* Jaques, presenting a single point on which true melancholy can dwell. . . . . (P. 75): Jaques thinks not of the baby deserted on the step of the inhospitable door, of the shame of the mother, of the disgrace of the parents, of the misery of the forsaken infant. His boy is at school, his soldier in the breach, his elder on the justice-seat. Are these the woes of life? Is there no neglected creature left to himself, or to the worse nurture of others whose trade it is to corrupt— who will teach him what was taught to swaggering Jack Chance, found on Newgate steps, and educated at the venerable seminary of St Giles's Pound, where

> 'They taught him to drink, and to thieve, and fight,
> And everything else but to read and write'?

Is there no stripling short of commons, but abundant in the supply of the strap or the cudgel?—no man fighting through the world in fortuneless struggles, and occupied by cares or oppressed by wants more stringent than those of love?—or in love itself does the current of that bitter passion never run less smooth than when sonnets to a lady's eyebrow are the prime objects of solicitude?—or may not even he who began with such sonneteering have found something more serious and sad, something more heart-throbbing and soul-rending, in the progress of his passion? Is the soldier melancholy in the storm and whirlwind of war? Is the gallant confronting of the cannon a matter to be complained of? The dolorous flight, the trampled battalion, the broken squadron, the lost battle, the lingering wound, the ill-furnished hospital, the unfed blockade, hunger, and thirst, and pain, and fatigue, and mutilation, and cold, and rout, and scorn, and slight,—services neglected, unworthy claims preferred, life wasted, or honour tarnished,—are all passed by! In peaceful life we have no deeper misfortune placed before us than that it is not unusual that a justice of the peace may be prosy in remark and trite in illustration. Are there no other evils to assail us through the agony of life? And when the conclusion comes, how far less tragic is the portraiture of mental imbecility, if considered as a state of misery than as one of comparative happiness, as escaping a still worse lot! Crabbe is sadder far than Jaques, when, after his appalling description of the inmates of a workhouse, he winds up by showing to us amid its victims two persons as being

> '*happier* far than they,
> The moping idiot, and the madman gay.'

(P. 81): Shakespeare designed Jaques to be a maker of fine sentiments, a dresser forth in sweet language of the ordinary common-places or the common-place mishaps of mankind, and he takes care to show us that he did not intend him for anything else beside. With what admirable art he is confronted with Touchstone! He enters merrily, laughing at the pointless philosophising of the Fool in the forest. His lungs crow like chanticleer when he hears him moralising over his dial, and making the deep discovery that ten o'clock has succeeded nine and will be followed by eleven. When Touchstone himself appears, we do not find in his own discourse any touches of such deep contemplation. He is shrewd, sharp, worldly, witty, keen, gibing, observant. It is plain that he has been mocking Jaques; and, as is usual, the mocked thinks himself the mocker. If one has moralised the spectacle of a wounded deer into a thousand similes, comparing his weeping into the stream to the conduct of worldlings in giving in their testaments the sum of more to that which had too much,—his abandonment, to the parting of the flux of companions from misery,—the sweeping by of the careless herd full of the pasture, to the desertion of the poor and broken bankrupt by the fat and greasy citizens,—and so forth; if such have been the common-places of Jaques, are they not fitly matched by the common-places of Touchstone upon his watch? . . . . The motley fool is as wise as the melancholy lord whom he is parodying. The shepherd Corin, who replies to the courtly quizzing of Touchstone by such apothegms as that ' it is the property of rain to wet, and of fire to burn,' is unconsciously performing the same part to the clown as *he* had been designedly performing to Jaques. Witty nonsense is answered by dull nonsense, as the emptiness of poetry had been answered by the emptiness of prose. There was nothing sincere in the lamentation over the wounded stag. It was only used as a peg on which to hang fine conceits. Had Falstaff seen the deer, his imagination would have called up visions of haunches and pasties, preluding an everlasting series of cups of sack among the revel riot of boon companions, and he would have instantly ordered its throat to be cut. If it had fallen in the way of Friar Lawrence, the mild-hearted man of herbs would have endeavoured to extract the arrow, heal the wound, and let the hart ungalled go free. Neither would have thought the hairy fool a subject for reflections which neither relieved the wants of man nor the pains of beast. Jaques complains of the injustice and cruelty of killing deer, but unscrupulously sits down to dine upon venison, and sorrows over the sufferings of the native burghers of the forest city, without doing anything further than amusing himself with rhetorical flourishes drawn from the contemplation of the pain which he witnesses with professional coolness and unconcern.

It is evident, in short, that the happiest days of his life are those which he is spending in the forest. His raking days are over, and he is tired of city dissipation. He has shaken hands with the world, finding, with Cowley, that 'he and it would never agree.' To use an expression somewhat vulgar, he has had his fun for his money; and he thinks the bargain so fair and conclusive on both sides that he has no notion of opening another. His mind is relieved of a thousand anxieties which beset him in the court, and he breathes freely in the forest. The iron has not entered into his soul; nothing has occurred to chase sleep from his eyelids; and his fantastic reflections are, as he himself takes care to tell us, but general observations on the ordinary and outward manners and feelings of mankind,—a species of taxing which 'like a wild goose flies, unclaim'd of any man.' Above all, in having abandoned station, and wealth, and country to join the faithful few who have in evil report clung manfully to their prince, he knows that he has played a noble and an honourable part; and they to whose lot it may have fallen to experience the happiness of having done a generous, disinterested, or self-denying action, or sacrificed temporary interests to undying principle, or shown to the world without that what are thought to be its great advantages can be flung aside or laid aside when they come in collision with the feelings and passions of the world within,—will be perfectly sure that Jaques, reft of land and banished from court, felt himself exalted in his own eyes, and, therefore, easy of mind, whether he was mourning in melodious blank verse or weaving jocular parodies on the canzonets of the good-humoured Amiens. . . . .

Is the jesting, revelling, rioting Falstaff, broken of fortunes, luckless in life, sunk in habits, buffeting with the discreditable part of the world, or the melancholy, mourning, complaining Jaques, honourable of conduct, high in moral position, fearless of the future, and lying in the forest away from trouble,—which of them, I say, feels more the load of care? I think Shakespeare well knew, and depicted them accordingly.

W. W. LLOYD (Singer's Edition, 1856, p. 122): Jaques assuredly is wonderfully imagined; his recurring title is the melancholy Jaques, but his melancholy, as he intimates himself, is the most wondrously original. We hear that he has been a libertine, and he has seen too much of the worser side of the world and of mankind, and is not too hopeful of the world in any form; he gives a sour and saturnine picture of its people and their proceedings, and even of the course of nature's dispensations. His faith has received too severe a shock for it to be harmonised and braced again, even by the influences of the forest of Arden. But, perhaps, his restoration is merely proceeding. He can be already so far compassionate, as to weep while he makes satirical application of the sorrows of the sobbing deer; he can so far sympathise as to mightily enjoy the satire of Touchstone, and to come in merrily after the excitement and in high intellectual exaltation. Again, we find 'him merry, hearing of a song.' In his advances to Orlando first, and afterward to Rosalind, he seems to have a certain craving for sympathy, and to seek it among the young, but he gets no encouragement; and with these cheerful souls his despondency and censoriousness seem the habits of either a fool or a cipher, or a very abominable fellow. We may not unnaturally think that they do him injustice; the banished Duke found more matter in him than that; but those of his temperament may never hope to fare better from the young, the lovely, and who are moreover lovers. Still, I would fain put in a good word for the humorist, who, whether from his own fierce though now exhausted passions, or from the world's cold manners and hard treatment, has conceived a disgust for society as it is for the most part to be met with, will never venture deep into its treacherous waters, but is content to skirt the margin, within reach of retirement at any time, and the more crowded company of his own thoughts. Much of this temper remains with him to the last, but we see that, if little disposed still for cheerful sociability, at least the venom has left the wound that he bears with him, when the tenor of his parting speech evinces his recognition and belief of the practical reality in the Duke of patience and virtue deserving the happiest restoration, in Orlando of love and true faith, when he wishes good speed with a sympathy that is unaffected to the marriage blessings of Oliver and Silvius, and reserves his only barbed shaft for Touchstone, his companion, and ally, and fellow-satirist, and in more than one respect a representative of himself.

FRANÇOIS-VICTOR HUGO (*Introduction*, 1860, p. 62): Des critiques ingénieux ont comparé Jacques à Alceste. Mais Jaques n'est pas un misanthrope; il ne hait pas les hommes, il les plaint; s'il les censure, c'est par sollicitude, non par animosité. Ce ne sont pas les considérations mondaines qui le rendent hypocondre. . . . . La mauvaise humeur d'Alceste tient à des causes accidentelles; il a perdu son procès, il a été dupé par une coquette, il est né au milieu d'une société frivole, hypocrite et corrumpue, et de là son antipathie contre l'espèce humaine. Supposez qu'il ait gagné sa cause, qu'il se soit fait aimer de Célimène, et que tous les abus dénoncés par lui aient été réformés, sa misanthropie n'aura plus de raison d'être. Transportez Alceste dans le milieu où Shakespeare a placé Jacques, et il y a tout lieu de croire qu' Alceste sera satisfait. Pourquoi donc Jacques ne l'est-il pas? D'où vient que la république primitive établie à l'ombre de la forêt des Ardennes n'a pas désarmé son opposition? Comment se fait-il que le retour de l'age d'or n'ait pas apaisé ses murmures? Ah! c'est que le spleen de Jacques est produit par des raisons profondes. Ce n'est pas contre la société qu'il a des griefs, c'est contre l'existence. Ce n'est pas à l'humanité qu'il rompt en visière, c'est à la nature.

Ce qui attriste Jacques, c'est ce drame monotone dont une omnipotence anonyme a fait le scénario et que tous successivement nous jouons sur le théâtre du monde; c'est cette tragédie lugubre qui commence par des gémissements et qui finit par des gémissements, dont la première scène est une enfance 'qui vagit et bave au bras d'une nourrice,' et dont 'la scène finale est une seconde enfance, état de pur oubli, sans dents, sans yeux, sans goût, sans rien!'—Jacques a connu toutes les joies de ce monde, il a épuisé la jouissance, il a bu de la volupté jusqu' à cette lie captieuse, la débauche. Et d'une satiété aussi complète, il n'a gardé qu' une insondable amertume. Toutes nos délices terrestres n'ont réussi qu' à l'écœurer. La plus haute des émotions humaines, l'amour, n'est plus pour lui qu'un malaise moral. *Le pire de vos défauts*, dit-il à Orlando, *c'est d'être amoureux*. Et il se détourne avec une sorte de rage de ce jeune affolé.—Nos appétits révoltent Jacques autant que nos inclinations.

Il n'est pas jusqu' au plus frugal repas dont le menu ne lui répugne ; il s'indigne de cette voracité sanguinaire que peut seule apaiser une boucherie ; il a horreur de cette cuisine vampire qui ne dépèce que des cadavres. Quand le vieux duc s'en va quérir à la chasse son souper du soir, il faut entendre Jacques s'apitoyer ' sur ces pauvres animaux tachetés, bourgeois natifs de cette cité sauvage, que les flèches fourchues atteignent sur leur propre terrain ;' il faut l'entendre dénoncer la cruauté du noble veneur et ' jurer que le vieux duc est un plus grand usurpateur que son frère.' Ainsi les exigences mêmes de la faim ' navrent le melancholique Jacques.' Il critique la vie dans ses nécessités élémentaires ; il attaque, dans l'ordre physique comme dans l'ordre moral, la constitution même de l'être. C'est au nom de l'âme hautaine qu' il s'insurge contre cette double servitude imposée à l'homme ici-bas : le besoin et la passion. Il est incorrigible mécontent qu' aucune réforme ne satisfera, qu' aucune concession ne ralliera. Sa mélancholie superbe est le dédaigneux reproche jeté par l'idée à la matière, par l'esprit au corps, par la créature à la création.

The COWDEN-CLARKES (*Note on* V, iv, 201) : To our thinking the manner of Jaques's departure is in perfect harmony with his character throughout. We first see him bluff and churlish to Amiens, who sings at his request ; we see him full of churlish and affected avoidance of the Duke, who inquires for him ; we see him indulging in conceited and churlish rebukes upon vices that he himself had wallowed in to satiety ; we see him trying to disgust Orlando with his young and hearty love ; meddling in Touchstone's affairs with Audrey ; attempting to persuade the shepherd-boy, Ganymede, that assumed madness is wisdom ; and we now see him giving an ill-natured fling at the jester's choice of the country-girl, and morosely declining to witness the wedding festivities,—affected and churlish from first to last. The fact is, Jaques has always been taken for what he professes to be,—a moralist ; but looked at as the Duke demonstrates him to be, and as Shakespeare has subtly drawn him, he is a mere lip-deep moraliser, a dealer in moral precepts, a morality-monger.

DOWDEN (p. 77) : Of real melancholy there is none in the play ; for the melancholy of Jaques is not grave and earnest, but sentimental, a self-indulgent humour, a petted foible of character, melancholy prepense and cultivated. . . . . Jaques has been no more than a curious experimenter in libertinism, for the sake of adding an experience of madness and folly to the store of various superficial experiences which constitute his unpractical foolery of wisdom. The haunts of sin have been visited as a part of his travel. By and by he will go to the usurping Duke who has put on a religious life, because ' out of these convertites there is much matter to be heard and learned.'

Jaques died, we know not how, or when, or where ; but he came to life again a century later, and appeared in the world as an English clergyman ; we need stand in no doubt as to his character, for we all know him under his later name of Lawrence Sterne. Mr Yorick made a mistake about his family tree ; he came not out of the play of *Hamlet*, but out of *As You Like It*. In Arden he wept and moralised over the wounded deer ; and at Namport his tears and sentiment gushed forth for the dead donkey. Jaques knows no bonds that unite him to any living thing. He lives upon novel, curious, and delicate sensations. He seeks the delicious *imprévu* so loved and studiously sought for by that perfected French egotist, Henri Beyle. . . . . Falstaff supposed that by infinite play of wit, and inexhaustible resource of a genius creative of splendid mendacity, he could coruscate away the facts of life, and always remain master of the situation by giving it a clever turn in the idea or by playing over it with an arabesque of arch waggery. . . . . Jaques in his own way supposes that he can dispense with realities. The world, not as it is, but as it mirrors itself in his own mind, which gives to each object a humourous distortion,—this is what alone interests Jaques. Shakspere would say to us : ' This egoistic, contemplative, unreal manner of treating life is only a delicate kind of foolery. Real knowledge of life can never be acquired by the curious seeker for experiences.' But this Shakspere says in his non-hortatory, undogmatic way.

FURNIVALL (*Introduction to* The Leopold Shakspere, p. lviii) : Jaques, ' compact of jars,' is always getting out of bed on the wrong side every morning and taking the world the wrong way. . . . . He has been a libertine, is soured, and like the rascal Don John in *Much Ado,* he hides his bad nature under the cloak of seeming honesty of plain-speaking. His mission is to set everything to rights ; but God forbid *he* should take the trouble to act. He wants liberty only to blow on whom he pleases ; he abuses everybody, moralises, weeps sentimentally, and is a kind of mixture of Carlyle in his bad Latter-day-Pamphlets mood, and water, with none of the grand positiveness of our Victorian biographer, historian, and moralist. Look at his philosophy of man's life, and what poor stuff it is ! Macbeth, the murderer, repeats it ; to them both, men and women are but players.

A. O. KELLOGG (*Shakespeare's Delineations of Insanity,* &c. 1866, p. 87) : Those who have carefully observed the phenomena of mind as warped by the more delicate shades of disease,—shades so delicate perhaps as to be scarcely recognised by the ordinary observer,—must have remarked that in certain cases there are mental conditions which appear at first sight almost incompatible and contradictory. This is most frequently illustrated in those mild, but nevertheless marked, cases of incipient melancholia, underlying which may frequently be found a vein or substratum of genuine humour ; so that the expression ' wrapped in a most humorous sadness ' is neither contradictory nor by any means paradoxical. . . . . Shakespeare, who observed everything, has furnished us some notable examples, none more so, if we except Hamlet, than Jaques. In the character of Jaques it is very evident that Shakespeare intended to represent a certain delicate shade of incipient melancholia. . . . . The melancholy of Jaques is not so much a fixed condition of disease as the gradual ingravescence of the melancholic state. . . . . After a careful examination of him, we confess our inability to discover anything more really morbid in his mental or moral organization than what is glanced at above as belonging to the initiatory stage of the disease. . . . . His character contrasts most favourably with that of the Duke, who indulges in the grossest personalities toward him, and thereby shows that if the one is the nobleman, the other is, in this respect, much more the gentleman. When Jaques asks, ' What, for a counter, would I do but good ?' the Duke replies in a tirade of most ungentlemanly personalities, and the way these are received and replied to by Jaques is characteristic of him and highly creditable to his temper and disposition. How charmingly he eschews all personalities, and a disposition to injure the feelings of individuals in his innocent railings, in his reply to the coarse railings and gross personalities of the Duke !

HUDSON (*Introduction,* p. 18, 1880) : *Jaques the Juicy.* Jaques is, I believe, an universal favourite, as, indeed, he well may be, for he is certainly one of the Poet's happiest conceptions. Without being at all unnatural, he has an amazing fund of peculiarity. Enraptured out of his senses at the voice of a song; thrown into a paroxysm of laughter at the sight of the motley-clad and motley-witted Fool; and shedding the twilight of his merry-sad spirit over all the darker spots of human life and character, he represents the abstract and sum-total of an utterly useless, yet perfectly harmless, man, seeking wisdom by abjuring its first principle. An odd choice mixture of reality and affectation, he does nothing but think, yet avowedly thinks to no purpose; or rather thinking is with him its own end. On the whole, if in Touchstone there is much of the philosopher in the Fool, in Jaques there is not less of the fool in the philosopher; so that Ulrici is not so wide of the mark in calling them 'two fools.' Jaques is equally wilful, too, with Touchstone, in his turn of thought and speech, though not so conscious of it; and as he plays his part more to please himself, so he is proportionably less open to the healing and renovating influences of Nature. We cannot justly affirm, indeed, that 'the soft blue sky did never melt into his heart,' as Wordsworth says of his Peter Bell; but he shows more of resistance than all the other persons to the poetries and eloquences of the place. Tears are a great luxury to him; he sips the cup of woe with all the gust of an epicure. Still, his temper is by no means sour; fond of solitude, he is, nevertheless, far from being unsocial. The society of good men, provided they be in adversity, has great charms for him. He likes to be with those who, though deserving the best, still have the worst; virtue wronged, buffeted, oppressed, is his special delight, because such moral discrepancies offer the most salient points to his cherished meditations. He himself enumerates nearly all the forms of melancholy except his own, which I take to be the melancholy of self-love. And its effect in his case is not unlike that of Touchstone's art; inasmuch as he greatly delights to see things otherwise than as they really are, and to make them speak out some meaning that is not in them; that is, their plain and obvious sense is not to his taste. Nevertheless, his melancholy is grateful, because free from any dash of malignity. His morbid habit of mind seems to spring from an excess of generative virtue. And how racy and original is everything that comes from him! as if it bubbled up from the centre of his being; while his perennial fulness of matter makes his company always delightful. The Duke loves especially to meet him in his 'sullen fits,' because then he overflows with his most idiomatic humour. After all, the worst that can be said of Jaques is, that the presence of men who are at once fortunate and deserving corks him up; which may be only another way of saying that he cannot open out and run over save where things are going wrong.

MACDONALD (*The Imagination*, 1883, p. 109): But what do we know about the character of Shakespeare? How can we tell the inner life of a man who has uttered himself in dramas, in which of course it is impossible that he should ever speak in his own person? No doubt he may speak his own sentiments through the mouths of many of his persons; but how are we to know in what cases he does so? At least we may assert, as a self-evident negative, that a passage treating of a wide question put into the mouth of a person despised and rebuked by the best characters in the play is not likely to contain any cautiously formed and cherished opinion of the dramatist. At first sight this may seem almost a truism; but we have only to remind our readers that one of the passages oftenest quoted with admiration is 'The Seven Ages of Man,' a passage full of inhuman contempt for humanity and unbelief in its destiny, in which not one of the seven ages is allowed to pass over its poor sad stage without a sneer; and that this passage is given by Shakespeare to the *blasé* sensualist Jaques, a man who, the good and wise Duke says, has been as vile as it is possible for man to be,—so vile that it would be an additional sin in him to rebuke sin; a man who never was capable of seeing what is good in any man, and hates men's vices *because* he hates themselves, seeing in them only the reflex of his own disgust. Shakespeare knew better than to say that all the world is a stage, and all the men and women merely players. He had been a player himself, but only on the stage; Jaques had been a player where he ought to have been a true man. The whole of his account of human life is contradicted and exposed at once by the entrance, the very moment when he had finished his wicked burlesque, of Orlando, the young master, carrying Adam, the old servant, upon his back. The song that immediately follows, sings true: 'Most friendship is feigning, most loving mere folly.' But between the *all* of Jaques and the *most* of the song, there is just the difference between earth and hell.—Of course, both from a literary and dramatic point of view, *The Seven Ages* is perfect.

CELIA

CHARLES COWDEN-CLARKE (p. 51): The whole of this 'love at first sight' on Celia's part is managed with Shakespeare's masterly skill. I have always felt those three little speeches to be profoundly true to individual nature, where the ladies are questioning Oliver respecting the incident of the lioness and the snake in the forest, and of Orlando's timely succour. Celia exclaims, in amazement, 'Are you his brother?' Rosalind says, 'Was it you he *rescued?*' And Celia rejoins, 'Was 't *you* that did so oft contrive to kill him?' Celia's first exclamation is surprised concern to find that this stranger, who interests her, is that unnatural brother of whom she had heard. Rosalind's thought is of her lover,—Orlando's *generosity* in rescuing one who has behaved so unnaturally towards himself; while Celia recurs to the difficulty she has in reconciling the image of one who has acted basely and cruelly with him she sees before her—who is speedily becoming to her the impersonation of all that is attractive, estimable, and lovable in man. Her affectionate nature cannot persuade itself to believe this villainy of him; she, therefore, incredulously reiterates, 'Was 't YOU that did so oft contrive to kill him?' And his reply is a beautiful evidence of the sweetness which beams transparent in her; since it already influences him, by effecting a confirmation of the virtuous resolves to which his brother's generosity has previously given rise, and by causing him to fall as suddenly in love with her as she with him. He says:

> ' 'Twas I; but 'tis not I;—I do not shame
> To tell you what I was, since my conversion
> So sweetly tastes, being the thing I am.'

It is one of the refined beauties that distinguish Shakespeare's metaphysical philosophy, to show us how a fine nature acting upon an inferior one through the subtle agency of love, operates beneficially to elevate and purify. At one process it proclaims its own excellence, and works amelioration in another. Celia's charm of goodness wins the unkind brother of Orlando (Oliver) to a passionate admiration of herself, at the same time that it excites *his* emulation to become worthy of her. It begins by teaching him the bravery of a candid avowal of his crime,—the first step towards reformation. Celia's loving-kindness, like all true loving-kindness, hath this twofold virtue and grace: it no less benefits her friends than adorns herself.

27

TOUCHSTONE

HAZLITT (p. 308, 1817): Touchstone is not in love, but he will have a mistress as a subject for the exercise of his grotesque humour and to show his contempt for the passion by his indifference about the person. He is a rare fellow. He is a mixture of the ancient cynic philosopher with the modern buffoon, and turns folly into wit, and wit into folly, just as the fit takes him. His courtship of Audrey not only throws a degree of ridicule on the state of wedlock itself, but he is equally an enemy to the prejudices of opinion in other respects. The lofty tone of enthusiasm which the Duke and his companions in exile spread over the stillness and solitude of a country life receives a pleasant shock from Touchstone's sceptical determination of the question in his reply to Corin, III, ii, 14–22. Zimmerman's celebrated work on *Solitude* discovers only *half* the sense of this passage.

GERMAN CRITICISMS

A. W. SCHLEGEL (*Lectures on Dramatic Literature*, trans. by Black, 1815, vol. ii, p. 172): It would be difficult to bring the contents of *As You Like It* within the compass of an ordinary relation: nothing takes place, or rather what does take place is not so essential as what is said; even what may be called the dénouement is brought about in a pretty arbitrary manner. Whoever perceives nothing but what is capable of demonstration will hardly be disposed to allow that it has any plan at all. Banishment and flight have assembled together in the Forest of Arden a singular society: a Duke dethroned by his brother, and, with his faithful companions in misfortune, living in the wilds on the produce of the chase; two disguised princesses, who love each other with a sisterly affection; a witty court fool; lastly, the native inhabitants of the forest, ideal and natural shepherds and shepherdesses. These lightly-sketched figures pass along in the most diversified succession; we see always the shady dark-green landscape in the background, and breathe in imagination the fresh air of the forest. The hours are here measured by no clocks, no regulated recurrence of duty or toil; they flow on unnumbered in voluntary occupation or fanciful idleness, to which every one addicts himself according to his humour or disposition; and this unlimited freedom compensates all of them for the lost conveniences of life. One throws himself down solitarily under a tree, and indulges in melancholy reflections on the changes of fortune, the falsehood of the world, and the self-created torments of social life; others make the woods resound with social and festive songs to the accompaniment of their horns. Selfishness, envy, and ambition have been left in the city behind them; of all the human passions, love alone has found an entrance into this wilderness, where it dictates the same language to the simple shepherd and the chivalrous youth, who hangs his love-ditty to a tree. A prudish shepherdess falls instantaneously in love with Rosalind, disguised in man's apparel; the latter sharply reproaches her with her severity to her poor lover, and the pain of refusal, which she at length feels from her own experience, disposes her to compassion and requital. The fool carries his philosophical contempt of external show and his raillery of the illusion of love so far, that he purposely seeks out the ugliest and simplest country wench for a mistress. Throughout the whole picture it seems to have been the intention of the poet to show that nothing is wanted to call forth the poetry which has its dwelling in nature and the human mind, but to throw off all artificial constraint and restore both to their native liberty. In the progress of the piece itself the visionary carelessness of such an existence is expressed; it has even been alluded to by Shakespeare in the title. Whoever affects to be displeased that in this romantic forest the ceremonial of dramatic art is not duly observed, ought in justice to be delivered over to the wise fool, for the purpose of being kindly conducted out of it to some prosaical region.

Gervinus (*Shakespeare*, 4th ed., Leipzig, 1872, i, 494): The sweetest salve in misery, so runs 'the golden legacy' of the *Novel*, is patience, and the only médicine for want is contentment. Misfortune is to be defied with equanimity, and our lot be met with resignation. Hence, both the women and Orlando mock at Fortune and disregard her power. All the three principal figures (or, including Oliver, four) have this fate in common, that to all their external misfortunes, to banishment and to poverty, there is added, as a new evil (for so it is regarded): love. Even this they strive to encounter with the same weapons, with control and with moderation, not yielding too much, not seeking too much, with more regard to virtue and nature than to wealth and position, just as Rosalind chooses the inferior (*nachgeborenen*) Orlando, and just as Oliver chooses the shepherdess Celia. It is in reference to this that the pair of pastoral lovers are brought into contrast: Silvius loves too ardently, while Phebe loves too prudishly. If this moral reflection be expressed in a word, it is Self-control, Equanimity, Serenity in outward sorrow and inward suffering, whereof we here may learn the price. That this thought lies at the core of Shakespeare's comedy is scarcely at the first glance conceivable. So wholly is every reflection eliminated, so completely is there, in the lightest and freest play of the action and of the dialogue, merely a picture sketched out before us.

Ulrici (*Shakespeare's Dramatic Art*, ii, 14, translated by L. Dora Schmitz, London, 1876): The general comic view of life is reflected throughout the whole play, and forms the foundation and platform upon which the action moves. . . . . The motives which set the whole in motion are merely chance, the unintentional encounter of persons and incidents, and the freaks, caprices, and humours, the sentiments, feelings, and emotions, to which the various personages recklessly give way in what they do and leave undone. Nowhere does the representation treat of conscious plans, definite resolves, decided aims and objects; nowhere do we find preconsidered or, in fact, deeper, motives proceeding from the inmost nature of the characters. The characters themselves, even though clearly and correctly delineated, are generally drawn in light, hurried outlines, but are full of life, gay and bold in action, and quick in decision; they appear, as already said, either inconstant, variable, going from one extreme to the other, or possess such a vast amount of imagination, sensitiveness, and love for what is romantic and adventurous that their conduct, to a prosaic mind, can only appear thoughtless, capricious, and arbitrary; and such a mind would be inclined to call them all fools, oddities, and fantastic creatures (in the same way as Sir Oliver Martext, in the play itself, calls the whole company in the forest 'fantastical knaves.' [A doubtful interpretation.—Ed.]) And, in fact, all do exactly what and as they please; each gives him or herself up, in unbridled wilfulness, to good or evil, according to his or her own whims, moods, or impulses, whatever the consequences may prove to be. Each looks upon and turns and shapes life as it pleases him or herself. The Forest of Arden is their stage; with its fresh and free atmosphere, its mysterious chiaroscuro, its idyllic scenery for huntsmen and shepherds, it is, at the same time, the fitting scene for the realisation of a mode and conception of life as is here described. . . . . At court, in more complicated relations, in a state of impure feelings and selfish endeavours, [such a life as just described] would lose its poetical halo, its innocence and gayety, and become untruth, hypocrisy, injustice, and violence, as is proved by the reigning Duke, his courtiers, and Oliver de Bois. The point of the piece seems to lie in this contrast; but care had to be taken not to make it too pointed, not to make it a serious moral conflict. . . . . Shakespeare's intention—that is, the sense in which he conceived Lodge's narrative and transformed it into a drama, which, as I think, is clearly enough manifested in the spirit and character of the whole, as well as reflected in the several points—is concentrated, and, so to say, condensed in the second and more personal contrast in which the two fools of the piece stand to one another. They, and the unimportant figure of the shepherdess whom Touchstone chooses as his sweetheart, are the only persons whom Shakespeare did not find in Lodge's narrative, but freely invented. This addition, however, is in so far of great importance, as it alone gives the original subject-matter a different character and colouring, and, so to say, forms the ideal norm, which determines the other alterations introduced by Shakespeare. The two fools, by virtue of the contrast in which they stand to each other, mutually complete each other. The melancholy Jaques is not the fool by profession; he appears rather to be a comic character *par excellence;* but his meditative superficiality, his witty sentimentality, his merry sadness have taken so complete a hold of his nature, that it seems to contradict itself, and, therefore, upon a closer examination, distinctly bears the impress of folly, although it certainly is an original kind of folly.

(P. 20): He, Touchstone, the professed Fool, may frankly be declared the most rational person of the whole curious company, for he alone invariably knows his own mind; in regarding everything as sheer folly, he, at the same time, takes it up in the humour in which it must be understood.

F. KREYSSIG (*Vorlesungen*, &c., vol. iii, p. 237, Berlin, 1862): Shakespeare took for the subject of his drama the Pastoral Romance of Lodge, whereof the ruling idea is the contrast between the over-refined worn-out state of society and health-giving freshness of Nature. In the drama, however, both sides of the picture stand out clear and contrasted, and vague dissolving portraiture rises to plastic dramatic representation.

[In III, i, where Oliver tells the usurping Duke that he never lov'd Orlando, and the Duke answers, 'More villain thou.—Well, push him out of doors,' &c., Kreyssig exclaims, 'What a significant contribution to the Natural History of political tyranny is contained in this answer of the Duke?' and then adds:] Just as the earnest gravity of the dramatic action is here directed against moral principles, so, the whole piece through, the arrows of wit are aimed at the follies and weaknesses of the world of rank and fashion, the target for the merriment of the fool as well as for the acrid sarcasm of the misanthrope; and, if without bitterness, at least one and all of the healthier natures there turn their backs on it.

(P. 242): And on this dark background of life [*i. e.* all Touchstone's descriptions of court manners] which the Poet has drawn, not in lackadaisical whinings and taffeta phrases, but with the vigorous colours of reality, he has painted a picture of a simple, natural mode of life as bright and fresh as ever quickened the weary soul of a worn-out citizen at the very first breath of the woods and the mountains. Through these scenes, in praise of which all lovers of Shakespeare unite, is wafted the refreshing earthy smell of the woods and the vivifying breeze from the mountains. Like the outlaws of the popular ballad, like Robin Hood and his comrades, the exiled Duke and his faithful friends forget under the boughs of the Forest of Ardennes loss and vexation, envy and ambition, with care and sorrow in their train.

(P. 243): For vigorous natures, temporarily out of tune, the Poet offers a wholesome medicine throughout this airy romantic life, which, however, is not to be regarded as the sentimental ideal of a normal condition which has been overwhelmed and lost in society. What the shepherds and shepherdesses in conventional pastoral poetry really are (without intending to appear so), namely, fugitives from a false social condition enjoying for a while a sort of masquerade and picnic freedom—in place of such, Shakespeare gives us honest and true his romantic dwellers in the Forest of Ardennes. And this is the very reason why he catches the genuine tone of this careless, free, natural existence, which in the case of the ideal shepherds of the Spaniards, French, or Italians is cabined and confined by merely another form of artificial intercourse.

[After having described the effect of the last words of Jaques: ' out of these convertites there is much matter to be heard and learned,' and how ' with these words the supersubtle, travelling man of the world takes a fresh comfortless start for new studies in his barren knowledge,' Kreyssig goes on to say:] (P. 250): Thus here in a romantic Arcadia, the law of life prevailing in a well-ordered moral condition of society maintains its sacred rights. And while the genius of the British Poet, conscious of its aim, rises high above the conventional forms of the South which it had borrowed, many of the scenes of this comedy are transformed into a diverting parody of the sentimentalism of pastoral poetry.

GEORGE SAND'S *COMME IL VOUS PLAIRA*

GEORGE SAND'S adaptation, *Comme il vous plaira*, is another illustration of the impossibility of transplanting *As You Like It;* it takes even less kindly to French than to German soil.

By way of Preface to her adaptation George Sand gives a letter which she wrote to Régnier, explaining her aims. From the tone of this letter, so outspoken and enthusiastic in its admiration of Shakespeare, it is easy to see that wherein George Sand does not follow her original, it is through no lack of reverence, but that in all sincerity she endeavoured to adapt her version to the usages of her own country, or rather (to be more correct) to the fashion of the hour. ' Whilst Shake- ' speare,' she says (I quote Lady Monson's translation), ' abandoned himself to the ' passionate transports or the delicious caprices of his inspiration, he trod under foot, ' along with the rules of composition, certain requirements which the mind legiti- ' mately demands—order, sobriety, the harmonies of action, and logic. But he was ' Shakespeare; therefore, he did well if such ebullitions were necessary to the pour- ' ing out of the most vast and vigorous genius that ever pervaded a theatre.' It is the contrasts in Shakespeare, the high lights and deep shades, it seems, which, to a mind educated in the inflexible laws of the French drama, prove almost insurmountable barriers to a due appreciation of Shakespeare. ' By a strange inconsistency,' she says in another place, ' which appears incomprehensible, he placed the most divine grace and ' chastity side by side with the most startling cynicism; the gentleness of the angel by

'the fury of the tiger; and the most piercing sorrow in juxtaposition with untranslat-
'able conceits of reckless license.' George Sand, therefore, deemed it 'neither a
'profanation nor an outrage to clothe this Colossus in borrowed garments—rather it is
'a homage, rendered to the impossibility of finding robes of modern French fashion
'sufficiently grand and majestic for him.'

It would be easy enough to be flippant and to make merry over the cut of the very
modern French garments in which George Sand has here clothed the characters of *As
You Like It*. To her, as to the Germans, the wit and charm of heavenly Rosalind are
lost; the melancholy Jaques fascinates her, and he becomes the hero of the play, far
eclipsing all the rest. The treatment of such a comedy by such a woman, in our own
day, presents so curious a problem that it is, I think, well worth while to ponder over
a sketch, at least, of her version.

We must bear in mind that in this adaptation George Sand is simply what her
public made her. She merely interprets the demands of the day and speaks to
French ears. Under this inspiration, let us trust, rather than under what is genuinely
her own, the Forest of Arden is transformed into the *Faubourg Saint-Germain*.

In the opening scene, which is laid on a lawn before the Ducal Palace, with the
ring prepared for the wrestling, Orlando declares to Adam his determination to stay
and see the games and the court, but, above all, the fair Rosalind; Oliver enters
and a quarrel ensues, wherein some of Shakespeare's phrases are used, such as
Orlando's demand for his patrimony and reproaches for his ill-treatment. Oliver calls
Orlando 'jeune drôle,' and threatens him with a switch, which the younger brother
snatches and flings away, but which Adam picks up and respectfully returns to Oliver,
who calls him, as is in the original, 'old dog,' and goes out leaving Orlando in tears.
Jaques, who had entered during the quarrel and been a silent spectator, now comes
forward and asks for an explanation of the scene from Adam, with the suggestion
that it may have been a rehearsal for the games at hand;—this, Orlando resents, and
at last demands who Jaques is: 'Qui je suis?' replies the latter, 'Hélas! un homme
bien las de l'être.' 'Si vous avez le spleen,' rejoins Orlando, 'ne dégoûtez pas les
jeunes gens de vivre.' After some bitter comments by Jaques on that style of 'living,'
Orlando departs, having expressed his determination to try a fall with the champion
Charles. Adam then reveals to Jaques that he has recognised him as an old adherent
of the banished Duke, and begs to know if a place could be found at the banished
Duke's court for Orlando. Before this point is settled Rosalind, Celia, and some pages
enter, and Adam and Jaques retire. Celia begs Rosalind to be gay, but the latter
explains her melancholy by revealing her suspicions that her uncle by his recent ill-
treatment of her intends shortly to banish her. Celia assures Rosalind that when the
succession to the throne falls to her she will restore it all again to Rosalind; 'Oh!
j'en fais le serment,' she adds, 'et, si j'y manque, puissé-je devenir un monstre de
laideur!' Touchstone enters (here called Pierre Touchard), and the original is
somewhat followed in the story of the knight and the pancakes, but before it is
finished Rosalind catches sight of Jaques and Adam at the back, and gazes intently
at Jaques, of whose features she has a dim memory. Adam kisses Jaques's hand
and retires; Jaques comes forward, and asks Touchstone which of the two ladies is
the daughter of the Duke. Celia advances and replies:

Je suis la fille du duc qui règne. (*Montrant Rosalinde.*) Elle est la fille de celui
qui devrait régner.

Jacques. Madame, vous dites plus vrai peut-être que vous ne pensez.

Celia (étonnée de la brusquerie de Jacques). Ah! ami, que ne prends-tu le bonnet de ce fou? Tu sembles fait pour le porter!

Jacques. Je sais qu' à la cour, il faut porter ce bonnet pour dire la vérité. (*A Rosalinde, en allant à elle.*) Madame, je vous apporte des nouvelles de votre père.

Rosalinde. Mon père! Ah! parlez vite! et parlez beaucoup!

Jacques. Il m'a chargé de vous dire qu' il vous souhaitait un printemps aussi vert que sa vieillesse.

Rosalinde (allant à Célia.) Embrasse-moi, chère Célia, et Dieu soit loué! (*A Jacques.*) Est-il toujours dans son château des Ardennes, et compte-t-il y rester encore?

Jaques is able to assure Rosalind that her father is contented and happy; and then becomes himself the object of the ladies' curiosity. 'Je ne suis plus ce que j'étais,' he says, 'ne me cherchez pas dans vos souvenirs; mon nom a changé de sens comme tout le reste. Autrefois, ici, j'étais pour tous Jacques le viveur et le magnifique; aujourd'hui, on m'appelle, là-bas, Jacques le rêveur et le solitaire.' He promises to carry a letter from Rosalind to her father, and Celia, as she retires, says of him: 'Son œil est encore vif et beau; mais sa bouche est une tombe où le sourire est enseveli.' While Jaques is waiting for this letter he overhears Oliver and Charles plotting the death of Orlando at the wrestling, and has time only to warn Adam of it before the Duke and his court enter and take their places to witness the games, and Rosalind gives Jaques the letter. Orlando, despite Adam's agonised entreaties, insists upon wrestling, and is of course victorious. The Duke is angered at hearing his name. Rosalind gives him a chain. The Duke recognises Jaques, and trembles. After the games are over, and Celia, Rosalind, and Jaques are in conversation, Touchstone enters hastily and announces that the Duke's suspicion against Rosalind is again aroused, and that, having marked her interest in Orlando, and detected her in giving a letter to Jaques, is convinced that she is in a conspiracy against him, and that he has therefore banished her. The First Act closes with the resolution of Celia and Rosalind to fly to the Forest of Ardennes under the escort of Jaques and of Touchstone, whose thoughts, by the way, are always engrossed by eating and drinking.

The Second Act opens in the Forest of Ardennes with the Duke, Amiens, and lords. A fire is lit at the back for an improvised kitchen, and valets are unpacking hampers and dishes.

Le Duc. Voici le lieu choisi pour notre halte. (*A ses gens.*) Amis, servez-nous la collation sous ces arbres. (*Aux seigneurs.*) Si Jacques revient aujourd'hui, il saura nous retrouver ici. Puissé-je recevoir aujourd'hui des nouvelles de ma fille chérie et revoir la figure d'un ami fidèle! Et vous, mes frères, mes compagnons d'exil, ne vous tarde-t-il point d'entendre soupirer ou gronder notre philosophe mélancholique? . . . . Pour moi, plus il me gourmande, plus il m'intéresse, et c'est dans ses plus grands accès de misanthropie que je trouve du profit à l'entendre. J'aime alors à le contredire et à le critiquer pour l'obliger à parler davantage; car, au fond de ses récriminations contre le genre humain, je vois toujours briller l'amour du vrai et la haine du mal, comme les claires étoiles derrière les nouages sombres.'

Audrey appears bringing in 'le lait de ses brebis et les fruits de son verger,' whereupon the Duke is touched and thus addresses her: 'Sois toujours la bienvenue, ma pauvre enfant! Ma fille est à peu près de son âge; mais combien je me la représente plus grande et plus belle!' Touchstone enters, much to Audrey's alarm, and while demanding to have the Duke pointed out to him falls to eating whatever he can lay his hands on. At last he takes an apple with the remark: 'Je prends cette pomme pour philosopher sur le destin de l'homme. Ce fruit n'est-il pas son image? Que faisait cette pomme sur son arbre, et que va-t-elle devenir si je ne la mange? (*Il mords dans la pomme.*) C'est ainsi que, d'heure en heure, nous mûrissons, mûrissons; et puis d'heure en heure, nous pourrissons, pourrissons, jusqu' à ce que la mort nous croque et que la terre nous avale.'

Jaques enters with Rosalind, clad as a young boy. 'Jacques!' exclaims the Duke, 'et ma fille? ma fille?

Jacques. Voici une lettre d'elle.

Le Duc. Une lettre?

Jacques. Vous attendiez-vous donc à la revoir?

Le Duc (ouvrant la lettre). Helas! non . . . . Si elle est heureuse, ... qu'elle reste où elle est bien!

Jacques (à Rosalinde, qui est restée loin derrière lui, à mi-voix). Approchez . . . . et parlez-lui avec précaution.

Rosalinde. Ah! je ne saurais lui parler!

Le Duc (lisant la littre). Elle espère qu'un jour on lui permettra. . . . . Ah! si j'étais moins vieux, j'aurais plus de patience. (*A Rosalinde, qui met un genou en terre devant lui.*) Que veux-tu mon enfant? Es-tu le fils ou le petit-fils de quelque ami de ma jeunesse? Et, pour cela, on te persécute peut-être à la cour de mon frère? (*Jacques fait un signe affirmatif.*) Si tu cherches un refuge auprès de moi, sois le bienvenu. Mais ne compte pas faire ici une brillante carrière. Nous avons perdu la pompe de notre rang et trouvé une vie plus rude pour le corps, plus saine pour l'âme. Ces bois nous offrent moins de dangers que les palais, séjour de l'envie. Ici, nous n'avons à subir que la peine infligée à notre premier père, le changement des saisons et la nécessité de devoir notre nourriture aux fatigues de la chasse; mais, brûlé par le soleil ou surpris par la tempête, je souris parfois en me disant: "Il n'y a point ici de flatteurs, car voilà des conseillers qui me font sentir qu'un prince est un homme, et un homme est bien peu de chose! . . . ." Mais pourquoi pleures-tu, mon enfant? car je sens tes larmes sur mes mains! Mon sort t'effraye, et tu regrettes d'être venu le partager?

Rosalinde. Ah! je veux vivre près de vous, monseigneur; ne me renvoyez pas!

Jacques (souriant). Gardez-le près de vous; il vous servira bien.

Le Duc. J'y consens; mais qu'il me dise son nom et me montre son visage.

(*Rosalinde se relève. Il la regarde avec émotion. Elle n'y peut tenir et se jette dans ses bras.*)

Rosalinde. Ah! mon père! c'est moi!

Le Duc. Ma fille, ma Rosalinde! sous ce déguisement! (*Surprise et movement général.*)

Rosalinde. La crainte de vous surprendre trop vite me l'avait fait prendre en voyage.

There is general rejoicing, which is restrained within due bounds by Jaques, who repeats, as the sum of his travels, the Seven Ages. Orlando breaks in, demanding food for himself and Adam pretty much as in Shakespeare. Rosalind speaks to him, and in an *aside* Orlando exclaims, 'O puissances célestes! Rosalinde!' but, aloud, addresses Rosalind as 'Monsieur,' who in turn, in an *aside*, says sadly, 'Je croyais qu'il m'aurait reconnue!' While still in doubt as to the reception which the exiled Duke would give to his niece, Celia, the daughter of his enemy, it is considered advisable to keep Celia in concealment in an old castle belonging to Jaques. Much time is now devoted to the conversion of Jaques from a misanthrope to a jealous lover of Celia. In the midst of a conversation between Jaques, Celia, Rosalind, and Orlando, in which Rosalind, still in a page's dress, endeavours in vain to make Orlando tell the name of his love, Touchstone enters hastily, crying to them to save themselves and fly. In the attempt to comply they are met face to face by Charles the wrestler, who at the head of 'une petite escorte de Gens Armés' has been sent by Duke Frederick to bring back his daughter. Out of complaisance to Orlando, his former antagonist and vanquisher, Charles chivalrously and gallantly declines to seize Celia, and, with a grace snatched beyond the bounds of truth, tells his soldiers that the object of their search is not present, and then retires.

The first two or three Scenes of the Third Act are taken up with the love-making of Touchstone, Audrey, and William, with Jaques as the guide, philosopher and friend of all parties. Jaques manifests his increasing devotion to Celia by his exertions to furbish up his old mansion, and while thus occupied Orlando begs his aid in correcting some love-verses which he had composed, beginning: 'Bonnes gens, oyez la merveille! L'Amour, petit comme une abeille, Est venu cacher dans mon cœur Et son venin et sa douceur,' &c. Celia enters, and by her coquetry with Orlando so stirs Jaques's jealousy that nothing less than an appeal to the duello will satisfy Jaques, convinced as he now is that Orlando's verses were intended for Celia, who in vain tries to allay the storm. Rosalind enters, and at a word from her Orlando sheaths his sword; thereupon Jaques does the like, but Orlando is still too bashful to acknowledge that the verses were meant for Rosalind. The Duke enters and announces that his brother has repented and restored to him his dominions. Celia salutes Rosalind as 'ma princesse, ma souveraine! Je te vais prêter foi et hommage! mais tu permettras . . . . (*elle fait signe à Roland*) qu'un de ses amis prenne place à tes genoux.' Hereupon the Duke interferes, and in severe tones expresses his doubts as to Orlando's honesty, and commands Oliver to approach, who accuses Orlando and old Adam of robbing him of a sum of money before they left home, and of having threatened his life. Old Adam swears that the money was his own, and Jaques testifies to the plot on Orlando's life which he overheard Oliver and Charles devise. Thereupon, the Duke commands Oliver to be thrown from a high rock; a fine chance is now given to Orlando to show his magnanimity in pleading for his brother's life; and he improves it. Oliver is pardoned. Rosalind is given to Orlando. William eclipses Touchstone and carries off Audrey. Jaques declares that he will not leave the forest, but will bid them all farewell—he cannot follow them. Thereupon, Celia, who is left alone with Jaques, gently confesses that her heart is his:

Jacques. Célia! . . . . Non! vous raillez! je ne suis plus jeune! . . . .

Célia. Aimez-vous?

Jacques. Je suis pauvre, triste, mécontent de toutes choses. . . . .

Célia. Vous n'aimez donc pas?

Jacques (*transporté*). Ah! tenez! vous avez raison! Je suis jeune, je suis riche, je suis gai, je suis heureux. Oui, oui, le firmament s'embrase là-haut et la terre fleurit ici-bas! Je respire avec l'amour une vie nouvelle, et mes yeux s'ouvrent à la vérité! Qui? moi, mélancholique? Non! je ne suis pas un impie! Le ciel est bon, les hommes sont doux, le monde est un jardin de délices et la femme est l'ange du pardon . . . . (*il tombe à ses pieds*), si je ne rêve pas que vous m'aimez!

Célia. Il doute encore! . . . . Jacques, par les roses du printemps, par la virginité des lis, par la jeunesse, par la foi, par l'honneur, je vous aime! A présent, voulez-vous me quitter?

Jacques. Non, jamais ! car je t'aime aussi ! Oh ! la plus belle parole que l'homme
puisse dire : Je t'aime ! ....

Célia. Eh bien, puisque mon père n'est plus ni riche ni puissant .... puisque,
grâce au ciel, je puis être à vous, ... suis-moi !

FIN DE COMME IL VOUS PLAIRA.

ACTORS

BOADEN (*Memoirs of Mrs Siddons*, 1827, vol. ii, p. 166) : The Rosalind of *As You
Like It* had been a favourite character of MRS SIDDONS on theatres nearer to the Forest
of Arden ; and for her second benefit this season [1785] she ventured to appear upon
the London stage in a dress which more strongly reminded the spectator of the sex
which she had laid down than that which she had taken up. .... Rosalind was one
of the most delicate achievements of MRS SIDDONS. The common objection to her
comedy, that it was only the smile of *tragedy*, made the express charm of Rosalind,—
her vivacity is understanding, not buoyant spirits,—she closes her brilliant assaults
upon others with a smothered sigh for her own condition. She often appears to my
recollection addressing the successful Orlando by the beautiful discrimination of
Shakespeare's feelings : '*Gentleman*, Wear this for me,' &c., I, ii, 241 ; '*Orlando*' had
been familiar, '*young man*' now coarse. And, on the discovery that modesty kept even
his encouraged merit silent, the graceful farewell faintly articulated was such a style
of comedy as could come only from a spirit tenderly touched. .... MRS SIDDONS
put so much soul into all the raillery of Ganymede as really to cover the very boards
of the stage. She seemed indeed brought up by a deep magician, and to be forest
born. But the return to the habiliments of Rosalind was attended with that happy
supplement to the poet's language, where the same terms are applied to different personages, and the meaning is expanded by the discrimination of look, and tone, and
action,—'To you I give myself, *for* I am YOURS.'

CAMPBELL (*Life of Mrs Siddons*, 1834, vol. ii, p. 68) : The new character which
she performed [30 April, 1785] was that of Rosalind. After a successful transition
from the greatest to the gentlest parts of tragedy, it would have been but one step
further, in the versatility of genius, to have been at home in the enchanting Rosalind ; and as the character, though comic, is not broadly so, and is as romantic and
poetical as anything in tragedy, I somewhat grudgingly confess my belief that her
performance of it, though not a failure, seems to have fallen equally short of a triumph. It appears that she played the part admirably in some particulars. But,
altogether, Rosalind's character has a gay and feathery lightness of spirits which
one can easily imagine more difficult for MRS SIDDONS to assume than the tragic
meekness of Desdemona. In *As You Like It* Rosalind is the soul of the piece ;
aided only by the Clown (and, oh that half the so-called wise were as clever as
Shakespeare's clowns !), she has to redeem the wildness of a forest and the dulness
of rustic life. Her wit and beauty have 'to throw a sunshine in the shady place.'
Abate but a spark of her spirit, and we should become, in the forest scenes, as melancholy and moralising as Jaques. Shakespeare's Rosalind, therefore, requires the
gayest and archest representative. In a letter from Mr Young, which I have before
me, he says, ' Her Rosalind wanted neither playfulness nor feminine softness ; but it

was totally without archness,—not because she did not properly conceive it; but how could such a countenance be arch?' Here alone, I believe, in her whole professional career, MRS SIDDONS found a rival who beat her out of a single character. The rival Rosalind was MRS JORDAN; but those who best remember MRS JORDAN will be the least surprised at her defeating her great contemporary in this one instance. MRS JORDAN was, perhaps, a little too much of the romp in some touches of the part; but, altogether, she had the *naïveté* of it to a degree that Shakespeare himself, if he had been a living spectator, would have gone behind the scenes to have saluted her for her success in it. ANNA SEWARD, who, though her taste was exceedingly bad in many points, had a due appreciation of our great actress, speaks of her as follows in the part of Rosalind: 'For the first time I saw the justly celebrated MRS SIDDONS in comedy, in the part of Rosalind; but though her smile is as enchanting as her frown is magnificent, as her tears are irresistible, yet the playful scintillations of colloquial wit, which most strongly mark that character, suit not the Siddonian form and countenance. Then her dress was injudicious. The scrupulous prudery of decency produced an ambiguous vestment, that seemed neither male nor female.' 'But,' MISS SEWARD adds, 'when she first came on as the Princess, nothing could be more charming, nor than when she resumed her original character, and exchanged comic spirit for dignified tenderness.'

THE SCOTSMAN :* Shakespeare has, in this character of Rosalind, left more to the creative genius of the actor than perhaps in any other of his female characters. Hence, the author and actor have not far from equal shares in the finished work; it is not merely that MISS FAUCIT, in her Rosalind, does justice to the reproduction of Shakespeare's creation; she completes and illuminates for us his conception. The singularly acute and subtle sympathy by which this complement is given to the work of the great dramatist, produces an effect like that of sunlight on some fair landscape,—beautiful before the delicate and generous light flows over it, but, after, glowing with the very perfection of theretofore unimagined loveliness. This exceptional partnership of author and actor imparts one of its great charms to MISS FAUCIT'S representation of Rosalind; there is so much of her own in it that we sometimes forget that there is in it anything not her own, and are brought back with a start to the remembrance that, after all, it is playing, and not real living and loving, that is going on before us. It may be a kind of conscientiousness of part-proprietorship in the character of Rosalind that in her representation of it heightens the always high finish, and refines the always delicate handling, which MISS FAUCIT bestows on her acting; certainly a more exquisite and graceful piece of dramatic art playgoers may fairly despair of seeing, and players of presenting. Even Shakespeare has given us no other such outline of an airy, romantic, sensitive female nature joined to great sprightliness, resolution, tenderness, and wit; and MISS FAUCIT'S filling in of this rare outline is perfectly harmonious. Not a word, or tone, or gesture jars upon us from first to last; nothing disturbs the ideal that, from Rosalind's earliest appearance, we represent to ourselves, but every touch adds new graces and new charms. Especially in the sudden mutations of mood and style that so frequently occur during the adventures of Ganymede in the forest, was the perfect congruity of MISS FAUCIT'S conception conspicuous; never by chance, in all these changes, did she show or hint in

---

* A newspaper cutting, undated, kindly sent to me by a correspondent. It certainly deserves preservation, if only for the two or three glimpses which it gives us of look, tone, or gesture in particular passages.—ED.

Rosalind aught that was not in harmony with everything that went before and was to come after. When, for example, after the mock marriage, Orlando is summoned away to attend the Duke, and Rosalind goes off in a fit of pouting and tears, the counterfeiting was so admirably done as to induce the momentary fancy that her character had broken down under the strain of self-denying deception. But in an instant a radiant smile, growing to a half-railing laugh, altered the whole current, and gave us back the arch yet earnest woman who overflows with gayety, because she has in her hand all that her heart desires, and can afford to torment herself by balking herself of it, because she is so sure of it. Another admirable touch of harmonising colour, so to speak, is conveyed in the partly involuntary and nervous laughter that the assumed Ganymede gives way to; with curious felicity expressing at once maidenly alarm lest her disguise should fail to screen her, and maidenly glee she can ill repress at the knowledge that the man she loves, loves her and is at her command.

THE GLASGOW CONSTITUTIONAL (17 February, 1847) : So prolific is MISS HELEN FAUCIT'S genius,—so entirely has she adopted and improved upon the conception of Shakespeare,—that above two-thirds of the charming image, which is painted indelibly on every mind which witnessed it, is entirely her own. It is quite Shakespearian, but it is not to be found in Shakespeare. Her pantomime would be nearly as effective if she never said a word. The step, the smile, the arch look, the exquisite playfulness, the uniform grace, the passing malice, and lasting kindness of heart, are all her own.

THE ART JOURNAL (January, 1867—cited by W. C. Russell, *Representative Actors*, p. 410) : Like all true artists, [LADY MARTIN] manifestly works from within outward. Whatever character she assumes has a truth and unity which could be produced in no other way. Consider her, for example, in *As You Like It*. It is clear that she has entered into the soul of Rosalind, nor realised that alone, but all the life of the woman and her surroundings as well. Rosalind's words, therefore, sparkle upon her lips as if they were the offspring of the moment, or deepen into tenderness as if her very Orlando were thrilling her heart with tones that are but faint echoes of her own emotion. All she says and does seems to grow out of the situation as if it were seen and heard for the first time. She takes us into Arden with her, and makes us feel, with the other free foresters of this glorious woodland, what a charm of sunshine and grace that clear, buoyant spirit diffused among its melancholy boughs. . . . . Her characters seem to be to her living things, ever fresh, ever full of interest, and on which her imagination is ever at work. They must mingle with her life, even as the thickcoming *fancies* of the poet mingle with his. As, therefore, her rare womanly nature deepens and expands, so do they take a deeper tone and become interfused with a more accomplished grace.

COSTUME

E. W. GODWIN (*The Architect*, 1 May, 1875) : This play refers distinctly to a time prior to the succession of Anne of Brittany, for her duchy was the last of the princedoms added to the crown by her marriage with the King of France. The time of the action, therefore, belongs to some period before the commencement of the sixteenth century, and the reign of Louis XI (1461–1483), contemporary with that of our Edward IV, is probably as late as we can safely place it. Architecture has very little to do with the scenery of this comedy. Indeed, there is no need of its introduction at all. The First Act gives: 1. An orchard near Oliver's house. 2. A lawn before the Duke's palace. 3. A room in the palace. Now there is nothing to call for any buildings in 1 and 2, and the 3d Scene may just as well be enacted on the lawn (2) as in a room. In the Second Act we have for the 2d Scene a room in the palace, occurring again in the 1st Scene of the Third Act. Both scenes are extremely short, and might be omitted without doing any violence to the conduct of the plot. So, too, the 3d Scene of the Second Act may be the same as the 1st of the First. And as all the rest of the action is in the Forest of Arden, there is really no need of any architectural scenery in *As You Like It*.

The costume of 1461–1483 was not so extravagant in France as it was in England. In the Court of Duke Frederick we should see doublets and gowns of silk velvet and cloth of gold; rich embroideries in Venice gold, chiefly of the net and pine-apple pattern; deep trimmings of fur or velvet to collars, cuffs, and skirts of Rosalind's and Celia's dresses; and various other things, [such as are required for the] plays of *Henry VI* and *Richard III*. But there are so many MSS of this time, especially in the Imperial and National Libraries in Paris, and their illuminations reveal so many different styles of toilette, that the power of selection to a certain extent and within certain limits is in our hands, and our decision in these matters must therefore be more or less influenced by the *physique* of the actor or actress. For the more we know of the costume of the past, the more satisfied we are that we can avoid, if we choose, those curiosities of dress where the ludicrous is predominant, and which, by arousing untimely laughter, interfere sadly with the dramatic action.

[Godwin has referred to the costume of the time of Edward IV as appropriate to this play, of which costume he wrote as follows in the same journal of 6 February:] Fashion in costume was now beginning that activity of life which is so acutely felt at present. Every new thing, no matter how inappropriate, provided only it were brought out in France, was sure to be received in England. Costly materials, such as silk, satin, velvet, cloth of gold, and fur of sables, were worn even by boys. Heavy chains of gold, and girdles of the same material and of silver gilt, were so common as to make it necessary to forbid the use of them, except to such persons as were possessed of 40*l*. a year. In 1464, Edward IV tried to govern the fashion by Act of Parliament, by which only lords had privilege of wearing the indecently short jackets or doublets hitherto worn by knights and squires. The pikes or points of the shoes and boots were limited to a length of 2 inches, excepting only those of the nobility, who had the privilege of wearing them from 6 to as much as 24 inches long. Stuffing of wool, or as we should call it *padding*, was used to such an extravagant degree by the fine young gentlemen of the period that their shoulders looked absolutely deformed. In the armour there is the same padded, bulging look which we recognise in the civil costume. . . . . The silk surcoat of earlier days was seldom or ever used, but instead of it they wore either a tabard of arms, as worn by heralds, or a long sleeveless cloak open at the sides. The costume of the ladies was as costly and extravagant as that of the gentlemen. The gowns had enormously wide borders of fur or velvet. Conical caps, as much as three-quarters of a yard high, were quite the correct thing; loose fine kerchiefs hung from the top of them, reaching nearly to the ground. One of these head-dresses, when bordered by wings, was known at the time by the name of 'butterfly;' and head-dresses of this kind, made of starched and wired lawn, may yet be seen in St. Lô, with the butterfly's wings and all complete as they were worn four centuries ago.

[In the costume of the time of Richard III there was very little change from that just described.] The embroidered pattern of this time was that composed of what was called 'the nett and pyne apple,' a decoration that seems to have been not only a great favourite, but a very long-lived one. For the head, men used hats of estate, the rolls behind and the beeks (peeks) before; little round caps or bonnets (*bonets*), with fur edging and a feather, something like a lady's modern pork-pie hat; and the cape with its hood. Top-boots, 9 or 10 inches higher than the knee and very long pointed toes, were commonly worn. The doublets and gowns were of satin, velvet, or cloth of gold lined with velvet, many of them being richly embroidered with personal badges or the fashionable pattern above mentioned. In the ladies' dresses we note first the disappearance of the tall head-gear, and in its place we see a reasonable caul or net of gold confining the hair at the back of the head, with a very fine kerchief stiffened into shape as in the preceding reign. . . . . On ordinary occasions the hair seems to have been worn loosely hanging over the shoulder, *au naturel*. It requires no wonderful wit to render such a costume eminently pleasing.

RICHARD GRANT WHITE (*Studies in Shakespeare*, 1886, p. 242): It would seem as if all the Rosalinds—all of them—laid themselves out to defy both Shakespeare and common sense in this matter [of costume] to the utmost of attainable possibility. When they come before us as Ganymede, they dress themselves not only as no man or boy in England, but as no human creature within the narrow seas, was dressed in Shakespeare's time. Instead of a doublet, they don a kind of short tunic, girdled at the waist and hanging to the knee. They wear long stockings, generally of silk, imagining them to be hose, and ignorant, probably, that in Shakespeare's time there were not a dozen pair of silk hose in all England. Nevertheless, they go about with nothing but light silk stockings upon their legs amid the underwood and brambles of the Forest of Arden. With some appreciation of this absurdity, one distinguished actress in this part wears long buttoned gaiters, which are even more anachronistic than the silk stockings. Upon their heads they all of them, without exception, wear a sort of hat which was unknown to the masculine head in the days of Elizabeth and James,—a low-crowned, broad-brimmed something, more like what is known to ladies of late years as a 'Gainsborough' than anything else that has been named by milliners. If a man had appeared in the streets of London at that day in such a hat, he would have been hooted at by all the 'prentices in Eastcheap. There was not in all the Forest of Arden a wolf or a bear, of the slightest pretension to fashion, that would not have howled at the sight of such a head-gear. Briefly, the Rosalinds of the stage are pretty impossible monsters, unlike anything real that ever was seen, unlike anything that could have been accepted by their lovers for what they pretend to be, and particularly unlike that which Shakespeare intended that they should be.

Let us see what Shakespeare did intend his Rosalind to be when she was in the Forest of Arden. . . . . Plainly, when the young princesses set forth on their wild adventure they did all that they could to conceal the feminine beauty of their faces. Celia puts herself in the dress of a woman of the lower classes. Rosalind assumes not merely the costume of a young man, but that of a martial youth, almost of a swashbuckler. She says that she will have 'a swashing and a martial outside,' as well as carry a boar-spear in her hand and have a curtle-axe upon her thigh. And, by the way, it is amusing to see the literalness with which the stage Rosalinds take up the text and rig themselves out in conformity with their construction, or it may be the conventional stage construction, of it. They carry, among other dangling fallals, a little axe in their belts or strapped across their shoulders. But Rosalind's ' curtle-axe ' was merely a short sword, which she should wear as any soldierly young fellow of the day would wear his sword.

Thus browned, and with her hair tied up in love-knots, after the fashion of the young military dandies of that time, with her boar-spear and her cutlass, she would yet have revealed her sex to any discriminating masculine eye had it not been for certain peculiarities of costume in Shakespeare's day. There were the doublet and the trunk-hose. Rosalind, instead of wearing a tunic or short gown, cut up to the knees, should wear the very garments that she talks so much about, and in which I never saw a Rosalind appear upon the stage. A doublet was a short jacket with close sleeves, fitting tight to the body, and coming down only to the hip or a very little below it. Of course its form varied somewhat with temporary fashion, and sometimes, indeed, it stopped at the waist. To this garment the hose (which were not stockings, but the whole covering for the leg from shoe to doublet) were attached by silken tags called points. But during the greater part of Shakespeare's life what were called trunk-hose were worn; and these, being stuffed out about the waist and the upper part of the thigh with bombast or what was called cotton-wool, entirely reversed the natural outline of man's figure between the waist and the middle of the thigh, and made it impossible to tell, so far as shape was concerned, whether the wearer was of the male or female sex. Rosalind, by the doublet and hose that Shakespeare had in mind, would have concealed the womanliness of her figure even more than by her umber she would have darkened, if not eclipsed, the beauty of her face. This concealment of forms, which would at once have betrayed her both to father and lover, was perfected by a necessary part of her costume as a young man living a forest life : these were boots. An essential part of Rosalind's dress as Gany-mede is loose boots of soft tawny leather, coming up not only over leg, but partly over thigh, and almost meeting the puffed and bombasted trunk-hose. To complete this costume in character, she should wear a coarse russet cloak and a black felt hat with narrow brim and high and slightly conical crown, on the band of which she might put a short feather and around it might twist a light gold chain or ribbon and medal. Thus disguised, Rosalind might indeed have defied her lover's eye or her father's. Thus arrayed, the stage Rosalind might win us to believe that she was really deluding Orlando with the fancy that the soul of his mistress had migrated into the body of a page. This Rosalind might even meet the penetrating eye of that old sinner Jaques, experienced as he was in all the arts and deceits of men and women in all climes and countries. With this Rosalind, Phebe indeed might fall in love; and a Phebe must love a man.

Nor are the perfection of Rosalind's disguise and concealment of her sex from the eyes of her companions important only in regard to her supposed relations with them. It is essential to the development of her character, and even to the real significance of what she says and does. . . . . Rosalind, for all her soft, sweet apprehensiveness and doubt about Orlando's value of that which she has given to him before he had shown that he desired it, enjoys the situation in which she is placed. She sees the fun of it, as Celia, for example, hardly sees it; and she relishes it with the keenest appetite. If that situation is not emphasized for the spectators of her little mysterious mask of love by what is, for them, the absolute and perfectly probable and natural deception of Orlando, Rosalind lacks the very reason of her being. To enjoy what she does and what she is, to give her our fullest sympathy, we must not be called upon to make believe very hard that Orlando does not see that she is the woman that he loves; while at the same time we must see that he feels that around this saucy lad there is floating a mysterious atmosphere of tenderness, of enchanting fancy, and of a most delicate sensitiveness. Moreover, we must see that Rosalind herself is at rest about her incognito, and that she can say her tender, witty, boy-masked sayings undisturbed by the least consciousness that Orlando's eyes can see through the doublet and hose, which at once become her first concern, her instant thought, when she is told plainly that he is in the Forest of Arden. The perfection of her disguise is thus essential to the higher purpose of the comedy. Rosalind was fair; but after having seen her in her brilliant beauty at the court of her usurping uncle, we must be content, as she was, to see it browned to the hue of forest exposure and deprived of all the pretty coquetries of personal adornment which set so well upon her sex, and to find in her, our very selves, the outward seeming of a somewhat overbold and soldierly young fellow, who is living, half-shepherd, half-hunter, in welcomed companionship with a band of gentlemanly outlaws. Unless all this is set very clearly and unmistakeably before us by the physical and merely external appearance of our heroine, there is an incongruity fatal to the idea of the comedy, and directly at variance with the clearly defined intentions of its writer.

That incongruity always exists in a greater or less degree in the performance of all the Rosalinds of the stage. I can make no exception. In case of the best Rosalinds I have ever seen, the supposition that Orlando was deceived, or that any other man could be deceived, in the sex of Ganymede was absurd, preposterous. They all dress the page in such a way, they all play the page in such a way, that his womanhood is salient. It looks from his eye, it is spoken from his lips, just as plainly as it is revealed by his walk and by the shape and action of the things he walks with. That they should dress the part with female coquetry is, if not laudable, at least admissible, excusable. The highest sense of art is perhaps not powerful enough to lead a woman to lay aside, before assembled hundreds, all the graces peculiar to her sex; but surely no artist, who at this stage of the world's appreciation of Shakespeare ventures to undertake the representation of this character, ought to fail in an apprehension of its clearly and simply defined external traits, or in the action by which those traits are revealed. . . . .

(P. 256): All this may be very true, our gently smiling manager replies; but do you suppose that you are going to get any actress to brown her face and rig herself up so that she will actually look like a young huntsman, and play her part so that a man might unsuspectingly take her for another man? O most verdant critic, do you not know why it is actresses come before the public? It is for two reasons, of which it would be hard to say which is the more potent: to have the public delight in them, and to get money. It is in themselves personally that they wish to interest their audiences, not in their author or his creations. . . . . She must have an opportunity to exhibit herself and her 'toilettes;' especially both, but particularly the latter. And, O most priggish and carping critic, with your musty notions about what Shakespeare meant and such fusty folly, the public like it as it is. They care more to see a pretty woman, with a pretty figure, prancing saucily about the stage in silk tights and behaving like neither man nor woman, than they would to see a booted, doubleted, felt-hatted Rosalind behaving now like a real man and now like a real woman. To which the critic replies, O most sapient and worldly-wise manager, I know all that; and, moreover, that it is the reason why, instead of a Rosalind of Shakespeare's making, we have that hybrid thing, the stage Rosalind.

JOHNSON'S *LOVE IN A FOREST*

In 1723, CHARLES JOHNSON, who apparently relieved his mind after the duties of keeping a tavern in Bow Street by unbending it over Shakespeare, had influence enough with Cibber and with Wilks to induce them to bring out at Drury Lane, where it ran for six nights, his version of *As You Like It*, which he re-named *Love in a Forest*.

This version or perversion, with its monstrous jumble of plays, would have received no notice here, were it not that, curiously enough, it anticipates GEORGE SAND in devising a love-match and marriage between Jaques and Celia. JOHNSON's *Dramatis Personæ* will, of themselves, give a sufficient indication of the composite character of this hodge-podge: 'Jaques; Orlando; Alberto, the banished Duke; Adam; Oliver; Duke Frederick; Amiens; Robert de Bois; Le Beu; Charles, Master of the Duke's Academy; Rosalind; Celia; Pyramus; Wall; Moonshine; Thisby.'

GENEST (iii, 101) gives a synopsis of the play which is more than amply full, and is as follows:

Act First: The wrestling between Orlando and Charles is turned into a regular combat in the Lists,—Charles accuses Orlando of treason; several speeches are introduced from *Richard II.*

Act Second: When Duke Alberto enters with his friends, the speech about the wounded stag is very properly taken from the First Lord and given to Jaques; an improvement [*sic*] which is still retained on the stage,—in the next scene between the same parties, notwithstanding Touchstone is omitted, yet Jaques gives the description of his meeting with a fool,—much, however, of his part in this scene is left out very injudiciously, as is still the case when *As You Like It* is acted.

Act Third: The verses which Celia ought to read are omitted, and Touchstone's burlesque verses are given her instead,—when Orlando and Jaques enter, they begin their conversation as in the original, and end it with part of the First Act of *Much Ado*,—Jaques speaking what Benedick says about women,—when Rosalind and Celia come forward, Jaques walks off with Celia,—Rosalind omits the account of time's different paces,—Jaques returns with Celia and makes love to her, after which he has a soliloquy patched up from Benedick and Touchstone, with some additions from C. Johnson.

Act Fourth begins with a conversation between Jaques and Rosalind, in which he tells her of his love to Celia,—in the scene between Orlando and Rosalind considerable omissions are made, and Viola's speech, ' She never told her love,' &c., is inserted, —Robert (Jaques) de Bois brings the bloody napkin to Rosalind, instead of Oliver, who does not appear after the *First Act*,—Robert says that he (not Oliver) was the person rescued from the lioness,—that Oliver had killed himself, &c.—the Act concludes with the Second Scene of Shakespeare's *Fifth Act*, in which Rosalind desires all the parties on the stage to meet her to-morrow,—Jaques and Celia are made in some degree to supply the place of Sylvius and Phebe.

Act Fifth consists chiefly of the burlesque tragedy of Pyramus and Thisbe from *Midsummer Night's Dream;* this is represented before the Duke, while Rosalind is changing her dress, instead of Touchstone's description of the quarrel,—when Rosalind returns, the play ends much as in the original, except that Jaques marries Celia, instead of going in quest of Duke Frederick, and that the Epilogue is omitted.

[See also the notice in ' Music,' *post*, of a composition by HENRY CAREY, called *The Huntsman's Song*, introduced in *Love in a Forest*.]

28

MUSIC

Vnder the greene wood tree.

Act II, Scene v, Lines 3–9.

ALFRED ROFFE (*Handbook of Shakespeare Music*, London, 1878, p. 6) : Before I speak for myself as to the music belonging to this beautiful pastoral, I wish to let Mr Linley be heard. The following are his words respecting the music for Amiens : ' In ' this charming play several songs are introduced, two of which have been delightfully ' set to music by DR ARNE. Of both these pieces the Doctor has omitted to notice ' some of the words; a circumstance greatly to be regretted, and difficult to be ' accounted for. The first song, " Under the greenwood tree," is in the play followed ' by a chorus, " Who doth ambition shun," which could not so well have been sung ' to the opening strain, but how easily, and with what superior characteristic effect, ' could he not have proceeded with the chorus in question.' Dr Arne's felicitous setting of Amiens's first song, ' Under the greenwood tree,' is of course well known to every one who cares for Shakespeare and for music. It had at first seemed to me, as to Mr Linley, singular that the Doctor had not included the words, ' Who doth ambition shun,' in his composition,—setting them to another, or varied, strain, of course; but it has since occurred to me, that at all events it does not follow, but that the Doctor may have composed ' Who doth ambition shun ' as a chorus, following the stage-direction of ' All together here,' and yet that *it may never have been printed.* All who are interested in old opera and oratorio music know how unmercifully choruses and recitatives are left *unprinted.* It must also be remembered that there is a certain amount of most characteristic dialogue, which takes place between the *close of* Amiens's song and the introduction of the chorus. [For the purpose of showing that ' *in the drama* " Under the greenwood tree " and " Who doth ambition shun " are really two distinct pieces,' Roffe here cites lines 10–37 of this same scene, and then continues :] Observe the expression used by Jaques, ' Come, sing; and you that ' will not, hold your tongues.' From this it plainly seems that Jaques looks for a chorus; and although Amiens replies, ' I'll end the song,' that would merely relate to the fact that he is the leader of the rest,—the solo singer whenever, not merely a *song* is required, but also the little piece of solo requirement which often belongs to a chorus.

The want which in this case MR LINLEY felt, he has in some measure supplied, so far as his own work was concerned, by composing music to the words, ' Who doth ambition shun ' as a chorus to follow at once upon Dr Arne's song. Still, the *dramatic* effect is not attained, as Mr Linley has written his chorus for first and second sopranos and bass (with a view to performance in the drawing-room only), and not for male voices entirely, as required by the stage situation.

Dr Arne's melody has been arranged as a glee for four male voices by SIR HENRY BISHOP, and in that form was introduced into the operatised *Comedy of Errors.* [He also arranged Dr Arne's melody for Voice and Piano in his *The whole of the Music in* As You Like It, 1824, pp. 34–37.—*New Shakspere Society*, p. 4.] There is a little three-voiced ' Under the greenwood tree ' in a book of vocal compositions by MARIA HESTER PARK (date, about 1790). Lastly, as far as I at present know, there is a very elaborate setting of the song by STAFFORD SMITH, 1792. The first soprano part of this composition, which is a glee for four voices, is of a somewhat florid character, and the glee altogether is one which I doubt not, if it were skilfully performed, would give much pleasure to the Shakespearian musician.

THE NEW SHAKSPERE SOCIETY (*List of Songs*, &c., Series VIII, *Miscellanies*, No. 3, p. 4) adds the following settings:

EDWARD SMITH BIGGS, about 1800. Three voices.

G. A. MACFARREN, 1869. Soprano, Alto, Tenor, Bass. Novello's *Part-Song Book.*

H. W. WAREING, 1878. Soprano, Alto, Tenor, Bass. Part-Song. Novello.

[In OECHELHÄUSER'S adaptation for the German stage (1870), a setting, as a duet, of this song is given, composed by ED. THIELE, Hofkapellmeister in Dessau.]

Blow, blow, thou winter winde.

Act II, Scene vii, Lines 185–197.

ROFFE (*Ibid*, p. 9): DR ARNE'S beautiful setting of this song is of course known to every one who thinks of Shakespeare and music. It does, however, really seem somewhat singular that the Doctor should have omitted to set the burthen ' Heigh, ho! the holly,' &c. It cannot but be considered as a great mistake not to have set the poem entire. MR LINLEY has remarked upon the fact of this omission, and has accordingly composed the music himself for the burthen, and has added it to Dr Arne's melody. Mr Linley, as I imagine, has executed his self-imposed task very felicitously, and it can hardly be conceived that any one, after hearing the song with Mr Linley's addition, would ever desire to hear the Doctor's beautiful melody without Shakespeare's ' Heigh, ho! the holly,' as made musical by Mr Linley. N. B.— Any baritone, desirous of singing Amiens's song with Linley's addition, will find the whole flow on very pleasantly by transposition into the key of Eb, which will then make the highest note fall on the upper F.

MR R. J. STEVENS has set this song in its entirety as a four-voiced glee, for soprano, alto, tenor, and bass, producing a very attractive composition of its kind; and SIR HENRY BISHOP, having harmonised Dr Arne's air for four male voices (to be introduced into the operatised *Comedy of Errors*), has added, with the proper acknowledgement to Mr Stevens, *the burthen* from *his* glee. In this case Sir Henry has raised the key from Bb, the original key, as sung by Mr Lowe (at least according to the printed copy), to C, so as to use an alto voice for the melody, accompanied by two tenors and a bass. Of Dr Arne's melody, strictly, there is another arrangement, as a glee for four male voices, by the eminent glee composer JOHN DANBY. In this case the original key is retained, so that the glee might be called one for three tenors and a bass.

In a collection of Vocal Music composed by SAMUEL WEBBE, the younger, published about 1830, will be found an elaborate setting of this song as a glee for five voices.

There is a setting of this song by the HON. MRS DYCE SOMBRE. This is a slow air (in the key of D), and suitable for either contralto or baritone, or, indeed, for any voice, the compass being only from the lower C♯ to D. The melody is simple, and not without a certain feeling, however remote from the merits of that of Dr Arne. The burthen ' Heigh, ho,' &c. is omitted.

There is also a setting of this song by AGNES ZIMMERMAN, which I find reviewed in *The Athenæum* for 27 June, 1863. I transcribe the words of the critic, who, of this and of another composition by Miss Zimmerman, writes that they ' go far to jus-' tify the reputation gained by this young lady in the Royal Academy.' The critic then goes on to give his view, that ' there is a certain ungraciousness of character in ' the Shakespeare song, referable, no doubt, to the words; but be it right, be it wrong, 'we prefer Arne's rendering. The mixture of melancholy, melody, and freshness in his setting is almost unparagoned in the library of Shakespeare's songs.'

The latest setting of this song, that I have heard of, is a 'part-song' composed by *R. SCHACHNER*, and published in 1865.

THE NEW SHAKSPERE SOCIETY :—

MRS A. S. BARTHOLOMEW (*first* MOUNSEY), 1857. Part Song. S., A., T., B. 'Six four-part Songs,' No. 3. Novello.

G. A. MACFARREN, 1864. Part Song. S., A., T., B. Novello. 'Choral Songs,' No. 7.

[In OECHELHÄUSER'S adaptation a setting of this song, as a Baritone Solo with male chorus, is given, composed by *ED. THIELE*, Hofkapellmeister in Dessau.]

From the east to westerne Inde.

Act III, Scene ii, Lines 87–92.

THE NEW SHAKSPERE SOCIETY (*Ib.* p. 5) :—

SIR ARTHUR S. SULLIVAN, 1865. Solo, Soprano. Called 'Rosalind.' Metzler & Co. He adds a spurious verse : 'Rosalind, of many parts,' &c. [See lines 148–153 of the same scene. It is hardly fair to call a verse 'spurious' which is Shakespeare's own. The composer merely transferred the verse, which, I think, is quite permissible.—ED.]

What shall he haue that kild the Deare ?

Act IV, Scene ii, Lines 12–20.

See notes and music *ad loc*, pp. 227–231.

ROFFE (p. 12) : *JOHN STAFFORD SMITH* set this song as a glee for alto, two tenors, and bass, and omitted the burthen [line 14]. This composition *MR LINLEY* has transferred to his work, adapting it, however, for two sopranos and a bass, apologising, at the same time, for the liberty of introducing a strain for this burthen : 'Then sing him home,' &c. *SIR HENRY BISHOP* has written for *The Comedy of Errors*, in his very effective and dramatic style, a setting of this song including the burthen. Of this work by Sir Henry Bishop, which is in E♭, and for men's voices only, in foui parts, it may be noted that in *The Shakespeare Album* it is reproduced, but transposed into A♭, and arranged for soprano, contralto, tenor, and bass, soli and chorus.

There is a composition by *HENRY CAREY*, called *The Huntsman's Song* in *Love in a Forest*, which is a setting of Shakespeare's song, with an alteration of certain words in the original. [Lines 16–18] are transformed into ' It was the crest thy father wore, Thy father's father long before.' This composition by Carey, as *printed*, is on only two lines, the one vocal and the other a simple bass. There appears no symphony either for the introduction or the close, and no parts are given for the chorus, which is merely indicated by the word 'Chorus.' . . . . No doubt this is the same piece of music of which mention may be found in an advertisement for a benefit at the Theatre Royal, Drury Lane, upon Tuesday, 12th of May, 1723, wherein we are promised : ' Several Entertainments of Singing and Dancing, particularly a Song 'on the Death of a Stag. The words by Shakespeare, set to music by Mr Henry 'Carey, and sung by Mr Ray, accompanied by French Horns, concluding with a Dance of Foresters.'

There is a three-part composition to this hunting-song by DR PHILIP HAYES. It is in a simple style, and I think has not the burthen, which is given by Carey.

There is also in Warren's Collection a setting of this song by R. J. STEVENS, with the burthen. The composition is for four male voices.

THE NEW SHAKSPERE SOCIETY (*Ib.* p. 6) :—
E. EDGAR, 1881. 'The horn, the horn.'

It was a Louer, and his lasse.

Act V, Scene iii, Lines 17–34.
See notes and music *ad loc.*, pp. 262–263.

ROFFE (p. 16) : [In addition to the setting of this song as a duet by LINLEY, there is also] a setting, as a glee, by R. J. STEVENS. This is one among that composer's favorite pieces. SIR HENRY BISHOP has likewise a setting in the solo form, which was sung by Miss M. Tree in the operatised *Comedy of Errors*.

Lastly, I find in a Catalogue a setting of this song put down as a 'part-song,' composed by S. REAY in 1862; and again, another 'part-song' setting by EDWARD LODER is to be found in the programme of a performance at St James's Hall on the 22nd of April, 1864.

THE NEW SHAKSPERE SOCIETY (*Ib.* p. 7) :—
F. STANISLAUS, 1868. Solo, Soprano or Tenor. Ashdown.
G. A. MACFARREN, 1869. Part Song, S., A., T., B. Novello.
H. HILES, 1870. S., A., T., B. Novello.
C. H. HUBERT PARRY, 1874. 'Spring Song.' 'A Garland,' No. 2. Contralto. Sung by Mad. Ant. Sterling. Boosey.
M. B. FOSTER, 1876. Solo, Contralto. Alfred Phillips. Kilburn.
J. MEISSLER, 1877.
C. LABUNEYER, 1881. 'In the spring-time.'
D. DAVIES. Part Song. First sung May 7, 1883, at the Highbury Philharmonic Society.
DR J. C. BRIDGE, Nov., 1883. Part Song. S., A., T., B. Novello.
B. LUARD SELBY. Part Song. Novello.
J. BOOTH. Part Song. Novello.
MICHAEL WATSON. Part Song. S., A., T., B. Ashdown.
[OECHELHÄUSER gives a setting, as a duet, of this song, by ED. THIELE, Hofkapellmeister in Dessau.]

Hymen. *Then is there mirth in heaven.*

Act V, Scene iv, Lines 111–118.
ROFFE (p. 17) : Mr Linley, after he has given the high praises due to Dr Arne's compositions for the songs of Amiens, goes on to assign his reasons for not allowing this song of Hymen to appear at all in his work. These are Linley's words, with a few italics of my own :—' There is another song of ARNE'S introduced when this play 'is performed, which begins : "Then is there mirth in Heaven;" but the *words are* '*not Shakespeare's*, neither does the tune bear any comparison with the pastoral air- 'iness and originality of the former pieces.' It is curious that Linley offers not the least authority for his assertion [as to the authenticity of the words]. As to his

remark upon Arne's setting of this Hymen song, as compared with that of Amiens's song, no one would dispute its truth.

Hymen's song has been set not only by ARNE, but also (much more happily, to my mind) by SIR HENRY BISHOP, whose composition I heard, when Sir Henry's operatised *As You Like It* [was first brought out], most attractively given by Master Longhurst, who personated Hymen. There are many triplets in the composition, which were executed with a most agreeable neatness.

THE NEW SHAKSPERE SOCIETY (*Ib.* p. 8): In his setting of the operatised *Two Gentlemen of Verona*, 1821, SIR H. BISHOP has, at pp. 81–91, first a Soprano Solo of the first four lines of *Sonnet 25*, then a Chorus made up [as follows: ' Good Duke ! receive thy daughter ! Hymen from Heaven brought her. Such is great Juno's crown : To Hymen, honour and renown !'], and then a duet, one soprano taking the first four lines of *Sonnet 25*, the other, the first four of *Sonnet 97*.

[I have a setting composed by C. DIBDIN, arranged for the Piano by J. Addison, published by Caulfield.—ED.]

Wedding is great Iunos crown.

Act V, Scene iv, Lines 144–149.

ROFFE (p. 18): This has been set by THOMAS CHILCOT, whose work, Linley writes, ' he should have gladly introduced had he found it in any degree expressive ' of the sense of the words.' LINLEY considered it ' too flippant for the dignity of the ' sentiments.' He has, therefore, set the words himself, and no doubt with infinite superiority. Chilcot's setting, which I have seen, I take to be of about the year 1740. [I have it arranged for the Piano by J. Addison, Caulfield.—ED.]

THE NEW SHAKSPERE SOCIETY (*Ib.* p. 9):—
B. TOURS, 1882. Part Song. Unpublished.

PLAN OF THE WORK, &c.

IN this Edition the attempt is made, to give, in the shape of TEXTUAL NOTES, on the same page with the Text, all the Various Readings of *As You Like It*, from the First Folio to the latest critical Edition of the play; then, as COMMENTARY, follow the Notes which the Editor has thought worthy of insertion, not only for the purpose of elucidating the text, but at times as illustrations of the history of Shakespearian criticism. In the APPENDIX will be found discussions of subjects, which on the score of length could not be conveniently included in the Commentary.

LIST OF EDITIONS COLLATED IN THE TEXTUAL NOTES.

THE FIRST FOLIO	$[F_1]$			1623
THE SECOND FOLIO	$[F_2]$			1632
THE THIRD FOLIO	$[F_3]$			1664
THE FOURTH FOLIO	$[F_4]$			1685
ROWE (First Edition)	[Rowe i]			1709
ROWE (Second Edition)	[Rowe ii]			1714
POPE (First Edition)	[Pope i]			1723
POPE (Second Edition)	[Pope ii]			1728
THEOBALD (First Edition)	[Theob. i]			1733
THEOBALD (Second Edition)	[Theob. ii]			1740
HANMER	[Han.]			1744
WARBURTON	[Warb.]			1747
JOHNSON	[Johns.]			1765
CAPELL	[Cap.]			(?) 1765
JOHNSON and STEEVENS	[Steev. '73]			1773
JOHNSON and STEEVENS	[Steev. '78]			1778
JOHNSON and STEEVENS	[Steev. '85]			1785
MALONE	[Mal.]			1790
STEEVENS	[Steev.]			1793
RANN	[Rann]			(?) 1794
REED'S STEEVENS	[Var. '03]			1803
REED'S STEEVENS	[Var. '13]			1813
BOSWELL'S MALONE	[Var.]			1821
CALDECOTT	[Cald.]			1832
KNIGHT	[Knt]			1841
COLLIER (First Edition)	[Coll. i]			1842
HALLIWELL (Folio Edition)	[Hal.]			1856
SINGER (Second Edition)	[Sing. ii]			1856
DYCE (First Edition)	[Dyce i]			1857
COLLIER (Second Edition)	[Coll. ii]			1858
STAUNTON	[Sta.]			1858
R. GRANT WHITE (First Edition)	[Wh. i]			1861
CAMBRIDGE (CLARK and WRIGHT)	[Cam.]			1863

GLOBE (CLARK and WRIGHT) ..	..	[Glo.]	..	..	..	.. 1864
KEIGHTLEY	..	[Ktly]	..	..	..	.. 1864
CHARLES and MARY COWDEN-CLARKE		[Clarke]	..	..	..	(?) 1864
DYCE (Second Edition) ..	..	[Dyce ii]	..	..	..	.. 1866
CLARENDON (WILLIAM ALDIS WRIGHT)		[Cla.]	..	..	..	.. 1877
DYCE (Third Edition) ..	..	[Dyce iii]	.	..	..	.. 1875
COLLIER (Third Edition)	..	[Coll. iii]	..	..	..	.. 1877
ROLFE	..	[Rlfe]	..	..	..	.. 1878
HUDSON	..	[Huds.]	..	..	..	.. 1880
R. GRANT WHITE (Second Edition) ..		[Wh. ii]	..	..	..	.. 1883

In the TEXTUAL NOTES the symbol Ff indicates the agreement of the Second, Third, and Fourth Folios.

The omission of the apostrophe in the F_2, a peculiarity of that edition, is not generally noted.

The sign + indicates the agreement of ROWE, POPE, THEOBALD, HANMER, WARBURTON, and JOHNSON.

When WARBURTON precedes HANMER in the Textual Notes, it indicates that HANMER has followed a suggestion of WARBURTON'S.

The words *et cet.* after any reading indicate that it is the reading of *all other* editions.

The words *et seq.* indicate the agreement of all subsequent editions.

The abbreviation (*subs.*) indicates that the reading is *substantially* given, and that immaterial variations in spelling, punctuation, or stage directions are disregarded.

An Emendation or Conjecture which is given in the Commentary is not repeated in the Textual Notes unless it has been adopted by a subsequent editor; nor is *conj.* added to any name in the Textual Notes unless the name happens to be that of an editor, in which case its omission would be misleading.

The colon is used as it is in German, as equivalent to ' namely.'

All citations of Acts, Scenes, and Lines in *Romeo and Juliet, Macbeth, Hamlet, Lear, Othello,* and *The Merchant of Venice* refer to this edition of those plays; in citations from other plays the GLOBE EDITION is followed.

I have not called attention to every little misprint in the Folio. The Textual Notes will show, if need be, that they are misprints by the agreement of all the Editors in their correction.

Nor is notice taken of the first Editor who adopted the modern spelling, or who substituted commas for parentheses, or changed ? to !.

COLL. (MS) refers to COLLIER'S annotated F_2.

QUINCY (MS) refers to an annotated F_4 in the possession of MR J. P. QUINCY.

In the Commentary, the CLARENDON PRESS EDITION is cited under the name of its Editor, WRIGHT.

ALLEN (MS), and sometimes simply ALLEN, refer to the marginal notes written by the late Professor GEORGE ALLEN, of *The University of Pennsylvania,* in his copy of the play, which was kindly given to me by his daughters, and is now one of my valued possessions.

To economise space in the Commentary, I have, in general, cited merely the name of an author and the page. In the following LIST OF BOOKS used in the preparation of this play, enough of the full title is given to serve as a reference.

COLLIER : *History of English Dramatic Poetry* (ed. ii, 1879) 1831
GALT : *Lives of the Players* 1831
MRS JAMESON : *Characteristics of Women* 1832
GENEST : *Some Account of the English Stage* 1832
HALLAM : *Introduction to the Literature of Europe* 1837
GUEST : *History of English Rhythms* 1838
THOMAS CAMPBELL : *Dramatic Works of Shakespeare* 1838
C. A. BROWN : *Shakespeare's Autobiographical Poems* 1838
COLLIER : *Shakespeare's Library* 1843
DYCE : *Remarks, &c.* 1844
HUNTER : *New Illustrations, &c.* 1845
VERPLANCK : *Shakespeare's Works*, New York 1847
FLETCHER : *Studies of Shakespeare* 1847
MARLOWE : *Works* (ed. Dyce) 1850
HARTLEY COLERIDGE : *Essays and Marginalia* 1851
COLLIER : *Notes and Emendations* 1852
SINGER : *Shakespeare's Text Vindicated* 1853
DYCE : *Few Notes, &c.* 1853
J. P. QUINCY : *MS Corrections in a Copy of the Fourth Folio*, Boston .. 1854
W. S. WALKER : *Shakespeare's Versification* 1854
R. G. WHITE : *Shakespeare Scholar* 1854
COLLIER : *Seven Lectures of Coleridge, &c.* 1856
BATHURST : *Remarks on the Differences in Shakespeare's Poetry, &c.* .. 1857
LILLY : *Dramatic Works* (ed. Fairholt) 1858
G. L. CRAIK : *English of Shakespeare* (ed. ii), London 1859
DYCE : *Strictures, &c.* 1859
WALKER : *Critical Examination of the Text, &c.* 1859
LORD CAMPBELL : *Shakespeare's Legal Acquirements*, New York 1859
S. JERVIS : *Proposed Emendations* 1860
DR J. C. BUCKNILL : *Shakespeare's Medical Knowledge* 1860
MAGINN : *Shakespeare Papers* 1860
F. KREYSSIG : *Vorlesungen über Shakespeare*, Berlin 1862
C. COWDEN-CLARKE : *Shakespeare Characters, &c.* 1863
BEISLY : *Shakspere's Garden* 1864
BISHOP WORDSWORTH : *Shakespeare and the Bible* 1864
R. CARTWRIGHT : *New Readings* 1866
W. W. SKEAT : *William of Palerne* (E. E. T. Soc.) 1867
KEIGHTLEY : *Shakespeare Expositor* 1867
H. GILES : *Human Life in Shakespeare* 1868
DINGELSTEDT : *Wie es euch gefällt* 1868
W. L. RUSHTON : *Shakespeare's Testamentary Language* 1869
ELLIS : *Early English Pronunciation* (E. E. T. Soc.) 1869
A. SCHMIDT (*Uebersetzt von Schlegel*), Berlin 1869
FRENCH : *Shakespeareana Genealogica* 1869
E. A. ABBOTT : *Shakespearian Grammar* (3d ed.) 1870
P. A. DANIEL : *Notes and Emendations* 1870
W. OECHELHÄUSER : *Wie es euch gefällt. Für die deutsche Bühne bearbeitet* 1870
RUSHTON : *Shakespeare's Euphuism* 1871
HERWEGH : *Wie es euch gefällt* 1871

A List of *Dictionaries* is added merely for the sake of their chronological order:

INDEX

445

29